HORNDEAN 2000
A History

Barry Stapleton

HORNDEAN PARISH COUNCIL

First published in the United Kingdom 1999.

HORNDEAN 2000. Copyright © Barry Stapleton 1999

All rights reserved. No part of this publication may be reproduced, stored in a retrieval system, or transmitted in any form or by any means, electronic, mechanical, photocopying, recording or otherwise without the prior written permission of the publishers and copyright holder.

ISBN   0 9537317 0 7

A catalogue record of this book is available from the British Library.

Printed by Hobbs the Printers, Ltd, Brunel Road, Totton, Hampshire

Contents

List of illustrations		5
Acknowledgements		7
Abbreviations		8
Preface		10
Chapter One	Prehistoric	11
Chapter Two	Roman to Saxon	15
Chapter Three	Medieval	19
Chapter Four	Tudor and Stuart	26
Chapter Five	The Eighteenth Century	39
Chapter Six	The Nineteenth Century	49
Chapter Seven	The Twentieth Century	61
Appendix		83
Illustrations		87
Glossary		189
Electoral Roll		190
Index		223

List of Illustrations

Map 1 Horndean and Forest Of Bere, 1810
Map 2 Enclosure Map, 1816
Map 3 Blendworth, Catherington & Horndean, 1870
Map 4 Blendworth, Catherington & Horndean, 1910
Map 5 Blendworth, Catherington & Horndean, 1933
Map 6 Blendworth, Catherington & Horndean, 1962
Map 7 Blendworth, Catherington & Horndean, 1982

Horndean
1. Toll House
2. Antigua Cottages
3. Antigua demolished, 1977
4. London Road looking north before 1914
5. London Road looking south about 1908
6. London Road about 1905
7. Brewery and *Ship and Bell* about 1905
8. Horndean Hill about 1908
9. The Square about First World War
10. Looking down Horndean Hill about 1915.
11. Looking up Blendworth Lane about 1916
12. Horndean in 1929
13. The Square in the late 1930s
14. Down Horndean Hill in the mid 1950s
15. Down Horndean Hill in 1977
16. Havant Road 1912
17. Seymour Cottage 1967
18. Bill for Seymour Cottage 1909
19. Westfield before Precinct 1960s
20. Five Heads Road early 20th century
21. Five Heads Road cottages
22. Five Heads Road & old *Brewers Arms*
23. Five Heads Road about 1913
24. Portsmouth Road looking towards Horndean about 1908
25. Looking south about 1908
26. Union Workhouse before demolition
27. Isolation Hospital
28. Merchistoun Hall 1968
29. Five Heads Road & new *Brewers Arms* late 1930s
30. Air Raid Precaution volunteers 1939
31. Portsmouth Road in Second World War
32. Portsmouth Road before D-Day
33. Keydell House
34. Causeway Stores
35. The Riggs
36. Bulls Copse Lane 1960s
37. Bulls Copse Lane 1960s

Catherington
38. View from Catherington Down
39. Pond & former vicarage
40. Tudor Cottages
41. Old blacksmith's
42. Cottages south of old forge
43. Old Kinches Farm
44. Kinches Farm after fire
45. Catherington House

Blendworth
46. Old Blendworth
47. St Giles Farm
48. Sky Lane about First World War
49. Former Blendworth Rectory
50. Blendworth in early 20th century
51. Blendworth in early 1950s
52. Cadlington House
53. Blendworth Lodge pre 1914
54. Blendworth Lodge after fire
55. Down Blendworth hill to Horndean
56. Crookley

Work
57. Reaping
58. Haymaking 1930
59. Haymaking at Five Heads Farm
60. Haymaking at Five Heads Farm
61. Harvesting at Hinton Daubney
62. Treadwheel at Kinches Farm
63. Jam making in Second World War
64. Fire Brigade
65. A.R.P. Wardens & First Aiders
66. Home Guard
67. Roadworkers
68. Cooperage, Gales Brewery
69. Turf Cutting

Commerce
70. Gales Brewery about 1910
71. *Ship and Bell* pre 1914
72. *Farmer Inn*
73. *Brewers Arms*
74. New *Brewers Arms*
75. *Good Intent*
76. The *Anchor*
77. *Red Lion*

78 Advertisements from 1911
79 Wiles the tailor
80 Hood boot & shoe repairs
81 Marsh's Garage
82 Horndean Pharmacy
83 Inside the Pharmacy
84 Woodlands Cafe
85 Cafe staff

Transport
86 Mitchell's delivery cart
87 Ox-drawn cart
88 Steam powered lorry
89 Horndean Light Railway tram
90 Plan of railway to Square
91 Trams at Terminus
92 Tram fares 1910
93 Tram timetable summer 1910
94 Early cars at Cadlington house
95 And at Catherington House
96 1920s Dennis lorry
97 Butser Turf Co. transport, early 1930s
98 Ex W D A.E.C. in late 1940s
99 Sixten and Cassey van post Second World War

Religion
100 Catherington Church pre 1914
101 All Saints Church 1912
102 Interior of Catherington Church
103 The Lych Gate
104 Catherington Retreat House
105 Horndean War Memorial
106 Old St Giles Church, Blendworth
107 Holy Trinity Church, Blendworth
108 Interior of Holy Trinity
109 Methodist Chapel, Horndean

Education
110 Grace Thompson
111 Blendworth School 1915
112 Blendworth School 1927
113 Catherington School mid 1920s
114 Horndean Boys School 1927
115 Horndean School 1956–57
116 Horndean School about 1960s
117 Coronation Party 1953
118 Needlework class

Leisure
119 Hazelton Woods
120 Sheepwash Lane
121 Rushmore Pond
123 The Lily Pond
123 The Holt
124 Sunny Horndean

125 Light in the night
126 Romance
127 Slowing the pace
128 Time flies
129 Romantic Horndean
130 *Ship and Bell* Tea Gardens
131 *Ship and Bell* Tea Rooms
132 *Good Intent* Tea Gardens
133 Causeway Farm Tea Gardens
134 Coronation Party at *Red Lion* 1902
135 Band of Hope outing
136 *Good Intent* charabanc outing
137 Hambledon Hunt 1910
138 Sports at Blendworth Lodge
139 Horndean Flower Show
140 Catherington Choir about 1893
142 Horndean W I Choir early 1930s
143 Horndean Marching Band
144 Horndean Amateur Dramatic Company
145 Street Party 1945
146 Victory Party, Drill Hall 1945
147 Old Folks Party, Parish Hall 1945
148 British Legion dinner 1945
149 Old Time Dance Club
150 Morris Dancers early 1960s
151 Morris Dancers early 1960s
152 Horndean Football Club 1953–54
153 Horndean Football Club 1969–70

Modern Horndean
154 Horndean Precinct
155 All Saints Church
156 Methodist Chapel before closure
157 Old Lovedean Mission
158 New Bethesda Mission
159 Dedication of new building Catherington School
160 Telephone Exchange
161 Kings Mede Stores
162 Oil rig, Pyle Farm
163 Dean Court, Five Heads Road
164 Catherington 1999
165 Horndean Square 1980s
166 London Road & village 1980s
167 War Memorial & Post Office 1990s
168 London Road & Brewery in 1990s
169 Prince Andrew at Brewery 1997
170 Aerial Photograph, Horndean 1990s

Acknowledgements

The writing of any book normally incurs debts of gratitude to many people, but the writing of local history especially so, since almost everybody not only proves extremely generous in sharing their knowledge of the community with a complete stranger but also happily provides whatever materials they may have collected about the locality. Thus, many people in Horndean have to be acknowledged. Councillors David Eaton and John Merrill were particularly helpful from the outset, as was Clerk to the Parish Council, Sally Hopgood. In the process of research and writing Cecilia Eastwood, Freya Green, Cynthia Porter, Jacqueline Smith, Christine Wagstaff, Maureen Williams, Bill Evershed, Mike Martin, Richard Rees, and John Roberts were all helpful. To Dodo Seward, David Eaton, Alec Peters and Ken Russell particular thanks for their generosity in providing illustrations. Brenda Worton not only provided a copy of her dissertation on Blendworth, but also her collection of old photographs. John Merrell's collection of illustrations is unsurpassable. Without the help of all these generous people this book would inevitably be the poorer.

In addition, former colleagues at the University of Portsmouth, Dr John Chapman and Dr James H Thomas provided valuable information from their own extensive researches, and David Sherren supplied maps of Horndean. I have also benefited from valuable assistance provided at Horndean Library by Carol Groom and Diana Francombe, and at Havant Museum, especially by Gavin Maidment. The staff of Hampshire County Record Office efficiently dealt with my many requests, as did those of Portsmouth's City Record Office. At Portsmouth Museum, Jenny Stevens of the Archaeology Department was particularly helpful, as was the staff of Portsmouth Central Library's Local Collection where Alan King's expertise was very valuable. A similar debt is due to Philippa Stevens of Hampshire County Library's Local Studies Collection at Winchester.

Finally, my grateful thanks to Carol Lacey who, at very short notice, with her usual efficiency, typed the last three chapters and Malcolm Rose of Hobbs who will be able to sleep soundly again, I hope, now this book is published. Should any errors remain, none of the above are to blame, the responsibility is mine alone.

There are no words which can adequately express the debt I owe to my wife, Sandie, not only for her advice and helpful comments on the chapters, but also for being the one constant thread in the tapestry of life.

Abbreviations

B L	British Library
D C	District Council
D N B	*Dictionary of National Biography*
Ec H R	*Economic History Review*
H C	*Hampshire Chronicle*
H L	Horndean Library
H M	Havant Museum
H R O	Hampshire Record Office
H T	*Hampshire Telegraph*
I P M	Inquisitions Post Mortem
P C	Parish Council
P C L	Portsmouth Central Library
P C R O	Portsmouth City Record Office
P R O	Public Records Office
Proc H F C	*Proceedings of the Hampshire Field Club and Archaeological Society*
R D C	Rural District Council
V C H	*The Victoria History of the Counties of England*
W I	Women's Institute

TO GRAHAM AND IAN

who grew up in Horndean
with fond memories of childhood

Preface

Following a meeting with Horndean Parish Council's Millennium Working Party in November 1997, a request was made in late January, 1998 to produce a commemorative book on the history of Horndean to mark the beginning of the third millennium. The Parish Council had already determined the title *Horndean 2000*, which was to be a history illustrated with photographs. Otherwise, the contents were not specified. The book, however, is in seven chapters, beginning some 200,000 years ago and ending at the present day, plus a section of illustrations at the end.

Ideally, another two years would have allowed a more comprehensive analysis of the surviving records and more time to meet and discuss with many more local residents, in order to improve the quality of this book. Consequently, this is not the definitive history of Horndean and future local historians may well add more or rewrite this story of local people. In the 200,000 years covered by this book there would have been 8,000 generations of our ancestors living in the parish, most of whom would have been hunter-gatherers, farmers or farm workers of one sort or another. Only the last six of these generations have lived in an industrial age and only the last two generations have experienced the overwhelming changes which the parish has undergone since the 1950s.

However, what all these generations had in common was the underlying physical structure of the land. Geologically Horndean parish is divided into two. The northern part of the parish forms part of the upper chalk, a white limestone, about 98 per cent pure calcium carbonate, apart from the characteristic flints which formed secondarily after the original chalk deposition. The southern part lies in the Reading Beds, formerly called the 'Red Clay', and is comprised mainly of mottled clays and thin sandstone,[1] which supported the early brick and tile kilns at Rowlands Castle and Padnell. The conjunction of the chalk with the clay ensured a favourable water supply, as surface water filtered through the chalk to the more impervious clay. Such a confluence provided an appropriate location for the sinking of wells to provide a relatively pure water supply for the local population.

The parish lies in a soil region classified as "strong flinty loams and hazel mould on chalk, occasionally veiled with peat, a rich soil ideal for the growing of wheat, barley and oats",[2] which was fortunate since most of our ancestors were tied to the soil, but also had the benefit of access to the Forest of Bere.

The parish within the brief of this book is the civil parish of Horndean, which includes Blendworth, Catherington and part of Lovedean. However, Horndean civil parish was created only in the early 1930s, hence records which survive before that time relate to different authorities and most frequently to Blendworth and Catherington ecclesiastical parishes. Thus, boundaries were not always the same and it is not always easy to determine who lived in what is now Horndean parish.

Even so, it is hoped that, since this book concentrates on the people of the past, it will provide the reader with some insight into how life was for many of our ancestors in this small corner of south-east Hampshire.

References
1   B Daley and D Carter in B Stapleton and J H Thomas *The Portsmouth Region*, 1989, pp. 123–26.
2   R A Pelham, 'The Agricultural Revolution in Hampshire', *Proc. H.F.C.*, XVIII, 1958, p. 140.

Chapter 1
Prehistoric

South-east Hampshire has probably been inhabited for approaching a quarter of a million years, archaeological evidence suggesting that the region's resources have been exploited for over 200,000 years. In the Old Stone Age (Palaeolithic) and Middle Stone Age (Mesolithic) early man was a nomadic hunter-gatherer using primitive stone implements and the known sites of his habitation have been discovered mainly in two groups. First, along the coast where man could have exploited the resources of both land and sea and secondly, those on hill tops which provided more easily defensible positions. Both the early settlement of Blendworth and Catherington could be placed in the latter category, although neither would have existed in Stone Age times.

Even so, the archaeological evidence for the presence of early man within the parishes is relatively thin, although more pronounced in the surrounding locality especially to the north. For the Old Stone Age, a period from about 200,000 to 8,300 years B.C. (which included two ice ages from 200,000 B.C. to 125,000 B.C. and from 70,000 to 8,300 B.C.), a hand axe was discovered near the summit of Butser Hill,[1] and a similar implement in Horndean (its exact location is unknown). For most of the period the nomadic people who used these tools almost certainly would have been Neanderthals—short, stocky, with small foreheads and heavyset features. Their speech, if they had any at all., would have been nasal-sounding and imprecise,[2] hindering development, yet they survived until some 30,000 years ago.

For the Middle Stone Age (8300 B.C. to 4500 B.C.) the evidence of human presence in the area is a little better, but mainly concentrated to the north on Butser Hill, Oxenborne Down and Windmill Hill. Archaeological finds, including flint axes and blades, suggest several Mesolithic sites on the crest of Butser Hill and Windmill Down. Nevertheless, near the southern boundary of the present Horndean parish, on the east side of Portsmouth Road, Mesolithic flint material, including an arrow head, has been located, with further evidence being uncovered at Hazleton Wood just west and south of Sheepwash Pond (now submerged under the A3M motorway). Additionally, the discovery of Mesolithic flakes on Blendworth Down, south-east of Snell's Corner, suggests contemporary implements were made there, within Horndean Parish.

None of this evidence from the Middle Stone Age suggests any change in the patterns of living of hunter-gatherer people and many of the archaeological finds from the New Stone Age (Neolithic) from 4500 B.C. to 2200 B.C. suggest that a similar lifestyle continued. Butser Hill, Windmill Hill and Oxenborne Down continued to provide evidence of occupation, especially with the discovery of axes, including a Cornish greenstone one on Oxenborne Down and the suggestion of the existence of an axe factory on Windmill Hill.

However, there were differences from the Middle Stone Age. To begin with, the period was characterised by ground or polished implements and weapons. Secondly, Neanderthal man disappeared some 30,000 years ago to be replaced by *homo sapiens* a taller, slimmer and more agile race who benefited from a small evolutionary change—the larynx was placed deeper in the throat and that brought the possibility of speech which was better articulated (and eventually more sophisticated).[3] Thirdly, whereas Neanderthals had hunted indiscriminately, *homo sapiens* did so more systematically and co-operatively, tracking particular kinds of game seasonally. Furthermore, their increasingly co-operative and linguistic skills led to the slow development of some breeds of wild animals into domestic ones. Hence, they could take animals with them to new locations in the woodland areas which dominated southern England. For, as conditions improved following the last ice age, forests spread so that 10,000 years ago most of the landscape of the claylands between Portsdown Hill to the south and the South Downs to the north was covered by forests in which oaks were predominant, whilst the Downs supported woodland in which elms and limes were most prevalent. Fourthly, they learned that the sowing of certain seeds could result in greater quantities being harvested and once this occurred so the basis for a less nomadic population was laid and small permanent settlements could develop.

Thus, about 4,000 years ago the earliest agriculturalists of the region settled on the downs to the north where the lighter soils were not only more easily cleared of trees, but also more easily tilled with the primitive stone tools available.[4] That farming occurred in the Horndean area in the New Stone Age is indicated by the finding of a finely worked, neolithic, white flint sickle in the garden of Down House on the northern border of Catherington parish with Clanfield parish,[5] verifying that harvesting was being carried out and the first farmers were established in that part of the parish nearest the higher downland. No doubt a greater element of social organisation was also being developed. If food surpluses could be produced, then the opportunity for trade would be created and thus explain the presence of a Cornish stone axe at Highfield Avenue, Waterlooville.

The evidence for settlement in the Bronze Age (2200 BC to 700 BC), to some extent, continues the pattern established in the New Stone Age with sites on Butser Hill, which included burials beneath round barrows, Oxenborne Down and north of Windmill Hill, a site with rectilinear field enclosures. Other round barrows were found east of Netherly Down on the very eastern edge of Blendworth parish and also close to the eastern side of the London Road (A 3) south of Hog's Lodge. However, around Chalton, another downland site was discovered with much Bronze Age material such as pottery and possible hut sites and cremations, implying an established community. Similarly, at Gravel Hill Bottom, just north of Horndean, a Middle Bronze Age hutted site, dated about 1540 BC, existed.[6] It seems to have been a small farmstead with two circular huts of six metres and four and half metres in diameter. A loom weight found at the site indicates that the inhabitants may have undertaken some weaving.

Clearly by Bronze Age times our ancestors had moved away from complete dependency on the wearing of skins and furs which would have clothed Stone Age man, to a wider range of materials which became possible only with the domestication of animals. Hence, flocks of sheep would supply coarse wool for cloth and long-haired cattle provide the raw material for haircloth, both of which would need to be woven.

Useful bronze items were left behind on the Gravel Hill Bottom site, suggesting a hurried departure—perhaps because being in a dry valley, although better for farming, it was a less defensible position. However, traces of Celtic field farming systems can be found on Butser Hill, at Chalton and just outside the north-western boundary of Horndean parish at Broadhalfpenny Down, and may be dated to the Middle Bronze Age about 1450 BC.

Despite the fact that the most important technological innovation of the Bronze Age was the development of bronze (an alloy of copper and tin) and copper founding for the production of implements and weapons, the use or Stone Age implements overlapped into the period as indicated by the finding of flint arrows on Butser Hill to the north, at Cowplain to the south and in Horndean itself.[7] Nevertheless, in the middle Bronze Age the Portsmouth area seems to have been important for metal working as bronze implements were produced there.[8]

The later Bronze Age saw further technological development with the introduction of a lead-bronze alloy which allowed the production of thinner walled castings and was the precursor of the last of the prehistoric periods, the Iron Age (700 BC to 100 AD), a period in which man increasingly used iron implements and weapons. Unsurprisingly, in the Horndean area, the sites of Iron Age occupation tend to be concentrated in those locations of Stone Age and Bronze Age settlement. It is possible that Butser Hill was an early hill-fort as probable Iron Age cross-dykes existed.[9] Around Chalton much evidence of Iron

Age pottery has been discovered on several sites, as well as a storage pit just to the north and a possible Iron Age enclosure to the north-west. On Broadhalfpenny Down two sites have disclosed pottery and on Windmill Hill, Iron Age hut hollows and earthworks have been found to the east and south-east, along with pottery and a circular enclosure to the north. More pottery was uncovered to the north of Horndean opposite the Hog's Lodge on the A3, just outside the north-east boundary of Blendworth parish near Netherly Farm, as well as on Idsworth Down just north-east of Idsworth House. It would thus seem that, by this time, the widespread nature of finds on the Downs indicates that they had been cleared of their native forest.

However, perhaps the most significant local archaeological evidence from the Iron Age comes from within Horndean parish. First, in the north at Snell's Corner, three late Iron Age burials were discovered (dated by pottery finds) on a site which suggested that burials occurred intermittently into the Anglo-Saxon era.[10] Secondly, in Blendworth parish, just east of Blendworth Down, fragments of early first century coarseware pots and flint-tempered blackware were found. Thirdly, fragments of Belgic[11] jars and bowls from the first half of the first century AD were found at Causeway Farm,[12] Catherington Lane, on a site probably occupied during the first four centuries AD, as Roman ware was also found. Most significantly, however, a little further North-west along Catherington Lane a Cheriton gold stater (coin),[13] one of only five known to be in existence, was found in the garden of number fifty-seven.

Two significant factors can be deduced from this Horndean evidence. First, that early Britons had already begun to extend their settlements and farming activities making inroads into the forested lowland areas and secondly, that the circulation of coinage proper indicates that our ancestors engaged in trade on a wider than local scale—local exchange could have been undertaken simply by barter. Coins, of course, began to carry the names of the rulers under which they were minted, thus introducing the first written records and terminating the prehistoric period. The landing near Chichester of a Roman legion in AD 43 brought a more literate and cultured people to southern England and the dawn of a new historical era for the residents of the Horndean area.[14]

References
1. D J Rudkin, 'Prehistoric' in B Stapleton & J H Thomas, *The Portsmouth Region*, Gloucester, 1989, p. 4.
2. See Bill Bryson, *Mother Tongue; The English Language*, 1990, pp. 11–13.
3. Ibid. p. 12.
4. R Burkmar, *The Wildlife and History of Hurstwood*, 1991, p. 3.
5. The majority of the references to Stone Age implements comes from the card index of the sites and monuments record in the Archaeology Department at the City of Portsmouth Museum. I am most grateful to Jenny Stevens for allowing me access to, and facilities for researching, the record. Further references are in Rudkin, *Portsmouth Region*, pp. 5–9 and J C Draper, Mesolithic Distribution in South-East Hampshire, *Proc. H F C*, 23, 1964–68, pp. 110–19.
6. It was destroyed by road widening of the A3 in 1968.
7. References to Bronze Age sites and implements come from the record in the Archaeology Department at the City of Portsmouth Museum and also from Rudkin, *Portsmouth Region*, pp. 9–11 and J P Williams-Freeman, 'Field Archaeology as Illustrated in Hampshire, 1915, pp. 276–77 and *The Archaeological Journal*, 20, 1863 pp. 371–72.
8. Rudkin, in *Portsmouth Region*, p. 11.
9. Ibid. p. 12.
10. G M Knocker, 'Early Burials and an Anglo-Saxon Cemetery at Snell's Corner near Horndean, Hampshire', *Proc. H F C*, 19, part 2, 1956, pp. 117–70.
11. The Belgae were an ancient tribe of southern England for whom Winchester (Venta Belgarum) was their main settlement.

12 Causeway Farm is now sheltered housing for the elderly.
13 Originally a Greek gold coin, later copied and developed by Celtic tribes.
14 References to Iron Age sites and implements are from the record in the Archaeology Department at the City of Portsmouth Museum and also from Rudkin, *Portsmouth Region*, pp. 11–14 and Barry Cunliffe, 'Report on a Belgic and Roman Site at the Causeway, Horndean' (1959), *Proc. H F C*, 22, part 1, 1961, pp. 25–9.

Chapter 2

Roman to Saxon

The arrival of the Romans was to bring Britain into the international trading pattern of the Roman Empire as well as to open up the country to the possibility of internal trade through the network of roads built to connect the most important Roman population centres. The nearest of these roads to Horndean was that east-west along the coast from Chichester to Bitterne and then north to Winchester, and which did not directly affect the local community. Nevertheless, the local archaeological evidence of Roman times is considerable, and indicates that the inhabitants tended to continue the established pattern of settlement with a preponderance of occupied sites on the downs. South-east of Butser Hill, north of Windmill Hill, and both north and south of Gravel Hill are sites which have disclosed Roman pottery, whilst between Gravel Hill and Windmill Hill to the east of the A3 trunk road and south-east of Windmill Hill are a scattering of sites of Romano-British pottery. Furthermore, sites of Roman buildings have been discovered in Holt Down Plantation east of Hogs Lodge and south-east of Windmill Hill, just north of Netherly Farm.

However, the greatest concentration of Roman discoveries in the locality was excavated at Chalton where an orderly-arranged Romano-British village of rectangular, timber-framed houses with, apparently, intensively cultivated gardens was uncovered.[1] Even so, it would appear that the village was basically a British one, since none of the fine Roman ware, which they imported and was usually associated with Roman occupied buildings, was found. The Chalton pottery was largely locally produced at the Rowlands Castle kilns, around which a further concentration of Roman occupation occurred and was undoubtedly associated with the pottery established on the Reading clay there. Even a minor road was built to link the kilns with the major coast road at Havant,[2] thus bringing closer access to the network for Horndean. Yet these developments, like the brick and tile kilns on the London clay at Crookhorn, where a veritable factory was established, were all peripheral to Horndean.

No such concentrations of Roman activity have been found within the parish to compare with those to the north, east and south-east. However, evidence of occupation has been revealed by the discovery of Romano-British pottery. North of Hinton Daubnay at Prew's Hanger several pieces were recovered from an oil exploration site and north of Hinton Manor coarseware pottery, thought to be from the third century AD, was found on the covered reservoir site. Other Romano-British coarsewares were discovered, along with a Roman coin, on the very northern border of the parish just east of the *Bat and Ball Inn*. More central to Horndean was the unearthing of Roman roof tiles in the garden of a house opposite Catherington School as well as pottery both south-west of the Old Vicarage and south of Catherington churchyard.[3] Aerial photographs of the latter site also revealed two square enclosures and embankments abutting on to the churchyard hedge, suggesting some concentrated agricultural development had taken place.

At the southern end of Catherington Lane, the Causeway Farm site continued to be occupied throughout the Roman period, probably into the fourth century, with pottery, a quern of the late Roman period and loomweights being disclosed. Continuing south-east into the Forest of Bere (now Hazleton Wood), [Horndean was located on the forest's northern fringe], a Roman site south of Sheepwash Pond revealed more Roman pottery and tiles.[4]

Hence, evidence of occupation in Roman times has been found from the northern to the southern boundary of the parish. Furthermore, the burial ground at Snell's Corner, established in the Iron Age, furnished six Romano-British burials plus three Roman coins[5] and north of Old Blendworth a dense concentration of Roman brick and tile indicates a probable Roman villa site.[6] Further east, just within the Blendworth parish boundary, near Netherly Down, plaster, pottery and parts of a rotary quern suggest a possible site of another Roman building. That the site of yet a further Roman building was found just south of the parish, in Gladys Avenue, Cowplain, testifies to a not inconsiderable occupation of the area in Roman times.

Apart from the fact that the neighbourhood saw increasing occupation in the Roman period, and not just on the higher downland areas, a number of further conclusions can be deduced from the evidence. First, living conditions, for some at least, would seem to have improved, since the existence of timber-framed buildings suggests somewhat superior accommodation to that of the hutted sites of Iron Age times. The existence of brick and tile works indicates that some buildings were even better constructed, but these were likely to be only for the upper echelons of the Roman hierarchy. Secondly, wells were a Roman innovation, and one was found just north of Horndean parish in Oak Road, Clanfield suggesting a better water supply not only for the population but also for crops. Thirdly, the references to quern stones, the finding of a twelve-inch long, iron-hafted, Roman bill south-west of Denmead and the presumed sites of intensive farming at Chalton and Catherington, all suggest that agricultural surpluses may well have been produced. Fourthly, the references to coins—a further one of the Emperor Diocletian was found in a garden in the parish[7] and 66 at the side of Glidden Lane, Hambledon,—indicate the growth of trade in surpluses and not barter. For local residents these surpluses could only be agricultural. In any case, the Roman administration imposed taxation, both in coin and kind, on the native farmers who were thus obliged to produce more than they could consume and therefore adjust agricultural practices to do so. Surpluses had to feed Roman legions and administrators in Britain and also the citizens of Rome. Britain became one of the great granaries of the Roman Empire. Certainly two residences of prosperous owners have been discovered near Rowlands Castle.[8] They may have been on a single large estate since large units were more effective in providing intensive farming surpluses. There is, of course, no way of knowing whether this estate would have spread into nearby Blendworth or Catherington. Undoubtedly the forested areas of the southern part of the parishes would have been exploited for timber for construction purposes and also fuel. Additionally, as charcoal was used in Roman times, it may have been produced by the practice of coppicing which continued into the modern era. Coppicing enabled a crop to be produced every decade. After the trees were cut close to the ground, regenerating shoots would grow to be cut (or stubbed) for charcoal ten years hence, thus providing the next crop. That this practice occurred in the Horndean parish area is virtually certain by the existence of Stubbins Down which derives its name from a place where trees have been stubbed or coppiced.[9]

Beginning in the third century, but increasingly in the fourth century AD, Roman Britain became threatened by raiders, hence the construction of the 'forts of the Saxon Shore' from the Wash to Portchester Castle in Portsmouth Harbour which, by the late fourth century was garrisoned by mercenary soldiers. By the evidence of their huts and pottery they appear to have been of Germanic origin.[10] It seems likely that towards the end of the era of Roman presence the whole of the Forest of Bere was included within a mercenary enclave centred on the fort at Portchester.[11] Thus, there may have been a gradual takeover of a disintegrating Empire rather than a mass replacement of people.

Increasing barbarian attacks on the Roman Empire meant that the imperial government decided it could no longer defend its far-flung possessions and in 410 AD it relinquished its control of Britain in favour of defending Rome. Thus began a period lasting until the Norman Conquest generally known as the Dark Ages of British history. In the fourth to the sixth centuries the Angles, Saxons and Jutes, Germanic tribes from southern Denmark and northern Germany settled in Britain. To the native Celtic Britons they were all Saxons and subsequent place names reveal the approximate date of some settlements. For instance, places with names which are a combination of a Roman and an Old English word indicate early Saxon settlements. Havant, an amalgam of the Saxon personal name *häma* and the Latin *funta* (spring) is clearly one such place. However, place names ending in 'ing', 'ton' or 'worth' are also Anglo-Saxon probably indicating secondary settlement in the mid- to late-Saxon period.[12] Thus, Catherington and Blendworth appear to be mid-Saxon settlements and were certainly secondary to that already established at Chalton, where 61 structures were uncovered in a remarkable Anglo-Saxon village with three varying types of rectangular buildings.[13]

For Horndean parish there is little doubt that the Anglo-Saxon period conformed to its name of the Dark Ages since few sites of the period have been discovered. It is thought that Rushmore Pond (Anglo-Saxon 'risc-meare')[14] dates back to the period and therefore could have been providing a water supply to the local population. North-east of Blendworth, just outside the parish (OS SU 734 143) a Saxon site revealed pottery, a loom weight and a quern stone. Inside the parish a late Saxon bone implement used to manipulate threads in weaving was found among the contents of a medieval rubbish pit located at Catherington (OS SU 695 144). Its contents suggested the site had been occupied from Roman times. Pottery from the pit indicated Saxon presence in the late 10th and 11th centuries.[15] The only other Anglo-Saxon site discovered in the parish was the burial ground at Snell's Corner. Bearing in mind that the two ecclesiastical parishes bear Saxon names this lack of sites is disappointing, particularly since the earliest known form of the name Catherington comes from the early 11th century as *Cateringatune*[16] which, it has been suggested, means 'the settlement of the people at the hill fort'. However, no evidence of a hill fort has been found on the crest of the ridge north of the Church, although the field name Turbery found in the Tithe Award in the first half of the 19th century, may suggest a hill fort similar to that on Torberry Hill, Harting in Sussex.

Nevertheless, despite the minimal nature of the surviving evidence the cemetery at Snell's Corner can provide some information about our Anglo-Saxon ancestors. Thirty-three Anglo-Saxon graves were found. Twenty of them contained thirteen males and seven females. Of the other thirteen, three contained two children and the others were too damaged to be certain, although two probably contained males and two more contained females. Generally, what they suggest is that the locality was populated by relatively poor people. There were neither silver items nor a single brooch in any of the graves. Bronze and iron buckles, bronze rings and a few beads were the only decoration. However, although ornaments were rare, eighteen of the graves contained knives and charcoal was found scattered in many of them, thus confirming the theory that charcoal burning was a possible occupation in the forest area. Five of the males were warriors, being buried with their spears and the graves of two old men contained shields with conical bosses, typical of the South Saxons, as also was a round black cooking pot found in one grave. Sadly, and not too differently from their modern counterparts, many of the Saxon folk buried here had suffered a life plagued with arthritis.

As a whole, the grave objects suggest that the cemetery was probably of the late 7th century, and the north-south orientation of the bodies with heads pointing south, indicates that they were pagans.[17] They were, undoubtedly, among the last of our pagan ancestors since in 634 AD Bishop Birinus, who probably landed at Portchester, began to convert the heathen west Saxons to Christianity, although paganism and the worship of heathen gods lingered on in parts of south Hampshire. Initially, Christianity was carried out by priests who undertook open air preaching, parish churches being built later. Hambledon Church has a nave with Saxon origins as does the important Titchfield Church which may, exceptionally, be dated back as far as the late 7th century and was the focal point of a large parish including Wickham and Fareham.[18]

Thus, the origins of the English ecclesiastical parish system can be dated to the mid-Saxon period. As for Blendworth and Catherington their beginnings remain unclear, although it seems likely that permanent settlements were named about this time. Even so, the two communities were part of a larger, more important Saxon holdings at Chalton, where the late Saxon estate would have had an influence on the shape of things to come.

References
1. B W Cunliffe, 'A Romano-British village at Chalton. Hants'., *Proc. H F C*, 33, 1976, pp. 45–67.
2. G Soffe and D E Johnston, 'Route 421 and other Roman roads in South Hampshire', *Rescue Archaeology in Hampshire*, II, 1974 pp. 99–118.
3. J S Pile and K J Barton, 'An Early Medieval Rubbish Pit at Catherington, Hampshire, *Proc. H F C*, 28, 1971, pp. 49–55; J S Pile 'Excavations near Catherington church', unpublished typescript, 1969, p. 2.
4. The site, just inside Horndean parish boundary, continues eastward disappearing beyond the motorway (A3M) boundary fence.
5. Knocker, 'Early Burials', pp. 117–70.
6. *V C H Hants.*, I, 1900, p. 310.
7. Its exact location is unknown. References to Romano-British sites and artefacts come from the record in the Archaeology Department at the City of Portsmouth Museum, except where otherwise stated.
8. *V C H Hants* I, 1900, p. 310.
9. See for example J S Pile, Aspects of the forest of Bere from the Later Iron Age to the Middle Ages', *Proc. H F C*, 45, 1989, p. 118. Charcoal burning continued in Catherington at least into the 18th century.
10. D E Johnston, 'Roman to Saxon', in *Portsmouth Region*, p. 19–20.
11. Pile, 'Aspects of Bere', p. 115.
12. Johnston in *Portsmouth Region*, p. 21.
13. P V Addyman and D. Leigh, 'The Anglo-Saxon village at Chalton Hampshire', *Medieval Archaeology*, 17, 1973, pp. 1–25; T. C. Champion 'Chalton', *Current Archaeology*, 59, 1977, pp. 354–71.
14. G Soffe, *The A3M Motorway*, typescript, South Hampshire Archaeological Rescue Group, 1974, p.5.
15. Pile and Barton, Rubbish Pit', p. 52.
16. E Ekwall (ed.), *the Concise Oxford Dictionary of English Place Names*, 4th ed., 1960.
17. Knocker, 'Early Burials', pp. 117–70.
18. M J Hare, 'The Anglo-Saxon Church of St. Peter, Titchfield', *Proc. H F C*, 32, 1975, pp. 5–48.

Chapter 3
Medieval

The death of Edward the Confessor in 1066 brought an end to the Anglo-Saxon period and heralded a major change in the administration of England. William, Duke of Normandy, considered that, in 1051, he had been given an informal promise that he would become King Edward's heir. Even so, before he died childless, Edward nominated Harold, son of the Anglo-Saxon Earl Godwin as his successor. William, however, pursued his claim and defeated Harold at Hastings, whereupon he proceeded to replace the Anglo-Saxon nobility with Norman barons, as Domesday Book clearly indicates.

In south-east Hampshire, prior to 1066, the Anglo-Saxon hierarchy was represented as land holders by King Edward, Queen Edith, Earl Godwin, Earl Harold and the Bishop of Winchester, whereas in 1086, when Domesday Book was produced, the land was held by a Norman aristocracy headed by William I, Hugh de Port, William Mauduit, William de Waren, the Earl of Shrewsbury, and the Norman Bishop of Winchester. Almost half the manors were, in fact, in ecclesiastical hands, indicating the power of the church.

Neither Blendworth nor Catherington was mentioned in Domesday Book, not because they did not exist, but because both were included under the extensive manor of *Ceptune*. Before the conquest this was held by Earl Godwin, but afterwards was granted by William to Roger de Montgomery, Earl of Shrewsbury who also held other land in south-east Hampshire. Thirty-two years later *Ceptune* was held by Roger de Montgomery's son Roger de Belesme, Earl of Arundel and Shrewsbury who, in 1102, rebelled against Henry I. This could have been the time of uncertainty when the motte and bailey castle at Motley's Copse, between Blendworth and Rowlands Castle, was built. Whatever the case, after the failure of de Belesme's rebellion his lands were confiscated, one result being the break-up of the large manor of *Ceptune*. It was divided into areas which approximated to the modern ecclesiastical parishes of Chalton, Idsworth, Clanfield, Blendworth and Catherington.[1] Thus it would seem we can date the two parishes forming most of Horndean to the early 12th century, although clearly, the communities already existed before that time. Archaeological evidence has shown the presence of the Anglo-Saxon village of Chalton although, along with the other local communities, it was not mentioned in Domesday Book. Thus, despite Domesday giving the best coverage of England for the medieval period it is an inadequate record. For example, it refers to an unspecified number of churches in *Ceptune* manor.[2] Presumably, one of these was in Chalton since it was the main Anglo-Saxon community and it is thought that Catherington Church, basically a late 12th century Norman construction, was erected on the site of a previous wooden Saxon structure. Whether there was a church at Blendworth is unknown. Similarly, the number of workers in each community remains a mystery, only the number for *Ceptune* as a whole, for which 104 are listed, over a fifth of whom were serfs.[3]

Each one of these *Ceptune* manor workers is thought to represent a household with an average size of 4.5 people. Thus, approximately 470 people, plus administrators, would have been living on *Ceptune* manor in the late 11th century. However, it has to be remembered that Domesday Book was intended to show William I what his recently acquired province was worth in taxable value and not to be a population census, hence, all figures are estimates only. Even so, it is possible to discover that the communities of Chalton, Idsworth, Clanfield, Catherington and Blendworth had population densities below the average for south-east Hampshire as a whole. Greater than average densities were to be found along the coastal strip south of the Forest of Bere (except for Portsea Island which was more thinly peopled than the downland parishes). As *Ceptune* manor contained approximately 12,400 acres giving an average density of 26.5 acres per person,[4] there was clearly the potential for population growth.

However, how many of these residents lived in Blendworth or Catherington it is impossible to say, but it could have been some 40 to 44 households—180 to 200 inhabitants. There is little doubt that the majority of these people would have been engaged in agricultural labour on behalf of their overlord on his demesne lands and, when the lord's work was completed, on their own land holdings, there being ten ploughlands in the lord's demesne and twenty-seven for the rest of the inhabitants.[5] How the landholdings were organised is unknown. The feudal system, then in operation, usually meant large open fields farmed in strips allocated between the lord and the peasant tenant farmers. However, the evidence for the existence of such fields in the Horndean parishes is negligible. What exists are the strip lynchets (cultivated terraces) extending on both sides of Lovedean Road. Those on the west side have been heavily ploughed over the centuries and are not now as prominent as those on Catherington Down where some are still well preserved, rising to a height of four metres. How old they are is debatable. They may well have been Celtic in origin, predating the Romans, and have been subsequently ploughed by the Saxons. On slopes, as at Catherington Down, the action of the plough tended to move earth downhill and to pile it against the lower field boundary to form a terrace called a lynchet. The steeper Celtic fields tend to be narrow and to follow the contours to form flights of terraces, as at Catherington. Most are earlier than the Celtic (that is Iron Age) period. Some are even from the New Stone Age and were in use through the Bronze Age.[6] Although these lynchets do not conform to the traditional medieval open fields perhaps, in the absence of other evidence, they were the common fields for Hinton Daubnay and Catherington. Certainly the latter community appears to have had a common field, since a lease of 1734 for Youles (Yoells) included " three several pieces [of land] lying dispersedly in the common field of Catherington".[7] As no evidence of traditional common fields exists for Catherington, the strip lynchets appear to be the only possible alternative.

Whatever was the reality, *Ceptune* contained more ploughlands than any other manor in south-east Hampshire,[8] thus confirming that much, if not all, of the northern downlands had been cleared of forest. Even so, *Ceptune* also contained woodland to support more pigs than any other south-east Hampshire manor, Droxford being the next largest with woods for forty pigs as again Ceptune's fifty.[9] Clearly, therefore, much of the southern half of the manor remained in the Forest of Bere where pasture for the pigs would be provided. Since *Ceptune* also contained pasturage for livestock valued at 10 shillings it would seem that the local communities contained all the elements of mixed farming in the late 11th century. What was not available for the inhabitants, however, was a mill. Whereas most of the manors in south-east Hampshire possessed a mill for grinding grain (e g Havant had two, Hambledon one and Droxford two) *Ceptune* had none.[10] Since the manor had more land under plough than any other, this is curious. Perhaps it was thought that the population was scattered too thinly to make it a profitable proposition and since Earl Roger of Shrewsbury was also the Lord of Hambledon, no doubt he instructed his peasants to have their grain ground at his neighbouring mill.

By the end of the 13th century, long after Blendworth and Catherington had been separately identified, the manor of Catherington alias Five Heads had its own mill. In 1302, part of the manor described as "a messuage, a mill, 300 acres of land, 24 acres of wood, and 20 shillings rent" was settled on Ralph de Hangleton and his wife Joan. The other part was settled on Joan's sister, Isabel,[11] whose daughter Joan probably married William Bonet who acquired the Hangleton's part of the manor. Bonet died in 1349 whilst his son Nigel was still a minor, so the King granted custody of William's property in Catherington to William de Fifhide until Nigel came of age. However, he died while still a minor leaving his fourteen year old brother, William, as his heir. Shortly after coming of age William also died without heirs hence, William de Fifhide appears to have taken over and died in possession of Catherington manor in 1361. His eighteen year old son inherited and held the manor until his death in 1387 and from this date the manor has frequently been called the manor of Fifhides or Catherington Fifhides after the family who owned it.[12]

When William de Fifhide died in 1361 the manor was described as "Two capital messuages, a dovecote, a windmill, 200 acres of arable land in severalty (privately owned); 150 acres of land in common of which 12 acres can be sown, and the rest lie uncultivated and cannot be valued because they are common; pasture in severalty containing six acres; eight acres of wood, the underwood and pasturage of which are worth eighteen pence, a certain profit of "housebote" (the right of wood from the forest to repair a house) and "haibote" (the right of wood for repair of fences) to be received from the wood of the lord of Chalton; rents of eight free tenants; rents of tenants at will (of the lord), 45 shillings and sixpence; pleas and perquisites of [manorial] court, three shillings and fourpence".[13]

Thus, by 1360, Catherington manor contained 221 acres individually owned and a further 150 acres of land in common. As twelve acres of this latter could be sown, it would seem that crops were being grown in a common field and the twelve acres would have been part of the lord's demesne land. This reference, therefore, seems to confirm the existence of a common field, just as the reference to a windmill confirms the previous mention in 1302. It is not easy to interpret these scraps of evidence. However, they do show that mixed arable and pastoral farming continued into the 14th century, but also imply that the output of the land and the population supported by it had risen. Greater output of grain would have required a mill which in turn suggests a greater concentration of local inhabitants as customers for the miller.

Such a rise in the numbers of people would simply reflect changes in the nation's medieval population as a whole. Generally, the period from 1086 to the early 14th century was one of growing numbers. Depending on assumed household size, England's population is variously estimated to have risen between 1086 and 1377 from either 1.1 million to 2.23 million or from 2.6 million to 3.4 million people.[14] Certainly, south-east Hampshire appears to have experienced population growth in the 12th and 13th centuries, as indicated by the establishment of Southwick Priory in the early 12th century and Portsmouth about 1180. In the 13th century urban and rural growth, and therefore increasing numbers of consumers, along the coastal strip was demonstrated by the creation of new markets at Havant (1200), Emsworth (1239) and Portchester (1294). Wickham also received the grant of a market in 1268. By contrast, the area between the South Downs and Portsdown, mainly the Forest of Bere, had no growing urban centres, although Chalton was granted a market in 1224, provided that it created no nuisance to other neighbouring ones, and Hambledon received a grant in 1256.[15] The establishment of markets in both of these communities implies both growing trading surpluses and rising population in the surrounding rural areas. Catherington and Blendworth were located between the two. Evidence of trading taking place over a wider area was provided by the cooking pots, dishes and bowls found in Catherington which were manufactured in 12th century Chichester. Wares from this pottery had a widespread distribution through south Hampshire and West Sussex.[16] The existence of a commercial pottery, superseding domestic production, is another indicator of a growing market.

Also testifying to rising numbers was the subdivision of larger peasant landholdings into smaller plots as happened on the estates of nearby Titchfield Abbey in the 13th century.[17] This was a clear indicator of the increasing land hunger as the numbers of people needing land rose faster than any new supply.

In an agricultural country, with a relatively static agricultural technology, such as England was in medieval times, feeding rising numbers of people could only be achieved either by an extension of the cultivated area or by more extensive use of existing farmland. New and growing settlements indicate that agricultural land was extended and subdivision of holdings implies more intensive farming was practised. Inevitably, however, subdividing landholdings will result in some plots of land being smaller than the ten acres considered to be the minimum requirement for the support of a peasant family at subsistence level.[18] Yet, by 1259 smallholders with under ten acres accounted for half the tenants on the Bishop of Winchester's estates in Hampshire, and Bishop's Waltham manor had an increase in those with less than ten acres from 42.6

per cent in 1259 to a 51.5 per cent in 1332.[19] If those peasants unable to inherit land because population outstripped supply are taken into account, then the average holding on the Bishop's estates fell to a mere two acres.[20] Thus, many peasants must have fallen perilously close to, if not below, the subsistence level in late 13th century south-east Hampshire. It seems unlikely that the peasant farmers of Blendworth and Catherington were not similarly affected. However, as both communities had below average population densities in the late 11th century, the pressure on land could have been less intense than in those places, like the market towns, which had grown faster. In any case, both parishes had the benefit of access to the Forest of Bere, thus the residents had considerable opportunity to exploit the woodland pasture. The pasturing of cattle and swine of those communities within or on the edge of the forest was a custom which was clearly established at least from Saxon times and probably before, and in 1792 the Royal Commission on Crown Woods and Forests listed Catherington among those parishes which were allowed to turn out into the forest horses, horned cattle and ringed swine at all times of the year, seemingly without restriction.[21] In addition, the forest could be exploited for its timber for buildings, fencing or for charcoal.

There is no doubt that the Forest of Bere came under increasing pressure. For instance, the medieval process of creating assarts—clearing an area of forest, enclosing it, using the timber for a homestead and cultivating it—took place as manorial lords found themselves with too many peasants who could be provided with holdings of land in the open fields. The tenant of an assart had the advantage of a land holding free of labour services which normally accrued to the lord from an open field tenancy. Not only was the assart free of the customs of the open field, it was also hereditary. Not surprisingly, therefore, the Forest of Bere was gradually reduced. Several perambulations (recording the boundaries of the Forest) were held between 1218 and 1301 and their frequency implies they were largely ineffective[22] and the forest was gradually reduced probably from about 30,000 acres to not much more than 10,000 by 1662.[23]

In England as a whole, the effect of rising population can be seen in the late 13th and 14th centuries when the inevitable years of inclement weather caused bad harvests. In those years increasing numbers died. Beginning with the poor harvest of 1272 mortality was substantially higher than normal and the experience was repeated in 1277, 1283, 1294 and especially in the successive bad harvest years of 1315–17, which affected most of Western Europe.[24] On the Winchester manors there was a steep rise in the number of poor dying in years of bad harvests from the 1290s and especially between 1316 and 1319.[25] This suggests that south-east Hampshire had become relatively overpopulated, with declining living standards leaving many of the less well-off particularly vulnerable to fluctuations in harvest yields. Thus, it seems more than likely that the rise in population ended not in 1348–49 with the arrival of the Black Death, but with the Great Famine of 1315–17. Such a view is supported by the movement of wages on Winchester manors. In the 13th century wages remained stable while agricultural prices rose so that the real value of wages fell by 25 per cent.[26] Population growth, providing an increased labour supply, had clearly kept wages from rising but, from the 1320s, money wages on the Bishop of Winchester's manors began to grow and kept on doing so for more than a century.[27] Since the famine of 1315–17 appears to have resulted in the deaths of some 10 to 15 per cent of the population of England,[28] it seems likely that the origins of rising wage levels lay in that period of crisis when the labour force was reduced. Even so, such a level of population loss seems small by comparison to that caused by the Black Death some 30 years later which decimated between 30 and 45 per cent of the nation's population.[29] In Droxford deanery, which included Blendworth and Catherington parishes, 47 per cent of the clergy died and at nearby Titchfield 80 per cent of the tenants perished.[30] The residents of Hayling Island were granted a reduction in taxation when they petitioned Edward III in May 1352 as a very great number of men had " been destroyed by the said mortal pestilence".[31]

Despite the evidence of substantial mortality in south-east Hampshire, the Black Death of 1348–49 could not alone have been responsible for the continued labour shortage which rising wage levels for the next three-quarters of a century reflected. Repeated plague epidemics meant population recovery was constantly thwarted. The first outbreak was in 1361–62, a second in 1369 and a further one in 1374–75 when many towns in southern England were said to have been ravaged by the "Fourth Pestilence".[32] There are no surviving figures for local mortality from these epidemics but estimates of national death rates suggest that 18 or 19 per cent of the population died.[33] Not only did population not recover after the Black Death but it declined even further. Yet more national epidemics occurred in 1390–91 and in 1405–07. Generally, the plague was endemic in England with frequent regional outbreaks in the late 14th and early 15th centuries,[34] so that it seems likely that demographic decline was not halted until around 1440 when, it is estimated, the national population had shrunk almost to its Domesday level with a decline perhaps of some 60 per cent.[35] Some places disappeared forever and the site of a deserted medieval village in Blendworth parish is a probable indicator of the local impact.[36]

Should such a loss of the workforce occur in a modern economy it would lead to economic chaos. The manorial lords of the late 14th and 15th centuries, operating a feudal system of labour services, were faced with similar chaos having insufficient labourers, not only to undertake the day-to-day farming activities, but especially at harvest time. Some landlords attempted to solve their problems by imposing greater labour services on the surviving tenants, others converted from direct farming of their demesne lands to leasing on rentals to peasants as tenant farmers. This discrepancy between the treatment of peasants, often on neighbouring manors, contributed to the growing resentment which exploded into the Peasants' Revolt of 1381. By then, for example, all but one of the acres of Titchfield Abbey's open fields were enclosed and leased to peasants. As enclosed lands fetched higher rents the Abbey had found a way to maintain its income whilst passing the problems of poor harvests on to tenants. At Fareham labour services were converted into money payments as labour became scarcer. Thus, the £1.12s 9d (£1.64) received from tenants in lieu of services in 1346 had become £9.6s (£9. 30) by 1352 after the Black Death, and £12.12s 6d (£12.63) by 1421,[37] suggesting that the labour supply remained inadequate at least until the 1420s. On the Winchester manors the demesne lands of the Bishop were leased out as they ceased to be cultivated directly and agricultural wages rose between the 1340s and the 1440s by 50 per cent.[38]

What was happening in response to the demographic crisis was the gradual collapse of the feudal system. Once labour services had been commuted to money rents it was most unlikely that tenant farmers would be prepared to return to the subservient positions of the pre-Black Death period. Many had opportunities to farm as never before with greater individual freedom and especially so in those places where few peasants had survived the successive plague outbreaks.

Blendworth and Catherington were similarly controlled by manorial lords. The former came under the lordship of Chalton while Catherington was affected by a number of manors, namely Catherington or Catherington Fifhide, Hinton Daubnay, the small manor of Hinton Markaunt and the 80 acre manor of Hinton Burrant.[39] No medieval records of the operations of these manors survive, but it seems highly unlikely that their manorial lords did not suffer the same problems which afflicted their contemporaries in the surrounding manors of south-east Hampshire.

There is no doubt that medieval governments, comprised largely of the major landowners, attempted to control the movement of labour by such methods as the Statute of Labourers, but economic forces were operating in the labourers' favour and such measures, although having some effect in the short run, were inevitably bound to fail as peasants discovered better opportunities on other manors or in nearby, or even more distant, towns. Some lords, in any case, desperate for labourers were prepared to offer incentives to attract workers. Thus, it seems safe to conclude that the residents of Blendworth and Catherington in the 15th century were experiencing greater freedom either in their ability to farm on their own account or as wage labourers. At the close of the Middle Ages peasant living standards were higher than they had ever been before or were to be again until after the Industrial Revolution,[40] hence governments passed sumptuary legislation aimed at ensuring that the lower orders of society did not ape their betters in style of dress in late 15th century England.

References

1. Margaret Hoad and John Webb in *Portsmouth Region*, pp. 46–50.
2. Ibid. p. 49.
3. Ibid.
4. Barry Stapleton in *Portsmouth Region*, pp. 84–5.
5. A ploughland (or carucate) was what one plough with eight oxen could plough in one year. This would vary considerably depending on the type of soil—more on lighter soils, less on heavy.
6. The *Hampshire Treasures Survey*, vol. 6, East Hampshire, 1982, surprisingly places the lynchets under the Post-Norman heading (p. 193); O. Rackham, *The History of the Countryside*, 1986, pp. 158–59.
7. H R O 6M59/Box2/2 Clarke-Jervoise Estate Papers. This is one of only two references to a common field that have been found. None were included in the Enclosure of 1816.
8. The next largest was Hayling Island with 28 ploughlands. See Hoad and Webb, *Portsmouth Region*, pp. 47–50.
9. Ibid.
10. Ibid.
11. P R O Feet of Fines, Hants., Trin. 30 Edw. I, (1302), quoted in *V C H Hants.*, Vol. III, p. 95.
12. P R O I. P. M. 35 Edw. III, pt. 1, no. 88, (1361); I. P. M. 10 Ric. II, no. 17, (1387) quoted in *V C H Hants.*, Vol. III. pp. 95–6. In 1431 the manor was referred to as 'Fyfehydes in Kateryngton and in 1591 as Kathrington *Alias* Kathrington Fyfhed. By 1736 it was Catherington alias Fiveheads and in 1774 the manor of Five Heads. (See *V C H* Vol. III, p. 96). It is still represented by Five Heads farm house and Five Heads Road, but it is not a reference to the five communities which came from *Ceptune* manor as stated in Soffe, *The A3M Motorway*. 1974, pp. 4–5. Similarly, in the 13th century, Hinton Daubney, a manor described as £10 of land in Catherington, was named after the Daubneys who held it from the late 13th century to 1383; Hinton Markaunt, a small manor, took its name from Sir Robert Markaunt who, with his family held it from 1384 to the 15th century. Hinton Burrant, a manor of 80 acres in 1283, was acquired by Roger de Boarhunt and remained in the de Boarhunt family, from which it took its name, until at least 1363. See *V C H Hants*, III, pp. 96–8.
13. P R O I.P.M. 35 Edw. III pt. 1, no. 88, quoted in *V C H, Hants*, III, p. 95.
14. J C Russell, *British Medieval Population*, 1948, pp. 34–54, 118–146; M M Postan (ed.) *The Cambridge Economic History of Europe*, 1, 1966, pp. 561–5; J T Krause, 'The Medieval Household: Large or Small?'. *Ec. H.R.*, IX, 1956, pp. 420–32; M M Postan, *The Medieval Economy and Society*, 1975, pp. 30–8; J Z Titow, *English Rural Society 1200–1350*, 1969, pp. 66–71. The wide variations in estimates of population size have depended on whether the average medieval household was considered to have contained as few as 3.5 or as many as 5.0 people. Generally historians have shown greater support for a larger household averaging about 4.5 people. The 1086 figure is derived from Domesday Book and that of 1377 from the Poll Tax, neither of which was intended to count the numbers of people.
15. Stapleton in *Portsmouth Region*, pp. 86–7; Hoad and Webb, p. 52. The nearest markets to Chalton would have been Petersfield and Havant.
16. Pile and Barton, 'Rubbish Pit', pp. 49–56.
17. D G Watts, 'A Model for the Early Fourteenth Century', *Ec.H.R.*, XX, 3, 1967, pp. 543–44.
18. Titow, *Rural Society*, pp. 80–90.
19. Ibid. pp. 78–9.
20. Postan (ed.) *Cambridge Econ. Hist. Europe*, I, p. 564.
21. See Gavin Maidment, 'An Analysis of Development and Change in the settlement and Land Use of the Forests of Bere and Stansted, circa A.D. 1550, with Speical Reference to the Village of Rowlands Castle and its Surrounding Area', unpublished dissertation for Advanced Certificate in Local History,

King Alfred's College, Winchester, 1992, p. 15 and Appendix to Thirteenth Report of the Commission on Crown Woods and Forests.
22 Ibid. pp. 17–18.
23 D J Carter, 'A Historical Geography of the Forest of Bere', *South Hampshire Geographer*, 1968, p. 81.
24 H S Lucas, 'The Great European Famine of 1315, 1316 and 1317', *Speculum*, v, 1930, reprinted in E M Carus-Wilson (ed.) *Essays in Economic History*, Vol. 2, 1962, pp. 49–72; Postan, *Cambridge Econ. Hist. Europe*, I, p. 564, J. M. Stratton, *Agricultural Records AD 220–1977*, 1978, pp. 25–8.
25 M M Postan and J Z Titow, 'Heriots and Prices on Winchester Manors', *Ec. H.R.*, XI. no. 2, 1958, pp. 392–410; Postan, *Medieval Economy*, p. 38.
26 Postan (ed.), *Cambridge Econ. Hist. Europe*, I, p. 566; *Medieval Economy*, p. 40.
27 W. Beveridge, 'Wages on the Winchester Manors', *Ec. H.R.*, VII, 1936, pp. 26–43; Postan (ed.) *Cambridge Econ. Hist. Europe*, I, pp. 566–7.
28 Postan, *Medieval Economy*, p. 41.
29 J Hatcher, *Plague, Population and the English Economy 1348–1530*, 1977, pp. 21–6.
30 J D F Shrewsbury, *A History of Bubonic Plague in the British Isles*, 1971, pp. 90–1; D G Watts (ed.) *Titchfield, a History*, 1982, p. 39.
31 Calendar of Close Rolls, Edw. III, IX 432, membrane 19 quoted in Shrewsbury, *Bubonic Plague*, p. 89; Originalia Roll, 29 Edw. III m.8, cited in P. Ziegler, *The Black Death*, 1970 p. 150.
32 V H Galbraith (ed.), *Anonimalle Chronicle 1333 to 1381*, 1927, p. 77.
33 T H Hollingsworth, *Historical Demography*, pp. 385–6.
34 Ibid. p. 358; C. Creighton, *A History of Epidemics in Britain*, 2 vols., 1891–4, reprinted 1964, I; Hatcher, *Plague, Population*, pp. 57–61.
35 Hollingsworth, *Hist. Demog.*, pp. 378–87; Hatcher, *Plague, Population*, pp. 26–8, 68–9.
36 *V C H Hants*. III, pp. 82–4.
37 *V C H Hants.*, V, pp. 421–2.
38 Beveridge, 'Wages in Winchester Manors', pp. 38–43.
39 *V C H Hants.*, III, pp. 94–8.
40 E W Phelps Brown and S. V. Hopkins, 'Seven Centuries of the Prices of Consumables Compared with Builders' Wage-Rates', *Economica*, 1956, reprinted in Carus-Wilson (ed.), *Essays*, Vol. 2, 1962, pp. 179–96.

Chapter 4

The Sixteenth and Seventeenth Centuries

The late 15th and early 16th centuries were ones which saw some recovery in the size of the nation's population but, starting from a very low base about 1440, there was little pressure on resources, hence the better standard of living for most people continued until the second quarter of the 16th century. Thereafter, the problems of a growing population in an agricultural country with a somewhat static technology again began to appear, so that by the 1550s bad harvests and plague were causing high death rates. Indeed the years 1558–59 were to see greater mortality than any until after Britain had industrialised in the 19th century. In 1554, 1555 and 1556 there were particularly poor harvests, exports of wheat being prohibited in 1554, and 1556 being a famine year with heavy mortality.[1] A weakened population was particularly vulnerable to disease and succumbed to what appeared to be an epidemic of influenza in the next three years.[2] Legislation repeatedly enacted against poverty was a clear indication that serious social problems existed; prices in the previous quarter of a century had risen whilst wages had not.

Thus, Queen Elizabeth acceded to the throne at a time of crisis and although her reign is always characterised as one of stability and prosperity in which the nation flourished politically—the growth of the nation state, militarily—the defeat of the Spanish Armada in 1588, and culturally—the age of Shakespeare, Marlowe, Spenser, and Hilliard, little is ever said about the economy. It was also an age when the population of England once more reached its pre-Black Death level and continued to grow into the early 17th century. This pressure of population on resources caused considerable inflation and consequent increasing levels of poverty among labourers, wage earners and peasant farmers, with many becoming dependent on poor law doles and charitable relief. The seriousness of the problems of poverty was regularly demonstrated by repeated legislation which was finally codified in the 1601 Act establishing the Tudor Poor Law, in which each parish had the responsibility for looking after its own poor.

However, an increasing division between rich and poor developed. Since large farmers and merchants with goods to sell at inflated prices grew richer, so the gap between them and the poor widened. Wage-earners fared badly with their real incomes being halved as money wages failed to match prices. Rising population also meant increasing unemployment,[3] and with political and religious uncertainties associated with the Reformation and counter-Reformation—for instance the vicar of Catherington was among those ejected in 1559 for refusing to recognise Queen Elizabeth's oath of Supremacy[4]—there were many problems facing the men and women of south-east Hampshire in the late 16th and early 17th centuries.

Blendworth and Catherington did not escape these problems, if only because they did not escape the growth of population. In 1525 Catherington is estimated to have been a community of about 180 people whilst Blendworth held around 117.[5] Thus, some 66 households are thought to have held almost 300 people. By 1603, this figure had risen to 517, a 74 per cent increase in just over threequarters of a century.[6] However, the effect on the two villages varied. Blendworh grew slowly with an easily absorbed increase of 15 per cent whereas Catherington's population rose by 112 per cent, almost double that of south-east Hampshire generally.[7] In the process it had become larger than Chalton, Wickham, Portchester and Warblington, all with greater numbers in 1525. It is inconceivable therefore, that the consequences of 16th and early 17th century price inflation were not felt in the parish. Prices in the last three-quarters of the 16th century rose some fourfold, peaking in 1597 when three years of bad harvests brought famine to

Europe and food riots to England, with prices over 1000 per cent higher than at the beginning of the century.[8] Such price increases were good for producers, but calamitous for consumers on fixed or reduced real incomes. Poverty must have been widespread for the majority, but equally landowners and large farmers would have prospered. Thus, when yeoman farmer Humphrey Aylward of Catherington died in 1598, he was living in a house with a hall, parlour and kitchen all with rooms above them, and in addition on the ground floor, a kitchen chamber, an entry chamber, a buttery, meal house and a well chamber. In all eleven rooms and his main room, the hall, had "glasse in the windowes", an unusual 16th century luxury and was wainscotted. He had a newly made joined bedstead and slept on a feather mattress with feather pillows and bolsters, as opposed to flock or the straw palliasses which the poor would have endured. The total value of the contents of his house was £38.17s 10d (£38.89), vastly more than the total possessions of most of his contemporaries. But he was one of Catherington's wealthiest residents, for in 1586 he had been taxed at, £4 on his goods, the third highest in the community—only Humphrey Brett at £7 and Nicholas Hunt £9, were more highly taxed. In fact, only nine Catherington residents were wealthy enough to pay the tax, plus seven more in Hinton Daubney. In Blendworth eleven people paid a total of £34. Catherington's nine paid £38 and Hinton Daubney's seven paid £41, making them on average the wealthiest taxpayers.[9] Even so, out of a population of over 500, only 27 taxpayers indicates the majority were too poor and exempted from payments. But it was not on the value of his household goods that Aylward was taxed. His real wealth lay in his farming activities. He had at least 34 acres sown with crops, the most important being barley (15 acres) and wheat (11 acres). Peas (four acres), oats (two acres), and vetches (two acres) were his other crops. Barley may well have been the main crop, not only because as a cheaper grain, it could have been better afforded by the poorer than wheat, but also for its use in brewing. Aylward had four and-a-half quarters (126lbs) of malt in his kitchen loft and was probably carrying out his own brewing, especially since he had his own supply of water in his well chamber. But arable farming was only one half of Aylward's farming activities, for he had over 120 sheep, 16 cattle, 16 pigs and four horses. Some of the cattle were oxen for ploughing and harrowing—he had three ploughs and five harrows -others would provide milk, butter, cheese and meat—he had two breasts of meat in his kitchen loft. The pigs are an indication of the use of the Forest of Bere for pasturing and were primarily to provide meat, especially bacon, of which six flitches hung in his kitchen loft.[10]

Along with the malted barley, meat and cheese and the dung in the yard outside, the smells of sixteenth-century houses must have been fairly strong if not noxious. Although well-off and living in a considerable house—Aylward's probate inventory value totalled over £176, he was not the wealthiest resident. The highest taxpayer in the two parishes in 1586 was John Foster of Hinton paying £10. When his father died in 1560, the Fosters were already wealthy but, because his household goods were not itemised room by room it is impossible to determine the size of their house. However, since it contained three feather mattresses and five flock ones it can be assumed it was not small, especially since the household goods, including 12 silver spoons, were valued at over £50. Yet again, as in Aylward's case, it was in the Fosters agricultural activities where their main wealth lay. Unfortunately, John Foster, somewhat uncooperatively, like many of the farmers, died in winter when only the winter wheat would have been sown.[11] Thus, only 30 acres of wheat are listed as being in the ground. However, there were 10 quarters (280lbs) of wheat stored in the barn from the previous year, plus 60 quarters (1,680lbs) of barley and three quarters (84 lbs) of oats. Whether this represents the reality of sown acreage is debatable. It seems unlikely that Foster would have grown six times more barley than wheat, but clearly he did grow more. As he also had a load each of peas and vetches stored and three acres of vetches sown, his farm was probably greater than 100 acres in size. On the pastoral side he possessed 500 sheep, over 40 cattle, 27 pigs and nine horses. His livestock alone were valued at nearly £120, whilst his crops and tools amounted to over £50. In his house he had 16 tods of wool stored. A tod equalled two stones and he thus had 32 stones valued at 8 shillings per stone. Also stored were six hogs of bacon and a quantity of cheese.[12] Foster was clearly farming on a much grander scale than most, if not all, of his contemporaries hence, the higher tax valuation.

John Foster's house also contained unspecified weapons and his bow and arrows, an indication that practice at the archery butts was still a legal requirement (hence Catherington's Butts Cottage). Similarly, his contemporary John Padwike, who also lived at Hinton and died in 1569, had a bow and arrows as well as a sword and dagger. John Padwike's son also paid tax in 1586, but only £3 and the reason for this can be seen in the value of his household goods—just over £10— and the scale of his farming. Padwike was a co-operative farmer, dying in June, thus all his crops were in the ground—his 23 acres of barley, 20 acres of wheat, 13 of peas and vetches and one acre of oats. He was also growing a little hemp. He too had livestock—84 sheep, 23 cattle, 27 pigs and five horses. Because of access to the pasture of the Forest of Bere for all the farmers, the number of pigs is clearly less varied. Like his contemporaries, Padwike's house contained produce—three and-a-half quarters of malt (98lbs), two and-a-half tods of wool (five stones or 50lbs) and nine bacon hogs at the roof. But the total value of his inventory was less than £70.[13]

As the century progressed and prices rose, so inventory valuations would increase. Hence, when Richard Barnard, another Catherington yeoman, died in June 1584, his inventory stated that he was leasing Hinton Burrant farm and his assets were valued at £228. He had 45 acres of barley, 40 acres of wheat and nine acres of peas and vetches in the ground. Clearly, with the land which would normally lie fallow each year, Barnard would have had a farm of well over 100 acres. His livestock was also substantial—350 sheep, 42 cattle and 32 pigs. His horses were valued at £10 but not specified by number. His arable crops were valued at £55 10s (£55.50) and his livestock at almost, £110.[14] A generation later when John Barnard died in January 1628, again with possessions worth over £100, the growing wealth of the family was demonstrated by the building of an extension comprising a new chamber and loft above, on to their existing two-storey house. As the yeoman farmers became wealthier, so they wanted more space and comfort hence, the Barnard's house became part of the rebuilding of rural England.

The Fosters, Aylwards, Barnards and Padwikes were the wealthy farmers, prospering because they had surpluses to sell at a time of rising prices. They may well have been good farmers, but even a poor one could still have made a profit when economic circumstances were all operating in his favour. Small farmers, on the other hand, would have experienced a different lifestyle. For example, John Shorter described as a husbandman, ie small farmer, when he died in June 1592 had household effects worth less than £8, lived in a three roomed house—hall, chamber and kitchen—and slept on a flock bed. Unlike his wealthier contemporaries his house contained a spinning wheel, indicating that spinning wool was carried out to earn extra income. Despite having a summer inventory, only one acre was sown with oats, demonstrating that his farm had been reduced below the 10 acres which would have been required for his subsistence. He seems to have been providing only for his livestock from the land and not his family. He had 20 sheep three cattle and three pigs. Even so, his house contained one quarter (28lbs) of malt, two hogs of bacon and 14 cheeses, though these were priced at only one shilling and sixpence. His total inventory was valued at only £7.14s 10d (£7.74).[15] Yet most Catherington residents would not have had enough possessions to require a probate inventory at all, and probably lived in a single room.

In Blendworth, a smaller parish and a smaller community, there was less evidence of the extremes of wealth and poverty. All the farmers for whom evidence has survived were described as husbandmen (small farmers). Thomas Foster, who died in August 1559, had a house with a feather bed, a bow and arrows, but an unspecified number of rooms with a total value of less than £4. As no acreages of crops were recorded, he clearly died after that year's harvest—an average one.[16] Thus, his crops are given in quarters -16 quarters of wheat, eight of barley, plus vetches and hay. Even so, as in Catherington, it was the livestock which were most valuable. He had 75 sheep, 6 cattle, 18 pigs and five horses and they were valued at over £22. However, there were indications that Foster was involved in other commercial activity for he had 18 yards of cloth in his house, though no loom. As he was not weaving, he may have been buying and selling cloth. Similarly, he had two bushels of bay salt (4437 cubic inches), an unusual presence in an inventory which suggests he could have been trading in the salt evaporated from the sea at the salterns which were a feature of Portsea Island's Langstone Harbour coast in Elizabethan times.[17] Salt was a commodity used in every household and therefore would have had a demand. Foster appears to have had something of an entrepreneurial spirit and consequently was a reasonably comfortably off husbandman, whose goods were valued at £43 14s 10d (£43.74).[18]

A generation later Richard Higgens senior, was another Blendworth husbandman with similar possessions to Foster, but without the commercial activities. Dying in early 1590, his household goods were valued at just under £5. Being winter, only wheat was in the ground, some 12 acres being sown. He had barley, wheat and peas in the barn unthreshed and also in store, and again the barley had a higher value than the other crops. But like his contemporary farmers the highest values were those of his livestock—37 sheep, 7 cattle, 9 pigs and 4 horses worth over £15 of his total value of £39.16s.[19] However, these two husbandmen contrast starkly with others found in late 16th century Blendworth. Richard Stephen, who died in April 1581, had a three roomed house, the contents of which were worth less than £2. He had two acres of wheat and a few vetches in the ground worth £1 and his livestock consisted of seven sheep, one bullock, eight pigs and two mares—that he had more pigs than sheep suggests he was also benefiting from the common pasture of the Forest of Bere. But the total value of his crops, livestock, tools and household goods was under £8.[20] Similarly, in November 1598 John Padwyck husbandman of Blendworth died with total assets of only £7 8s 2d (£7.41). His house had two rooms and a loft. Unusually, he had no sheep, one cow and a calf, five pigs, but three horses were worth alone more than half (£4) the value of his assets. There was no mention of any crops in the field though he had a bushel of wheat and 14lbs of dredge (oats and barley sown together) in store.[21] It would seem that the small farmer was finding life increasingly difficult in the inflationary late 16th century.

However, in the pecking order of late 16th and early-seventeenth century rural society there were those who came even below the husbandmen, the agricultural labourers who had no land and few possessions and consequently rarely left behind evidence of their existence. Fortunately, William Hall, a labourer from Catherington, who died in March, had made a will. He possessed "little goods, but all the goods he had he willed to his pore wife". He appears to have lived with her in one room, containing the dining furniture, one flock bed, two bushels of corn (presumably mixed grain), 1 bushel of malt, one flitch of bacon and a few hops. Outside he had three pigs. The sum total of his possessions was £2 10s 11d (£2.54), but he was owed money £9 15s (£9 75) so that his inventory was valued at £12. 5s 11d. (£12.29)[22] No doubt as a poor man he carried far too little weight to insist on payment of the debts owing to him. Thus they were 384 per cent greater than the value of his possessions. No doubt some of the money owing was as a result of labour he had provided, but William Hall is an example of those at the bottom of rural society, which demonstrably was hierarchical with many at the base, the husbandman above and the yeomen farmers and landowners near or at the apex.

From the late 14th century to the early seventeenth century the apex at Catherington Fifhides manor was the Sandys family, as a result of the surviving Fifhides family heir being the wife of Sir John Sandys. However, Lord Sandys, lord of the manor in 1602, sold it in November that year to his principal tenant Humphrey Brett for £750. Brett was a wealthy man, being the second highest taxpayer in Catherington in 1586 and in 1665 the family still lived in a house with four hearths. Nine years after purchase Brett sold the property to the Earl of Worcester, then Lord of Chalton manor. Thus, from 1611, Catherington manor was in the hands of the Chalton manorial lord. Similarly, in the early seventeenth century Hinton Daubney manor was sold to probably its most distinguished owner Sir Nicholas Hyde, Chief Justice of the Court of King's Bench, and it remained with the Hyde family and their descendants until the 20th century (Sir Nicholas Hyde's family tomb is in the Hyde chapel in Catherington church). Curiously enough, the late 16th and early 17th centuries seemed to be a significant period for other manorial owners in

Catherington, for in 1594 Isabel Norton was granted lands in Catherington parish by her brother Anthony. Isabel married Thomas Lovedean of East Meon after which the land became the manor of Lovedean and in 1635 was described as a cottage and 50 acres in Catherington, a messuage called Lovedean and five and-a-half acres in Catherington. Subsequently, in the 18th century, it was bought by the lord of Hinton Daubney and this formed part of the Hinton Daubney estate. Also becoming part of the Hinton estate was Ludmore which, when sold by John Chatfield in 1629, was described as a messuage, a close called the Home Close of 10 acres, a close called Constables of 26 acres (Constable Copse still exists), a close called Credies of 12 acres, a close north of the Mansion House of Sir Nicholas Hyde in Hinton Daubney (where Ludmore still is) and a close of pasture and wood called Harecroft of 10 acres; over 58 acres in all, which also subsequently was acquired by Sir Nicholas Hyde.[23]

Table 4.1

	Fireplaces in Houses 1665							
Hearths	1	2	3	4	5	6	14	17
Catherington	31	8	9	4	2	1		
Hinton Daubney	18	5	5	4	3	1	1	1
Blendworth	22	9	7	4	2	1		
Total	71	22	21	12	9	3	1	1
Percentage	52	16	15	9	5	2	0.5	0.5

Sources: PRO E179/176/565 Hearth Tax Assessment, Easter 1665; Elizabeth Hughes and Philippa White, *The Hampshire Hearth Tax Assessment 1665*, Hampshire Record Series, Vol. 11, 1991, pp. 126–27.

That this society was becoming increasingly polarised in the 16th and 17th centuries seems undeniable. In the last 30 years of the 16th century the probate records list four yeoman and seven husbandmen in Catherington and Blendworth. In the first half of the 17th century the number of yeomen rose to 14 whilst husbandmen numbered 10. But between 1650 and 1700 the number of yeomen increased to 25 whilst the husbandmen fell to six.[24] Large farmers were clearly progressing at the expense of smaller ones. The central government's taxation by hearths in houses provides clear evidence of society's divisions in Catherington and Blendworth parishes. Over half of the houses had only one fireplace and of these 71 houses, 33 were occupied by those who were so poor they were exempt from paying the tax, 12 of them were widows. With little except the Poor Law in the form of social security, being widowed was clearly distressing in more ways than one and especially so if children were involved. Over two-thirds of premises had two hearths or less and above that level was the third of the population who were wealthy enough to create probate records. Demonstrating the real extremes of society were the two houses at Hinton Daubney with 14 and 17 hearths (see table 4.1). The largest was that of Lawrence Hyde, second son of Sir Nicholas Hyde of Hinton Manor and the other that of Mistress Englefield of Hinton Markaunt manor. Their ostentatious wealth contrasts starkly with those, often living in one room, at the opposite end of the social scale. Slowly the peasant farmer was being squeezed out as the modern structure of rural society emerged—landlord, tenant farmer and agricultural labourer with many husbandmen sinking to labourer status whilst their lands were acquired by a few.

However, it is clear that the picture of mixed farming which had been gleaned from archaeological and other evidence such as Domesday Book was substantially correct. All farmers, large and small, were engaged in mixed farming and the crops grown were primarily barley, followed by wheat, with much smaller acreages of peas, vetches and oats. The description of Hinton Markaunt manor lands in 1621 with fields called "Barlie Asted, Wheate Asted, Fetch Asted... and Oate Purrocke" confirms this form of arable farming.[25] The large quantities of livestock maintained would have the benefit of producing substantial amounts of manure for spreading on the arable fields, hence the two forms of farming were mutually beneficial. Numerically, sheep formed the largest group of livestock and their wool would have been in demand by the woollen textile industry which, in the 16th century, flourished in the towns of northern Hampshire from Andover in the west to Odiham in the east.[26] These large numbers of sheep, grazing on the thin, chalky soil of the downs, were much more valued for their wool and manure than for their meat. Cattle were kept for milk, and hence butter and cheese, as well as meat, but the primary source of meat was the pig, as can be seen by the number of houses which had bacon hanging within. The popularity of pigs in the parishes is undoubtedly the result of the availability of common pasture in the Forest of Bere, a fact clearly indicated in the description of Hinton Markaunt manor which specified ", common of pasture in the Forest of East Bere".[27] There appear to have been no changes in agricultural practice within the records of any of these farmers, large or small, and that remained the case into the 18th century.

There was no evidence of the introduction of root crops such as turnips, or clover and artificial grasses such as sainfoin for fodder. Although these had been written about and recommended from the 1650s by publicists such as Richard Weston and John Worlidge of Petersfield,[28] it appears that local farmers had not thought it necessary to change their methods and introduce the new crops in a rotation which eliminated the need to leave fields fallow for a year and therefore raised productivity. It could hardly be expected that small farmers with inadequate resources would lead the way in experimenting with new crops, particularly when the pressure was for them to give up their landholdings, as Catherington farmers, husbandmen Richard Pink and Robert Bryant, dying respectively in July 1680 and April 1691 must have done. Pink had only five sheep and Bryant no livestock. Neither had evidence of any crops.[29] However, Richard Poate a yeoman farmer of Hinton Daubney, living in an eight roomed house with five fireplaces[30] and a servant chamber, was farming on a large scale when he died in March 1671. He had 95 acres of crops sown, but there was absolutely no change in his farming methods from his predecessors a century before. Wheat consumed 39 acres, oats 22, peas 22 and vetches 12. His barn contained 60 quarters of barley, 18 quarters of wheat and eight quarters of oats. Presumably, so early in the year, he had yet to sow his barley which, the evidence in the barn suggests, was his main crop. If so, it could well be he was harvesting from at least 150 acres. In addition, he had a flock of 220 sheep, 25 cattle, only seven pigs and six horses, the value of his livestock being over £153. His crops in the fields and in the barn almost equalled the value of his livestock, being worth over £128. His total moveable possessions were valued at over £314.[31] Similarly, when yeoman William Biden of Catherington died in June 1685, he was the occupant of a two-storey, seven roomed house with three fireplaces.[32] He had 79 sheep, nine cattle, four pigs and three horses. In both his barn and his fields he had only wheat, barley and oats. The only noticeable difference for these two yeomen farmers was the reduction in the number of pigs kept, which perhaps indicates that the forested area of the parish had been reduced by population pressure and less was available for pasture.

Although the vast majority of the people in Blendworth and Catherington, as in most other villages in 16th and 17th century Britain, would have been engaged in farming of one sort or another, there were a minority employed in other activities. Some of these provided services to farmers and foremost among them was the blacksmith, required for shoeing horses, repairing ploughs, harrows and cartwheels and some of the edged tools like bills and scythes. In the late 16th century an Elizabethan blacksmith in Blendworth was William Kent who lived in a house with three rooms and a loft, plus a shop. Since his bed chamber contained a feather bed he could afford to live in some comfort.[33] Fortunately, the contents of his shop were described in some detail, affording a glimpse of the operation of an Elizabethan blacksmith's business. The shop contained two anvils, one swage, two pairs of bellows, two vices, a buckhorn, eight nail tools, seven sledges, two hand hammers, a binding hammer, two riveting hammers, a shoeing hammer, nine pairs of tongs, two dozen files, two stakes, two bolsters, a cart pritchel, a horseshoe pritchel, a round pritchel,, four other pritchels, two tempes, a gouge, a fuller, a cleft, a print, two dogs, pincers, a drawing knife, three tool irons, a hearthstaff, a pan, two coulters, a shophalter, beam and weights, old iron, grindstone, 132lbs of new iron, ware and stores and two chaldrons of sea coals. Some of the contents are recognisable today. Others are described by words that have long disappeared from the language. Thus, a swage was an anvil with a groove, a buckhorn was a goat's horn for blowing a blast (presumably for the forge), a sledge was a sledgehammer, a pritchel was a sharp, pointed instrument for punching holes, especially nail holes in a horseshoe, a tempe was a wedge, a gouge was a stamping tool for cutting out and making holes, a fuller was a grooved tool in which iron was shaped by being driven into the grooves, a cleft was probably a tool for splitting, a print was an instrument producing a mark by pressing, a stamp or die; a dog was a tool for gripping or holding, a hearthstaff was for stirring the coals of the furnace, a shophalter was a rope with a noose for leading horses into the shop and a chaldron was a weight of 36 bushels of coal.[34] The total value of the contents of William Kent's shop was £23.10s 6d (£23 53). His anvils, bellows, vices, wares and stores in the shop accounted for half this total. Whereas his estimated two chaldron of "sea coles", were valued at £2 2s, his 132lbs of new iron was worth only 12s 6d (63 p), just over 1 penny per pound. What the source of his iron was remains unknown. It could have been northern England or the Baltic, but his sea coals were almost certainly imported from Newcastle or Sunderland in the north-east, through Chichester or Portsmouth which was then beginning to grow.[35] Kent was clearly connected to the local agricultural activities by the use of tools for replacing iron bands on cartwheels and making horseshoes. But he also was in another way. In a small community like Blendworth it would be very unlikely that he would have found enough blacksmith's work to either keep him fully occupied or to provide a living wage. Hence, apart from an acre of vetches sown in the ground, he had an estimated 10 quarters (280lbs) of wheat and barley in his barn. He also had 24 sheep, seven cattle, and seven pigs, but no horse. Presumably he used his four bullocks to pull his carts and ploughs. Dual occupations were common among those whose main activities were outside agriculture just as, in north Hampshire, many small farmers had secondary occupations weaving Hampshire kerseys.

As everyone had to be clothed and shod, other essential services were provided by tailors and shoemakers. A contemporary of William Kent, Nicholas Cover, a tailor of Blendworth, died in March 1597. If he was typical of late sixteenth-century tailors then it would seem that they were not among the wealthy of a community. He lived in a three roomed house, sparsely furnished, but with absolutely no evidence of his tailoring occupation—not even to a pair of scissors. However, he farmed in a small way having wheat in the ground valued at 10 shillings (50 p) and had a calf and two pigs, but his total assets came only to a little over £9.[36] By contrast, Thomas Pitt a Catherington shoemaker, who died in January 1633 had a two-storey house with at least six rooms downstairs and three above. It was well stocked with food having 40 cheeses, two pots of butter and in the milk house fresh butter and lard, five hogs of bacon and a small pig. One of the downstairs rooms was his shoemaker's shop which contained shoes and leather (and presumably tools) to the value of £3.16s 4d (£3.82), but more than £25 was due to him on bonds and bills on his shopbook and in debts. Yet Thomas Pitt farmed on quite a large scale as well. He had 124 sheep, no cattle, 11 pigs, including 10 young ones and four horses, presumably to pull his two ploughs, four harrows and one roller. He had sown 11 acres of wheat and two acres of vetches and in the barn were seven quarters of wheat, eight of barley and eight bushels of peas and oats, suggesting he had a substantial landholding, more so than many farmers, yet his primary occupation was making footwear.[37] He was certainly better off than shoemakers who lived later in seventeenth-century Catherington. Thomas Kinch, who died in 1680 had a shoemaker's shop, the contents of which were valued at only £1[38] and George Hawtrell who died early in 1671 lived in a two-storey house not dissimilar from Thomas Pitt's in size and the shoes, tools and leather in his shop were valued at £5, rather more than Pitt's. But his farming was on a much smaller scale, having five-and-a-half acres of wheat and one acre of vetches sown, with his sole livestock being 10s worth of pigs. The total value of his possessions came to £22 16s 6d (£22 82), but he clearly had not managed his affairs successfully, since he owed debts to eleven people, including a tanner who presumably supplied his leather, of over £40.[39]

In the second half of the seventeenth-century and the first half of the 18th century the pressure of population in England receded as growth slowed down. In 1650 the population was five and one quarter million people and actually fell to five millions by 1700, afterwards rising to five and three-quarter millions by 1750. In Blendworth and Catherington the Compton Census of 1676 suggests that the population might have fallen slightly since 1603 to 125 and 377 respectively.[40] In Britain agricultural output, aided by better methods of production, began to increase and by the end of the 17th century England was exporting grain surpluses to Western Europe, while the price of grain was beginning to fall. Exports of grain helped to offset the increasing imports of commodities for general consumption. In previous centuries trade had been mainly inter-European, except for such commodities as spices, but the opening up of the New World led to growing imports of goods which were difficult to produce in Europe. Foremost among these were sugar and tobacco, followed by tea, coffee and cocoa especially in the early 18th century. But large quantities of imported groceries at the ports had to be distributed inland and the traditional weekly markets and annual fairs were inadequate mechanisms. What was needed were premises which could hold stocks of the imported goods and retail them daily—hence the growth of shops in the 17th century, especially in larger towns and then gradually into villages.

The first of these recorded at Catherington was as early as January 1675 when shopkeeper Richard Biggs died.[41] Not surprisingly, his was a general store—there would have been insufficient demand for specialist shops except in a few cases such as butcher, shoemaker or mercer. Such establishments had only a limited range of commodities for sale and thus give little clear picture of life generally, for instance when William Souter, father of Biggs Souter died in Catherington in June 1685, he was a mercer with a shop, the contents of which were described as "small wares and other cloth of wool and linen" all valued at £10. By comparison, Richard Biggs' shop contained a variety of goods including textiles of greater value than those of William Souter. Fortunately, they were all listed. He had

30 yards of woollen cloth in low priced remnants,	£3 15s 0d
3 remnants of serge and two of linsey wolsey (mixed flax and wool)	£1 2s 0d
6 remnants of cotton being 40 yards	£2 13s 4d
50 ells[42] (62.5 yards) of canvas some at 10d some at 12d	£2 10s 0d
30 ells (37.5 yards) of locram[43] (linen) in remnants	£1 10s 0d
Thread and buttons and silk (thread?) and other small things	£1 10s 0d
Stockings and tape } Pitch and tar	£1 0s 0d
Crocks (earthen pots), oyl (olive oil?), soap, sugar	£1 2s 4d
Fruit and strong water (alcoholic spirits)	9s 6d
Glasses and brooms	2s 6d
Additionally, in the house were four tods (112lbs) of olive oil	£2 16s 0d
½ hundred of cheese and 3lbs (59lbs)	12s 0d

quantities which suggest they were for retailing.

It is noticeable that, although textiles formed the bulk of the value apart from the canvas, all the cloths were remnants which, presumably, would not compete with the mercer and also be cheaper and, for those customers making their own clothes, the haberdashery items—thread, buttons, silk, presumably for embroidery, and tape -would obviously be useful. The rest of the listed stock was very varied. Pitch and tar were used for preserving timber and seemed more like the materials of a builder. Crocks would be for cooking pots and the oil for cooking. Fruit may have been fresh or dried, probably the latter as the listing was made in January when little or no fresh fruit would have been available. Alcoholic spirits normally would have been found in an inn, but were sold along with the glasses from which to drink them. Sugar was one of the new imports and clearly had made its way to this small shop in rural Hampshire—though noticeably without tea or coffee. It was most likely being used as a sweetener in cooking.

Missing from the shop's contents were such staple items as bread, butter and milk because most people, in an agricultural community, would have produced their own. Unusually, however, Biggs seemed to have very little to do with farming. There was no reference to crops being grown or to livestock. Only in his room over the hall, where three-quarters of barley and one quarter of malt were stored and in his room above the shop where he had 59lbs of cheese, were there indications of farming. Both of these upper rooms also contained feather beds, so it would seem that sleeping in smelly rooms was quite common, especially in an agricultural village which, more than likely, contained more livestock than people with their associated odours and manure. With no piped water or sewage, the human condition would not have been much different. Larger communities such as Petersfield or Havant would have been even smellier, containing tallow chandlers and soap boilers, each rendering down animal fat by boiling to make their products. Oddly Biggs' shop had no candles, but it does offer a rare glimpse into the lives of our 17th century ancestors.

However, probate inventories only provide a look at the lives of those who were wealthy or made wills—often the same group. As today, many people did not make a will hence, some two-thirds of those who were included as householders on the Hearth Tax of 1665 did not appear in the probate records. Almost all those who did not pay tax (24 per cent of the households) and many others were, therefore, excluded from this glimpse of life in 17th century Horndean. For it is in this century that the name of Horndean is found in the records. There is, of course, the oft quoted 14th century charter stating that "the men of the Manor of Chalton have the right to pasture their beasts in the Forest of Bere from Rolokscatel (Rowlands Castle) to Dene".[44] Even so, this does not say Horndean, nor does it confirm that there was a centre of population, however small. But in 1615, when John Padwick died, his probate inventory stated that he was of Horndean. Three years later came a second reference in the will of Robert Randoll.[45] That two men of property were living in the one place at the same time suggests the presence of an already established community, hence Horndean certainly existed in the 16th century, which coincidentally is when Portsmouth began to grow from about 450 people in 1552 to about 800 in 1603, its expansion being encouraged by the naval development of the port. Horndean was fortunately placed on the road from London at a junction, which meant travellers could go via Havant if they wished to avoid the hazards of the long unbroken stretch through the forest of Bere. As it happens, the prudent did, as indicated by Samuel Pepys who wrote on 23 April 1662 "up early, and to Petersfield; and thence got a countryman to guide us to Havant, to avoid going through the forest." However, this junction could have been the vital location which made the seventeenth century parish rather different from the sixteenth century one. Whereas in the 16th century the occupations from the probate records were almost entirely agricultural, in seventeenth-century Catherington blacksmiths, shoe makers, carpenters, bricklayers, shopkeepers, and a wine taster and bottler could be found, altogether suggesting a broadening economy, moving slowly away from an entirely agricultural society. The appearance of bricklayers indicates that the buildings too were changing from the timber framed houses of medieval and Tudor times, such as the Tudor cottages in Catherington Lane, to brick built ones, bricks being supplied from kilns at Rowlands Castle and Padnell. Even so, Thomas Hobbs, the bricklayer, who died in 1685, was still involved in farming, having four acres of wheat in the field and 17 sheep, four cattle, one horse and two pigs. Giles Freeborne, who died in 1668, was a carpenter whose connection with the land was limited to two pigs and one horse, on which he would have travelled to work. Carpentry was clearly his main activity since almost half (48 per cent) of his total possessions, valued at £11 16s (£11.80 p) was the value of his wood—boards and planks—and his working tools. New brick built houses would need wooden floors and window frames at least. He lived in a two-storey house of at least six rooms.[46]

Also living in a two-storey house was yeoman Richard Quallett. He had a hall, parlour, kitchen, buttery and milk house downstairs and further rooms above his hall and parlour. As there were five fire places in his house, it would seem to have been well appointed. His total possessions were valued at over £70, so he was not among the richest farmers, possibly because, somewhat unusually, his pastoral activities were secondary to his arable. He had only eight sheep, eight cattle, five horses and 13 pigs, the latter suggesting he had access to the Forest. His livestock were valued at over £28, but his grain in the barn was worth £30. Quallett died in October 1666, shortly after harvest time, so had no crops in the fields to indicate his land holding. His real significance lies in the fact that he gave his family name to his holding—Quallett's Grove—and that became the location of Merchistoun Hall[47] in the south of the parish and hence, near or in the Forest of Bere.

Apart from Francis Searle, wine cooper, a person employed in sampling and bottling wine, there is an absence of representatives of the drinks trade in the probate records and Searle's seems an unlikely occupation for a small agricultural community. Perhaps when he died in 1696, he had come to Catherington to retire—there were certainly no Searles listed in the Hearth Tax assessment of 1665.[48] Perhaps innkeepers were not wealthy enough or did not usually produce wills, for property deeds show that an old *Katryngton Inne* existed.[49] Probably a 16th century inn, it was bought by John Frie, an East Meon surgeon, for £85 with John Chamberlen continuing as the tenant. Its use as an inn appears to have declined in the late seventeenth-century, part of it being used as a blacksmith's shop. It was located where the northern driveway into St Catherine's now exists and presumably began to suffer from the establishment of the newer *Farmer Inn* across the road.

Liquid refreshment was also essential for the large number of livestock in the parishes. The larger farms had their own ponds, as also had the villages, but for the people there would have to be wells, since neither village had the benefit of running water by means of stream or river. As populations grew, more wells would be needed and this process can be seen in an indenture of February 1616, when William Kenche, husbandman, son of John the elder of Catryngton, agreed to pay six pence a year for access to a well dug on the land of John Bridger, coverletmaker of Catryngton.[50]

John Kenche probably lived a little further south in Catherington Lane than the old inn, but was not the first to live there, for in 1603 a John Kinch, yeoman of Catherington died. He was the first of a series of John Kenchs (or Kinch) who died in Catherington—in 1625, 1685 and 1719. All were described as yeomen and have left their name at Kinches Farm where they were almost certainly responsible for the building of the "great wheeled well" mentioned in 1692, which was a man operated treadwheel for raising water from the well in an outhouse next to the farm. The last John Kinch died leaving his nephew John Kinch of Pulborough in Sussex as his heir. The nephew sold "the dwelling house, formerly an inn, malthouse, barns, stables, Garden, Orchard, Wells and rents from wells to Biggs Souter for £80.[51] The treadwheel was essential because of the depth from which water had to be raised, particularly in dry summers. Catherington being some 400 ft above sea level often required wells of up to 300 ft deep, so raising water was not easy, hence the use of treadwheels. They, however, were rare most wells raising water by winding up a bucket on a rope or chain. All the major farms and houses in the parishes had their wells and parish wells were dug too for the benefit of those with no access to a personal well. Horndean had one in the Square and at least 28 are known to have existed in Catherington and Horndean, a further nine in

Blendworth and 11 in Lovedean.[52] Their depths ranged from the 298 feet of the well at St Catherine's House to 13 feet at Causeway Farm Cottage. There, the water level was only two feet below the surface whilst that at St Catherine's was 266 feet below.

Despite evidence of some change in 17th century Catherington, there was little evidence of change in the smaller village of Blendworth,—known occupations remaining those of an agricultural community. In any case, the Duke of Beaufort who became lord of the manor of Chalton in 1699, when he had a survey of his new manor carried out, still retained considerable power, the extent of which can be judged by comparing the 36 households of the Hearth Tax of 1665 with the 33 copyholdings—land held by a person having a copy of a manorial court roll, indicating a right to hold the property. Clearly, very few, if any, in Blendworth fell outside the direct influence of the manorial lord. Additionally, there were 11 freeholds of Chalton manor in the parish. Not all these holders of land would be residents of Blendworth, but the fact that the total acreage of the copyholds came to over 900, gives some indication of the power of the manorial lord, since Blendworth was composed of just over a total of 2300 acres and some was common downland and forest. Similarly, Catherington had 19 copyholders with a total of over 1250 acres under manorial control and 22 freeholders in the manor of Five Heads as well as further freeholders in the Catherington tithing of Chalton manor. It was not feudal England, but the manorial lord still expected his rents and some of the tenants still had to pay the annual rental sum plus two capons! Rents for copyholds tended to be small, but these were offset by the payment of much larger sums as an entry fine for a new tenant on the death of the previous one. In the Court Survey of Chalton manor in 1699, Pyle Farm was the largest copyholding in Blendworth parish, it being 154 acres and let at an annual rent of £46, but had an entry fine of £480. Furthermore, the survey shows that on Blendworth Down there was a windmill, its lease stating "the windmill situate on Blendworth Down within the parish of Blendworth, and all the Mill Wheels, Coggs, Stones and every utensil and implement for the grinding of corn". Thus, at least by the 17th century, Blendworth had its own mill.

In Catherington, the largest copyhold was Five Heads Farm, an undertaking of a considerable 306 acres by 1687 and leased to Robert Brett for £75 per annum with an entry fine of a massive £820. Brett must have hoped both for good harvests and a long life in order to save the money. But the community was less dominated by the lord of Chalton than was Blendworth, for Catherington had over 5250 acres and a much smaller proportion controlled directly by the manorial lord. Hence, opportunities for change would be greater, especially with large quantities of common land and forest.[53]

In any case, by the close of the 17th century another force was beginning to bring change from outside. During this century Portsmouth had grown from less than 800 people to over 5000 and Gosport from under 600 to over 2500. Situated on either side of Portsmouth Harbour, they had grown to dominate south-east Hampshire. Not even massive plague deaths in 1665–66 could prevent Portsmouth's growth, fuelled by the Admiralty decision to expand Portsmouth as the nation's premier naval base. In 1687 the Dockyard employed 294 men, by 1711 more than 2000 worked there.[54] It was Catherington's, or more accurately Horndean's good fortune, to lay at a crucial point on the main road from the Admiralty in London to the naval and military town which was developing nine miles south—just the distance for the last change of horses on the London-Portsmouth carriage route, or where thirsty soldiers and sailors could stop for a drink. The *Anchor, Red Lion* and *Ship and Bell Inn*, established before 1695, were ready to assist them in this process. Thus, it was Horndean which was to become the parishes' focal point of development in the 18th century.

References

1. Stratton, *Agricultural Records*, p. 41.
2. F J Fisher, 'Influenza and Inflation in Tudor England', *Ec.H.R.* 2nd ser., XVIII (1965), pp. 120–9; Wrigley and Schofield, *Population History*, pp. 212, 336.
3. A. L. Beier, *Masterless Men. The vagrancy problem in England 1560–1640*, pp. 17–9, 38–9.
4. *V C H Hants*, II, p. 73.
5. PRO E179/181 Lay Subsidy Roll, 1525, which lists taxed heads of households. Catherington had 40 and Blendworth 26. A multiplier of 4.5 was used to convert these to population totals.
6. The figure for 1603 is obtained from BL Harleian 495 ff237–39 Liber Cleri communicants list, using a multiplier of 5/3 to convert adult communicants to total population.
7. Stapleton in *Portsmouth Region*, p. 90.
8. Stratton, *Agricultural Records*, p. 74; J. Thirsk (ed.), *The Agrarian History of England and Wales 1500–1600*, IV, p. 820.
9. C R Davey (ed.), *The Hampshire Lay Subsidy Rolls, 1586*, Hampshire Record Series, IV, 1981, pp. 20–21.
10. HRO 1598A/5/2 probate inventory of Humphrey Aylward.
11. For historians it was helpful if farmers died in summer before harvest, when all the crops recorded in the probate inventory would have been in the fields, thus giving a good indication of the range of produce and size of the farm.
12. HRO 1561U/17, inventory of John Foster.
13. HRO 1569B/57/2, inventory of John Padwicke. Later inventories contained no references to weapons.
14. HRO 1591A/5/2, inventory of Nicholas Barnard; 1628A/4/2, inventory of John Barnard; W G Hoskins, 'The Rebuilding of Rural England 1570–1640, *Past and Present*, IV, 1953, reprinted in Hoskins *Provincial England*, 1963, pp. 131–48.
15. HRO 1592AD/92, inventory of John Shorter.
16. Stratton, *Agricultural Records*, p. 41.
17. Hoad and Webb in *Portsmouth Region*, pp. 35–56.
18. HRO 1559U/74/2 inventory of Thomas Foster.
19. HRO 1584A/33/2 inventory of Richard Higgens.
20. HRO 1581B/109/2 inventory of Richard Stephen.
21. HRO 1598AD/54, inventory of John Padwycke.
22. HRO 1605A/35/ 1–2, will and inventory of William Hall.
23. *V C H Hants*, III, pp. 96–99; Davey, *Lay Subsidy, 1586*, p. 20; Elizabeth Hughes and Philippa White (eds.), *The Hampshire Hearth Tax Assessment 1665*, Hampshire Record Series, II, 1991, p. 126.
24. HRO Index to probate records by place name 1570–1700.
25. *V C H Hants*, III, p. 97.
26. Barry Stapleton, *Hampshire of 100 Years Ago*, 1993, p. 9.
27. *V C H Hants*, III, p.97.
28. Weston's *A Discours of Husbandrie used in Brabant and Flanders*, was first published in 1650 and Worlidge's *Systema Agriculturae, in 1669*.
29. HRO 1679AD/94/2, inventory of Richard Pink; 1690B/8/2, inventory of Robert Bryant.
30. PRO E179 /176/565 Hearth Tax Assessment, Easter 1665; Hughes and White, *Hearth Tax Assessment, 1665*, pp. 126–27.
31. HRO 1671A/94/2, inventory of Richard Poate.
32. PRO E179/176/565 Hearth Tax 1665; Hughes and White, *Hearth Tax*, p. 126; HRO 1685A9/2 inventory of William Biden.
33. HRO 1592A/65/2, inventory of William Kent.
34. Definitions from the Oxford English Dictionary, 10 vols.

35 Stapleton, *Portsmouth Region*, pp. 91–93.
36 HRO 1597AD/27, inventory of Nicholas Cover.
37 HRO 1633A/60/2, inventory of Thomas Pitt.
38 HRO 1680B/29/2, inventory of Thomas Kinch.
39 HRO 1671A/63/2, inventory of George Hawtrell.
40 Wrigley and Schofield, *Population History*, pp. 528–29; Stapleton, *Portsmouth Region*, p. 91; William Salt Library, Stafford, MS. Salt 33, Compton Census communicants list using multiplier of 5/3 to convert adults to total population; HRO B/2/A 1725 Visitation Return; 21/M/65 1788 Visitation Return.
41 HRO 1675A/9/2, inventory of Richard Biggs
42 An English ell, a measurement of the length of cloth, equalled 45 inches.
43 Lockram took its name from a Brittany village which was known for the production of linen.
44 See for example *Horndean Conservation Area*, E.H.D.C., 1977, p. 1.
45 HRO 1615AD/62, inventory of John Paddick; 1618A/54/1, will of Robert Randoll.
46 HRO 1684AD/78, inventory of Thomas Hobbs; 1668B/24/2, inventory of Giles Freeborne.
47 HRO 1666A/73/2, inventory of Richard Quallett; Hughes and White, *Hearth Tax*, p. 126, Anon. *Merchiston Hall*, typescript, p. 3.
48 HRO 1696A/89/2, inventory of Francis Searle; Hughes and White, *Hearth Tax*, pp. 126–27.
49 PCRO 170A/1/3–13, deeds relating to *Old Catherington Inn*.
50 PCRO 170A/1/1, indenture between John Bridger and William Kenche.
51 HRO 1603B/35/1, will of John Kench; 1625B/32/1, will John Kench; 1681B/26 will of John Kinch senr.; 1719AD/74, inventory of John Kench; HRO 57M92/2 Clarke-Jervoise Estate Papers. The tread-wheel was removed to the Weald and Downland Museum, Singleton, in the late 1960s.
52 HRO 43M75/F/B87; 57M92/4 Clarke-Jervoise Estate Papers.
53 HRO 6M59/Box2/2; 18M64/Box3/22; 43M75/M3; 57M92/2 Clarke-Jervoise Estate Papers.
54 Stapleton in *Portsmouth Region*, pp. 91–95.
55 HRO 57M92/1 Clarke-Jervoise Estate Papers.

Chapter 5

The Eighteenth Century

England in the eighteenth century was a nation in transformation. Agriculture, the main occupation, continued its change from medieval open fields to enclosed ones, a process increasing in pace in the later decades of the century, when major innovations altered the textile and iron and steel industries and technological inventions saw the application of steam power. Turnpike roads and canals improved the speed and quality of travel and the numbers of people in the country began to increase slowly from 5 to 5.75 millions in the first half of the century, but at an unprecedented rate in the second half so that by 1800 some 8 million people lived in England and Wales.[1]

For the most part Blendworth and Catherington were only marginally affected by the changes. Blendworth's population remained relatively stable until the last 20 years of the century when baptisms rose and, in 1800, the population was 174. Catherington's fluctuated until the 1770's when large increases in baptisms began and, by 1801, its population was estimated at over 550.[2] Thus, population changes were more noticeable only in the last quarter of the eighteenth century. However, whereas the nation's population had grown by 80 per cent between 1700 and 1800, that of the two parishes had risen by only just over half that amount, all of which could be accounted for in the surplus of baptisms over burials in the registers of the parishes during the century's last two decades. Apart from the fact that the majority of the parishes' residents would still be either landholders or landworkers it would seem that the development of the London Road did little to enhance growth and perhaps it has to be accepted that the road could just have easily been the means of people's departure as to encourage them to stay, hence the fluctuations in Catherington's population before 1770. It was not that opportunities were not present in nearby Portsmouth, as demonstrated by the growth of Portsea Island's population from some 6 or 7,000 people in 1700 to 33,000 by 1800, vastly outpacing the growth of the nation's population.[3] In the process of this possible 500 per cent increase, many employment opportunities would have been created to entice the young and more adventurous to leave their local communities. But it was a two way process since the growth of such a centre of population would have made increasing demands upon the surrounding district, especially for food, so local large farmers would have a ready market for milk, butter, cheese, meat and grain. Similarly, as Portsmouth's naval dockyard expanded and more ships were built or repaired, so the Forest of Bere supplied thousands of mature oaks for the wooden warships, so much so that when a Royal Commission surveyed the Forest in 1792 it discovered very few mature oaks for the navy were left. Undoubtedly, some of the local residents had benefited from this process. Thus, yeoman like John Kench of Catherington, who died in January 1720, and Joseph Padwick of Blendworth, who died in 1732, had inventories with higher values—over £700 and almost £270 respectively.[4] Interestingly Kench appears to have supplemented his farming activities, valued at some £240, with money lending. He had loaned £200 on bonds on which interest of just over £8 was due. Thus, he was lending at 4 per cent per annum, but to put his interest earnings in perspective, they represented more than 50% of a labourer's annual wage of £14 to £15! Kench was a good example of how rural credit was provided in an age before banks were established outside London. The wealthier members of society would find it profitable to use surplus capital in loans to those wishing to expand or even maintain their farms in difficult times. His loans to six people were between £10 and £100 each and, in addition, he was renting property too. The Kenches had obviously done so well that, not only did they live in a three storey house, (it had a cellar) with at least ten rooms, but they could also act as unofficial bankers to some of their neighbours. The need for such credit could imply that there was some economic growth in the parish.

By comparison, Blendworth's Joseph Padwick lived in similar comfort in a house also with a cellar but with eleven other rooms, including a mill house and a brew house. But the rest of Padwick's wealth was tied up in his farm on which he had 151 sheep, 18 cattle, 7 horses and 13 pigs, plus 74 acres sown with crops. He died in May, hence all his crops were in the ground—23 acres of wheat, 28 acres of barley, 17 acres of oats and 6 acres of peas and vetches. The wheat was worth £30 and the rest together £35. His livestock were valued at £88.10s (£88.50). He had bacon and pork in the house and wheat, barley, peas and oats in the barn. His farming activities were, thus, indistinguishable from any of his predecessors in the previous 200 years. The same crops, the same livestock, the same house contents, only the values had risen and inflation in 200 years would have caused much of that. What this indicates is that Blendworth, where Padwick resided, had remained a small, unchanging community whereas Catherington, or more accurately Horndean, was demonstrating more clearly the growing capitalism in society. However, one other similarity was that both yeomen had invested some of their wealth in new houses since previously, no mention of cellars had appeared. Now, new brick built houses with excavated cellars and, no doubt, greater space were being constructed for the better off.

Another house with a cellar was that of Catherington widow Elizabeth Pledger, who died in June 1715.[5] She too, therefore, lived in a 'modernised' house, but her income came from her shop and its contents show how much consumer choice had expanded in the 40 years since shopkeeper Richard Biggs died in 1685. Again it was a general store which sold several different kinds of tape including stout cotton, coarse tape and linen tape, five different types of thread including three qualities of silk thread, coventry—a blue thread also for embroidery, and ordinary threads. In addition, gartering (presumably elastic), remnants of worsted, whipcord and other cloths along with laces, needles, pins, thimbles, thread buttons and brass buttons were all provided for those, usually ladies, who wished to make and embroider their own clothes. Indigo, a blue dye, and alum, a dyestuff fixative, were also stocked, along with blue starch, and ordinary starch for treating the clothing when completed. Other household goods were 20 lbs of candles, soap, beeswax, resin and brimstone, and 4d combs were additionally available. Two different qualities of paper were sold as well as wrapping paper (cap paper).

In groceries there was much more evidence of imported goods than 40 years earlier. A wide range of spices—pepper, cloves, mace, ginger, allspice (a mixture of cinnamon, nutmeg or cloves) and caraway seeds were all provided. Three different qualities of sugar as well as treacle and candy were stocked, as was tobacco. Thus the two major imports of the late seventeenth and early eighteenth centuries were being consumed locally, but it seems that people still preferred to brew their own beer rather than drink tea or coffee since neither appear in the stock of Elizabeth Pledger's shop. Of course, there may have been other shops which sold them, along with other goods, nevertheless the contents of the widow's shop gives an unusual insight into some of the items which our ancestors were purchasing in the early eighteenth century.

In November 1756, came the last of the surviving probate inventories for the two parishes and it was significant in two ways. First, it confirmed the existence of a mill in Blendworth for it was the inventory of John Taylor, miller[6] who lived in an eight roomed house, plus a cellar. He also had flour and wheat in the mill with sacks and dressing cloths. He had a brewing room and also a chamber containing hops plus 1000 hop poles, so it would appear that he was growing a new crop in the area. But he also farmed in the traditional way, although on a smaller scale, having corn and hay in his barn and 7 sheep, 1 bullock, 2 horses and 5 pigs. But it was not in relation to his farming that the miller was significant in a second way, but to a particular item listed in his house, for in his kitchen he had a clock in its case. More than any other item in all the inventories this indicated the separation of the ancient parishes from modern times.

John Taylor is the only person who is known to have had a clock by the middle of the eighteenth century, but it seems likely that he would not have been the only one. Clocks began to be more widely used in the last decades of the seventeenth century and they represent the ability to measure time. Until then it was not possible to make appointments or have meetings at specific times—meetings could be in the morning or afternoon. Perhaps the only time in the week when people had to be at a particular place at a particular time was attendance at church on Sunday, hence the necessity of church bells to let the parishioners know when the services were about to start. For most the daily grind of work began at dawn and ended at dusk, with a much longer working day in summer. With the advent of clocks John Taylor, and others like him, were able to make appointments at specific times and thus more economically use their days. Even so, they would have been a minority of the wealthier members of the community who could have afforded a timepiece.

The measurement of time also became important for those who used the London-Portsmouth road through Horndean, as throughout the eighteenth century, increasing coach services were introduced to cater for the rising number of travellers. All the coaches operated to timetables giving starting times, usually from inns in Holborn, and departure times from similar ones in Portsmouth. Thus the landlord of the *Ship and Bell* would need to be aware of the approximate time of arrival in order that a change of horses would be ready and travellers would also need to know departure and arrival times. Not only was there an increase in coaches, but journey times were shortened. By the 1770s they were down to sixteen hours, still an arduous trek, but had been reduced to nine by 1805.

The growing volume of traffic was undoubtedly linked to Portsmouth's rise as a major naval and military town which necessitated an improvement in the road. Accordingly, in 1710 a Turnpike Trust was established to improve the southern end of the direct route to Portsmouth by creating a turnpike road between Sheet Bridge, north of Petersfield and Portsmouth. Shortly after the first meeting of the Trust, in June 1911, travellers along the road would have been expected to pay at tollbooths on Sheetbridge and Portsbridge and also at the toll house and toll gate built across the road at the Petersfield end of the village (it was demolished in 1965).[7] The Turnpike Trust used the income from the tolls to keep the road repaired to a reasonable standard, hence the reduction in journey times. But the increasing use of the road meant increasing repairs. In June 1711, it was estimated that £2,816 was required to repair the road between Horndean and Wait Lane End (now Waterlooville).[8] Yet in the 1720s and 1730s the highway surveyor was to repair the "most Broken and Dangerous parts of the High way leading through the Forest from Wait Lane End to Horndeane....." The flints, used in prehistoric times for axes and weapons, were now provided from Horndean for road repairs. Apart from the regular coaches, carrier and wagon services, mail carriers and marching troops, as well as local farmers and others all placed the road under constant strain. A great diversity of travellers passed through the village to its economic benefit and especially to that of the three inns along the road, especially where the last change of horses occurred.[9]

Perhaps the need for the turnpike road was emphasised in July 1706 when some 400 Swiss and Walloon troops passed through Horndean on their way to the Isle of Wight, since wagons with ordnance may well have been needed too. Certainly, in 1759, wounded Scots soldiers from the battle at Ticonderoga were transported through and no doubt the injured Highlanders would have been grateful for the better surface of the turnpike road.[10] Two years later 50 wagons of ordnance rumbled through the village on their way to Portsmouth for an expedition in the Seven Years' War and the following year in 1762, twenty wagons guarded by 40 marines carrying £616,000 worth of booty, captured from the ship Hermione, rolled by.[11] In 1787 1,000 Hessian soldiers marched through Horndean on their way to Portsmouth before embarking for India.[12] Times of war clearly substantially increased the volume of traffic through the village and since almost half the eighteenth century was spent at war, many additional travellers were recorded on the road.

With the eighteenth century growth of empire and the consequent increasing importance of the navy and army, the Portsmouth road must have become one of the major arterial roads of England. There are numerous recorded travellers, but vastly more in coaches, wagons, on horseback or foot must have passed unrecorded through Horndean, bringing rising economic prosperity and change.

While the wooded valley in which Horndean lay was experiencing some transformation, the two villages of Blendworth and Catherington remained relatively unchanged being still dominated by both church and manor. The church organised not only ecclesiastical affairs but also lay parochial matters, being involved in the appointment of parish officers—overseers of the poor and surveyors of the highways, as well as churchwardens, at the annual Easter vestry meetings. Thus, in small communities such as Blendworth and Catherington, the church exerted a considerable influence. At Blendworth, since rectors have been appointed since 1303, a church must have existed from at least that time. Even so, no trace of an early building remains, although a Churchwardens Account and Vestry Minute Book survives from 1705.[13] It indicates that a new and enlarged church of St Giles was built in 1759 on the road leading from Chalton to the manorial lands. In November, 1759 John Marman was paid £96 12s (£96.60) for building it and William Minchin Jnr received £35 5s 5d (£36.27) for all "the carpentering work". Why such a small community needed a new church the Vestry Book does not say. Perhaps, the previous building had become an old and unsafe structure. Certainly, the previous half century had been one of some severe gales, the worst of which had been in 1703. In November, eighteen days of windy weather culminated in a hurricane on Friday 26th and Saturday 27th. Many houses, barns and trees were blown down. Eddystone Lighthouse was washed away and twelve warships sunk off the coast. Many lives were lost in what was thought to be the most violent gale ever recorded in England, but in the south it was surpassed by another on December 7th and 8th, and the year ended with more violent gales on December 27th and 28th. In the years 1712, 1729, 1736, 1739 and 1753 there were more gales.[14] Old structures would have taken a battering and were much more likely to have suffered severely than new ones. Perhaps the weather also offers a further explanation for the building of houses with cellars. Sixteen years before the new church was built, however, the church wardens produced an account in 1743 of seating in the old church.[15] It showed that the building held about 60 people, plus the poor, who sat or stood at the back. This was because the others bought their 'seat rooms' within the church and were allocated pew spaces accordingly. Thus, seating tended to be hierarchical—the wealthiest, usually the manorial lord, having the best seats. As no manorial lord lived in Blendworth, no seat was needed for him. However, although Blendworth Church had pews allocated according to landholdings, it was segregated differently—by sex. The men sat in one set of pews and the women in another, but being a male dominated society, all the women's pews were allocated under their menfolk's names so, largely, the names in the women's pews reiterated those in the men's!

When the new church was built it appears to have been little or no larger than the old one, since a new seating plan for the parish church when built, was produced in January 1759.[16] It also showed seating for about 60 people plus benches at the back, and a gallery presumably for the poor. However, although retaining the purchasing of seats by landholdings, a normal practice in eighteenth century parish churches, it did attempt some Christian progress by mixing men and women together on the same pews—sexual segregation was not a usual practice. The only other change was to move the pulpit from the centre to the front of the church, indicating the growing importance of sermons in the church service. From the later Middle Ages the priest had the assistance of two lay churchwardens, one chosen by the priest and the other elected annually. From the sixteenth century, with the introduction of the poor law, they were joined by overseers of the poor and also by surveyors of the highways once parishes became responsible for the upkeep of roads in Elizabethan times. In many communities those duties were undertaken by a relatively small number of the more prominent landholders or small businessmen. Blendworth was no exception, in some cases the official positions passing through generations of the same family. Thus, members of the Padwick family held the office of churchwarden for some 30 years in the eighteenth century and the Hoares for 20 years.[17] Frequently, they were also overseers of the poor. The churchwardens were responsible for the maintenance of the fabric of the church and churchyard, and for assisting poor travellers on their way, for example in March 1714 they paid "to a woman with a child that has ye smal poxe", one shilling. They were also responsible for the control of vermin—in Blendworth's case, foxes and sparrows. Almost every year between 1714 and 1750 they paid sums for the destruction of foxes and, from 1731 into the nineteenth century, for sparrows' heads.

One major function of the churchwardens was to levy and collect the church rate which raised money for church and churchyard repairs. In 1705 the rate was 2d in the £ and 25 contributors were listed, some having to pay on both leasehold and freehold land. The rate fluctuated depending on the need for church repairs, but had become 2s 3d in the £ by 1810 when 28 people paid, suggesting that any growth in population had not been among the landholders, but among the poor and landless. The building of a gallery in the new church in 1759 for the poor, suggests they may have been increasing in number, but firmer evidence comes from the existence of a parish poor house which was built on the Western corner of the junction of Woodhouse Lane (from St Giles Church past Pyle Farm) and Greenhook Lane (now Rowlands Castle Road) and would have been the responsibility of the overseers.

There is little doubt that, were the evidence to survive, the churchwardens and overseers of the poor of Catherington would have been seen to carry out very similar duties in very similar ways. The Norman church seems to have had few, if any, of the problems of Blendworth church being well maintained and having a new red-brick storey added to the tower in 1750, to accommodate a peal of bells. Thus, money was collected by the churchwardens to develop the existing church. These local unpaid officials were the local authority of their times and were regarded as such, thus frequently when wealthier residents died and wished to establish a charity, they left sums of money to be administered by the churchwardens and overseers of the poor. For instance, William Appleford left £200 in his will "to the Churchwardens and Overseers of the Poor of the Parish of Blendworth....to the intent that the Interest and Profits....shall be layed out....in putting out Poor Children to School and buying off Books for them."[18] Seventeen acres of land and a house in Lovedean were purchased and the rents used for running a school, which was opened in 1702.[19] Similarly, Appleford left money for a school in Catherington, an estate of 12 acres in Barton Stacey producing £10 p.a. to help to defray the expenses.[20] Goodwives, usually married, local women of humble background, were paid for schooling the children and primers and bibles were bought periodically. Occasionally, local residents would contribute thus, in 1704, Biggs Sowter, a yeoman farmer, paid 11s 4d (57p) for books for poor children at the recently opened Blendworth school.[21] However, the administration of the finances of the schools remained with the churchwardens, but at least in the eighteenth century, poorer children were beginning to get some basic education, although much of it would have been in religious instruction.

Apart from the church, the other institution which continued relatively unchanged in eighteenth century communities was the manor. Hinton Daubnay was to remain in the Hyde family until the mid-eighteenth century when it passed to a cousin, Mr Tooker, whose family held it until the late twentieth century. Catherington Manor (Five Heads), sold to the Earl of Worcester, Lord of Chalton Manor in 1611, became part of the Chalton Manor estate which, including Blendworth and Catherington, was bought by the Duke of Beaufort in 1699 and sold to Jervoise Clarke-Jervoise in 1780 whose family held the manor until 1974.

At the beginning of the eighteenth century the manorial lands in Blendworth amounted to approximately 978 acres, and in Catherington, 336 acres with a further 300 acres in Five Heads manor. By 1774 the Blendworth acreage had risen to 1,187 and by the end of the century to 1,278, of which 970 acres were enclosed and 308 were commons on downs or pasture. Manorial lands in Catherington had also increased; in 1774 to 540 acres plus 325 in Five Heads and in 1799 to 590 acres and 425 respectively, a total of 1,015 acres.[22] Thus, the Lord of the manor's estate in Catherington had increase by 60 per cent, exactly double the rate in Blendworth. However, such figures hide the reality of lordship, for while the manorial lands in Catherington accounted for only just under 20 per cent of the total acreage of the parish, in Blendworth they amounted to more than half—57 per cent.[23] Hence, manorial influence was likely to be much more pervasive in the smaller community than the larger one. Blendworth parish had 32 copyholds and 26 copyholders. One resident had two copyholds and George Foster had six.[24] In addition, there were eleven freeholds in the parish, yet five of the freeholders also held copyholds, and three cottages at Woodhouse Ashes. One of the copyholds confirmed the existence of the "Windmill situate on Blendworth Down in the parish of Blendworth and all the Mill Wheel, Coggs, Stones and every utensil and implement for the grinding of corn".[25] Another copyhold, a blacksmith's shop in 1699 was a plot of some 360 square yards adjoining the west end of the *Red Lion* Inn. By 1735, the blacksmith's shop had gone, having been replaced by a stable, in 1769 the land had been reduced by a third to just over 240 square yards, because the *Red Lion* "hath lately been extended in length by 20 feet". Even so, eleven years later the extension had become 28 feet, and the remaining land transformed into a garden. Presumably, the *Red Lion* had been extended until it was adjacent to the London Road, demonstrating clearly the effect on one building of the growing importance of the road.

In Catherington Five Heads Manor the Lord of Chalton had 19 copyholds and 22 freeholds. Most of the holders of these lands were involved in the traditional mixed farming but occasionally other occupations are mentioned. Thus, a six acre freehold of Five Heads Manor situated in Lovedean also included the blacksmith's forge of Edward Barnard at the beginning of the eighteenth century. Similarly, a three acre freehold in Catherington was held by Richard Aldred, blacksmith. Both holdings were too small to be farmed on any scale and presumably only produced food for the families concerned. When Eleanor Randall inherited the Butts, a 27 acre freehold in Catherington, on the death of her husband Thomas, she leased it out provided she had access to her house and shop. Curiously, when Jervoise Clarke-Jervoise became Lord of Chalton Manor he bought all these three properties in the 1780s, offering one explanation for the growth in manorial acreage.

The copyholds of Five Heads Manor also shed a little light on eighteenth century Horndean. One copyhold of three acres had a house and workshop against the *Ship and Bell*, presumably where the cycle shop is now. In 1739 it was leased to William Carter, a tailor in Horndean. William's mother Ann had leased a nearby small copyhold described as 'at the lower end of Horndean Lane against the Smith's shop', (presumably this would now be Blendworth Hill and would be near the foot on the north side) and this passed to William on her death, staying in the Carter family until 1791, during which time it changed from a tailor's shop to a general store and in 1802 was taken on by Thomas Bettesworth. When the last William Carter died in 1791, one of the executors of his will, who had to see that the interest and properties went to his daughter Susannah, was Robert Luckens, wheelwright, who was also a copyholder of the manor and had leased one and a half acres adjacent to Catherington Down in Lower Petersfield Way (now Whitedirt Lane) where he had his wheeler's shop.

In 1733 when Thomas Randall, who held the Butts freehold died, he was also the tenant of Great and Little Wycocks. Copyholds of 40 and 25 acres respectively (they became the 65 acres Wecocks Farm), his widow Eleanor took on his tenancy. Thomas was a butcher in Catherington as was his son Thomas, so presumably the shop to which Eleanor retained access was a butcher's. Her son, however, was no businessman. Despite owning a considerable amount of property he was always in debt and the legacies in his father's will of 1733 remained unpaid for 42 years until 1775, and all the properties were mortgaged. By the 1790's the copyhold was in the hands of Henry Padwick and the freehold had been sold to the Lord of the Manor.

John Kinch, who farmed at Broadway Farm, not a manorial holding, at the beginning of the eighteenth century, took on two 38 acre copyholds in Catherington one by Parsonage Farm on the east side of Catherington Lane and the other by Roads Lane (now Roads Hill). Although these were held by the Kinch family for only 26 years until they died out, their name remained attached to the second of these copyholds (now Kinches Farm).

The largest of the Catherington copyholds was Five Heads Farm, which was estimated to have 224 acres of arable land, 22 acres of meadow and 30 acres of wood and coppices, a considerable farm by any standards at the beginning of the eighteenth century. In Blendworth the largest copyhold was Pyle Farm in Forest Lane, of 154 acres in 1700. By coincidence both these farms were held by the Rev. Thomas Franklyn, rector of Chalton, from the last years of the seventeenth century. Presumably, the rector was well known to the lord of the manor and most probably sub-let these two farms since he could hardly have carried out his spiritual duties and run two large farms. Franklyn died in 1710 and his widow, Thomasina, took over them both until her death when her widowed daughter Elizabeth Bramston took over the leases, until her death in 1753. It was then reported at the Manorial Court that "both Pile and Fiveheads Farmhouses were in ruinous condition". Why had the steward or bailiff of the manor allowed such circumstances to arise? No other copyhold was ever so described. It can only be assumed that this was a reflection of the influence of a family strongly connected to the church and thus, it was not thought appropriate to raise the subject of the state of the farmhouses, or that, because of their position in society, the Franklyn's simply felt able to ignore any requests for them to maintain the farmhouses properly. Whatever the position it explains why both Pyle and Fiveheads Farmhouses are eighteenth century buildings since both would have had to be rebuilt after 1753.[26]

Regulations for the way in which these manorial holdings would be operated by the tenants were issued from the Manorial Court. The number of horses, pigs and sheep on the commons were controlled—each copyhold had the specific number of sheep that could be folded on the commons clearly stated. Sheep were obviously of importance in the mixed farming economy. Not surprisingly, in Blendworth in 1710 George Foster, who had six copyholds, had the largest flock of 320 sheep but the average for each farmer was 65. Almost half a century later in 1756 when twelve farmers—owners, tenants and copyholders—were granted permission by the Duke of Beaufort, Lord of Chalton Manor, to plough over 200 acres of Blendworth Down, retaining 92 acres for pasture, there was seen to be very little change in sheep farming,[27] although the indication was that arable farming was of increasing importance. Since the local population was stable, perhaps this was an example of cereal growing for the rapidly expanding Portsmouth market.

Certainly, in the first half of the eighteenth century, English agriculture became more productive, so much so that England became one of the granaries of Europe with increasing quantities of surplus grain, mainly wheat, exported, and grain prices remaining low. However, by 1768, wheat prices which had averaged under 34s per quarter (28 lbs) in the 1740's, had risen to 53s 9d per quarter, and food riots occurred in many places.[28] Partly the cause was national population growth and partly inclement weather which was to continue, for in 1774 Gilbert White, of nearby Selborne, wrote of the previous decade "Such a run of wet seasons, a century or two ago, would, I am persuaded, have occasioned famine."[29] Even more rapid population growth in the second half of the eighteenth century, periodic bad harvests and war with France were to make matters worse, so that wheat prices rose to 75s per quarter in 1795, food was scarce and food riots widespread.[30] In wartime such economic and social distress was worrying for the government, which had no accurate knowledge of agricultural output in Britain. Thus, it was decided to request each parish incumbent to submit a return of the number of acres of each crop grown. Clover and artificial grasses for fodder were omitted. This census of crops was produced in 1801 and shows that in Blendworth parish 83 per cent of farmland was growing grain—171 acres of wheat, 90 acres of barley, 53 acres of oats, plus eight of peas. But some changes had occurred for there was an acre of potatoes and 55 acres (14.6 per cent) of turnips. Thus, the agricultural revolution, beginning in the seventeenth century had begun to have an impact in Blendworth by the second half of the eighteenth century. In Catherington, 1346 acres were cultivated with 1070 acres (79.5 per cent) being grain crops and 213 acres (15.8 per cent) being turnips. Thus, Catherington, had a very similar pattern of farming to that in Blendworth, which, since both shared the same manorial lord, is not surprising.[31]

These acreages included non-manorial, as well as manorial, holdings of land. However, for non-manorial farms, unless the individual farmers kept records which have survived, there is no information. Broadway Farm, was non-manorial, and that John Kinch was its farmer in the early eighteenth century is known only because he took on the two manorial copyholds. Horndean Windmill reported to have been built in 1729, was also non-manorial. It was a tower mill similar to Chalton and was in a state of disrepair by the early twentieth century.[32] Its location is unknown.

The eighteenth century growth of Horndean meant that the village began to be commented upon. Whereas travellers like Celia Fiennes in the late seventeenth century and Daniel Defoe in the early eighteenth century made no mention of the village, the Rev. Shaw travelling in 1788 wrote

> "From hence we approach the Forest of Bear, a large tract of woodland. Pass through the village of Hamden (Horndean), beyond which the country changes to extensive downs, the road widening through a deep vale, surrounded by noble hills of verdure, heaped in various forms; while the fleecy flocks, that strayed along their sides, with each a shepherd, with his crook and dog, made the same truly Arcadian."

At the turn of the century Horndean was described as a 'pretty little village'.[33] Not surprisingly, therefore, the parishes with their rural charm and good communications became attractive to those, especially naval officers, who found Portsmouth increasingly crowded. Thus, on August 20th 1764 Lieutenant (later Admiral) Samuel Hood, in search of a home near Portsmouth, leased a copyhold farmhouse and one acre with a promise of a newly built dwelling house and 36 acres from the Duke of Beaufort for 99 years.[34] The newly built dwelling house, plus a coach house, became the Georgian, Catherington House and was to be the Hood's family home even after Admiral Lord Hood, created Viscount Hood of Catherington in 1796, had retired from naval service and become Governor of Greenwich Hospital where he spent the last 20 years of his life. In 1770 Captain Hood, as he had become, being Governor of the Naval Academy at Portsmouth leased a manorial freehold, and in 1778, another copyhold the 38 acre Kinch's Farm, by which time Hood was Commander in Chief at Portsmouth.[35] Catherington House was to become a centre for entertaining some of the great and famous such as the Younger Pitt, Earl Howe the Lord Chief Justice and possibly Nelson.[36] Lord Hood's son, the Hon. Henry Hood, took on the house after his father's move to be Governor of Greenwich in 1796 and involved himself in farming. By the end of the century, by amalgamating six copyholds together, he had created a holding of 160 acres. It was the first example in Catherington of a trend which had been common throughout eighteenth century England—the amalgamation of a number of small farms into large units thus creating the modern farming structure of landlord, tenant farmer and agricultural labourer. The Horndean area was clearly late in joining in this activity.

Other large properties which were established in the parishes and helping to create an air of gentility around Horndean were Blendworth Cottage (now Lodge) built by John Hopper, and what is now Merchistoun Hall. This was in the hands of the Franklin family at least from 1699 until 1804, when it was known as Qualletts Grove, a 40 acre farm, from at least 1763 when it was held by Joseph Franklin.[37] One of the attractions for some, no doubt, was that a pack of harriers had been kept in Horndean, during the second half of the eighteenth century and it was presumed to be "a scenting and sporting country to be surpassed by very few".[38]

Large farms and large houses needed servicing. The large farms would have employed living-in farm servants hired by the year, who were in a better position than the agricultural day labourer. But, towards the end of the eighteenth century hiring-in declined as farmer's wives and daughters demanded greater privacy and segregation from servants and labourers as social class pretensions grew. Furthermore, farmers began to prefer, except for the more skilled jobs of cowherd and shepherd, casual labourers whom they could employ and dismiss at will, rather than ones who had to be housed and fed.

For the last twenty years of the century as wheat prices doubled [39] so labourers, both agricultural and general, found life increasingly difficult, as demonstrated in Blendworth Vestry Book which stated in November 1785 that parishioners had agreed to employ only labourers of their own parish,[40] an obvious reference to a growing problem of unemployment. Five years later it seems the problem had not been solved since rising poverty led to a proposition to establish a "Generall Workhouse for the Support of the Poor". But by 1795 it was the Speenhamland System, introduced at Speen in Berkshire, which was to be widely operated in southern England. It tied poor relief payments to the price of bread and the size of the family and acted as a disincentive to employers to pay adequate wages and thus passed the problem to all those in each parish who paid the poor rates, which were inevitably raised. Small farmers employing only family members came to be subsidising large ones who underpaid their labourers. Poor houses existed in both parishes, Catherington's being opposite the junction of Five Heads Road with the Portsmouth Road immediately north of the location of the Union Workhouse established in the next century.

At this time Britain was in the midst of the Industrial Revolution with steam powered factories growing in the North and Midlands and urban centres like Manchester, Birmingham, Sheffield, Leeds and Newcastle growing rapidly. Both Blendworth and Catherington's populations were also beginning to grow, but there was no evidence of an Industrial Revolution in the two communities. Indeed, it would seem that the Agricultural Revolution had only recently arrived.

References

1 Wrigley and Schofield, *Population History*, pp. 528–29.
2 Stapleton in *Portsmouth Region*, p. 102.
3 Ibid.
4 HRO 1719AD/74 inventory of John Kench; 1732AD/86 inventory of Joseph Padwick.
5 HRO 1715B/31/2 inventory of Elizabeth Pledger.
6 HRO 1757A/95/2 inventory of John Taylor.
7 Soffe, *The A3M Mortorway*, p. 4.
8 Barry Stapleton, *Waterlooville a Pictorial History*, 1996, n.p.
9 W Albert and P D A Harvey (eds.), *Portsmouth and Sheet Bridge Turnpike Commissioners' Minute Book 1711–54*, Portsmouth Record Series, 2, 1973, pp. 2, 65, 89, 97.
10 N Luttrell, *A Brief Historical Relation of State Affairs from September 1678 to April 1714* 6 vols., 1857, VI, pp. 53, 66; *Annual Review for 1759*, 8th edn., 1802, p. 77.
11 *Gentlemen's Magazine*, XXXI, 1761, p. 236.
12 *H C*, 759, 9 April 1787; D M Low (ed.), *Gibbon's Journal to January 28th, 1763*, 1929, pp. 110–11.
13 PCRO CHU40/2/1 Blendworth Churchwardens' Account and Vestry Minute Book, 1705–84, accounts for 1759–60.
14 Stratton, *Agricultural Records*, pp. 65–78.
15 PCRO CHU40/2/1 Vestry Book, accounts for 1743.
16 Ibid., accounts for 1758–59.
17 Ibid.; CHU40/2/2 Vestry Book, 1785–1862.
18 PCRO CHU40/4/4, papers re Appleford Charity.
19 PCRO CHU40/3/1, Blendworth Free School Account Book, 1702–1827.
20 HRO 21M65 B4/3/28, Visitation Return, 1788. The Barton Stacey land, four pieces of meadow bringing in £16 per annum, was sold in 1937 and the money invested in trust funds. (Horndean Parish Council Minutes).
21 PCRO CHU40/3/1, School Account Book, 1702–1827, passim.
22 HRO 57M92/2, Clarke-Jervoise Estate Papers.
23 The Inclosure Award of 1815 gives the acreage of Catherington as 5,139 and Blendworth as 2,232, HRO Q23/1/1 pp. 249–392.
24 HRO 6M59 Box2/2, Clarke-Jervoise Estate Papers, Manor of Chalton Court of Survey, 1699.
25 HRO 6M59 Box2/2, Clarke-Jervoise Estate Papers.

26 All the references to manorial freeholds and copyholds in Blendworth and Catherington are from HRO 57M92/1–2.
27 B Worton, 'The Parish of Blendworth, Hampshire 1700–1851, unpublished dissertation for Diploma in English Local History, Portsmouth Polytechnic (now University), 1986, pp. 22–23.
28 Stratton, *Agricultural Records*, pp. 75–81.
29 Gilbert White quoted in Stratton, *Agricultural Records*, p. 83.
30 Stratton, *Agricultural Records*, p.91.
31 R A Pelham, 'The Agricultural Revolution in Hampshire', *Proc. H F C*, XVIII, 1952, pp. 150–51.
32 A Keeble Shaw, 'Windmills and Watermills in Hampshire', *Proc. H F C*, XXI, 1958, pp. 108–09.
33 Rev. S. Shaw, 'A Tour to the West of England in 1788', in J Pinkerton (ed.), *A general collection of the best and most interesting voyages and travels in all parts of the world*, (17 vols., 1808–14), vol. 11, p. 312; L. Wolf (ed.), *Essays in Jewish History*, 1934, pp. 251–2, quoted in B. Stapleton and J. H. Thomas, *Gales, a Brewing, Business and Family History*, 2000, forthcoming.
34 HRO 57M92/2 Clarke-Jervoise Estate Papers.
35 Ibid.
36 *D N B* p. 1469. He was created Baron Hood of Catherington in 1782, a Lord of the Admiralty from 1788 to 1793, Admiral in 1794 and Viscount Hood in 1796.
37 HRO 57M92/2, Clarke-Jervoise Estate Papers.
38 *HT*, 298, 24 June 1805.
39 J D Chambers and G. E. Mingay, *The Agricultural Revolution 1750–1880*, 1966, pp. 112–13.
40 PCRO CHU40/2/2 Blendworth Churchwardens' Account and Vestry Minute Book 1784–1862, 10 November 1785.
41 Ibid., 24 November 1790.

Chapter 6
The Nineteenth Century

The nineteenth century opened inauspiciously, with grain prices at heights which would have been considered famine prices a decade or so earlier. Wheat prices averaged 113s 10d (£5.59) per quarter, 200 per cent higher than 15 years previously and more than twice the price of two years earlier. It was mostly a consequence of a run of wet summers and bad harvests in the late 1790s and 1800 was no better, with rains coming in August. Food was scarce and food riots occurred. Understandably, the following year saw prices even higher before a good harvest brought about a rapid fall but only to an average of 74s (£3.70) per quarter over the next seven years. Afterwards, bad harvests returned from 1809 to 1812, by which year wheat prices reached the highest annual average recorded in the Napoleonic Wars—126s 6d (£6.33) per quarter. A fine dry summer and good harvest in 1813 brought prices down by the end of the year, when wheat averaged 109s 9d per quarter (£5.48). In Portsmouth wheat prices fell from 123s 10d (£6.64) in January to 67s 10d (£3.39) in November.[1]

This rise in grain prices was also assisted by the continuance of the Napoleonic Wars and the increasing rate of growth of population. As a result of the price increases, the number of small farmers in England, which had been declining in the eighteenth century, actually rose, as more land was brought under grain and landlords issued increasing numbers of leases at higher rents which the higher prices covered. However, wars end and harvests improve and 1815 saw both, with the result that as prices tumbled, so did farmers incomes and leases had to be given up because rents were then too high and could not be paid.[2] An agricultural depression set in. Landlords, using their influence in Parliament, passed the Corn Laws in 1815, designed to artificially maintain high prices by preventing imports unless wheat was over 80 shillings per quarter—a famine price before the wars. It was not a policy which endeared itself to the poor, who had suffered badly throughout the high priced war years and hoped for some relief from cheaper grain. Not only was this not to be, but the numbers of poor rose as soldiers and sailors were demobilised, and Portsmouth's dockyard workforce was reduced from its peak of 4,000 to half that by the 1830's. Thus, pressure on the Poor Law authorities increased and so did their disbursements to the poor, enhanced by the continuingly growing population which doubled between 1800 and 1850 from eight to sixteen million people.[3] There were clearly too many people for the available employment opportunities once the Wars were over. In 1816 there was much distress and food riots and by the autumn of 1818 severe unemployment existed among the agricultural labourers of southern and eastern England, up to 60 per cent being unemployed.[4] Expenditure on poor relief was rising rapidly, exacerbating problems for small farmers who had to pay the poor rates.

Certainly this seems to have been the case in Blendworth which, contrary to the national experience, saw the number of owners and occupiers of land decline in the Napoleonic War period. In 1800 there were 31 landholders and 42 occupiers of whom 16 were owner-occupiers. Jervoise Clarke-Jervoise, the first lord of the manor to live within the Manor of Chalton at Idsworth House, along with his son Rev. Samuel Clarke, held more than half (53.3 per cent) the cultivated land. George Foster was the only other holder of significance with 13.5 per cent of the farmland. By 1811 the number of landholders had declined to 25 and the occupiers to 36.[5] The eighteenth century trend appears to have arrived late at Blendworth.

The enclosure of over 2000 acres of land in Chalton, Catherington, Clanfield, Blendworth and Idsworth in 1816[6] could only have assisted the decline of small farmers, since it was largely common lands which were enclosed for the benefit of a single individual, thus dispensing with the rights of common pasture of livestock which small farmers had enjoyed from time immemorial. Some 935 acres were enclosed in Catherington parish, mainly Catherington Common and Horndean and Catherington Downs, of which 540 were allocated to the Clarke-Jervoises, 132 acres being added to Five Heads Farm and 15 to Wecocks. A further 227 acres went to the Tookers, lords of the manor of Hinton Daubnay. Thus 82 per cent of the enclosed area was granted to the manorial lords, of which 58 per cent went to the Lord of Chalton. In Blendworth some 587 acres, mainly of Blendworth Common and Down, were enclosed. Of these 570 acres went to the Trustees of the late Thomas Clarke-Jervoise—a massive 97 per cent, only small fractions being left to others.[7] It should come as no surprise, therefore, to discover that the number of landowners in Blendworth had fallen to eighteen by 1821 and the number of tenants to 25.[8] Thus, over 40 per cent of both owners and occupiers had disappeared within 20 years. It was not only the enclosure of common land which encouraged this trend, but also the post-war agricultural depression which continued, and at least one of Catherington's copyholders found life too difficult. Thomas Harfield had taken on the Hon. Henry Hood's combined copyhold of approximately 150 acres and in 1816 was paying a rent of £122 per annum. Despite the fact that the rent was reduced in 1817 (£113), 1820 (£103), 1821 (£93) and 1822 (£70), Harfield was 'insolvent' in 1823 and the copyhold was split up, part going to Five Heads Farm and part to William Pescott's copyhold.[9] By 1851 in Blendworth, four men only owned over 96 per cent of the cultivated land, Sir Jervoise Clarke-Jervoise (61.7 per cent), the Reverend Edward Langton-Ward, rector of Blendworth (15 per cent), the Reverend John Astley, rector of Chalton (10 per cent) and a relative newcomer, Sir William Knighton (10 per cent). Five small landowners held the remaining 3.3 per cent. Only nine proprietors of land indicated that a decrease of 71 per cent had taken place since 1801. The number of tenants had fallen from 42 to 15 in the same period, a 64 per cent decline.[10] Only three farmers were listed in the 1851 census, but 40 men employed mainly as labourers, in agriculture.[11]

Most of those who disappeared joined the increasing number of agricultural labourers for whom employment opportunities fell in Blendworth by 28% between 1821 and 1831.[12] The more adventurous headed for the less healthy confines of Portsmouth and hoped for work in the town. Unfortunately, the reduction of the dockyard workforce, after the Napoleonic Wars, created a decline which continued until 1832. What made matters worse was that farmers, faced with high rents from the wartime period of expansion, bad harvests and inflation, reduced labourers' wages after the wars. In 1814 labourers had been paid between 12s and 15s a week, but by 1822 they were receiving only 9s to 10s a week,[13] rates that were to change little for the next 20 years. Labourers in work were thus under considerable pressure so, when threshing machines were introduced, threatening to reduce their limited opportunities for winter earnings from hand threshing, hostility grew. Poor harvests in 1828 and 1829[14] meant further reduced earnings for labourers' families, thus the spring of 1830 saw many hungry, cold and unemployed. Labourers, unwilling to have their incomes reduced in the coming winter of 1830-31, took to threshing machine breaking and the so-called Swing Riots occurred throughout southern England. Between 1830 and 1832, forty-five machines were smashed in Hampshire alone. In addition, riots, assaults and incendiarism took place.[15] A mob of 1,000 was reported, in November 1830, to have passed through Chichester and Emsworth destroying all the machinery it could find and then headed for Horndean and the Petersfield Road.[16] Local labourers may well have joined in and, at the least, witnessed the progress of the mob.

Jervoise Clarke-Jervoise, Lord of the Manor, was clearly alarmed by having such disturbances in his manorial enclave, and in June 1831 wrote to the Duke of Wellington, as Lord Lieutenant of Hampshire, asking for permission to raise a troop of yeomanry "for the preservation of the peace of this district consisting of part of the two counties of Hants and Sussex and comprising the towns of Horndean, Havant and Emsworth; with the adjacent villages. During the disturbances of last Autumn, considerable inconvenience was felt in the absence of any available force in the part of the country to which I refer,..."[17]

His request was granted but his fears of a repeat of the disturbances of the previous autumn were unwarranted as the Hampshire riots had largely died out. However, the labourers constant struggle against poverty had not. Increasingly, in the post-Napoleonic War decades the burden fell upon the poor rates. Both Catherington and Blendworth had established poor houses, the latter being on the north west corner of the junction of Green Hook Road (now Rowlands Castle Road) and Forest Road (now Pyle Farm Road) and a cottage for the poor was erected adjoining its west end in 1809.[18]

However, both poor houses were to become redundant following the Poor Law Amendment Act of 1834 which led to the establishment of Poor Law Unions and the erection in 1836 of a Union Workhouse just south of the existing Catherington poor house. A meeting at Blendworth in November 1790 had taken a decision to establish one "Generall Workhouse for the support of the Poor" for the combined parishes of Chalton, Catherington, Blendworth, Clanfield and Idsworth. It took 46 years, a growing problem of poverty and an Act of Parliament to accomplish it, but in its treatment of the poor the New Poor Law was decidedly worse, the poor being regarded as feckless and unwilling to work and hence, confined in the workhouse.

Catherington workhouse was located on the London Road and, presumably as such, was a warning to all itinerant travellers that it was better to keep moving through Horndean than look for assistance within the parish. For as the road got busier and enhanced Horndean's economy, so it also brought problems to the pleasant village. The wealthier a place may become, the more likely to attract undesirables. The Forest of Bere, in any case, had a reputation as a haunt of footpads. Gipsies used to pitch their tents in the most remote parts of the woods and descend upon the highways after dusk to prey upon travellers. Discharged sailors often indulged in a few days robbery by way of pastime after a long voyage, and Horndean was just about the distance the hangers on of a regiment on the march would go from Portsmouth. Girls abandoned by soldiers had an unpleasant habit of creeping into outhouses about the village and hanging themselves. Thus, on 28 April 1810 it was reported that "an unfortunate girl of the name of Neale, who had followed some soldiers that were going to London, in a fish-cart was abandoned by them at Horndean. Being intoxicated, and without any money, she wandered about the lanes till day-light when she went into a farmer's outhouse, and attempted to hang herself, with the strings of her pocket. Early in the morning a labourer discovered her, in a senseless state, hanging with her feet upon the ground. After several hours process the functions of life were restored, and she was taken to the Poor House". It was reported in November 1802, two gentlemen travelling to Petersfield were robbed on Horndean Down, by three fellows in sailors clothing and on 20 December 1805 that "Last night Mr Mills, miller of Lyss, near Petersfield, was stopped in the Forest [of Bere], near Horndean, by a man who had a gun and a dog with him; the fellow put the gun to Mr Mill's breast, and swore he would shoot him if he did not deliver to him his money.—Mr M terrified at his appearance and imprecations gave him his purse, containing in gold and silver about fifty shillings. The same fellow soon after robbed a servant of Mr Mullen's of Hambledon, of a watch; and a higgler of eight shillings. An alarm was soon given at Horndean when Mr Marner, a peace-officer and several other persons went in search of the depredator, and were successful in taking him. He belongs to a gang of gipseys, who he stated were concerned with him, and that they had a tent in the midst of the Forest, almost a mile from the Turnpike Road, which the constable, etc. searched, and there found ten others of the gang whom they also secured."[19]

But it was not only the danger on the road that travellers had to be wary of, for stopping at an inn could produce its disagreements. In the first decade of the nineteenth century when William Bell, an ensign in the 89th Foot, was on the road he wrote "At one place on the last march from Petersfield our breakfast cost 2/10 each, and a bad dinner the same day at Horndean a small village about 8 miles further on, was charged 5/- each".[20] He makes it clear that a good dinner should only have cost between 3s and 3s 6d. Clearly Horndean was not free from bad landlords who, realising the potential of the road, were exploiting the travellers.

There is an interesting difference between William Bell's description of Horndean in the early years of the nineteenth century and that of Jervoise Clarke-Jervoise in his letter to the Duke of Wellington in 1831. Bell describes it as a small village, Clarke-Jervoise as a town and compares it with Havant and Emsworth. Since it is unlikely that the manorial lord who lived locally would have misconceptions about the community, it seems that Horndean had grown substantially in the first 30 years of the nineteenth century. Some of this growth may well have been due to its pleasant surroundings. Admiral Hood's second son, Samuel, had married Nelson's niece in 1810 and continued to live at Catherington. Few distinguished naval or military officers visited Portsmouth without calling on them in Catherington and the Gosport Division of the Portsdown Yeomanry Cavalry, long commanded by Samuel Hood had many a field day and pleasant entertainment in the grounds until the house was sold to a retired Indian civil judge, Francis Morgan. When it became known that the Princess of Wales would spend August 1805 in Catherington there was a tremendous demand for houses in the neighbourhood. At that time there were numerous sporting boxes in the district usually occupied in the hunting season. One of the prettiest was Mr Cross's house at Blendworth. He had been the owner of the fashionable *Crown Inn* at Portsmouth and a large coaching company, before retiring to Blendworth and in 1805 bought Joseph Franklin's 77 acre property, Qualletts Grove, for £2,500, advertised in the delightful village of Horndean.[21] He was offered the highest rent ever paid for a house in the county for the month of the Princess's visit, and accepted. Clearly, some enhancement of the local economy should have been experienced. Furthermore, in 1822 Edmund Kean, the famous actor, while playing in Portsmouth, drove out to Catherington, was enraptured by the beauty of the surrounding country and bought Keydell House. Similarly, Sir William Knighton bought James Hopper's Blendworth Cottage in Coppid Hall Lane (now Church Path), and built Blendworth Lodge.[22]

Another Horndean attraction was cricket played by the Horndean team on Horndean Down prior to enclosure, after which it moved to Bulls Copse Corner.[23] Horse racing also took place and in 1818 the races from Portsdown Hill were integrated with the Horndean Down Races, but only for that year, as the course was thought to be bad and the meeting moved to Hambledon Down the following year.[24] Other celebrations in 1810 were the ringing and singing for George III's golden jubilee.[25] There were therefore, clearly attractions to life in Horndean but mainly, it has to be said, for those with the money to be able to enjoy them and also to build or buy attractive houses in their own substantial grounds, usually on the outskirts of the villages.

Wealth of other sorts came the way of individual members of the community. In May 1813 "a labourer working for Mr Bettesworth and digging on his premises in Horndean discovered a few feet down a bag containing a quantity of silver coins of the reign of Edward VI and Henry VIII. In a more perfect state than can be imagined", and in June 1816 "five labouring men, who had scraped together a few shillings with which to buy a sixteenth part of a lottery ticket, learned to their delight that the number had won a £20,000 prize and in due time received £1,250 between them in return for their modest outlay. It is feared that the incident had an unsettling effect on the villagers of Horndean. Certain it is that Mr Bettesworth who was the principal tradesman in the village, did a roaring trade in lottery tickets for many years after, and certain it is that an undue proportion of the prize found its way into the pocket of the landlord of the comfortable and highly esteemed hostelry, the *Ship and Bells* (sic)".[26] Shades of the 1990s!

However, these were isolated events and would not sustain a community, let alone encourage its population growth, which from 1801 to 1831, was almost 70%. It must have been this sort of expansion which had caused Clarke-Jervoise's remark. By the early 1830s there were at least four baker's shops, two grocers and general shops, two boot and shoe makers, a butcher, two wheelwrights, a carpenter, a painter, plumber and glazier, a corn dealer, a tailor, a land surveyor and two surgeons in Horndean.[27] By the early 1830s, the three inns of the neat little village had become four, with the addition of *The Woodman*,[28] soon to be *The Good Intent*. The decadal censuses show that Catherington's population continued to grow through the nineteenth century until 1891 (see Table 6.1). By contrast Blendworth after growing by 43 per cent in the first 20 years of the nineteenth century had a fluctuating population which never reached 300. Thus, whereas Catherington's population in 1811 was only two and a half times larger than Blendworth's,

Table 6.1   **Population 1801–1901**

	1801	1811	1821	1831	1841	1851	1861	1871	1881	1891	1901
Blendworth	174	236	249	246	280	236	219	284	298	291	268
Catherington	559*	607	798	944	1003	1094	1151	1293	1321	1413	1356
Total	733	843	1047	1190	1283	1330	1370	1577	1619	1704	1624

*estimate   Source: Censuses of Great Britain 1801–1901.

by 1901 it was five times bigger. It was not that Catherington village was growing substantially, but that Horndean was developing on the London Road, and much of Blendworth's 54 per cent nineteenth century growth was located in that part of the parish which butted on to Horndean, at the foot of Blendworth Hill, for example Crookley Cottages were built in 1863, Crookley at the end of the 1870s and Flint Cottage in 1888.

The 1841 Census gives a clearer picture of Horndean's growth—at least the main part along the valley, but the area around Five Heads Road, the Workhouse, *Good Intent* and Merchistoun Hall do not appear. Causeway, Keydell and Prochurch Farm all along the main road are included in Catherington. Some 300 people however lived in Horndean from around the Toll House at the Petersfield end to around the Square at the Portsmouth end and they could be divided into distinct groups. The innkeepers and victuallers (5), the wheelwrights (4), blacksmiths (4), harness makers (2), the carter and the toll collector could all be said to obtain their main living from travellers along the road. Certainly, four wheelwrights and four blacksmiths could not have been kept busy simply by local users or agricultural activity, since only one farmer lived in Horndean. A second group including bricklayers (5), carpenters (5), painters (2), plumber, thatcher and sawyer could be associated with a burgeoning building industry, for many houses were built in nineteenth century Horndean such as Westfield, Southfield and Crookley as well as cottages. Shops were a third group. Four grocers, three butchers, three tailors, one general shop, one draper, one baker and three shoemakers. In addition to the numerous labourers, there were also three surgeons, one dealer, one tea hawker, one corn merchant, one postman and a schoolmaster. If, however, Horndean is incorporated into the whole of Catherington parish the picture changes dramatically for then about 40 per cent of males were engaged in farming, a little over 20 per cent in trade, under 10 per cent in building and over 10 per cent in domestic service. Of working women 80 per cent were in domestic service, indicating the growing number of large houses appearing in the parishes. In Blendworth this element was even stronger, since over 90 per cent of working women were in domestic service, demonstrating the growth of houses such as Blendworth Lodge and Cadlington, as well as the existence of large farms. Blendworth men, too, were more involved in domestic service as grooms and gardeners. Nearly 28 per cent of the male workforce were so engaged, while over 45 per cent were in agriculture. By the last decade of the century these proportions had not changed much—40 per cent being employed in agriculture, 24 per cent in domestic service and 16 per cent in trade, an area of increasing importance in the last decade of the century, as it was for Blendworth women, some 14 per cent then being in trade. Even so, 81 per cent of working women were still employed in domestic service. In Catherington, by 1891, the proportion of occupied males in agriculture had fallen from 40 to 30 per cent, risen slightly in building to 13 per cent and domestic service to 16 per cent, but fell in trade to 18 per cent. For women, opportunities in trade increased from 20 to 30 per cent and correspondingly fell in domestic service from 80 to 63 per cent.[29] The two major trends, therefore, appear to be the decline in opportunities for men in agriculture and the rise in the numbers of women occupied in trade. The former of these trends has been well documented with the growth of mechanisation in farming—the first reaper appeared as early as 1860 and the first transatlantic grain shipments came in 1875. Furthermore, pastoral farming began to suffer from the imports of chilled and refrigerated meat from the United States and Australia in the 1870s. Thus, both aspects of mixed farming were being adversely affected, leading to a depression in agriculture in the last quarter of the nineteenth century.

The effect on nineteenth century Horndean, despite population growth, was that the number employed in agriculture fell between 1851 and 1891 from 160 to 129. Even so, despite England having long passed through her Industrial Revolution (1760-1830), there were few signs in Catherington, or Blendworth of the effects of industrialisation. By 1891, there was one agricultural engine driver (farm tackle), William Knight, who lived on Horndean Hill. Other indications of 'modernisation' were the presence at Causeway (now Catherington Lane) of an insurance agent, with the appropriate name of George Money, an inland revenue officer and a telegraphist who lived at Antigua Cottages. Finally, living along the Havant Road was Charles Hall, engine driver of a stationary engine. The likelihood was that Hall worked at the Brewery which had the only known stationary steam engine in Horndean.

The Horndean Brewery had by the 1890's already become Horndean's most familiar landmark with its Victorian tower. Its development had resulted from the purchase of the *Ship and Bell* in May 1847 by Richard Gale, son of Ann Gale, shopkeeper at the corner of Five Heads Road (where Dean Court now is). Richard Gale was himself a successful shopkeeper having built a grocer's shop with bakery (now Horndean Post Office) in 1836 and then, putting his eldest son Henry in charge, became a corn merchant. He had four sons, three of whom died in their twenties between late 1847 and 1854, leaving only the youngest son George Alexander, who returned from his job as a commercial traveller in Portsmouth, to take over the *Ship and Bell* in 1853. Most small country inns brewed their own beer and the *Ship and Bell* was no exception, but Gale decided to expand brewing at Horndean, for by 1861 he employed at least nine men and two boys, and in the early 1860's installed a stationary steam engine as well as further enlarging the premises in 1863. However, in March 1869 disaster struck.

> "A serious fire broke out early on Saturday morning 6th March at Mr. G. A. Gale's steam brewery and spirit stores, Horndean. A plentiful supply of water being at hand the fire had considerably abated before the arrival of the fire engine from Havant. The office, engine room, grinding room and a considerable portion of the brewery, however, were destroyed. Fortunately the fire was discovered in time to save the stock of ale and beer, as well as the spirit store and a very large quantity of malt and barley. The malt house, through the exertions of the workmen, was not much damaged. Providentially there was very little wind, or the whole of the buildings and stock must have been destroyed".[30]

It was clearly a sizeable building, but with the insurance company paying out only ten days after the fire, an even larger building with an imposing tower was built in the same year. In the new building double the number of workers were employed, some twenty men and two boys and by 1881 that number had risen to about thirty. A note in the 1871 census stated that "Additional labourers' cottages have been provided in Catherington parish, and the increase of population is stated to be owing to the employment of more persons at the brewery".[31] Supporting this statement was the fact that twenty-nine houses were built between the 1861 and 1871 censuses. Gales Brewery survived the increasing concentration in the brewing industry in the late nineteenth century and became an incorporated company in 1888 when it owned eighteen tied public houses, four off licences and sixteen brewery cottages. The Brewery also leased a further pub. In 1894 George Gale was 65, all his three sons had died in childhood, and his three daughters were married well. Thus, having no one to inherit his business, he sold it in 1896 to Herbert Frederick Bowyer of Guildford. It was a flourishing concern, which he had created and was an important factor in the growth of the numbers employed in trade in Horndean.[32]

The growth of population also necessitated changes in both religious and educational life in the villages. Although Catherington parish had the largest growth in the numbers of people its All Saints Church remained relatively unchanged. It was restored in 1883 when its three galleries were removed. The north gallery had been occupied by the gentry, the south by schoolchildren and the west held the organ and choir—girls on one side boys on the other. It is doubtful, therefore, whether the restoration work in 1883 increased rather than reduced its capacity. Perhaps this was because changes elsewhere in the parishes were beginning to cater for the spiritual needs of others. The late eighteenth and early nineteenth centuries had seen a considerable growth of non-conformity in Britain especially in the growing towns of the north and midlands, where whole new communities grew without any new Anglican churches. This movement was not confined to the industrial areas, however, there being substantial non-conformity in Portsmouth and in 1830 a small Independent Methodist chapel was erected on the Portsmouth Road almost opposite the lodge gate of Merchistoun Hall.

The major change, however, was to occur in Blendworth. Having had a new St Giles Church built in 1759 it seems the community had failed to look after it too well, so that by the 1840s it needed considerable repairs. Perhaps Blendworth, having been polarised into a community of mainly agricultural labourers and a handful of farmers had not been able to afford its upkeep. Fortunately, its delightful rural setting had attracted the wealthy to construct mansions like Blendworth Lodge and Cadlington House within the parish, but relatively close to the facilities that Horndean and the London Road offered. Thus, when the committee established to survey St Giles' Church came to a decision, it was to build a new larger church on a site provided by Sir William Knighton at the top of Blendworth Hill.[33] A sum of over £2,100 was needed and raised by subscription, with the Queen Dowager, the Marquis of Cholmondeley, W.E. Gladstone and Lady Seymour, widow of Sir Michael Seymour of Cadlington House, being among the benefactors. However, most of the money was provided by Sir William Knighton,[34] and the foundation stone laid by Lady Knighton on 26 April 1850, with the new church consecrated in 1852. William Bettesworth, builder of Horndean agreed to undertake "to pull down the chancel of the old church at Blendworth and fill in the archway at the east end with a flint wall plastering the inside. His bill for this was £8-1-0 but the rector expected a payment of £9-16-0 for the tiles, flint, stones, bricks, paving, wood etc. which Bettesworth removed. Thus he had to pay £1-15-0 to the Rev. E.L. Ward.[35]

It would seem that the centre of Blendworth was being redefined, away from the old road to Chalton—an indication perhaps of the declining importance of Chalton Manor, which had sold off some 2,400 acres of the estate in and around Horndean in 1820 for £30,000.[36] Certainly, Sir Jervoise Clarke-Jervoise, who had contributed £200 to the church building, took little interest in the foundation ceremony and did not attend.[37] Furthermore, the new larger church was both much closer to the mansions of the Knightons and Seymour families and, auspiciously, to the burgeoning centre of Horndean. With its construction, going to Holy Trinity Church became a shorter walk for the parishioners of Catherington living in Horndean, than their own parish church of All Saints at Catherington. Thus, many must have found it more convenient to take the shorter journey, especially in inclement weather. It seems unlikely that Sir William Knighton had not considered this probability when he provided the new site. Similarly, a new location was provided for the Rector, the Rev. Edward Langton Ward, whose parsonage house was on the opposite side of the road in which the Knightons lived at Blendworth Lodge. The new rectory, (Blendworth House) was closer to the church but remoter from the parishioners. Rev. Ward was still at his parsonage house with its own glebe lands in 1841[38], but since the Tithe Commutation Act of 1836 had abolished the payment of tithes in favour of a rent charge the parson no longer needed to farm his own glebe lands and these were bought by the Knightons, the old rectory demolished and a kitchen garden established.

In Lovedean, a Sunday School for the village children, the Lovedean Mission, was begun in 1879 by Mrs Lucy Stares, wife of Horndean's relieving officer and rate collector, and her daughter Elizabeth. It began in the summer house of their home Lovedean Cottage Farm (now 143-5 Lovedean Lane) and in the following year they purchased the village blacksmith's shop and enlarged it both for worship and to accommodate the growing number of children attending. The Keans, who lived at Keydell, used to pay the school fees for some poor children in the neighbourhood. They were only taught to read and write by Miss Stares. When the children had finished at her school they went on to Catherington National School, but felt somewhat inferior by comparison to the education received there.[39]

The Catherington National School was established in 1852. Before then there had been a Dame School held in the lower part of Ivy Cottage by a Mrs Wells who could read but not write and another Dame School in Horndean.[40] There was also a Sunday and day school with a master and four mistresses who were teachers for the Sunday school. Presumably this was the school established under the Appleford Charity's bequest of an estate of twelve acres in Barton Stacey. The school was reported on in the National Society's survey of schools in 1846 when it was said to have 65 boys and 66 girls and the master was paid £42 a year. The National Society's full title was the National Society for Promoting the Education of the Poor in the Principles of the Established Church throughout England and Wales. Those who wished to have their schools united to the National Society had to declare that

1. The Children are to be instructed in the Holy Scriptures, and in the Liturgy and Catechism of the Established Church.
2. With respect to such instruction, the Schools are to be subject to the superintendence of the Parochial Clergymen.
3. The children are to be regularly assembled for the purpose of attending Divine Service in the Parish Church, or other place of worship under the Establishment, unless such reason be assigned for their non-attendance as is satisfactory to the Managers of the School.
4. The masters and mistresses are to be members of the Church of England.
5. A Report on the state and progress of the Schools is to be made, at Christmas in every year, to the Diocesan Board, the District Society, or the National Society; and the Schools are, with the consent of the Managers, to be periodically inspected by persons appointed by the Bishop of the Diocese, the National Society, or the Diocesan Board of Education.
6. In case any difference should arise between the Parochial Clergy and the Managers of the Schools, with reference to the preceding Rules, respecting the religious instruction of Scholars, or any regulation connected therewith, an appeal is to be made to the Bishop of the Diocese, whose decision is to be final.

It is clear from these rules where the emphasis on education was to lay and equally clear that authority did not lie with the teachers, but with the clergy.

The Catherington National School opened in 1852 for 106 pupils on a site donated by the manorial lord, the Rev. Samuel Clarke-Jervoise. Two rooms were built, a larger one for girls and a smaller one for infants and the total cost, including a teacher's house built on the premises, was £670. The teacher appointed in 1861 was Miss Hannah Thomson who taught for 10 years before leaving to marry, becoming Mrs. Mitchell, the wife of the baker and grocer whose shop was in Horndean Square (now the Indian Restaurant).

Eight years after the opening of Catherington School, Horndean Church of England School for boys opened for 147 pupils[41] on the site now occupied by the library. However, neither of these was the first new school established in the community, for Blendworth National School pre-dated both, despite seemingly having less pupils. In 1819 only 17 pupils attended the Blendworth Free School[42] and when the one room National School was built for £287 in 1840, intending to receive 66 to 77 pupils,[43] it had only 38, fifteen boys and twenty-three girls, in May 1841.[44] From 1860, when Horndean School opened, boys over infant age attended there thus, like Catherington, Blendworth became a girl's school.

By 1879, when Blendworth school came under Government control, it had three rooms, one being newly built. When Mrs. Williams, the new teacher took over in April 1879, her first comment was "Found the children very deficient in order and discipline—backward in their lessons, especially in Arithmetic—and irregular in Attendance".[45] However, by February 1880, less than a year later, when the school had its first inspection, the Inspector's report said "This little school has done very nicely at its first Inspection. More desks, books and apparatus needed". Five new desks arrived the following month. In 1885, the report said that "the infants have been carefully taught but they should be made to march more than at present" a comment which seems to say more about the Inspector than the school. That year, however, work was seriously disrupted in the autumn by typhoid fever which closed the school for a few weeks. Many children were sick into January 1886 and the Inspector commented "considering the amount of sickness and the closing of the school for so long the results of the examination are very creditable." The following year he remarked that the infants room was much too crowded "being only large enough for twelve when there were often double that number present". In 1888 he was able to say that the addition to the classroom was most successful.

Sickness among the children was a perennial problem. Apart from the typhoid fever, measles, whooping cough, diphtheria, chicken pox, and influenza were all responsible more than once in the 1880s and 1890s for absences, as were severe colds. Measles was particularly bad in early 1889 halving the attendance and the teacher Mrs. Williams was also ill. The Inspector reported that "the school had suffered considerbaly from sickness both among the children and the teacher". In August 1890, after another bout of illness, Mrs. Williams resigned. Her replacement lasted only until the next Inspection when the report was critical of the teacher and she was replaced.

In 1896 Catherington School, having been found too small for the ever increasing number of children, was enlarged and twelve girls from there were temporarily admitted to Blendworth, from mid September to 13 November, while the work was carried out. The following January a new teacher Miss Maria Elizabeth Knight arrived at Blendworth stating that the children's attainments were "anything but satisfactory. Tables were not well known, children murmured at writing and counted on their fingers in arithmetic". Five weeks later, on 18th February, she resigned and left, but not before six pupils had already departed for Catherington School! The new teacher, Miss Smith, appears to have been conscientious and hard working. She attempted to improve attendance by introducing an incentive scheme—a ticket given for every ten attendances and prizes distributed at the end of the year, according to the number of tickets obtained. It did help, but illness, bad weather, harvesting, hay making, blackberry picking and having no boots, were all causes of absence. Poor families required children either to work in periods of concentrated labour in the harvest year or look after younger children while mothers worked in the fields.

Even in the Victorian era when everyone was supposed to know their place in society there came the unpleasant parent. Thus, when Miss Smith kept two girls in for quarter of an hour in July 1898 the mother of Daisy Gast came up to the school "in a great passion, shook her fist and 'dared' me ever to keep her child in again". Despite such unpleasantries it seems the school was generally well thought of since when it first came under Government control in 1879 it had 34 on roll, but by the end of the century this had risen to 50.[46]

There is little doubt that the majority of these children were from poor homes. Every time there was heavy rain, stormy weather, ice or snow attendance was seriously affected because children did not have appropriate clothing or footwear. But at least they were in family homes unlike the orphans, children of unmarried mothers, or the children of those families whose poverty had driven them into the new workhouse, beside the old one which was still standing in 1870.[47] The Union Workhouse was built to take a capacity of 90 inmates but census returns indicate that between 1841 and 1891 it did not hold more than 27 (1881) and in 1891 held only nineteen. The number of males varied between ten and nineteen and the females were always eight, nine or ten. Clearly, since the early years of the century standards for most had risen and hence, the poor were fewer and the workhouse was never full. However, males and females were segregated, being so entered in the census of 1871. Thus couples married for a long time, but now elderly and infirm, would be separated in the closing years of their lives.[48] Their lot constrasts starkly with the standard of living achieved by those who lived in the recently erected mansions in Horndean and Blendworth. In June 1885 the executors of the late Sir William Knighton arranged a sale of the contents of Blendworth Lodge and the catalogue itemises them room by room. There were thirteen ground floor rooms, eleven bedrooms, three bathrooms and a dressing room, two servants rooms and an attic. Below ground were three cellars. Apart from the fact that all rooms were fully furnished, there were over 250 wine glasses listed, presumably essential for consuming the over 1,000 bottles of wine, many of them quarts, in two of the cellars. Port, sherry, madeira and claret were the most common. There were 77 lots of linen ending the first day of the sale. The second day saw the sale, among other things, of 35 paintings, engravings and prints. China and ornaments filled more than another three pages of items. In total, over three days, there were approaching 1,000 lots sold. A fourth day was taken to sell the 6,000 volumes of books!

It seems unlikely that the occupants of such houses, living in considerable luxury, even by today's standards, would have needed or wanted to mix with the ordinary people of the villages. Certainly, with so much wine and spirits in the house it was unlikely they would need to visit the nearby *Ship and Bell*, even though it was something of a social centre for local residents. It was the venue for auction sales of houses, land or estates, farms, farm stock and implements and timber. After 150 volunteers had mustered for drill they were taken to the *Ship and Bell* for refreshments provided by Sir William Knighton and each year an annual ball took place in January. In 1862 about forty couples danced from 9 o' clock throughout the night in the ballroom, which was tastefully decorated with flowers and evergreens, refreshments being supplied by the landlord Mr. W.J. Edney.[49] Horndean had no church which could act as a social centre and it seems the *Ship and Bell* provided that role. Although it was unlikely to attract the very wealthy, some clearly did not forget the poor for, when Lady Knighton died in 1862, business was suspended in Horndean for the funeral of a "beloved and amiable lady" who "liberally supported schools and charitable institutions and was always ready to relieve the poor and those in distress. Her death will be deeply felt by the poor of this district".[50] Lady Knighton, clearly a compassionate lady, made attempts to reduce the problem of poverty and the chasm between rich and poor in nineteenth century England. It was to be hoped that the formation of the Catherington Parish Council in 1894 under the chairmanship of G.A. Gale,[51] would continue to find ways of assisting the less fortunate of the community, although the major contributor, since the 1840s, to the reduction of poverty had been the British economy. Being the first industrial nation had given Britain an economic lead, so much so that most people had better standards of living by the end of the century. The rise of mass markets in machine-made clothes and shoes, the appearance of packaged foods like tea and condensed milk, growing imports of grain, meat, fruit and dairy produce together with machine-produced furniture and cheap rail excursions widened consumers' choices at a time of rising real incomes. But it was to be a relatively short period before other nations such as the United States and Germany were themselves to become industrialised competitors. Before the end of the nineteenth century both these nations were producing more coal and steel and had begun to erode Britain's share of world trade and economic lead.

References
1. Stratton, *Agricultural Records*, pp.88–97.
2. Chambers and Mingay, *Agricultural Revolution*, pp.91–92.
3. Stapleton in *Portsmouth Region*, p.105 for dockyard workforce; Wrigley and Schofield, *Population History*, pp.528–529.
4. Stratton, *Agricultural Records*, pp.98–99.
5. Worton, 'Blendworth', p.26.

6 HRO Q23/1/2/, Enclosure Act, pp.249–392.
7 I am most grateful to Dr John Chapman of the Department of Geography, University of Portsmouth, for supplying me with details of the enclosure allotments for the Chalton Enclosure Act.
8 Worton, 'Blendworth' p.26.
9 HRO 57M92/2, Clarke-Jervoise Estate Papers.
10 Worton, 'Blendworth', pp.26–27.
11 HRO Microfilm No. 36, 1851 Census of Great Britain, Blendworth.
12 PCL Abstracts of Census Returns 1801–1901.
13 Chambers and Mingay, *Agricultural Revolution*, p.130.
14 Stratton, *Agricultural Records*, p.102.
15 E J Hobsbawm and G Rudé, *Captain Swing*, 1973, p.262.
16 Ibid., p.89.
17 HRO 25M61/3/3/22, Jervoise Clarke-Jervoise to Arthur, Duke of Wellington, June 1831, quoted in Worton, 'Blendworth'.
18 PCRO CHU40/3/1, Free School Account Book 1702–1827.
19 PCL Pescott Frost Cuttings, vol.1 (1899), pp.145–46; *HT.* 551, 30 April 1810; 163, 22 Nov. 1802; 302 22 July 1805.
20 Brigadier B W Webb-Carter, 'The Letters of William Bell, 89th Foot 1808-10', *Journal of the Society for Army Historical Research*, XLVIII, 1970, p.80.
21 *HT.* 298, 24 June 1805.
22 PCL Pescott Frost Cuttings pp.144-45.
23 Ibid., p.145.
24 G O'Connell, *Secretive Southwick*, Domesday to D-Day, 2nd ed., 1994, pp.118–19.
25 PCRO CHU41/2A/1, Catherington Churchwardens' Account Book 1807–92.
26 *HT.* 712, 31 May 1813; Pescott Frost Cuttings, p.146.
27 Pigot and Co. Directory 1831-32, pp.422-23.
28 See HRO 21M65/F7/43/1–2, Catherington Tithe Map 1838 and Award 1843 for *Woodman* Public House.
29 The above figures have been extracted from PRO HO/107/396/10-11, Census of Great Britain 1841; 1851; RG9/699 1861; RG10/1219 1871; RG11/1239, 1881; RG12/944, 1891.
30 *HT.* 3815, 10 March 1869.
31 PRO RG10/1219 Census of Great Britain 1871.
32 Information about Gales Brewery is taken from Barry Stapleton, *Gales of Horndean The Hampshire Brewers 1847–1997*, 1997, and B Stapleton and J H Thomas *Gales, a Brewing, Business and Family History*, 2000 forthcoming.
33 PCRO CHU40/4/3, papers concerning building of new church. Sir William Wellesley Knighton of Blendworth Lodge, was the son of the first baronet, who had been physician to George IV.
34 Ibid.
35 Ibid.
36 HRO 6M59 Box 1/11; Box 3/13-14; 57M92/2 Clarke-Jervoise Estate Papers.
37 HRO 18M64 Box 1, diaries of Jervoise Clarke-Jervoise.
38 PRO HO/107/396/10, Census of Great Britain, 1841.
39 PCRO CHU41/5/E3, notes by Miss Briggs.
40 Ibid.
41 *VCH Hants.*, III, p.397.
42 PCRO CHU40/4/4.
43 *VCH Hants.*, III, p.396.

44 Terms of the Union of Blendworth School with the National Society.
45 Blendworth School Log Book, I, 21 April 1879–14 April 1904. I am most grateful to the former head teacher of Blendworth School, Christine Wagstaff, for allowing me use of the School Logbooks.
46 This section about Blendworth School is taken from entries in Log Book No. 1 up to 1900.
47 PCRO CHU41/3/A/1, Catherington Vestry Minute Book, 25 March 1848–30 March 1921. On 14 April 1870, an offer was made to sell the old workhouse and lands to the existing Workhouse Guardians for £200.
48 Censuses of Great Britain 1841–91.
49 *HT.* 298, 24 June 1805; 302, 22 July 1805; 376, 22 Dec. 1806; 1069, 3 April 1820; 1071, 17 April 1820; 1353, 12 Sept. 1825; 3252, 1 Feb. 1862.
50 *HT.* 3252, 1 Feb. 1862.
51 HRO 20M81/A/DX1, Catherington Parish Council Minutes. Note that the Council took the name of the ecclesiastical parish and was not named after, what was by then accepted as, the major population centre, Horndean.

Chapter 7

The Twentieth Century

At the beginning of the century Horndean was described as being a place where almost anything could be bought or obtained. It was said to have two bakers, Streets (where the Post Office is now) and Mitchells (now Indian Restuarant in the Square) who had very good bread and lardy cakes and Horndean residents who made large pies at home, took them to be baked in Mitchell's large ovens, two butchers—Mr. Pruce at the western side of the foot of Blendworth Hill (now the Main Bakery) and Pesketts, Mr. Hobbs blacksmith's shop and forge opposite the Brewery. A tailor, Mr. Wile, lived opposite Marsh's garage and specialised in riding clothes for the gentry; a saddler and harness maker; a shoemaker; a chairmaker and repairer, Fred Burgess, who was blind after being hit by a cricket ball; a builder, Bert Edney whose bell rang at seven o'clock for the men to go to work; an undertaker and registrar of births, deaths and marriages, Henry Bettesworth, who was also the local chemist and a grocer and lived on the eastern side of the foot of Blendworth Hill (now hairdressers). There was also Mr. Warrilow's drapery store with mens' clothes on one side and womens' on the other and which sold virtually everything (now cycle shop); a newsagent and photographer, Harry Thompson who lived in Merchistoun Lodge, opposite the Methodist Chapel; Mr. Luff who sold fruit, vegetables and flowers and George Edney's grocery store (on a site now occupied by the Co-op store) where on Saturday evenings men would congregate to buy tobacco and then cross the road to the *Red Lion*.[1]

In the 1891 census there were, in addition, a wheelwright, a watchmaker and also a carpenter situated where the parish hall was at the end of Five Heads Road. A second blacksmith was also located near the junction of Five Heads Road with the Portsmouth Road.[2] Blacksmiths were kept busy since almost everything was delivered by horse vans or wagons. Henry Adams hired out carriages, took people to Petersfield Station by horse and trap and delivered milk by horse and cart, the milk being in a large pail with half pint, pint and quart measures for emptying into the customer's jug. His father had a long white beard, walked about the village in a smock and old hat driving four or five cows which provided the milk. There were carriers also to Portsmouth. Mr. Edney had a horse and van, collected parcels from individuals or shops and after delivering them, shopped in Portsmouth for those in Horndean who had given him lists of groceries. John Pearson of Causeway Farm (now sheltered housing) was also a regular carrier to Portsmouth five times a week returning at 10 o'clock in the evening, and Mr. Sherring who lived down Causeway had an old horse and wagon and went to Portsmouth three times a week, usually walking—his wagon always had a load of buns. Later, when his draper's shop had been established in Waterlooville, Mr. Wadham brought a horse van round with all varieties of clothing and drapery items. Dr. Nash also visited by pony and trap and the Post Office had a horse drawn coach from Petersfield in which the letters were sorted. Clearly there would have been work for two blacksmiths, but already signs of change had arrived in the village for Gales Brewery had acquired, by 1895, a steam traction engine to be followed in 1903 by Foden steam lorries.[3] Another form of delivery was by bicycle. Each week end a man with a basket on the front of his cycle rode from Emsworth to sell fresh fish and winkles, there being no fresh fish shop in Horndean. It would not have been an easy ride since the roads were of packed flints and more like today's tracks.

For the most part, however, ordinary people had neither cycles nor horses and tended to walk everywhere, even to get water. There were two pumps in the village for those without a well, of which there

HORNDEAN AND ITS INHABITANTS.

A HUMOROUS SKIT.

To a village I am going
Where a *Gale* is always blowing,
Where everything is nice and sweet,
In every corner of the *Street*.
If a townsman tried to cod 'em
He would be introduced to *Wadham*.
He'd mend your motor car or bike,
And do it just as you would like.
Were you to have a spill or smash,
There is a surgeon, Doctor *Nash*.
He'd set your bones if they were broken,
So highly are his praises spoken.
He'd heal a wound, or mend your chest,
At least, I know he'd do his best.
If you would know Horndean affairs,
You must consult our friend, *John Stares*.
He deals with all affairs of state,
Relieves the poor, collects the rate.
His energy, it never slacks,
When gathering in the income tax.
Then builder *Edney*, you will find
He has a cultivated mind.
It is an intellectual treat
To converse with him when you meet.

There is a "Lion" painted red,
Who offers you a well aired bed.
Host *Biden*, he will treat you well,
If full, there is the " Ship and Bell."
If "Good Intent" should be your lot,
The proprietor is *R. J. Scott*.
If restaurants you're looking for,
I recommend " Excelsior."
It is the very best I've seen,
And is a credit to Horndean.
The Postmaster is *Bettesworth*,
A man of very noble birth.
He'll serve you well and stamp your letter,
No man alive could do it better.
Just for a moment hold your breath,
He registers a birth or death.
And then the butcher, *Mr. Pruce*,
His meat is always full of juice;
His beef and mutton it is prime,
I've tasted both, ah, many a time.
But *Pescott's* meat perhaps you favour,
It has the splendid Horndean flavour.
Then *Warlow*, at the drapery stores,
Ah, the successes that he scores.
He'll fit you out from head to feet,
And make you look both smart and neat.
Hats, caps, and bonnets, boots and shoes,
A splendid stock from which to choose.
And *Harry Thompson* to be sure,
He will supply your literature;
Dispatch with promptitude I ween,
Your paper or a magazine.
Your photograph he'd like to take,
A splendid job of it he'd make;
His work will bear the strictest test,
And it is always of the best.
My friend and neighbour, *Mr. Luff*,
So jovial, kindly hearted, bluff,
He uses all his skill and powers
With vegetables, fruit and flowers.
He'd sell a Button hole or spray,
Fit to wear on your wedding day;
A shower bouquet or pretty posies,
His speciality is roses.
A lady next; ah, who could spurn her?
Her name you know is *Mrs. Turner*.
She, visitors supplies with teas,
And always manages to please.
Then *Pearson*, he a carrier bold,
Who many a jolly tale has told,
His friendship you of course will seek—
He goes to town five times a week.
Hobbs is the blacksmith, you will find
He has a most contented mind.
A man that's not too tall or short,
But just about the poet's sort;
A man that everyone must like,
Although he's always on the strike.
The *Mitchells* you must understand,
Are always genial, kind, and bland;
Their bread is wholesome, good and sweet,
And fit for any king to eat.
George Edney's grocery store you see
Is noted for the splendid tea
And the good bacon, butter, cheese,
He always studies how to please.
A rival? That he never fears,
Established now for many years.
Milk, milk, when you require any,
You'll be well served by *Mrs. Penny*,
Or *Henry Adams*, truth to say,
Would sell it to you any day.
Smart carriages he has for hire,
Quite fit for any duke or squire;
His charges are so just and fair,
He always acts upon the square.
There are some others without doubt
The poet ought to write about,
They all deserve both fame and glory,
But that would make too long a story.
Then peace and plenty all around,
May trade and commerce 'ere abound,
With loyalty to King and Queen,
And double loyalty to Horndean.

Composed by

W. J. BOOKER,

Booker lived at Newton along Havant Road. His skit was written about 1910 and echoes many of Bessie Catchlove's memories.

were eighteen in Horndean, nine in Blendworth, thirteen in Lovedean and five in Catherington. There were three at Causeway Farm and its cottages and four at Merchistoun Hall, Farm and cottages. The Workhouse had its own well as did Mitchells, bakers and grocers, Antigua cottages and Five Heads Farm and a new one was dug at Prochurch Farm in 1908.[4] But the best known was at the Brewery from which ordinary people obtained their water, men carrying it in buckets. Alternatively, water had to be fetched from the springs at Rushmore or Sheepwash in Hazleton Wood. All had to be boiled before it was drunk. Cadlington House had water from the Brewery brought in a two-wheeled horse drawn large barrel, and three or four servants took turns to bath in the same water.

In the homes of working people there was insufficient room to keep much water, so it was stored outside. Piped mains water and drains were still in the distant future and toilet facilities were outside privies. Emptying them involved digging a large hole in the garden, then plying the men with beer before emptying the large adult and small children's canisters. Those at the *Farmer Inn* were replaced by earth closets in 1905. Waste water similarly had to be disposed of. House keeping was a full time job. Cooking was on an open range fire so everything had to be cooked in one pot—bacon, pork, vegetables and potatoes—and a long handled skimmer was kept by the fire to take off the scum. Baking was done in an oven beside the fire, which was drawn underneath. The whole range had to be black leaded each week. Fires had to be laid each morning after the previous day's ashes had been cleared out and probably spread on the garden. Wood was the main fuel. Lighting was by oil lamps downstairs and candles were used to go upstairs to bed. As there was no water laid on to houses there were no bathrooms. Baths were taken in a tub often in front of the fire.

Despite the problems of running the home there were occasions to enjoy, particularly as most went to Church and enjoyed the Easter festival, when ordinary eggs were decorated, and Christmas, when children received gifts of oranges, which were a luxury imported item. All the big mansions, Hinton Daubnay, Hinton Manor, St. Catherines, Keydell, Merchistoun, Crookley, Cadlington and Blendworth Lodge, held servants' balls. Mr. Adams took people in a glass fronted horse drawn brougham, the women inside and men outside. They were great dances for the domestic servants, grooms, coachmen and stable hands. Concerts were held in the Brewery engine sheds—the Foden engines were pushed out—a rather sooty job—and then brewery men recited monologues, had a minstrel troupe and sang Horndean ditties. More refined concerts were held in the Boys School (now Library). In the summer an annual flower show was held. Many women made cakes which were put on show for prizes, and the show ended with a wonderful firework display. There were also the annual fairs at Petersfield and Havant as well as Portsdown.

Perhaps the biggest day of entertainment each year, however, was the Amalgamated Clubs day organised by the Foresters, Oddfellows and all the benefit societies, the schoolchildren being given a half-day holiday. It began with a procession to church in the morning with the Hambledon band playing, followed by a public lunch at the *Red Lion* of roast meats and fruit pies from Mitchells with all the dignitaries—parsons, doctors and gentry. In the afternoon there were sports in the meadow along Havant Road, and swinging boats and roundabouts in the meadow behind the *Red Lion*. In the Square (where the War Memorial now is) were side shows, a whelk stall, and coconut shies. All the villagers turned out and it finished with an excellent firework display. In winter evenings most stayed in and if they had a piano would have a sing song or practice. In the summer there was cricket on the pitch by South Road, Horndean having its own team.[5]

However, the twentieth century was destined to be one of great change and Horndean was not to be excepted. Before the Second World War the century saw the growth of public transport but after World War Two it was dominated by the expansion of private transport. However, from 21 December 1901 to 10 October 1902 the Portsdown and Horndean Light Railway was constructed from Cosham, where it linked with Portsmouth Corporation tramways, to Waterlooville. The continuation to Horndean was completed by the beginning of March 1902 and the line opened at 11 am on 2 March with a procession of six of the emerald and green cars. Services for the public began the next day, the first car leaving Horndean terminus, by the Methodist Chapel, at 7.50 a.m. In winter, the cars ran every twenty minutes and in summer every ten minutes, the return fare from Horndean to Cosham being fixed at 6d.[6] It was intended to continue the line, along the centre of the road, from the terminus to Horndean Square, but this stretch of the line was never constructed (see illustration no. 90).

Nevertheless, Horndean residents had a transit system to Portsmouth changing at Cosham—few rural areas could claim to have trams and perhaps the company hoped, by providing better access, it would encourage development along the route and thus create more passengers. At the beginning of the century beyond Horndean, on the way to Portsmouth, were few houses. After Causeway only Prochurch Farm existed, before the terrace of cottages at Cowplain. The rest was still forest. But by September 1905 the company was doing poorly so a regular service in the winter was suspended.[7] In addition, the trams seem to have lacked reliability. Frequently they broke down and it could take much of the day to get to Portsmouth. Coming back to Horndean prospective passengers often had to hire a pony and trap in Cosham when Horndean trams were not running.[8] For Horndean, curiously, the benefits accrued in the other direction for the village became an attraction for those seeking a day out in the pleasant rural, woodland area. Many people would ride out of the confines of Portsmouth to Waterlooville then walk towards Stakes, turn left into Lovers Walk (now Hurstville Drive) and thence through Hurst and Hazleton Woods to Horndean. The effect on Horndean was substantial. In summer large queues stretched back from the tram terminus and the *Good Intent*, especially at times like Easter weekend when many walked through Rushmore and returned by tram having had a great day out.[9] The response in Horndean was rapid. One of the houses by the terminus opened a tea garden; so did the *Good Intent*, the *Red Lion* and the *Ship and Bell*, as well as Causeway Farm! John Street's grocers and bakers shop (now Post Office) became the 'Excelsior' Restaurant, advertised as three minutes walk from the Light Railway Terminus.[10] Both the *Ship and Bell* and *Red Lion* inns became hotels with accommodation, and the village began to get the reputation only reserved for seaside resorts, with the publication of slightly risqué postcards of 'Sunny Horndean' (see illustrations nos. 124–29).

Thus, in 1910 Horndean was described as "deservedly popular as a holiday resort; it still bears a quaint old-fashioned aspect, and a very picturesque one...Horndean is simply crowded at holiday times, but their wants are well looked after, and there are many places, where teas and refreshments can be obtained at strictly commercial prices; there are cosy 'Tea Gardens', in pleasant and convenient locations, good Public Houses, with every accommodation, and small cottages with the well-known sign 'Teas' ".

At the terminus was "the entrance to Hazleton Wood, through which a delightful stroll of barely a mile takes us to the lily pond in a really beautiful piece of water—well stocked with gold fish". Walking towards Horndean from the terminus was, set back on the right, the Isolation Hospital and a little further along the road, Catherington Workhouse "...it seems a pity that the name 'Workhouse' or 'Union' cannot be expunged altogether,...there is something revolting and grating in these names to the susceptibilities of those who have to accept the charity, and the many, who have not deserved so ill of the world, and whom at the thin end of their careers, have the skeleton of the Workhouse or Union constantly before them; surely some other name might be devised more euphoneous, and less hurtful to the feelings of the *genuine* poor,—why not "home or rest"?[11]

This was a perceptive view of a system which had many years to go before it was replaced by the social security system. It was not that the Workhouse was increasingly being filled for, in 1907 and 1908, there were only eleven inhabitants, but in the first two weeks of 1908 seventy-two had been casually relieved and a year later 109, an indication of the scale of seasonal poverty—winter being the time when least agricultural work was available—and fewer waitresses and assistants required in the tea shops.[12]

Catherington was described as a "charming little village" and Blendworth and Lovedean as "pretty", the countryside around "healthy and invigorating", and the Holt along the Rowlands Castle Road—"once a portion of Bere Forest—retains a great deal of its ancient character, the magnificent avenue of great trees, is nearly a mile in length, and leads almost directly to Rowlands Castle, it is a most popular walk".[13]

There seems little doubt that Horndean, in its setting of woodland to the south and the downs to the north had an idyllic charm which attracted many. The trams were a novelty which meant a smooth ride, as opposed to the slow and jolting horse buses from Waterlooville to Cosham. The 1910 guidebook had advertisements for the 'Excelsior' Restaurant and Gardens offering Teas, Luncheons, Minerals and Ices with a choice variety of Pastries and Chocolates, as well as for the *Red Lion* with Pleasure Grounds and Tea Gardens good stabling and accommodation for cyclists and others. Along with these developments came a sign of modernisation—a telephone exchange was established in the front room of a cottage (now 56 London Road) in 1912.

Even so, many of the residents of Horndean were not entirely engaged in catering for visitors, but were busy making plans for community developments. A fund was established for building a Parish Hall on a site provided by the manorial lord, near the junction of Five Heads Road with the London Road. The amount of £650 was required and a number of events were organised to raise the money, among which was a Garden Fete and Bazaar at Blendworth Lodge in September 1911.

> Careful and well-thought out arrangements—beautiful grounds—with two such keen enthusiasts as Mrs. and Miss Long at the head of affairs—could not fail to bring success to any undertaking of the nature of an outdoor social gathering, provided that one thing was added which is beyond human power to add—a fine day. Fortunately September 6th was brilliant, and a sucessful result was assured; there was no doubt of it from the very beginning that the Parish Hall Fund was going to make a big jump. Punctually at 2.30p.m. Mrs. W.G. Nicholson declared the Bazaar open, and Admiral Bayly having thanked her for so doing, the afternoon's enjoyment commenced in earnest to the strains of the Royal Naval Barracks' Band. There need not have been, and we do not think there was, a flagging moment for any one of the large numbers who had come together evidently with one set purpose—to find enjoyment in furthering a good cause. The various stalls—including Plain-work, Fancy, Scotch woollen goods, and Pottery and Toy stalls—were all well patronized. Meanwhile a Tennis Tournament (won by Mr. F. Walley-Tooker and Miss Smith), Progressive Games (won by Miss V. and Mr. H.L. Holbrook of Southsea), Skittles (pig won by Mr. Pocock), Live Aunt Sally and various other side shows were in full swing: the doll dressing competition was won by Miss Wright of Southsea. But provision had also been made for the less energetic: exhibitions of ju-jitsu wrestling by two naval experts were given twice during the afternoon and created a great deal of interest, especially as each "lock" and "throw" were carefully explained by the chief petty officer in command.
>
> Two excellent Concerts were also given at intervals by Miss Grace Hoskyns and Miss D. Stubbington in the Drawing Room—the former charming everyone as usual with her pretty rendering of old English Folk songs, and the latter displaying equally well her skill on the violin. Then there was the lady Palmist! who was in great demand—hardly without a break—from 2.30 to 7.30: we cannot vouch for her accuracy as regards any details she may have given as to the future, but we feel sure that all who, with somewhat quaking hearts, laid their hands palms upward upon the little table, can testify as to the accuracy of her descriptions of character and will have much to think about for some time to come. A museum Tent was also in evidence, in which one might while away a few quiet moments from the outside excitement: and its contents were well worth an inspection.
>
> In summing up, we cannot do better than quote the words of an outside critic as given in the "Portsmouth Times" of September 9th: "Nothing that could possibly add to the enjoyment of

such functions was omitted, and no end of trouble had been taken by Mrs. and Miss Long to see that it should be a real success". The hope, too, that the writer expressed in the same article that "the efforts of these ladies and the many friends who helped in the organisation of the many side shows will meet with their reward when the takings are counted up", was amply fulfilled. Our highest hopes did not reach to more than £70; but when over that amount was counted out in solid gold, and the full amount totalled up to just over £110, well—there was nothing else to do but to shake hands over it. Since then a few more pounds have dribbled in, which brings the grand total to £120! Expenses? NIL!—at least so Mrs. Long said. Can't you see that Hall beginning to take shape in your mind's eye on the top of Horndean Hill?
(Catherington Parish Magazine, September 1911.)

By June 1912 over £480 had been collected and it was decided to go ahead, John Edney being asked to undertake the construction. The opening ceremony took place later that year on 6 November—Mrs. Long of Blendworth Lodge donated a billiard table, Mrs. Livingstone Learmouth of Cadlington House gave a piano and Miss Briggs a bagatelle board. In December a Mens Club opened in the Hall and by April 1913 it had 191 members.

Meanwhile, in April 1911, a rifle range was built and inaugurated on 24 May with Catherington and District Rifle Club being formed with Admiral Bayly as president and the vicar of Catherington, the Rev. E.J. Kefford, vice-president.[14] In 1913 the Clarke-Jervoise estate provided a site north of the cottages built on the east side of Five Heads Road between 1900 and 1903, on which the Drill Hall was built.[15]

A different sort of community spirit was demonstrated against a man often drunk, who was a habitual wife beater and lying in bed would bellow 'Bring up the bucket Annie', a reference to the privy. Eventually, in 1912, decent people in Horndean had had enough and arranged to show their disgust at his brutal behaviour. Effigies of the wife batterer and his current female friend were paraded through the village to the sound of 'rough music' played on kettles, tin cans, buckets, horse collar bells and drums. A banner bearing the phrase 'Bring up the bucket Annie' was carried at the head of the procession, along with a mock coffin, up Horndean Hill and past the offender's cottage. After three nights of this treatment the effigies were hanged from a finger post in the Square, a mock sermon read, then the effigies cut down and placed in the coffin. This was then carried to the back of the offender's cottage where a bonfire was lit and the coffin placed on it, to the sound of more rough music, boos and jeers and the following verse spoken

> There is a man who lives in this place
> Who beats his wife in sad disgrace
> He beats her black he beats her blue
> He beats her till the blood comes through
> And if this man don't mend his manners
> We'll send his hide to the tanners
> And if the tanner don't tan it well
> We'll hang it on a nail in Hell.

Sadly the bully did not mend his ways.[16]

Nevertheless, it is clear that, in the early years of the twentieth century, Horndean was economically thriving, assisted by expanding output at Gales Brewery. More employment would have been created, although much of it would have been for women. At both the *Good Intent* and the *Red Lion* on busy summer weekends six or seven waitresses were employed and increases in bar and kitchen staff would have been required. Many women would have been glad of the additional income and there is no doubt many had to work despite family commitments, as Miss Smith, teacher at Blendworth School discovered in March

1900 when visiting one family whose two daughters had been absent five times each week. She found the mother very ill with seven children at home and the eleven year old eldest daughter having to look after the others. It was a bad year for the schools generally with epidemics of measles, whooping cough and scarlet fever. The latter closed Catherington School in early September to late October. Even then, the scarlet fever did not clear up and eventually, in late January 1901, Blendworth School was also closed, staying so for nine weeks until 25 March. There were, however, celebratory days for the children. The relief of Ladysmith saw them all given an orange and a holiday on 1 March 1900 and in May another holiday was granted to celebrate both the Queen's birthday and the Relief of Mafeking. The Amalgamated Clubs day resulted in another day off school on 5 July. It did not take Blendworth School long to use the facilities of the Horndean Light Railway for a day out—thus reversing the trend of people coming from Portsmouth. Miss Smith had urged children to save pennies for the day and on 17 July 1903 they took the 9.25 tram car to Clarence Pier and on the way took flowers to the Children's Ward at the Royal Hospital Portsmouth (now the site of Sainsbury's store and car park). But the girls at Blendworth had to work as well and were being taught decimal fractions and averages. Miss Smith, however, was advised by the H.M.I. to omit these and do simple interest and proportion, so that the pupils would "be able to make out a bill and that would be sufficient in a school for girls"! A male chauvinistic view, unfortunate in an H.M.I., but which still had many years to run, with a common opinion that it did not really matter about educating girls since they were only going to get married. A curious attitude which seemed to ignore entirely the influence of mothers on small children. As it happens, Miss Smith continued to teach decimals to the girls.

There were recurrent outbreaks of measles, chicken pox, whooping cough, and scarlet fever, one pupil being removed to the Isolation Hospital up Horndean Hill in January 1903. Diphtheria, however, was the most feared of the diseases and that appeared in April 1905. On 1 June, entered in the logbook was "Harry Pinnock dear little scholar three and a half years old died on Good Friday after six days illness". Two other pupils were sent to the Isolation Hospital, one dying on 8 June, an event sadly repeated in July 1912, when Dr. Nash closed the school. Parents kept their children at home for fear of contagion. Miss Smith herself had clearly caught some infection having had periods of illness since 1904 with a sore throat which affected her for most of 1906 and which was not helped by the school stove being inadequate in the intense cold of January 1907—a new stove was fitted in February. But her problems were compounded by those in authority. She was reprimanded for sending scholars to the Doctor in December 1906 and, after being congratulated by the County Medical Officer in January 1910 on having the cleanest school he had visited (no head lice!), she was then informed by the Rector that he wanted the pupils to enter the school by the front door. Miss Smith objected as the front lobby opened on to her sitting room, thus both dirt and cold air would come in. The Rector's response, hardly a christian one, was to send the girls from the back door to come in at the front. Nor surprisingly, following this incident, the Doctor recommended the far from well Miss Smith to take two months rest for health reasons. When she returned at the end of April, Miss Smith discovered the Rector had given her house key to the replacement supply teacher, so that she could use the house in the lunch hour. Miss Smith had not been informed, nor her permission sought and she was understandably upset as her private papers about personal affairs had been left in the room. When she gently remonstrated, the Rector expected and received an apology for her action. It would have been interesting to see how the Rector would have reacted had a similar circumstance arisen at the Rectory. The effect on a far from well Miss Smith was that, later in the year, she had to take enforced leave as a result of a breakdown, and was still suffering from nervous trouble a year later. In February 1913, she resigned through bad health after nearly 15 years at the school.

It was not the last the girls were to see of her, however, for she called in November to say goodbye as she was going to live in Worcestershire. Two and a half years later, in May 1916, she visited the school when 'the girls were pleased to see her'. That so long afterwards, in the middle of a war, Miss Smith was prepared to visit the school implies something about her dedication, and that the girls were pleased to see her, after so long, suggests that she had left a considerable and favourable impact on her pupils. Her time at the school had seen attendances affected badly by inclement weather and illnesses as well as harvests, gathering blackberries—eight in September 1905—and birdnesting (April 1910). On the other hand she had received a weighing machine and weighed and measured all children from November 1908 and in March 1909, gave the first cookery lesson to the girls. She also took in girls from the Workhouse in 1904 and still had workhouse girls in 1910.[17]

When Miss Smith resigned the clouds of war were gathering in Europe. Territorial army members drilled in Horndean Square and sent a cycle corps to France after war was declared. In September 1914, the Parish Hall was open every evening from 8p.m. to 9.30p.m. for drill instruction and rifle practice, the Rifle Club shootings being suspended. In January 1914, the Bishop of Winchester's letter to the Catherington Parish Magazine referred to "the inflamed and dangerous condition of opinion". However, this was not a refence to the political situation and the possibility of war but "to the claims of women for the franchise"! It was "a matter specially needing our prayers", said the Bishop. Six months earlier, suffragette Emily Davison had died under the hooves of the King's horse in the Derby.

Village women meeting at the Parish Hall in August 1914 decided to make garments for the forces under the direction of the Red Cross every Friday afternoon. In February 1915, they were asked to supply 800 shirts to the King's Royal Rifles—Hampshire's Regiment, so their Friday afternoons were then spent concentrating on fulfilling the request. By September they had made 104.[18] Their children at Blendworth School enjoyed two novel experiences in the summer of 1914. For the first time the Girls Choir sang in the Petersfield Choral Music Festival and won the novice banner, and also came the first mention of the choir and school being photographed. In June many went by tram to the Agricultural Show at Southsea—unofficially, thus attendance at school was poor. The first mention of the effect of war on the pupils came in September when the geography syllabus was altered to Europe. The girls followed the troop movements and marked their positions each day on a map. In addition, in needlework they made flannel petticoats and overalls for those children who had become the orphans of soldiers. At times, being able to see either a map or a needle must have been difficult—in January 1914 it was impossible to see the lines in exercise books towards the end of the afternoon in very dull and overcast weather—clearly the school had no lighting and remained so until February 1915, when a hanging lamp was provided. It was so beneficial that a second, "both giving a very good light" arrived the following month. Also in 1915, as a result of the war, came an unwelcome financial imposition. "These poor children are asked to bring in pennies for Lord Roberts fund for workshops for disabled soldiers and subscribe to the Christmas Fund for the Overseas Club". Clearly, the teacher considered it a burden many could not afford. But this was as nothing compared to the costs of war upon four of the girls in late September 1916. The classic World War I recruiting poster of Lord Kitchener saying your country needs you with pointing finger straight at the onlooker had clearly had its desired effect on at least two local men, with disastrous results for their families. On 27 September was written "Ethel Hilda and Margaret Merritt and Elsie and Ethel Gough have left the school today. As their fathers have now joined the Army and their places taken by other men, their cottages were required. Unfortunately, no houses were to be obtained near and the two families have gone to Clanfield to live. The children are a loss to the school as they are bright and intelligent". What an indictment on the society of the time, that agricultural labourers who performed a patriotic duty should find their families evicted from their tied cottages in favour of others who stayed at home. Thus these bright girls had to have their education disrupted, leave their schoolfriends and neighbours and their families commence life elsewhere. Obviously, should their fathers survive the war, they would have no jobs to return to either.

For the pupils who remained at the school there was an unusual cause of excitement in September 1917, when an aeroplane landed in a field close by—it was so rare an event that the children were allowed out to see it start. The following month one of the girls was sent to her cousin's on account of the air raids! The end of the war, late the following year received no mention, because the school had been closed once again through illness, this time an influenza epidemic—it had previously been closed in 1917 through a joint measles and whooping cough outbreak. That year there were no Xmas festivities as many fathers and brothers were away in the forces,[19] in fact children were exhorted to take school dinners which had been started to save on bread consumption. A real shortage of flour and cereals existed, but children still went to school with bread and biscuits. However, on Monday 11 November 1918 at 8 o' clock in the evening the Blendworth and Catherington church bells rang peals of joy and thanksgiving to herald peace and in June 1919 three of the men who had been prisoners of war in Germany, Frank Tilbury, George White and Henry Jerrum returned.[20]

The real cost of the war on the local communities, however, is clearly to be seen on the War Memorial, largely paid for by Sir Dudley Clarke-Jervoise who contributed £343, and erected in the Square. There 74 names of local men who fought and died for their country are inscribed.[21] In November 1916 the Parish Magazine stated that 76 men were at the front in the Army and 64 at home or foreign stations and a further 62 in the Royal Navy. Including another 18 in the Territorial Army there were a total of 220 men enlisted.[22] That number must have represented the vast majority of Horndean men between the ages of 19 and 38 whom Kitchener had urged to join up, and it means that a third of them were never to return. There could hardly have been a family who did not suffer a loss or whose neighbours and friends had not done so. It is not surprising that the village wished to celebrate the cessation of hostilities memorably. The Parish Council proposed in May 1919 to raise a 3d rate to cover the cost of peace celebrations and on Saturday 19 July all the school children had a tea and sports. Typically, for an English holiday, rain fell and all had to adjourn to the Parish Hall with the sports being completed on the following Monday—a day which was a holiday for all pupils. On the 8 December a dinner was held at the *Good Intent*, the *Ship and Bell* and the *Red Lion* for all returning members of the forces followed by a smoking concert at the Parish Hall.[23]

During the war the last link of the Napier family to Merchistoun Hall was broken with the death of Mrs. Eloisa Jodrell, daughter of Admiral Sir Charles Napier, who had given the name of his birthplace to the Hall when he had bought Qualletts Grove in 1836 and lived there until his death, in November 1860, and burial in Catherington Churchyard.[24] Another sad event was the destruction, on Friday 27 January, of the greater part of Blendworth Lodge, the home of widowed Mrs. Long. The fire had started in a chimney and "fire brigades were called from Havant and Emsworth but only the latter arrived with a steamer about 5 o' clock the horses being driven by Miss Isabel Silver the eighteen year old daughter of Mr. R. Silver. The fire began about 3 p.m. The Petersfield Brigade could not attend because, although they were ready, they had no horses"![25] The necessity of Horndean having its own fire station was becoming obvious.

Shortly before the end of the war, in August 1918, the Clarke-Jervoise family sold off over 2,200 acres of the western part of the Idsworth estate. The properties sold included Five Heads Farm, Kinches Farm (51 acres), Butts Farm (20 acres), Yoells Farm (65 acres), Prochurch Cottage, the smith's and wheelwright's shops, Tollgate Cottage, Southfield and two cottages in Horndean and the *Farmer Inn* in Catherington, which was bought by Gales Brewery. All the properties were auctioned and Austin and Wyatt, the auctioneers, were asked to interview tenants who were interested in buying at the *Ship and Bell*. Five Heads Farm was acquired by E.A. Edney and in 1921 he bought the cricket field which was no longer wanted by the club. The Idsworth estate retained Blendworth Farm of 496 acres, Pyle Farm 302 acres, Pyle Knapp Farm 126 acres and Prochurch Farm 10 acres, the first being sold after World War II in 1948 and the last in 1929 to George Grant. In 1921 and 1922 land at Cowplain from Park Lane to Padnell Road and London Road to Prochurch Lane was sold by the estate and in 1923 land from Prochurch Farm to the Causeway and then along to the tram terminus was sold in 50 feet wide lots to a depth of 200 to 400 feet with restrictions placed on the number of houses per plot. A central section opposite Causeway was excluded.

Only from this time on would it be possible to develop housing between Causeway and Prochurch Farm or between Causeway and the tram terminus.[26] There would, however, be problems associated with development as no mains water, drainage or lighting was available.

The first of these problems was solved in 1924 when land at Prochurch Farm was leased for a reservoir and pumping station for Catherington Rural District Council and from this year Horndean received mains water. "To have a tap and a sink was wonderful".[27] But outlying areas were not so fortunate. Extensions of the water main to Havant Road took place in 1928 and Pyle Farm received mains water in 1930. St. Giles Farm, created from the break up of the large Blendworth Farm after the death of James Goldsmith in 1931, had to wait until 1933 for mains water. New Buildings had water in 1937 and Nobles Buildings, Hook Lane, received water and electricity in 1938-39.[28] Electricity did not arrive until 1933, Blendworth being lit up on 1 October.[29] In May 1929, Catherington residents petitioned for a water supply. They were successful and where the rather grandly titled 'Garden Suburb' of Catherington, planned in 1932 for 115 houses, was built on Glamorgan Road in 1933 water was available in all the new properties. Similarly, mains drainage did not arrive until the early 1930s. In May 1931, a tender for the Horndean and Blendworth Sewerage Extension Scheme was accepted at a cost of £24,666, although Drill Hall Road (now Queen's Crescent) and Glamorgan Road were not linked until 1936 and Five Heads Road in 1937.

The village in the 1920s was, nevertheless, not substantially different from that of 1900. In fact some of the same families still traded. Bettesworth, however, had become a stationer and ironmonger, but Edney, grocer, as well as Edney, builder, remained as did Mitchell, grocer, Pearson the carrier, Penny builders and both butchers Pruce and Pescott. In 1921, however, the blacksmith had become Walter Lovick who was kept busy making shoes for the carthorses and hunters and the iron rims on all the cartwheels. Most of the businesses still delivered by horse and cart.[30] But times were beginning to change. From 1919 buses started to run on solid tyres, turning round at the *Good Intent*, competing with the Light Railway. They were operated by the Safety Tourist Company, but later taken over by the Southdown Bus Company.[31] In the village the sign of change was the establishment of the garage of Sidney George Marsh, motor engineer, where, in the 1930s, his manual pumps exhibited the price of petrol as 1s 9d (9p) a gallon.[32] His success was partly based on the fact that Gales Brewery introduced petrol-engined lorries from 1908 and cars from 1912, as well as expanding their numbers of tied public houses. Under Herbert Bowyer, the Brewery was outstandingly successful in the first 40 years of the twentieth century. While the British brewing industry suffered a period of declining output up to the Second World War, losing approximately half of national production, Gales completely bucked the trend and increased output by 140 per cent. Brewers generally had to compete with the growth of consumer expenditure in other directions—radios, cinemas, the shops, coffee bars and spectator sports. In the 1930s a Government cheap money policy resulted in over 4 million houses being built, and meant much expenditure went on homes and their contents—cookers, vacuum cleaners, refrigerators, furniture and furnishings. Yet Gales carried on increasing their sales, the Wall Street crash of 1929 and the subsequent Great Depression of the early 1930s, leaving the Company's output virtually untouched. It certainly suggests that Gales beers which won many awards in the 1920s and 1930s were part of consumers' choices.[33]

The development of motorised transport inevitably led to the need to improve roads and the A3 was widened on the east side from Horndean to Chalton Lane in 1926 and from Chalton Lane to Gravel Hill in 1929. Much of the new traffic was commercial, either for business or public transport. The increase in private cars was restricted to the wealthy, most people travelling by bus or beginning to enjoy the comfortable new motor coaches, as J.B. Priestley noted in 1933 when travelling through the Hampshire countryside en route to Southampton. "They offer luxury to all but the most poverty-stricken" he wrote. "They have annihilated the old distinction between rich and poor travellers. No longer can the wealthy go splashing past in their private conveyances, driving the humble pedestrian to the wall, leaving him to shake his fist and curse the proud pampered crew. The children of these fist shakers now go thundering by in their own huge coaches and loll in velvet as they go. Perhaps it is significant that you get the same sort of overdone comfort, the same sinking away into a deep sea of plush, in the vast new picture theatres.....It is the decaying landed country folk, with their rattling old cars, their draughty country houses, their antique bathrooms and cold tubs who are the spartans of our time". Priestley was commenting not only on ordinary people's ability to travel more widely but also on the social changes which the First World War had brought about as well as the growth of the new mass entertainment, the cinema, the nearest for Horndean residents being the Curzon built in Waterlooville in the 1930s. The new post-war England was one of "filling stations and factories that look like exhibition buildings, of giant cinemas and dance-halls and cafes, bungalows with tiny garages, cocktail bars, Woolworths, motor-coaches, wireless, hiking, factory girls looking like actresses, greyhound racing and dirt tracks, swimming pools, and everything given away for a cigarette coupon".[34] But this ignored the fact that there were two million unemployed and many families suffering real hardship.

Even so, it was the road to Portsmouth not London which seemed to maintain its volume of traffic. The Light Railway tramcars may have disappeared, but buses now came into the village centre and on most summer Sunday evenings in the 1930s, queues of day trippers would form along the whole frontage of Gales Brewery to wait for extra buses to take them back to Portsmouth. The walks through the woods by Sheepwash and Rushmore Ponds were still unspoilt and the woodland remnants of the Forest of Bere undeveloped. On most days boys could be seen walking along the Portsmouth Road to the secondary school in Hartplain Avenue, Cowplain. These came from the old Union Workhouse which had been converted into a remand home until its use as a Civil Defence post in the Second World War. Another conversion came in June 1929, when the isolation hospital was sold to Mr. Edney for £750 (now Acacia Nursing Home), and three months later a further change with the demolition of the old *Brewer's Arms* in Five Heads Road and the building of the existing one, while Catherington House, Lord Hood's old home, was converted into a retreat house in June 1922 after Mr. Ernest Edney had sold it at a small price to the Church.[35]

Another post World War One development of note was the decision by Blendworth and Catherington parishes to have some war memorial of their own. Blendworth opted for a clock in the church and Catherington's War Memorial Committee decided in June 1919, on a lych-gate and chose to have a copy of that at Felpham Church, Bognor Regis, as opposed to the vicar, the Rev. Kefford's design. In July, the vicar wrote condemning the decision in that month's Parish Magazine. On July 9, he chaired a meeting of all the subscribers to the War Memorial Fund, which rejected the Felpham design. As a result the War Memorial Committee resigned. The following month the Committee's treasurer Admiral Bayly of Hinton Manor, stated that only the vicar's views were given in the Parish Magazine and had the vicar fallen into line with everyone else there would have been peace. Additionally, Admiral Bayly refused to hand over the funds and books to the new treasurer.

In January 1920 it was said that the vicar's chosen architect Mr. Romney Green was preparing final plans and the lych gate was consecrated on 24 August 1921 with the architect present. The Bishop of Winchester, carrying out the consecration said "I hope Catherington will remain a happy and United Parish".[36] Unfortunately the Rev. Kefford never saw the lych gate opened, for he died at the early age of 48 on 6 March 1920.

A further community development was the acquisition of a parish recreation ground. After two abortive attempts of acquiring land in 1927 and 1928, Mr. Edney of Five Heads Farm offered six acres of land for recreation on 2 July 1928. On 3 December Hampshire County Council gave consent for Catherington Parish Council to borrow £779 repayable over 30 years for purchase of the land, which was conveyed on 23 May 1929. Swings and a see-saw were installed in June 1933.[37]

But, from the point of view of this volume, the most significant inter-war development was the demise of Catherington Parish Council on 31 March 1932 and the appearance of Horndean Parish Council on 1 April.[38] The Civil parish had replaced the ecclesiastical one with Horndean being recognised as the major centre of population, having outgrown Catherington. At the same time Catherington Rural District Council was replaced by Petersfield Rural District Council. Some 3,000 people lived in the civil parish in the 1930s and between 1935 and 1939 over 200 new houses were built in Horndean. As well as Glamorgan Road, development of housing in the early 1930s had taken place along the London Road towards Snell's Corner, the northern end of Whitedirt Lane, the east side of Downhouse Road, Five Heads Road, Drill Hall Road (Queen's Crescent) and St. Ann's Road, the Causeway and Catherington Lane south end, Victory Avenue, Bulls Copse and Frogmore Lane, the Portsmouth Road south of the Methodist Chapel and north from Prochurch Farm. In the late 1930's it was these locations which were to see more development. Even so, population growth could not save the Portsdown and Horndean Light Railway, for it ceased on 3 October 1934 having been bought out by the Southdown Motor Company.

The period also saw changes in the local schools. From 1 October 1930 Catherington and Blendworth Girls' schools were reorganised as Junior Girls', all the girls over eleven years of age being transferred to the newly built Senior School in Hartplain Avenue, Cowplain. The infants were supplied with tables and the junior girls with dual desks. Catherington had 92 children on roll and, following an inspection it was described as having a "delightful atmosphere and the outlook considered good". Horndean Boys School would have similarly changed. Catherington School was subject to a further reorganisation in April 1939 when boys were admitted and it became a junior mixed and infants school, which was a great advantage for those families whose sons and daughters could now attend the same school.[39] Presumably, Horndean did the same. A new excuse for non-attendance also appeared in December 1921 when Blendworth children were absent in the two weeks prior to Christmas "to see the shops in Portsmouth and Southsea". Ten years later in December 1931 attempts to learn at Blendworth must have been improved by the installation of electric light—'a beautiful light and a great improvement on the two lamps'. Even so, it was not good enough for one girl who returned to Portsmouth complaining that "this place is too quiet for her". In December 1934, the school had lavatories and wash basins installed. Mains drainage resulted in the demise of the sanitary buckets and ashpit closets, and in 1937 the playground was asphalted during the summer holidays, thus reducing the amount of dirt brought into the school, especially on rainy days. By September 1938, the growing international crisis had anxious parents arriving at Catherington School enquiring about gas masks for their children and on the 29th they were all fitted with them.[40] Preparations for war had begun as early as February 1937, with discussion of an air raid precautions scheme. By January 1939, detailed evacuation schemes had been produced and in March, 1,200 houses were canvassed about the billeting of children.

There is little doubt that the Second World War had a greater impact directly on Horndean residents than the first one. The schools were affected from the beginning with the problem of housing and educating an evacuated London School. Blendworth girls spent half a day in Nash Hall and half in the School, alternating with the London Belleville Junior School. Catherington took in evacuated girls while the boys went to Horndean. Many houses in the village accommodated the children and most built Anderson air raid shelters in their gardens. A public air raid shelter for the village was completed in September 1941. Schools had their windows painted with anti-splinter liquid and were provided with air raid first aid kits. Keydell House, Merchistoun Hall and Cadlington House were all requisitioned by the army in 1940. Blackout restrictions affected everyone, travelling after dark being particularly difficult and in winter school began at 9.30 so that children would not have to leave home in the dark. Air raids disrupted classes and on the night of 25 June 1941 a parachute bomb fell about 200 yards from Blendworth School blowing in several windows and bringing down part of the ceiling. Even so the structure was sound, so lessons were held a day later. Two months earlier, however, Horndean residents were less fortunate when, during an air raid, a stick of bombs fell demolishing one house in Bulls Copse and another in Causeway. Five people in two families were killed.[41] This was bringing the war home with a vengeance to the community and must have concerned all those who had vacated Portsmouth for the safety of the countrywide. In September

1940, Petersfield Rural District Council rented a four acre field at Horndean and created a camping site to accommodate people coming from Portsmouth to avoid the blitz. By May 1941 they had to lease another one and a half acres in Drift Road for an additional site as the original one was full. In addition about forty squatters moved into Catherington Lith in 1940 to escape the blitz in Portsmouth, some even building semipermanent hutments.[42] In June 1940 'squatters' of a different sort filled Hazleton Wood, when some of the 335,000 men evacuated from Dunquerque camped in tents there and others replaced some of the evacuated children in various homes. Similarly, before D Day exactly four years later, 6 June 1944, Hazleton Wood was again full of soldiers as was Queen's Enclosure, and Portsmouth and Havant Roads had tanks and DUKWs lined up along their lengths ready for the invasion. American forces were included in the latter location and they used Nash Hall for a cinema in the evenings before, one night, they all departed in total secrecy, leaving messages of thanks behind.

One other inconvenience of the war was the rationing of food and clothing, even more so for Horndean residents as, until May 1943, two thirds of the way through the war, they had to collect their ration books (and identity cards) from Petersfield. From the 20 May, an office was opened in Horndean.[43] Another development as a result of the war, was the commencement of school dinners on 24 June 1944. For Horndean they were supplied in containers from kitchens in Portchester! With the first severe icy weather in January 1945 no dinners were delivered and schools were closed.[44] For most people there were inconveniences and the wartime spirit of all pulling together to defeat the enemy was generally foremost and perhaps best epitomised, in September 1941, when War Weapons Week was declared. Horndean's target was to raise £3,000 in the week—that sum was raised on the first day and the week's final figure was £14,000.[45] But the real cost of the war to many was the additional 40 names of soldiers, sailors and airmen, which were inscribed on Horndean's war memorial. It was a war which worldwide, however, claimed the lives of more civilians than members of the forces. Yet no civilian names appear on the memorial. The names of the three members of the Jordan family, and the two Rileys, killed by German bombs in Bulls Copse and Causeway are not remembered. Two other deaths occurred late in the war when an RAF Mosquito with a crew of two Australians, flying low between the Brewer's Arms and the cottages at the junction of Five Heads Road and the Portsmouth Road, hit the centre of the roof of the Parish Hall and careered on to hit a row of elm trees across the Portsmouth Road. Wreckage was scattered down to the Havant Road.[46]

The end of the war V E Day (Victory in Europe) 8 May 1945 was marked by jubilant celebrations in Horndean, as elsewhere in Allied countries. Two days holiday was given to all schoolchildren and Catherington, Blendworth and Horndean schools combined at Horndean School for a joint sports day. Children from Catherington School marched in procession carrying flags and banners. A splendid tea was provided by the parents and the events closed at 6.30 p.m.[47] Street parties were everywhere. On 15 August V J Day (Victory over Japan), Japan surrendered and the Second World War was over. From 1 October street lighting was restored with 22 lights on the A3 through Horndean. Despite the celebrations, the years of austerity and rationing were to continue for some time—well into the 1950's though the Festival of Britain in 1951 was intended to brighten up the austere years and celebrate the peace. The coronation of Queen Elizabeth II in 1953 was also a celebratory occasion with two days holiday for the schools and village sports meetings. Catherington schoolchildren had the treat of being taken to Waterlooville's Curzon cinema to see the newsreel of the Coronation and four days later, on 12 June, children from all three local schools went to the Odeon Cinema, Cosham, to see the full length coronation film "A Queen is Crowned".[48]

Meanwhile, the end of the war brought no immediate change to Horndean residents. Building licences were restricted and raw materials scarce, so little development occurred in the immediate post-war years. Residents of Broadway Lane Cottages must have felt a sense of relief in 1946, not just over the end of the war, but because they at last received mains water. The following year Bulls Copse residents were asking for a connection to the mains. But it was 1947 which presaged the first post war housing development when in July the Rural District Council bought the Merchistoun Estate for £14,335 17s 0d. By April 1948 there were 101 applicants on the list for what was to be a major council house development. The tender for the first eight houses was issued in July 1948, shortly after the District Council had sold 2.6 acres of the land to the recently formed Horndean Community Association.[49]

With the help of a grant the Community Association were able to build three tennis courts and a pavilion on the land, and when Merchistoun Hall came back on the market in the early 1950s the Association worked hard to raise the capital. Thus in 1955, for £5,000, they were the happy new owners of the Hall. Much work had to be carried out to clean and restore the Hall but everybody gave their free time, being rewarded on Saturday, 31 January 1956, when the Horndean Community Centre was officially opened. The Association fetes became the highlight of the Horndean year, being opened by nationally known stars like Arthur English, Harry Secombe and Peter Sellers. In the early years, perhaps the most influential force behind the Centre was Admiral Murray, who had bought Cadlington House at the end of 1937, and who chaired the committee which established the Community Association.[50]

The Merchistoun council housing estate was to be the first of many housing developments which were to change the face of post-war Horndean and remove the tranquil village atmosphere for ever. It was built with no garages, there being no anticipation on the part of the District Council that its tenants may one day become owners of private transport other than cycles or motor bikes. But it was the growth in ownership of motor cars which was to be the real catalyst for change.

The first substantial private development was the estate built on Keydell Farm lands. Keydell House a Georgian mansion, with gardens and farm had been bought in the 1880s by Lieutenant General Drury-Lowe and in 1912 his widow leased the farm to John and Elizabeth Strange. The place was lovely with bluebells and buttercups in profusion. The garden meadow had a view to Portsdown Hill and, except for a single cottage, no buildings interrupted the view. John Strange died in January 1932, and his funeral was probably the last of its type. The coffin covered with greenery and yew branches surrounded by wreaths was placed on one of his own farm carts, drawn by his horse Polly, which was led by the cowman along the two miles of country road to Catherington Church. The family followed in, by then, the traditional cars. His son Ron and daughter-in-law Margaret took over the farm.

The year before, the 85 year old widowed Lady Drury-Lowe had died and the estate was divided and sold, the Stranges eventually buying the farm and converting the old coach house into a larger home which had electricity and mains water supplied in 1934. The Second World War saw stray bombs fall there at the first bombings of Portsmouth and Keydell House occupied by the army. The Stranges sold the farm in 1953 but retained the nursery, which their son John was running as a market garden. Keydell House was demolished in the 1960s and was replaced by a housing estate up to the boundaries of the nursery.[51]

The selling of the farm in 1953 was the catalyst for the building of the Keydell estate. In late 1957 and early 1958 the development had drainage problems causing flooding in Blenheim Road, Bulls Copse and Frogmore Lane. Bulls Copse itself was to begin to expand in late 1958. A further estate of 140 houses, which was to be linked to the Keydell one, was begun at Kings Mede, with an entrance from Causeway (Catherington Lane). It was developed southward to join the Keydell estate.

Meanwhile, in 1948, the Idsworth Estate sold off over 600 acres, mainly woodland, between the Havant, Portsmouth and Padnell Roads for £23,400. This part of the estate comprised Hazleton Wood, a former part of Prochurch Farm, Blendworth Common, Pyle Knapp Farm and Rushmore Cottages.[52] The value of most of the land lay in its timber, but once that had been harvested then it was clearly of greater value for housing development. It was from Cowplain's Padnell Road that the large Hazleton estate was being developed northwards, in the late 1950s, and beginning to eat away at both the Common and Hazleton Wood. The popular ramble from Waterlooville through the woods to Horndean was no more.

But all this development was to have its effect on the small Horndean School which could not cope with the rising numbers of children. Thus, in March 1959, the new Horndean Junior School opened at the eastern end of Merchistoun Estate, and in September of the previous year Catherington Junior School had erected a prefabricated classroom (hut) allowing juniors to be separated from infants. Only two years earlier they had come up to date with flush sanitation installed![53] Blendworth School had to wait until 1966 for its old toilets to be demolished and new ones, with wash basins, erected.[54] Not only was it necessary to cater for growing educational needs but also spiritual ones. Thus, in the mid 1950s, a Hall was erected in Napier Road as a Mass Centre for Roman Catholic worshippers, looked after by the Waterlooville Catholic Church, before it became the independent St. Edmund's Catholic Parish Church in 1968.[55]

Thus, from the mid 1950s, when electric street lighting replaced gas, came the beginning of the population expansion and housing development in Horndean. By the 1961 census more than 5,500 lived in the civil parish. But by comparison with what was to come this was a relatively muted beginning. As in most of south-east Hampshire, the 1960s were to see a veritable orgy of building. Already in 1960 there were ominous signs. Horndean's new Junior School could not cope with the numbers of children and an overflow had to be taught in the old school (now library). The emergency would end, it was said, when the new Padnell Junior School opened at Cowplain in January 1962. Meanwhile, as numbers of children rose from 344 in March 1961 to 424 in June that year, plans had to be made to use the Drill Hall and the Parish Hall for teaching additional children. Conditions at the school worsened throughout 1962. Not until November 1962 was there any relief when 100 pupils left for Cowplain. In November 1961, it was said that, since 1950, some 964 additional dwellings had been erected in Horndean, and it was estimated that in the next six or seven years a further 1,400 would be constructed.

In the north of the parish, in the early 1960s, Hawthorn Road and the Southdown Road area were subject to rapid development and a new estate near to Snells Corner had its names, Godwin Crescent, Wessex, Draycote and Francis Roads and Wode Close approved in March 1962. North Road and St. Michael's Way were also under construction. At the rear of Merchistoun Hall another estate, comprising Murray Road, Bourne and Dorset Closes was a further 1962 development. A new road (now Hazleton Way) being driven into the Hazleton Estate had created an obstruction on the footpath and before the end of 1960 motorists using the road were complaining that the adjacent bus shelter obstructed their view. Despite the fact that the estate was far from complete, its road was. The Parish Council were concerned because of the creation of problems in health, education and burial provision (Catherington Churchyard had to be extended) and in 1963 came the problem of overloading on the telephone exchange with real problems telephoning Portsmouth, particularly between 9 and 10 a.m.—of particular concern was the inability to make emergency calls rapidly.

In July 1964 the Parish Council wrote to the County education authority pointing out the need for a secondary school in Horndean, but the reply "not in the near future" was discouraging. Instead, in December, came a proposal from Hampshire County Council for a new infants school for 240 five to seven year old pupils. Horndean Junior School numbers had risen to over 400 again. Built for 380 it had 434 pupils in February 1965. However, 80 places were to be provided by temporary classrooms so that, with the new infants school intended to be built on the same site there would be 700 small children on one site. But the use of the Parish Hall by two classes would no longer be necessary. Catherington school was taking its share, by having a second wooden classroom added in 1964.

Meanwhile, in the south of the parish the large, 500 house Hazleton estate continued to be built and the Parish Council were concerned about the length of time the development was taking. Their request for a terminal date elicited the response that it would be finished in 1966. While all those larger estates were being built small builders were busily infilling with limited developments such as in 1965 at the rear of Cross Lane—between the Kings Mede and Keydell Estates, and off Catherington Lane where the cottages known as the Riggs disappeared to make way for Cheriton Close—beyond which was still trees and fields to Frogmore Lane. In 1966 Benbow Close, residences for the elderly were also constructed off the Merchistoun Estate and permission was given for three shops to be built on the corner of Kings Mede and Catherington Lane.

But development did not stop there in the 1960s. In the north of the parish 300 houses bounded by Southdown Road and Hawthorn Crescent needed some open space. In October 1966 a plan to build 210 dwellings on 30 acres of Hazleton Farm was opposed by Petersfield Rural District Council, concern being expressed about lack of open space and schools. In 1967 came a new development on the south-east side of Murray Road four new closes being named. Open space was becoming important,. thus the developers of Kings Mede estate were refused permission to build on the only open space within the site and, similarly, the Parish Council proposed to preserve the Dell in Hazleton Way as the only substantial open space in the Hazleton Estate.[56]

The resulting population growth of Horndean Parish from all these developments can be seen in the census figures. From 5,555 in 1961 the number of people rose by a massive 57 per cent to 8,724 by 1971. An increase of 3,169 meant more than 300 additional people each year were making their residences in Horndean. The consequences were considerable. Both the Parish Council and its representation on the Rural District Council were increased in 1965, the former from 11 to 15 and the latter from four to five. In 1967 planning permission was given for a new secondary school off Bridle Path and late that year the new infant school opened to relieve some of the pressure on educational space. At the other end of the age scale, it was proposed to build old people's flatlets at the junction of Portsmouth Road with Five Heads Road on the site of the row of cottages where Ann Gale had once had her shop. New services were also required and on Blendworth Hill the new Fire Station, built at a cost of £15,000, opened in 1964 and a new telephone exchange was erected on the Westfield site, indicating that one of Horndean's larger houses had been demolished to make way for this progress. Completed in 1971 it stood empty and inoperative until 1975, when it replaced the exchange in what is now Napier Hall, acquired by the Parish Council in 1984. Just north of the telephone exchange on Horndean Hill planning permission was granted in January 1969 for a shopping precinct and car park. In the same year new play equipment for children was installed in the recreation ground.

Road widening was necessary to accommodate the increasing volume of traffic which all the new development helped to create, but it meant the loss of the early eighteenth century Toll House in 1965. Catherington Lane, a narrow but attractive road with stately poplar trees, was altered beyond recognition by widening on the very side where the trees grew, so all were lost in 1968, the year in which it was agreed to widen Havant Road. The following year came the first references to problems of car parking in Merchistoun Road, with a request for lay-byes to be created.[57]

The last three items are all a reflection of the growth of personal motorised transport. Many of the new arrivals in Horndean, in the age of the motor car, were commuters to Portsmouth, especially since few jobs had been created in Horndean. Gales Brewery still survived but only just. Its post-war performance between 1945 and 1959 had been the opposite of its pre-war experience. From an output of 25,000 barrels per annum production fell to less than 11,000 in 1959, some 58 per cent of output had been lost, a performance twice as poor as the brewing industry's average. Clearly there was no scope for increased employment at Gales—exactly the reverse was true. From 1959 output did begin to improve led by the introduction of Horndean Special Bitter (HSB) in that year, but from such a low base any improvement would need to take up the slack in Gales operation before additional workers were required.[58] There is of course no doubt that the population growth itself must have been a blessing to producers such as Gales, just as the building of hundreds of houses must have meant that the 1960s was an excellent decade of trading for the Butser Turf and Timber Company. Founded by E.A. Edney in 1929 and incorporated in 1933, the company was the first to cultivate permanent pasture professionally and to produce turf which had been fertilised and weed treated. Most of the houses built in the 1960s had gardens which builders turfed to make them attractive to prospective buyers. Butser Turf were well placed to benefit from this trend as well as the clearing of woodland, not only in Horndean, but also in Clanfield, Cowplain and Waterlooville all of which experienced the building boom.[59]

In October 1967, a suggestion at a Parish Council meeting that an area might be put aside within the parish for industrial development met with the response that there were no plans. Clearly it was considered that Horndean was becoming a dormitory of Portsmouth. Even though its population was growing so fast, one large open space was provided for the public when in 1963 Captain Long presented 32 acres of Catherington Down to Hampshire County Council on condition it was preserved in its natural state for the benefit of all. The following year it was proposed to build a village hall for Catherington at the rear of the Village School.

Late in 1964 it was discovered that the statue of Victory and its base surmounting the War Memorial were in a dangerous condition and beyond repair. On 11 December, after 43 years, the statue was removed and in June 1965 work began to raise the memorial by one foot and to surmount it with a lamp.

Although the 1970s saw population growth continue it was at a much lower rate. In 1981 Horndean had 10,181 people in the parish, a rise of under 1,500 for the decade 1971-81, less than half that of the 1960s. The major development of the 1970s was the opening of Horndean's first secondary school called Horndean Bilateral School, quickly becoming Horndean Comprehensive and then in the late 1980s Horndean Community School. It opened in September 1970 and when it reached its full complement in the mid 1970s, there would be 1,500 pupils, a number assisted by the raising of the school leaving age in September 1973 to 16.[60] At least some employment for Horndean residents would be created. The other major development of the 1970s was literally to cut the village in two. This was the proposal, to begin in 1973, for a new arterial road of motorway standard from Horndean to Bedhampton, which was opened at the end of 1979. In the process Antigua cottages were demolished in April 1977. It was a clear indication of the impact of the motor car on the local area, for the journey to work in Portsmouth had become one of attempting to avoid the inevitable traffic jams along the Portsmouth Road.

In addition, housing development continued into the 1970s. Phase two of the First Avenue site, was completed in 1970, as was Hillside Close. Tarberry Crescent, opposite the Drill Hall, was built in 1971, when 58 more council houses were constructed in First Avenue. Durland Road on the site of Durham House in 1972, St. Hugh's Close and St. Hilda's Avenue in 1973, among others, were also completed. Dean Court, the old people's flatlets were subject to many delays, but eventually would open in 1974, nearly six years after the tenders were put out.

As a result of the continued population growth Horndean Junior School had not only to continue to use the old school building, but also to import two transportable classrooms in 1972. The presence of two large schoosl in the Merchistoun estate area was inevitably to lead to traffic and parking problems. The County Council refused a request for parking bays to be installed but accepted that one should be placed in Merchistoun Road outside the Junior School. Parking problems were to plague Barton Cross residents for many years and pointed to the inadequacy of a small cul-de-sac as the only entrance to a major secondary school. As early as 1973 the School and the Parish Council unsuccessfully attempted to obtain a second entrance.

Close to, but outside the parish, came the development of Queen Elizabeth Country Park. For Horndean residents, this expanse of natural woodland had been a pleasant week-end family picnic and rambling spot, replacing the lost walks through Hazleton Wood. Its conversion, with a Visitors Centre and pay car park, removed local residents' free access and the unspoilt nature of the entrance area. But open space outside the parish needed to be matched by open space within. After several years of intensive residential development, with little thought of open or amenity space, the Parish Council wanted the County Council to address the matter. In March 1972, a resident of Viking Way had referred to the lack of playing space—the only field which local children had used had been taken over by the development of council houses in First Avenue. The first result of this increasing awareness was that the Dell, in Hazleton Way became a recreational area after agreement between the developers and the Rural District Council in 1973.[61] And the 1980s development between Frogmore Lane, Victory Avenue and Catherington Lane which commenced in Stonechat Road had open space planned into it.

The early 1980s also saw the development of the Horndean oilfield, the site for oil exploration at Pyle Farm being levelled in November 1982, drilling commencing in 1983 with a 150 foot high rig and nodding donkeys becoming part of Horndean's skyline since. Meanwhile, Gales Brewery had recovered its lost output, having record production levels in the late 1970s, thus, in the economic recession of 1979-81, the decision was taken to increase productive capacity. The cramped Horndean site would not allow a lateral spread so the decision was taken to build upwards. A new process floor costing £600,000 was constructed in 1983 on top of the existing building, but sympathetically blending with the original. As Gales expanded, elsewhere in Horndean permanent construction took place. In August 1982 a familiar landmark was to disappear when the old Union Workhouse, which had been built in 1835 on London Road, was demolished. For a short period of its recent history it had housed Horndean's only swimming pool and also been the home of Sixten and Cassey for lampshade manufacture, their main fabric wholesaling being carried on at Crookley, where they had acquired the old Gales residence. The Workhouse was replaced by a light industrial estate, bringing more employment to the parish. A permanent home for Horndean Library was to be a further product of the early 1980s. It began in February 1967 in Nash Hall, now the Brewery offices, and on 26 March 1969, transferred to the Parish Hall in Five Heads Road, when opening hours were extended from 10 to 14 per week. On 2 November 1981 it moved into the old Junior School building, which had, at last, been freed from overflow pupils, and remains there to this day. Apart from providing books and information it holds storytimes and activities for children.

The early 1980s was also to see a major change along the Havant Road for John Strange's Keydell Nurseries began to develop a new site in 1982 on the south side, which included Rushmore Cottages and Pond. Five years later, the new and larger Keydell Nurseries opened and the old site sold, Cherry Tree Gardens being built on the former nursery.

Meanwhile, 1986 saw the opening of the New Blendworth Centre, which aimed to give youngsters with special needs and disabilities an interest and a sense of achievement in their teenage and adult lives. Like Keydell it is a horticultural centre, although with charitable status. It has its own nursery, in what was part of the grounds of Cadlington House, and labour force of youngsters helping to keep Horndean tidy, trimming hedges, repairing fences and clearing footpaths. The almost forty disabled youngsters enjoy the achievement of growing their own produce and have recreational and learning facilities. Next door, Cadlington House was sold by Admiral Murray's widow at a bargain price to Mencap and since 1978 has been the home for some 27 young adults with severe learning disabilities and mental handicaps, where the staff provide a quality of life which would be unlikely in an institution or mental hospital.[62]

When the Horndean Area Local Plan was produced in 1984 it envisaged that almost another 500 residential dwellings would be built before 1991. West of Frogmore Lane would be a site for 65 houses but the vast majority, 370 were to be on the land between Catherington and Frogmore Lanes, with three other building sites. Fortunately, the main building did not begin before 16 October 1987, for early that morning Horndean was hit by a full scale hurricane leaving a swathe of damage and destruction. Countless fallen trees, blocked roads and damaged houses testified to the powerful winds which swept through Southern England. The major development began with Stonechat Road in the late 1980s and continued in the early 1990s and finally the north side of Stonechat Road in 1999. Similarly, land put aside for industrial development to the south of Portsmouth Road and west of the A3M became the Lakesmere Road site, adjoining the old workhouses site and intended to meet employment needs to 1996. Smaller light industrial estates had been developed earlier in Enterprise Road and behind the new telephone exchange on the Westfield site.

The plan also indicated a public open space at Wessex Road in north Horndean, a large recreational area north of the feeder road to the A3M from Catherington Lane, and playing fields off Frogmore Lane, plus a recreation area at Yoells Copse. A village centre proposed for the junction of White Dirt Lane and Drift Road was developed.[63]

The 1990s were to prove a remarkable decade for Horndean's largest company Gales. The number of public houses they owned rose to around 120, while the company evolved from being solely a brewing concern to a broader retailing enterprise, giving it a broader base for the future. The effect could be seen in the company's turnover which doubled from £10 million to over £20 million between 1990 and 1994 with profits approaching £3 million. In 1997 Gales celebrated their 150th anniversary with the publication of their history. Since 1847 the number of breweries in Britain has fallen from about 45,000 to under 100 and brewing companies to 65. Gales has both survived and expanded—a remarkable achievement, which for Horndean residents has meant generations of employment, and also a rare visit of a member of the royal family to the village when HRH Prince Andrew opened their 150th anniversary celebrations.[64]

While Gales successfully continued, 1999 saw the end of an even older Horndean institution for on 31 March the Independent Methodist Chapel closed its doors. Riddled with dry rot its restoration was too expensive to justify, thus another landmark, part of Horndean for 169 years and known not only to its worshippers, but also particularly to generations of travellers on the Light Railway because it stood close to the terminus, was, seemingly, to be no more. Its worshippers were to transfer to the chapel in Drift Road. Similarly the end came in the summer of 1999 for the Parish Hall at the end of Five Heads Road when it was demolished. A new one was to be built between Catherington Church and the vicarage, the first sod being cut on 1 August.

A decade after the 1984 Local Plan, East Hampshire District Council produced a district local plan in March 1994, indicating that, between 1991 and 2001, some 4,600 additional dwellings would be built in East Hampshire. The only new allocation to affect Horndean was for 30 houses west of Lovedean Lane, apart from infilling or conversion or sub division of properties. However, the east side of Portsmouth Road, Horndean was to be protected, as an area of low density with substantial homes set in large plots with mature trees, from further intensification or development.

The plan stated that Horndean was poorly provided with recreational facilities thus Dell Piece West was allocated for informal recreation and kickabout areas plus commercial recreational facilities. So were the remaining strip of Hazleton Wood between the Hazleton estate and the A3M, playing fields off Catherington Lane, north of Stonechat Road, an informal recreation area with kickabout facilities south of the caravan park west of London Road and north of Horndean village, and Yoells Copse, which was regarded as of nature conservation importance. Additionally, the well wooded Catherington Lith was thought best in Council ownership in order to implement the management scheme for the area, devised to ensure nature conservation and informal use. Areas of undeveloped land between Horndean and Blendworth, Horndean and Catherington and Horndean and Clanfield were designated as local gaps as they formed important breaks between the different communities and therefore help to retain their separate identities.[65] Thus it seems, as the people of Horndean approach the year 2000 there will be a pause in the residential building which saw the population rise from over 5,500 in 1961 to 11,985 in 1991. There is little doubt that by the millennium it will be well over 12,000 a growth of over 116 per cent in 30 years. Quite enough.

Even so Horndean residents should not be too depressed by this. Unlike Waterlooville, where virtually all traces of the attractive village photographed by Herbert Marshall in the early years of the twentieth century, have long since disappeared, visitors to Horndean, Blendworth and Catherington would still be able to recognise much of the centres of these communities as being similar to those they would have seen one hundred years ago. It says much for the local authorities that these village centres can still be enjoyed—Blendworth and Catherington still demonstrate the rural charm that brought those myriads of day trippers by tram in the early years of the century and Horndean, by virtue of the transfer of traffic to the A3M roaring close by, similarly retains much of its early twentieth century structure.

Finally, the 1990s also saw the development of probably the largest builing in Horndean, with the opening of the Safeway supermarket in Lakesmere Road. For those readers who wonder how much progress has been made in modern times it would be instructive to turn back the pages of this volume and look again at the contents of the community's shops in the seventeenth and eighteenth centuries. Then it was possible to describe all their contents. Should an attempt be made here to do the same for the contents of Safeway then this book would at least double in size. In three hundred years consumer choice has widened astronomically so that it is possible for one customer to leave the supermarket with a trolley full of more goods than the total contents of the seventeenth century shop. That also says something of the growth in consumer wealth—that one person can afford to buy so much. Similarly, Safeway's car park is vastly bigger than Horndean's old bus station, situated mid-way along the village on the west side of the road, ever was. It demonstrates that whereas in the past only the rich with their carriage and pair could afford personal transport, now most people can and their transport is equivalent to the power of ten horses or more. Few eighteenth century wealthy could have afforded the fifteen horse equivalent of a 1500cc motor car. And this progress has almost entirely been in the second half of the twentieth century.

History is a continuum and there is no doubt that the twenty-first century will see the accelerating rate of change of the past continue to transform lives at an even faster pace, especially with the revolution in information technology. Even so, it seems very likely that future generations will still be able to enjoy the increasingly ageing charm of the three communities which form the parish of Horndean. If not, then it is just as well that the Parish Council commissioned this book, so that the images in its words and pictures will be there for generations of children still to come.

References

1 Extracted from *Horndean as it was*, tapes made by the Horndean Women's Institute in 1968, when Bessie Catchlove and Mrs. Edney were asked for their recollections of Horndean at the beginning of the twentieth century. Miss Catchlove, born in Blendworth in 1876, the daughter of Edmund Catchlove, sawyer, and his wife Jane would have been 92 when her voice was recorded. She was 24 at the beginning of the century. The original tapes are at the HRO Wessex Film and Sound Archive.
2 PRO RG12/944, Census of Great Britain, 1891.
3 Stapleton, *Gales of Horndean*, p.29; Stapleton and Thomas, *Gales*, forthcoming.
4 HRO 43M75/F/B87, Clarke-Jervoise Estate Papers, list of wells Jan. 1905; 43M75 E/C 1-25.
5 HRO Wessex Film and Sound Archive, W I Tapes; 43M75 E/C 1-25, Clarke-Jervoise Estate Papers for reference to *Farmer Inn*.
6 L Bern, *The Portsdown and Horndean Light Railway*, 1980, pp.1-2.
7 *HT.* 6465, 23 Sept. 1905.
8 HRO Wessex Film and Sound Archive, W I Tapes.
9 Ibid.
10 *Bennett's Business Directory*, 1907, p.108.
11 J C Todd, *William's Guide to some of the Beauty Spots on the Portsdown and Horndean Light Railway*, 1910, pp.19-21.
12 *HT.* 6367, 16 Jan. 1909.
13 Todd, *William's Guide*, pp. 3, 18, 19, 21. The booklet described fifty walks.
14 PCRO CHU41/5/A1, Catherington Parish Magazine, Feb. 1911–12.
15 HRO 57M92/4, Clarke-Jervoise Estate Papers.

16 W I Tapes; *Hampshire*, April 1984, p. 54. This may well have been the last case of 'Rough Music' in England.
17 This account of school and educational activities is taken from entries in Blendworth School Log Books, No.1, 21 April 1879–14 April 1904; No.2, 4 April 1905–22 Dec. 1916. The Log Books are now at the HRO.
18 PCRO CHU41/5/A2, Catherington Parish Magazine, 1913–26.
19 Blendworth School Log Book, No.2, 4 April 1905–22 Dec. 1916; No.3, 8 Jan. 1917–31 March 1925.
20 PCRO CHU41/5/A2, Catherington Parish Magazine, 1913–26.
21 See Appendix 1.
22 PCRO CHU41/5/A2, Catherington Parish Magazine, 1913–26.
23 HRO 20M81/A/PX1, Catherington Parish Council Minutes; Blendworth School Log Book No 3, 8 Jan. 1917–31. Mar. 1925.
24 PCRO CHU41/5/A2 Catherington Parish Magazine 1913–26; 'Merchistoun Hall', typescript history, anon.
25 *HT.* 7052, 2 Feb. 1917.
26 HRO 43M75/E/C 15a, 15b, Clarke-Jervoise Letter Books; 57M92/4, Clarke-Jervoise Estate Papers.
27 W I Tapes.
28 HRO 57M92 Clarke-Jervoise Estate Papers.
29 HL Horndean Parish Council Minutes.
30 *Kelly's Directory of Hampshire*, 1923, pp.160–62.
31 W I Tapes.
32 *Kelly's Directory*, 1923, p.162.
33 Stapleton, *Gales of Horndean*, pp.25–41; Stapleton and Thomas *Gales*, chapters 4 and 5 forthcoming.
34 HRO 42M75/E/C 1–25, Clarke-Jervoise Estate Papers; J B Priestley, *English Journey*, 1934, pp.3–4, 401.
35 HL Catherington Rural District Council Minutes, 13 Sept. 1927–29 March 1932; *HT.* 3829, 2 June 1922.
36 PCRO CHU41/5/A2, Parish Magazine, 1913–26.
37 HRO 20M81/A/PX1, Catherington Parish Council Minutes; HL, Horndean Parish Council Minutes.
38 HL Horndean P C Minutes.
39 Blendworth School Log Book, No 4, 1 April 1925–31 March 1941; Catherington Junior Girls' School Log Book, 1 Oct. 1930–25 March 1964. I am most grateful to the headteacher Mrs. M. Williams for allowing me access to the Log Book.
40 Catherington School Log Book, 1930-64.
41 Blendworth School Log Book, No.4, 1 April 1925–31 March 1941; No.5, 1 April 1941–13 May 1981; HM 451A/3 Mortuary Register Book.
42 HL Petersfield Rural District Council Minutes; Parish Council Minutes.
43 HL Horndean P C Minutes.
44 Blendworth School Log Book No.5, 1 April 1941–13 May 1981.
45 HL Horndean P C Minutes.
46 *The News*, 4 April 1996.
47 Blendworth School Log Book No.5, 1941–81; Catherington Junior Girls' School Log Book, 1930–64.
48 Catherington School Log Book, 1930–64.
49 Petersfield R D C Minutes.
50 'Merchistoun Hall', typescript, anon., n.d., pp.10–12.
51 HM notes from Margaret Strange's autobiographical notebook.

52 HL Horndean P C Minutes; Sale Particulars of part of Idsworth Estate, 19 Feb. 1948. I am most grateful to Alec Peters for drawing the sale catalogue to my attention and allowing me use of his copy.
53 HL Ibid.; Catherington School Log Book, 1930–64.
54 Blendworth School Log Book No.5, 1941–81.
55 I am most grateful to Fr Lawrence Flinn for kindly providing this information.
56 Information on all these developments comes from Horndean P C Minutes.
57 Ibid.
58 Stapleton, *Gales of Horndean*, pp. 47–52; Stapleton and Thomas, *Gales*, Chapter 6 forthcoming.
59 *Petersfield Post*, 29 Dec. 1993, Stapleton, *Waterlooville*, n.p.
60 Horndean P C Minutes.
61 Ibid.; *Petersfield Post*, 15 Feb. 1973.
62 Information on the New Blendworth Centre kindly supplied by Mike Martin and on Cadlington House by Cecilia Eastwood.
63 East Hampshire District Council, Horndean Area Local Plan, 1984.
64 Stapleton, *Gales of Horndean*, pp.71–76; Stapleton and Thomas, *Gales*, chapter 7 forthcoming.
65 East Hampshire D C, East Hampshire District Local Plan, First Review, March 1994.

Appendix 1

HORNDEAN WAR MEMORIAL

Front Inscription

ERECTED
BY PUBLIC SUBSCRIPTION
TO THE MEMORY OF THE
MEN WHOSE NAMES ARE INSCRIBED
WHO WENT FROM THIS COUNTRY-SIDE

AT THE CALL OF DUTY
AND LAID DOWN THEIR LIVES
IN THE GREAT WAR

1914–1919

"IN THE EVENING AND IN THE MORNING
WE WILL REMEMBER THEM."

ALSO
TO THOSE WHO FELL
IN THE WORLD WAR

1939–1945

Right side panel 1 (Great War 1914–1919)
AUSTIN N.	MAJ.
ATTWOOD W. H.	P.O.
BUDDEN W. F.	Pte
BIGNELL W. H.	TELEGst
BULBECK G.	Pte
CAYME B. C.	..
CROCKFORD H. S.	..
CLARK F.	Cpl
CLARK-JERVOIS Sir E. Bart.	MAJ.
CROUCH N.	Pte
CLARK H. J.	Ch COOK
DARBY R. M.	Pte
DOBSON E. W.	Q.M. SGt
EDNEY C.	Pte
GEOGHEGAN H.	FLEET SGn
GIBBINS W.	Pte
GOBLE C. L.	Pte
GOLDSMITH F.	MAJ. M.C. & BAR
GRAFHAM C. G.	Pte
HOLDAWAY C. F.	GNr
HARDEN J. P.	A.B.
HATCH H.	Pte
HOLLOWAY P. C.	GNr
HADAWAY J. W.	Cpl

Right side panel 2 (World War 1939–1945)
BERRY T. J. A.	Mne
BUTLER R.	P.O.
CHAPPELL D.	SGT Pilot
CORNELIUS C. C. L.	C.E.R.A.
CRESSWELL H.R.	Mne
CROWDER A.	A.B.
CULLIMORE H. T.	P.O.
de PASS A. P.	Lieut
DAVIS F. J.	Sto P.O.
GOFFIN W.	Sto
GOWING G. R.	E.R.A.

Right side panel 3 (World War 1939–1945)
DENHAM G. C.	Lieut
HIGGINS H. C.	Lieut Comdr
MATTHEWS A.	Sto
HUDSON N. J.	W.O. R.A.F.

Right side panel 4
Probably sculptors name:
G. MAILLE & SONS.
(unreadable line)

Rear panel 1 (Great War 1914–1919)
HATCH G. F.	Pte
HOUSE W.	..
JACOBS J. A.	..
LEWIS J. M.	Cpl
LARCOMBE F. G.	..
MERRITT E.R.	Sgt
MERRETT E.	Pte
MARCHANT F.	MUSn
MASTERS P.	DVr
OLIVER T.	Pte
PANNEL J. F.	GNr
PARKS G. E. H.	Lt
PARVIN F.	Gnr
PARVIN H.G.	Pte
PATRICK V. R.	L/Cpl
PEARSON N. P.	..
PEARSON A.	GNr
PRIOR E. R. S.	Lt Col D.S.O. M.C.
PEARCE F.	Pte
PIPER L. G.	..
PIPER F.	..
PATERSON C. J.	CAPT
PATTENDEN J.	Pte
STONE A. E.	Pte
HUDSON E. C.	Pte

Rear panel 2 (World War 1939–1945)
HARPER V.	C.E.R.A.
HIBBERT F.	L.S.
HOLLAND W. E.	Pte
HONEY G. P.	L.A.M.
KERLEY A.	Corp
LANGDOWN F. D. K.	M.S.
LONG H. E.	Ch COOK
LONG J. P.	LIEUT
MILLER R.	L.A.C.
MATTHEWS A.	Pte
OUSGOOD F.	C.E.R.A.

Appendix 1

Left side panel 1   (Great War 1914–1919)

REED E. G.	Pte
SPENCER S.	. .
STANLEY W. G.	GNr
SHIER A.	Cpl
SHEPPARD W. J.	A.B.
SMITH J. A.	Pte
SPENCER A. E.	L.S.
SULIVAN G. H.	CAPT
TARRANT G.	L/Cpl
TARRANT W. J.	SPr
TILBURY G. V.	Pte
TREMLETT J. H.	. .
THOMPSON H.	. .
TRIBE W.	. .
TREAGUS G.	Cpl
TULLEY G.	. .
TURNER. C. G.	M.GNr
VINCENT E. J.	GNr
WEST S.	TPr
WELLS G.	Cpl
WICKENS W.	Pte
WILDS W.	Cpl
WOODS W.T.	Pte
TAYLOR W. H.	Pte
HORTON F. H.	A.B.

Left side panel 2   (World War 1939–1945)

PRATT F. C.	Pte
PURDY E. L. F.	Pte
RAYMOND A. J.	L.S.
SMITH E. E.	Cdsm
SMITH S. K.	P.O.
SPACEY A. E.	L.S.
SPARKES F. V.	L/Sgt
VALLOR W. R.	A.B. rnvr
VENN T.	Pte
VYSE G. W.	Spr
WARD L. G. W.	Flt Lieut

Left side panel 3   (World War 1939–1945)

RICH G. F.	Mne
ROOME D. A. W.	A.M. f.a.a.
WEAVING R. J.	P.O.
YATES W.	PAY Comdr

Acknowledgements for Illustrations

A number of local residents have been very generous in allowing their collections of photographs to be used in this book. for permission to publish illustrations, gratitude is expressed to the following;

Dodo Seaward:	1, 5, 19, 27, 34, 44, 54, 58, 60, 61, 65, 82, 86, 87, 88, 94, 95, 105, 114, 117, 134, 135, 137, 140, 141, 142, 143, 160, 161.
Brenda Worton:	46, 50, 120, 122, 124, 125, 126, 127, 128, 129.
Maureen Williams:	110, 113.
David Eaton:	4, 16, 48, 101, 119, 121, 123.
John Merrill:	8, 11, 12, 13, 22, 23, 24, 28, 29, 31, 32, 33, 35, 38, 39, 41, 42, 43, 45, 51, 59, 62, 64, 66, 67, 70, 72, 74, 75, 76, 79, 80, 81, 84, 85, 91, 100, 106, 107, 108, 111, 118, 133, 144, 149, 150, 151, 152, 153, 155, 156, 157, 158, 159, 162, 163, 164, 165, 166, 167, 168, 169, 170.
Alec Peters:	7, 14, 20, 21, 30, 47, 49, 52, 53, 56, 69, 71, 83, 89, 96, 97, 98, 102, 103, 104, 136, 138, 139. (Most of these are from the Bill Hammond collection.)
Ken Russell:	63, 112, 115, 116, 145, 146, 147, 148.
John Roberts:	17, 18, 154.
Ray Sadler:	109.
Paul Turner:	26.
Gales Brewery:	68.
Horndean Library:	2, 3, 15.

The remainder are from the author's collection.

Maps 1, 3, 4, 5, 6 & 7 are reproduced by kind permission of the Ordnacne Survey and Map 2 by permission of Hampshire Record Office

Map 1 Shows the Forest of Bere stretching unbroken from Horndean to Waitland End (now just south of Waterlooville) in 1810.

Map 2 The Enclosure Map of 1816 showing Horndean as a small ribbon development along the London Road with a cluster around the Square. Opposite the end of Five Heads Road is the long slim outline of the old Workhouse.

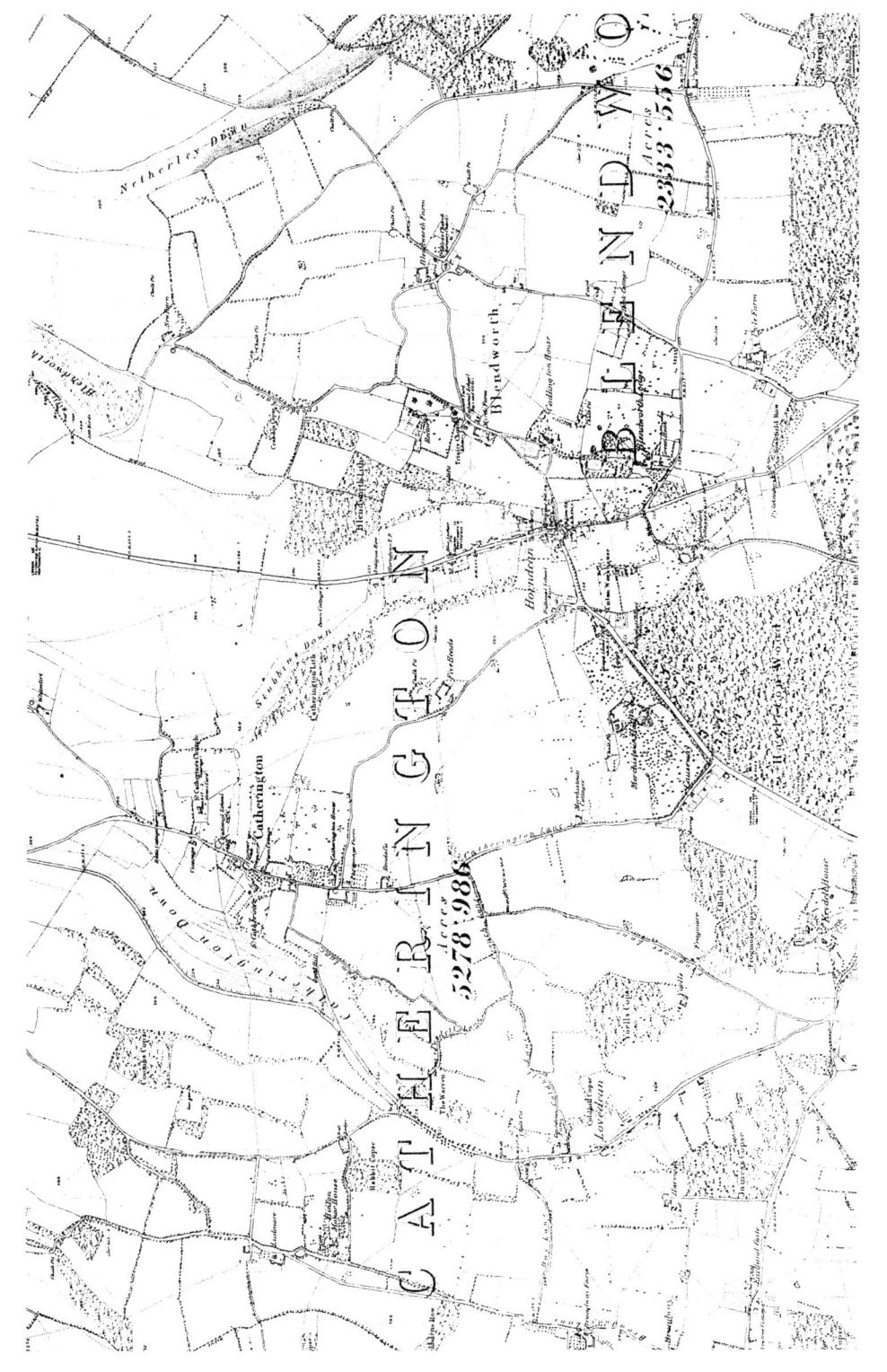

Map 3 By 1870 Keydell House, Merchistoun Hall, Blendworth Lodge and Cadlington House are all prominently indicated, as are the new rectory and Trinity Church at Blendworth and the Union Workhouse.

Map 4 Forty years later only minor development has occurred. A few houses at Causeway and Five Heads as well as Westfield and Crookley, but most significantly, since this is 1910, the Horndean Light Railway is shown along the Portsmouth Road.

Map 5 By 1933 clear signs of growth can be seen in Catherington Lane, Drill Hall Road (now Queen's Crescent), Havant Road, and in north Horndean in North and South Roads, London Road and Whitedirt Lane.

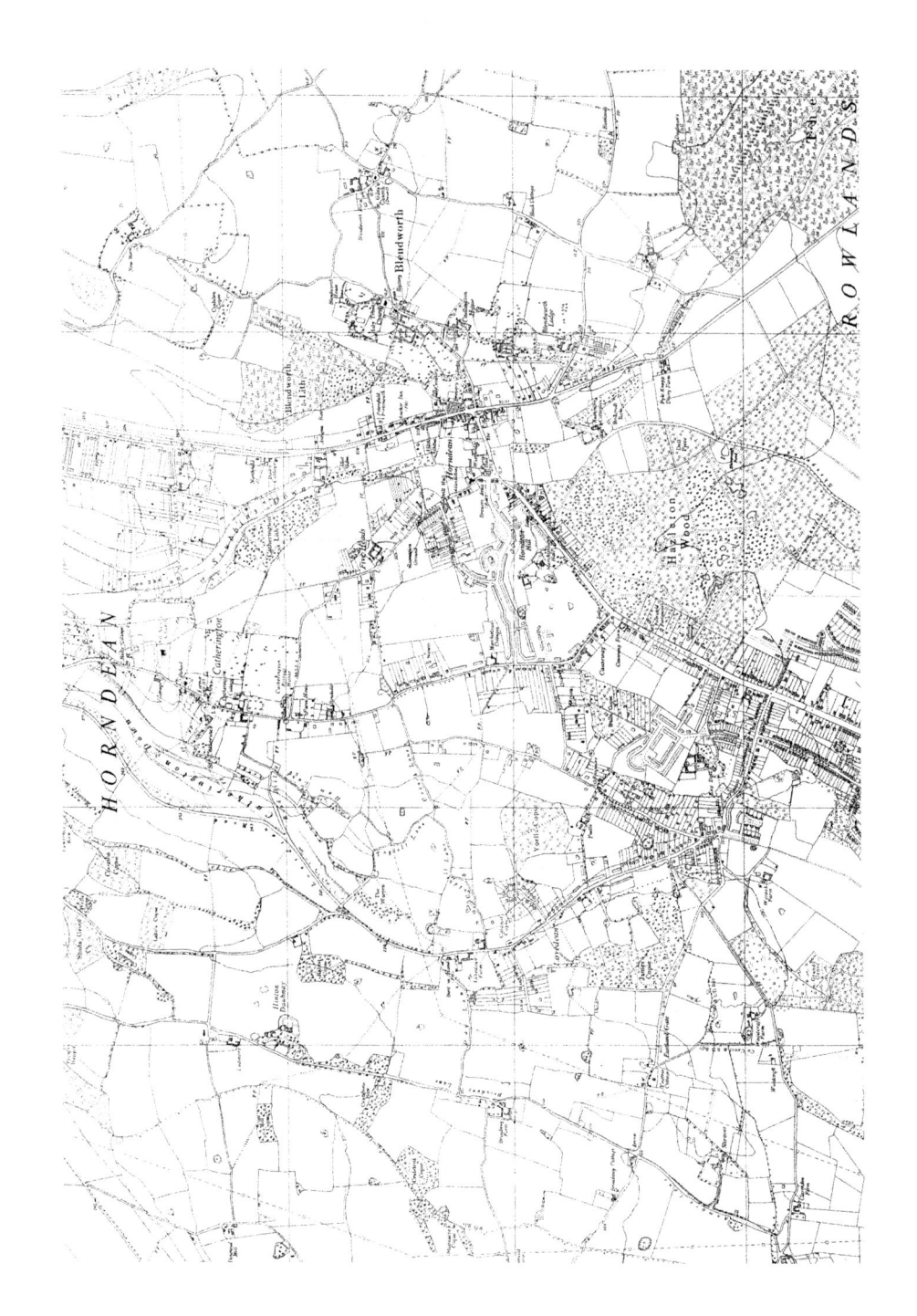

Map 6 The major development by 1962 was the Merchistoun Council Housing estate with open space designed in. The Keydell estate was also being developed to link in with that at Bulls Copse.

Map 7 By 1982 both north and south Horndean are heavily built-up areas and Catherington and Blendworth appear as untouched oases. The most conspicuous feature is the A3M slicing through Horndean although the mapmakers forgot to complete the link to the Portsmouth Road.

Horndean

1 The Horndean Toll House built c1710 by the Portsmouth and Sheet Bridge Turnpike Trust to the north of Horndean where the A3M now crosses the London Road. Travellers had to pay a toll to use the road before they were allowed to pass through the toll gate which adjoined the house. It was demolished about 1965.

2 Antigua—a row of Victorian cottages to the north of the village pictured on a dull April day in 1977

3 All that remained on 4 May 1977 when all but the cottage on the right were demolished to make way for the A3M.

4 Looking north along the London Road. The number of telephone wires indicate it is before the First World War.

5 The reverse direction—looking south. The brickwork of the house on the left is just visible on the right of the previous photograph. The blind covering the window of the next building protects the workshop of Mr Wiles, tailor. Fewer telephone wires indicate an earlier date—c1908.

6 An even earlier photograph showing Street's grocers and Excelsior Restaurant (now Post Office), the building which became the Nash Memorial Hall (now Brewery offices) and on the left, Dendy's butchers shop (now Main Bakery) with delivery cart outside. Beyond are the *Ship and Bell* and Brewery tower. Probably around 1905.

7 A closer view of the Brewery and *Ship and Bell* about the same time. The gate to the right of the pub led into the tea gardens. On the right is Warrilow's drapers shop.

8 A Marshall photograph looking up Horndean Hill, the *Red Lion* on the left and Street's protected from the morning sunshine as is Edney's grocers further up the hill. Cycling was a growing activity and Street was advertising accordingly, c. 1908.

9 Looking into the Square showing Mitchell's grocers and bakers and the *Red Lion* from a postcard dated 8 August 1916 and quite a few telephone wires by then.

10 Looking down Horndean Hill at about the same time. Edney advertises Colman's Mustard on the right and the butchers facing the hill was then Pruce's. Beyond, on Blendworth Lane was Pescott's butchers.

11 A view up the Blendworth Road. On the left is Warrilow's drapers, then cattle perhaps being taken to either Pruce's or Pescott's butchers. On the right is Bettesworth's stationers and newsagents which was also Horndean post Office, c. 1916.

12 A generation later—1929. The only constant factor is Bettesworth's. The butcher is now Gray and the horse drawn carts have given way to petrol lorries. Another new feature is the First World War memorial. Many more telephone wires.

13 Late 1930s and little change in the Square with Mitchells and the *Red Lion* as before. On the left, however Bayly's cycle shop has replaced Warrilow the draper.

14 The mid 1950s show some changes down Horndean Hill. Apart from more traffic—six private cars already—the first building has become Horndean Pharmacy, the next is Lloyd's Bank and beyond, where Edney's was is the new Co-operative store. Pescott's, now the butchers at the foot of the hill, has become double fronted.

15 January 1977. Behind the Co-operative delivery van is the current Post Office. Steve Bee has replaced Bayly at the cycle shop but Pescott is still the butcher. The telephone wires have disappeared underground.

16 Along Havant Road three pairs of Victorian houses were built and named New Town. This postcard picture shows the road outside the cottages looking towards Horndean and is dated 6 April 1912, so the picture predates then.

ESTABLISHED 40 YEARS

HORNDEAN, HANTS.

Mr. A. Mitchell   August   1909

Dr. to JOHN EDNEY,
Builder, Contractor, Undertaker, etc.

1909				
April	As to Building New House Building Wash house & Apple Room			
	1 New Trellis Gate and fencing painted green			
	Fencing in front from yard Oak Post & Rail			
	Coved with 6 foot Iron Hard Galvd: Iron 24 gauge			
	fitted with door hinges latch bolt & fastenings			
	all painted green			
	Low fence from house to front oak post rails			
	and Wales Painted white			
	1 New Dresser in Kitchen fitted with doors			
	Drawers Shelves with Brass knobs brass			
	Sitting Room 1 set of Cupboards with doors shelves			
	Dining Room 1 set of Cupboards with Drawers			
	1 do Upstairs with dome full length of Room			
	Bedroom fitted with Picture Rail ...			
	Tiles on Hearth to Range to Water ...			
	Lining with white tile Round Scullery			
	Range & Forced Pump —			
	Cutting down drawing front of house			
	and Altering and rebuilding wall to design			
	New Red Brick work 9 long on both sides of and			
	& half round Coping on top fitted with			
	New Gate 2 Oak Post Oak Bell and New Iron			
	fencing on top of wall and Oak hinge & Latch			
	Painted Complete with Labour and			
	Materials Complete. —	260	=	=
		40 = 0 = 0		
	Received by Cash on a/c £ 200 = 0 = 0 £	300 = 0 = 0		
	Balance £	100 = 0 = 0		

18 Builder John Edney's bill for the building of Seymour Cottage. The extras show that the house had its own well and was fenced. All this and built-in cupboards for £300!

17 Seymour Cottage, Havant Road in 1967. It was built for Mr Mitchell, the grocer in the Square in 1909.

19 Westfield House, which had been the home of the Bowyers after they had bought the Brewery from G. A. Gale, was demolished for the A3M. The space being cleared in the centre was for the Precinct for which planning permission was granted in 1969.

20 An ancient tree, originally part of the Forest of Bere, partially hides the cottages at the junction of Five Heads Road with Portsmouth Road in the early twentieth century.

21 A few years later, a Marshall photograph shows the tree has gone revealing all the cottages, including Bignell's grocers which was probably where Ann Gale, mother of Richard, had her shop.

22 Five Heads Road with a gentleman's carriage and pair and top hatted coachman having just passed the old *Brewer's Arms*. An early photograph.

23 A later and wider view of Five Heads Road with the new Parish Hall, probably in 1913.

24 Portsmouth Road looking north towards Five heads Road from the tram terminus. The large building in the background is the Union Workhouse and beyond it the single storey building is almost certainly the old Workhouse.

25 Looking south towards the tram terminus about 1908. The last building on the left is the Methodist Chapel and the grounds of Merchistoun Hall are on the right.

26 The Union Workhouse just before demolition to make way for an industrial estate.

27 The Isolation Hospital with Mrs Lamming, the matron, her caretaker husband and Lilian, their daughter. It lay down the driveway south of the Workhouse. After the hospital's closure it became a private residence, 'The Gables' and is now the Acacia Nursing Home.

28 Merchistoun Hall in the winter snow of 1968.

29 Five Heads Road in the late 1930s with the new *Brewers Arms* and new houses between the Parish Hall and the old cottages.

30 At the corner of Five Heads Road schoolboys read about the volunteers required for air raid precautions in 1939. The view is down Horndean Hill with Westfield House on the left.

31 The Portsmouth Road during the Second World War. Note the telegraph posts painted white to assist drivers in the black-out.

32 The same road just before the D-Day landings in Normandy lined with tanks and military vehicles.

33 Keydell House in its splendid grounds. A Marshall photograph of the early twentieth century. Demolished for housing development.

34 Causeway Stores at the corner of Catherington Lane and Kings Mede. Pulled down in 1968 and three shops built there.

35 The Riggs, a pair of old cottages in Catherington Lane demolished in 1964 and Cheriton Close built on the site.

36 Bulls Copse Lane a quagmire in October 1967. Milkmen and residents alike had to wear Wellingtons. The car on the left must have been marooned.

37 The same road in May 1968 now completed with pavements and lighting to the relief of all.

Catherington

38 Looking towards Clanfield from Catherington Down. Development has already affected Catherington Hill and some of Downhouse Road, but beyond are open fields.

39 A view across a partially overgrown village pond to the old vicarage in the early twentieth century.

40 Catherington's Tudor Cottages and early twentieth century Catherington Lane with horses being led to the blacksmith's next door—entrance in the foreground.

41 The blacksmith's shop south of Tudor Cottages (now Forge Cottage). In the foreground is the apparatus for putting iron rims onto cart wheels.

42 South of the blacksmith was this pair of cottages, now converted into a single residence, St Catherine's Cottage.

43 The old Kinchs Farm with thatched roof in what was then called Catherington Causeway.

44 Kinchs Farm after a disastrous fire which resulted in its demolition and rebuilding in its current form.

45 Catherington House after it had become a retreat house for the diocese of Portsmouth. It had begun life as the family home of Admiral Lord Hood.

Blendworth

4 Old Blendworth with the now demolished St Giles Church behind the tree on the left.

47 The old thatched St Giles Farm Old Blendworth.

48 Sky Lane, north of Blendworth. A picture postcard dated 1917 demonstrating the rural attraction of the area which brought many visitors who sent the postcards—this one to Peckham, south-east London.

49 The former Blendworth Rectory built in the mid-nineteenth century. Now Blendworth House.

50 Early twentieth century postcard of Blendworth with Holy Trinity Church in the background and the girls of Blendworth School on the road, with the school on the left.

51 An early 1950s photograph showing new cottages on the right the large tree obscuring the church having disappeared. The climber covering the school has also gone.

52 Cadlington House in the early twentieth century taken by Marshall.

53 Blendworth Lodge before the First World War. It seemed to be the fashion for buildings to be covered with climbing plants.

54 The ruins of Blendworth Lodge after the disastrous fire of January 1917.

55 Blendworth Road looking downhill towards Horndean Square on a postcard dated 23 August 1916 and sent by someone who had just enjoyed 'a nice tram ride'.

56 Crookley was built in the late nineteenth century for Richard Gale's retirement. Now the home of Sixten and Cassey's Blendworth Fabrics.

Work

57 Traditionally most workers in Horndean were employed in agriculture. Here a trio of horses pull an early mechanical reaper which replaced scythes in the late nineteenth century. This Marshll photograph was taken near Lovedean.

58 Haymaking in 1930 at the foot of Catherington Down near Downhouse Road. Note the unusual hay raking machines pulled by a horse on each side.

59 The same activity at Five Heads Farm somewhat later when the hay raking machine was pulled by a single horse.

60 Harvesting at Hinton Daubney with the 'Squire', Mr Whalley Tooker (holding his dog), and his farmworkers, one holding the two pronged pitchfork for pitching the sheaves of corn onto the two horse cart.

61 Threshing machines were introduced in the early nineteenth century. Here, in 1921, Edney's threshing machine is driven by a steam powered traction engine. Sacks of grain, weighing two and a quarter hundredweights await collection.

62 A boy stands inside the great treadwheel at Kinches Farm in the late 1960s before its removal and reconstruction at The Weald and Downland Museum at Singleton

63 Surplus home grown fruit being used for jam making in the *Farmer Inn* hut during the Second World War. The ladies are Mrs G Samways, Mrs V Russell, Mrs Cookson, Mrs Farnham and Mrs Turner.

64 Horndean had a long wait to get its Fire Brigade. Here with shiny engine are—*Back Row*; A. Jeram, H. Dobson, A. Hughs, C. Foster, F. Bayly, B. Fox. *Front Row*; T. Longhurst, G. Hammond, H. Feben, W. Moon, B. Weston.

65 Air Raid Precaution Wardens and First Aid Personnel in 1940.

66 Members of the Home Guard 1939–45. *Back row*; middle two Bill Over and George Pescott. *Middle row*; Bert Thatcher second, James Hatch fourth, Charlie Foster sixth. *Front row*; Reg Benians, Bill Dawtry, Jack Tilbury,———, Jack Rolls, Harry Heath, Harry Craven.

67 Roadworkers realigning the A3 at the top of Horndean Hill. The Parish Hall clearly shows the repaired roof following it being struck by an aircraft in the Second World War. Westfield House is in the background.

68 The cooperage at Gales Brewery where wooden barrels were both manufactured and repaired before the advent of metal casks which saw such work disappear.

69 Manual turf cutting in the mid-1950s. Bob Pratt working for Butser Turf and Timber Company.

Commerce

70 Gales Victorian Brewery about 1910. Note the horse drawn delivery wagons and on the left the oast house indicating that Gales at one time malted their own barley.

71 The *Ship and Bell* Family and Commercial Hotel before the First World War. The entrance gate to the tea gardens is on the right.

72 Catherington's *Farmer Inn* attractively marooned in the snow of the hard winter of 1963. Customers on foot only!

73 An early twentieth century postcard of the old *Brewer's Arms*. Did customers have to park their carriages?

74 The new *Brewers Arms*, a more functional building. Like the *Farmer* it was owned by Gales. Recently the Five Heads Road building was sold and is now a 'free' house.

75 The *Good Intent* in the early twentieth century. It was owned by R.J.Scott, seen standing to the right of the centre doorway. The gateway to the tea gardens is on the right. Scott also owned the *Wellington Inn*, Waterlooville.

76 *The Anchor* stands at the Petersfield end of the village and, unlike the *Good Intent* at the opposite end of Horndean, has changed little from this photograph.

77 Horndean's central pub the *Red Lion* in the Square after the Second World War. Its tea garden at the rear had now become a beer garden.

GEO. GALE & Co., Ltd.
HORNDEAN.

PRIZE MEDAL ALES AND STOUTS
IN
Casks, Bottles, and 4 Quart Crates.

☞ A TRIAL SOLICITED. ☜

FINEST QUALITY GOODS ONLY.

G. EDNEY'S
Grocery & Provision Stores,
HORNDEAN.

Noted for Bacon, Butter & Cheese.

National Telephone, No. 2 X, Horndean.

— THE —
EXCELSIOR RESTAURANT,
HORNDEAN.

LUNCHEONS, TEAS, MINERALS, ICES.

PARTIES CATERED FOR.

NATIONAL TELEPHONE No. 6.

W. A. STREET.

Public National Telephone, No. 5.

F. WARRILOW, Horndean.
FAMILY DRAPER AND GENERAL OUTFITTER.

Departments.

Dress Fabrics	Shirtings	Ribbons	Shoes	Collars
Corsets	Blankets	Gloves	Hats	Ties
Underclothing	Sheeting	Hosiery	Caps	Braces
Calicoes	Flowers	Boots	Umbrellas	Shirts, &c.

☞ Boys,' Youths' and Men's Clothing ready made, also to measure.
Linos, Carpets, Matting and Rugs.

Agent for Drs. JAEGER & LAHMANN.   Agent for BRUNSWICK DYEING & CLEANING.

The "Ship & Bell,"
FAMILY & COMMERCIAL HOTEL,
LARGE OR SMALL PARTIES CATERED FOR.

LUNCHEONS, DINNERS, TEAS.

TEA GARDEN, GOOD TENNIS LAWN.

78 Advertisements from Catherington Parish Magazine of 1911 for some of Horndean's major businesses. Notably the *Ship and Bell* had a lawn tennis court.

79 Almost opposite Marsh's garage was Wiles the tailor. Here Albert Levy, chauffeur to the Learmouth family at Cadlington House, arrives to be measured for a new livery.

80 Hood's boot and shoe repairs in the cottage south of Marsh's garage.

81 Marsh's Garage with old style BP petrol pumps and second hand cars for sale inside the left hand building, priced at £149 and £175.

82 Horndean Pharmacy on the Hill where the car park is now. Before it was the pharmacy it had been Bessie Catchlove's shop. Behind are a clothes shop and Horndean Motors. The building on the right is Lloyds Bank.

83 Inside the pharmacy in 1959 with a smiling Sue Ripper (now Peters) ready to serve with some still familiar brands.

84 Woodlands Cafe on the Portsmouth Road would have been near the tram terminus had it not closed in the early 1930s. It is now a sports shop and previously was Horndean D I Y.

85 The size of the staff of the cafe suggests it must have been, at one time, a thriving enterprise.

Transport

86 Most deliveries in the early twentieith century were by horse-drawn cart. Pictured here is the cart of Mitchell's grocers and bakers in the Square. A basket for bread sits on top of the cart.

87 Not all carts were horse-drawn. Here, in front of Mitchell's shop is a rare ox-drawn cart. The two oxen were perhaps intended as an endorsement of the product being delivered, 'Atora' beef suet.

88 Steam powered lorries were popular for a brief period and Edneys, who began the Butser Turf Company, had a Sentinel, a fine example of the type.

89 In 1903 the Portsdown and Horndean Light Railway opened, bringing its green and cream trams to Horndean. Passengers could choose to enjoy the views from the open top or travel downstairs in the curtained interior. This one waits at the terminus near Horndean Methodist Chapel.

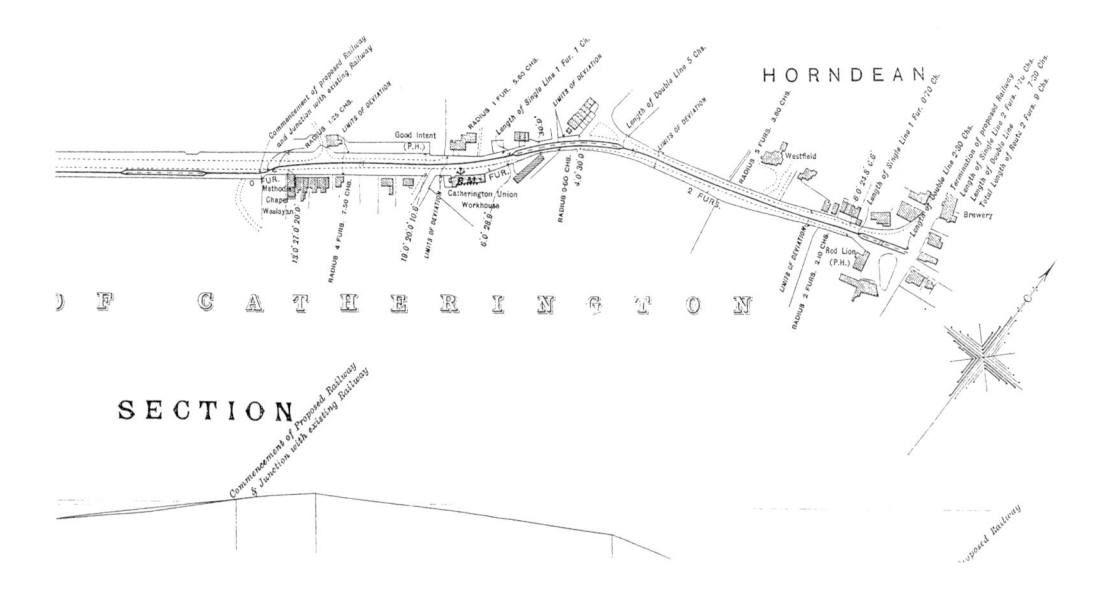

90 It had been the intention of the company to continue the service to the centre of Horndean. This plan shows how the continuation was intended to occupy the centre of the road with double tracks at the end of Five Heads Road and in the Square. In the event it was never built.

91 Trams 1 and 2 await at the Horndean terminus on the Portsmouth Road about 1908. In the distance are both the old and new Workhouses (shown on the plan number 90).

PORTSDOWN & HORNDEAN LIGHT RAILWAY.
—:o:—
List of Revised Fares.
—:o:—

Cosham and the George Inn	1d.
George Inn and Purbrook (Leopard)	1d.
Purbrook (Leopard) and Waterloo (Hambledon Road)	1d.
Waterloo (Hambledon Road) and Spotted Cow (Cow Plain)	1d.
Park Lane (Car Shed) and Horndean	1d.
Cosham and Purbrook (Leopard)	2d.
George Inn and Waterloo (Hambledon Road) ...	2d.
Waterloo (Hambledon Road) and Horndean ...	2d.
Cosham and Waterloo (Hart Plain Siding) ...	3d.
Purbrook (Leopard) and Horndean	3d.
Cosham and Spotted Cow (Cow Plain)	4d.
Cosham and Horndean, single	5d.
Cosham and Horndean, return	8d.

The above returns are issued on any car throughout the day, and are available to return by any car the same day only; they are not transferable, and passengers cannot break and resume their journey with the same ticket.

Children under 12, one Penny for a 1d. or 2d. section, and Twopence for a 3d., 4d., or 5d. section.

School Tickets for Children under 16 years of age, available between 8 and 9.30 a.m., 12 and 2 p.m., and 4 and 6 p.m., as under:—

1d. Tickets (1s. a dozen) available for the full journey, to be had of the Inspector.

½d. Tickets, available in a 2d. section, issued on the cars.

Return Tickets are issued before 9.30 a.m.:
Cosham and Park Lane ... ... 4d.
Cosham and Horndean ... ... 6d.

J. FEREDAY GLENN,
MANAGER,
COSHAM, HANTS.

For Rates and Particulars of Special Cars apply to above address.

xxi

92 The revised fare structure for 1910 showing the day out to the splendours of rural Horndean cost 8d (3p) from Cosham.

PORTSDOWN & HORNDEAN LIGHT RAILWAY.
—:o:—
Summer Service.
—:o:—

On and after Thursday, July 11th,
the Car Service will be re-arranged to work to the following times.

DOWN CARS FOR COSHAM LEAVE:

Horndean—8.0, 8.20, 8.40. 9.0, 9.20, 9.40, 10.0, 10.20, 10.40, 11.0 a.m., and every 10 minutes until 9.0 p.m., then 9.20, 9.40, 10.0, and 10.18.

Park Lane—7.50, 8.7, 8.27, 8.47, 9.7, 9.27, and every 10 minutes until 9.7 p.m., then 9.27, 9.47, 10.7, and 10.22.

Waterloo—7.55, 8.15, 8.35, 8.55, 9.15, 9.35, 10.7, and 10.22, a.m. and every 10 minutes until 9.15 p.m., then 9.35, 9.55, 10.15 and 10.30.

— SUNDAYS. —

Horndean—10.10, 11.40, 1.0
Park Lane—8.30, 10.17, 11.45, 1.7 } and every 10 minutes as on week days—the last car being { 10 p.m.
Waterloo—8.35, 10.25, 11.50, 1.15 } { 10.7
Purbrook—Depart 5 Minutes after Waterloo. { 10.15

UP CARS FOR HORNDEAN LEAVE:

Cosham—8.30, 8.50, 9.10, 9.30, 9.50, 10.10 a.m., and every 10 minutes until 9.40 p.m., then 9.50, 10.10, 10.30, 10.50, and 11.5.

Purbrook—Departure Times: 15 Minutes after Cosham.

Waterloo—8.55, 9.15, 9.35, 9.55, 10.15, 10.35 a.m., and every 10 minutes until 10.5 p.m., then 10.15, 10.35, 10.55, 11.15, and 11.25.

Park Lane—7.52, 8.12, 8.32, 8.52, 9.2, 9.22, 9.42, 10.2, 10.22, 10.42 a.m., and every 10 minutes until 10.12 p.m., the 10.22, 10.42, 11.2, 11.22, and 11.30 will only proceed if they have passengers for Horndean.

— SUNDAYS. —

Cosham—9.10, 11.5, 12.20, 1.50
Waterloo—9.35, 11.35, 12.40, 2.15 } and every 10 minutes as on week days—the last car being { 10.50
Park Lane—9.42, 11.32, 12.47, 2.22 } { 11.15

J. FEREDAY GLENN, MANAGER.

xxv

93 The summer service, timed to commence shortly before the school holidays, shows that trams ran every ten minutes to and from Horndean.

94 Early motor cars at Cadlington House in 1906. Mr Livingstone-Learmouth's AA 1446 chauffered by Trussler; Mr Somerville-Learmouth's AA 1445 chauffered by Albert Levy and Captain of the Royal Yacht, Norman Palmer's BP 649 chauffered by Milhall.

95 A few years later, outside Catherington House, before leaving for Goodwood Races. Albert Levy on the right.

96 A shiny new Dennis lorry delivered to Butser Turf Company in the 1920s.

97 Joe Parvin, Dick Woods and Ted Pocock are the Butser Turf Company's staff in this early 1930s picture of a Guys Motors lorry towing a trailer with tracked vehicle.

98 An ex War Department A E C converted in the company's workshops with a home made trailer outside the Portsmouth Road offices of Butser Turf and demonstrating the timber hauling aspect of the company's work in the late 1940s.

99 A post Second World War Sixten and Cassey van from the time when the showroom was next door to the Palladium in London's Argyle Street and the works in the old Union Workhouse in Portsmouth Road.

Religion

100 Catherington Church with a much smaller church yard before the First World War. The section in the foreground lay between the churchyard and the road.

101 A very rural scene looking over the village pond to All Saints church from a card postmarked 1912.

102 A Marshall picture postcard from the early twentieth century showing the interior of All Saints.

103 The Lych Gate, erected at the entrance to Catherington churchyard was the village's memorial to those residents who had died in the First World War. The ceremony of blessing took place on 24 August 1921 with George Edney, churchwarden, the Bishop of Portsmouth, the Bishop of Winchester and Dick Taylor, churchwarden.

104 A gathering containing a number of churchmen at Catherington Retreat House, thought to be in 1923.

105 The unveiling of Horndean War Memorial in 1920. The four principals were Mr Whalley-Tooker, Lady Lowe, Rev. Sheppard and Rev. Nelson.

106 Old St Giles Church, Old Blendworth in a deteriorating state not long before its demolition.

107 Holy Trinity Church, Blendworth after the First World War. The clock in the tower was Blendworth's First World War Memorial.

108 The interior of Holy Trinity thought to be from the same period.

109 The Methodist Chapel on the Portsmouth Road in the early 1960s. Built in 1830 renovation was then necessary. There was clearly a considerable and active congregation.

Education

110 Grace Thompson was born in 1837 and was schoolmistress at Catherington about 1870 until her marriage to Albert Mitchell, the grocer in Horndean Square, on 4 September 1871.

111 Blendworth School 1915 with the Novice Banner which they had won at Petersfield Choral Music Festival in 1914. *Back row;* Margaret Merritt, Kathy Austin, Daisy Murrant, Ella Pearson, Gladys Pearson, Ethel Merritt. *Second row;* Dolly Kingsbury, Eileen Pearson, Norah Pattenden, Dorothy Adams, Ivy Parfoot, Alice Weston. *Third row;* Millicent Luff, Mabel Cooper, Muriel Causby, Brenda Pearson (teacher), Mrs Wilkins (governess), Ivy Sherlock, Dorah Cobb, Lily Tribe. *Front row;* Grace Adams, Edie Luff, Frances Gillett,—Tribe, Eileen Fleet. The Merritt girls had to leave when evicted in First World War.

112 Blendworth School in 1927. Mrs Wilkins remains.

113 Catherington School in the mid 1920s

114 Horndean Boys School in 1927

115 Horndean School 1956–57. Fred Bushell was the teacher.

116 Horndean School, taken on the playing field of the school which opened in 1959. Probably a 1960s photograph. The school had certainly grown in numbers.

117 A schoolchildren's Coronation Party in 1953 with their own picture of Queen Elizabeth II.

118 Mrs Spencer's needlework class on the field which was to become the playing field of the new Horndean Junior School.

Leisure

119 The following five photographs give an evocative indication of why so many visitors came to Horndean on the trams in the early twentieth century. The walk through Hazelton Wood was justifiably popular.

120 Through Hazelton Wood the visitor came to Sheepwash Lane. Here, in 1913, the Lane passes through Rushmore, now the site of Keydell Nurseries. The Pond is on the left.

157

121 The quiet and peaceful calm of Rushmore Pond is captured in this picture postcard sent in July 1911.

122 The Lily Pond at Horndean was a very similar attraction to Rushmore Pond.

123 Along the Havant Road the Holt offered a walk very characteristic of that through Hazelton.

124 The popularity of Horndean led to the growth of somewhat risqué picture postcards reminiscent of seaside resorts. It is not easy to think of Horndean in these terms but the next six illustrations clearly show that is how it was. The first advertises the resort of Sunny Horndean! Sent in 1913 by a young man to a young lady in Southsea.

126 Romance definitely seemed to be in the Horndean air in the early twentieth century.

125 Not only the moon sheds a little light on a Horndean night in Hazelton Wood.

127 But not all the young ladies would appear to have been totally co-operative. Some needed to slow the pace.

128 Others found that time passed only too quickly, especially when the man had both hands full, as in this card from 1908.

129 It seems everyone came to Horndean for romance as shown by the ten pairs depicted here. There was also a complete lack of colour prejudice. Quite refreshing for a card sent in 1914.

130 Presumably after all the excitement and exercise the visitors would require some refreshment. Horndean had a variety of places to provide it. One was the tea gardens beside the *Ship and Bell*.

131 If the weather was inclement then visitors could move to the tea rooms inside.

132 Not to be outdone the *Good Intent* also had its tea gardens which had lighting for the summer evenings. Here the staff are photographed awaiting their customers.

133 Causeway Farm, a small one, like many similar ones in the West Country today, decided to attract visitors by opening its own tea garden and very successfully it seems.

134 Believed to be the village party for the Coronation of Edward VII in the *Red Lion* gardens 9 August 1902.

135 In the days before motor vehicles the Band of Hope annual outing from Horndean to Hayling Island. Local farmers lent their wagons, the centre one being provided by James Goldsmith of Blendworth Farm. Some preferred to cycle.

136 Outings a little later on were by charabanc. This was a *Good Intent* one probably in the 1920s. The boy under the cap in the front seat was Bill Hammond.

137 The Hambledon Hunt meeting in the Square about 1910. Edney's shop advertises Fry's cocoa and the cottages at the end of Five Heads Road can be seen at the top of the hill.

138 The gardens of Blendworth Lodge were the location of sports at Horndean before the First World War

139 Horndean Flower Show was the great event of the year in the early twentieth century. In the grounds of Blendworth Lodge a slow bicycle race was one of the attractions.

140 There appears to have been a long musical tradition in the parish. Here is the Catherington Choir about 1893.
Back row;
Harry Attwood, Mr Carter (schoolmaster), Mr Godfrey, Bert Edney, Tom Edney, Mr Barber, Fred Edney, W. Bignell.
Second row; sixth from left George Coles, seventh Bert Pearson.
Front left Bert Carter (schoolmaster's son).

141 Horndean Choir in the early 1930s.
Back left; Edie Wharton and Rose Twine.
Back centre; George Vivian and Mr Linton.
Second row; Mrs Merritt, Miss Pearson, Alice Bacon, Mr Collins (conductor), Rene Tilbury, ———, Nell Soffley.
Front row; ———, Mrs Bettesworth, Elsie Edney, Mrs Knight, Mrs Lenton, Miss Read, Mrs Read.

142 Horndean W I Choir at Petersfield Music Festival in the early 1950s. *Second from left at back* Iris Jolliffe. *Middle row;* ———, May Duffell, Rose Twine, Daisy Hawkey, Phoebe May, ———, Edie Wharton, ———, ———.

Front row; Mrs Ash, Ivy Sheppard, Win Pescott, Marjorie Bushell (Leader), ———, Nellie Bey.

143 Horndean Marching Band being presented with new trumpets by D. Cork, P. Boyd (Fire Service), Ted Hibberd (Southern Press), M. Mann (Band Leader) receiving.

144 An early twentieth century Marshall photograph of Horndean Amateur Dramatic Company whose successor still performs at Merchistoun Hall.

145 The street party in Drill Hall Road (Now Queen's Crescent) to celebrate V E Day at the end of the Second World War in 1945.

146 The childrens Victory Party held in the Drill Hall in 1945.

147 Party for the 'Old Folks' held in the Parish Hall (demolished 1999) after the Second World War.

148 Post Second World War British Legion dinner held in the Nash Memorial Hall (now Brewery offices).

149 Horndean Old Time Dance Club enjoying themselves in the Parish Hall.

150 Morris dancers in the Square probably in the early 1960s, in front of Mitchells Stores (now Indian Restaurant) and flanked by Smith and Vosper, the bakers (now Horndean Travel).

151 The reverse direction reveals new street lighting on the A3 and across the road Horndean Post Office with a branch of Barclays Bank, then one of two banks in the village.

152 The village football team won the Portsmouth League, Division Two in the 1953-54 season and proudly display their trophy. Back row; E.Barge, P.Whitlock, T.Heath, A.Turner, J.Berry, A.Oakland, H.Berry, A.Horton. Front row; R.Newman, Mr H.Heath, W.Turner, H.Green, T.Purdy.

153 Going from strength to strength, Horndean Football Club won the Portsmouth Premier League in 1968-69, 1969-70 and 1970-71. Not a single game was lost in the 1969-70 season. *Back row;* H.Thomason (Manager), E.Edney, E.Langton, R.Burgess, C.Smith, R.Bennett, D.Greaves, A.Doughty. *Front row;* R.Bevis, C.Main, J.Holland (Captain), M.Wallis, K.Turner, R.Thomas.

Modern

154 The newly built Horndean Precinct dwarfs the pharmacy and Lloyds Bank, both soon to be demolished for the car park, in this photograph of about 1970. Lloyds Bank was formerly Edney's Store.

155 A recent wintry scene of the enduring and unchanging All Saints Church, Catherington.

156 How the Methodist Chapel looked after the early 1960s renovations, the mellow brick and flint being covered. This was how it looked when it closed in 1999.

157 The old blacksmiths shop which became the Lovedean Mission

158 It was demolished for this new Bethesda Mission which, somehow, does not have the same character.

159 The dedication, by the Rev. Beardsley of the new building at Catherington Infants School on 26 September 1995. The thatched roof of Tudor Cottages in the background.

160 The demolition of Westfield House provided the site for the brick and concrete cube of the new telephone exchange and the Westfield Industrial Estate behind it, photographed here in 1987.

161 Replacing the old Causeway Stores was another featureless building of three shops at the corner of Catherington Lane and Kings Mede. They now form the One Stop Stores, replacing a general store, a greengrocers and Grovers butcher's shop all shown here in 1983.

162 The exploration for oil began with the erection of this oil rig at Pyle Farm seen here in the 1980s

163 The junction of the Portsmouth Road and Five Heads Road showing Dean Court on the left, built as sheltered housing for the elderly, now being converted into flats for rent. Behind is the Brewers Arms, now a free house and just visible behind the pub is the old Horndean Boys School, now the Library. On the right is the Village Hall demolished in 1999. The photograph is from the 1990s.

164 A picture showing the rural charm that is still Catherington. Behind the tree on the left is the Infants School with the Farmer Inn beyond. On the right are School Cottages and thatched Tudor cottages.

165 Horndean Square in the 1980s. Horndean Travel has replaced Smith and Vospers and The Indian Cottage Restaurant is where Mitchells was for many decades. The Red Lion has been extended at its eastern end.

166 The same period and probably photographed from the same location, the tower of Gales Brewery. A view of the village looking north along the London Road.

167 The modified War Memorial restored in the 1960s standing in the attractive little garden created around it. Behind, in this 1990s photograph are the Post Office and the Brewery offices in what was formerly Nash Hall.

168 Another 1990s photograph with Gales Victorian Brewery tower dominating the picture. In the foreground the corner shop, having been a butchers for a century, has become the Main Bakery.

169 In 1997 Gales celebrated 150 years in business and H R H Prince Andrew, seen here with Brewery Managing Director, Nigel Atkinson, came to inaugurate the festivities.

170 A 1990s aerial photograph showing the A3M bisecting the village and the Westfield Industrial Estate to its right and Gales Brewery land and buildings to its right with the London Road dividing them.

Glossary

assart	a piece of forest land converted into arable
bushel	a measure of corn equalling eight gallons
carucate	ploughland
copyhold	tenure of land at the will of the manorial lord and held by copy of the manorial court roll
dredge	a mixture of grain, usually oats and barley sown together
gallon	a dry measure for corn—$277\frac{1}{4}$ cubic inches
haybote	the right to take wood or thorns for repair of fences
housebote	the right to wood for repair of a house
messuage	a dwelling house and its appurtenances. Capital messuage—a property containing several messuages including that of the owner
ploughland	what one plough and eight oxen could plough in one year
pannage	pasturage for swine in a forest or wood
quarter	measure of grain equalling eight bushels; a fourth part of a hundredweight
tare	some species of vetch
vetch	plant of bean family used for forage especially tares
virgate	early English land measure varying in extent but in many cases averaging 30 acres

Electoral Roll

HORNDEAN (MURRAY)
CROZIER, JANET E, 1, BARTON CROSS, HORNDEAN
GROOMBRIDGE, PAMELA M, 3, BARTON CROSS, HORNDEAN
GROOMBRIDGE, PHILIP J, 3, BARTON CROSS, HORNDEAN
GROOMBRIDGE, RUTH P, 3, BARTON CROSS, HORNDEAN
MILLARD, MATTHEW R, 5, BARTON CROSS, HORNDEAN
MILLARD, RAYMOND I, 5, BARTON CROSS, HORNDEAN
MILLARD, ROSEMARY, 5, BARTON CROSS, HORNDEAN
PARRY, WINIFRED E, 7, BARTON CROSS, HORNDEAN
COOMBES, OLIVE B, 9, BARTON CROSS, HORNDEAN
COOMBES, RAYMOND J, 9, BARTON CROSS, HORNDEAN
CHALLEN, RICHARD J, 11, BARTON CROSS, HORNDEAN
MOIGNARD, BARRY J, 13, BARTON CROSS, HORNDEAN
MOIGNARD, JOY L, 13, BARTON CROSS, HORNDEAN
MOIGNARD, ROY H, 13, BARTON CROSS, HORNDEAN
SMYTH, GLADYS M, 15, BARTON CROSS, HORNDEAN
HOLLINGWORTH, ADELE, 17, BARTON CROSS, HORNDEAN
HALL, ALLEN, 19, BARTON CROSS, HORNDEAN
MOLE, FREDERICK J, 21, BARTON CROSS, HORNDEAN
PETERS, JAMES E, 21, BARTON CROSS, HORNDEAN
STONE, APRIL, 21, BARTON CROSS, HORNDEAN
COX, MARY A, 23, BARTON CROSS, HORNDEAN
COX, WILLIAM J, 23, BARTON CROSS, HORNDEAN
KING, GEORGE H, 2, BARTON CROSS, HORNDEAN
STEVENSON, KEVIN M, 4, BARTON CROSS, HORNDEAN
STEVENSON, PAULA J, 4, BARTON CROSS, HORNDEAN
PEARSON, JOHN E, 6, BARTON CROSS, HORNDEAN
PEARSON, PATRICIA M, 6, BARTON CROSS, HORNDEAN
GILL, JACK, 8, BARTON CROSS, HORNDEAN
KELL, BRENDA J, 10, BARTON CROSS, HORNDEAN
WATTS, PETER J, 12, BARTON CROSS, HORNDEAN
BARNACLE, EILEEN E, 14, BARTON CROSS, HORNDEAN
BARNACLE, THOMAS W, 14, BARTON CROSS, HORNDEAN
WHITTAKER, ANNETTE C, 16, BARTON CROSS, HORNDEAN
GARVIN, PHILLIP J, 18, BARTON CROSS, HORNDEAN
KING, LEONARD D, 20, BARTON CROSS, HORNDEAN
KING, RUBY, 20, BARTON CROSS, HORNDEAN
GREEN, DOUGLAS I, 22, BARTON CROSS, HORNDEAN
GREEN, JAYNE M, 22, BARTON CROSS, HORNDEAN
HARRIS, DAVID K, 24, BARTON CROSS, HORNDEAN
HARRIS, FIONA, 24, BARTON CROSS, HORNDEAN
HARRIS, TIMOTHY C, 24, BARTON CROSS, HORNDEAN
SANG, MARGARET J, 1, BENBOW CLOSE, HORNDEAN
THOMAS, ELEANOR E.M, 3, BENBOW CLOSE, HORNDEAN
HARRIS, HAZEL H, 5, BENBOW CLOSE, HORNDEAN
NEWMAN, PEGGY, 7, BENBOW CLOSE, HORNDEAN
TURNER, HILDA M, 9, BENBOW CLOSE, HORNDEAN
DAVEY, IRENE, 11, BENBOW CLOSE, HORNDEAN
STREET, HENRY J, 11, BENBOW CLOSE, HORNDEAN
COBB, AGNES M, 13, BENBOW CLOSE, HORNDEAN
COBB, PETER J, 13, BENBOW CLOSE, HORNDEAN
CANNINGS, PHYLLIS J, 2, BENBOW CLOSE, HORNDEAN
CHARLES, ELSIE, 2, BENBOW CLOSE, HORNDEAN
WOODWARD, ALFRED H, 4, BENBOW CLOSE, HORNDEAN
WHITE, ANTHONY L, 6, BENBOW CLOSE, HORNDEAN
WHITE, CHRISTOPHER, 6, BENBOW CLOSE, HORNDEAN
WHITE, JUNE D, 6, BENBOW CLOSE, HORNDEAN
BUTLER, JOYCE E, 8, BENBOW CLOSE, HORNDEAN
GRAYER, MOLLY J, 10, BENBOW CLOSE, HORNDEAN
ANDREWS, MAURICE, 12, BENBOW CLOSE, HORNDEAN
ROBERTS, EVELYN M, 14, BENBOW CLOSE, HORNDEAN
ROBERTS, RONALD, 14, BENBOW CLOSE, HORNDEAN
GOODHAND, DAVID C, 1, BENTLEY CLOSE, HORNDEAN
GOODHAND, EMILY A, 1, BENTLEY CLOSE, HORNDEAN
GOODHAND, SIMON A, 1, BENTLEY CLOSE, HORNDEAN
SELLERS, EDITH A, 3, BENTLEY CLOSE, HORNDEAN
SELLERS, NORMAN R, 3, BENTLEY CLOSE, HORNDEAN
TAYLOR, GEOFFREY R, 5, BENTLEY CLOSE, HORNDEAN
TAYLOR, HELEN J, 5, BENTLEY CLOSE, HORNDEAN
SANDERS, ELIZABETH A, 7, BENTLEY CLOSE, HORNDEAN
SANDERS, SIMON J, 7, BENTLEY CLOSE, HORNDEAN
JOHNSTONE, ALEX G, 9, BENTLEY CLOSE, HORNDEAN
JOHNSTONE, ALEXANDRA J, 9, BENTLEY CLOSE, HORNDEAN
JOHNSTONE, SIMON A, 9, BENTLEY CLOSE, HORNDEAN
GUNATILLAKA, ASANGA C, 15, BENTLEY CLOSE, HORNDEAN
GUNATILLAKA, JAYANTHA C, 15, BENTLEY CLOSE, HORNDEAN
GUNATILLAKA, MAHESWARI, 15, BENTLEY CLOSE, HORNDEAN
STEVENS, DAVID S, 17, BENTLEY CLOSE, HORNDEAN
STEVENS, RACHEL G, 17, BENTLEY CLOSE, HORNDEAN
LOVELL, PATRICIA A, 19, BENTLEY CLOSE, HORNDEAN
LOVELL, RAYMOND J, 19, BENTLEY CLOSE, HORNDEAN
DE LA PERRELLE, JOHN P, 2, BENTLEY CLOSE, HORNDEAN
DE LA PERRELLE, LINDA, 2, BENTLEY CLOSE, HORNDEAN
LOVESY, KELLY R, 2, BENTLEY CLOSE, HORNDEAN
GREEN, DAVID I, 4, BENTLEY CLOSE, HORNDEAN
GREEN, TIFFANY E, 4, BENTLEY CLOSE, HORNDEAN
TEBBUTT, RONALD E, 6, BENTLEY CLOSE, HORNDEAN
TEBBUTT, SHIRLEY W, 6, BENTLEY CLOSE, HORNDEAN
DURBIN, CHRISTOPHER J, 8, BENTLEY CLOSE, HORNDEAN

COCHRANE, IAN M, 12, BENTLEY CLOSE, HORNDEAN
COCHRANE, SUSAN L, 12, BENTLEY CLOSE, HORNDEAN
DAVISON, CLAIRE I, 14, BENTLEY CLOSE, HORNDEAN
DAVISON, PHILIP A, 14, BENTLEY CLOSE, HORNDEAN
DAVISON, TERESA M, 14, BENTLEY CLOSE, HORNDEAN
DRAYCOTT, CLARE E, 18, BENTLEY CLOSE, HORNDEAN
DRAYCOTT, IRVIN, 18, BENTLEY CLOSE, HORNDEAN
DRAYCOTT, SYLVIA, 18, BENTLEY CLOSE, HORNDEAN
PRICE, ALAN J, 20, BENTLEY CLOSE, HORNDEAN
PRICE, HELEN E, 20, BENTLEY CLOSE, HORNDEAN
ROBSON, AMANDA S, 105, BLENDWORTH
ROBSON, ROBERT N, 105, BLENDWORTH
SMITH, DAVID C, MOUSE COTTAGE, 107, BLENDWORTH
CROUGHAN, MARGARET A, PEPPERCORN COTTAGE, 109, BLENDWORTH
CROUGHAN, PETER S, PEPPERCORN COTTAGE, 109, BLENDWORTH
PICKLES, DAVID, 111, BLENDWORTH
PICKLES, ELAINE, 111, BLENDWORTH
EDMONDS, EDWIN T, 115, BLENDWORTH
EDMONDS, JANICE M, 115, BLENDWORTH
BROWN, ERIC J, FOX COTTAGE, 117, BLENDWORTH
BROWN, MARIANNE A, FOX COTTAGE, 117, BLENDWORTH
THIMBLEBY, ANTONY L, 104, BLENDWORTH
THIMBLEBY, MARY, 104, BLENDWORTH
DALBY, DAVID, ST. GILES FARM BUNGALOW, 106, BLENDWORTH
DALBY, CECIL J, ST. GILES FARM COTTAGE, 106, BLENDWORTH
BENNETT, PATRICIA M, 108, BLENDWORTH
LOVETT, JANE E, 110, BLENDWORTH
LOVETT, SPENCER B, 110, BLENDWORTH
OAKLAND, DORIS M, 112, BLENDWORTH
OAKLAND, HERBERT, 112, BLENDWORTH
MINKER, JEAN H, 116, BLENDWORTH
MINKER, ROBERT F, 116, BLENDWORTH
WITTCOMB, LOUISA E, BLENDWORTH FARM, BLENDWORTH
WITTCOMB, MARY L, BLENDWORTH FARM, BLENDWORTH
WITTCOMB, STANLEY R, BLENDWORTH FARM, BLENDWORTH
LANG, RICHARD B.D, BLENDWORTH FARMHOUSE, BLENDWORTH
LANG, SARAH H, BLENDWORTH FARMHOUSE, BLENDWORTH
DEBACKER, MARK E.P, THE ANNEXE, BLENDWORTH FARMHOUSE, BLENDWORTH
DEBALKER, EMILY J, THE ANNEXE, BLENDWORTH
READER, ALEXANDRA L, BLENDWORTH RECTORY, BLENDWORTH
READER, KRISTINA L, BLENDWORTH RECTORY, BLENDWORTH
READER, LESLEY S, BLENDWORTH RECTORY, BLENDWORTH
READER, SAMANTHA J, BLENDWORTH RECTORY, BLENDWORTH
READER, TREVOR A, BLENDWORTH RECTORY, BLENDWORTH
TODD, MICHAEL J, PEAK REVS, BROXBURN NURSERIES, BLENDWORTH
TODD, VALERIE P, PEAK REVS, BROXBURN NURSERIES, BLENDWORTH
EASON, CHRISTOPHER W, CHURCH COTTAGE, BLENDWORTH
EASON, ISOLDE V.S, CHURCH COTTAGE, BLENDWORTH
ROBERTSON, IAN B, CHURCH COTTAGE, BLENDWORTH
ESCOTT, JULIE C, COPPERFIELD, BLENDWORTH
ESCOTT, SIMON P, COPPERFIELD, BLENDWORTH
PEACOCK, MATTHEW, GUNTLES BOYES BELL ROAD, BLENDWORTH
YOUNG, JAMES R, GUNTLES BOYES BELL ROAD, BLENDWORTH
YOUNG, SUSAN C, GUNTLES BOYES BELL ROAD, BLENDWORTH
LOVETT, ETHEL, HEATHER LEY, BLENDWORTH
SISSON, EDNA G, HEDGE CORNER, BLENDWORTH
PALMER, CHRISTOPHER P.H, HOOK COTTAGE, BLENDWORTH
PALMER, JOSEPH H, HOOK COTTAGE, BLENDWORTH
NAGLER, CORRINNE F, LITTLE HOOK COTTAGE, BLENDWORTH
NAGLER, MARK A, LITTLE HOOK COTTAGE, BLENDWORTH
NAGLER, MERVYN M, LITTLE HOOK COTTAGE, BLENDWORTH
HAWKES, MARJORIE, 121, NEW BARN FARM, BLENDWORTH
SMITH, RUTH, 121, NEW BARN FARM, BLENDWORTH
HAWKES, DALE R, HAWQUINS, NEW BARN FARM, BLENDWORTH
HAWKES, LESLIE, HAWQUINS, NEW BARN FARM, BLENDWORTH
HAWKES, VALERIE A, HAWQUINS, NEW BARN FARM, BLENDWORTH
HAWKINS, EDITH K, PERRYMEAD, BLENDWORTH
HAWKINS, JOHN, PERRYMEAD, BLENDWORTH
WEEKS, IRENE, SIX BELLS FARM, BLENDWORTH
WEEKS, ROGER N, SIX BELLS FARM, BLENDWORTH
WEEKS, STEPHEN R, SIX BELLS FARM, BLENDWORTH
BURDA, STEFAN, ASHBOURNE, CADLINGTON HOUSE, BLENDWORTH LANE, BLENDWORTH
BUSSEY, NEAL, ASHBOURNE, CADLINGTON HOUSE, BLENDWORTH LANE, BLENDWORTH
HARTIGAN, DECLAN, ASHBOURNE, CADLINGTON HOUSE, BLENDWORTH LANE, BLENDWORTH

MCCULLEY, STUART, ASHBOURNE, CADLINGTON HOUSE, BLENDWORTH LANE, BLENDWORTH
FOSTER, AMANDA, BEECHES, CADLINGTON HOUSE, BLENDWORTH LANE, BLENDWORTH
KELLY, NOEL, BEECHES, CADLINGTON HOUSE, BLENDWORTH LANE, BLENDWORTH
LENFESTEY, MARIE, BEECHES, CADLINGTON HOUSE, BLENDWORTH LANE, BLENDWORTH
OLIVER, MICHELLE, BEECHES, CADLINGTON HOUSE, BLENDWORTH LANE, BLENDWORTH
WHEELER, ANDREW, BEECHES, CADLINGTON HOUSE, BLENDWORTH LANE, BLENDWORTH
BURNHAM, GRAHAM, OAKDENE, CADLINGTON HOUSE, BLENDWORTH LANE, BLENDWORTH
CHALK, NICOLA, OAKDENE, CADLINGTON HOUSE, BLENDWORTH LANE, BLENDWORTH
CONN, ROBBIE M, OAKDENE, CADLINGTON HOUSE, BLENDWORTH LANE, BLENDWORTH
STEVENS, CORINNA, OAKDENE, CADLINGTON HOUSE, BLENDWORTH LANE, BLENDWORTH
BUGG, CHRISTINE, SYCAMORES, CADLINGTON HOUSE, BLENDWORTH LANE, BLENDWORTH
DE-MICHAEL, MICHAEL, SYCAMORES, CADLINGTON HOUSE, BLENDWORTH LANE, BLENDWORTH
QUIGLEY, ANDREW, SYCAMORES, CADLINGTON HOUSE, BLENDWORTH LANE, BLENDWORTH
WOODHEAD, KAREN, SYCAMORES, CADLINGTON HOUSE, BLENDWORTH LANE, BLENDWORTH
BICETTE, DAVID, THE CEDARS, CADLINGTON HOUSE, BLENDWORTH LANE, BLENDWORTH
BOTTERO, PATRIZIA, THE CEDARS, CADLINGTON HOUSE, BLENDWORTH LANE, BLENDWORTH
MORAN, KAREN, THE CEDARS, CADLINGTON HOUSE, BLENDWORTH LANE, BLENDWORTH
NZEOGU, FELICIA, THE CEDARS, CADLINGTON HOUSE, BLENDWORTH LANE, BLENDWORTH
PRATT, ELIZABETH, THE CEDARS, CADLINGTON HOUSE, BLENDWORTH LANE, BLENDWORTH
BROOKE, JEMIMA, WILLOWS, CADLINGTON HOUSE, BLENDWORTH LANE, BLENDWORTH
JOHNSON, CLAIRE, WILLOWS, CADLINGTON HOUSE, BLENDWORTH LANE, BLENDWORTH
MINDERIDES, KOSTAS, WILLOWS, CADLINGTON HOUSE, BLENDWORTH LANE, BLENDWORTH
VALENTINE, RACHEL, WILLOWS, CADLINGTON HOUSE, BLENDWORTH LANE, BLENDWORTH
ADAMS, DAISY M, 1, CROOKLEY COTTAGES, BLENDWORTH LANE, BLENDWORTH
TOMSEN, JOHN P, 2, CROOKLEY COTTAGES, BLENDWORTH LANE, BLENDWORTH
PRIVETT, ANNABEL P, CROOKLEY POOL, BLENDWORTH LANE, BLENDWORTH
PRIVETT, FRANK S.K, CROOKLEY POOL, BLENDWORTH LANE, BLENDWORTH
PRIVETT, JENNIFER P, CROOKLEY POOL, BLENDWORTH LANE, BLENDWORTH
PRIVETT, RUPERT K, CROOKLEY POOL, BLENDWORTH LANE, BLENDWORTH
EDMONDS, CLARE L, 1, FLINT COTTAGES, BLENDWORTH LANE, BLENDWORTH
BUTT, IVY E, 2, FLINT COTTAGES, BLENDWORTH LANE, BLENDWORTH
SKINNER, RUSSELL, 3, FLINT COTTAGES, BLENDWORTH LANE, BLENDWORTH
WEBBER, DAWN, 3, FLINT COTTAGES, BLENDWORTH LANE, BLENDWORTH
HATCH, EDITH M, 1, MYRTLE COTTAGES, BLENDWORTH LANE, BLENDWORTH
HATCH, GEORGE T, 1, MYRTLE COTTAGES, BLENDWORTH LANE, BLENDWORTH
WHITLOCK, TERENCE G, 2, MYRTLE COTTAGES, BLENDWORTH LANE, BLENDWORTH
HOLMES, STEPHEN R, 3, MYRTLE COTTAGES, BLENDWORTH LANE, BLENDWORTH
BRIDGER, DENIS, MYRTLE FARM, BLENDWORTH LANE, BLENDWORTH
BRIDGER, PAMELA L, MYRTLE FARM, BLENDWORTH LANE, BLENDWORTH
CRADDOCK, HANNELORE, 1, SEYMOUR COTTAGES, BLENDWORTH LANE, BLENDWORTH
ROGERS, CAROL J, 2, SEYMOUR COTTAGES, BLENDWORTH LANE, BLENDWORTH
ROGERS, MICHAEL, 2, SEYMOUR COTTAGES, BLENDWORTH LANE, BLENDWORTH
SILLS, HARRY W, 3, SEYMOUR COTTAGES, BLENDWORTH LANE, BLENDWORTH
SILLS, IRIS M, 3, SEYMOUR COTTAGES, BLENDWORTH LANE, BLENDWORTH
BUTLER, ADRIAN F, 4, SEYMOUR COTTAGES, BLENDWORTH LANE, BLENDWORTH
RALPH, ALISON M, 4, SEYMOUR COTTAGES, BLENDWORTH LANE, BLENDWORTH

Electoral Roll

HICKMAN, CHRISTOPHER T, THE LODGE, BLENDWORTH LANE, BLENDWORTH
HICKMAN, LARRAINE, THE LODGE, BLENDWORTH LANE, BLENDWORTH
LEDINGHAM, LILY M, YEW TREE COTTAGE, BLENDWORTH LANE, BLENDWORTH
MULLEN, ANNIE, 3, BOURNE CLOSE, HORNDEAN
MULLEN, NORMAN H, 3, BOURNE CLOSE, HORNDEAN
FRANCE, LOUISA E, 5, BOURNE CLOSE, HORNDEAN
SILVESTER, EDITH M, 7, BOURNE CLOSE, HORNDEAN
WARHURST, DAVID J.R, 9, BOURNE CLOSE, HORNDEAN
WARHURST, JOHN D, 9, BOURNE CLOSE, HORNDEAN
PALMER, JOHN W.J, 2, BOURNE CLOSE, HORNDEAN
KNIGHT, ANDREW C, 4, BOURNE CLOSE, HORNDEAN
KNIGHT, SUSAN, 4, BOURNE CLOSE, HORNDEAN
STRETEN, DAVID M, 6, BOURNE CLOSE, HORNDEAN
STRETEN, DENISE L, 6, BOURNE CLOSE, HORNDEAN
CRAWLEY, MARIA A, 1, BOWES-LYON COURT, HORNDEAN
CRAWLEY, ROBERT J, 1, BOWES-LYON COURT, HORNDEAN
WALLACE, BROOKE L, 2, BOWES-LYON COURT, HORNDEAN
WALLACE, MARK W, 2, BOWES-LYON COURT, HORNDEAN
TRIGGS, IAIN C, 3, BOWES-LYON COURT, HORNDEAN
TRIGGS, MICHELLE A, 3, BOWES-LYON COURT, HORNDEAN
PHILLIPS, BRIAN G, 4, BOWES-LYON COURT, HORNDEAN
PHILLIPS, LINDA C, 4, BOWES-LYON COURT, HORNDEAN
COLLIS, CECIL G, 5, BOWES-LYON COURT, HORNDEAN
SPACEY, JEANNE M, 5, BOWES-LYON COURT, HORNDEAN
REES, JULIE C, 6, BOWES-LYON COURT, HORNDEAN
REES, PETER D, 6, BOWES-LYON COURT, HORNDEAN
GREEN, DONALD, 7, BOWES-LYON COURT, HORNDEAN
GREEN, SALLY-ANN, 7, BOWES-LYON COURT, HORNDEAN
OSBORNE, RUTH, 8, BOWES-LYON COURT, HORNDEAN
MATTHEWS, KERRY L, 9, BOWES-LYON COURT, HORNDEAN
MATTHEWS, PATRICIA K, 9, BOWES-LYON COURT,
MATTHEWS, THOMAS J, 9, BOWES-LYON COURT, HORNDEAN
NEWMAN, GERALDINE E, 10, BOWES-LYON COURT,
NICHOLS, MICHEAL C, 10, BOWES-LYON COURT, HORNDEAN
THOMSON, ROSEANNE, 11, BOWES-LYON COURT, HORNDEAN
CRANE, EMMA V, 14, BOWES-LYON COURT, HORNDEAN
BONIFACE, SALLY-ANN, 15, BOWES-LYON COURT, HORNDEAN
COOK, SAMANTHA, 16, BOWES-LYON COURT, HORNDEAN
BURROWS, SHAWN, 17, BOWES-LYON COURT, HORNDEAN
RENNIE, LINDSEY, 17, BOWES-LYON COURT, HORNDEAN
SMITH, HAYLEY, 18, BOWES-LYON COURT, HORNDEAN
SMITH, WAYNE D, 1, BRIDGET CLOSE, HORNDEAN
SMITH, YVONNE M, 1, BRIDGET CLOSE, HORNDEAN
ATTWOOD, DAVID J, 3, BRIDGET CLOSE, HORNDEAN
MCLEAN, JACQUELINE, 5, BRIDGET CLOSE, HORNDEAN
MCLEAN, PHILIP M, 5, BRIDGET CLOSE, HORNDEAN
MCLEAN, STEWART J, 5, BRIDGET CLOSE, HORNDEAN
ANDERSON, DARREN, 7, BRIDGET CLOSE, HORNDEAN
ANDERSON, SAMANTHA J, 7, BRIDGET CLOSE, HORNDEAN
LEE, MARION I, 9, BRIDGET CLOSE, HORNDEAN
LEE, MARTIN, 9, BRIDGET CLOSE, HORNDEAN
SIMPSON, ADRIAN J, 2, BRIDGET CLOSE, HORNDEAN
STAINTON, CRAIG A, 4, BRIDGET CLOSE, HORNDEAN
STAINTON, JANETTE A, 4, BRIDGET CLOSE, HORNDEAN
HOOPER, PATRICIA Y, 6, BRIDGET CLOSE, HORNDEAN
LYNN, SHARON, 8, BRIDGET CLOSE, HORNDEAN
TROY, PAUL M, 8, BRIDGET CLOSE, HORNDEAN
FRANKLAND, DAVID J, 10, BRIDGET CLOSE, HORNDEAN
FRANKLAND, HAZEL L, 10, BRIDGET CLOSE, HORNDEAN
HEATH, GARETH L, 1, BRIDLE PATH, HORNDEAN
HEATH, JOHNATHON, 1, BRIDLE PATH, HORNDEAN
HEATH, MARIE D, 1, BRIDLE PATH, HORNDEAN
HEATH, TREVOR, 1, BRIDLE PATH, HORNDEAN
HISCOCK, CECIL G.W, 1A, BRIDLE PATH, HORNDEAN
HISCOCK, SHEILA M, 1A, BRIDLE PATH, HORNDEAN
MILL, BRIAN R, 2, BRIDLE PATH, HORNDEAN
MILL, PAULA, 2, BRIDLE PATH, HORNDEAN
TREACHER, ANTHONY L, LAURELDENE, 4, BRIDLE PATH,
TREACHER, JOHANNAH, LAURELDENE, 4, BRIDLE PATH,
FITT, BARRY, CASTLEMEAD KENNELS AND CATTERY, BRIDLE PATH, HORNDEAN
FITT, MARGARET R, CASTLEMEAD KENNELS AND CATTERY, BRIDLE PATH, HORNDEAN
FITT, MICHAEL R, CASTLEMEAD KENNELS AND CATTERY, BRIDLE PATH, HORNDEAN
BRADY, DANIELLE, DELLHAVEN, BRIDLE PATH, HORNDEAN
BRADY, MARILYN, DELLHAVEN, BRIDLE PATH, HORNDEAN
BRADY, RODNEY J, DELLHAVEN, BRIDLE PATH, HORNDEAN
PULLEN, DANIEL J, DOMUS DIANDI, BRIDLE PATH,
PULLEN, DOROTHY L, DOMUS DIANDI, BRIDLE PATH,
ASTLE, JOHN W, HAZELWOOD, BRIDLE PATH, HORNDEAN
ASTLE, PATRICIA A, HAZELWOOD, BRIDLE PATH, HORNDEAN
MABB, MAUDIE, THE BUNGALOW, BRIDLE PATH, HORNDEAN
MABB, WINIFRED M, THE BUNGALOW, BRIDLE PATH,
PEEK, LEON C, 32, CATHERINGTON LANE, HORNDEAN
PEEK, LINDA A, 32, CATHERINGTON LANE, HORNDEAN
HARFIELD, BRIAN G, 36, CATHERINGTON LANE, HORNDEAN
CORNISH, PAUL, 38, CATHERINGTON LANE, HORNDEAN
HICKS, MARION, 38, CATHERINGTON LANE, HORNDEAN
CHITTENDEN, SUSAN, 40, CATHERINGTON LANE, HORNDEAN
KING, DOROTHY R.A, 42, CATHERINGTON LANE, HORNDEAN
KING, JOHN A, 42, CATHERINGTON LANE, HORNDEAN
BEASLEY, GEOFFREY W, 44, CATHERINGTON LANE,
BEASLEY, JOAN O, 44, CATHERINGTON LANE, HORNDEAN
MATHIESON, IRENE, 46, CATHERINGTON LANE, HORNDEAN
PHILLIPS, ALICE S, 48, CATHERINGTON LANE, HORNDEAN
MACLACHLAN, MURIEL, 50, CATHERINGTON LANE,
MACLACHLAN, NEIL, 50, CATHERINGTON LANE, HORNDEAN
MCINTYRE, GEORGINA, 52, CATHERINGTON LANE,
MCINTYRE, JOHN G, 52, CATHERINGTON LANE, HORNDEAN
ILLINGWORTH, DAVID M, 54, CATHERINGTON LANE,
ILLINGWORTH, MURIEL T, 54, CATHERINGTON LANE,
ILLINGWORTH, NICHOLAS D, 54, CATHERINGTON LANE,
JOYNER, ALAN P, 56, CATHERINGTON LANE, HORNDEAN
JOYNER, HAZEL R, 56, CATHERINGTON LANE, HORNDEAN
ANDREWS, ANGELA C, 58, CATHERINGTON LANE,
ANDREWS, PHILIP J, 58, CATHERINGTON LANE, HORNDEAN
HORTON, JOAN C, 60, CATHERINGTON LANE, HORNDEAN
HORTON, MICHAEL J, 60, CATHERINGTON LANE, HORNDEAN
HORTON, TRACEY L, 60, CATHERINGTON LANE, HORNDEAN
JERAM, ANDREW, 62, CATHERINGTON LANE, HORNDEAN
JERAM, KATHLEEN, 62, CATHERINGTON LANE, HORNDEAN
CORNISH, FRANK R, 64, CATHERINGTON LANE, HORNDEAN
CORNISH, PATRICIA L, 64, CATHERINGTON LANE,
RICHARDSON, GERTRUDE A, 64, CATHERINGTON LANE,
SIMMONS, KAY V, 66, CATHERINGTON LANE, HORNDEAN
SIMMONS, MICHAEL E, 66, CATHERINGTON LANE,
CHESTNUTT, ANDRENIA D, 68, CATHERINGTON LANE,
CHESTNUTT, ANDREW D, 68, CATHERINGTON LANE,
BENBOW, ALAN M, 70, CATHERINGTON LANE, HORNDEAN
BENBOW, MARIAN T, 70, CATHERINGTON LANE, HORNDEAN
SMITH, BARBARA, 72, CATHERINGTON LANE, HORNDEAN
SMITH, GORDON, 72, CATHERINGTON LANE, HORNDEAN
HERRIDGE, HECTOR F.D, 74A, CATHERINGTON LANE,
HERRIDGE, JEAN D.S, 74A, CATHERINGTON LANE,
SMITH, SHANE P, 74B, CATHERINGTON LANE, HORNDEAN
ANTHONY, RONALD, 76A, CATHERINGTON LANE, HORNDEAN
ANTHONY, VERA M, 76A, CATHERINGTON LANE, HORNDEAN
CHAMBERLAIN, NATASHA J, 76B, CATHERINGTON LANE,
LAMONT, GARY R, 76B, CATHERINGTON LANE, HORNDEAN
PLUM, MARGARET A, 78A, CATHERINGTON LANE,
GIDDINGS, DOROTHY R, 78B, CATHERINGTON LANE,
READ, TERENCE P, 80A, CATHERINGTON LANE, HORNDEAN
READ, YVONNE D, 80A, CATHERINGTON LANE, HORNDEAN
SHAW, MARK P, 80B, CATHERINGTON LANE, HORNDEAN
EDWARDS, ALFRED, 90, CATHERINGTON LANE, HORNDEAN
EDWARDS, DOROTHY E, 90, CATHERINGTON LANE,
HISCUTT, MICHAEL H, 92, CATHERINGTON LANE,
HISCUTT, PATRICIA, 92, CATHERINGTON LANE, HORNDEAN
GARLIKE, FRANK E, 94, CATHERINGTON LANE, HORNDEAN
GARLIKE, MURIEL C, 94, CATHERINGTON LANE, HORNDEAN
PODMORE, DAVID E, 96, CATHERINGTON LANE, HORNDEAN
PODMORE, JANICE R, 96, CATHERINGTON LANE, HORNDEAN
PODMORE, VICTOR F, 96, CATHERINGTON LANE,
WOODWARD, GERDA S, 98, CATHERINGTON LANE,
ROSE, EDNA M, 102, CATHERINGTON LANE, HORNDEAN
THOMPSON, ANTHONY L, 104, CATHERINGTON LANE,
THOMPSON, BRENDA J, 104, CATHERINGTON LANE,
THOMPSON, LEOPOLD R, 106, CATHERINGTON LANE,
HAXELL, FLORA A, 108, CATHERINGTON LANE, HORNDEAN
HAXELL, PETER R, 108, CATHERINGTON LANE, HORNDEAN
COPLAND-MANDER, CAROL A, 108A, CATHERINGTON LANE,
LUCAS, JOYCE E, 110, CATHERINGTON LANE, HORNDEAN
LUCAS, ROYAL, 110, CATHERINGTON LANE, HORNDEAN
ALLINSON, BRIAN W, 112, CATHERINGTON LANE, HORNDEAN
ALLINSON, MOIRA V, 112, CATHERINGTON LANE, HORNDEAN
COYLE, MURIEL V, 114, CATHERINGTON LANE, HORNDEAN
SPARSHOTT, MARTIN C, 116, CATHERINGTON LANE,
SPARSHOTT, ROSEMARY, 116, CATHERINGTON LANE,
RUDLING, ADAM J, 122, CATHERINGTON LANE, HORNDEAN
RUDLING, MARTIN J, 122, CATHERINGTON LANE, HORNDEAN
HOWES, BRUCE, 122A, CATHERINGTON LANE, HORNDEAN
HOWES, ESTELLE, 122A, CATHERINGTON LANE, HORNDEAN
HOWES, MARIE-CLAUDE, 122A, CATHERINGTON LANE,
BAXTER, TANIA D, 124, CATHERINGTON LANE, HORNDEAN
LIGHT, DAVID E, 124, CATHERINGTON LANE, HORNDEAN
TUDOR, HAZEL, 126, CATHERINGTON LANE, HORNDEAN
TUDOR, MICHAEL J, 126, CATHERINGTON LANE, HORNDEAN
TUDOR, RUSSELL, 126, CATHERINGTON LANE, HORNDEAN
MUNDEN, BRENDA M, 128, CATHERINGTON LANE,
MUNDEN, JACK, 128, CATHERINGTON LANE, HORNDEAN
POPE, EDNA D, 130, CATHERINGTON LANE, HORNDEAN
POPE, ROBERT W, 130, CATHERINGTON LANE, HORNDEAN
STEVENSON, CLIFFORD J, 132, CATHERINGTON LANE,
STEVENSON, FRANCES G, 132, CATHERINGTON LANE,
STEVENSON, ROGER, 132, CATHERINGTON LANE,
SCHILLEMORE, PAUL C, 134, CATHERINGTON LANE,
SCHILLEMORE, SARA E, 134, CATHERINGTON LANE,
HARRIS, JAMES, 136, CATHERINGTON LANE, HORNDEAN
HARRIS, LYNDA D, 136, CATHERINGTON LANE, HORNDEAN
IRWIN, MYRTLE, 138, CATHERINGTON LANE, HORNDEAN
ROBINSON, CAROLYN M, 142, CATHERINGTON LANE,
ROBINSON, KENELM J, 142, CATHERINGTON LANE,
ALNER, PATRICIA A, 144, CATHERINGTON LANE, HORNDEAN
ALNER, SEAN D, 144, CATHERINGTON LANE, HORNDEAN
FRY, SHIRLEY B.E, 148, CATHERINGTON LANE, HORNDEAN
FRY, WALTER E.H, 148, CATHERINGTON LANE, HORNDEAN
WEST, CHARLES W, 1, CHALK HILL ROAD, HORNDEAN
MARCH, CLIVE, 3, CHALK HILL ROAD, HORNDEAN
MARCH, KERRY, 3, CHALK HILL ROAD, HORNDEAN
MARCH, SUSAN R, 3, CHALK HILL ROAD, HORNDEAN
HALL, ANN P, 2, CHALK HILL ROAD, HORNDEAN
HALL, MARTIN R, 2, CHALK HILL ROAD, HORNDEAN
HALL, RICHARD A, 2, CHALK HILL ROAD, HORNDEAN
HALL, RODNEY A, 2, CHALK HILL ROAD, HORNDEAN
SMITH, DAVID A, 4, CHALK HILL ROAD, HORNDEAN
SMITH, HILARY L, 4, CHALK HILL ROAD, HORNDEAN
SMITH, LAURA, 4, CHALK HILL ROAD, HORNDEAN
BEEDLE, MIRIAM A, 1, CHANTRY ROAD, HORNDEAN
BEEDLE, STEPHEN P, 1, CHANTRY ROAD, HORNDEAN
JONES, ANITA, 3, CHANTRY ROAD, HORNDEAN
JONES, STEPHEN C, 3, CHANTRY ROAD, HORNDEAN
SINCLAIR, DAVID A, 5, CHANTRY ROAD, HORNDEAN
BEST, SIMON R, 2, CHANTRY ROAD, HORNDEAN
DUNCAN, STEPHEN M, 4, CHANTRY ROAD, HORNDEAN
BURR, JOSEPHINE, 6, CHANTRY ROAD, HORNDEAN
BURR, PHILIP C, 6, CHANTRY ROAD, HORNDEAN
WATKINS, JOHN P, 1, CRISSPYN CLOSE, HORNDEAN
WATKINS, UNA J, 1, CRISSPYN CLOSE, HORNDEAN
HALL, GERALD P, 3, CRISSPYN CLOSE, HORNDEAN
HALL, SANDRA J, 3, CRISSPYN CLOSE, HORNDEAN
HUSSAIN, MOMTAR, 5, CRISSPYN CLOSE, HORNDEAN
MIAH, KELON N, 5, CRISSPYN CLOSE, HORNDEAN
MIAH, TUHIL, 5, CRISSPYN CLOSE, HORNDEAN
GLAZIER, CORAL J, 7, CRISSPYN CLOSE, HORNDEAN
GLAZIER, JOHN N, 7, CRISSPYN CLOSE, HORNDEAN
GLAZIER, STEPHEN J, 7, CRISSPYN CLOSE, HORNDEAN
CRATHERN, LYN M, 9, CRISSPYN CLOSE, HORNDEAN
CRATHERN, PATRICIA M, 9, CRISSPYN CLOSE, HORNDEAN
CRATHERN, PAUL E, 9, CRISSPYN CLOSE, HORNDEAN
HANCOCK, ALAN G, 2, CRISSPYN CLOSE, HORNDEAN
HANCOCK, YVONNE L, 2, CRISSPYN CLOSE, HORNDEAN
PUDDY, PAUL, 4, CRISSPYN CLOSE, HORNDEAN
RENSHAW, ROBERT E, 4, CRISSPYN CLOSE, HORNDEAN
FIELD, JOHN A.S, 6, CRISSPYN CLOSE, HORNDEAN
MACNAUGHTON, DORIS I, 6, CRISSPYN CLOSE, HORNDEAN
OVERINGTON, JOHN C, 8, CRISSPYN CLOSE, HORNDEAN
PETTITT, CELIA M, 10, CRISSPYN CLOSE, HORNDEAN
PETTITT, COLIN T, 10, CRISSPYN CLOSE, HORNDEAN
MUNDAY, GLADYS M, 1, CUNNINGHAM ROAD, HORNDEAN
DULAKE, PHYLLIS B, 3, CUNNINGHAM ROAD, HORNDEAN
DULAKE, REGINALD J, 3, CUNNINGHAM ROAD, HORNDEAN
HAMPSON, ANITA M, 5, CUNNINGHAM ROAD, HORNDEAN
HAMPSON, COLIN J, 5, CUNNINGHAM ROAD, HORNDEAN
HAMPSON, MARK S, 5, CUNNINGHAM ROAD, HORNDEAN
HOOPER, TRACEY J, 7, CUNNINGHAM ROAD, HORNDEAN
RANDALL, ROY R, 7, CUNNINGHAM ROAD, HORNDEAN
CHURLISH, JOAN, 2, CUNNINGHAM ROAD, HORNDEAN
CHURLISH, STEPHEN, 2, CUNNINGHAM ROAD, HORNDEAN
VENTON, KEITH R, 4, CUNNINGHAM ROAD, HORNDEAN
VENTON, SARAH J, 4, CUNNINGHAM ROAD, HORNDEAN
RIDLER, PAUL J, 6, CUNNINGHAM ROAD, HORNDEAN
RIDLER, TREVOR G, 6, CUNNINGHAM ROAD, HORNDEAN
ROGERS, DAVID A, 6, CUNNINGHAM ROAD, HORNDEAN
ROGERS, MERCIA P, 6, CUNNINGHAM ROAD, HORNDEAN
MCLEOD, BARRYMORE R, 8, CUNNINGHAM ROAD,
MCLEOD, PAULINE E, 8, CUNNINGHAM ROAD, HORNDEAN
JENKINS, HELEN, 1, DORSET CLOSE, HORNDEAN
HICKS, FLORENCE M, 3, DORSET CLOSE, HORNDEAN
HICKS, REGINALD H, 3, DORSET CLOSE, HORNDEAN
GILLIES, CYRIL J, 5, DORSET CLOSE, HORNDEAN
GILLIES, DORIS M, 5, DORSET CLOSE, HORNDEAN
CLEIFE, JUNE A, 7, DORSET CLOSE, HORNDEAN
CLEIFE, VERNON W, 7, DORSET CLOSE, HORNDEAN
STAINTON, DENISE, 9, DORSET CLOSE, HORNDEAN
STAINTON, RAYMOND I, 9, DORSET CLOSE, HORNDEAN
DAVISON, JOHN R, 13, DORSET CLOSE, HORNDEAN
LANGHAM, CHRISTOPHER E, 15, DORSET CLOSE,
LANGHAM, NICHOLAS E, 15, DORSET CLOSE, HORNDEAN
LANGHAM, SUSAN A, 15, DORSET CLOSE, HORNDEAN
ROBINSON, KEITH T, 17, DORSET CLOSE, HORNDEAN
ROBINSON, SHEILA A, 17, DORSET CLOSE, HORNDEAN
WAY, IVY, 2, DORSET CLOSE, HORNDEAN
HERMITAGE, MAVIS, 4, DORSET CLOSE, HORNDEAN
CHEATLE, HARVEY J, 12, DORSET CLOSE, HORNDEAN
CHEATLE, PHYLLIS A, 12, DORSET CLOSE, HORNDEAN
DAWSON, PETER J, 14, DORSET CLOSE, HORNDEAN
THORNCROFT, MARGARET A, 14, DORSET CLOSE,
WINDEL, ALEXANDER J, 16, DORSET CLOSE, HORNDEAN
WINDEL, EDWARD C, 16, DORSET CLOSE, HORNDEAN
WINDEL, HELEN P, 16, DORSET CLOSE, HORNDEAN
BUTLAND, GEOFFREY J.G, 1, DURLANDS ROAD, HORNDEAN
BUTLAND, RITA, 1, DURLANDS ROAD, HORNDEAN
FEHRENBACH, RAYMOND, 3, DURLANDS ROAD, HORNDEAN
PHILLIPS, KENNETH J, 3, DURLANDS ROAD, HORNDEAN
PHILLIPS, SHEILA E, 3, DURLANDS ROAD, HORNDEAN
MORSE, CHRISTOPHER D, 5, DURLANDS ROAD, HORNDEAN
MORSE, DEREK M, 5, DURLANDS ROAD, HORNDEAN
MORSE, JANET E, 5, DURLANDS ROAD, HORNDEAN
MORSE, MATTHEW J, 5, DURLANDS ROAD, HORNDEAN
HANCOCK, DAVID J, 6, DURLANDS ROAD, HORNDEAN
HANCOCK, JANET E, 6, DURLANDS ROAD, HORNDEAN
STEVENS, FRANCES M, 7, DURLANDS ROAD, HORNDEAN
STEVENS, MARTIN S, 7, DURLANDS ROAD, HORNDEAN
STEVENS, TERENCE K, 7, DURLANDS ROAD, HORNDEAN
AYLING, JOHN M, 9, DURLANDS ROAD, HORNDEAN
AYLING, RICHARD J, 9, DURLANDS ROAD, HORNDEAN
AYLING, SALLY A, 9, DURLANDS ROAD, HORNDEAN
JENKINS, CHRISTINE E, 1, FIVE HEADS ROAD, HORNDEAN
JENKINS, MICHAEL P, 1, FIVE HEADS ROAD, HORNDEAN
JENKINS, PHILLIP M, 1, FIVE HEADS ROAD, HORNDEAN
NEWMAN, YVONNE, 4, FIVE HEADS ROAD, HORNDEAN
DRUMMOND, ADRIAN A, 5, FIVE HEADS ROAD, HORNDEAN
DRUMMOND, SHEILA L, 5, FIVE HEADS ROAD, HORNDEAN
NEWMAN, CHARLOTTE A, 6, FIVE HEADS ROAD, HORNDEAN
NEWMAN, NICHOLAS W, 6, FIVE HEADS ROAD, HORNDEAN
NEWMAN, SUSAN A, 6, FIVE HEADS ROAD, HORNDEAN
PETTIT, MATTHEW, 6, FIVE HEADS ROAD, HORNDEAN
LINDSAY, DENISE A, 7, FIVE HEADS ROAD, HORNDEAN
LINDSAY, JOHN, 7, FIVE HEADS ROAD, HORNDEAN
ALLEN, DEBRA J, 8, FIVE HEADS ROAD, HORNDEAN
ALLEN, MARK J, 8, FIVE HEADS ROAD, HORNDEAN
PALMER, IAN, 9, FIVE HEADS ROAD, HORNDEAN
PALMER, ISABEL, 9, FIVE HEADS ROAD, HORNDEAN
WILKINSON, MARK, 10, FIVE HEADS ROAD, HORNDEAN
WILKINSON, SARA J, 10, FIVE HEADS ROAD, HORNDEAN

HEMSWORTH, KENNETH J, 11, FIVE HEADS ROAD,
HEMSWORTH, SUSAN, 11, FIVE HEADS ROAD, HORNDEAN
STREET, ROBERT W, 12A, FIVE HEADS ROAD, HORNDEAN
STREET, SHEILA M, 12A, FIVE HEADS ROAD, HORNDEAN
HANSON, ROGER W, 12B, FIVE HEADS ROAD, HORNDEAN
HANSON, SUSAN M.C, 12B, FIVE HEADS ROAD, HORNDEAN
HUSKINSON, HOWARD P, 13, FIVE HEADS ROAD, HORNDEAN
EASON, MARGARET, 13A, FIVE HEADS ROAD, HORNDEAN
EASON, ROGER B, 13A, FIVE HEADS ROAD, HORNDEAN
HERBERTSON, PENELOPE A, 14, FIVE HEADS ROAD,
HERBERTSON, RICHARD P, 14, FIVE HEADS ROAD,
MORRIS, JOHN, 15, FIVE HEADS ROAD, HORNDEAN
MORRIS, MARION S, 15, FIVE HEADS ROAD, HORNDEAN
POPE, CAROL L, 16, FIVE HEADS ROAD, HORNDEAN
POPE, CHARLES D, 16, FIVE HEADS ROAD, HORNDEAN
WILSON, JEAN O, 17, FIVE HEADS ROAD, HORNDEAN
MOHAMMED, ASHAFF, 18, FIVE HEADS ROAD, HORNDEAN
MOHAMMED, JUDITH D, 18, FIVE HEADS ROAD, HORNDEAN
SMITH, RAYMOND A, 19, FIVE HEADS ROAD, HORNDEAN
JONES, CARLA J, 20, FIVE HEADS ROAD, HORNDEAN
JONES, SIMON E, 20, FIVE HEADS ROAD, HORNDEAN
PHILLIPS, JUNE, 21, FIVE HEADS ROAD, HORNDEAN
HUGHES, ROBERT, 22, FIVE HEADS ROAD, HORNDEAN
HUGHES, RUSSELL, 22, FIVE HEADS ROAD, HORNDEAN
HUGHES, SUZANNE E, 22, FIVE HEADS ROAD, HORNDEAN
CROOK, NICOLA J, 23, FIVE HEADS ROAD, HORNDEAN
CROOK, NORMAN A, 23, FIVE HEADS ROAD, HORNDEAN
LEOTTA, SALVATORE V, 24, FIVE HEADS ROAD, HORNDEAN
MIROY, CAROLINE J, 24, FIVE HEADS ROAD, HORNDEAN
MIROY, CHRISTINE, 24, FIVE HEADS ROAD, HORNDEAN
MIROY, ROGER H, 24, FIVE HEADS ROAD, HORNDEAN
HARRIS, KATHLEEN J, 25, FIVE HEADS ROAD, HORNDEAN
HARRIS, MICHAEL G, 25, FIVE HEADS ROAD, HORNDEAN
BENFORD, VICTORIA S, 26, FIVE HEADS ROAD, HORNDEAN
REDPATH, IAN, 26, FIVE HEADS ROAD, HORNDEAN
REDPATH, TANIA A, 26, FIVE HEADS ROAD, HORNDEAN
THOMPSON, BRIDGET, 27, FIVE HEADS ROAD, HORNDEAN
THOMPSON, STEPHEN, 27, FIVE HEADS ROAD, HORNDEAN
STOKES, PATRICIA R, 29, FIVE HEADS ROAD, HORNDEAN
STOKES, ROBERT A, 29, FIVE HEADS ROAD, HORNDEAN
SACKETT, IVY K, 31, FIVE HEADS ROAD, HORNDEAN
SACKETT, MICHAEL A, 31, FIVE HEADS ROAD, HORNDEAN
WILLIAMS, JOANNE E, 32, FIVE HEADS ROAD, HORNDEAN
HOBBS, ANDREW W, 33, FIVE HEADS ROAD, HORNDEAN
HOBBS, ELSIE W, 33, FIVE HEADS ROAD, HORNDEAN
ALLERY, JAYNE, 34, FIVE HEADS ROAD, HORNDEAN
BARKER, IAN, 34, FIVE HEADS ROAD, HORNDEAN
KING, AILEEN K, 35, FIVE HEADS ROAD, HORNDEAN
KING, DONNA M, 35, FIVE HEADS ROAD, HORNDEAN
HOLLOWAY, PERCY, 36, FIVE HEADS ROAD, HORNDEAN
HOLLOWAY, ROSEMARY V, 36, FIVE HEADS ROAD, HORNDEAN
HOLLOWAY, STEVEN J, 36, FIVE HEADS ROAD, HORNDEAN
KNIGHT, ARTHUR, 37, FIVE HEADS ROAD, HORNDEAN
LONGHURST, DOREEN S, 38, FIVE HEADS ROAD, HORNDEAN
LONGHURST, EDWARD A.G, 38, FIVE HEADS ROAD,
LONGHURST, TREVOR P, 38, FIVE HEADS ROAD, HORNDEAN
CRACKNELL, DOROTHY S, 39, FIVE HEADS ROAD,
REYNOLDS, EVELYN, 39, FIVE HEADS ROAD, HORNDEAN
REYNOLDS, WILLIAM E, 39, FIVE HEADS ROAD, HORNDEAN
TUCKER, PAUL F, 40, FIVE HEADS ROAD, HORNDEAN
BARLOW, JEFFERY L, 40A, FIVE HEADS ROAD, HORNDEAN
BARLOW, LYNDA M, 40A, FIVE HEADS ROAD, HORNDEAN
BORROW, BENJAMIN P, 40B, FIVE HEADS ROAD, HORNDEAN
BORROW, MEDE W, 40B, FIVE HEADS ROAD, HORNDEAN
CHARMAN, BETTY, 41, FIVE HEADS ROAD, HORNDEAN
CHARMAN, ERIC, 41, FIVE HEADS ROAD, HORNDEAN
GRAY, JANE E, 42, FIVE HEADS ROAD, HORNDEAN
STEINSON, MARK M, 42, FIVE HEADS ROAD, HORNDEAN
BROWN, CAROLYN S, 44, FIVE HEADS ROAD, HORNDEAN
MARTIN, JOHN D, 46, FIVE HEADS ROAD, HORNDEAN
MARTIN, MARY P, 46, FIVE HEADS ROAD, HORNDEAN
MARTIN, RICHARD J, 46, FIVE HEADS ROAD, HORNDEAN
PAFFETT, ALAN H, 48, FIVE HEADS ROAD, HORNDEAN
PAFFETT, JEAN M, 48, FIVE HEADS ROAD, HORNDEAN
BURGESS, RONALD G, 50, FIVE HEADS ROAD, HORNDEAN
WHITE, DAVID B, 52, FIVE HEADS ROAD, HORNDEAN
ATTREE, DAVID A, 52A, FIVE HEADS ROAD, HORNDEAN
ATTREE, ROSEMARY M, 52A, FIVE HEADS ROAD, HORNDEAN
MIDDLETON, DOUGLAS T, 56, FIVE HEADS ROAD, HORNDEAN
MIDDLETON, JANET E, 56, FIVE HEADS ROAD, HORNDEAN
ASHTON, KATHLEEN M, 58, FIVE HEADS ROAD, HORNDEAN
ASHTON, MICHAEL J, 58, FIVE HEADS ROAD, HORNDEAN
WARMAN, AINA I, 60, FIVE HEADS ROAD, HORNDEAN
WARMAN, RICHARD K, 60, FIVE HEADS ROAD, HORNDEAN
WARMAN, ROBERT J, 60, FIVE HEADS ROAD, HORNDEAN
HEATH, MARGARET G, 61, FIVE HEADS ROAD, HORNDEAN
PURKIS, IAN R, 61, FIVE HEADS ROAD, HORNDEAN
EMERY, CHRISTOPHER W, 62, FIVE HEADS ROAD, HORNDEAN
EMERY, PENNY A, 62, FIVE HEADS ROAD, HORNDEAN
FOWLER, LLOYD A.M, 63, FIVE HEADS ROAD, HORNDEAN
FOWLER, LYN, 63, FIVE HEADS ROAD, HORNDEAN
WALKER, EVE A, 64, FIVE HEADS ROAD, HORNDEAN
WALKER, STEPHEN H, 64, FIVE HEADS ROAD, HORNDEAN
BEAUMONT, JULIE M, 66, FIVE HEADS ROAD, HORNDEAN
BOWYER, DAVID, 68, FIVE HEADS ROAD, HORNDEAN
BARRETT, ALAN A, 70, FIVE HEADS ROAD, HORNDEAN
BARRETT, SUSAN, 70, FIVE HEADS ROAD, HORNDEAN
BARRETT, TIMOTHY A, 70, FIVE HEADS ROAD, HORNDEAN
EMMERSON, CHRISTINE E, 1A, HAVANT ROAD, HORNDEAN
EMMERSON, RODNEY J, 1A, HAVANT ROAD, HORNDEAN
DONALD, ALASTAIR J, 3, HAVANT ROAD, HORNDEAN
DONALD, IAIN A, 3, HAVANT ROAD, HORNDEAN
DONALD, ROBERT A, 3, HAVANT ROAD, HORNDEAN
DONALD, ROSEMARY A, 3, HAVANT ROAD, HORNDEAN
MEDCALF, BENJAMIN T, 1, HEATH CLOSE, HORNDEAN
MEDCALF, ERICA J, 1, HEATH CLOSE, HORNDEAN
MEDCALF, TERENCE A, 1, HEATH CLOSE, HORNDEAN
NEALE, DORIS M.P, 1A, HEATH CLOSE, HORNDEAN
STEVENS, CECIL E, 2, HEATH CLOSE, HORNDEAN
MULLIGAN, BETTY B, 3, HEATH CLOSE, HORNDEAN
MULLIGAN, FREDERICK T, 3, HEATH CLOSE, HORNDEAN
DOODY, ALISON C, 4, HEATH CLOSE, HORNDEAN
DOODY, GARETH J, 4, HEATH CLOSE, HORNDEAN
DOODY, JOHN, 4, HEATH CLOSE, HORNDEAN
TAYLOR, CLAIRE L, 5, HEATH CLOSE, HORNDEAN
TAYLOR, MARILYN L, 5, HEATH CLOSE, HORNDEAN
TAYLOR, STUART C, 5, HEATH CLOSE, HORNDEAN
BROTHERTON, ANDREW R, 6, HEATH CLOSE, HORNDEAN
BROTHERTON, DOREEN R, 6, HEATH CLOSE, HORNDEAN
BROTHERTON, JOHN M, 6, HEATH CLOSE, HORNDEAN
MARTIN, COLIN C, 8, HEATH CLOSE, HORNDEAN
MARTIN, GERALD W.S, 8, HEATH CLOSE, HORNDEAN
MARTIN, WENDY A, 8, HEATH CLOSE, HORNDEAN
WHITTAKER, ADAM J, 9, HEATH CLOSE, HORNDEAN
WHITTAKER, COLIN L, 9, HEATH CLOSE, HORNDEAN
WHITTAKER, SUSAN E, 9, HEATH CLOSE, HORNDEAN
HART, ALISON, 10, HEATH CLOSE, HORNDEAN
HART, REBECCA, 10, HEATH CLOSE, HORNDEAN
HART, RICHARD M.S, 10, HEATH CLOSE, HORNDEAN
HART, SUSAN, 10, HEATH CLOSE, HORNDEAN
LAYTON, ANTHONY N, 11, HEATH CLOSE, HORNDEAN
MCLAUGHLAN, HAZEL L, 12, HEATH CLOSE, HORNDEAN
MCLAUGHLAN, JAMES W, 12, HEATH CLOSE, HORNDEAN
MCLAUGHLAN, JAMES Y, 12, HEATH CLOSE, HORNDEAN
MCLAUGHLAN, STUART L, 12, HEATH CLOSE, HORNDEAN
FISK, LINDA J, 14, HEATH CLOSE, HORNDEAN
FISK, PETER A, 14, HEATH CLOSE, HORNDEAN
ELLIS, LINDA J, 15, HEATH CLOSE, HORNDEAN
ELLIS, MARTIN J, 15, HEATH CLOSE, HORNDEAN
ELLIS, RONALD, 15, HEATH CLOSE, HORNDEAN
PATTEN, JACQUELINE, 16, HEATH CLOSE, HORNDEAN
PATTEN, TERENCE R, 16, HEATH CLOSE, HORNDEAN
ROBERTSON, ANDREW J, 18, HEATH CLOSE, HORNDEAN
ROBERTSON, KATHRYN A, 18, HEATH CLOSE, HORNDEAN
ROBERTSON, PHILIP W, 18, HEATH CLOSE, HORNDEAN
ROBERTSON, STEVEN M, 18, HEATH CLOSE, HORNDEAN
PHILLIPS, JEAN A, 1, HIGHCROFT LANE, HORNDEAN
HELYER, JOHN A, 15, HIGHCROFT LANE, HORNDEAN
HELYER, TANIA L, 15, HIGHCROFT LANE, HORNDEAN
MCGROARTY, ARTHUR, 17, HIGHCROFT LANE, HORNDEAN
MCGROARTY, HEATHER, 17, HIGHCROFT LANE, HORNDEAN
KITTREDGE, ANTHONY K, 19, HIGHCROFT LANE,
KITTREDGE, CHRISTINE, 19, HIGHCROFT LANE, HORNDEAN
KITTREDGE, DANIEL W, 19, HIGHCROFT LANE, HORNDEAN
KITTREDGE, MICHAEL K, 19, HIGHCROFT LANE, HORNDEAN
CLARE, EDWARD J, 21, HIGHCROFT LANE, HORNDEAN
DEAN, GURTHA M, 23, HIGHCROFT LANE, HORNDEAN
DEAN, JOHN E, 23, HIGHCROFT LANE, HORNDEAN
BRAME, DANIEL J, 25, HIGHCROFT LANE, HORNDEAN
BRAME, JOHN, 25, HIGHCROFT LANE, HORNDEAN
BRAME, JUDITH A, 25, HIGHCROFT LANE, HORNDEAN
BRAME, PAUL M, 25, HIGHCROFT LANE, HORNDEAN
BARNETT, JOHN K, 27, HIGHCROFT LANE, HORNDEAN
BARNETT, JOYCE M, 27, HIGHCROFT LANE, HORNDEAN
BARNETT, STRUAN S, 27, HIGHCROFT LANE, HORNDEAN
HAYDEN, GEMMA E, 29, HIGHCROFT LANE, HORNDEAN
HAYDEN, GEOFFREY E, 29, HIGHCROFT LANE, HORNDEAN
HAYDEN, SANDRA J, 29, HIGHCROFT LANE, HORNDEAN
HAYDEN, STEPHEN G, 29, HIGHCROFT LANE, HORNDEAN
WRIGHT, EVA D, 31, HIGHCROFT LANE, HORNDEAN
RISING, ANNE, 33, HIGHCROFT LANE, HORNDEAN
RISING, BARRY D, 33, HIGHCROFT LANE, HORNDEAN
WINSOR, MALCOLM R, 35, HIGHCROFT LANE, HORNDEAN
WINSOR, ROSE M.K, 35, HIGHCROFT LANE, HORNDEAN
YOUREN, CHARLES E, 37, HIGHCROFT LANE, HORNDEAN
YOUREN, HELEN, 37, HIGHCROFT LANE, HORNDEAN
O'CONNOR, KATHERINE, 39, HIGHCROFT LANE, HORNDEAN
O'CONNOR, STEVEN J, 39, HIGHCROFT LANE, HORNDEAN
HICKS, ENID E, 41, HIGHCROFT LANE, HORNDEAN
TURNER, SONIA R, 41, HIGHCROFT LANE, HORNDEAN
HAMMOND, ANDREW F, 43, HIGHCROFT LANE, HORNDEAN
HAMMOND, PETER J, 43, HIGHCROFT LANE, HORNDEAN
HAMMOND, SARAH J, 43, HIGHCROFT LANE, HORNDEAN
HAMMOND, WENDY A, 43, HIGHCROFT LANE, HORNDEAN
PINK, JOHN H.D, 45, HIGHCROFT LANE, HORNDEAN
PINK, PENELOPE A, 45, HIGHCROFT LANE, HORNDEAN
PINK, PETER C, 45, HIGHCROFT LANE, HORNDEAN
BLICK, JACQUELINE V, 47, HIGHCROFT LANE, HORNDEAN
BLICK, NORMAN J, 47, HIGHCROFT LANE, HORNDEAN
DEAN, CHRISTOPHER R, 49, HIGHCROFT LANE, HORNDEAN
DEAN, JANE C, 49, HIGHCROFT LANE, HORNDEAN
MEAD, JILL E, 51, HIGHCROFT LANE, HORNDEAN
MEAD, TREVOR E, 51, HIGHCROFT LANE, HORNDEAN
GRAYSTON, KAREN L, 53, HIGHCROFT LANE, HORNDEAN
COOK, GARY F, 55, HIGHCROFT LANE, HORNDEAN
PURVIS, DAVID, 57, HIGHCROFT LANE, HORNDEAN
PURVIS, MILDRED A, 57, HIGHCROFT LANE, HORNDEAN
PURVIS, REBECCA, 57, HIGHCROFT LANE, HORNDEAN
HEFFER, MARGARET G, 59, HIGHCROFT LANE, HORNDEAN
SAUNDERS, WENDY, 59, HIGHCROFT LANE, HORNDEAN
BALLAM, JOHN, 61, HIGHCROFT LANE, HORNDEAN
BALLAM, JUDITH, 61, HIGHCROFT LANE, HORNDEAN
DENTON, CHRISTOPHER G, 63, HIGHCROFT LANE,
DENTON, JAMES P, 63, HIGHCROFT LANE, HORNDEAN
DENTON, JEAN E, 63, HIGHCROFT LANE, HORNDEAN
POTTS, EDDA A, 65, HIGHCROFT LANE, HORNDEAN
POTTS, GEOFFREY, 65, HIGHCROFT LANE, HORNDEAN
BROOKS, ADRIAN W, 67, HIGHCROFT LANE, HORNDEAN
BROOKS, CAROLE J, 67, HIGHCROFT LANE, HORNDEAN
CROTHALL, JOY S, 2, HIGHCROFT LANE, HORNDEAN
CROTHALL, NEIL C, 2, HIGHCROFT LANE, HORNDEAN
MILLER, JACK A.H, 4, HIGHCROFT LANE, HORNDEAN
MILLER, LINDA, 4, HIGHCROFT LANE, HORNDEAN
LORD, JOHN C, 8, HIGHCROFT LANE, HORNDEAN
LORD, WENDY M, 8, HIGHCROFT LANE, HORNDEAN
SMART, CHRISTOPHER E, 10, HIGHCROFT LANE, HORNDEAN
SMART, DAVID E, 10, HIGHCROFT LANE, HORNDEAN
SMART, LESLEY A, 10, HIGHCROFT LANE, HORNDEAN
SMART, MATHEW R, 10, HIGHCROFT LANE, HORNDEAN
WALKER, ROGER A, 12, HIGHCROFT LANE, HORNDEAN
CHANDLER, DOREEN M, 14, HIGHCROFT LANE, HORNDEAN
COYNE, DOUGLAS C, 16, HIGHCROFT LANE, HORNDEAN
COYNE, PATRICIA J, 16, HIGHCROFT LANE, HORNDEAN
BURGESS, ALAN F, 18, HIGHCROFT LANE, HORNDEAN
BURGESS, PATRICIA, 18, HIGHCROFT LANE, HORNDEAN
MCTEER, JOSEPH R, 20, HIGHCROFT LANE, HORNDEAN
MCTEER, ROSEMARY E, 20, HIGHCROFT LANE, HORNDEAN
GILLHAM, JOAN, 22, HIGHCROFT LANE, HORNDEAN
GILLHAM, RONALD W, 22, HIGHCROFT LANE, HORNDEAN
DE MELLOW, CHRISTINE M, 28, HIGHCROFT LANE,
DE MELLOW, CHRISTOPHER J, 28, HIGHCROFT LANE,
HOLLINGSHEAD, GEOFFREY J, 30, HIGHCROFT LANE,
HOLLINGSHEAD, SHIRLEY H, 30, HIGHCROFT LANE,
HOLLINGSHEAD, WENDY A, 30, HIGHCROFT LANE,
LEWIS, EILEEN A, 32, HIGHCROFT LANE, HORNDEAN
LEWIS, MICHAEL J, 32, HIGHCROFT LANE, HORNDEAN
KNIGHT, DAVID S, 34, HIGHCROFT LANE, HORNDEAN
KNIGHT, MARILYN A, 34, HIGHCROFT LANE, HORNDEAN
DEACON, ERNEST J, 36, HIGHCROFT LANE, HORNDEAN
DEACON, PAULINE A, 36, HIGHCROFT LANE, HORNDEAN
TARRANT, ANN-MARIE, 50, HIGHCROFT LANE, HORNDEAN
GROSMAIRE-LORIER, BRIGITTE M, 52, HIGHCROFT LANE,
LORIER, PHILIPPE C, 52, HIGHCROFT LANE, HORNDEAN
MCCANN, EDWARD R, 56, HIGHCROFT LANE, HORNDEAN
MCCANN, LINDA E, 56, HIGHCROFT LANE, HORNDEAN
REEVES, MARK, 58, HIGHCROFT LANE, HORNDEAN
REEVES, SUE, 58, HIGHCROFT LANE, HORNDEAN
PRESCOTT, PAULINE, 1, JODRELL CLOSE, HORNDEAN
PRESCOTT, STEPHEN, 1, JODRELL CLOSE, HORNDEAN
CLARK, HENRY W, 2, JODRELL CLOSE, HORNDEAN
CLARK, NELLIE L, 2, JODRELL CLOSE, HORNDEAN
LARKHAM, MARGARET H, 3, JODRELL CLOSE, HORNDEAN
FREEMANTLE, CLARE A, 4, JODRELL CLOSE, HORNDEAN
FREEMANTLE, ELAINE M, 4, JODRELL CLOSE, HORNDEAN
FREEMANTLE, KEVIN E, 4, JODRELL CLOSE, HORNDEAN
FREEMANTLE, TRACY C, 4, JODRELL CLOSE, HORNDEAN
GOOD, CHRISTINA J, 5, JODRELL CLOSE, HORNDEAN
O'BOYLE, AMANDA J, 6, JODRELL CLOSE, HORNDEAN
WILSON, ANITA D, 6A, JODRELL CLOSE, HORNDEAN
PACKHAM, SHEILA A, 7, JODRELL CLOSE, HORNDEAN
PACKHAM, STEVEN P, 7, JODRELL CLOSE, HORNDEAN
HOSKINS, GRAHAM, 8, JODRELL CLOSE, HORNDEAN
HOSKINS, REBECCA M, 8, JODRELL CLOSE, HORNDEAN
WHEELER, TONY M, 9, JODRELL CLOSE, HORNDEAN
WHEELER, WENDY J, 9, JODRELL CLOSE, HORNDEAN
HOWELL, BARBARA, 10, JODRELL CLOSE, HORNDEAN
HOWELL, JANET, 10, JODRELL CLOSE, HORNDEAN
HOWELL, JEANETTE, 10, JODRELL CLOSE, HORNDEAN
HOWELL, RICHARD, 10, JODRELL CLOSE, HORNDEAN
HOWELL, SIMON, 10, JODRELL CLOSE, HORNDEAN
THOMPSETT, ANGELA J, 11, JODRELL CLOSE, HORNDEAN
THOMPSETT, MICHAEL J, 11, JODRELL CLOSE, HORNDEAN
NEL, STEPHEN M, 12, JODRELL CLOSE, HORNDEAN
NEL, SUSAN, 12, JODRELL CLOSE, HORNDEAN
TUPPER, DANIEL C, 13, JODRELL CLOSE, HORNDEAN
TUPPER, EDWIN J, 13, JODRELL CLOSE, HORNDEAN
TUPPER, JOSEPHINE M, 13, JODRELL CLOSE, HORNDEAN
CHALMERS, CLAIRE L, 14, JODRELL CLOSE, HORNDEAN
CHALMERS, HERBERT H, 14, JODRELL CLOSE, HORNDEAN
CHALMERS, IVY, 14, JODRELL CLOSE, HORNDEAN
CHALMERS, SARAH J, 14, JODRELL CLOSE, HORNDEAN
DAY, NIGEL J, 15, JODRELL CLOSE, HORNDEAN
DAY, SARAH E, 15, JODRELL CLOSE, HORNDEAN
HUGHES, GILLIAN J.P, 16, JODRELL CLOSE, HORNDEAN
HUGHES, KEITH P, 16, JODRELL CLOSE, HORNDEAN
MAY, SIMON, 17, JODRELL CLOSE, HORNDEAN
SMITH, LISA M, 17, JODRELL CLOSE, HORNDEAN
CHAPMAN, DAWN, 18, JODRELL CLOSE, HORNDEAN
DAVIES, VIRGINIA, 19, JODRELL CLOSE, HORNDEAN
SANG, PATRICK N, 20, JODRELL CLOSE, HORNDEAN
TRINDER, ANNE A, 22, JODRELL CLOSE, HORNDEAN
TRINDER, TREVOR R, 22, JODRELL CLOSE, HORNDEAN
SMITH, REBECCA L, 24, JODRELL CLOSE, HORNDEAN
BROUGH, BRIAN, 26, JODRELL CLOSE, HORNDEAN
BROUGH, MARY, 26, JODRELL CLOSE, HORNDEAN
BAXTER, DONALD H, 28, JODRELL CLOSE, HORNDEAN
MAJOR, JENNIFER, 30, JODRELL CLOSE, HORNDEAN
PURCELL, NOEL P, 32, JODRELL CLOSE, HORNDEAN
HODGETT, LESLEY G, 34, JODRELL CLOSE, HORNDEAN
TURVEY, GWENDOLINE L, 36, JODRELL CLOSE, HORNDEAN
BUTT, JEAN M, 38, JODRELL CLOSE, HORNDEAN
BUTT, RONALD F, 38, JODRELL CLOSE, HORNDEAN
DOUGHTY, ARTHUR J.L, 40, JODRELL CLOSE, HORNDEAN
STUBBS, BRIAN E, 1, KEFFORD CLOSE, HORNDEAN
EDWARDS, GWEN E, 1A, KEFFORD CLOSE, HORNDEAN
ROSS, JOAN W, 2, KEFFORD CLOSE, HORNDEAN
SPENDLOVE, DENNIS E.J, 2, KEFFORD CLOSE, HORNDEAN
WALTERS, JOE, 4, KEFFORD CLOSE, HORNDEAN
WALTERS, LISA, 4, KEFFORD CLOSE, HORNDEAN

Electoral Roll

WALTERS, MARY, 4, KEFFORD CLOSE, HORNDEAN
POFFLEY, LISA A, 5, KEFFORD CLOSE, HORNDEAN
CAMILLERI, LAURA, 6, KEFFORD CLOSE, HORNDEAN
RAPSON, BRIAN, 6, KEFFORD CLOSE, HORNDEAN
JENKINS, DEREK P, 7, KEFFORD CLOSE, HORNDEAN
BOWBRICK, HILDA C, 8, KEFFORD CLOSE, HORNDEAN
PRATT, EDWARD J, 10, KEFFORD CLOSE, HORNDEAN
PRATT, RHONDA, 10, KEFFORD CLOSE, HORNDEAN
WILLIAMS, JOY A, 11, KEFFORD CLOSE, HORNDEAN
WHITE, JOHN T, 12, KEFFORD CLOSE, HORNDEAN
TUNGATT, COLIN P, 13, KEFFORD CLOSE, HORNDEAN
TUNGATT, SUSAN J, 13, KEFFORD CLOSE, HORNDEAN
HADDRELL, DAVID P, 14, KEFFORD CLOSE, HORNDEAN
HADDRELL, NICOLA L, 14, KEFFORD CLOSE, HORNDEAN
AMBIA, TANIA, 15, KEFFORD CLOSE, HORNDEAN
NESSA, SHAFIUN, 15, KEFFORD CLOSE, HORNDEAN
HEWITT, MARY E, 16, KEFFORD CLOSE, HORNDEAN
COOK, KENNETH J, 17, KEFFORD CLOSE, HORNDEAN
MEALE, ALEXANDRA I, 17, KEFFORD CLOSE, HORNDEAN
MEALE, LEWIS A, 17, KEFFORD CLOSE, HORNDEAN
MEALE, LLEWELLYN R, 17, KEFFORD CLOSE, HORNDEAN
GAMBLE, KATHRYN, 18, KEFFORD CLOSE, HORNDEAN
KERSLEY, MALCOLM P, 18, KEFFORD CLOSE, HORNDEAN
NEWMAN, GEORGE W, 5, LONDON ROAD, HORNDEAN
FRISBY, ANDREW M, SHIP AND BELL HOTEL, LONDON ROAD,
MOREADO, CLAUDIA F, SHIP AND BELL HOTEL,
SHORTMAN, LINDA E, 7, LONDON ROAD, HORNDEAN
SHORTMAN, PHILIP R, 7, LONDON ROAD, HORNDEAN
BUDD, JESSIE V, 9, LONDON ROAD, HORNDEAN
COLES, DUDLEY R, 14, LONDON ROAD, HORNDEAN
BLAKE, ALAN W, 16, LONDON ROAD, HORNDEAN
SPENCER, DEREK W, 18, LONDON ROAD, HORNDEAN
LOVICK, AUBREY E, 19, LONDON ROAD, HORNDEAN
HAWTHORNE, IAN, 20, LONDON ROAD, HORNDEAN
HAWTHORNE, MARK, 20, LONDON ROAD, HORNDEAN
HAWTHORNE, PAMELA R, 20, LONDON ROAD, HORNDEAN
HAWTHORNE, PETER J, 20, LONDON ROAD, HORNDEAN
MARTIN, SHAUN, 23, LONDON ROAD, HORNDEAN
WARD, FIONA L, 23, LONDON ROAD, HORNDEAN
BATES, WINIFRED J, 24, LONDON ROAD, HORNDEAN
BENIAMS, LEILA M, 26, LONDON ROAD, HORNDEAN
CRIDDLE, SALLY E, 28, LONDON ROAD, HORNDEAN
KNIGHT, RICHARD W, 28, LONDON ROAD, HORNDEAN
BOYD, MAUREEN A, 29, LONDON ROAD, HORNDEAN
BOYD, PETER W, 29, LONDON ROAD, HORNDEAN
BOYD, SHEENA A, 29, LONDON ROAD, HORNDEAN
INGRAM, KAREN N, 30, LONDON ROAD, HORNDEAN
INGRAM, RONALD J, 30, LONDON ROAD, HORNDEAN
BRITT, DAVID, 31, LONDON ROAD, HORNDEAN
BRITT, DONNA, 31, LONDON ROAD, HORNDEAN
CHATFIELD, SADIE J, 32, LONDON ROAD, HORNDEAN
SHEPHERD, JAY A, 32, LONDON ROAD, HORNDEAN
CROAD, DUNCAN R, 33, LONDON ROAD, HORNDEAN
CROAD, JANET E, 33, LONDON ROAD, HORNDEAN
CROAD, JONATHAN J, 33, LONDON ROAD, HORNDEAN
CROAD, PAULA E, 33, LONDON ROAD, HORNDEAN
ATTA, ROSANNA, 34, LONDON ROAD, HORNDEAN
WARE, PHILIP, 34, LONDON ROAD, HORNDEAN
BAZELEY, PATRICIA A, 35, LONDON ROAD, HORNDEAN
BAZELEY, ROY W, 35, LONDON ROAD, HORNDEAN
COMLAY, MICHAEL P, 37, LONDON ROAD, HORNDEAN
COMLAY, REBECCA W, 37, LONDON ROAD, HORNDEAN
MILLAR, SIAN M, 38, LONDON ROAD, HORNDEAN
PERRYMAN, NIGEL R, 39, LONDON ROAD, HORNDEAN
BARKER, DAVID, 39A, LONDON ROAD, HORNDEAN
BARKER, IRENE J, 39A, LONDON ROAD, HORNDEAN
SHARPE, PETER R, 41A, LONDON ROAD, HORNDEAN
SKILLING, SAMANTHA L, 41A, LONDON ROAD, HORNDEAN
LEE, IAN J, 41B, LONDON ROAD, HORNDEAN
LEE, LINDA J, 41B, LONDON ROAD, HORNDEAN
LEE, SARAH C, 41B, LONDON ROAD, HORNDEAN
TUTT, MELISSA J, 41C, LONDON ROAD, HORNDEAN
TUTT, STEVEN R, 41C, LONDON ROAD, HORNDEAN
HICKMAN, JULIA V, 41D, LONDON ROAD, HORNDEAN
HICKMAN, VALERIE A, 41D, LONDON ROAD, HORNDEAN
SMITH, JOYCE L, 42, LONDON ROAD, HORNDEAN
HUMPHREYS-DAVIES, ALENA, 43, LONDON ROAD, HORNDEAN
HUMPHREYS-DAVIES, WILLIAM P, 43, LONDON ROAD,
MCPHEE, KEN D, 44, LONDON ROAD, HORNDEAN
HOLT, IAN, 46, LONDON ROAD, HORNDEAN
REANEY, HELEN D, 46, LONDON ROAD, HORNDEAN
BARNFIELD, BRYAN A, 47, LONDON ROAD, HORNDEAN
BARNFIELD, MICHELE J, 47, LONDON ROAD, HORNDEAN
HOLLOWAY, MABEL I, 48, LONDON ROAD, HORNDEAN
WILKINS, TREVOR M, 50, LONDON ROAD, HORNDEAN
WORRALL, LINDSEY R, 50, LONDON ROAD, HORNDEAN
BROWN, LINDA, 52, LONDON ROAD, HORNDEAN
CALDER, STEVE, 52, LONDON ROAD, HORNDEAN
INMAN, MOLLIE R, 53, LONDON ROAD, HORNDEAN
LOVICK, LILLIAN M, 54, LONDON ROAD, HORNDEAN
BALE, RICHARD M, 55, LONDON ROAD, HORNDEAN
MERRELL, JOHN G, 56, LONDON ROAD, HORNDEAN
MERRELL, MAURICE G, 56, LONDON ROAD, HORNDEAN
ASKER-BROWNE, DAVID M, 57, LONDON ROAD, HORNDEAN
LYON, JUDY, 57, LONDON ROAD, HORNDEAN
TURNER, DAVID, 58, LONDON ROAD, HORNDEAN
TURNER, ELISABETH E, 58, LONDON ROAD, HORNDEAN
TURNER, TRACEY, 58, LONDON ROAD, HORNDEAN
GREENHOUSE, SALLY A, 62, LONDON ROAD, HORNDEAN
TURNER, ARTHUR E, 65, LONDON ROAD, HORNDEAN
BENNETT, LESLIE L, 67, LONDON ROAD, HORNDEAN
THURLOW, EMMA H, 68, LONDON ROAD, HORNDEAN
THURLOW, RUTH M.H, 68, LONDON ROAD, HORNDEAN
THURLOW, STEVEN E, 68, LONDON ROAD, HORNDEAN
STURGE, DAVID W, 70, LONDON ROAD, HORNDEAN
WARD, ANNE R, 72, LONDON ROAD, HORNDEAN
WARD, ANTHONY J, 72, LONDON ROAD, HORNDEAN
ISAAC, GILLIAN M, 74, LONDON ROAD, HORNDEAN
ISAAC, KENNETH A, 74, LONDON ROAD, HORNDEAN
ISAAC, NIKKI L, 74, LONDON ROAD, HORNDEAN
CHATFIELD, JAN M, 76, LONDON ROAD, HORNDEAN
BARKER, MARGARET, 78, LONDON ROAD, HORNDEAN
BARKER, WILL G, 78, LONDON ROAD, HORNDEAN
MCGOLDRICK, CHERYL J, 80, LONDON ROAD, HORNDEAN
MCGOLDRICK, PHILIP J, 80, LONDON ROAD, HORNDEAN
BROOKS, MONICA, 82, LONDON ROAD, HORNDEAN
HAUGHTON, DOREEN, 82, LONDON ROAD, HORNDEAN
ISON, DORIS, 82, LONDON ROAD, HORNDEAN
LEACH, VIOLET, 82, LONDON ROAD, HORNDEAN
LINKHORN, FRANK, 82, LONDON ROAD, HORNDEAN
SHERIFF, ESME, 82, LONDON ROAD, HORNDEAN
SUNDBORG, ELIZABETH, 82, LONDON ROAD, HORNDEAN
WOODEN, EDITH, 82, LONDON ROAD, HORNDEAN
CLARE, FRANCES M, 84, LONDON ROAD, HORNDEAN
CLARE, HENRIETTA L, 84, LONDON ROAD, HORNDEAN
CLARE, MALCOLM J, 84, LONDON ROAD, HORNDEAN
POPE, DEREK A, 86, LONDON ROAD, HORNDEAN
POPE, RICHARD J, 86, LONDON ROAD, HORNDEAN
POPE, SUSAN A, 86, LONDON ROAD, HORNDEAN
EASTWOOD, BARRY T, 88, LONDON ROAD, HORNDEAN
EASTWOOD, SHEILA A, 88, LONDON ROAD, HORNDEAN
ELLEKER, DARREN, 90, LONDON ROAD, HORNDEAN
PAYNE, LAURA E, 1, LYCHGATE DRIVE, HORNDEAN
PAYNE, LINDA J, 1, LYCHGATE DRIVE, HORNDEAN
PAYNE, STEPHEN, 1, LYCHGATE DRIVE, HORNDEAN
KEEBLE, MICHAEL J, 2, LYCHGATE DRIVE, HORNDEAN
BREWITT, CHRISTOPHER G, 3, LYCHGATE DRIVE, HORNDEAN
BREWITT, JENEVE A, 3, LYCHGATE DRIVE, HORNDEAN
BREWITT, ZEINA J, 3, LYCHGATE DRIVE, HORNDEAN
WILKINSON, ANDREW J.R, 5, LYCHGATE DRIVE, HORNDEAN
WILKINSON, RACHEL Y, 5, LYCHGATE DRIVE, HORNDEAN
WOOLLEY, ANDREW C, 6, LYCHGATE DRIVE, HORNDEAN
WOOLLEY, ANNE L, 6, LYCHGATE DRIVE, HORNDEAN
WOOLLEY, JOHN A, 6, LYCHGATE DRIVE, HORNDEAN
WOOLCOCK, CHRISTINE M, 7, LYCHGATE DRIVE,
WOOLCOCK, PENELOPE J, 7, LYCHGATE DRIVE, HORNDEAN
WOOLCOCK, STEPHEN T, 7, LYCHGATE DRIVE, HORNDEAN
TRYB, DOMINIC R, 8, LYCHGATE DRIVE, HORNDEAN
TRYB, RICHARD, 8, LYCHGATE DRIVE, HORNDEAN
TRYB-MILERSKA, JADWIGA M, 8, LYCHGATE DRIVE,
GLANVILLE, HILARY M, 9, LYCHGATE DRIVE, HORNDEAN
GLANVILLE, MICHAEL W, 9, LYCHGATE DRIVE, HORNDEAN
STACK, DAVID J, 10, LYCHGATE DRIVE, HORNDEAN
STACK, RUTH I, 10, LYCHGATE DRIVE, HORNDEAN
WILSON, ANDREW J, 11, LYCHGATE DRIVE, HORNDEAN
WILSON, SIOBHAN E.H, 11, LYCHGATE DRIVE, HORNDEAN
MARTIN, EDWARD A, 12, LYCHGATE DRIVE, HORNDEAN
MARTIN, FRANCES M, 12, LYCHGATE DRIVE, HORNDEAN
MARTIN, TIMOTHY, 12, LYCHGATE DRIVE, HORNDEAN
SLARK, LEE E, 14, LYCHGATE DRIVE, HORNDEAN
SLARK, SANDRA H, 14, LYCHGATE DRIVE, HORNDEAN
YOUNG, MICHAEL J, 15, LYCHGATE DRIVE, HORNDEAN
SLEEMAN, JULIE, 17, LYCHGATE DRIVE, HORNDEAN
SLEEMAN, PETER T, 17, LYCHGATE DRIVE, HORNDEAN
BUSHNELL, CHRISTINE A, 18, LYCHGATE DRIVE, HORNDEAN
BUSHNELL, TERENCE A, 18, LYCHGATE DRIVE, HORNDEAN
WILLIS, EMMA L, 19, LYCHGATE DRIVE, HORNDEAN
WILLIS, LYNNE P, 19, LYCHGATE DRIVE, HORNDEAN
WILLIS, ROBERT A, 19, LYCHGATE DRIVE, HORNDEAN
MILTON-POLLEY, JOHN M, 20, LYCHGATE DRIVE, HORNDEAN
LIKE, GRAHAM H, 21, LYCHGATE DRIVE, HORNDEAN
LIKE, LESLEY M, 21, LYCHGATE DRIVE, HORNDEAN
BOLDERSTON, PETER J, 22, LYCHGATE DRIVE, HORNDEAN
MACDONALD-ROBINSON, LUCINDA J, 23, LYCHGATE DRIVE,
MACDONALD-ROBINSON, NICHOLAS U.S, 23, LYCHGATE DRIVE,
HOLTER, ROGER J, 24, LYCHGATE DRIVE, HORNDEAN
KANE, MICHAEL S, 25, LYCHGATE DRIVE, HORNDEAN
KANE, REBECCA C, 25, LYCHGATE DRIVE, HORNDEAN
WATERMAN, DAVID G, 26, LYCHGATE DRIVE, HORNDEAN
WATERMAN, PENELOPE A, 26, LYCHGATE DRIVE, HORNDEAN
THOMSON, ANDREW, 27, LYCHGATE DRIVE, HORNDEAN
THOMSON, FRANCES, 27, LYCHGATE DRIVE, HORNDEAN
MARSLAND, JOHN S, 29, LYCHGATE DRIVE, HORNDEAN
MARSLAND, KATHRYN, 29, LYCHGATE DRIVE, HORNDEAN
WILLIAMS, ANNE K, 31, LYCHGATE DRIVE, HORNDEAN
MARKS, JANE M, 33, LYCHGATE DRIVE, HORNDEAN
MARKS, NEIL A, 33, LYCHGATE DRIVE, HORNDEAN
PARKIN, JEAN V, 35, LYCHGATE DRIVE, HORNDEAN
PINKNEY, AMANDA J, 37, LYCHGATE DRIVE, HORNDEAN
PINKNEY, SIMON C, 37, LYCHGATE DRIVE, HORNDEAN
STEVENS, CRAIG, 39, LYCHGATE DRIVE, HORNDEAN
STEVENS, JANETTE, 39, LYCHGATE DRIVE, HORNDEAN
HENDERSON, STEPHEN G, 41, LYCHGATE DRIVE, HORNDEAN
WALLER, AMANDA J, 41, LYCHGATE DRIVE, HORNDEAN
JENKINS, LUCY E, 43, LYCHGATE DRIVE, HORNDEAN
JENKINS, MICHAEL T, 43, LYCHGATE DRIVE, HORNDEAN
JENKINS, SARAH J, 43, LYCHGATE DRIVE, HORNDEAN
MILLWATER, PHILIP S, 45, LYCHGATE DRIVE, HORNDEAN
LOVETT, MARK R, 47, LYCHGATE DRIVE, HORNDEAN
LOVETT, SUZANNE, 47, LYCHGATE DRIVE, HORNDEAN
HOLDWAY, ANTHONY, 49, LYCHGATE DRIVE, HORNDEAN
HOLDWAY, ANTONY, 49, LYCHGATE DRIVE, HORNDEAN
HOLDWAY, SANDRA A, 49, LYCHGATE DRIVE, HORNDEAN
BARNES, JULIA C, 51, LYCHGATE DRIVE, HORNDEAN
BARNES, NICHOLAS J, 51, LYCHGATE DRIVE, HORNDEAN
GIBBS, GILLIAN M, 53, LYCHGATE DRIVE, HORNDEAN
GIBBS, PHILIP N.C, 53, LYCHGATE DRIVE, HORNDEAN
EVERETT, MICHELLE D, 55, LYCHGATE DRIVE, HORNDEAN
EVERETT, RICHARD, 55, LYCHGATE DRIVE, HORNDEAN
BELL, DAVID J, 1, MAYNARD PLACE, HORNDEAN
BELL, ELIZABETH A, 1, MAYNARD PLACE, HORNDEAN
HEDGES, KEITH P, 2, MAYNARD PLACE, HORNDEAN
HEDGES, MARY E, 2, MAYNARD PLACE, HORNDEAN
DOWN, JOHN J, 3, MAYNARD PLACE, HORNDEAN
DOWN, URSULA M, 3, MAYNARD PLACE, HORNDEAN
STEVENS, CRAIG W, 4, MAYNARD PLACE, HORNDEAN
STEVENS, DANIEL P, 4, MAYNARD PLACE, HORNDEAN
STEVENS, JULIE R, 4, MAYNARD PLACE, HORNDEAN
STEVENS, SCOTT C, 4, MAYNARD PLACE, HORNDEAN
ANDREWS, JAMES P, 5, MAYNARD PLACE, HORNDEAN
ANDREWS, JENNIFER M, 5, MAYNARD PLACE, HORNDEAN
ANDREWS, PETER, 5, MAYNARD PLACE, HORNDEAN
MCGINTY, DIANE, 6, MAYNARD PLACE, HORNDEAN
MCGINTY, IAN, 6, MAYNARD PLACE, HORNDEAN
MCGINTY, MARIE, 6, MAYNARD PLACE, HORNDEAN
CLARK, BARBARA D, 8, MAYNARD PLACE, HORNDEAN
CLARK, THOMAS, 8, MAYNARD PLACE, HORNDEAN
ATHERTON, DARRELL J, 9, MAYNARD PLACE, HORNDEAN
ATHERTON, JASON M, 9, MAYNARD PLACE, HORNDEAN
ATHERTON, JOHN, 9, MAYNARD PLACE, HORNDEAN
ATHERTON, SANDRA A, 9, MAYNARD PLACE, HORNDEAN
RADBOURNE, JOHN V, 10, MAYNARD PLACE,
RADBOURNE, MARGARET A, 10, MAYNARD PLACE,
THURMAN, JOHN P, 11, MAYNARD PLACE, HORNDEAN
THURMAN, THERESA J, 11, MAYNARD PLACE, HORNDEAN
MOORE, PAMELA E, 12, MAYNARD PLACE, HORNDEAN
WILLIAMS, IAN R, 14, MAYNARD PLACE, HORNDEAN
WILLIAMS, LYNN J, 14, MAYNARD PLACE, HORNDEAN
TOMSETT, PAUL J, 14A, MAYNARD PLACE, HORNDEAN
TOMSETT, SALLY J, 14A, MAYNARD PLACE, HORNDEAN
EVANS, DEBORAH, 15, MAYNARD PLACE, HORNDEAN
EVANS, STEPHEN J, 15, MAYNARD PLACE, HORNDEAN
LASKEY, FRANCIS J, 16, MAYNARD PLACE, HORNDEAN
LASKEY, TRACY D, 16, MAYNARD PLACE, HORNDEAN
CONEY, DENISE, 18, MAYNARD PLACE, HORNDEAN
CONEY, TIMOTHY D, 18, MAYNARD PLACE, HORNDEAN
EVANS, GWYN, 1, MERCHISTOUN ROAD, HORNDEAN
EVANS, GWYN (JNR), 1, MERCHISTOUN ROAD, HORNDEAN
EVANS, JAMIE, 1, MERCHISTOUN ROAD, HORNDEAN
EVANS, MARY L, 1, MERCHISTOUN ROAD, HORNDEAN
EVANS, TRACY, 1, MERCHISTOUN ROAD, HORNDEAN
GIBSON, BERYL M, 3, MERCHISTOUN ROAD, HORNDEAN
GIBSON, HANNAH L, 3, MERCHISTOUN ROAD, HORNDEAN
GIBSON, KARL H, 3, MERCHISTOUN ROAD, HORNDEAN
GIBSON, PATRICIA C, 3, MERCHISTOUN ROAD, HORNDEAN
MOSLEY, KEVIN, 5, MERCHISTOUN ROAD, HORNDEAN
GREENAWAY, MARK, 7, MERCHISTOUN ROAD, HORNDEAN
GALLAGHER, DIANE L, 9, MERCHISTOUN ROAD, HORNDEAN
ROWE, CECILLE M.L, 11, MERCHISTOUN ROAD, HORNDEAN
MAY, REGINALD J, 13, MERCHISTOUN ROAD, HORNDEAN
MILLS, MARJORIE M, 13, MERCHISTOUN ROAD, HORNDEAN
MILLS, WILLIAM A, 13, MERCHISTOUN ROAD, HORNDEAN
PRESCOTT, CAROLINE L, 15, MERCHISTOUN ROAD,
PRESCOTT, PATRICIA, 15, MERCHISTOUN ROAD, HORNDEAN
PRESCOTT, WILLIAM N, 15, MERCHISTOUN ROAD,
WEAVER, COLIN S, 17, MERCHISTOUN ROAD, HORNDEAN
WEAVER, GARY P, 17, MERCHISTOUN ROAD, HORNDEAN
WEAVER, JUDITH A, 17, MERCHISTOUN ROAD, HORNDEAN
WEAVER, PAUL S, 17, MERCHISTOUN ROAD, HORNDEAN
WALKER, BARBARA J, 19, MERCHISTOUN ROAD, HORNDEAN
WALKER, LAUREN A, 19, MERCHISTOUN ROAD, HORNDEAN
WEEKS, CHRISTOPHER N, 19, MERCHISTOUN ROAD,
VOLLER, DOREEN J, 21, MERCHISTOUN ROAD, HORNDEAN
SADLER, CARL S, 23, MERCHISTOUN ROAD, HORNDEAN
SADLER, PAULINE E, 23, MERCHISTOUN ROAD, HORNDEAN
DAVIS, BRENDA D, 25, MERCHISTOUN ROAD, HORNDEAN
DAVIS, EDWARD, 25, MERCHISTOUN ROAD, HORNDEAN
DAVIS, SIMON P, 25, MERCHISTOUN ROAD, HORNDEAN
PROWTING, DENNIS J, 27, MERCHISTOUN ROAD, HORNDEAN
PROWTING, SYLVIA A, 27, MERCHISTOUN ROAD, HORNDEAN
CHEWTER, JOSEPHINE I, 29, MERCHISTOUN ROAD,
CHEWTER, LESLIE W, 29, MERCHISTOUN ROAD, HORNDEAN
DALE, ROBERT A, 29, MERCHISTOUN ROAD, HORNDEAN
DALE, WENDY M, 29, MERCHISTOUN ROAD, HORNDEAN
HOOD, DIANA I, 31, MERCHISTOUN ROAD, HORNDEAN
HOOD, JOHN W, 31, MERCHISTOUN ROAD, HORNDEAN
BANTING, TREVOR P, 33, MERCHISTOUN ROAD, HORNDEAN
BENNETT, DEBORAH S, 33, MERCHISTOUN ROAD, HORNDEAN
HIBBERT, CHARLES E, 35, MERCHISTOUN ROAD, HORNDEAN
HIBBERT, PATRICIA M, 35, MERCHISTOUN ROAD, HORNDEAN
BRAMHALL, DANIEL J, 37, MERCHISTOUN ROAD, HORNDEAN
BRAMHALL, JOHN D, 37, MERCHISTOUN ROAD, HORNDEAN
BRAMHALL, MARIE J, 37, MERCHISTOUN ROAD, HORNDEAN
BRAMHALL, MARILYN J, 37, MERCHISTOUN ROAD,
COUZENS, PHILIPPA, 39, MERCHISTOUN ROAD, HORNDEAN
COUZENS, RICHARD, 39, MERCHISTOUN ROAD, HORNDEAN
WEAVING, SALLY T, 41, MERCHISTOUN ROAD, HORNDEAN
WEAVING, WAYNE G, 41, MERCHISTOUN ROAD, HORNDEAN
BONIFACE, LEONARD J, 43, MERCHISTOUN ROAD,
BONIFACE, SYLVIA R, 43, MERCHISTOUN ROAD, HORNDEAN
LINKHORN, DAVID, 45, MERCHISTOUN ROAD, HORNDEAN
LINKHORN, JOANNE E, 45, MERCHISTOUN ROAD, HORNDEAN
LINKHORN, NEIL E, 45, MERCHISTOUN ROAD, HORNDEAN
MALENDEWICZ, ANNA, 47, MERCHISTOUN ROAD, HORNDEAN
DOWNHAM, GEORGE W, 49, MERCHISTOUN ROAD,
DOWNHAM, REBECCA, 49, MERCHISTOUN ROAD, HORNDEAN
PARKER, JUNE M, 51, MERCHISTOUN ROAD, HORNDEAN
PARKER, NEVILLE A, 51, MERCHISTOUN ROAD, HORNDEAN

WILLIAMS, HENRY J, 53, MERCHISTOUN ROAD, HORNDEAN
WILLIAMS, INA M, 53, MERCHISTOUN ROAD, HORNDEAN
HATCH, COLIN, 55, MERCHISTOUN ROAD, HORNDEAN
HATCH, SHEILA M, 55, MERCHISTOUN ROAD, HORNDEAN
HATCH, SUZANNE, 55, MERCHISTOUN ROAD, HORNDEAN
BRAMHALL, JOHN R, 57, MERCHISTOUN ROAD, HORNDEAN
BRAMHALL, JOY, 57, MERCHISTOUN ROAD, HORNDEAN
BRAMHALL, PAUL J, 57, MERCHISTOUN ROAD, HORNDEAN
OSGOOD, MICHAEL S, 59, MERCHISTOUN ROAD, HORNDEAN
OSGOOD, SHIRLEY A, 59, MERCHISTOUN ROAD, HORNDEAN
HAWTHORNE, SUSANNE E, 61, MERCHISTOUN ROAD,
LOWTHER, RICHARD W, 61, MERCHISTOUN ROAD,
WESTON, TERESA C, 63, MERCHISTOUN ROAD, HORNDEAN
DOUGHTY, DRINA V, 65, MERCHISTOUN ROAD, HORNDEAN
DOUGHTY, MICHAEL T, 65, MERCHISTOUN ROAD,
HUGHES, PAT, 67, MERCHISTOUN ROAD, HORNDEAN
STANLEY, ALBERT E, 69, MERCHISTOUN ROAD, HORNDEAN
HURKETT, ETHEL G, 71, MERCHISTOUN ROAD, HORNDEAN
POWELL, DOROTHY E, 73, MERCHISTOUN ROAD, HORNDEAN
PURDY, KATHLEEN L, 75, MERCHISTOUN ROAD, HORNDEAN
PURDUE, BETTY, 77, MERCHISTOUN ROAD, HORNDEAN
LEGGAT, BEVERLEY A, 79, MERCHISTOUN ROAD, HORNDEAN
LEGGAT, JAMES C, 79, MERCHISTOUN ROAD, HORNDEAN
FLEWIN, BEATRICE N, 81, MERCHISTOUN ROAD, HORNDEAN
FLEWIN, HARRY, 81, MERCHISTOUN ROAD, HORNDEAN
BUCKLE, CHRISTOPHER R, 83, MERCHISTOUN ROAD,
BUCKLE, SUSAN L, 83, MERCHISTOUN ROAD, HORNDEAN
ELCOME, HEATHER M, 83, MERCHISTOUN ROAD, HORNDEAN
CROUCH, KENNETH B, 85, MERCHISTOUN ROAD, HORNDEAN
CROUCH, MARY J, 85, MERCHISTOUN ROAD, HORNDEAN
HOGBEN, EDITH J, 87, MERCHISTOUN ROAD, HORNDEAN
MARTIN, HAYLEY P, 89, MERCHISTOUN ROAD, HORNDEAN
MARTIN, JANE A, 89, MERCHISTOUN ROAD, HORNDEAN
MARTIN, MALCOLM P, 89, MERCHISTOUN ROAD, HORNDEAN
KERSLEY, IRIS M, 91, MERCHISTOUN ROAD, HORNDEAN
KERSLEY, LEONARD H, 91, MERCHISTOUN ROAD, HORNDEAN
RATCLIFFE, TIM E, 93, MERCHISTOUN ROAD, HORNDEAN
WILTSHIRE, JANE, 93, MERCHISTOUN ROAD, HORNDEAN
DOREY, MARK L, 95, MERCHISTOUN ROAD, HORNDEAN
DOREY, TRACY, 95, MERCHISTOUN ROAD, HORNDEAN
DUNNING, HILDEGARD, 97, MERCHISTOUN ROAD,
DUNNING, MAURICE P, 97, MERCHISTOUN ROAD, HORNDEAN
HUSSELBREE, ANDREW, 99, MERCHISTOUN ROAD,
HUSSELBREE, MICHAEL, 99, MERCHISTOUN ROAD,
HUSSELBREE, PAUL, 99, MERCHISTOUN ROAD, HORNDEAN
HUSSELBREE, SEAN, 99, MERCHISTOUN ROAD, HORNDEAN
HUSSELBREE, SUSAN, 99, MERCHISTOUN ROAD, HORNDEAN
CHAPMAN, CAROLE A, 101, MERCHISTOUN ROAD,
CHAPMAN, KATHRYN M, 101, MERCHISTOUN ROAD,
CHAPMAN, LEONARD R, 101, MERCHISTOUN ROAD,
HEATHER, DAVID E, 103, MERCHISTOUN ROAD, HORNDEAN
NICHOLAS, KIM-SUZANNE, 103, MERCHISTOUN ROAD,
BAKER, LINDA R, 105, MERCHISTOUN ROAD, HORNDEAN
BAKER, MALCOLM, 105, MERCHISTOUN ROAD, HORNDEAN
MILLARD, CHRISTOPHER R, 107, MERCHISTOUN ROAD,
MILLARD, LANA E, 107, MERCHISTOUN ROAD, HORNDEAN
RILEY, DOROTHY F, 2, MERCHISTOUN ROAD, HORNDEAN
RILEY, EDWARD K, 2, MERCHISTOUN ROAD, HORNDEAN
ANDERSON, MICHAEL J, 4, MERCHISTOUN ROAD, HORNDEAN
ANDERSON, SHEILA K, 4, MERCHISTOUN ROAD, HORNDEAN
HALL, NANCY W, 6, MERCHISTOUN ROAD, HORNDEAN
HALL, PETER R.M, 6, MERCHISTOUN ROAD, HORNDEAN
TANNER, FREDRICK S, 8, MERCHISTOUN ROAD, HORNDEAN
TODD, ANN J, 10, MERCHISTOUN ROAD, HORNDEAN
DULAKE, JEAN I, 12, MERCHISTOUN ROAD, HORNDEAN
DULAKE, PETER J, 12, MERCHISTOUN ROAD, HORNDEAN
CAINES, JENNIFER A, 14, MERCHISTOUN ROAD, HORNDEAN
PARFOOT, BRYAN C, 14, MERCHISTOUN ROAD, HORNDEAN
PARFOOT, SHANE W, 14, MERCHISTOUN ROAD, HORNDEAN
HUMPHREY, STEPHEN R, 16, MERCHISTOUN ROAD,
HUMPHREY, SUSAN, 16, MERCHISTOUN ROAD, HORNDEAN
KELLETT, EILEEN I, 18, MERCHISTOUN ROAD, HORNDEAN
KELLETT, MARTIN K, 18, MERCHISTOUN ROAD, HORNDEAN
CHAPMAN, JENNIFER J, 20, MERCHISTOUN ROAD, HORNDEAN
WILKINS, ADRIAN C, 20, MERCHISTOUN ROAD, HORNDEAN
HOWARD, DONALD L, 22, MERCHISTOUN ROAD, HORNDEAN
HOWARD, PATRICIA S, 22, MERCHISTOUN ROAD, HORNDEAN
MULLONEY, NELLIE F, 22, MERCHISTOUN ROAD, HORNDEAN
MUSTON, BRIAN E, 24, MERCHISTOUN ROAD, HORNDEAN
MUSTON, RITA M.E, 24, MERCHISTOUN ROAD, HORNDEAN
SANDY, KATHLEEN M, 26, MERCHISTOUN ROAD, HORNDEAN
CHARLTON, PHILIP A.R, 28, MERCHISTOUN ROAD,
GREEN, GILLIAN A.C, 30, MERCHISTOUN ROAD, HORNDEAN
GREEN, ROBERT, 30, MERCHISTOUN ROAD, HORNDEAN
WHITE, DENNIS L, 32, MERCHISTOUN ROAD, HORNDEAN
WHITE, LESLIE D, 32, MERCHISTOUN ROAD, HORNDEAN
WHITE, PATRICIA H, 32, MERCHISTOUN ROAD, HORNDEAN
CAMILLERI, ANTHONY, 34, MERCHISTOUN ROAD,
CAMILLERI, SPIRO, 34, MERCHISTOUN ROAD, HORNDEAN
BARNES, BRENDA N, 36, MERCHISTOUN ROAD, HORNDEAN
PETERS, BEN, 38, MERCHISTOUN ROAD, HORNDEAN
PETERS, KARL, 38, MERCHISTOUN ROAD, HORNDEAN
PETERS, MANDY J, 38, MERCHISTOUN ROAD, HORNDEAN
FAWCETT, VERA D, 40, MERCHISTOUN ROAD, HORNDEAN
FAWCETT, WILLIAM S, 40, MERCHISTOUN ROAD, HORNDEAN
WEAVING, BERTIE E, 42, MERCHISTOUN ROAD, HORNDEAN
LIBBY, ELIZABETH M, 44, MERCHISTOUN ROAD, HORNDEAN
SMITH, KATHLEEN A, 46, MERCHISTOUN ROAD, HORNDEAN
SMITH, RICHARD J, 46, MERCHISTOUN ROAD, HORNDEAN
MAYNARD, GRAHAM W, 48A, MERCHISTOUN ROAD,
MAYNARD, SUSAN E, 48A, MERCHISTOUN ROAD, HORNDEAN
WARREN, CHRISTINE A, 48B, MERCHISTOUN ROAD,
MANLEY, ROSE, 50A, MERCHISTOUN ROAD, HORNDEAN
ROGERS, CHARLES D, 50B, MERCHISTOUN ROAD, HORNDEAN
ROGERS, JEAN, 50B, MERCHISTOUN ROAD, HORNDEAN
DAVIS, JACK W, 52, MERCHISTOUN ROAD, HORNDEAN
DAVIS, MARGARET, 52, MERCHISTOUN ROAD, HORNDEAN
WOOD, STELLA, 54, MERCHISTOUN ROAD, HORNDEAN
BOX, CLAIRE, 56, MERCHISTOUN ROAD, HORNDEAN
MUIR, ALISON, 58, MERCHISTOUN ROAD, HORNDEAN
ALESBURY, DAVID A, 60A, MERCHISTOUN ROAD, HORNDEAN
ROGERS, CAROL J, 60A, MERCHISTOUN ROAD, HORNDEAN
BLABY, CHRISTINE A, 60B, MERCHISTOUN ROAD, HORNDEAN
BLABY, GEORGE E, 60B, MERCHISTOUN ROAD, HORNDEAN
NICHOLS, BETTY E, 62A, MERCHISTOUN ROAD, HORNDEAN
OVER, KAREN J, 62B, MERCHISTOUN ROAD, HORNDEAN
LOCKLEY, JACQUELINE, 64, MERCHISTOUN ROAD,
LOCKLEY, LINDA A, 64, MERCHISTOUN ROAD, HORNDEAN
SHEPHARD, ALISON, 66, MERCHISTOUN ROAD, HORNDEAN
SHEPHARD, CARMEL, 66, MERCHISTOUN ROAD, HORNDEAN
SHEPHARD, MOLLY A, 66, MERCHISTOUN ROAD, HORNDEAN
PRESCOTT, DEBORAH, 68, MERCHISTOUN ROAD, HORNDEAN
PRESCOTT, JOHN, 68, MERCHISTOUN ROAD, HORNDEAN
SPARKS, COLIN E, 70, MERCHISTOUN ROAD, HORNDEAN
YOUNGS, GARY A, 72, MERCHISTOUN ROAD, HORNDEAN
YOUNGS, JANET M, 72, MERCHISTOUN ROAD, HORNDEAN
BEVES, ARTHUR F, 74, MERCHISTOUN ROAD, HORNDEAN
BEVES, GRACE, 74, MERCHISTOUN ROAD, HORNDEAN
CHAMBERLAIN, JUDITH A, 76A, MERCHISTOUN ROAD,
CHAMBERLAIN, TERENCE J, 76A, MERCHISTOUN ROAD,
SAUNDERS, JUNE, 76B, MERCHISTOUN ROAD, HORNDEAN
PRESCOTT, JENNIFER, 78A, MERCHISTOUN ROAD,
DAVIS, FREDERICK, 78B, MERCHISTOUN ROAD, HORNDEAN
BENNETT, HAZEL E.M, 80, MERCHISTOUN ROAD, HORNDEAN
LINKHORN, ALLEN, 82, MERCHISTOUN ROAD, HORNDEAN
LINKHORN, TINA, 82, MERCHISTOUN ROAD, HORNDEAN
FARMER, GEOFFREY H.J, 84, MERCHISTOUN ROAD,
FARMER, JILL, 84, MERCHISTOUN ROAD, HORNDEAN
FARMER, WENDY R, 84, MERCHISTOUN ROAD, HORNDEAN
HILLIER, EILEEN P, 86, MERCHISTOUN ROAD, HORNDEAN
HILLIER, RONALD F, 86, MERCHISTOUN ROAD, HORNDEAN
HARROP, FLORENCE W, 88, MERCHISTOUN ROAD,
HARROP, JOHN L, 88, MERCHISTOUN ROAD, HORNDEAN
HARROP, PETER R, 88, MERCHISTOUN ROAD, HORNDEAN
MCEWAN, JAMES J, 90, MERCHISTOUN ROAD, HORNDEAN
MCEWAN, JUNE R, 90, MERCHISTOUN ROAD, HORNDEAN
FALLOWS, CHRISTOPHER, 92, MERCHISTOUN ROAD,
FALLOWS, JACQUELINE, 92, MERCHISTOUN ROAD,
SARGEANT, TANYA, 92, MERCHISTOUN ROAD, HORNDEAN
HEATH, ANDREW M, 94, MERCHISTOUN ROAD, HORNDEAN
HEATH, CAROL E, 94, MERCHISTOUN ROAD, HORNDEAN
HEATH, DOREEN F, 94, MERCHISTOUN ROAD, HORNDEAN
HEATH, ERIC R, 94, MERCHISTOUN ROAD, HORNDEAN
HEATH, KATHLEEN G, 94, MERCHISTOUN ROAD, HORNDEAN
HEDGCOCK, LESLEY A, 96, MERCHISTOUN ROAD,
SALMON, PAUL A, 96, MERCHISTOUN ROAD, HORNDEAN
CHAMBERS, DOMINIC R.J, 98, MERCHISTOUN ROAD,
CHAMBERS, SALLY E, 98, MERCHISTOUN ROAD, HORNDEAN
ALLEN, ANTHONY G, 100, MERCHISTOUN ROAD, HORNDEAN
ALLEN, FRANCES C, 100, MERCHISTOUN ROAD, HORNDEAN
ALLEN, KENNETH G, 100, MERCHISTOUN ROAD, HORNDEAN
LINKHORN, JOAN, 102, MERCHISTOUN ROAD, HORNDEAN
CANNINGS, JANET, 104, MERCHISTOUN ROAD, HORNDEAN
CANNINGS, MALCOLM L, 104, MERCHISTOUN ROAD,
CANNINGS, RAY J, 104, MERCHISTOUN ROAD, HORNDEAN
CANNINGS, RICHARD J, 104, MERCHISTOUN ROAD,
CANNINGS, STUART R, 104, MERCHISTOUN ROAD,
JOHNSON, BARRY, 106, MERCHISTOUN ROAD, HORNDEAN
JOHNSON, CAROLE A, 106, MERCHISTOUN ROAD, HORNDEAN
TUKE, EDWARD K.D, 1, MURRAY ROAD, HORNDEAN
TUKE, WINIFRED, 1, MURRAY ROAD, HORNDEAN
WEST, LUCIA, 3, MURRAY ROAD, HORNDEAN
BAZLEY, PAMELA M, 5, MURRAY ROAD, HORNDEAN
SULLIVAN, COLIN B, 7, MURRAY ROAD, HORNDEAN
SULLIVAN, JOHN P, 7, MURRAY ROAD, HORNDEAN
SULLIVAN, KEVIN J, 7, MURRAY ROAD, HORNDEAN
SULLIVAN, MARGARET R, 7, MURRAY ROAD, HORNDEAN
SHIRLAW, EDMUND J, 9, MURRAY ROAD, HORNDEAN
SHIRLAW, HANNAH, 9, MURRAY ROAD, HORNDEAN
GUTTERIDGE, ELIZABETH, 11, MURRAY ROAD, HORNDEAN
GUTTERIDGE, RONALD J, 11, MURRAY ROAD, HORNDEAN
ROWETT, DANIEL J, 13, MURRAY ROAD, HORNDEAN
ROWETT, JENNY R, 13, MURRAY ROAD, HORNDEAN
ROWETT, KEITH L, 13, MURRAY ROAD, HORNDEAN
WESTON, ANDREW M, 15, MURRAY ROAD, HORNDEAN
WESTON, COLIN C, 15, MURRAY ROAD, HORNDEAN
WESTON, EILEEN S, 15, MURRAY ROAD, HORNDEAN
WESTON, MARK C, 15, MURRAY ROAD, HORNDEAN
WILKINSON, SARA J, 17, MURRAY ROAD, HORNDEAN
WILKINSON, SCOTT, 17, MURRAY ROAD, HORNDEAN
MCELHINNEY, BARBARA, 19, MURRAY ROAD, HORNDEAN
MCELHINNEY, NOEL, 19, MURRAY ROAD, HORNDEAN
MCELHINNEY, SHAUN, 19, MURRAY ROAD, HORNDEAN
MCELHINNEY, TERESA, 19, MURRAY ROAD, HORNDEAN
BOWES, JAMES J, 21, MURRAY ROAD, HORNDEAN
SHORE, GAIL, 23, MURRAY ROAD, HORNDEAN
SHORE, KATHERINE L, 23, MURRAY ROAD, HORNDEAN
SHORE, MAUREEN, 23, MURRAY ROAD, HORNDEAN
WILKINSON, DOREEN M, 25, MURRAY ROAD, HORNDEAN
WILKINSON, KENNETH, 25, MURRAY ROAD, HORNDEAN
MOULD, BARRY E, 27, MURRAY ROAD, HORNDEAN
MOULD, KELLY E, 27, MURRAY ROAD, HORNDEAN
MOULD, MARIE G, 27, MURRAY ROAD, HORNDEAN
BASCAL, ZAINAB A, 29, MURRAY ROAD, HORNDEAN
SABIR, KHATAB O, 29, MURRAY ROAD, HORNDEAN
HEATH, GRAHAM, 31, MURRAY ROAD, HORNDEAN
HEATH, WILMA E, 31, MURRAY ROAD, HORNDEAN
FOOTMAN, CAROL, 33, MURRAY ROAD, HORNDEAN
FOOTMAN, MICHAEL H, 33, MURRAY ROAD, HORNDEAN
LONG, KERRIE I, 35, MURRAY ROAD, HORNDEAN
LONG, KEVIN, 35, MURRAY ROAD, HORNDEAN
LONG, GEORGE W, THE ANNEXE, 35, MURRAY ROAD,
LONG, GWENDOLINE J, THE ANNEXE, 35, MURRAY ROAD,
CULLUM, ALBERT V, 37, MURRAY ROAD, HORNDEAN
EDDY, DAVID A, 37, MURRAY ROAD, HORNDEAN
BIRD, ROY H, 39, MURRAY ROAD, HORNDEAN
BIRD, VERA W, 39, MURRAY ROAD, HORNDEAN
SCARD, BRIAN A, 41, MURRAY ROAD, HORNDEAN
SCARD, PATRICIA A, 41, MURRAY ROAD, HORNDEAN
SWAN, MARY K, 43, MURRAY ROAD, HORNDEAN
SWAN, ROBERT A, 43, MURRAY ROAD, HORNDEAN
JARVIS, ALAN C, 45, MURRAY ROAD, HORNDEAN
JARVIS, KATHLEEN G, 45, MURRAY ROAD, HORNDEAN
WALKER, AMY C, 47, MURRAY ROAD, HORNDEAN
WALKER, EILEEN, 47, MURRAY ROAD, HORNDEAN
WALKER, LINSEY J, 47, MURRAY ROAD, HORNDEAN
GRINYER, BRUCE, 49, MURRAY ROAD, HORNDEAN
GRINYER, JEAN, 49, MURRAY ROAD, HORNDEAN
POLSON, JUNE L, 51, MURRAY ROAD, HORNDEAN
POLSON, KEITH M, 51, MURRAY ROAD, HORNDEAN
EVERSHED, CHRISTINE S, 53, MURRAY ROAD, HORNDEAN
EVERSHED, VICTOR, 53, MURRAY ROAD, HORNDEAN
HOMEWOOD, MICHAEL I.J, 55, MURRAY ROAD, HORNDEAN
HOMEWOOD, SARAH J.C, 55, MURRAY ROAD, HORNDEAN
WALLACE, PATRICIA A, 57, MURRAY ROAD, HORNDEAN
WALLACE, WALTER G, 57, MURRAY ROAD, HORNDEAN
DUKOFF-GORDON, BARBARA M, 59, MURRAY ROAD,
DUKOFF-GORDON, LENNOX C, 59, MURRAY ROAD,
OLIVER, HEIDI J, 61, MURRAY ROAD, HORNDEAN
OLIVER, TERRY D, 61, MURRAY ROAD, HORNDEAN
MONK, ANNE M, 63, MURRAY ROAD, HORNDEAN
MONK, ROBERT, 63, MURRAY ROAD, HORNDEAN
STREET, STEVE, 65, MURRAY ROAD, HORNDEAN
STREET, WENDY, 65, MURRAY ROAD, HORNDEAN
HOLDEN, GARETH J, 67, MURRAY ROAD, HORNDEAN
HOLDEN, LINDA C, 67, MURRAY ROAD, HORNDEAN
HOLDEN, ROGER A, 67, MURRAY ROAD, HORNDEAN
GILL, DOREEN B, 69, MURRAY ROAD, HORNDEAN
GILL, LANCE, 69, MURRAY ROAD, HORNDEAN
GILL, NIGEL C, 69, MURRAY ROAD, HORNDEAN
KEOGH, DOROTHY M, 73, MURRAY ROAD, HORNDEAN
KEOGH, GERARD M, 73, MURRAY ROAD, HORNDEAN
GEORGE, JULIE, 75, MURRAY ROAD, HORNDEAN
GEORGE, PAUL G, 75, MURRAY ROAD, HORNDEAN
HICKS, JOAN A, 77, MURRAY ROAD, HORNDEAN
HICKS, MICHAEL A, 77, MURRAY ROAD, HORNDEAN
HICKS, MICHAEL A (JNR), 77, MURRAY ROAD, HORNDEAN
SAYER, DOROTHY A, 79, MURRAY ROAD, HORNDEAN
SCOREY, CHRISTINA, 81, MURRAY ROAD, HORNDEAN
SCOREY, ROBERT, 81, MURRAY ROAD, HORNDEAN
ADAMS, ANTHONY J, 83, MURRAY ROAD, HORNDEAN
ADAMS, LINDA J, 83, MURRAY ROAD, HORNDEAN
JOHNSTONE, CHRISTINE H, 4, MURRAY ROAD, HORNDEAN
KING, JOYCE, 6, MURRAY ROAD, HORNDEAN
MARSDEN, ERIC, 8, MURRAY ROAD, HORNDEAN
MARSDEN, MARGARET O, 8, MURRAY ROAD, HORNDEAN
WALTERS, JOHN E, 10, MURRAY ROAD, HORNDEAN
WILLIAMS, MELVINA E, 10, MURRAY ROAD, HORNDEAN
SHOTTON, SUSAN P, 12, MURRAY ROAD, HORNDEAN
SWANTON, RACHEL L, 16, MURRAY ROAD, HORNDEAN
SWANTON, SHAW J, 16, MURRAY ROAD, HORNDEAN
OXFORD, FIONA C, 18, MURRAY ROAD, HORNDEAN
WHITMAN, HOWARD M, 20, MURRAY ROAD, HORNDEAN
REARDON, MICHAEL, 22, MURRAY ROAD, HORNDEAN
REARDON, SHARON M, 22, MURRAY ROAD, HORNDEAN
KEOGH, NADINE M, 24, MURRAY ROAD, HORNDEAN
STANDEN, CRAIG L, 24, MURRAY ROAD, HORNDEAN
MABON, ANN M, 26, MURRAY ROAD, HORNDEAN
MABON, JOHN B, 26, MURRAY ROAD, HORNDEAN
DEXTER, ALAN J, 28, MURRAY ROAD, HORNDEAN
DEXTER, CAROL M, 28, MURRAY ROAD, HORNDEAN
LIGHTFOOT, SYLVIA R, 46, MURRAY ROAD, HORNDEAN
MOUNTY, JACQUELINE M, 48, MURRAY ROAD, HORNDEAN
TINDORF, ERIC, 50, MURRAY ROAD, HORNDEAN
TINDORF, ERIKA, 50, MURRAY ROAD, HORNDEAN
TINDORF, SHEILA, 50, MURRAY ROAD, HORNDEAN
FARMER, RAYMOND J, 52, MURRAY ROAD, HORNDEAN
FARMER, RYAN J, 52, MURRAY ROAD, HORNDEAN
FARMER, SUSAN M, 52, MURRAY ROAD, HORNDEAN
REDMOND, ANDREW, 54, MURRAY ROAD, HORNDEAN
REDMOND, HILDA, 54, MURRAY ROAD, HORNDEAN
REDMOND, PETER R, 54, MURRAY ROAD, HORNDEAN
BAWLER, JACQUELINE A, 56, MURRAY ROAD, HORNDEAN
BAWLER, JOHN N, 56, MURRAY ROAD, HORNDEAN
RUSSELL, DONALD, 58, MURRAY ROAD, HORNDEAN
RUSSELL, SYLVIA M, 58, MURRAY ROAD, HORNDEAN
RELPH, CLARE E, 60, MURRAY ROAD, HORNDEAN
RELPH, GEOFF J.F, 60, MURRAY ROAD, HORNDEAN
RELPH, JUNE S, 60, MURRAY ROAD, HORNDEAN
RELPH, KATHERINE A, 60, MURRAY ROAD, HORNDEAN
TAYLOR, LESLIE, 60B, MURRAY ROAD, HORNDEAN
TAYLOR, PATRICIA A, 60B, MURRAY ROAD, HORNDEAN
CRAMER, IRIS C, 60C, MURRAY ROAD, HORNDEAN
CRAMER, WILLEM H.J, 60C, MURRAY ROAD, HORNDEAN
PINE, ANDREW O.J, 64, MURRAY ROAD, HORNDEAN
PINE, LYNDA J, 64, MURRAY ROAD, HORNDEAN
PINE, VICTORIA L, 64, MURRAY ROAD, HORNDEAN
ANSELL, DAVID S, 64A, MURRAY ROAD, HORNDEAN
ANSELL, MARGARET M, 64A, MURRAY ROAD, HORNDEAN

Electoral Roll

BONELL, MARGARET A, 64B, MURRAY ROAD, HORNDEAN
BONELL, STANLEY B, 64B, MURRAY ROAD, HORNDEAN
GOBLE, GLENDA, 66, MURRAY ROAD, HORNDEAN
HILLMAN, DAVID, 66A, MURRAY ROAD, HORNDEAN
PULLEN, ALISON M, 68, MURRAY ROAD, HORNDEAN
PULLEN, KIM D, 68, MURRAY ROAD, HORNDEAN
DAVIES, FRANK, 70, MURRAY ROAD, HORNDEAN
DAVIES, MARGARET E, 70, MURRAY ROAD, HORNDEAN
WELD, ANTHONY E, 72, MURRAY ROAD, HORNDEAN
WELD, MABEL, 72, MURRAY ROAD, HORNDEAN
PETERS, CAROLINE A, 74, MURRAY ROAD, HORNDEAN
PETERS, NIGEL C, 74, MURRAY ROAD, HORNDEAN
MACKFALL, IAN D, 76, MURRAY ROAD, HORNDEAN
MACKFALL, SHEREE J, 76, MURRAY ROAD, HORNDEAN
YOUNG, ALLEN M, 78, MURRAY ROAD, HORNDEAN
YOUNG, ELIZABETH W.J, 78, MURRAY ROAD, HORNDEAN
OPEN, JOAN L, 1, NAPIER ROAD, HORNDEAN
FOX, EDWARD J, 2, NAPIER ROAD, HORNDEAN
STRUGNELL, ROSEMARY E, 3, NAPIER ROAD, HORNDEAN
NORMAN, ENID R, 4, NAPIER ROAD, HORNDEAN
WEDGEWORTH, CAROLAN, 5, NAPIER ROAD, HORNDEAN
CLARE, JEFFERY D, 7, NAPIER ROAD, HORNDEAN
BAKER, COLIN L, 9, NAPIER ROAD, HORNDEAN
BAKER, JUSTINE F, 9, NAPIER ROAD, HORNDEAN
FREEMAN, DAVID R, 10, NAPIER ROAD, HORNDEAN
FREEMAN, MICHAEL R, 10, NAPIER ROAD, HORNDEAN
FREEMAN, SHARON P, 10, NAPIER ROAD, HORNDEAN
ALLMAN, DEBORAH J, 11, NAPIER ROAD, HORNDEAN
MARTIN, DONALD R, 12, NAPIER ROAD, HORNDEAN
MARTIN, JOYCE A, 12, NAPIER ROAD, HORNDEAN
KINGE, KATHLEEN M, 13, NAPIER ROAD, HORNDEAN
KINGE, PERCY G, 13, NAPIER ROAD, HORNDEAN
SHUTE, JOYCE A, 14, NAPIER ROAD, HORNDEAN
CHURCHILL, BRIAN, 15, NAPIER ROAD, HORNDEAN
CHURCHILL, VALERIE G, 15, NAPIER ROAD, HORNDEAN
WRIGHT, PAULINE F, 16, NAPIER ROAD, HORNDEAN
ROBINSON, MICHAEL P, 17, NAPIER ROAD, HORNDEAN
SEARLE, SUZANNE L, 17, NAPIER ROAD, HORNDEAN
CRESSWELL, VICTORIA, 18, NAPIER ROAD, HORNDEAN
FROST, ANDREW M, 18, NAPIER ROAD, HORNDEAN
SMITH, CYNTHIA M, 19, NAPIER ROAD, HORNDEAN
SMITH, JULIA A, 19, NAPIER ROAD, HORNDEAN
WEIGHTMAN, VIOLET E.M, 20, NAPIER ROAD, HORNDEAN
RANDALL, PATRICIA N, 1, NELSON CRESCENT, HORNDEAN
RANDALL, RONALD D.A, 1, NELSON CRESCENT, HORNDEAN
CHAMBERLAIN, GRAHAM B, 2, NELSON CRESCENT, HORNDEAN
KILLICK, GRAHAM D, 2, NELSON CRESCENT, HORNDEAN
KILLICK, HEATHER E, 2, NELSON CRESCENT, HORNDEAN
KILLICK, JOSEPH G, 2, NELSON CRESCENT, HORNDEAN
KILLICK, SUZANNE P, 2, NELSON CRESCENT, HORNDEAN
RAYMENT, BRIAN H, 3, NELSON CRESCENT, HORNDEAN
RAYMENT, KAREN J, 3, NELSON CRESCENT, HORNDEAN
WHITE, DAVID J, 4, NELSON CRESCENT, HORNDEAN
WHITE, HELEN D, 4, NELSON CRESCENT, HORNDEAN
STUBBINGTON, CARRIE, 5, NELSON CRESCENT, HORNDEAN
STUBBINGTON, GILLIAN, 5, NELSON CRESCENT, HORNDEAN
IRONS, TREVOR, 7, NELSON CRESCENT, HORNDEAN
CULLUM, BRYAN R, 8, NELSON CRESCENT, HORNDEAN
CULLUM, MARGARET R, 8, NELSON CRESCENT, HORNDEAN
KNOTT, DAVID D, 9, NELSON CRESCENT, HORNDEAN
KNOTT, MARION J, 9, NELSON CRESCENT, HORNDEAN
KNOTT, PAUL D, 9, NELSON CRESCENT, HORNDEAN
BONE, ALFRED J, 10, NELSON CRESCENT, HORNDEAN
BONE, SHEILA H, 10, NELSON CRESCENT, HORNDEAN
LANGRISH, ENA P, 11A, NELSON CRESCENT, HORNDEAN
WILD, PAMELA M, 11B, NELSON CRESCENT, HORNDEAN
PARSON, DAVID J, 12A, NELSON CRESCENT, HORNDEAN
PARSON, SUSAN E, 12A, NELSON CRESCENT, HORNDEAN
ROGERS, STUART J, 12A, NELSON CRESCENT, HORNDEAN
EASTLAND, ANN, 12B, NELSON CRESCENT, HORNDEAN
HOWGILL, GEORGE R, 1, PRINCESS GARDENS, HORNDEAN
HOWGILL, JOANNA, 1, PRINCESS GARDENS, HORNDEAN
HOWGILL, JONATHAN, 1, PRINCESS GARDENS, HORNDEAN
HOWGILL, SIMON C, 1, PRINCESS GARDENS, HORNDEAN
HOWGILL, VIVIENNE, 1, PRINCESS GARDENS, HORNDEAN
HOWGILL, ZOE, 1, PRINCESS GARDENS, HORNDEAN
DOBSON, KIM C, 2, PRINCESS GARDENS, HORNDEAN
DOBSON, ROY, 2, PRINCESS GARDENS, HORNDEAN
GREEN, JOHN H, 3, PRINCESS GARDENS, HORNDEAN
WENT, PATRICIA A, 3, PRINCESS GARDENS, HORNDEAN
SOWDEN, KATRINA L, 4, PRINCESS GARDENS, HORNDEAN
SOWDEN, PATRICIA, 4, PRINCESS GARDENS, HORNDEAN
SOWDEN, PAUL J, 4, PRINCESS GARDENS, HORNDEAN
SOWDEN, ROBERT J, 4, PRINCESS GARDENS, HORNDEAN
HANDLEY, ALAN L, 5, PRINCESS GARDENS, HORNDEAN
HANDLEY, KIM A, 5, PRINCESS GARDENS, HORNDEAN
NELSON, DAVID, 6, PRINCESS GARDENS, HORNDEAN
NELSON, RACHEL E, 6, PRINCESS GARDENS, HORNDEAN
THOMPSON, MARILYN P, 7, PRINCESS GARDENS, HORNDEAN
THOMPSON, MICHELLE, 7, PRINCESS GARDENS, HORNDEAN
THOMPSON, RICHARD C, 7, PRINCESS GARDENS, HORNDEAN
THOMPSON, RICHARD D, 7, PRINCESS GARDENS, HORNDEAN
HEBBERD, BARRY R, 8, PRINCESS GARDENS, HORNDEAN
HEBBERD, MAXINA N, 8, PRINCESS GARDENS, HORNDEAN
HEBBERD, MICHAEL J, 8, PRINCESS GARDENS, HORNDEAN
BLOY, NICHOLAS J, 9, PRINCESS GARDENS, HORNDEAN
BLOY, SARAH J, 9, PRINCESS GARDENS, HORNDEAN
FARR, PAUL A, 10, PRINCESS GARDENS, HORNDEAN
FARR, TERESA J, 10, PRINCESS GARDENS, HORNDEAN
HOSKINS, ADAM S.J, 11, PRINCESS GARDENS, HORNDEAN
HOSKINS, JANE, 11, PRINCESS GARDENS, HORNDEAN
HOSKINS, STEPHEN T, 11, PRINCESS GARDENS, HORNDEAN
BROWN, ESME J, 12, PRINCESS GARDENS, HORNDEAN
BROWN, LESLIE D, 12, PRINCESS GARDENS, HORNDEAN
EMPSON, JAMES C, 1, QUEENS CRESCENT, HORNDEAN
EMPSON, RYAN, 1, QUEENS CRESCENT, HORNDEAN
EMPSON, SARA, 1, QUEENS CRESCENT, HORNDEAN
GREENALL, CATHERINE L.J, 2, QUEENS CRESCENT,
GREENALL, STEVEN D, 2, QUEENS CRESCENT, HORNDEAN
GREENALL, VICTORIA M, 2, QUEENS CRESCENT, HORNDEAN
GREENALL-NEW, LESLEY M, 2, QUEENS CRESCENT,
GREENALL-NEW, MALCOLM M.C, 2, QUEENS CRESCENT,
POWELL, NIGEL B, 3, QUEENS CRESCENT, HORNDEAN
POWELL, SARA J, 3, QUEENS CRESCENT, HORNDEAN
POPE, MARION J, 4, QUEENS CRESCENT, HORNDEAN
POPE, SHAUN T, 4, QUEENS CRESCENT, HORNDEAN
POPE, TREVOR C, 4, QUEENS CRESCENT, HORNDEAN
CRAVEN, DOROTHY E, 6, QUEENS CRESCENT, HORNDEAN
CRAVEN, RONALD W, 6, QUEENS CRESCENT, HORNDEAN
SHIMBART, ANDREA C, 8, QUEENS CRESCENT, HORNDEAN
SHIMBART, JEFFERY, 8, QUEENS CRESCENT, HORNDEAN
HUGHES, CAROLE W, 9, QUEENS CRESCENT, HORNDEAN
HUGHES, DAVID K, 9, QUEENS CRESCENT, HORNDEAN
YOULDON, ALLAN D, 10, QUEENS CRESCENT, HORNDEAN
YOULDON, LAURA A, 10, QUEENS CRESCENT, HORNDEAN
BROWN, KAREN, 11, QUEENS CRESCENT, HORNDEAN
GOFF, KAREN T, 12, QUEENS CRESCENT, HORNDEAN
GOFF, KEVIN, 12, QUEENS CRESCENT, HORNDEAN
TAYLOR, DAMIEN, 14, QUEENS CRESCENT, HORNDEAN
TAYLOR, REBECCA, 14, QUEENS CRESCENT, HORNDEAN
HILLS, MARTIN R, 15, QUEENS CRESCENT, HORNDEAN
HILLS, MARY W, 15, QUEENS CRESCENT, HORNDEAN
SPRATT, BARBARA, 16, QUEENS CRESCENT, HORNDEAN
SPRATT, LAWRENCE, 16, QUEENS CRESCENT, HORNDEAN
POWELL, MARIA A, 17, QUEENS CRESCENT, HORNDEAN
POWELL, PETER W, 17, QUEENS CRESCENT, HORNDEAN
MECHEN, GLORIA J, 18, QUEENS CRESCENT, HORNDEAN
MECHEN, ROBERT, 18, QUEENS CRESCENT, HORNDEAN
MECHEN, SUSANNAH K, 18, QUEENS CRESCENT, HORNDEAN
DUGAN, FREDERICK E, 19, QUEENS CRESCENT, HORNDEAN
DUGAN, MARIE E, 19, QUEENS CRESCENT, HORNDEAN
BLACKWELL, DENISE, 20, QUEENS CRESCENT, HORNDEAN
BLACKWELL, MARK, 20, QUEENS CRESCENT, HORNDEAN
CUSHION, CLIVE R, 21, QUEENS CRESCENT, HORNDEAN
HOGG, DOROTHY, 21, QUEENS CRESCENT, HORNDEAN
WARE, KEITH, 22, QUEENS CRESCENT, HORNDEAN
WARE, LORRAINE J, 22, QUEENS CRESCENT, HORNDEAN
LIPSCOMBE, PAUL, 23, QUEENS CRESCENT, HORNDEAN
LIPSCOMBE, RYAN N.P, 23, QUEENS CRESCENT, HORNDEAN
FITCH, GIDEON O, 24, QUEENS CRESCENT, HORNDEAN
WALKER, SHARON E, 24, QUEENS CRESCENT, HORNDEAN
WHITE, PAULINE M, 25, QUEENS CRESCENT, HORNDEAN
HELLIER, MARK E, 26, QUEENS CRESCENT, HORNDEAN
HELLIER, PAULA M, 26, QUEENS CRESCENT, HORNDEAN
SAMSON, DOROTHY H, 28, QUEENS CRESCENT, HORNDEAN
HEXT, JOANNE C, 30, QUEENS CRESCENT, HORNDEAN
HEXT, MARK J, 30, QUEENS CRESCENT, HORNDEAN
KINDUR, PIOTR, 32, QUEENS CRESCENT, HORNDEAN
PONTING, ANNA, 32, QUEENS CRESCENT, HORNDEAN
PONTING, STEPHEN J, 32, QUEENS CRESCENT, HORNDEAN
KELLETT, SIMON J, 33, QUEENS CRESCENT, HORNDEAN
LEMM, BRIAN C, 33, QUEENS CRESCENT, HORNDEAN
LEMM, FRANCES M, 33, QUEENS CRESCENT, HORNDEAN
SANDY, WILLIAM J.C, 34, QUEENS CRESCENT, HORNDEAN
WEBB, LYNNE M, 35, QUEENS CRESCENT, HORNDEAN
WEBB, RICHARD W, 35, QUEENS CRESCENT, HORNDEAN
STRADLING, JENNIFER K, 36, QUEENS CRESCENT,
CONWAY, AMY L, 37, QUEENS CRESCENT, HORNDEAN
CONWAY, ANDREW N, 37, QUEENS CRESCENT, HORNDEAN
CONWAY, PAMELA J, 37, QUEENS CRESCENT, HORNDEAN
CONWAY, STEPHEN B, 37, QUEENS CRESCENT, HORNDEAN
HART, GARY D, 38, QUEENS CRESCENT, HORNDEAN
HART, KIRSTY, 38, QUEENS CRESCENT, HORNDEAN
RALLS, PAMELA, 39, QUEENS CRESCENT, HORNDEAN
STRICKLAND, JOHN A, 41, QUEENS CRESCENT, HORNDEAN
STRICKLAND, JULIE, 41, QUEENS CRESCENT, HORNDEAN
ANDREWS, FRANCES A, 41A, QUEENS CRESCENT, HORNDEAN
ANDREWS, KELVIN B, 41A, QUEENS CRESCENT, HORNDEAN
CLEARY, ROSEMARY A, 41B, QUEENS CRESCENT, HORNDEAN
POOLMAN, MARK R, 41B, QUEENS CRESCENT, HORNDEAN
LAWRENCE, MAUREEN B, 42, QUEENS CRESCENT,
LAWRENCE, SARAH-JANE A, 42, QUEENS CRESCENT,
LAWRENCE, TERENCE G, 42, QUEENS CRESCENT, HORNDEAN
ADEY, CHRISTINE, 44, QUEENS CRESCENT, HORNDEAN
ADEY, COLIN S, 44, QUEENS CRESCENT, HORNDEAN
ADEY, MARK, 44, QUEENS CRESCENT, HORNDEAN
ADEY, MICHAEL, 44, QUEENS CRESCENT, HORNDEAN
LOWE, YVONNE J, 45A, QUEENS CRESCENT, HORNDEAN
SMITH, KATHLEEN M, 45B, QUEENS CRESCENT, HORNDEAN
JOYCE, SUSAN V, 46, QUEENS CRESCENT, HORNDEAN
ABBINNETT, CATHERINE B, 47A, QUEENS CRESCENT,
ABBINNETT, RAYMOND J, 47A, QUEENS CRESCENT,
THOMPSON, HAILEY L.V, 47B, QUEENS CRESCENT,
MEW, SHARON, 48, QUEENS CRESCENT, HORNDEAN
OTHEN, DAWN, 48, QUEENS CRESCENT, HORNDEAN
OTHEN, GARRY A, 48, QUEENS CRESCENT, HORNDEAN
WINGHAM, SALLY A, 49, QUEENS CRESCENT, HORNDEAN
ALTOFT, IRIS M, 50, QUEENS CRESCENT, HORNDEAN
ALTOFT, RAYMOND, 50, QUEENS CRESCENT, HORNDEAN
TAYLOR, EDITH, 51, QUEENS CRESCENT, HORNDEAN
TAYLOR, MICHAEL J, 51, QUEENS CRESCENT, HORNDEAN
HOWELL, BARBARA J, 52, QUEENS CRESCENT, HORNDEAN
HOWELL, JANET G, 52, QUEENS CRESCENT, HORNDEAN
HOWELL, RICHARD J, 52, QUEENS CRESCENT, HORNDEAN
GAYLARD, EDNA E, 53, QUEENS CRESCENT, HORNDEAN
HUGHES, KATHLEEN, 54, QUEENS CRESCENT, HORNDEAN
STACEY, ARTHUR G, 55, QUEENS CRESCENT, HORNDEAN
STACEY, IVY V, 55, QUEENS CRESCENT, HORNDEAN
KEARVELL, GLADYS, 56, QUEENS CRESCENT, HORNDEAN
COOK, BERNARD L.R, 57, QUEENS CRESCENT, HORNDEAN
COOK, HERBERT J, 57, QUEENS CRESCENT, HORNDEAN
COOK, SHEILA H.W, 57, QUEENS CRESCENT, HORNDEAN
HARFIELD, MURIEL K, 58, QUEENS CRESCENT, HORNDEAN
PHILLIPS, EVELYN M, 59, QUEENS CRESCENT, HORNDEAN
NICOLS, IRENE D, 60, QUEENS CRESCENT, HORNDEAN
BARKER, TREVOR, 61A, QUEENS CRESCENT, HORNDEAN
HOLLOWAY, ETHEL, 61B, QUEENS CRESCENT, HORNDEAN
NICHOLSON, EDNA L, 62, QUEENS CRESCENT, HORNDEAN
HORBURY, KEVIN M, 63A, QUEENS CRESCENT, HORNDEAN
KINGE, CHRISTOPHER J, 63B, QUEENS CRESCENT,
SCAIFE, JULIET E, 63B, QUEENS CRESCENT, HORNDEAN
MOON, CHERYL E.P, 64, QUEENS CRESCENT, HORNDEAN
BACON, CARLA M, 66, QUEENS CRESCENT, HORNDEAN
BACON, KERRY L, 66, QUEENS CRESCENT, HORNDEAN
BACON, LORRAINE D, 66, QUEENS CRESCENT, HORNDEAN
BACON, MICHAEL K, 66, QUEENS CRESCENT, HORNDEAN
BACON, MICHAEL T, 66, QUEENS CRESCENT, HORNDEAN
TURNER, BRIAN M, 68, QUEENS CRESCENT, HORNDEAN
TURNER, MARIE, 68, QUEENS CRESCENT, HORNDEAN
COLES, ADAM C, 70A, QUEENS CRESCENT, HORNDEAN
ALLAN, TOM, 70B, QUEENS CRESCENT, HORNDEAN
NEWELL, DIANE K, 72A, QUEENS CRESCENT, HORNDEAN
GRANT, IAN S, 72B, QUEENS CRESCENT, HORNDEAN
TUPPER, ELIZABETH, 1, RODNEY WAY, HORNDEAN
TUPPER, KEITH M, 1, RODNEY WAY, HORNDEAN
TUPPER, SIDNEY M, 1, RODNEY WAY, HORNDEAN
TUPPER, WILLIAM E, 1, RODNEY WAY, HORNDEAN
STANLEY, ROBIN C, 2, RODNEY WAY, HORNDEAN
BOND, ANNETTE, 3, RODNEY WAY, HORNDEAN
BOND, ASHLEY, 3, RODNEY WAY, HORNDEAN
BRUMPTON, GEORGE E, 4, RODNEY WAY, HORNDEAN
BRUMPTON, RITA M, 4, RODNEY WAY, HORNDEAN
DOWN, ALBERTA B, 5, RODNEY WAY, HORNDEAN
DE LUCHI, ANTHONY, 6, RODNEY WAY, HORNDEAN
DE LUCHI, IRIS U, 6, RODNEY WAY, HORNDEAN
BUICK, ROBERT M, 7, RODNEY WAY, HORNDEAN
ELPHICK, EDWIN R, 8, RODNEY WAY, HORNDEAN
BLACK, DORCAS A, 9, RODNEY WAY, HORNDEAN
DICKINSON, ARTHUR T, 10, RODNEY WAY, HORNDEAN
DICKINSON, BETTINA W, 10, RODNEY WAY, HORNDEAN
GILES, EDITH A, 11, RODNEY WAY, HORNDEAN
GILES, JAMES E, 11, RODNEY WAY, HORNDEAN
COLEMAN, FRANK O, 12, RODNEY WAY, HORNDEAN
HARTLEY, GWEN, 1, ROLAND CLOSE, HORNDEAN
HARTLEY, JAMES M, 1, ROLAND CLOSE, HORNDEAN
THOMPSON, MICHELLE, 1, ROLAND CLOSE, HORNDEAN
ANDRE, DANNIELLA K, 2, ROLAND CLOSE, HORNDEAN
ANDRE, MARILYN P, 2, ROLAND CLOSE, HORNDEAN
ANDRE, MIA J, 2, ROLAND CLOSE, HORNDEAN
FLYNN, KATRINA, 3, ROLAND CLOSE, HORNDEAN
FLYNN, ROGER V, 3, ROLAND CLOSE, HORNDEAN
CHARMAN, MARK A, 4, ROLAND CLOSE, HORNDEAN
WOODLEY, IAN J, 5, ROLAND CLOSE, HORNDEAN
WOODLEY, JOHN W, 5, ROLAND CLOSE, HORNDEAN
WOODLEY, SYLVIA F, 5, ROLAND CLOSE, HORNDEAN
WATKINSON, HELEN M, 6, ROLAND CLOSE, HORNDEAN
MORRIS, ERIC W, 7, ROLAND CLOSE, HORNDEAN
MORRIS, GAWAIN R, 7, ROLAND CLOSE, HORNDEAN
MORRIS, JEAN M, 7, ROLAND CLOSE, HORNDEAN
JARMAN, MARGARET, 8, ROLAND CLOSE, HORNDEAN
JARMAN, ROBERT, 8, ROLAND CLOSE, HORNDEAN
JARMAN, STEVE, 8, ROLAND CLOSE, HORNDEAN
LINFORD, JOANNE S, 9, ROLAND CLOSE, HORNDEAN
LINFORD, PAUL R, 9, ROLAND CLOSE, HORNDEAN
LINFORD, SIMON P, 9, ROLAND CLOSE, HORNDEAN
LINFORD, SUSAN, 9, ROLAND CLOSE, HORNDEAN
TRUMPER, PAMELA L, 10, ROLAND CLOSE, HORNDEAN
HATFIELD, LOUISE A, 11, ROLAND CLOSE, HORNDEAN
SHERBORNE, PAUL W, 11, ROLAND CLOSE, HORNDEAN
DARAZ, CRAIG D, 12, ROLAND CLOSE, HORNDEAN
DARAZ, JAMES J, 12, ROLAND CLOSE, HORNDEAN
DARAZ, NICOLA D.C, 12, ROLAND CLOSE, HORNDEAN
MAIDENS, ANDREW J, 12, ROLAND CLOSE, HORNDEAN
ROBERTS, KAREN A, 14, ROLAND CLOSE, HORNDEAN
ROBERTS, LEE, 14, ROLAND CLOSE, HORNDEAN
PEARSON, JACQUELINE K, 15, ROLAND CLOSE, HORNDEAN
PEARSON, JOHN, 15, ROLAND CLOSE, HORNDEAN
PEARD, BEATRICE D, 16, ROLAND CLOSE, HORNDEAN
PEARD, JONATHAN L, 16, ROLAND CLOSE, HORNDEAN
PEARD, KENNETH, 16, ROLAND CLOSE, HORNDEAN
PAYNTER, ALAN, 17, ROLAND CLOSE, HORNDEAN
PAYNTER, EILEEN M, 17, ROLAND CLOSE, HORNDEAN
PAYNTER, PAUL T, 17, ROLAND CLOSE, HORNDEAN
BUTTERY, CONRAD D, 1, ROOKES CLOSE, HORNDEAN
BUTTERY, MARY A, 1, ROOKES CLOSE, HORNDEAN
LUKER, KARIN J, 2, ROOKES CLOSE, HORNDEAN
ELVIN, ADRIAN J, 3, ROOKES CLOSE, HORNDEAN
POWELL, RONALD E, 3, ROOKES CLOSE, HORNDEAN
EAMES, ANGELA C, 4, ROOKES CLOSE, HORNDEAN
EAMES, JOHN W, 4, ROOKES CLOSE, HORNDEAN
CARR, LOLA C, 5, ROOKES CLOSE, HORNDEAN
GREEN, SALLY J, 6, ROOKES CLOSE, HORNDEAN
BAKER, IVY M, 7, ROOKES CLOSE, HORNDEAN
BYATT, VICTOR G, 8, ROOKES CLOSE, HORNDEAN
TOOMBS, JOYCE D, 9, ROOKES CLOSE, HORNDEAN
POORE, MICHAEL J, 10, ROOKES CLOSE, HORNDEAN
CLARKE, JANE L, 11, ROOKES CLOSE, HORNDEAN
CLARKE, ROBERT T, 11, ROOKES CLOSE, HORNDEAN

MEW, SHARON E, 12, ROOKES CLOSE, HORNDEAN
ANDREWS, CHRISTOPHER J, 13, ROOKES CLOSE, HORNDEAN
ANDREWS, JENNIFER M, 13, ROOKES CLOSE, HORNDEAN
ANDREWS, LAURA E, 13, ROOKES CLOSE, HORNDEAN
ANDREWS, LOUISE, 13, ROOKES CLOSE, HORNDEAN
ANDREWS, RICHARD J, 13, ROOKES CLOSE, HORNDEAN
STAFFORD, JANE, 14, ROOKES CLOSE, HORNDEAN
YOUNGS, CAROLE J, 15, ROOKES CLOSE, HORNDEAN
YOUNGS, KEVIN, 15, ROOKES CLOSE, HORNDEAN
YOUNGS, TRUDIE, 15, ROOKES CLOSE, HORNDEAN
WOODLAND, PAULINE, 1, ST. ANN'S ROAD, HORNDEAN
WOODLAND, PHILLIP W, 1, ST. ANN'S ROAD, HORNDEAN
BRYSON, JOHN T, 3, ST. ANN'S ROAD, HORNDEAN
BRYSON, MARGARET E, 3, ST. ANN'S ROAD, HORNDEAN
BRYSON, MICHAEL J, 3, ST. ANN'S ROAD, HORNDEAN
SHAW, ROSINA, 5, ST. ANN'S ROAD, HORNDEAN
SADLER, DORA A, 2, ST. ANN'S ROAD, HORNDEAN
SADLER, RAYMOND F, 2, ST. ANN'S ROAD, HORNDEAN
COUSINS, MARY E, 4, ST. ANN'S ROAD, HORNDEAN
COUSINS, TREVOR F, 4, ST. ANN'S ROAD, HORNDEAN
WILKINSON, EDITH M, 6, ST. ANN'S ROAD, HORNDEAN
WILKINSON, ROY N, 6, ST. ANN'S ROAD, HORNDEAN
SCARBROUGH, JEANETTE L, 8, ST. ANN'S ROAD, HORNDEAN
SCARBROUGH, MICHAEL L, 8, ST. ANN'S ROAD, HORNDEAN
PUMFREY, ARTHUR A, 10, ST. ANN'S ROAD, HORNDEAN
PALMER, BARRY F, 21, ST. VINCENT CRESCENT, HORNDEAN
PALMER, MARGARET S, 21, ST. VINCENT CRESCENT,
SANDERS, ADRIAN G, 23, ST. VINCENT CRESCENT,
SANDERS, SUSAN M, 23, ST. VINCENT CRESCENT,
HARRIS, NICOLA J, 25, ST. VINCENT CRESCENT, HORNDEAN
HARRIS, RONALD J, 25, ST. VINCENT CRESCENT, HORNDEAN
HARRIS, SANDRA B, 25, ST. VINCENT CRESCENT, HORNDEAN
BROWN, LILY E, 27, ST. VINCENT CRESCENT, HORNDEAN
WEST, ELIZABETH E, 29, ST. VINCENT CRESCENT, HORNDEAN
WEST, MARGARET C, 31, ST. VINCENT CRESCENT,
WITHERS, ALAN J, 33, ST. VINCENT CRESCENT, HORNDEAN
WITHERS, DOROTHY, 33, ST. VINCENT CRESCENT,
BRAMBLEY, WILLIAM A, 35, ST. VINCENT CRESCENT,
GLENDENNING, DAVID R, 37, ST. VINCENT CRESCENT,
GLENDENNING, JOHN, 37, ST. VINCENT CRESCENT,
GLENDENNING, JOYCE L, 37, ST. VINCENT CRESCENT,
GLENDENNING, MARK E, 37, ST. VINCENT CRESCENT,
FORD, BARBARA J, 39, ST. VINCENT CRESCENT, HORNDEAN
DAVIES, ENA D, 61, ST. VINCENT CRESCENT, HORNDEAN
CHILDS, ALFRED J, 63, ST. VINCENT CRESCENT, HORNDEAN
STONE, AMY J, 63, ST. VINCENT CRESCENT, HORNDEAN
HARMSWORTH, PETER, 65, ST. VINCENT CRESCENT,
HARMSWORTH, SUSAN M, 65, ST. VINCENT CRESCENT,
WICKHAM, CATHERINE J, 67, ST. VINCENT CRESCENT,
WICKHAM, PAUL M, 67, ST. VINCENT CRESCENT, HORNDEAN
TOMLINSON, BRIAN, 2, ST. VINCENT CRESCENT, HORNDEAN
TOMLINSON, HELEN C, 2, ST. VINCENT CRESCENT,
JONES, DOROTHY M, 4, ST. VINCENT CRESCENT, HORNDEAN
JONES, TREVOR A, 4, ST. VINCENT CRESCENT, HORNDEAN
FROOM, CLARE, 6, ST. VINCENT CRESCENT, HORNDEAN
FROOM, WILLIAM G, 6, ST. VINCENT CRESCENT, HORNDEAN
GREENWOOD, PATRICIA A, 8, ST. VINCENT CRESCENT,
LOVICK, FRANK W, 10, ST. VINCENT CRESCENT, HORNDEAN
LOVICK, MURIEL E, 10, ST. VINCENT CRESCENT, HORNDEAN
SMITH, JENNIFER R, 12, ST. VINCENT CRESCENT, HORNDEAN
SMITH, RAYMOND J, 12, ST. VINCENT CRESCENT, HORNDEAN
GLOVER, GEMMA L, 14, ST. VINCENT CRESCENT, HORNDEAN
GLOVER, NICOLA J, 14, ST. VINCENT CRESCENT, HORNDEAN
GLOVER, PATRICIA A, 14, ST. VINCENT CRESCENT,
GLOVER, RONALD, 14, ST. VINCENT CRESCENT, HORNDEAN
ANCHOR, ANN, 16, ST. VINCENT CRESCENT, HORNDEAN
LIGERTWOOD, JOYCE A, 18, ST. VINCENT CRESCENT,
COURTNAGE, ROY S, 20, ST. VINCENT CRESCENT, HORNDEAN
COURTNAGE, WENDY A, 20, ST. VINCENT CRESCENT,
HOBBS, PAULINE J, 22, ST. VINCENT CRESCENT, HORNDEAN
HOBBS, STEPHEN D, 22, ST. VINCENT CRESCENT, HORNDEAN
HOLLAND, IAN M, 24, ST. VINCENT CRESCENT, HORNDEAN
HOLLAND, MAVIS, 24, ST. VINCENT CRESCENT, HORNDEAN
EDWARDS, CHRISTINE H, 26, ST. VINCENT CRESCENT,
EDWARDS, HELEN C, 26, ST. VINCENT CRESCENT, HORNDEAN
EDWARDS, RONALD W, 26, ST. VINCENT CRESCENT,
BREAM, BERYL M, 28, ST. VINCENT CRESCENT, HORNDEAN
BREAM, GEORGE L, 28, ST. VINCENT CRESCENT, HORNDEAN
BURTON, DOREEN, 30, ST. VINCENT CRESCENT, HORNDEAN
SWAN, CHRISTINE E.A, 32, ST. VINCENT CRESCENT,
SWAN, GORDON R, 32, ST. VINCENT CRESCENT, HORNDEAN
TERRY, JASON M, 32, ST. VINCENT CRESCENT, HORNDEAN
CRUTTWELL, JANE S, 34, ST. VINCENT CRESCENT,
WHAMOND, NORAH, 36, ST. VINCENT CRESCENT, HORNDEAN
HANMAN, JENNIE A, 38, ST. VINCENT CRESCENT, HORNDEAN
HANMAN, ROBERT B, 38, ST. VINCENT CRESCENT,
STEVEN, ALFRED, 40, ST. VINCENT CRESCENT, HORNDEAN
STEVEN, EILEEN P, 40, ST. VINCENT CRESCENT, HORNDEAN
DUNFORD, DENZIL K, 42, ST. VINCENT CRESCENT,
DUNFORD, FRANCES R, 42, ST. VINCENT CRESCENT,
TURNBULL, DANIEL J, 44, ST. VINCENT CRESCENT,
TURNBULL, MATTHEW B, 44, ST. VINCENT CRESCENT,
TURNBULL, NICOLA J, 44, ST. VINCENT CRESCENT,
TURNBULL, NIKOLAS P, 44, ST. VINCENT CRESCENT,
TURNBULL, RICHARD F, 44, ST. VINCENT CRESCENT,
TURNBULL, SIMON J, 44, ST. VINCENT CRESCENT,
BURDEN, GAVIN, 46, ST. VINCENT CRESCENT, HORNDEAN
BURDEN, JACQUELINE, 46, ST. VINCENT CRESCENT,
BURDEN, JEFFREY, 46, ST. VINCENT CRESCENT, HORNDEAN
CRONEY, LYNETTE, 48, ST. VINCENT CRESCENT,
CRONEY, STEPHEN P, 48, ST. VINCENT CRESCENT,
FINDLAY, ANDREW I, 50, ST. VINCENT CRESCENT, HORNDEAN
FINDLAY, ZOE H.A, 50, ST. VINCENT CRESCENT, HORNDEAN
KNIGHT, ANDREW J, 52, ST. VINCENT CRESCENT, HORNDEAN
KNIGHT, SHIRLEY A, 52, ST. VINCENT CRESCENT, HORNDEAN
WIGMORE, ANTHONY P, 54, ST. VINCENT CRESCENT,
WIGMORE, LYNDA J, 54, ST. VINCENT CRESCENT, HORNDEAN
HUTCHINS, LEONARD R, 56, ST. VINCENT CRESCENT,
ETHERINGTON, GEORGINA B, 58, ST. VINCENT CRESCENT,
ETHERINGTON, MICHAEL D, 58, ST. VINCENT CRESCENT,
BELL, BETTY E, 60, ST. VINCENT CRESCENT, HORNDEAN
BELL, EDWARD J, 60, ST. VINCENT CRESCENT, HORNDEAN
BARKER, ARTHUR W, 62, ST. VINCENT CRESCENT,
BARKER, KATHLEEN M, 62, ST. VINCENT CRESCENT,
BARKER, STEPHEN, 62, ST. VINCENT CRESCENT, HORNDEAN
RANDALL, IVY L, 64, ST. VINCENT CRESCENT, HORNDEAN
MILES, CAROLINE E, 1, STAGSHORN ROAD, HORNDEAN
MILES, SIMON P, 1, STAGSHORN ROAD, HORNDEAN
SAUNDERS, GILLIAN, 5, STAGSHORN ROAD, HORNDEAN
SAUNDERS, STEPHEN D, 5, STAGSHORN ROAD, HORNDEAN
KING, DAVID J, 7, STAGSHORN ROAD, HORNDEAN
KING, MARIA, 7, STAGSHORN ROAD, HORNDEAN
WELLS, JENNA L, 2, STAGSHORN ROAD, HORNDEAN
WELLS, MATTHEW J, 2, STAGSHORN ROAD, HORNDEAN
WELLS, STEPHEN J, 2, STAGSHORN ROAD, HORNDEAN
ADKINS, PAUL S, 4, STAGSHORN ROAD, HORNDEAN
ADKINS, SUSAN, 4, STAGSHORN ROAD, HORNDEAN
CORKINDALE, MARTIN, 4, STAGSHORN ROAD, HORNDEAN
ENDERBY, BELINDA J, 6, STAGSHORN ROAD, HORNDEAN
BAGYURA, BRENDA M, 8, STAGSHORN ROAD, HORNDEAN
BAGYURA, SABINE A, 8, STAGSHORN ROAD, HORNDEAN
WOOTTON, ANTHEA J, 10, STAGSHORN ROAD, HORNDEAN
HANDFORD, IAN D, 12, STAGSHORN ROAD, HORNDEAN
JAMES, BEVERLY, 14, STAGSHORN ROAD, HORNDEAN
SPONG, PAUL, 14, STAGSHORN ROAD, HORNDEAN
STONER, DAVID J, 16, STAGSHORN ROAD, HORNDEAN
STONER, VALERIE B, 16, STAGSHORN ROAD, HORNDEAN
SHARP, ANDREW J, 5, TARBERY CRESCENT, HORNDEAN
SHARP, ANTHEA P, 5, TARBERY CRESCENT, HORNDEAN
SHARP, PETER J, 5, TARBERY CRESCENT, HORNDEAN
PAGE, GEOFFREY, 7, TARBERY CRESCENT, HORNDEAN
PAGE, RITA E, 7, TARBERY CRESCENT, HORNDEAN
SIBLEY, JOAN K, 9, TARBERY CRESCENT, HORNDEAN
SIBLEY, KENNETH K, 9, TARBERY CRESCENT, HORNDEAN
WALKER, DAVID J, 11, TARBERY CRESCENT, HORNDEAN
WALKER, JANE L, 11, TARBERY CRESCENT, HORNDEAN
WALKER, JANET I, 11, TARBERY CRESCENT, HORNDEAN
WALKER, PHYLLIS M, 11, TARBERY CRESCENT, HORNDEAN
MACH, SHEILA C, 23, TARBERY CRESCENT, HORNDEAN
MACH, ZBIGNIEW J, 23, TARBERY CRESCENT, HORNDEAN
COLE, JAMES F, 25, TARBERY CRESCENT, HORNDEAN
COLE, VALERIE J, 25, TARBERY CRESCENT, HORNDEAN
COLLIER, BERYL, 27, TARBERY CRESCENT, HORNDEAN
COLLIER, FREDERICK W, 27, TARBERY CRESCENT,
BARFOOT, MARIAN A, 2, TARBERY CRESCENT, HORNDEAN
BARFOOT, MELVYN G, 2, TARBERY CRESCENT, HORNDEAN
LAMBERT, ALEXANDER G, 4, TARBERY CRESCENT,
LAMBERT, ANGELA M, 4, TARBERY CRESCENT, HORNDEAN
LAMBERT, GEOFFREY N, 4, TARBERY CRESCENT, HORNDEAN
STOCKLEY, GAVIN P, 6, TARBERY CRESCENT, HORNDEAN
STOCKLEY, MARK P, 6, TARBERY CRESCENT, HORNDEAN
STOCKLEY, PAUL M, 6, TARBERY CRESCENT, HORNDEAN
STOCKLEY, SUZANNE, 6, TARBERY CRESCENT, HORNDEAN
NEWTON, ALAN F.R, 8, TARBERY CRESCENT, HORNDEAN
NEWTON, JUDITH M, 8, TARBERY CRESCENT, HORNDEAN
NEWTON, RUTH E, 8, TARBERY CRESCENT, HORNDEAN
THOMPSON, ANDREW, 8, TARBERY CRESCENT, HORNDEAN
ALLERY, MARION C, 10, TARBERY CRESCENT, HORNDEAN
ALLERY, ROGER J, 10, TARBERY CRESCENT, HORNDEAN
ROGERS, JAMES W, 12, TARBERY CRESCENT, HORNDEAN
ROGERS, LEANNE E, 12, TARBERY CRESCENT, HORNDEAN
ROGERS, LYNDA, 12, TARBERY CRESCENT, HORNDEAN
ROGERS, TREVOR, 12, TARBERY CRESCENT, HORNDEAN
FODEN, DIANA M, 14, TARBERY CRESCENT, HORNDEAN
FODEN, JOHN E, 14, TARBERY CRESCENT, HORNDEAN
FODEN, MARK R, 14, TARBERY CRESCENT, HORNDEAN
FODEN, MICHAEL I, 14, TARBERY CRESCENT, HORNDEAN
FODEN, ROBERT G, 14, TARBERY CRESCENT, HORNDEAN
RONAN, HELEN M, 16, TARBERY CRESCENT, HORNDEAN
RONAN, JAMES E, 16, TARBERY CRESCENT, HORNDEAN
RONAN, MARTIN E, 16, TARBERY CRESCENT, HORNDEAN
RONAN, TOMAS J, 16, TARBERY CRESCENT, HORNDEAN
MUNRO, HILARY S, 18, TARBERY CRESCENT, HORNDEAN
MUNRO, JOHN G, 18, TARBERY CRESCENT, HORNDEAN
NOL, PAUL N, 20, TARBERY CRESCENT, HORNDEAN
NOL, PAULINE B.D, 20, TARBERY CRESCENT, HORNDEAN
BARKER, EDITH M, 22, TARBERY CRESCENT, HORNDEAN
RUSSELL, KENNETH G, 22, TARBERY CRESCENT, HORNDEAN
GOODENOUGH, ALAN J, 24, TARBERY CRESCENT, HORNDEAN
GOODENOUGH, JULIE E, 24, TARBERY CRESCENT,
COOPER, JAMES P, 26, TARBERY CRESCENT, HORNDEAN
ROBERTS, KAY T, 26, TARBERY CRESCENT, HORNDEAN
PHIPPS, DORIS I, 28, TARBERY CRESCENT, HORNDEAN
PHIPPS, HARRY R, 28, TARBERY CRESCENT, HORNDEAN
WOODARD, ELAINE, 30, TARBERY CRESCENT, HORNDEAN
WOODARD, KATHARINE, 30, TARBERY CRESCENT,
WOODARD, MICHAEL, 30, TARBERY CRESCENT, HORNDEAN
WOODARD, VICTORIA E, 30, TARBERY CRESCENT,
ROBINSON, CAROLINE J, 1, WALDEN GARDENS, HORNDEAN
ROBINSON, TERENCE N, 1, WALDEN GARDENS, HORNDEAN
BRIDGER, KERRY L, 3, WALDEN GARDENS, HORNDEAN
BRIDGER, REGINALD J, 3, WALDEN GARDENS, HORNDEAN
BRIDGER, YVONNE, 3, WALDEN GARDENS, HORNDEAN
HARRISON, ERNEST, 5, WALDEN GARDENS, HORNDEAN
HARRISON, JOAN M, 5, WALDEN GARDENS, HORNDEAN
LACEY, CAROL J, 7, WALDEN GARDENS, HORNDEAN
LACEY, DAVID J, 7, WALDEN GARDENS, HORNDEAN
LACEY, JOHN A, 7, WALDEN GARDENS, HORNDEAN
ALDRIDGE, ALEXANDER J, 9, WALDEN GARDENS, HORNDEAN
ALDRIDGE, CHERYL L, 9, WALDEN GARDENS, HORNDEAN
ALDRIDGE, DAVID R, 9, WALDEN GARDENS, HORNDEAN
CORN, CHRISTINE L, 11, WALDEN GARDENS, HORNDEAN
CORN, DAVID J, 11, WALDEN GARDENS, HORNDEAN
CORN, JEFFERY M, 11, WALDEN GARDENS, HORNDEAN
CORN, LINDA J, 11, WALDEN GARDENS, HORNDEAN
HONEY, ROSS, 15, WALDEN GARDENS, HORNDEAN
KING, DAVID, 17, WALDEN GARDENS, HORNDEAN
KING, JANETTE, 17, WALDEN GARDENS, HORNDEAN
CAHILL, CAROLINE G, 19, WALDEN GARDENS, HORNDEAN
CAHILL, IVOR W, 19, WALDEN GARDENS, HORNDEAN
GILBERT, JOAN E, 2, WALDEN GARDENS, HORNDEAN
GILBERT, JULIE M, 2, WALDEN GARDENS, HORNDEAN
GILBERT, PATRICK J, 2, WALDEN GARDENS, HORNDEAN
GILBERT, SUSAN J, 2, WALDEN GARDENS, HORNDEAN
PANG, KAM T, 4, WALDEN GARDENS, HORNDEAN
PANG, YOK L, 4, WALDEN GARDENS, HORNDEAN
SMITH, ANGELA M, 6, WALDEN GARDENS, HORNDEAN
SMITH, CHRISTOPHER P, 6, WALDEN GARDENS, HORNDEAN
SMITH, ERIC A, 6, WALDEN GARDENS, HORNDEAN
SMITH, NICOLA L, 6, WALDEN GARDENS, HORNDEAN
JACKSON, MARGARET J, 8, WALDEN GARDENS, HORNDEAN
JACKSON, STEPHEN D, 8, WALDEN GARDENS, HORNDEAN
OWEN, DAVID S, 10, WALDEN GARDENS, HORNDEAN
OWEN, SUSAN, 10, WALDEN GARDENS, HORNDEAN
BIRTLES, LYNDA V, 12, WALDEN GARDENS, HORNDEAN
BICKERTON, DAVID M, 24, WALDEN GARDENS, HORNDEAN
BICKERTON, DOROTHY, 24, WALDEN GARDENS, HORNDEAN
BICKERTON, JULIE C, 24, WALDEN GARDENS, HORNDEAN
MITCHELL, DIANE, 26, WALDEN GARDENS, HORNDEAN
MITCHELL, STEVEN, 26, WALDEN GARDENS, HORNDEAN
STEERE, GARY, 28, WALDEN GARDENS, HORNDEAN
STEERE, SALLY C, 28, WALDEN GARDENS, HORNDEAN
HELE, HILARY J, 1, WENTWORTH DRIVE, HORNDEAN
HELE, ROBERT J, 1, WENTWORTH DRIVE, HORNDEAN
SHOTTON, HUGH L, 3, WENTWORTH DRIVE, HORNDEAN
SWATRIDGE, NICOLA S, 3, WENTWORTH DRIVE, HORNDEAN
HARLEY, JACQUELINE, 7, WENTWORTH DRIVE, HORNDEAN
HARLEY, STUART J, 7, WENTWORTH DRIVE, HORNDEAN
RICHARDS, PATRICIA L, 11, WENTWORTH DRIVE,
RICHARDS, PHILIP W, 11, WENTWORTH DRIVE, HORNDEAN
RICHARDS, SIAN L, 11, WENTWORTH DRIVE, HORNDEAN
PANLEY, WENDY L, 15, WENTWORTH DRIVE, HORNDEAN
DEAN, BARBARA J, 17, WENTWORTH DRIVE, HORNDEAN
DEAN, LESLIE H, 17, WENTWORTH DRIVE, HORNDEAN
JACK, DENIS R, 19, WENTWORTH DRIVE, HORNDEAN
JACK, MARGARET K, 19, WENTWORTH DRIVE, HORNDEAN
CROOKES, ALAN F.J, 21, WENTWORTH DRIVE, HORNDEAN
CROOKES, MATTHEW B.J, 21, WENTWORTH DRIVE,
CROOKES, SHEILA A, 21, WENTWORTH DRIVE, HORNDEAN
CASTLE, CHRISTOPHER R, 2, WENTWORTH DRIVE,
CASTLE, SUSAN M, 2, WENTWORTH DRIVE, HORNDEAN
SMITH, JACQUELINE D, 4, WENTWORTH DRIVE, HORNDEAN
SMITH, STEPHEN G, 4, WENTWORTH DRIVE, HORNDEAN
FISHER, CHRISTOPHER M, 6, WENTWORTH DRIVE,
FISHER, SHARON C, 6, WENTWORTH DRIVE, HORNDEAN
RICE, DAVID R, 8, WENTWORTH DRIVE, HORNDEAN
RICE, PAMELA A, 8, WENTWORTH DRIVE, HORNDEAN
MORFEY, STEPHEN F, 10, WENTWORTH DRIVE, HORNDEAN
MORFEY, TRUDI H, 10, WENTWORTH DRIVE, HORNDEAN
FLETCHER, DIANA M, 12, WENTWORTH DRIVE, HORNDEAN
FLETCHER, EMILY L, 12, WENTWORTH DRIVE, HORNDEAN
FLETCHER, HAYDN G, 12, WENTWORTH DRIVE, HORNDEAN
FLETCHER, MATTHEW J, 12, WENTWORTH DRIVE,
POOLE, ADRIAN R, 14, WENTWORTH DRIVE, HORNDEAN
POOLE, KAREN L, 14, WENTWORTH DRIVE, HORNDEAN
MOORES, DAMIEN J, 16, WENTWORTH DRIVE, HORNDEAN
MOORES, JANET E, 16, WENTWORTH DRIVE, HORNDEAN
MOORES, PETER, 16, WENTWORTH DRIVE, HORNDEAN
MARSH, FRANK D, 18, WENTWORTH DRIVE, HORNDEAN
GEE, ANTONY W, 20, WENTWORTH DRIVE, HORNDEAN
GEE, MARY E, 20, WENTWORTH DRIVE, HORNDEAN
HICKS, CHRISTOPHER K, 22, WENTWORTH DRIVE,
HICKS, DAVID J, 22, WENTWORTH DRIVE, HORNDEAN
HICKS, SHEILA, 22, WENTWORTH DRIVE, HORNDEAN
MOULD, LOUISE M, 1, THE YEWS, HORNDEAN
PRISTON, DAREN J, 2, THE YEWS, HORNDEAN
ADAM, HAZEL, 3, THE YEWS, HORNDEAN
ADAM, PAUL J, 3, THE YEWS, HORNDEAN
BONNER, CHRISTINE, 5, THE YEWS, HORNDEAN
BONNER, LEE, 5, THE YEWS, HORNDEAN
FRAME, NATALIE, 6, THE YEWS, HORNDEAN
MORGAN, GARY, 6, THE YEWS, HORNDEAN
SANDY, PETER D, 8, THE YEWS, HORNDEAN
EVANS, SUSAN A, 9, THE YEWS, HORNDEAN
DAVISON, JOANNA C, 10, THE YEWS, HORNDEAN
TEASDALE, ZOE E, 11, THE YEWS, HORNDEAN
WILSON, DANIEL A, 11, THE YEWS, HORNDEAN
PENNELL, PETER E, 12, THE YEWS, HORNDEAN
FUDGE, TREVOR J, 14, THE YEWS, HORNDEAN
THOMPSON, WAYNE A, 15, THE YEWS, HORNDEAN
NEW, MICHAEL G, 16, THE YEWS, HORNDEAN
HUGHES, DIANE, 17, THE YEWS, HORNDEAN
SADLER, MARTIN B, 17, THE YEWS, HORNDEAN
MAYS, ANGELA M, 18, THE YEWS, HORNDEAN
MAYS, PETER A, 18, THE YEWS, HORNDEAN
GRIMSHAW, DEREK S, 19, THE YEWS, HORNDEAN
GRIMSHAW, SUSAN J, 19, THE YEWS, HORNDEAN
ASHWELL, AMANDA J, 20, THE YEWS, HORNDEAN
ASHWELL, NORMAN M, 20, THE YEWS, HORNDEAN

Electoral Roll

LOVEMAN, MARTIN, 21, THE YEWS, HORNDEAN
WELSH, HELEN M, 21, THE YEWS, HORNDEAN
STILWELL, JILLIAN M, 22, THE YEWS, HORNDEAN
JOHNSTON, CYRIL R, 23, THE YEWS, HORNDEAN
MCCAFFERY, SUSAN B, 23, THE YEWS, HORNDEAN
KILBY, JANET K, 24, THE YEWS, HORNDEAN
WOLFE, STEPHEN G, 26, THE YEWS, HORNDEAN
BOWLES, SIMON R.D, 27, THE YEWS, HORNDEAN
BOWLES, WENDY H, 27, THE YEWS, HORNDEAN
STRANGE, GRAHAM, 28, THE YEWS, HORNDEAN
STRANGE, RAYMOND R, 28, THE YEWS, HORNDEAN
STRANGE, TERRY R, 28, THE YEWS, HORNDEAN
GALYER, DEAN, 29, THE YEWS, HORNDEAN
STEVENS, AMANDA T, 29, THE YEWS, HORNDEAN
WEST, CHRISTINA M, 30, THE YEWS, HORNDEAN
CAMERON, ROBERT D, 31, THE YEWS, HORNDEAN
BRETT, PATRICIA M, 32, THE YEWS, HORNDEAN
BRETT, RONALD J, 32, THE YEWS, HORNDEAN
THOMAS, ANGELA, 33, THE YEWS, HORNDEAN
THOMAS, ROLAND, 33, THE YEWS, HORNDEAN
TURNER, MELANIE P.A, 33, THE YEWS, HORNDEAN
BURCHELL, JEAN E, 34, THE YEWS, HORNDEAN
BURCHELL, PETER H, 34, THE YEWS, HORNDEAN
AUSTIN, JENNIFER M, 35, THE YEWS, HORNDEAN
AUSTIN, LOUISE L, 35, THE YEWS, HORNDEAN
AUSTIN, MATTHEW R, 35, THE YEWS, HORNDEAN
AUSTIN, ROBERT C, 35, THE YEWS, HORNDEAN
DYER, GRAHAM P, 36, THE YEWS, HORNDEAN
DYER, JENNIFER J, 36, THE YEWS, HORNDEAN
COLLIER-DEANE, JANE C, 37, THE YEWS, HORNDEAN
BURGESS, CYRIL A, 38, THE YEWS, HORNDEAN
BURGESS, PEGGY, 38, THE YEWS, HORNDEAN
THOMSON, IAN D, 39, THE YEWS, HORNDEAN
CHARMAN, JENNIFER B, 40, THE YEWS, HORNDEAN
CHARMAN, JONATHAN A, 40, THE YEWS, HORNDEAN
CHARMAN, MATTHEW J, 40, THE YEWS, HORNDEAN
CHARMAN, PETER A, 40, THE YEWS, HORNDEAN
COMPTON, LORRAINE T, 41, THE YEWS, HORNDEAN
COMPTON, MALCOLM P, 41, THE YEWS, HORNDEAN
YOUELL, DEBORAH M, 42, THE YEWS, HORNDEAN
YOUELL, NICHOLAS A, 42, THE YEWS, HORNDEAN
LOWE, JANE, 42A, THE YEWS, HORNDEAN
LOWE, MARK N, 42A, THE YEWS, HORNDEAN
COX, CHERYL M, 43, THE YEWS, HORNDEAN
COX, GEOFFREY I, 43, THE YEWS, HORNDEAN
COX, KAY M, 43, THE YEWS, HORNDEAN
COX, NEIL C, 43, THE YEWS, HORNDEAN
MUNDY, PAMELA, 43A, THE YEWS, HORNDEAN
MUNDY, PETER, 43A, THE YEWS, HORNDEAN
BOLTON, GARY, 44A, THE YEWS, HORNDEAN
BOLTON, JEAN E, 44A, THE YEWS, HORNDEAN
BOLTON, JOANNA, 44A, THE YEWS, HORNDEAN
BOLTON, ROGER W, 44A, THE YEWS, HORNDEAN
CLEVERLEY, DARREN A, 45, THE YEWS, HORNDEAN
CLEVERLEY, LORRAINE, 45, THE YEWS, HORNDEAN
CLEVERLEY, PETER A, 45, THE YEWS, HORNDEAN
WADE, MARSHALL A, 46, THE YEWS, HORNDEAN
MASSINK, JULIA F, 47, THE YEWS, HORNDEAN
MASSINK, STEVEN L, 47, THE YEWS, HORNDEAN
LOCKIE, LUCY L, 48, THE YEWS, HORNDEAN
LOCKIE, NORMAN C, 48, THE YEWS, HORNDEAN
MCMANUS, ALLAN R, 49, THE YEWS, HORNDEAN
MCMANUS, HELEN J, 49, THE YEWS, HORNDEAN
YEATES, PAUL C, 50, THE YEWS, HORNDEAN
PONSFORD, MAUREEN D, 51, THE YEWS, HORNDEAN
ANDREWS, JOHN D, 52, THE YEWS, HORNDEAN
PATTERSON, LESLEY A, 52, THE YEWS, HORNDEAN
BYNG, ALLAN F, 54, THE YEWS, HORNDEAN
GLANVILLE, KERRI, 55, THE YEWS, HORNDEAN
MUGRIDGE, SCOTT E, 55, THE YEWS, HORNDEAN
WISE, ROSEMARY, 56, THE YEWS, HORNDEAN
PRIOR, JANET B, 57, THE YEWS, HORNDEAN
ILES, GEORGE C.L, 58, THE YEWS, HORNDEAN
PURRINGTON, SUZANNE I, 59, THE YEWS, HORNDEAN
BEVAN, CHRISTOPHER M.A,,
HOUSE, CAROL A,,
MCGILLIVRAY, KAREN A,,
PRICE, PAUL F,,
TYRRELL, STEPHEN L,,
WALL, ANDREW

HORNDEAN (KINGS)

HELLEN, ANN E, 1, ACORN GARDENS, HORNDEAN
HELLEN, JOHN, 1, ACORN GARDENS, HORNDEAN
STEWART, NEIL M, 2, ACORN GARDENS, HORNDEAN
MOORE, RICHARD W, 3, ACORN GARDENS, HORNDEAN
SOUTH, ALISON M, 3, ACORN GARDENS, HORNDEAN
HANDEL, GEOFFREY G, 4, ACORN GARDENS, HORNDEAN
HANDEL, SARAH L, 4, ACORN GARDENS, HORNDEAN
FOSTER, JACQUELINE M, 5, ACORN GARDENS, HORNDEAN
HARRISON, ANDREW L, 5, ACORN GARDENS, HORNDEAN
COX, WILLIAM K, 6, ACORN GARDENS, HORNDEAN
PIKE, KATHLEEN, SHROVER COTTAGE, ANMORE LANE, DENMEAD, PORTSMOUTH
SESSIONS, LILIAN A, 1, SHROVER HALL, ANMORE LANE, DENMEAD, PORTSMOUTH
FOX, PAUL K, 2, SHROVER HALL, ANMORE LANE, DENMEAD, PORTSMOUTH
WATSON, DAVID A, 3, SHROVER HALL, ANMORE LANE, DENMEAD, PORTSMOUTH
WATSON, MARGARET J, 3, SHROVER HALL, ANMORE LANE, DENMEAD, PORTSMOUTH
LEWIS, JEREMY R, 1, SHROVER LODGE, ANMORE LANE, DENMEAD, PORTSMOUTH
LEWIS, KAY D, 1, SHROVER LODGE, ANMORE LANE, DENMEAD, PORTSMOUTH
MUGRIDGE, HEATHER M, 1, ASHLEY CLOSE, LOVEDEAN
MUGRIDGE, PETER E, 1, ASHLEY CLOSE, LOVEDEAN
SHENTON, EDNA J, 2, ASHLEY CLOSE, LOVEDEAN
DALLAS, COLIN D, 2A, ASHLEY CLOSE, LOVEDEAN
DALLAS, JANE A, 2A, ASHLEY CLOSE, LOVEDEAN
POWELL, DENNIS C, 3, ASHLEY CLOSE, LOVEDEAN
POWELL, JEANETTE P, 3, ASHLEY CLOSE, LOVEDEAN
POWELL, JOHN, 3, ASHLEY CLOSE, LOVEDEAN
DAY, JAMES A, 4, ASHLEY CLOSE, LOVEDEAN
FEBEN, ANGELA, 4A, ASHLEY CLOSE, LOVEDEAN
FEBEN, HUBERT E, 4A, ASHLEY CLOSE, LOVEDEAN
BARTLETT, APRIL, 5, ASHLEY CLOSE, LOVEDEAN
BARTLETT, MARK T, 5, ASHLEY CLOSE, LOVEDEAN
BEAZLEY, REBECCA L, 6, ASHLEY CLOSE, LOVEDEAN
PUMFREY, ALAN D, 6, ASHLEY CLOSE, LOVEDEAN
NASH, STEVEN J, 7, ASHLEY CLOSE, LOVEDEAN
GRANGE, PETER, 8, ASHLEY CLOSE, LOVEDEAN
HARRIS, ANGELA M, 9, ASHLEY CLOSE, LOVEDEAN
HARRIS, SIMON J, 9, ASHLEY CLOSE, LOVEDEAN
STACEY, GRAHAM M.P, 10, ASHLEY CLOSE, LOVEDEAN
DAVIDSON, ANNE J, 11, ASHLEY CLOSE, LOVEDEAN
HARRISON, JOHN M, 11, ASHLEY CLOSE, LOVEDEAN
HAZLEHURST, PETER J, 12, ASHLEY CLOSE, LOVEDEAN
HUNT, KAREN L, 12, ASHLEY CLOSE, LOVEDEAN
HOATH, BARBARA J, 14, ASHLEY CLOSE, LOVEDEAN
HOATH, PHILIP, 14, ASHLEY CLOSE, LOVEDEAN
FIRBY, CYNTHIA L, 15, ASHLEY CLOSE, LOVEDEAN
MARTIN, ANDREW W, 16, ASHLEY CLOSE, LOVEDEAN
MARTIN, NOELA M, 16, ASHLEY CLOSE, LOVEDEAN
MCDERMOTT, HEATHER M.W, 17, ASHLEY CLOSE, LOVEDEAN
MCDERMOTT, RUSSELL J, 17, ASHLEY CLOSE, LOVEDEAN
DAWSON, AILEEN B, 18, ASHLEY CLOSE, LOVEDEAN
DAWSON, DAVID J, 18, ASHLEY CLOSE, LOVEDEAN
CRANE, EILEEN A, 19, ASHLEY CLOSE, LOVEDEAN
CRANE, GERALD J.V, 19, ASHLEY CLOSE, LOVEDEAN
BOWN, GLADYS M, 20, ASHLEY CLOSE, LOVEDEAN
BOWN, THOMAS C, 20, ASHLEY CLOSE, LOVEDEAN
HOBBS, MICHELINE B, 21, ASHLEY CLOSE, LOVEDEAN
HOBBS, NICHOLAS R, 21, ASHLEY CLOSE, LOVEDEAN
WALTON, LUCIENNE A, 22, ASHLEY CLOSE, LOVEDEAN
BUCKEE, JAMES W, 23, ASHLEY CLOSE, LOVEDEAN
BUCKEE, MARGARET, 23, ASHLEY CLOSE, LOVEDEAN
WADE, MARION D, 24, ASHLEY CLOSE, LOVEDEAN
WADE, TERENCE A, 24, ASHLEY CLOSE, LOVEDEAN
CLARK, ALBERT E.J, 25, ASHLEY CLOSE, LOVEDEAN
CLARK, BERYL I, 25, ASHLEY CLOSE, LOVEDEAN
VERNON, BRIAN R, 27, ASHLEY CLOSE, LOVEDEAN
VERNON, JULIE, 27, ASHLEY CLOSE, LOVEDEAN
ROBINSON, VERA L, 29, ASHLEY CLOSE, LOVEDEAN
EDWARDS, PAUL R, 27, BEVAN ROAD, LOVEDEAN
NORTH, CLAIRE J, 27, BEVAN ROAD, LOVEDEAN
STEVENS, LYNN D, 29, BEVAN ROAD, LOVEDEAN
MARTIN, WINIFRED M, 31, BEVAN ROAD, LOVEDEAN
SUMNER, ANDREA J, 33, BEVAN ROAD, LOVEDEAN
VOYSEY, KAY, 1, BIRDLIP CLOSE, HORNDEAN
VOYSEY, TERENCE P, 1, BIRDLIP CLOSE, HORNDEAN
MULCOCK, BRIAN M, 2, BIRDLIP CLOSE, HORNDEAN
MULCOCK, PAULINE J, 2, BIRDLIP CLOSE, HORNDEAN
JERVIS, HELEN E, 3, BIRDLIP CLOSE, HORNDEAN
JOHNSON, LESLEY H, 4, BIRDLIP CLOSE, HORNDEAN
STANLEY, ALAN M, 5, BIRDLIP CLOSE, HORNDEAN
STANLEY, LINDA M, 5, BIRDLIP CLOSE, HORNDEAN
CUTTING, ROGER, 6, BIRDLIP CLOSE, HORNDEAN
CUTTING, SANDRA J, 6, BIRDLIP CLOSE, HORNDEAN
CASSELL, CHANTAL R.P, 7, BIRDLIP CLOSE, HORNDEAN
CASSELL, TERENCE M, 7, BIRDLIP CLOSE, HORNDEAN
MANLEY, KAREN M, 8, BIRDLIP CLOSE, HORNDEAN
MANLEY, LINDA, 8, BIRDLIP CLOSE, HORNDEAN
MANLEY, PETER, 8, BIRDLIP CLOSE, HORNDEAN
OVER, JEAN A, 9, BIRDLIP CLOSE, HORNDEAN
OVER, JOHN F, 9, BIRDLIP CLOSE, HORNDEAN
RILEY, JOANNE L, 10, BIRDLIP CLOSE, HORNDEAN
RILEY, RICHARD J, 10, BIRDLIP CLOSE, HORNDEAN
RILEY, SUSAN A, 10, BIRDLIP CLOSE, HORNDEAN
KAY, BARBARA, 11, BIRDLIP CLOSE, HORNDEAN
KAY, MARTIN A, 11, BIRDLIP CLOSE, HORNDEAN
KAY, SAMUEL A, 11, BIRDLIP CLOSE, HORNDEAN
WIGGINS, ANDREW J, 12, BIRDLIP CLOSE, HORNDEAN
WIGGINS, FIONA O, 12, BIRDLIP CLOSE, HORNDEAN
HILLIAM, IRIS E.O, 15, BIRDLIP CLOSE, HORNDEAN
HILLIAM, JOHN L, 15, BIRDLIP CLOSE, HORNDEAN
LOVETT, ROBIN J, 16, BIRDLIP CLOSE, HORNDEAN
LOVETT, WENDY A, 16, BIRDLIP CLOSE, HORNDEAN
ROBINSON, DEBORAH, 17, BIRDLIP CLOSE, HORNDEAN
ROBINSON, PHILIP, 17, BIRDLIP CLOSE, HORNDEAN
MOST, BRIAN H.R, 2, BLENHEIM ROAD, HORNDEAN
MOST, THERESA M, 2, BLENHEIM ROAD, HORNDEAN
DANE, JOAN W, 3, BLENHEIM ROAD, HORNDEAN
DANE, NEVILLE, 3, BLENHEIM ROAD, HORNDEAN
NASH, DAVID F, 4, BLENHEIM ROAD, HORNDEAN
NASH, DEBRA A, 4, BLENHEIM ROAD, HORNDEAN
NASH, DEIDRE Y, 4, BLENHEIM ROAD, HORNDEAN
THOMPSON, GEORGE, 5, BLENHEIM ROAD, HORNDEAN
HARRISON, DENNIS, 6, BLENHEIM ROAD, HORNDEAN
HARRISON-BROWN, MIRANDA J, 6, BLENHEIM ROAD,
TILLER, ROSEMARIE A, 7, BLENHEIM ROAD, HORNDEAN
WILSON, DAVID J, 7, BLENHEIM ROAD, HORNDEAN
WILSON, SUSAN J, 7, BLENHEIM ROAD, HORNDEAN
WHITBREAD, GLADYS M, 8, BLENHEIM ROAD, HORNDEAN
LEE, MILDRED, 9, BLENHEIM ROAD, HORNDEAN
CLOSE, FREDERICK R, 10, BLENHEIM ROAD, HORNDEAN
CLOSE, HELEN A, 10, BLENHEIM ROAD, HORNDEAN
BROWN, JEREMY J, 11, BLENHEIM ROAD, HORNDEAN
NORTH, SUZANNE E, 11, BLENHEIM ROAD, HORNDEAN
BAKER, DOUGLAS H, 12, BLENHEIM ROAD, HORNDEAN
PYSDEN, GEOFFREY A, 13, BLENHEIM ROAD, HORNDEAN
PYSDEN, VALERIE M, 13, BLENHEIM ROAD, HORNDEAN
BARRETT, ANTONY J, 14, BLENHEIM ROAD, HORNDEAN
BARRETT, CLARE, 14, BLENHEIM ROAD, HORNDEAN
BARRETT, LYNNE J, 14, BLENHEIM ROAD, HORNDEAN
BARRETT, SIMON, 14, BLENHEIM ROAD, HORNDEAN
FORD, MARIE E, 15, BLENHEIM ROAD, HORNDEAN
BENFORD, MARILYN, 16, BLENHEIM ROAD, HORNDEAN
BENFORD, MICHAEL G, 16, BLENHEIM ROAD, HORNDEAN
BEETON, JANET M, 17, BLENHEIM ROAD, HORNDEAN
BEETON, JOHN, 17, BLENHEIM ROAD, HORNDEAN
BROWN, JAMES L, 18, BLENHEIM ROAD, HORNDEAN
BROWN, JUNE E, 18, BLENHEIM ROAD, HORNDEAN
WOOLSTON, DENNIS G, 19, BLENHEIM ROAD, HORNDEAN
WOOLSTON, LESLEY M.K, 19, BLENHEIM ROAD, HORNDEAN
WOOLSTON, ROBERT J, 19, BLENHEIM ROAD, HORNDEAN
WOOLSTON, STUART D, 19, BLENHEIM ROAD, HORNDEAN
SINGLETON, ERIC J, 20, BLENHEIM ROAD, HORNDEAN
SINGLETON, RAE A, 20, BLENHEIM ROAD, HORNDEAN
SHAW, JEAN D, 21, BLENHEIM ROAD, HORNDEAN
MOORE, CHRISTOPHER, 22, BLENHEIM ROAD, HORNDEAN
PETERS, CHRISTOPHER A.R, 23, BLENHEIM ROAD,
PETERS, MARGARET A, 23, BLENHEIM ROAD, HORNDEAN
CUFFLING, GAIL, 24, BLENHEIM ROAD, HORNDEAN
CUFFLING, RONALD H, 24, BLENHEIM ROAD, HORNDEAN
EDGE, DOROTHY, 25, BLENHEIM ROAD, HORNDEAN
EDGE, IAN S, 25, BLENHEIM ROAD, HORNDEAN
ROBERTS, GRAHAM L, 26, BLENHEIM ROAD, HORNDEAN
ROBERTS, JEAN I, 26, BLENHEIM ROAD, HORNDEAN
ELLISON, LESLEY A, 28, BLENHEIM ROAD, HORNDEAN
HILLEBRANDT, MICHAEL J, 28, BLENHEIM ROAD, HORNDEAN
BURCHER, BRYAN H, 30, BLENHEIM ROAD, HORNDEAN
BURCHER, JUNE, 30, BLENHEIM ROAD, HORNDEAN
JARVIS, HARRY L, 32, BLENHEIM ROAD, HORNDEAN
JARVIS, VERA F, 32, BLENHEIM ROAD, HORNDEAN
GASTON, MARGUERITE F, 34, BLENHEIM ROAD, HORNDEAN
GASTON, RAYMOND H.E, 34, BLENHEIM ROAD, HORNDEAN
DEACON, PHYLLIS M, 36, BLENHEIM ROAD, HORNDEAN
SMITH, ANTHONY F, 38, BLENHEIM ROAD, HORNDEAN
SMITH, JENNIFER R, 38, BLENHEIM ROAD, HORNDEAN
PURSER, ALEXANDRA J.V, 40, BLENHEIM ROAD, HORNDEAN
PURSER, HARRY, 40, BLENHEIM ROAD, HORNDEAN
WATERS, DOROTHY M, 42, BLENHEIM ROAD, HORNDEAN
KEIR, COLIN A.K, 44, BLENHEIM ROAD, HORNDEAN
KEIR, DUNCAN R, 44, BLENHEIM ROAD, HORNDEAN
KEIR, VALERIE R, 44, BLENHEIM ROAD, HORNDEAN
KEIR, VERITY R, 44, BLENHEIM ROAD, HORNDEAN
CHAPMAN, CAROLINE G, 46, BLENHEIM ROAD, HORNDEAN
CHAPMAN, MILES P, 46, BLENHEIM ROAD, HORNDEAN
GRIFFEN, COLIN D, 1, BRIARFIELD GARDENS, HORNDEAN
GRIFFEN, SHARON J, 1, BRIARFIELD GARDENS, HORNDEAN
RUSHFORTH, CAROLINE A, 2, BRIARFIELD GARDENS,
RUSHFORTH, MATTHEW P, 2, BRIARFIELD GARDENS,
WARMAN, MARK R, 2, BRIARFIELD GARDENS, HORNDEAN
DOWNEY, ROBERT, 2A, BRIARFIELD GARDENS, HORNDEAN
DOWNEY, VIRGINIA E, 2A, BRIARFIELD GARDENS,
CULLEN, GEORGE A, 3, BRIARFIELD GARDENS, HORNDEAN
CULLEN, JEANETTE A, 3, BRIARFIELD GARDENS, HORNDEAN
GREEN, KENNETH R, 4, BRIARFIELD GARDENS, HORNDEAN
WILLIAMS, ABBIE, 4, BRIARFIELD GARDENS, HORNDEAN
WILLIAMS, BRYONY, 4, BRIARFIELD GARDENS, HORNDEAN
WILLIAMS, LINDA, 4, BRIARFIELD GARDENS, HORNDEAN
ENGKVIST-PARR, MONICA A.M, 5, BRIARFIELD GARDENS,
PARR, RICHARD L, 5, BRIARFIELD GARDENS, HORNDEAN
SCUTT, ALISON B, 6, BRIARFIELD GARDENS, HORNDEAN
SCUTT, ROBERT W, 6, BRIARFIELD GARDENS, HORNDEAN
COOK, GEOFFREY D, 7, BRIARFIELD GARDENS, HORNDEAN
COOK, KATHRYN E, 7, BRIARFIELD GARDENS, HORNDEAN
BUTT, ANDREW F.R, 8, BRIARFIELD GARDENS, HORNDEAN
BUTT, MAUREEN A, 8, BRIARFIELD GARDENS, HORNDEAN
WOODWARD, ARTHUR R.H, 9, BRIARFIELD GARDENS,
WOODWARD, NADINE J, 9, BRIARFIELD GARDENS,
QUINN, KATHERINE S, 10, BRIARFIELD GARDENS,
WALL, MARILYN T, 10, BRIARFIELD GARDENS, HORNDEAN
WHITTEAR, TRUDY E, 10, BRIARFIELD GARDENS, HORNDEAN
CHALMERS, GEOFFREY F, 10A, BRIARFIELD GARDENS,
CHALMERS, NANCY, 10A, BRIARFIELD GARDENS, HORNDEAN
ANDERSON, LINDSEY E, 11, BRIARFIELD GARDENS,
SMITH, BRENDA, 11, BRIARFIELD GARDENS, HORNDEAN
FISHER, DAVID J, 12, BRIARFIELD GARDENS, HORNDEAN
FISHER, SAMANTHA, 12, BRIARFIELD GARDENS, HORNDEAN
STEPHENS, KATHRYN J, 12, BRIARFIELD GARDENS,
STEPHENS, SAMUEL J, 12, BRIARFIELD GARDENS, HORNDEAN
HUGHES, PAUL A, 14, BRIARFIELD GARDENS, HORNDEAN
DOUGHTY, GRAHAM, 15, BRIARFIELD GARDENS, HORNDEAN
DOUGHTY, LISA J, 15, BRIARFIELD GARDENS, HORNDEAN
RAVEN, CAROLE A, 16, BRIARFIELD GARDENS, HORNDEAN
GRIFFIN, BARRY F, 17, BRIARFIELD GARDENS, HORNDEAN
GRIFFIN, MARK P, 17, BRIARFIELD GARDENS, HORNDEAN
GRIFFIN, WENDY A, 17, BRIARFIELD GARDENS, HORNDEAN
TUVEY, PHILLIP, 18, BRIARFIELD GARDENS, HORNDEAN
TUVEY, TRACY S, 18, BRIARFIELD GARDENS, HORNDEAN
EASTLAND, DAVID W, 19, BRIARFIELD GARDENS, HORNDEAN
WILDIG, JANETTE J.P, 19, BRIARFIELD GARDENS, HORNDEAN
NEW, MARILYN E, 20, BRIARFIELD GARDENS, HORNDEAN
NEW, MICHAEL D.M, 20, BRIARFIELD GARDENS, HORNDEAN
NEW, STEPHEN C.J, 20, BRIARFIELD GARDENS, HORNDEAN

ROUTLEY, ALAN F, 21, BRIARFIELD GARDENS, HORNDEAN
ROUTLEY, KATHLEEN, 21, BRIARFIELD GARDENS,
LINKHORN, STEPHEN R, 22, BRIARFIELD GARDENS,
PINHORNE, SARAH L, 22, BRIARFIELD GARDENS, HORNDEAN
CHERRY, JOHN S, 24, BRIARFIELD GARDENS, HORNDEAN
HANSELL, MARGARET E.R, 26, BRIARFIELD GARDENS,
WINTLE, PETER T.H, 26, BRIARFIELD GARDENS, HORNDEAN
FRICKER, ALFRED, 28, BRIARFIELD GARDENS, HORNDEAN
HOLMES, DIANE, 30, BRIARFIELD GARDENS, HORNDEAN
HOLMES, STEPHEN J, 30, BRIARFIELD GARDENS, HORNDEAN
NICHOLL, JUNE-ANNE, 32, BRIARFIELD GARDENS,
NICHOLL, VINCENT D, 32, BRIARFIELD GARDENS,
GIBSON, KENNETH N, 34, BRIARFIELD GARDENS, HORNDEAN
GIBSON, PATRICIA J, 34, BRIARFIELD GARDENS, HORNDEAN
HARRIS, DENE G, 36, BRIARFIELD GARDENS, HORNDEAN
WARREN, DIANA F, 38, BRIARFIELD GARDENS, HORNDEAN
SHEPPARD, JOYCE G.G, 1, BROADWAY COTTAGES, BROADWAY LANE, LOVEDEAN
SHEPPARD, ROBERT J, 1, BROADWAY COTTAGES, BROADWAY LANE, LOVEDEAN
FORD, JAYNE, 2, BROADWAY COTTAGES, BROADWAY LANE,
JEFFERIES, COLIN, 2, BROADWAY COTTAGES, BROADWAY LANE, LOVEDEAN
BOWELL, FLORENCE E, BROADWAY FARM HOUSE, BROADWAY LANE, LOVEDEAN
BOWELL, KENNETH A, BROADWAY FARM HOUSE, BROADWAY LANE, LOVEDEAN
PUNCHARD, CHRISTINA, BROADWAY FARMHOUSE ANNEXE, BROADWAY LANE, LOVEDEAN
HODELL, CATHERINE, BROADWAYS, BROADWAY LANE,
HODELL, JAMES A, BROADWAYS, BROADWAY LANE,
HODELL, KATHERINE G, BROADWAYS, BROADWAY LANE,
COLES, JASON K, HIGHFIELD COTTAGE, BROADWAY LANE,
COLES, KEITH D.P, HIGHFIELD COTTAGE, BROADWAY LANE,
COLES, LORAINE E, HIGHFIELD COTTAGE, BROADWAY LANE,
COLES, MARK D, HIGHFIELD COTTAGE, BROADWAY LANE,
EDWARDS, MATHEW D, THE COACH HOUSE, HINTON DAUBNAY, BROADWAY LANE, LOVEDEAN
MUNNOCH, GAVIN R.C, THE COACH HOUSE, HINTON DAUBNAY, BROADWAY LANE, LOVEDEAN
MUNNOCH, KATHRYN M, THE COACH HOUSE, HINTON DAUBNAY, BROADWAY LANE, LOVEDEAN
TURNER, HAZEL V, HOLME COTTAGE, BROADWAY LANE,
TURNER, JOHN C, HOLME COTTAGE, BROADWAY LANE,
WARREN, JEREMY F, LOWER CHAPTER, BROADWAY LANE,
WARREN, PHILIPPA J, LOWER CHAPTER, BROADWAY LANE,
LINKHORN, CHRISTOPHER J, 2, LUDMORE COTTAGES, BROADWAY LANE, LOVEDEAN
PANNELL, MARY G, 2, LUDMORE COTTAGES, BROADWAY LANE, LOVEDEAN
THORNS, BRIAN, NORTHORN, BROADWAY LANE, LOVEDEAN
THORNS, PATRICIA, NORTHORN, BROADWAY LANE,
SMITH, JANE E, THE ARROWS, BROADWAY LANE, LOVEDEAN
SMITH, SIMON R, THE ARROWS, BROADWAY LANE,
KERNAN, DAVID J, 1, BULLS COPSE LANE, HORNDEAN
KERNAN, EMMA J, 1, BULLS COPSE LANE, HORNDEAN
KERNAN, GILLIAN M, 1, BULLS COPSE LANE, HORNDEAN
KERNAN, JEREMY J, 1, BULLS COPSE LANE, HORNDEAN
PLATTS, MAUREEN M, 3, BULLS COPSE LANE, HORNDEAN
SAYNER, JOHN, 3, BULLS COPSE LANE, HORNDEAN
MULLIS, JULIE, 5, BULLS COPSE LANE, HORNDEAN
MCWHIRR, ALISON G, 7, BULLS COPSE LANE, HORNDEAN
MCWHIRR, IAN, 7, BULLS COPSE LANE, HORNDEAN
MCWHIRR, JUNE V, 7, BULLS COPSE LANE, HORNDEAN
DAUGHTREY, CHARLOTTE A.F, 9, BULLS COPSE LANE,
DAUGHTREY, JOHN C, 9, BULLS COPSE LANE, HORNDEAN
MORFORD, DAVID P, 11, BULLS COPSE LANE, HORNDEAN
MORFORD, LYNNE S, 11, BULLS COPSE LANE, HORNDEAN
BENHAM, CAROLINE J, 13, BULLS COPSE LANE, HORNDEAN
BENHAM, PETER L, 13, BULLS COPSE LANE, HORNDEAN
HAWKING, JOYCE, 14, BULLS COPSE LANE, HORNDEAN
HAWKING, RICHARD A, 14, BULLS COPSE LANE, HORNDEAN
STUBBS, ALISON M, 15, BULLS COPSE LANE, HORNDEAN
STUBBS, NEIL G, 15, BULLS COPSE LANE, HORNDEAN
CUNLIFFE, HARRY, 17, BULLS COPSE LANE, HORNDEAN
CUNLIFFE, PAULINE M, 17, BULLS COPSE LANE, HORNDEAN
DANIELLS, ANTHONY E, 21, BULLS COPSE LANE, HORNDEAN
DANIELLS, JULIE C, 21, BULLS COPSE LANE, HORNDEAN
DANIELLS, LISA J, 21, BULLS COPSE LANE, HORNDEAN
DANIELLS, SHIRLEY C, 21, BULLS COPSE LANE, HORNDEAN
COMLEY, GILLIAN R, 22, BULLS COPSE LANE, HORNDEAN
COMLEY, STEPHEN J, 22, BULLS COPSE LANE, HORNDEAN
HAYTER, SHEILA M, 23, BULLS COPSE LANE, HORNDEAN
COOPER, GORDON A, 25, BULLS COPSE LANE, HORNDEAN
COOPER, JEAN M, 25, BULLS COPSE LANE, HORNDEAN
COOPER, TIMOTHY C, 25, BULLS COPSE LANE, HORNDEAN
PARRY, JUNE T, 27, BULLS COPSE LANE, HORNDEAN
WALKER, ANNETTE J, 29, BULLS COPSE LANE, HORNDEAN
WALKER, IAN, 29, BULLS COPSE LANE, HORNDEAN
RAFFERTY, PATRICIA C, 31, BULLS COPSE LANE, HORNDEAN
RAFFERTY, PETER J, 31, BULLS COPSE LANE, HORNDEAN
BROWN, BETTY, 31A, BULLS COPSE LANE, HORNDEAN
BROWN, RONALD, 31A, BULLS COPSE LANE, HORNDEAN
BIDDLECOMBE, SELINA A, 33, BULLS COPSE LANE,
GRIFFIN, BERNARD J, 33A, BULLS COPSE LANE, HORNDEAN
GRIFFIN, SUSAN J, 33A, BULLS COPSE LANE, HORNDEAN
ESCOTT, JOYCE, 34, BULLS COPSE LANE, HORNDEAN
HIBBERD, KENNETH J, 35, BULLS COPSE LANE, HORNDEAN
HIBBERD, SHEILA V, 35, BULLS COPSE LANE, HORNDEAN
COCKING, BRIDGET A, 36, BULLS COPSE LANE, HORNDEAN
COCKING, JOHN E, 36, BULLS COPSE LANE, HORNDEAN
NORRIS, ALEXANDRA J, 37, BULLS COPSE LANE, HORNDEAN
NORRIS, ISOBEL R, 37, BULLS COPSE LANE, HORNDEAN
NORRIS, SIMON P, 37, BULLS COPSE LANE, HORNDEAN
NORRIS, STEPHEN A, 37, BULLS COPSE LANE, HORNDEAN
SADLER, GREGORY L, 38, BULLS COPSE LANE, HORNDEAN
SADLER, JULIE, 38, BULLS COPSE LANE, HORNDEAN
TODD, JANE, 38, BULLS COPSE LANE, HORNDEAN
DHILLON, GURNAM S, 39, BULLS COPSE LANE, HORNDEAN
DHILLON, RANVINDER K, 39, BULLS COPSE LANE,
DHILLON, VARINDER K, 39, BULLS COPSE LANE,
ORMONDE-DOBBIN, CHARLES A, 39A, BULLS COPSE LANE,
ORMONDE-DOBBIN, KATHERINE E, 39A, BULLS COPSE LANE,
ORMONDE-DOBBIN, VALERIE E, 39A, BULLS COPSE LANE,
HERBERT, ANNE R, 40, BULLS COPSE LANE, HORNDEAN
HERBERT, COLIN F, 40, BULLS COPSE LANE, HORNDEAN
HELLINGS, PATRICIA A, 41, BULLS COPSE LANE, HORNDEAN
RAINE, ARTHUR, 42, BULLS COPSE LANE, HORNDEAN
RAINE, WINIFRED E, 42, BULLS COPSE LANE, HORNDEAN
BENNETT, JACQUELYNNE L, 43, BULLS COPSE LANE,
BENNETT, JENNA L, 43, BULLS COPSE LANE, HORNDEAN
GRIFFITHS, DAVID, 44, BULLS COPSE LANE, HORNDEAN
GRIFFITHS, SONIA, 44, BULLS COPSE LANE, HORNDEAN
BARNES, DAVID J, 44A, BULLS COPSE LANE, HORNDEAN
BARNES, MARGARET J, 44A, BULLS COPSE LANE, HORNDEAN
BARNES, PETER J, 44A, BULLS COPSE LANE, HORNDEAN
GOODALL, DAVID N, 56, BULLS COPSE LANE, HORNDEAN
ROBINSON, CLAIRE J, 56, BULLS COPSE LANE, HORNDEAN
AYLWARD, LENA H, 57, BULLS COPSE LANE, HORNDEAN
AYLWARD, RONALD M, 57, BULLS COPSE LANE, HORNDEAN
BARTLETT, DAVID L, 58, BULLS COPSE LANE, HORNDEAN
BARTLETT, JOHN D, 58, BULLS COPSE LANE, HORNDEAN
BARTLETT, PAULINE M, 58, BULLS COPSE LANE, HORNDEAN
SEARLE, DIONE J, 59, BULLS COPSE LANE, HORNDEAN
SEARLE, MARK, 59, BULLS COPSE LANE, HORNDEAN
SWANDELL, CLAIRE, 60, BULLS COPSE LANE, HORNDEAN
SWANDELL, DOROTHY H, 60, BULLS COPSE LANE,
SWANDELL, MARTIN R, 60, BULLS COPSE LANE, HORNDEAN
SWANDELL, PATRICK, 60, BULLS COPSE LANE, HORNDEAN
SCOTT, ANNETTE, 61, BULLS COPSE LANE, HORNDEAN
SWALLOW, JONATHAN P, 62, BULLS COPSE LANE, HORNDEAN
SWALLOW, MICHAEL B, 62, BULLS COPSE LANE, HORNDEAN
SWALLOW, VALERIE, 62, BULLS COPSE LANE, HORNDEAN
TURNBULL, LAURENCE S, 63, BULLS COPSE LANE,
TURNBULL, RITA J.M, 63, BULLS COPSE LANE, HORNDEAN
KABIR, HUSNARA B, 64, BULLS COPSE LANE, HORNDEAN
KABIR, MUHAMMAD, 64, BULLS COPSE LANE, HORNDEAN
KABIR, MUHAMMAD Z, 64, BULLS COPSE LANE, HORNDEAN
KABIR, NADIA, 64, BULLS COPSE LANE, HORNDEAN
SCANLON, MARILYN D, 65, BULLS COPSE LANE, HORNDEAN
SCANLON, ROY, 65, BULLS COPSE LANE, HORNDEAN
GRAHAM, KENNETH J, 65A, BULLS COPSE LANE, HORNDEAN
NAGLER, FRIEDRICH, 68, BULLS COPSE LANE, HORNDEAN
NAGLER, MURIEL V, 68, BULLS COPSE LANE, HORNDEAN
SPENCER, JEANETTE E, 69, BULLS COPSE LANE, HORNDEAN
SPENCER, JENIFER M, 69, BULLS COPSE LANE, HORNDEAN
HAWKINS, DAMIAN P, 69A, BULLS COPSE LANE, HORNDEAN
HAWKINS, JENNIFER R, 69A, BULLS COPSE LANE, HORNDEAN
HAWKINS, PHILIP F, 69A, BULLS COPSE LANE, HORNDEAN
TRICKER, KAREN, 70, BULLS COPSE LANE, HORNDEAN
TRICKER, RAYMOND, 70, BULLS COPSE LANE, HORNDEAN
LINFIELD, CHRISTINE B, 71, BULLS COPSE LANE, HORNDEAN
LINFIELD, GREGORY T, 71, BULLS COPSE LANE, HORNDEAN
LINGFIELD, STUART D, 71, BULLS COPSE LANE, HORNDEAN
ELLIS, GEORGINA L, 71A, BULLS COPSE LANE, HORNDEAN
ELLIS, SANDRA C, 71A, BULLS COPSE LANE, HORNDEAN
HARRIS, ANGELA, 72, BULLS COPSE LANE, HORNDEAN
HARRIS, MARK P, 72, BULLS COPSE LANE, HORNDEAN
HERTING, CHARLES E, 73, BULLS COPSE LANE, HORNDEAN
HERTING, DORIS F, 73, BULLS COPSE LANE, HORNDEAN
FRY, ANTHONY J, 74, BULLS COPSE LANE, HORNDEAN
FRY, THERESA M, 74, BULLS COPSE LANE, HORNDEAN
WEST, ANNE, 75, BULLS COPSE LANE, HORNDEAN
DODGE, JOAN T, 76, BULLS COPSE LANE, HORNDEAN
ROBINSON, JENNIFER A, 77, BULLS COPSE LANE, HORNDEAN
VOKES, HAYLEY A, 77, BULLS COPSE LANE, HORNDEAN
HYAMS, SCOTT J, 78, BULLS COPSE LANE, HORNDEAN
INGAL, CHRISTOPHER, 78, BULLS COPSE LANE, HORNDEAN
PERKINS, KENNETH J, 79, BULLS COPSE LANE, HORNDEAN
PERKINS, PAMELA J, 79, BULLS COPSE LANE, HORNDEAN
LACEY, ANTHONY R, 80, BULLS COPSE LANE, HORNDEAN
LACEY, LYNN, 80, BULLS COPSE LANE, HORNDEAN
WADE, ANNETTE S.R, 82, BULLS COPSE LANE, HORNDEAN
PETERS, ALEC A, 84, BULLS COPSE LANE, HORNDEAN
PETERS, SUSAN J, 84, BULLS COPSE LANE, HORNDEAN
RADCLIFFE, DAVID J.C, HINTON BUNGALOW, CATHERINGTON
RADCLIFFE, PAULA, HINTON BUNGALOW, CATHERINGTON
COOPER, HANNAH J, HINTON HEIGHTS, CATHERINGTON
COOPER, MARION, HINTON HEIGHTS, CATHERINGTON
COOPER, MICHAEL S, HINTON HEIGHTS, CATHERINGTON
EVANS, ANNE R, HINTON MANOR COTTAGE, CATHERINGTON
EVANS, LAURA A, HINTON MANOR COTTAGE, CATHERINGTON
EVANS, RICHARD M.W, HINTON MANOR COTTAGE, CATHERINGTON
PINHORN, CHRISTINE, HINTON MANOR HOUSE, CATHERINGTON
PINHORN, WALTER E, HINTON MANOR HOUSE, CATHERINGTON
MORTON, JENNIFER C, LONE BARN FARM, CATHERINGTON
MORTON, JOHN E, LONE BARN FARM, CATHERINGTON
MORTON, RICHARD M, LONE BARN FARM, CATHERINGTON
FENNELL, CLAIRE M, 1, CATHERINGTON LANE, HORNDEAN
FENNELL, LEONARD E, 1, CATHERINGTON LANE, HORNDEAN
HAYDEN, HELEN L, 1A, CATHERINGTON LANE, HORNDEAN
MCDERMOTT, MARIE, 1B, CATHERINGTON LANE,
MAY, ANTONY M, 3, CATHERINGTON LANE, HORNDEAN
MAY, GILLIAN H, 3, CATHERINGTON LANE, HORNDEAN
HALL, GLENN R, 5, CATHERINGTON LANE, HORNDEAN
HEIGHTLEY, CINDY, 5, CATHERINGTON LANE, HORNDEAN
CHILDS, DAVID E, 7, CATHERINGTON LANE, HORNDEAN
FERRIS, PATRICIA A, 7, CATHERINGTON LANE, HORNDEAN
BUDD, MAUREEN L, 9, CATHERINGTON LANE, HORNDEAN
BUDD, RAYMOND J, 9, CATHERINGTON LANE, HORNDEAN
RIVOALLON, JEROME, 11, CATHERINGTON LANE, HORNDEAN
RIVOALLON, SANDRA, 11, CATHERINGTON LANE,
BEVES, FREDERICK D, 13, CATHERINGTON LANE,
COUZENS, PAMELA, 13, CATHERINGTON LANE, HORNDEAN
BOWERS, CHRISTOPHER A, 15, CATHERINGTON LANE,
BOWERS, GERALDINE I, 15, CATHERINGTON LANE,
BOWERS, REBECCA A, 15, CATHERINGTON LANE, HORNDEAN
HOOPER, JOSEPH J, 15, CATHERINGTON LANE, HORNDEAN
CARY, HELENA M, 15A, CATHERINGTON LANE, HORNDEAN
CARY, IAN D, 15A, CATHERINGTON LANE, HORNDEAN
PAYNE, JOANNE, 21, CATHERINGTON LANE, HORNDEAN
ABEL, IAN T, 23, CATHERINGTON LANE, HORNDEAN
ABEL, LINDA T, 23, CATHERINGTON LANE, HORNDEAN
NIMMONS, MICHAELA J, 23A, CATHERINGTON LANE,
CAMERON, MARY, 25, CATHERINGTON LANE, HORNDEAN
WORRALL, JULIE A, 27, CATHERINGTON LANE, HORNDEAN
BARNETT, DANIEL G, 31, CATHERINGTON LANE, HORNDEAN
BOYLAND, MICHELLE, 37B, CATHERINGTON LANE,
TYLER, JAMES H, 39, CATHERINGTON LANE, HORNDEAN
COLE, ALBERT P, 41, CATHERINGTON LANE, HORNDEAN
KEY, JANET M, 43, CATHERINGTON LANE, HORNDEAN
KEY, SHAUN M, 43, CATHERINGTON LANE, HORNDEAN
PECKHAM, DORIS M, 45, CATHERINGTON LANE, HORNDEAN
THOMAS, DAVID G, 47, CATHERINGTON LANE, HORNDEAN
THOMAS, RITA, 47, CATHERINGTON LANE, HORNDEAN
MACRAE, ANDREW C, 51, CATHERINGTON LANE, HORNDEAN
MACRAE, SARAH L, 51, CATHERINGTON LANE, HORNDEAN
STEEL, MARINA C, 53, CATHERINGTON LANE, HORNDEAN
EAMES, DAPHNE M.N, 55, CATHERINGTON LANE, HORNDEAN
MERRIVALE, IRIS I, 57, CATHERINGTON LANE, HORNDEAN
MERRIVALE, MICHAEL A, 57, CATHERINGTON LANE,
MERRIVALE, SIMON A, 57, CATHERINGTON LANE,
FENN, ALAN D, 59, CATHERINGTON LANE, HORNDEAN
FENN, PAULINE A, 59, CATHERINGTON LANE, HORNDEAN
KEWELL, KEVIN J, 61, CATHERINGTON LANE, HORNDEAN
KEWELL, SUSAN C, 61, CATHERINGTON LANE, HORNDEAN
CROUCH, BARTON K, 63, CATHERINGTON LANE, HORNDEAN
CROUCH, BERYL R, 63, CATHERINGTON LANE, HORNDEAN
KELLY, KATHLEEN M, 67, CATHERINGTON LANE, HORNDEAN
KINSELLA, LORETTA M, 69, CATHERINGTON LANE,
HERRINGTON, MARJORIE M, 71, CATHERINGTON LANE,
HOBBS, PAMELA J, 73, CATHERINGTON LANE, HORNDEAN
KOHLER, DOROTHY J, 75, CATHERINGTON LANE,
KOHLER, REGINALD D, 75, CATHERINGTON LANE,
BARBER, DIANE, 77, CATHERINGTON LANE,
BARBER, ROBERT D.C, 77, CATHERINGTON LANE,
TURNER, JANE, 77, CATHERINGTON LANE,
WICKHAM, RONALD C, 77, CATHERINGTON LANE,
BROWN, JEAN V, 79, CATHERINGTON LANE, HORNDEAN
BROWN, LEONARD R, 79, CATHERINGTON LANE, HORNDEAN
SAUNDERS, WINIFRED R, 81, CATHERINGTON LANE,
FLETCHER, GRAHAM, 83, CATHERINGTON LANE, HORNDEAN
FLETCHER, SHEILA R, 83, CATHERINGTON LANE, HORNDEAN
REYNOLDS, AVRIL J, 89, CATHERINGTON LANE, HORNDEAN
REYNOLDS, CHRISTOPHER J, 89, CATHERINGTON LANE,
ANDERSON, CAROLINE M, 91, CATHERINGTON LANE,
ANDERSON, THOMAS R, 91, CATHERINGTON LANE,
LOFTUS, BRENDAN P, 93, CATHERINGTON LANE, HORNDEAN
LOFTUS, PAULINA A, 93, CATHERINGTON LANE, HORNDEAN
PLIMMER, JOHN F, 95, CATHERINGTON LANE, HORNDEAN
PLIMMER, PENELOPE J, 95, CATHERINGTON LANE,
TITHERADGE, ELSIE, 97, CATHERINGTON LANE, HORNDEAN
TITHERADGE, JOAN L, 97, CATHERINGTON LANE,
ALLEN, STANLEY R, 99, CATHERINGTON LANE, HORNDEAN
ALLEN, SUSANNAH G, 99, CATHERINGTON LANE, HORNDEAN
ROZZELL, BRENDA E, 101, CATHERINGTON LANE,
ROZZELL, BRIAN, 101, CATHERINGTON LANE, HORNDEAN
ROZZELL, SIMON L, 101, CATHERINGTON LANE, HORNDEAN
MALLISON, MARK J, 103, CATHERINGTON LANE, HORNDEAN
LANGDON, JILL H, 105, CATHERINGTON LANE, HORNDEAN
LANGDON, TREVOR P, 105, CATHERINGTON LANE,
RICH, DAVID L, 107, CATHERINGTON LANE, HORNDEAN
RICH, DONALD M.J, 107, CATHERINGTON LANE, HORNDEAN
BLAKELEY, PATRICIA, 109, CATHERINGTON LANE,
BLAKELEY, TREVOR, 109, CATHERINGTON LANE, HORNDEAN
ROBERTS, CHRISTOPHER H, 111, CATHERINGTON LANE,
ROBERTS, MARGARET P.O, 111, CATHERINGTON LANE,
TARIQ, SALINA, 113, CATHERINGTON LANE, HORNDEAN
TARIQ, SYED M, 113, CATHERINGTON LANE, HORNDEAN
BUTT, ELEANORE R, 115, CATHERINGTON LANE, HORNDEAN
OLIVER, GORDON, 1, CHERITON CLOSE, HORNDEAN
OLIVER, JULIE A, 1, CHERITON CLOSE, HORNDEAN
FRANKLIN, CELIA M, 2, CHERITON CLOSE, HORNDEAN
FRANKLIN, PETER H, 2, CHERITON CLOSE, HORNDEAN
LEECH, JOHN F, 3, CHERITON CLOSE, HORNDEAN
LEECH, MARGARET E, 3, CHERITON CLOSE, HORNDEAN
ROBERTS, KATHLEEN, 4, CHERITON CLOSE, HORNDEAN
THOM, GRAEME J.A, 5, CHERITON CLOSE, HORNDEAN
THOM, LAURA M.V, 5, CHERITON CLOSE, HORNDEAN
THOM, RUTH E, 5, CHERITON CLOSE, HORNDEAN
PEMBERTON, HOWARD J, 6, CHERITON CLOSE, HORNDEAN
PEMBERTON, JENNIFER K, 6, CHERITON CLOSE, HORNDEAN
DUGGAN, JOY K, 7, CHERITON CLOSE, HORNDEAN

Electoral Roll

DUGGAN, RACHEL E, 7, CHERITON CLOSE, HORNDEAN
DUGGAN, TERENCE V, 7, CHERITON CLOSE, HORNDEAN
EFFORD, COLIN J, 8, CHERITON CLOSE, HORNDEAN
EFFORD, GABRIELLE N, 8, CHERITON CLOSE, HORNDEAN
STAPLETON, ALEXANDRA C, 9, CHERITON CLOSE, HORNDEAN
STAPLETON, BARRY, 9, CHERITON CLOSE, HORNDEAN
WHITE, JOAN W, 10, CHERITON CLOSE, HORNDEAN
MANN, DAVID R, GRANDVIEW, CLANFIELD
MANN, TRACEY F, GRANDVIEW, CLANFIELD
MCKNIGHT, SIMONE, TIPLEN GREEN FARM HOUSE, CLANFIELD
WHITE, ANTHONY D, TIPLEN GREEN FARM HOUSE,
WHITE, MARGARET E, TIPLEN GREEN FARM HOUSE,
BENDA, FRANK, COLDHILL FARM HOUSE, COLDHILL LANE, LOVEDEAN
BRAND, CHRISTOPHER N, HAYBARN HOUSE, COLDHILL LANE, LOVEDEAN
BRAND, DIANA, HAYBARN HOUSE, COLDHILL LANE,
SMITH, FELIX J.W, HEDGEROWS, COLDHILL LANE,
RASHID, JOSEPHINE E.D, HIGH TREES, COLDHILL LANE,
RASHID, KHAN G, HIGH TREES, COLDHILL LANE, LOVEDEAN
RASHID, SAEED K, HIGH TREES, COLDHILL LANE, LOVEDEAN
CHARLTON, ESMEE F.M, HILL VIEW, COLDHILL LANE,
CHARLTON, PETER W.N, HILL VIEW, COLDHILL LANE,
LEWIS, CAROLINE A, HILL VIEW, COLDHILL LANE, LOVEDEAN
LEWIS, JACQUELINE A.F, HILL VIEW, COLDHILL LANE,
LEWIS, ROBERT G, HILL VIEW, COLDHILL LANE, LOVEDEAN
HORNE, JANE, RINSEY COTTAGE, COLDHILL LANE,
HORNE, NICHOLAS J, RINSEY COTTAGE, COLDHILL LANE,
ROSE, MATTHEW G, WESSEX, COLDHILL LANE, LOVEDEAN
ROSE, MICHELLE V, WESSEX, COLDHILL LANE, LOVEDEAN
PACKER, KAREN L, 1, THE COPPICE, HORNDEAN
PACKER, WILLIAM, 1, THE COPPICE, HORNDEAN
KNOTT, CAROL A, 2, THE COPPICE, HORNDEAN
KNOTT, RAYMOND E, 2, THE COPPICE, HORNDEAN
MOORE, ALAN, 3, THE COPPICE, HORNDEAN
MOORE, BENJAMIN A, 3, THE COPPICE, HORNDEAN
MOORE, LESLEY P, 3, THE COPPICE, HORNDEAN
SAUNDERS, LORRAINE, 4, THE COPPICE, HORNDEAN
SAUNDERS, RAYMOND V, 4, THE COPPICE, HORNDEAN
BOWMAN, RAYMOND J, 5, THE COPPICE, HORNDEAN
MITCHELL, SUSAN C, 5, THE COPPICE, HORNDEAN
ADEY, SIMON, 6, THE COPPICE, HORNDEAN
GARNETT, SANDRA E, 7, THE COPPICE, HORNDEAN
GARNETT, TERENCE J, 7, THE COPPICE, HORNDEAN
KONIECZNY, ANTHONY J, 8, THE COPPICE, HORNDEAN
KONIECZNY, FELICITY A, 8, THE COPPICE, HORNDEAN
PETERS, BRIAN P, 9, THE COPPICE, HORNDEAN
PETERS, HAYLEY L, 9, THE COPPICE, HORNDEAN
PETERS, SUSAN M, 9, THE COPPICE, HORNDEAN
HARDING, GARRY P, 10, THE COPPICE, HORNDEAN
HARDING, LINDA G, 10, THE COPPICE, HORNDEAN
MOORE, NICOLA, 11, THE COPPICE, HORNDEAN
O'CONNOR, MARGARET C, 12, THE COPPICE, HORNDEAN
TUCKER, NEILL, 13, THE COPPICE, HORNDEAN
HOLLANDS, DAPHNE P.A, 14, THE COPPICE, HORNDEAN
HOLLANDS, STANLEY A.W, 14, THE COPPICE, HORNDEAN
WHEELER, ANDREW R, 15, THE COPPICE, HORNDEAN
WHEELER, JULIE A, 15, THE COPPICE, HORNDEAN
WERNHAM, ANDREW J, 16, THE COPPICE, HORNDEAN
WERNHAM, HELEN M, 16, THE COPPICE, HORNDEAN
LINDSTEDT, GAVIN R, 17, THE COPPICE, HORNDEAN
LINDSTEDT, LYNDA A, 17, THE COPPICE, HORNDEAN
INWOOD, DAVID, 18, THE COPPICE, HORNDEAN
INWOOD, TINA L, 18, THE COPPICE, HORNDEAN
HEDGELAND, JANE C, 19, THE COPPICE, HORNDEAN
HEDGELAND, PETER J, 19, THE COPPICE, HORNDEAN
MACNALLY, AMANDA L, 1, CHURCHILL COURT, THE COPPICE, HORNDEAN
MACNALLY, KEIR, 1, CHURCHILL COURT, THE COPPICE,
ELLIS, NICOLA G, 2, CHURCHILL COURT, THE COPPICE,
ELLIS, NORMAN, 2, CHURCHILL COURT, THE COPPICE,
HARD, CHRISTOPHER M, 3, CHURCHILL COURT, THE COPPICE, HORNDEAN
HARD, DEBORAH A, 3, CHURCHILL COURT, THE COPPICE,
ROBERTS, BRENDAN F, 4, CHURCHILL COURT, THE COPPICE,
ROBERTS, PAULA J, 4, CHURCHILL COURT, THE COPPICE,
SPARROW, PETER W, 21, THE COPPICE, HORNDEAN
SPARROW, SHEILA, 21, THE COPPICE, HORNDEAN
CAKE, DENISE J, 22, THE COPPICE, HORNDEAN
DONALDSON, EMMA J, 24, THE COPPICE, HORNDEAN
DONALDSON, HELEN L, 24, THE COPPICE, HORNDEAN
DONALDSON, MALCOLM J, 24, THE COPPICE, HORNDEAN
DONALDSON, MARGARET E, 24, THE COPPICE, HORNDEAN
WHITE, ANTHONY G, 25, THE COPPICE, HORNDEAN
WHITE, VALERIE J, 25, THE COPPICE, HORNDEAN
CARPENTER, JULIE L, 26, THE COPPICE, HORNDEAN
SCUTT, DONALD G.J, 26, THE COPPICE, HORNDEAN
COCKETT, MARK A, 27, THE COPPICE, HORNDEAN
COCKETT, ROSEMARY, 27, THE COPPICE, HORNDEAN
BALL, ROGER, 28, THE COPPICE, HORNDEAN
BALL, SANDRA A, 28, THE COPPICE, HORNDEAN
SMY, BARBARA C, 29, THE COPPICE, HORNDEAN
SMY, ROBERT M, 29, THE COPPICE, HORNDEAN
SMY, TREVOR, 29, THE COPPICE, HORNDEAN
HALES, RODNEY H, 30, THE COPPICE, HORNDEAN
SIMPSON, AMY E, 30, THE COPPICE, HORNDEAN
SIMPSON, CAROLYN A, 30, THE COPPICE, HORNDEAN
ASTLE, HELEN, 31, THE COPPICE, HORNDEAN
ASTLE, SIMON P, 31, THE COPPICE, HORNDEAN
GURNEY, JONATHAN J.H, 32, THE COPPICE, HORNDEAN
GURNEY, LINDSEY J, 32, THE COPPICE, HORNDEAN
WARWICKER, COLIN H, 33, THE COPPICE, HORNDEAN
WARWICKER, VALERIE P, 33, THE COPPICE, HORNDEAN
MCPHEE, DAVID J, 34, THE COPPICE, HORNDEAN
MCPHEE, GWENDOLINE F, 34, THE COPPICE, HORNDEAN
BALL, JACQUELINE, 35, THE COPPICE, HORNDEAN
BALL, NICHOLAS 5-11-1999, 35, THE COPPICE, HORNDEAN
ORCHARD, DARREN B, 36, THE COPPICE, HORNDEAN
ROBERTSON, ROBERT, 36, THE COPPICE, HORNDEAN
ROBERTSON, VIVIENNE M, 36, THE COPPICE, HORNDEAN
BARRESI, MARGARET, 37, THE COPPICE, HORNDEAN
WILDIG, EDWARD G, 1, CROSS LANE, HORNDEAN
WILDIG, ISABELLA, 1, CROSS LANE, HORNDEAN
RUDDOCK, GWYNETH M, 2, CROSS LANE, HORNDEAN
RUDDOCK, LESLIE M, 2, CROSS LANE, HORNDEAN
TURNER, JENNIFER A, 3, CROSS LANE, HORNDEAN
TURNER, KENNETH W, 3, CROSS LANE, HORNDEAN
COTTON, PATRICIA J, 4, CROSS LANE, HORNDEAN
COTTON, RAYMOND H, 4, CROSS LANE, HORNDEAN
STEVENSON, LAVINIA J, 5, CROSS LANE, HORNDEAN
STEVENSON, PETER, 5, CROSS LANE, HORNDEAN
HARRIS, LILIAN K, 6, CROSS LANE, HORNDEAN
NORMAN, GEORGE C, 7, CROSS LANE, HORNDEAN
MORT, BERYL J, 8, CROSS LANE, HORNDEAN
MORT, COLIN J, 8, CROSS LANE, HORNDEAN
WICKES, ANDREW W, 9, CROSS LANE, HORNDEAN
WICKES, GLORIA F, 9, CROSS LANE, HORNDEAN
FOSTER, EUNICE M, 10, CROSS LANE, HORNDEAN
FOSTER, THOMAS W, 10, CROSS LANE, HORNDEAN
NEVITT, CELIA M, 11, CROSS LANE, HORNDEAN
NEVITT, TERENCE F, 11, CROSS LANE, HORNDEAN
MCDERMOTT, LILIAN R, 12, CROSS LANE, HORNDEAN
MCDERMOTT, VICTOR J, 12, CROSS LANE, HORNDEAN
GROVE, ARTHUR G, 13, CROSS LANE, HORNDEAN
GROVE, GERALDINE L.E, 13, CROSS LANE, HORNDEAN
HUTCHINSON, ERICA A, 14, CROSS LANE, HORNDEAN
HUTCHINSON, WILLIAM, 14, CROSS LANE, HORNDEAN
LIMBURN, EMMA-CLAIRE, 1, CROSSBILL CLOSE, HORNDEAN
LIMBURN, JACQUELINE J, 1, CROSSBILL CLOSE, HORNDEAN
LIMBURN, KENNETH R, 1, CROSSBILL CLOSE, HORNDEAN
MAJOR, ALAN D, 2, CROSSBILL CLOSE, HORNDEAN
MAJOR, MARILYN, 2, CROSSBILL CLOSE, HORNDEAN
MENDONCA, DEREK O, 3, CROSSBILL CLOSE, HORNDEAN
MENDONCA, KIM M, 3, CROSSBILL CLOSE, HORNDEAN
WASHTELL, SUSAN A, 4, CROSSBILL CLOSE, HORNDEAN
HOLDER, KELLY-MARIE, 5, CROSSBILL CLOSE, HORNDEAN
KEEN, GRACE, 6, CROSSBILL CLOSE, HORNDEAN
CAMPBELL, ANDREW, 7, CROSSBILL CLOSE, HORNDEAN
HINGSTON, FIONA A, 7, CROSSBILL CLOSE, HORNDEAN
FRASER, JENNIFER A, 8, CROSSBILL CLOSE, HORNDEAN
CARTER, BARBARA A, 9, CROSSBILL CLOSE, HORNDEAN
CARTER, BENJAMIN C, 9, CROSSBILL CLOSE, HORNDEAN
HOWARD, CHARLES W, 10, CROSSBILL CLOSE, HORNDEAN
HOWARD, DORIS E, 10, CROSSBILL CLOSE, HORNDEAN
BLUNT, JOANNA F, 12, CROSSBILL CLOSE, HORNDEAN
BLUNT, SUSAN E, 12, CROSSBILL CLOSE, HORNDEAN
HEASMAN, DOUGLAS A, 14, CROSSBILL CLOSE, HORNDEAN
HEASMAN, GWYNETH L, 14, CROSSBILL CLOSE, HORNDEAN
HENDERSON, JANE L, 14, CROSSBILL CLOSE, HORNDEAN
HAMBLIN, EMILY J, 15, CROSSBILL CLOSE, HORNDEAN
CUSHION, JOHN, 1, THE CURVE, LOVEDEAN
CUSHION, SUSAN A, 1, THE CURVE, LOVEDEAN
TRIPP, BRIAN D, 1A, THE CURVE, LOVEDEAN
TRIPP, GERALDINE A, 1A, THE CURVE, LOVEDEAN
CHRISTIE, ARTHUR W, 1B, THE CURVE, LOVEDEAN
CHRISTIE, RITA M.G, 1B, THE CURVE, LOVEDEAN
WRIGHT, HELEN A.W, 2, THE CURVE, LOVEDEAN
WRIGHT, STEPHANIE J, 2, THE CURVE, LOVEDEAN
WRIGHT, TREVOR L, 2, THE CURVE, LOVEDEAN
HOLDSWORTH, IAN D, 3, THE CURVE, LOVEDEAN
HOLDSWORTH, JENNIFER A, 3, THE CURVE, LOVEDEAN
BUCKNOLE, ANDREW I, 4, THE CURVE, LOVEDEAN
BUCKNOLE, SUSAN C, 4, THE CURVE, LOVEDEAN
MURRAY, AMANDA L, 5, THE CURVE, LOVEDEAN
MURRAY, PAUL C, 5, THE CURVE, LOVEDEAN
HARVEY, BETTY I, 6, THE CURVE, LOVEDEAN
WALKER, BRIAN, 7, THE CURVE, LOVEDEAN
WALKER, MARGARET E, 7, THE CURVE, LOVEDEAN
TASKER, MOLLY I, 7A, THE CURVE, LOVEDEAN
TASKER, VAUGHAN O, 7A, THE CURVE, LOVEDEAN
BROOK, ANGELA J, 8, THE CURVE, LOVEDEAN
BROOK, COLIN A, 8, THE CURVE, LOVEDEAN
MEW, FREDERICK J, 9, THE CURVE, LOVEDEAN
MEW, ROSEMARY, 9, THE CURVE, LOVEDEAN
LOGAN, RONALD, 10, THE CURVE, LOVEDEAN
LOGAN, ROSE, 10, THE CURVE, LOVEDEAN
DENNETT, ALAN, 11, THE CURVE, LOVEDEAN
DENNETT, SUSANNE R, 11, THE CURVE, LOVEDEAN
BERRY, DAVID T, 12, THE CURVE, LOVEDEAN
BERRY, NICOLA J, 12, THE CURVE, LOVEDEAN
BEADLE, JACK A.E, 13, THE CURVE, LOVEDEAN
BEADLE, VERA E, 13, THE CURVE, LOVEDEAN
COOPER, RHONDDA M, 13, THE CURVE, LOVEDEAN
COOPER, ROBERT D, 13, THE CURVE, LOVEDEAN
CLARKE, ROLAND L, 14, THE CURVE, LOVEDEAN
BATE, ROBERT J, 15, THE CURVE, LOVEDEAN
SMITH, SHEILA A, 15, THE CURVE, LOVEDEAN
HOPKINS, ROBIN J, 16, THE CURVE, LOVEDEAN
GORMAN, CELIA M, 17, THE CURVE, LOVEDEAN
GORMAN, ROBIN V.G, 17, THE CURVE, LOVEDEAN
RUSSELL, ELIZABETH A, 18, THE CURVE, LOVEDEAN
RUSSELL, JOHN, 18, THE CURVE, LOVEDEAN
RUSSELL, KATE M, 18, THE CURVE, LOVEDEAN
LOVERSIDGE, JEANNE D.E, 19, THE CURVE, LOVEDEAN
THORNHILL, MARK J, 20, THE CURVE, LOVEDEAN
MUNDEN, ARTHUR D, 21, THE CURVE, LOVEDEAN
MUNDEN, DAVID M, 21, THE CURVE, LOVEDEAN
MUNDEN, JOAN F, 21, THE CURVE, LOVEDEAN
STRAY, ANTHONY D, 22, THE CURVE, LOVEDEAN
STRAY, DENISE M, 22, THE CURVE, LOVEDEAN
STRAY, JOHN D.A, 22, THE CURVE, LOVEDEAN
STONE, MARTIN D, 23, THE CURVE, LOVEDEAN
STREET, ALISON J, 25, THE CURVE, LOVEDEAN
STREET, DAVID, 25, THE CURVE, LOVEDEAN
CRAUFURD, SALLY A, 26, THE CURVE, LOVEDEAN
RYDER, PETER J, 27, THE CURVE, LOVEDEAN
RYDER, SUSAN M, 27, THE CURVE, LOVEDEAN
DOPSON, KAREN E, 28, THE CURVE, LOVEDEAN
DOPSON, PAUL R, 28, THE CURVE, LOVEDEAN
USHER, DEREK M.S, 29, THE CURVE, LOVEDEAN
USHER, PAULINE J, 29, THE CURVE, LOVEDEAN
NICHOLS, LILIAN R, 30, THE CURVE, LOVEDEAN
WILTSHIRE, DAVID J, 31, THE CURVE, LOVEDEAN
WILTSHIRE, ELAINE T, 31, THE CURVE, LOVEDEAN
SANDY, MARIA, 32, THE CURVE, LOVEDEAN
SANDY, PAUL A, 32, THE CURVE, LOVEDEAN
O'BYRNE, PATRICK, 1, CYPRESS CRESCENT, LOVEDEAN
O'BYRNE, THERESA M, 1, CYPRESS CRESCENT, LOVEDEAN
LANGWORTHY, LORRAINE, 2, CYPRESS CRESCENT,
LANGWORTHY, PETER L, 2, CYPRESS CRESCENT, LOVEDEAN
O'SMOTHERLY, CHRISTOPHER D, 3, CYPRESS CRESCENT,
O'SMOTHERLY, PETER J, 3, CYPRESS CRESCENT, LOVEDEAN
O'SMOTHERLY, RICHARD J, 3, CYPRESS CRESCENT,
O'SMOTHERLY, SHARON, 3, CYPRESS CRESCENT, LOVEDEAN
STOCKTON, SUSAN K, 4, CYPRESS CRESCENT, LOVEDEAN
JACKSON, MARK, 5, CYPRESS CRESCENT, LOVEDEAN
JACKSON, TINA H.L, 5, CYPRESS CRESCENT, LOVEDEAN
COOPER, KEITH L.R, 6, CYPRESS CRESCENT, LOVEDEAN
BEWICK, SUZANNE M, 7, CYPRESS CRESCENT, LOVEDEAN
CHAPPELL, KERRY A, 7, CYPRESS CRESCENT, LOVEDEAN
RIDLEY, EMMA L, 9, CYPRESS CRESCENT, LOVEDEAN
RIDLEY, PAULINE E, 9, CYPRESS CRESCENT, LOVEDEAN
THUNDERCLIFFE, LEE D, 10, CYPRESS CRESCENT, LOVEDEAN
THUNDERCLIFFE, NICOLA J, 10, CYPRESS CRESCENT,
DRINAN, PAT, 11, CYPRESS CRESCENT, LOVEDEAN
DRINAN, THOMAS P, 11, CYPRESS CRESCENT, LOVEDEAN
BURROUGHS, JACQUELINE, 12, CYPRESS CRESCENT,
HASKELL, ADAM L, 13, CYPRESS CRESCENT, LOVEDEAN
HASKELL, IAIN G, 13, CYPRESS CRESCENT, LOVEDEAN
HASKELL, SHARON C, 13, CYPRESS CRESCENT, LOVEDEAN
MORREY, MARGARET E, 14, CYPRESS CRESCENT, LOVEDEAN
MORREY, VIVIAN G.C, 14, CYPRESS CRESCENT, LOVEDEAN
STEWART, GRAEME A, 15, CYPRESS CRESCENT, LOVEDEAN
STEWART, MARGARET S, 15, CYPRESS CRESCENT, LOVEDEAN
STEWART, NICOLA C, 15, CYPRESS CRESCENT, LOVEDEAN
BRIGHT, JEFFREY J, 16, CYPRESS CRESCENT, LOVEDEAN
EVERITT, BARBARA A, 17, CYPRESS CRESCENT, LOVEDEAN
FOOKS, MARC J, 18, CYPRESS CRESCENT, LOVEDEAN
FOOKS, PAULINE, 18, CYPRESS CRESCENT, LOVEDEAN
GRIFFITHS, CAROL A, 24, CYPRESS CRESCENT, LOVEDEAN
GRIFFITHS, JAMES P, 24, CYPRESS CRESCENT, LOVEDEAN
WHITLOCK, CLAIRE L, 25, CYPRESS CRESCENT, LOVEDEAN
WHITLOCK, SUSAN M, 25, CYPRESS CRESCENT, LOVEDEAN
WRIGHT, ANDREW S, 26, CYPRESS CRESCENT, LOVEDEAN
WRIGHT, MICHAEL, 26, CYPRESS CRESCENT, LOVEDEAN
WATKYN, ANTHONY J, 27, CYPRESS CRESCENT, LOVEDEAN
WATKYN, SARAH J, 27, CYPRESS CRESCENT, LOVEDEAN
ARMSTRONG, HEIDI M, 28, CYPRESS CRESCENT, LOVEDEAN
MCEWAN, ANDREW A, 28, CYPRESS CRESCENT, LOVEDEAN
DOWBAKIN, PETER M, 29, CYPRESS CRESCENT, LOVEDEAN
DOWBAKIN, SALLY, 29, CYPRESS CRESCENT, LOVEDEAN
KELLY, CHRISTINE, 30, CYPRESS CRESCENT, LOVEDEAN
WESTON, DAVID, 30, CYPRESS CRESCENT, LOVEDEAN
WESTON, IAN D, 30, CYPRESS CRESCENT, LOVEDEAN
CAINE, DENISE, 33, CYPRESS CRESCENT, LOVEDEAN
CAINE, NICHOLAS J, 33, CYPRESS CRESCENT, LOVEDEAN
CARTER, ANDREW J, 34, CYPRESS CRESCENT, LOVEDEAN
CARTER, DAWN L, 34, CYPRESS CRESCENT, LOVEDEAN
SACKETT, CARL M, 35, CYPRESS CRESCENT, LOVEDEAN
SACKETT, JUDY L, 35, CYPRESS CRESCENT, LOVEDEAN
DUFFIELD, SUZANNE E, 36, CYPRESS CRESCENT, LOVEDEAN
FERRONI, JULIE, 37, CYPRESS CRESCENT, LOVEDEAN
FERRONI, PAUL A, 37, CYPRESS CRESCENT, LOVEDEAN
HALL, ANDREW J, 38, CYPRESS CRESCENT, LOVEDEAN
HALL, JEAN A, 38, CYPRESS CRESCENT, LOVEDEAN
GRIFFIN, KRISTELLE S, 39, CYPRESS CRESCENT, LOVEDEAN
GRIFFIN, MICHAEL R, 39, CYPRESS CRESCENT, LOVEDEAN
PROCTOR, ROSEMARY A, 40, CYPRESS CRESCENT, LOVEDEAN
PROCTOR, STEPHEN, 40, CYPRESS CRESCENT, LOVEDEAN
SLARK, DENISE, 41, CYPRESS CRESCENT, LOVEDEAN
SLARK, STEVEN J, 41, CYPRESS CRESCENT, LOVEDEAN
SHIPTON, ALAN M, 42, CYPRESS CRESCENT, LOVEDEAN
SHIPTON, DAVID J, 42, CYPRESS CRESCENT, LOVEDEAN
SHIPTON, MARK, 42, CYPRESS CRESCENT, LOVEDEAN
SHIPTON, SUSAN P, 42, CYPRESS CRESCENT, LOVEDEAN
MAXFIELD, GEOFFREY C, 43, CYPRESS CRESCENT, LOVEDEAN
MAXFIELD, MARGARET P, 43, CYPRESS CRESCENT,
HANSON, MALCOLM A.D, BOUNDARY COTTAGE, DAY LANE,
HANSON, MAUREEN J, BOUNDARY COTTAGE, DAY LANE,
HANSON, ROBERT D, BOUNDARY COTTAGE, DAY LANE,
RAWSON, KATHLEEN M, GLENGARRY, DAY LANE, LOVEDEAN
HALL, COLIN D, HILLCROFT, DAY LANE, LOVEDEAN
HARVEY, ERIC C, HILLSIDE, DAY LANE, LOVEDEAN
HARVEY, URSULA E, HILLSIDE, DAY LANE, LOVEDEAN
FURNAESS, ANTHONY B, WAYSIDE, DAY LANE, LOVEDEAN
TURNER, BARRY S, WHITE GATE, DAY LANE, LOVEDEAN
TURNER, HANNAH K, WHITE GATE, DAY LANE, LOVEDEAN

TURNER, PAULINE J, WHITE GATE, DAY LANE, LOVEDEAN
TURNER, STUART B, WHITE GATE, DAY LANE, LOVEDEAN
MILLAR, JOHN R, 1, EASTLAND GATE, LOVEDEAN
MILLAR, ROSEMARY M, 1, EASTLAND GATE, LOVEDEAN
ALEXANDER, RAYMOND J, 3, EASTLAND GATE, LOVEDEAN
ALEXANDER, SHEILA M, 3, EASTLAND GATE, LOVEDEAN
GRANT-SMITH, MAUREEN A, 2, EASTLAND GATE, LOVEDEAN
SMITH, STEPHEN J, 2, EASTLAND GATE, LOVEDEAN
WILSON, ANDREW H, BROADWAY LODGE, EASTLAND GATE,
WILSON, CHRISTINE P, BROADWAY LODGE, EASTLAND GATE,
WILSON, EMILY C, BROADWAY LODGE, EASTLAND GATE,
BELL, PETER D.O, EASTLAND GATE HOUSE, EASTLAND GATE,
FARWELL, DENISE A, EASTLAND GATE HOUSE, EASTLAND GATE, LOVEDEAN
NICHOLS, CHRISTOPHER, YEW TREE COTTAGE, EASTLAND GATE, LOVEDEAN
NICHOLS, ROGER, YEW TREE COTTAGE, EASTLAND GATE,
NICHOLS, YVONNE V, YEW TREE COTTAGE, EASTLAND GATE, LOVEDEAN
WEST, GARY K, 1, ELMESWELLE ROAD, LOVEDEAN
WEST, LYN, 1, ELMESWELLE ROAD, LOVEDEAN
COLWELL, CATHERINE L, 2, ELMESWELLE ROAD, LOVEDEAN
COLWELL, STEPHEN M, 2, ELMESWELLE ROAD, LOVEDEAN
OATES, IAN M, 3, ELMESWELLE ROAD, LOVEDEAN
OATES, JOAN E, 3, ELMESWELLE ROAD, LOVEDEAN
OATES, PAUL R, 3, ELMESWELLE ROAD, LOVEDEAN
OATES, RICHARD H, 3, ELMESWELLE ROAD, LOVEDEAN
OATES, SARAH J, 3, ELMESWELLE ROAD, LOVEDEAN
SALTER, KAREN J, 4, ELMESWELLE ROAD, LOVEDEAN
EVANS, ALISON J, 5, ELMESWELLE ROAD, LOVEDEAN
EVANS, NORMAN, 5, ELMESWELLE ROAD, LOVEDEAN
WINGATE, DOREEN, 6, ELMESWELLE ROAD, LOVEDEAN
BARNETT, JAMES C, 7, ELMESWELLE ROAD, LOVEDEAN
BARNETT, MARIA L, 7, ELMESWELLE ROAD, LOVEDEAN
PARRY, CHRISTOPHER M, 8, ELMESWELLE ROAD, LOVEDEAN
COLEMAN, JENNIFER M, 9, ELMESWELLE ROAD, LOVEDEAN
ROBERTSON, CRAIG R, 9, ELMESWELLE ROAD, LOVEDEAN
VOLLER, DAVID J, 10, ELMESWELLE ROAD, LOVEDEAN
VOLLER, JEAN R, 10, ELMESWELLE ROAD, LOVEDEAN
VOLLER, PAUL E, 10, ELMESWELLE ROAD, LOVEDEAN
KIERSTENSON, JANET, 11, ELMESWELLE ROAD, LOVEDEAN
KIERSTENSON, JEFFREY, 11, ELMESWELLE ROAD, LOVEDEAN
CURTIS, STEPHEN M, 12, ELMESWELLE ROAD, LOVEDEAN
LOGAN, BARRY W, 12, ELMESWELLE ROAD, LOVEDEAN
LOGAN, EMMA-JANE, 12, ELMESWELLE ROAD, LOVEDEAN
RIGBY, TAMMY L, 13, ELMESWELLE ROAD, LOVEDEAN
RIGBY, TERENCE, 13, ELMESWELLE ROAD, LOVEDEAN
HARRIS, NEIL P, 14, ELMESWELLE ROAD, LOVEDEAN
TAYLOR, JEANETTE S, 14, ELMESWELLE ROAD, LOVEDEAN
TAYLOR, PHILIP A, 14, ELMESWELLE ROAD, LOVEDEAN
SIMMONS, DEBORAH A, 15, ELMESWELLE ROAD, LOVEDEAN
SNASHALL, KEITH J, 16, ELMESWELLE ROAD, LOVEDEAN
SNASHALL, VALERIE, 16, ELMESWELLE ROAD, LOVEDEAN
RAWLINGS, NIGEL D, 17, ELMESWELLE ROAD, LOVEDEAN
RAWLINGS, SALLY A, 17, ELMESWELLE ROAD, LOVEDEAN
WARWICK, MARGARET E, 18, ELMESWELLE ROAD, LOVEDEAN
WARWICK, ROBERT K, 18, ELMESWELLE ROAD, LOVEDEAN
MAYE, ELAINE, 19, ELMESWELLE ROAD, LOVEDEAN
MAYE, JOHNATHAN L, 19, ELMESWELLE ROAD, LOVEDEAN
PETHER, BRIAN, 20, ELMESWELLE ROAD, LOVEDEAN
PETHER, JEAN A, 20, ELMESWELLE ROAD, LOVEDEAN
PETHER, LISA A, 20, ELMESWELLE ROAD, LOVEDEAN
FYTCHE, BRYAN E, 21, ELMESWELLE ROAD, LOVEDEAN
FYTCHE, DAVID R, 21, ELMESWELLE ROAD, LOVEDEAN
FYTCHE, SUSAN E.J, 21, ELMESWELLE ROAD, LOVEDEAN
WOODWARD, DEBORAH J, 22, ELMESWELLE ROAD,
WOODWARD, STEWART R, 22, ELMESWELLE ROAD,
LEE, SHIRLEY H, 23, ELMESWELLE ROAD, LOVEDEAN
TAYLOR, JOHN M, 24, ELMESWELLE ROAD, LOVEDEAN
TAYLOR, TRACEY L, 24, ELMESWELLE ROAD, LOVEDEAN
MARLOW, CAROL, 25, ELMESWELLE ROAD, LOVEDEAN
MARLOW, JOY-ANNE H, 25, ELMESWELLE ROAD, LOVEDEAN
MARLOW, TREVOR G, 25, ELMESWELLE ROAD, LOVEDEAN
GALLOWAY, MARTIN D, 26, ELMESWELLE ROAD, LOVEDEAN
GALLOWAY, TINA M, 26, ELMESWELLE ROAD, LOVEDEAN
JOHNS, ANTHONY M, 27, ELMESWELLE ROAD, LOVEDEAN
JOHNS, KIM E, 27, ELMESWELLE ROAD, LOVEDEAN
HANSLER, ROSALIND W, 28, ELMESWELLE ROAD, LOVEDEAN
HANSLER, SILVIA H, 28, ELMESWELLE ROAD, LOVEDEAN
BRAMHALL, CLARE E, 29, ELMESWELLE ROAD, LOVEDEAN
BRAMHALL, DAVID S, 29, ELMESWELLE ROAD, LOVEDEAN
BRAMHALL, PATRICIA J, 29, ELMESWELLE ROAD, LOVEDEAN
THOMSON, PAUL, 31, ELMESWELLE ROAD, LOVEDEAN
STOCK, ALEXANDER L, 33, ELMESWELLE ROAD, LOVEDEAN
STOCK, WENDY P, 33, ELMESWELLE ROAD, LOVEDEAN
MILLARD, JASON P, 35, ELMESWELLE ROAD, LOVEDEAN
MILLARD, KERRIE 21-12-1999, 35, ELMESWELLE ROAD,
MILLARD, PETER E, 35, ELMESWELLE ROAD, LOVEDEAN
MILLARD, RUSSELL, 35, ELMESWELLE ROAD, LOVEDEAN
MILLARD, YVONNE E, 35, ELMESWELLE ROAD, LOVEDEAN
DANN, ROBERT T, 1, EPERSTON ROAD, LOVEDEAN
CARPENTER, MARTIN R, 2, EPERSTON ROAD, LOVEDEAN
CARPENTER, VERA D, 2, EPERSTON ROAD, LOVEDEAN
GIBBONS, GEORGINA L, 4, EPERSTON ROAD, LOVEDEAN
GIBBONS, JANET M, 4, EPERSTON ROAD, LOVEDEAN
WHEELER, COLIN L, 6, EPERSTON ROAD, LOVEDEAN
WHEELER, ROBERT L, 6, EPERSTON ROAD, LOVEDEAN
WHEELER, ROSEMARY A, 6, EPERSTON ROAD, LOVEDEAN
HARPER, IVY W, 8, EPERSTON ROAD, LOVEDEAN
HARPER, REGINALD E.G, 8, EPERSTON ROAD, LOVEDEAN
BEVES, ANITA, 10, EPERSTON ROAD, LOVEDEAN
BEVES, ROGER J, 10, EPERSTON ROAD, LOVEDEAN
EKBERG, JUNE L, 12, EPERSTON ROAD, LOVEDEAN
CRESSWELL, ERICA, 14, EPERSTON ROAD, LOVEDEAN
CRESSWELL, VICTOR M, 14, EPERSTON ROAD, LOVEDEAN
O'CONNOR, DUANE M, 14, EPERSTON ROAD, LOVEDEAN
HORROCKS, CHRISTOPHER C, 1, FALCON ROAD, HORNDEAN
HORROCKS, MARION E, 1, FALCON ROAD, HORNDEAN
BOUGHTON, KAREN, 2, FALCON ROAD, HORNDEAN
BOUGHTON, PETER A.R, 2, FALCON ROAD, HORNDEAN
BATTEN, MICHAEL J, 3, FALCON ROAD, HORNDEAN
BATTEN, WENDY J, 3, FALCON ROAD, HORNDEAN
DENT, EMILY C, 4, FALCON ROAD, HORNDEAN
DENT, FRANCES M, 4, FALCON ROAD, HORNDEAN
DENT, FREDERICK E, 4, FALCON ROAD, HORNDEAN
DENT, SOPHIE M, 4, FALCON ROAD, HORNDEAN
NELSON, GRANT A, 6, FALCON ROAD, HORNDEAN
NELSON, MARGARET E, 6, FALCON ROAD, HORNDEAN
NELSON, TIMOTHY B, 6, FALCON ROAD, HORNDEAN
MOULD, TERENCE, 8, FALCON ROAD, HORNDEAN
SOUTHWELL, DEBORAH Y, 8, FALCON ROAD, HORNDEAN
WADE, ELIZABETH G, 10, FALCON ROAD, HORNDEAN
WADE, MARK C, 10, FALCON ROAD, HORNDEAN
ROMASZ, ANTONI M, 11, FALCON ROAD, HORNDEAN
ROMASZ, YVETTE N, 11, FALCON ROAD, HORNDEAN
ORTON, IAN W, 12, FALCON ROAD, HORNDEAN
ORTON, JULIET, 12, FALCON ROAD, HORNDEAN
SOUTHWELL, BARRY, 12, FALCON ROAD, HORNDEAN
EBDON, ALISON J, 14, FALCON ROAD, HORNDEAN
EBDON, BARRY G, 14, FALCON ROAD, HORNDEAN
HARRIS, HELEN L, 15, FALCON ROAD, HORNDEAN
HARRIS, PAUL J, 15, FALCON ROAD, HORNDEAN
FITZGERALD, ANTHONY P, 16, FALCON ROAD, HORNDEAN
FITZGERALD, OLIVE R, 16, FALCON ROAD, HORNDEAN
FITZGERALD, PAUL A, 16, FALCON ROAD, HORNDEAN
MCMILLAN, CLAIRE D, 17, FALCON ROAD, HORNDEAN
MCMILLAN, PETER R, 17, FALCON ROAD, HORNDEAN
HUNT, ANN T, 18, FALCON ROAD, HORNDEAN
HUNT, IAN P, 18, FALCON ROAD, HORNDEAN
WHITEHOUSE, CAROLINE L, 1, FARMHOUSE WAY, HORNDEAN
WHITEHOUSE, DAVID E, 1, FARMHOUSE WAY, HORNDEAN
WHITEHOUSE, PETER C, 1, FARMHOUSE WAY, HORNDEAN
BARR, MARK L, 2, FARMHOUSE WAY, HORNDEAN
BARR, SUSAN J, 2, FARMHOUSE WAY, HORNDEAN
BACK, JONATHAN P, 3, FARMHOUSE WAY, HORNDEAN
HARPER, ALAN, 4, FARMHOUSE WAY, HORNDEAN
HARPER, JUDITH C, 4, FARMHOUSE WAY, HORNDEAN
BARLOW, LORNA A, 5, FARMHOUSE WAY, HORNDEAN
HERBERT, CHARLES V, 6, FARMHOUSE WAY, HORNDEAN
HERBERT, MURIEL, 6, FARMHOUSE WAY, HORNDEAN
THOMPSON, HAZEL C, 7, FARMHOUSE WAY, HORNDEAN
THOMPSON, ROGER D, 7, FARMHOUSE WAY, HORNDEAN
PUDDICK, KAREN L, 8, FARMHOUSE WAY, HORNDEAN
PUDDICK, KEVIN R, 8, FARMHOUSE WAY, HORNDEAN
ROTHERAM, DAVID J, 8A, FARMHOUSE WAY, HORNDEAN
ROTHERAM, THERESA, 8A, FARMHOUSE WAY, HORNDEAN
BEE, CHERYL A, 9, FARMHOUSE WAY, HORNDEAN
BEE, MICHAEL J, 9, FARMHOUSE WAY, HORNDEAN
PITCHFORD, DAVID A, 9, FARMHOUSE WAY, HORNDEAN
PITCHFORD, RACHEL, 9, FARMHOUSE WAY, HORNDEAN
BARRETT, BEVERLEY J, 10, FARMHOUSE WAY, HORNDEAN
FOTHERGILL, GEORGE R, 10, FARMHOUSE WAY, HORNDEAN
FOTHERGILL, ZOE L, 10, FARMHOUSE WAY, HORNDEAN
GANTER, STEPHEN A, 10A, FARMHOUSE WAY, HORNDEAN
GANTER, SUSAN F, 10A, FARMHOUSE WAY, HORNDEAN
COUCH, ANNA M, 11, FARMHOUSE WAY, HORNDEAN
ANDERSON, IRENE T, 11A, FARMHOUSE WAY, HORNDEAN
ANDERSON, PETER J, 11A, FARMHOUSE WAY, HORNDEAN
EMERY, FRANCIS M, 12, FARMHOUSE WAY, HORNDEAN
EMERY, VICTOR P, 12, FARMHOUSE WAY, HORNDEAN
FOY, LINDA A, 12A, FARMHOUSE WAY, HORNDEAN
FOY, MICHAEL C, 12A, FARMHOUSE WAY, HORNDEAN
CLARKSON, CAROLINE L, 14, FARMHOUSE WAY, HORNDEAN
CLARKSON, KRISTIAN E, 14, FARMHOUSE WAY, HORNDEAN
EDGELL, JASON P, 14A, FARMHOUSE WAY, HORNDEAN
BANFIELD, MARTIN, 15, FARMHOUSE WAY, HORNDEAN
MOLLOY, MANDY J, 15, FARMHOUSE WAY, HORNDEAN
WASS, KEVIN M, 15A, FARMHOUSE WAY, HORNDEAN
PRATT, SUSAN C, 16, FARMHOUSE WAY, HORNDEAN
LAWRENCE, RICHARD J, 16A, FARMHOUSE WAY, HORNDEAN
DONOVAN, CHRISTOPHER J, 17, FARMHOUSE WAY,
DONOVAN, LYNN, 17, FARMHOUSE WAY, HORNDEAN
DONOVAN, PAUL, 17, FARMHOUSE WAY, HORNDEAN
TAYLOR, CHARLES L, 18, FARMHOUSE WAY, HORNDEAN
TAYLOR, NORMA E, 18, FARMHOUSE WAY, HORNDEAN
MCBRIDE, KAREN M, 19, FARMHOUSE WAY, HORNDEAN
MCBRIDE, MARTIN, 19, FARMHOUSE WAY, HORNDEAN
FITZGERALD, BRIAN K, 20, FARMHOUSE WAY, HORNDEAN
FITZGERALD, CRAIG, 20, FARMHOUSE WAY, HORNDEAN
FITZGERALD, DENISE, 20, FARMHOUSE WAY, HORNDEAN
EASON, CLAIRE E, 21, FARMHOUSE WAY, HORNDEAN
TAYLOR, RICHARD C, 21, FARMHOUSE WAY, HORNDEAN
POPE, LOUISE S, 22, FARMHOUSE WAY, HORNDEAN
POPE, PAUL D, 22, FARMHOUSE WAY, HORNDEAN
WORLEY, GRAHAM A, 23, FARMHOUSE WAY, HORNDEAN
WORLEY, RACHEL, 23, FARMHOUSE WAY, HORNDEAN
GOULD, ELIZABETH P, 24, FARMHOUSE WAY, HORNDEAN
GOULD, MAURICE, 24, FARMHOUSE WAY, HORNDEAN
BROWN, ADRIAN C, 75, FROGMORE LANE, LOVEDEAN
BROWN, JUDITH E, 75, FROGMORE LANE, LOVEDEAN
EDWARDS, STEVEN P, 77, FROGMORE LANE, LOVEDEAN
EVERED, KIM M, 77, FROGMORE LANE, LOVEDEAN
FINCH, IAN J, 79, FROGMORE LANE, LOVEDEAN
PARKER, CAROL A, 79, FROGMORE LANE, LOVEDEAN
PARKER, JANE C, 79, FROGMORE LANE, LOVEDEAN
PARKER, RONALD D, 79, FROGMORE LANE, LOVEDEAN
REEVE, DAVID, 81, FROGMORE LANE, LOVEDEAN
REEVE, IRENE, 81, FROGMORE LANE, LOVEDEAN
DALE, LILIAN, 83, FROGMORE LANE, LOVEDEAN
DALE, MALCOLM F.G, 83, FROGMORE LANE, LOVEDEAN
SCHRIMSHAW, DAVID H, 85, FROGMORE LANE, LOVEDEAN
SCHRIMSHAW, GAIL M, 85, FROGMORE LANE, LOVEDEAN
HIGGINS, INEZ, 87, FROGMORE LANE, LOVEDEAN
BROTHERTON, JULIAN, 113, FROGMORE LANE, LOVEDEAN
BROTHERTON, MAUREEN, 113, FROGMORE LANE, LOVEDEAN
BROTHERTON, STUART A, 113, FROGMORE LANE, LOVEDEAN
LESTER, CHRISTOPHER, 115, FROGMORE LANE, LOVEDEAN
LESTER, HANDAN, 115, FROGMORE LANE, LOVEDEAN
ATKINS, GARY C, 117, FROGMORE LANE, LOVEDEAN
ATKINS, VALERIE E, 117, FROGMORE LANE, LOVEDEAN
BOXALL, DEREK J, 121, FROGMORE LANE, LOVEDEAN
BOXALL, THERESA M, 121, FROGMORE LANE, LOVEDEAN
BEUZEVAL, JULIA A, 123, FROGMORE LANE, LOVEDEAN
BEUZEVAL, TERENCE G, 123, FROGMORE LANE, LOVEDEAN
RUSHTON, LIDIA D, 123, FROGMORE LANE, LOVEDEAN
RUSHTON, NICOLA A, 123, FROGMORE LANE, LOVEDEAN
BELL, ANDREW K, 125, FROGMORE LANE, LOVEDEAN
BELL, PATRICIA, 125, FROGMORE LANE, LOVEDEAN
TOLLIDAY, JANET P, 127, FROGMORE LANE, LOVEDEAN
TOLLIDAY, RAYMOND G, 127, FROGMORE LANE, LOVEDEAN
HALLINGTON, CHRISTINE, 129, FROGMORE LANE,
HALLINGTON, JAMES A, 129, FROGMORE LANE, LOVEDEAN
GIBBS, JOANNE L, 131, FROGMORE LANE, LOVEDEAN
GIBBS, LORRAINE, 131, FROGMORE LANE, LOVEDEAN
GIBBS, MICHELLE T, 131, FROGMORE LANE, LOVEDEAN
GIBBS, ROY, 131, FROGMORE LANE, LOVEDEAN
BALDWIN, KEVIN, 133, FROGMORE LANE, LOVEDEAN
BALDWIN, SUSAN V, 133, FROGMORE LANE, LOVEDEAN
MORRISON, IAN C, 135, FROGMORE LANE, LOVEDEAN
MORRISON, MOLLIE, 135, FROGMORE LANE, LOVEDEAN
MARTIN, PETER H, 137, FROGMORE LANE, LOVEDEAN
MARTIN, REBECCA S, 137, FROGMORE LANE, LOVEDEAN
MARTIN, SUSAN C, 137, FROGMORE LANE, LOVEDEAN
PEARCEY, ERIC R, 139, FROGMORE LANE, LOVEDEAN
KIRK, HELEN L, 143, FROGMORE LANE, LOVEDEAN
KIRK, JOHN F, 143, FROGMORE LANE, LOVEDEAN
KIRK, SIMON J, 143, FROGMORE LANE, LOVEDEAN
KIRK, STEPHEN J, 143, FROGMORE LANE, LOVEDEAN
WILLIAMS, CHRISTOPHER V, 145, FROGMORE LANE,
WILLIAMS, SUSAN C, 145, FROGMORE LANE, LOVEDEAN
FISHER, CAROL V, 147, FROGMORE LANE, LOVEDEAN
PINNOCK, DAVID J, 147, FROGMORE LANE, LOVEDEAN
FOLEY, FRANK A, 149, FROGMORE LANE, LOVEDEAN
FOLEY, VIOLET, 149, FROGMORE LANE, LOVEDEAN
FORD, TREVOR R, 153, FROGMORE LANE, LOVEDEAN
MURRAY, HEATHER L, 153, FROGMORE LANE, LOVEDEAN
MURRAY, LYNDSAY V, 153, FROGMORE LANE, LOVEDEAN
RENTON, ANTHONY D, 153, FROGMORE LANE, LOVEDEAN
RENTON, MARGARET L, 153, FROGMORE LANE, LOVEDEAN
EARLY, DAVID J, 155, FROGMORE LANE, LOVEDEAN
EARLY, VALERIE A, 155, FROGMORE LANE, LOVEDEAN
HUGHES, JOHN, 157, FROGMORE LANE, LOVEDEAN
HUGHES, SHEILA D, 157, FROGMORE LANE, LOVEDEAN
PETTER, MADELEINE D, 161, FROGMORE LANE, LOVEDEAN
WATT, CAROLINE H.F, 161, FROGMORE LANE, LOVEDEAN
CAVEY, DAVID W, 163, FROGMORE LANE, LOVEDEAN
CAVEY, MARGARET I.C, 163, FROGMORE LANE, LOVEDEAN
CAVEY, PAUL E, 163, FROGMORE LANE, LOVEDEAN
DOMMERSEN, BRIAN R, 165, FROGMORE LANE, LOVEDEAN
DOMMERSEN, SHEILA M, 165, FROGMORE LANE, LOVEDEAN
MACAULAY, BEN, 167, FROGMORE LANE, LOVEDEAN
MACAULAY, DONALD A.M, 167, FROGMORE LANE, LOVEDEAN
MACAULAY, JOAN, 167, FROGMORE LANE, LOVEDEAN
MACAULAY, MATTHEW A, 167, FROGMORE LANE, LOVEDEAN
MACAULAY, ROBERT W, 167, FROGMORE LANE, LOVEDEAN
HOPKINS, GRAHAM P, 169, FROGMORE LANE, LOVEDEAN
HOPKINS, COLIN R, 171, FROGMORE LANE, LOVEDEAN
HOPKINS, JOAN M, 171, FROGMORE LANE, LOVEDEAN
BEECH, PAUL C, 173, FROGMORE LANE, LOVEDEAN
SMITH, SHARON, 173, FROGMORE LANE, LOVEDEAN
LOCKWOOD, DENNIS, 175, FROGMORE LANE, LOVEDEAN
LOCKWOOD, PENELOPE A, 175, FROGMORE LANE,
STOCKS, JOAN, 175, FROGMORE LANE, LOVEDEAN
BLACK, IAN G, 72, FROGMORE LANE, LOVEDEAN
BLACK, LETITIA A.G, 72, FROGMORE LANE, LOVEDEAN
REYNOLDS, ELSPETH J, 74, FROGMORE LANE, LOVEDEAN
REYNOLDS, KEVIN A, 74, FROGMORE LANE, LOVEDEAN
TOWNSEND, VICTOR F.G, 76, FROGMORE LANE, LOVEDEAN
TOWNSEND, VIVIENNE R, 76, FROGMORE LANE, LOVEDEAN
MCCHEYNE, JACQUELINE, 78, FROGMORE LANE, LOVEDEAN
MCCHEYNE, JOHN S, 78, FROGMORE LANE, LOVEDEAN
LEE, ANNE K, 80, FROGMORE LANE, LOVEDEAN
PALMER, LUISA A, 80A, FROGMORE LANE, LOVEDEAN
PALMER, MATTHEW D, 80A, FROGMORE LANE, LOVEDEAN
UPTON, DENNIS R, 82, FROGMORE LANE, LOVEDEAN
MANSFIELD, MICHAEL J, 84, FROGMORE LANE, LOVEDEAN
WILLIAMS, PAUL M, 1, APPLEGATE PLACE, FROGMORE LANE,
WILSON, SARAH L, 1, APPLEGATE PLACE, FROGMORE LANE,
SPINKS, GEOFFREY A, 2, APPLEGATE PLACE, FROGMORE LANE, LOVEDEAN
CASSELL, CLAIRE L, 3, APPLEGATE PLACE, FROGMORE LANE,
LONG, ANTHONY S, 3, APPLEGATE PLACE, FROGMORE LANE,
EMERY, CLARE J, 4, APPLEGATE PLACE, FROGMORE LANE,
EMERY, MARK C, 4, APPLEGATE PLACE, FROGMORE LANE,
GALAVERNA, LINA, 5, APPLEGATE PLACE, FROGMORE LANE,
GALAVERNA, SERGIO, 5, APPLEGATE PLACE, FROGMORE LANE, LOVEDEAN
DUFFY, RIA J, 1, GOLDCREST CLOSE, HORNDEAN

Electoral Roll

DUFFY, ROBERT W, 1, GOLDCREST CLOSE, HORNDEAN
DUFFY, SUSAN C, 1, GOLDCREST CLOSE, HORNDEAN
ENGLISH, CRAIG J, 2, GOLDCREST CLOSE, HORNDEAN
ENGLISH, LISA J, 2, GOLDCREST CLOSE, HORNDEAN
BRINDLEY, DAVID, 3, GOLDCREST CLOSE, HORNDEAN
BRINDLEY, JOANNE L, 3, GOLDCREST CLOSE, HORNDEAN
DICKIE, GRAHAM T, 4, GOLDCREST CLOSE, HORNDEAN
SHARPE, TREVOR, 5, GOLDCREST CLOSE, HORNDEAN
EVANS, HELEN L, 6, GOLDCREST CLOSE, HORNDEAN
EVANS, IESTYN W, 6, GOLDCREST CLOSE, HORNDEAN
STRUGNELL, LISA J, 7, GOLDCREST CLOSE, HORNDEAN
STUBBS, GARY, 7, GOLDCREST CLOSE, HORNDEAN
PACE, SAMANTHA, 8, GOLDCREST CLOSE, HORNDEAN
PACE, STEPHEN J, 8, GOLDCREST CLOSE, HORNDEAN
PICKEN, JANE F, 9, GOLDCREST CLOSE, HORNDEAN
WELBY, NICHOLAS J, 9, GOLDCREST CLOSE, HORNDEAN
PINHORN, KATHLEEN W, 10, GOLDCREST CLOSE, HORNDEAN
PINHORN, LEONARD, 10, GOLDCREST CLOSE, HORNDEAN
FORD, KEVIN, 11, GOLDCREST CLOSE, HORNDEAN
FORD, KIM, 11, GOLDCREST CLOSE, HORNDEAN
BUTLER, ANITA B, 12, GOLDCREST CLOSE, HORNDEAN
BUTLER, KEITH R, 12, GOLDCREST CLOSE, HORNDEAN
STILES, KATE R, 14, GOLDCREST CLOSE, HORNDEAN
MEIKLE, MARGARET S, 15, GOLDCREST CLOSE, HORNDEAN
COPPING, REBECCA J, 16, GOLDCREST CLOSE, HORNDEAN
LUFF, CHRISTOPHER M, 16, GOLDCREST CLOSE, HORNDEAN
BOXALL, ALISON L, 17, GOLDCREST CLOSE, HORNDEAN
SMITH, WAYNE R, 17, GOLDCREST CLOSE, HORNDEAN
FRANCIS, GAVIN I, 18, GOLDCREST CLOSE, HORNDEAN
HOLDING, JEFFREY T, 18, GOLDCREST CLOSE, HORNDEAN
CASTLE, SUSAN J, 19, GOLDCREST CLOSE, HORNDEAN
CREAMER, GILLIAN, 20, GOLDCREST CLOSE, HORNDEAN
GRUNDY, DARRELL, 20, GOLDCREST CLOSE, HORNDEAN
BROWN, JEAN M, 21, GOLDCREST CLOSE, HORNDEAN
STRANGE, DAVID J, THE SWALLOWS, HAM LANE, CATHERINGTON
STRANGE, HELEN E, THE SWALLOWS, HAM LANE,
DE SILVA, DEBORAH L, 1, HARRIER CLOSE, HORNDEAN
DE SILVA, GEOFFREY T, 1, HARRIER CLOSE, HORNDEAN
ATWAL, MAJOR S, 2, HARRIER CLOSE, HORNDEAN
ATWAL, MANJEET K, 2, HARRIER CLOSE, HORNDEAN
HILLMAN, LYNN H, 3, HARRIER CLOSE, HORNDEAN
HILLMAN, MARK S, 3, HARRIER CLOSE, HORNDEAN
HILLMAN, STEPHEN D, 3, HARRIER CLOSE, HORNDEAN
BALL, JANICE M, 4, HARRIER CLOSE, HORNDEAN
BALL, MICHAEL J, 4, HARRIER CLOSE, HORNDEAN
CATON, JOHNATHAN J, 5, HARRIER CLOSE, HORNDEAN
CATON, JONATHAN L, 5, HARRIER CLOSE, HORNDEAN
CATON, LAURA J, 5, HARRIER CLOSE, HORNDEAN
CATON, SUSAN, 5, HARRIER CLOSE, HORNDEAN
KEMBLE, CAROLYN J, 6, HARRIER CLOSE, HORNDEAN
KEMBLE, SIMON P, 6, HARRIER CLOSE, HORNDEAN
BOWER, GLYN K, 7, HARRIER CLOSE, HORNDEAN
BOWER, JACQUELINE E, 7, HARRIER CLOSE, HORNDEAN
PAVEY, TRUDI A, 8, HARRIER CLOSE, HORNDEAN
TULL, BARRY P, 8, HARRIER CLOSE, HORNDEAN
THOMSON, KATHRYN, 9, HARRIER CLOSE, HORNDEAN
PROSSER, DEREK J, 10, HARRIER CLOSE, HORNDEAN
PROSSER, NICOLA J, 10, HARRIER CLOSE, HORNDEAN
PARKINS, STEPHEN J, 11, HARRIER CLOSE, HORNDEAN
PARKINS, VIVIENE F, 11, HARRIER CLOSE, HORNDEAN
WARE, KEITH W, 12, HARRIER CLOSE, HORNDEAN
WARE, TERESA A, 12, HARRIER CLOSE, HORNDEAN
PRIOR, JANE, 14, HARRIER CLOSE, HORNDEAN
PRIOR, KEVIN, 14, HARRIER CLOSE, HORNDEAN
TRIVEDI, MANEESHI, 15, HARRIER CLOSE, HORNDEAN
TRIVEDI, SHASHI, 15, HARRIER CLOSE, HORNDEAN
HARTLEY, DAVID, 16, HARRIER CLOSE, HORNDEAN
HARTLEY, LISA, 16, HARRIER CLOSE, HORNDEAN
HARTLEY, SUSAN E, 16, HARRIER CLOSE, HORNDEAN
BRACHER, BRIAN E, 17, HARRIER CLOSE, HORNDEAN
BRACHER, LOUISE J, 17, HARRIER CLOSE, HORNDEAN
CHARTER, DANIEL L, 18, HARRIER CLOSE, HORNDEAN
CHARTER, HOWARD J, 18, HARRIER CLOSE, HORNDEAN
CHARTER, LISA C, 18, HARRIER CLOSE, HORNDEAN
CLOUD, ANDREW J, 19, HARRIER CLOSE, HORNDEAN
CLOUD, JANICE, 19, HARRIER CLOSE, HORNDEAN
TEGG, CHRISTOPHER M, 20, HARRIER CLOSE, HORNDEAN
MASON, CHRISTOPHER P, 21, HARRIER CLOSE, HORNDEAN
MASON, HELEN, 21, HARRIER CLOSE, HORNDEAN
MASON, TERENCE C, 21, HARRIER CLOSE, HORNDEAN
SCOTT, BARBARA, 22, HARRIER CLOSE, HORNDEAN
SCOTT, WILLIAM, 22, HARRIER CLOSE, HORNDEAN
GUY, BRIAN E, 23, HARRIER CLOSE, HORNDEAN
GUY, CHRISTOPHER B, 23, HARRIER CLOSE, HORNDEAN
GUY, DAVID E, 23, HARRIER CLOSE, HORNDEAN
GUY, GLYNIS E, 23, HARRIER CLOSE, HORNDEAN
GUY, HANNAH, 23, HARRIER CLOSE, HORNDEAN
SAMPSON, JUNE M, 24, HARRIER CLOSE, HORNDEAN
SAMPSON, KELLY M, 24, HARRIER CLOSE, HORNDEAN
SAMPSON, MARK K, 24, HARRIER CLOSE, HORNDEAN
SAMPSON, TERENCE M, 24, HARRIER CLOSE, HORNDEAN
DUCK, CATHERINE A, 25, HARRIER CLOSE, HORNDEAN
DUCK, MARTIN P, 25, HARRIER CLOSE, HORNDEAN
BROOKFIELD, CATHERINE S, 26, HARRIER CLOSE,
BROOKFIELD, GORDON F, 26, HARRIER CLOSE, HORNDEAN
BROOKFIELD, JONATHON P, 26, HARRIER CLOSE, HORNDEAN
BROOKFIELD, YVONNE C, 26, HARRIER CLOSE, HORNDEAN
STRAWBRIDGE, ANDREW, 27, HARRIER CLOSE, HORNDEAN
STRAWBRIDGE, DEBORAH S, 27, HARRIER CLOSE,
WEST, JOHN R, 28, HARRIER CLOSE, HORNDEAN
WEST, MARY A, 28, HARRIER CLOSE, HORNDEAN
WEST, ROBERT M, 28, HARRIER CLOSE, HORNDEAN

SHOLTO-DOUGLAS, NEAL A, 29, HARRIER CLOSE,
SHOLTO-DOUGLAS, VIVIEN C, 29, HARRIER CLOSE,
WITHERS, ANDREW, OLD LODGE, HINTON DAUBNAY, LOVEDEAN
WITHERS, BRIAN W, OLD LODGE, HINTON DAUBNAY,
WITHERS, STEVEN, OLD LODGE, HINTON DAUBNAY,
WITHERS, WENDY M, OLD LODGE, HINTON DAUBNAY,
HUNT, MARION J, LITTLE LODGE FARM, HINTON MANOR ROAD, LOVEDEAN
HUNT, NICOLA J, LITTLE LODGE FARM, HINTON MANOR ROAD, LOVEDEAN
HUNT, RACHEL S, LITTLE LODGE FARM, HINTON MANOR ROAD, LOVEDEAN
HUNT, RONALD J, LITTLE LODGE FARM, HINTON MANOR ROAD, LOVEDEAN
MANSBRIDGE, STEVEN, 2, JAMES COPSE ROAD, LOVEDEAN
HUMPHREYS, ELSE S, 4, JAMES COPSE ROAD, LOVEDEAN
HUMPHREYS, PETER M, 4, JAMES COPSE ROAD, LOVEDEAN
KOPECKY, ARNOST, 6, JAMES COPSE ROAD, LOVEDEAN
KOPECKY, GILLIAN, 6, JAMES COPSE ROAD, LOVEDEAN
TUCKER, AMY, 8, JAMES COPSE ROAD, LOVEDEAN
TUCKER, CHRISTOPHER J, 8, JAMES COPSE ROAD, LOVEDEAN
TUCKER, MARIE I.M, 8, JAMES COPSE ROAD, LOVEDEAN
STRAW, MARIA J, 10, JAMES COPSE ROAD, LOVEDEAN
STRAW, MICHAEL, 10, JAMES COPSE ROAD, LOVEDEAN
WOODS, PETER W, 12, JAMES COPSE ROAD, LOVEDEAN
WOODS, SUSAN I, 12, JAMES COPSE ROAD, LOVEDEAN
MACDONALD, CHRISTINE M, 14, JAMES COPSE ROAD,
MACDONALD, ERIC J, 14, JAMES COPSE ROAD, LOVEDEAN
GOODE, ALAN E, 16, JAMES COPSE ROAD, LOVEDEAN
GOODE, BARBARA A, 16, JAMES COPSE ROAD, LOVEDEAN
HAYNES, RYAN P, 18, JAMES COPSE ROAD, LOVEDEAN
HAYNES, STEPHEN R, 18, JAMES COPSE ROAD, LOVEDEAN
WIMBLETON, VICTORIA J, 18, JAMES COPSE ROAD,
DARGON, NEIL S, 20, JAMES COPSE ROAD, LOVEDEAN
DARGON, STEVEN M, 20, JAMES COPSE ROAD, LOVEDEAN
DARGON, SUSAN A.P, 20, JAMES COPSE ROAD, LOVEDEAN
PRATLEY, CHRISTINA J, 22, JAMES COPSE ROAD, LOVEDEAN
PRATLEY, STEPHEN J, 22, JAMES COPSE ROAD, LOVEDEAN
CAMFIELD, MARK R, 24, JAMES COPSE ROAD, LOVEDEAN
CAMFIELD, SHIRLEY A, 24, JAMES COPSE ROAD, LOVEDEAN
KNIGHT, DAVID E, 26, JAMES COPSE ROAD, LOVEDEAN
KNIGHT, ELAINE J, 26, JAMES COPSE ROAD, LOVEDEAN
KNIGHT, PETER I, 26, JAMES COPSE ROAD, LOVEDEAN
STONE, LINDA M, 28, JAMES COPSE ROAD, LOVEDEAN
STONE, PAUL J, 28, JAMES COPSE ROAD, LOVEDEAN
GOODALL, SHELLY M, 30, JAMES COPSE ROAD, LOVEDEAN
PENNYCOOK, CHRISTOPHER P, 30, JAMES COPSE ROAD,
PENNYCOOK, LESLEY A, 30, JAMES COPSE ROAD, LOVEDEAN
HEPPLE, KAREN, 32, JAMES COPSE ROAD, LOVEDEAN
HEPPLE, PAUL N, 32, JAMES COPSE ROAD, LOVEDEAN
JONES, DAVID L, 34, JAMES COPSE ROAD, LOVEDEAN
JONES, ROSEMARY C, 34, JAMES COPSE ROAD, LOVEDEAN
NORTH, AMANDA J, 36, JAMES COPSE ROAD, LOVEDEAN
NORTH, FRANCESCA E, 36, JAMES COPSE ROAD, LOVEDEAN
NORTH, GILLIAN A, 36, JAMES COPSE ROAD, LOVEDEAN
NORTH, JULIE M, 36, JAMES COPSE ROAD, LOVEDEAN
NORTH, MICHAEL J, 36, JAMES COPSE ROAD, LOVEDEAN
WARDER, BERYL G, 38, JAMES COPSE ROAD, LOVEDEAN
WARDER, GRAHAM L, 38, JAMES COPSE ROAD, LOVEDEAN
WARDER, STEPHEN L, 38, JAMES COPSE ROAD, LOVEDEAN
HAYWARD, SHIRLEY D, 40, JAMES COPSE ROAD, LOVEDEAN
RIDLEY, SIMEON N.G, 40, JAMES COPSE ROAD, LOVEDEAN
GALLAWAY, CLARE V, 42, JAMES COPSE ROAD, LOVEDEAN
GALLAWAY, PAUL M, 42, JAMES COPSE ROAD, LOVEDEAN
GALLAWAY, STEPHEN A, 42, JAMES COPSE ROAD, LOVEDEAN
MOUNTENEY, BEVERLY R, 44, JAMES COPSE ROAD,
MOUNTENEY, DEAN, 44, JAMES COPSE ROAD, LOVEDEAN
MUNN, DAVID L, 46, JAMES COPSE ROAD, LOVEDEAN
MUNN, GILLIAN E, 46, JAMES COPSE ROAD, LOVEDEAN
PIDDUCK, EDNA M, 48, JAMES COPSE ROAD, LOVEDEAN
PIDDUCK, MAUREEN A, 48, JAMES COPSE ROAD, LOVEDEAN
ROBERTS, PATRICIA A, 1, JAY CLOSE, HORNDEAN
ROBERTS, PHILIP, 1, JAY CLOSE, HORNDEAN
AL-GHABBAN, MAUREEN, 2, JAY CLOSE, HORNDEAN
AL-GHABBAN, MOHAMMED R, 2, JAY CLOSE, HORNDEAN
KNIGHT, DIANA J, 3, JAY CLOSE, HORNDEAN
WARREN, PAUL, 4, JAY CLOSE, HORNDEAN
PETHER, ANNA M, 5, JAY CLOSE, HORNDEAN
PETHER, MARK D, 5, JAY CLOSE, HORNDEAN
ALEXANDER, BARRY N, 6, JAY CLOSE, HORNDEAN
ALEXANDER, DAVID, 6, JAY CLOSE, HORNDEAN
ALEXANDER, PATRICIA M, 6, JAY CLOSE, HORNDEAN
HOWES, VALERIE A, 7, JAY CLOSE, HORNDEAN
ALLEN, RAYMOND W, 8, JAY CLOSE, HORNDEAN
DAWSON, ELIZABETH, 9, JAY CLOSE, HORNDEAN
DICKENSON, IAN J, 10, JAY CLOSE, HORNDEAN
DONALD, DEBORAH M, 11, JAY CLOSE, HORNDEAN
PICKARD, IVY M, 12, JAY CLOSE, HORNDEAN
COOMBES, ANGELA, 14, JAY CLOSE, HORNDEAN
HUTSON, NORMAN, 15, JAY CLOSE, HORNDEAN
PARKER, TRUDIE R.T, 15, JAY CLOSE, HORNDEAN
GRAHAM, NEIL, 16, JAY CLOSE, HORNDEAN
PURVIS, MARTIN J, 17, JAY CLOSE, HORNDEAN
PURVIS, SARAH L, 17, JAY CLOSE, HORNDEAN
CAMPBELL, GLADYS, 1, KEYDELL AVENUE, HORNDEAN
DEVINE, LIAM A.J, 2, KEYDELL AVENUE, HORNDEAN
DEVINE, SARAH T, 2, KEYDELL AVENUE, HORNDEAN
GRIMMER, DAVID, 3, KEYDELL AVENUE, HORNDEAN
GRIMMER, PATRICIA A, 3, KEYDELL AVENUE, HORNDEAN
ASHWELL, ALFRED N, 4, KEYDELL AVENUE, HORNDEAN
ASHWELL, PAULINE A, 4, KEYDELL AVENUE, HORNDEAN
WATSON, ANGELA H, 5, KEYDELL AVENUE, HORNDEAN

WATSON, CHRISTOPHER C, 5, KEYDELL AVENUE, HORNDEAN
TAYLOR, ANN P, 6, KEYDELL AVENUE, HORNDEAN
TAYLOR, GORDON J, 6, KEYDELL AVENUE, HORNDEAN
TAYLOR, NEIL J, 6, KEYDELL AVENUE, HORNDEAN
CLUTTON, HAZEL M, 7, KEYDELL AVENUE, HORNDEAN
CLUTTON, IYSHA, 7, KEYDELL AVENUE, HORNDEAN
CLUTTON, NEAL D, 7, KEYDELL AVENUE, HORNDEAN
LEWIS, CHRISTOPHER G, 8, KEYDELL AVENUE, HORNDEAN
LEWIS, SUZANNE M, 8, KEYDELL AVENUE, HORNDEAN
WARD, CHRISTOPHER G, 9, KEYDELL AVENUE, HORNDEAN
WARD, DANIEL C, 9, KEYDELL AVENUE, HORNDEAN
WARD, WENDY K, 9, KEYDELL AVENUE, HORNDEAN
CORLETT, DAVID, 10, KEYDELL AVENUE, HORNDEAN
SHORTER, DAVID R, 10, KEYDELL AVENUE, HORNDEAN
SHORTER, HEATHER, 10, KEYDELL AVENUE, HORNDEAN
SHORTER, KEVIN M, 10, KEYDELL AVENUE, HORNDEAN
BROWNE, DOUGLAS, 11, KEYDELL AVENUE, HORNDEAN
GREEN, SANDRA, 11, KEYDELL AVENUE, HORNDEAN
WILMSHURST, MARGARET H, 12, KEYDELL AVENUE,
WILMSHURST, NIGEL, 12, KEYDELL AVENUE, HORNDEAN
LINDSAY, GERALD M, 13, KEYDELL AVENUE, HORNDEAN
BURRIDGE, JOANNA M, 14, KEYDELL AVENUE, HORNDEAN
BURRIDGE, MARYANN, 14, KEYDELL AVENUE, HORNDEAN
BURRIDGE, MICHAEL D.F, 14, KEYDELL AVENUE, HORNDEAN
BURRIDGE, SEAN R, 14, KEYDELL AVENUE, HORNDEAN
BANFIELD, PAULA Y, 15, KEYDELL AVENUE, HORNDEAN
POOK, STUART M, 15, KEYDELL AVENUE, HORNDEAN
FRECKLETON, LLEWELLYN W, 16, KEYDELL AVENUE,
MCELROY, MIRIAM P, 16, KEYDELL AVENUE, HORNDEAN
CHURCHILL, BERYL M, 17, KEYDELL AVENUE, HORNDEAN
CHURCHILL, HAROLD R, 17, KEYDELL AVENUE, HORNDEAN
JENNINGS, BRIAN H, 19, KEYDELL AVENUE, HORNDEAN
JENNINGS, MARGARET A, 19, KEYDELL AVENUE, HORNDEAN
SEYMOUR, CATHERINE M, 20, KEYDELL AVENUE,
TURNER, FRANK A, 21, KEYDELL AVENUE, HORNDEAN
TURNER, MURIEL M.M, 21, KEYDELL AVENUE, HORNDEAN
CLEVERLEY, BRIAN, 22, KEYDELL AVENUE, HORNDEAN
CLEVERLEY, CLARE C, 22, KEYDELL AVENUE, HORNDEAN
CLEVERLEY, GILES A, 22, KEYDELL AVENUE, HORNDEAN
CLEVERLEY, MONIKA F, 22, KEYDELL AVENUE, HORNDEAN
BARCLAY, PAOLA A, 23, KEYDELL AVENUE, HORNDEAN
BARCLAY, RICHARD D, 23, KEYDELL AVENUE, HORNDEAN
RICKWOOD, CAROL J, 24, KEYDELL AVENUE, HORNDEAN
RICKWOOD, JAMES W.A, 24, KEYDELL AVENUE, HORNDEAN
RICKWOOD, LEE J, 24, KEYDELL AVENUE, HORNDEAN
RICKWOOD, TARA M, 24, KEYDELL AVENUE, HORNDEAN
HOBDAY, EMMA J, 26, KEYDELL AVENUE, HORNDEAN
HOBDAY, IAN L, 26, KEYDELL AVENUE, HORNDEAN
HOBDAY, SUSAN, 26, KEYDELL AVENUE, HORNDEAN
PRATER, JEMMA, 27, KEYDELL AVENUE, HORNDEAN
PRATER, JOHN L, 27, KEYDELL AVENUE, HORNDEAN
PRATER, JULIE, 27, KEYDELL AVENUE, HORNDEAN
PLUMMER, MARGARET I, 28, KEYDELL AVENUE, HORNDEAN
PLUMMER, MICHAEL J, 28, KEYDELL AVENUE, HORNDEAN
DYKE, JOHN F, 29, KEYDELL AVENUE, HORNDEAN
DYKE, JOHN S, 29, KEYDELL AVENUE, HORNDEAN
DYKE, MATTHEW J, 29, KEYDELL AVENUE, HORNDEAN
UPSALL, JOAN E, 29A, KEYDELL AVENUE, HORNDEAN
THATCHER, COLIN, 29B, KEYDELL AVENUE, HORNDEAN
THATCHER, LARYSA, 29B, KEYDELL AVENUE, HORNDEAN
BYFORD, ANDREW J, 30, KEYDELL AVENUE, HORNDEAN
LEACH, RACHEL C, 30, KEYDELL AVENUE, HORNDEAN
POPLE, JULIE D, 31, KEYDELL AVENUE, HORNDEAN
POPLE, PETER C.R, 31, KEYDELL AVENUE, HORNDEAN
PRATT, DENIS H, 32, KEYDELL AVENUE, HORNDEAN
PRATT, DIANA K, 32, KEYDELL AVENUE, HORNDEAN
BARHAM, BRENDA D, 33, KEYDELL AVENUE, HORNDEAN
BARHAM, ROBERT A, 33, KEYDELL AVENUE, HORNDEAN
MARDLE, ALFRED, 34, KEYDELL AVENUE, HORNDEAN
MARDLE, JEAN K, 34, KEYDELL AVENUE, HORNDEAN
LACEY, DENNIS, 35, KEYDELL AVENUE, HORNDEAN
ROBERTS, KERRY D, 36, KEYDELL AVENUE, HORNDEAN
ROBERTS, STEPHEN J, 36, KEYDELL AVENUE, HORNDEAN
BUTLER, ELIZABETH M, 38, KEYDELL AVENUE, HORNDEAN
BUTLER, JEAN M, 38, KEYDELL AVENUE, HORNDEAN
BUTLER, PETER B, 38, KEYDELL AVENUE, HORNDEAN
BUTLER, ROBIN J, 38, KEYDELL AVENUE, HORNDEAN
CRAWFORD, ALBERT E, 39, KEYDELL AVENUE, HORNDEAN
CRAWFORD, DAWN E, 39, KEYDELL AVENUE, HORNDEAN
NEWMAN, LAWRENCE P, 40, KEYDELL AVENUE, HORNDEAN
SELWOOD, EVA M, 41, KEYDELL AVENUE, HORNDEAN
SELWOOD, MARTIN O.W, 41, KEYDELL AVENUE, HORNDEAN
MANNING, LUCY H, 42, KEYDELL AVENUE, HORNDEAN
MANNING, STEVER R, 42, KEYDELL AVENUE, HORNDEAN
HINTON, PAUL A, 1, KEYDELL CLOSE, HORNDEAN
HINTON, VICTORIA J.B, 1, KEYDELL CLOSE, HORNDEAN
JULL, KARIN A, 2, KEYDELL CLOSE, HORNDEAN
JULL, RANDALL L, 2, KEYDELL CLOSE, HORNDEAN
JULL, RICHARD A, 2, KEYDELL CLOSE, HORNDEAN
JULL, STEPHEN R, 2, KEYDELL CLOSE, HORNDEAN
HOLDING, CLIVE R, 3, KEYDELL CLOSE, HORNDEAN
HOLDING, NICOLA J, 3, KEYDELL CLOSE, HORNDEAN
JARRETT, CHRISTINE A, 4, KEYDELL CLOSE, HORNDEAN
JARRETT, PAULINE A, 4, KEYDELL CLOSE, HORNDEAN
JARRETT, SEAN, 4, KEYDELL CLOSE, HORNDEAN
JARRETT, TONY P, 4, KEYDELL CLOSE, HORNDEAN
HARRIS, DAWN A, 5, KEYDELL CLOSE, HORNDEAN
HARRIS, PATRICK J, 5, KEYDELL CLOSE, HORNDEAN
HARRIS, SYLVIA J, 5, KEYDELL CLOSE, HORNDEAN
SEWELL, JULIAN J, 6, KEYDELL CLOSE, HORNDEAN
SEWELL, RUPERT J, 6, KEYDELL CLOSE, HORNDEAN
KILBY, FRANCES M, 7, KEYDELL CLOSE, HORNDEAN
KILBY, IAN R, 7, KEYDELL CLOSE, HORNDEAN

KILBY, ROYSTON H, 7, KEYDELL CLOSE, HORNDEAN
HERN, IVY G, 8, KEYDELL CLOSE, HORNDEAN
WARMAN, MARY, 8, KEYDELL CLOSE, HORNDEAN
VINE, NIGEL I, 9, KEYDELL CLOSE, HORNDEAN
VINE, TRACEY M.J, 9, KEYDELL CLOSE, HORNDEAN
CLARK, ROBERT C, 10, KEYDELL CLOSE, HORNDEAN
CLARK, ROSANNA V, 10, KEYDELL CLOSE, HORNDEAN
SYKES, KIMBERLEY L, 11, KEYDELL CLOSE, HORNDEAN
SYKES, NIGEL R, 11, KEYDELL CLOSE, HORNDEAN
EDWARDS, JOHN M, 12, KEYDELL CLOSE, HORNDEAN
EDWARDS, KAREN A, 12, KEYDELL CLOSE, HORNDEAN
GOUGH, BRIAN G, 13, KEYDELL CLOSE, HORNDEAN
GOUGH, MARY C, 13, KEYDELL CLOSE, HORNDEAN
AUSTING, EDNA M, 14, KEYDELL CLOSE, HORNDEAN
AUSTING, HAROLD H, 14, KEYDELL CLOSE, HORNDEAN
WATTS, PEARL D, 15, KEYDELL CLOSE, HORNDEAN
WATTS, STANLEY C, 15, KEYDELL CLOSE, HORNDEAN
MCNIVEN, ALAN G, 16, KEYDELL CLOSE, HORNDEAN
MCNIVEN, IRENE M, 16, KEYDELL CLOSE, HORNDEAN
SOLLARS, ANDREW T, 17, KEYDELL CLOSE, HORNDEAN
SOLLARS, JEANETTE R, 17, KEYDELL CLOSE, HORNDEAN
SOLLARS, PETER M.A, 17, KEYDELL CLOSE, HORNDEAN
SOLLARS, RUTH E, 17, KEYDELL CLOSE, HORNDEAN
GRACE, JOHN E, 18, KEYDELL CLOSE, HORNDEAN
HARRISON, ANTHONY J, 19, KEYDELL CLOSE, HORNDEAN
HARRISON, WENDY E, 19, KEYDELL CLOSE, HORNDEAN
GOTT, TRACY, 20, KEYDELL CLOSE, HORNDEAN
HODDER, VALERIE, 20, KEYDELL CLOSE, HORNDEAN
SADDINGTON, AMANDA, 20, KEYDELL CLOSE, HORNDEAN
VALLOR, MARGERY J, 21, KEYDELL CLOSE, HORNDEAN
HARCOURT, ANITA M, 22, KEYDELL CLOSE, HORNDEAN
HARCOURT, BARRY G, 22, KEYDELL CLOSE, HORNDEAN
HARCOURT, PAUL B, 22, KEYDELL CLOSE, HORNDEAN
MURPHY, EVELYN J, 23, KEYDELL CLOSE, HORNDEAN
BALLARD, ENA E.D, 25, KEYDELL CLOSE, HORNDEAN
NETHERCOTT, ANGELA M, 27, KEYDELL CLOSE, HORNDEAN
NETHERCOTT, MARK S, 27, KEYDELL CLOSE, HORNDEAN
PIPER, JAMES E, 27, KEYDELL CLOSE, HORNDEAN
PIPER, SARAH, 27, KEYDELL CLOSE, HORNDEAN
SEYMOUR, FREDERICK J, 29, KEYDELL CLOSE, HORNDEAN
SEYMOUR, JEANETTE, 29, KEYDELL CLOSE, HORNDEAN
NICHOLLS, MABEL E, 1, KINGS MEDE, HORNDEAN
HUNT, GILLIAN A, 2, KINGS MEDE, HORNDEAN
HUNT, JOHN A, 2, KINGS MEDE, HORNDEAN
TAYLOR, CHRISTOPHER C, 4, KINGS MEDE, HORNDEAN
TAYLOR, MURIEL A, 4, KINGS MEDE, HORNDEAN
REYNOLDS, CRAIG, 6, KINGS MEDE, HORNDEAN
REYNOLDS, DENNIS J, 6, KINGS MEDE, HORNDEAN
REYNOLDS, SUSAN D, 6, KINGS MEDE, HORNDEAN
TAYLOR, GERALD B, 8, KINGS MEDE, HORNDEAN
TAYLOR, PATRICIA, 8, KINGS MEDE, HORNDEAN
WILLIAMS, NORMAN J, 10, KINGS MEDE, HORNDEAN
WILLIAMS, PATRICIA, 10, KINGS MEDE, HORNDEAN
COLLINS, BRIAN W, 12, KINGS MEDE, HORNDEAN
COLLINS, MAISIE B, 12, KINGS MEDE, HORNDEAN
FOYLE, KENNETH R, 14, KINGS MEDE, HORNDEAN
HELLIER, ANTHONY W, 16, KINGS MEDE, HORNDEAN
HELLIER, DOREEN J, 16, KINGS MEDE, HORNDEAN
FOSTER, EILEEN G, 18, KINGS MEDE, HORNDEAN
SMITH, EILEEN R.C, 20, KINGS MEDE, HORNDEAN
SMITH, IAN F, 20, KINGS MEDE, HORNDEAN
CANNON, PHILIP S, 22, KINGS MEDE, HORNDEAN
NEW, CATHERINE, 22, KINGS MEDE, HORNDEAN
MANTELL, EDNA J, 24, KINGS MEDE, HORNDEAN
KEMPSTER, FIONA G, 26, KINGS MEDE, HORNDEAN
KEMPSTER, GRAHAM K, 26, KINGS MEDE, HORNDEAN
WALKER, PAMELA I, 28, KINGS MEDE, HORNDEAN
PIGDON, PEGGY J, 30, KINGS MEDE, HORNDEAN
WALKER, CAROLE, 31, KINGS MEDE, HORNDEAN
WALKER, ERIC J, 31, KINGS MEDE, HORNDEAN
BRETTELL, JOANNAH L, 32, KINGS MEDE, HORNDEAN
BRETTELL, MARK I, 32, KINGS MEDE, HORNDEAN
WHITE, CYRIL A.E, 33, KINGS MEDE, HORNDEAN
WHITE, SHEILA M, 33, KINGS MEDE, HORNDEAN
PLANT, BEATRICE J, 34, KINGS MEDE, HORNDEAN
MOSS, DEIRDRE E, 35, KINGS MEDE, HORNDEAN
MOSS, GREGORY L, 35, KINGS MEDE, HORNDEAN
MOSS, JOHN T, 35, KINGS MEDE, HORNDEAN
WILSON, ANDREW P, 36, KINGS MEDE, HORNDEAN
WILSON, ANGELA J, 36, KINGS MEDE, HORNDEAN
SKYRME, BRENDA E, 37, KINGS MEDE, HORNDEAN
RUDD, ANDREW I, 38, KINGS MEDE, HORNDEAN
RUDD, ANNA M, 38, KINGS MEDE, HORNDEAN
DUNCAN, BERNARD H.F, 39, KINGS MEDE, HORNDEAN
DUNCAN, CAROLE A, 39, KINGS MEDE, HORNDEAN
DORN, PATRICIA A, 40, KINGS MEDE, HORNDEAN
MEAGHAN, BRIAN, 40, KINGS MEDE, HORNDEAN
GILBERT, GRAHAM R, 41, KINGS MEDE, HORNDEAN
GILBERT, JANET P, 41, KINGS MEDE, HORNDEAN
MORRIS, GERALD P, 42, KINGS MEDE, HORNDEAN
MORRIS, MARGARET, 42, KINGS MEDE, HORNDEAN
HUGHES, GORDON S, 43, KINGS MEDE, HORNDEAN
HUGHES, JOYCE H, 43, KINGS MEDE, HORNDEAN
HARRISON, BARBARA M, 44, KINGS MEDE, HORNDEAN
HARRISON, BRIAN C, 44, KINGS MEDE, HORNDEAN
STOCKLEY, PETER T, 45, KINGS MEDE, HORNDEAN
DANIEL, JENNIFER L, 46, KINGS MEDE, HORNDEAN
DANIEL, LORNA G, 46, KINGS MEDE, HORNDEAN
BLAKE, JOSEPH V, 47, KINGS MEDE, HORNDEAN
PULLIN, HENRIETTA B, 47, KINGS MEDE, HORNDEAN
TOMKINS, KEITH B, 48, KINGS MEDE, HORNDEAN
TOMKINS, SALLY A, 48, KINGS MEDE, HORNDEAN
GOODMAN, GRACE C, 49, KINGS MEDE, HORNDEAN
GOODMAN, JANET P, 49, KINGS MEDE, HORNDEAN
ATKINSON, ALICE M, 50, KINGS MEDE, HORNDEAN
TRENAMAN, MAISIE L.L, 51, KINGS MEDE, HORNDEAN
WATTS, MICHAEL P, 51, KINGS MEDE, HORNDEAN
BRAMBLE, HENRY J, 52, KINGS MEDE, HORNDEAN
BRAMBLE, PATRICIA K, 52, KINGS MEDE, HORNDEAN
BLAKE, PAMELA R, 53, KINGS MEDE, HORNDEAN
BLAKE, ROGER D, 53, KINGS MEDE, HORNDEAN
BARKER, ANTHONY P, 54, KINGS MEDE, HORNDEAN
EVELIN, SHARON, 54, KINGS MEDE, HORNDEAN
SELL, ANTHONY F, 55, KINGS MEDE, HORNDEAN
SELL, NOREEN R, 55, KINGS MEDE, HORNDEAN
NINEHAM, ANDREW J, 56, KINGS MEDE, HORNDEAN
NINEHAM, SHARON T, 56, KINGS MEDE, HORNDEAN
BUDD, ANDREW D, 57, KINGS MEDE, HORNDEAN
BUDD, DAVID O, 57, KINGS MEDE, HORNDEAN
BUDD, DIANE E, 57, KINGS MEDE, HORNDEAN
BUDD, SARAH C, 57, KINGS MEDE, HORNDEAN
SAMSON, CLAIRE E, 58, KINGS MEDE, HORNDEAN
SAMSON, DAVID M, 58, KINGS MEDE, HORNDEAN
SAMSON, ELIZABETH S, 58, KINGS MEDE, HORNDEAN
BRAITHWAITE, PAULA A, 59, KINGS MEDE, HORNDEAN
BERNARD, JEAN, 60, KINGS MEDE, HORNDEAN
REED, KEVIN R, 61, KINGS MEDE, HORNDEAN
REED, SUZANNE J, 61, KINGS MEDE, HORNDEAN
GARDNER, JOAN V, 62, KINGS MEDE, HORNDEAN
GARDNER, JOHN L, 62, KINGS MEDE, HORNDEAN
FINCH, EILEEN M, 63, KINGS MEDE, HORNDEAN
FINCH, ERNEST J, 63, KINGS MEDE, HORNDEAN
LONG, CAROLE A, 64, KINGS MEDE, HORNDEAN
LONG, KEITH E, 64, KINGS MEDE, HORNDEAN
ELCOME, JESSIE K, 65, KINGS MEDE, HORNDEAN
CORNELL, SUSAN, 66, KINGS MEDE, HORNDEAN
WADDELL, WILLIAM J, 66, KINGS MEDE, HORNDEAN
BLAKE, SUSAN L, 67, KINGS MEDE, HORNDEAN
BOWBRICK, ANDREW P, 67, KINGS MEDE, HORNDEAN
SMITH, DAVID R.P, 68, KINGS MEDE, HORNDEAN
SMITH, DEBORAH S, 68, KINGS MEDE, HORNDEAN
SMITH, PAUL J, 68, KINGS MEDE, HORNDEAN
SMITH, SUSAN M, 68, KINGS MEDE, HORNDEAN
CAREY, ANDREW J, 70, KINGS MEDE, HORNDEAN
CAREY, JOHN H, 70, KINGS MEDE, HORNDEAN
CAREY, MARGARET B, 70, KINGS MEDE, HORNDEAN
HOWES, DAVID G, 72, KINGS MEDE, HORNDEAN
HOWES, MAISIE, 72, KINGS MEDE, HORNDEAN
RUTTER, MARCUS W, 74, KINGS MEDE, HORNDEAN
RUTTER, NITA O, 74, KINGS MEDE, HORNDEAN
RUTTER, PETER C, 74, KINGS MEDE, HORNDEAN
WAKEFORD, OLIVE I, 74, KINGS MEDE, HORNDEAN
RUSSELL, URSULA G.A, 76, KINGS MEDE, HORNDEAN
HARLAND, JEAN A, 78, KINGS MEDE, HORNDEAN
WOOD, STEPHEN T, 78, KINGS MEDE, HORNDEAN
HARVEY, BARRY, 80, KINGS MEDE, HORNDEAN
BENTLEY, GARY L, 82, KINGS MEDE, HORNDEAN
BENTLEY, JOANNE, 82, KINGS MEDE, HORNDEAN
WICKHAM, PATRICIA A, 1, LAPWING CLOSE, HORNDEAN
BONSOR, GLENN, 2, LAPWING CLOSE, HORNDEAN
BONSOR, JACQUELINE, 2, LAPWING CLOSE, HORNDEAN
LEGG, KIM, 3, LAPWING CLOSE, HORNDEAN
TESH, GARY D, 4, LAPWING CLOSE, HORNDEAN
TESH, SERETA, 4, LAPWING CLOSE, HORNDEAN
HAWKES, TIMOTHY P.A, 5, LAPWING CLOSE, HORNDEAN
GOSS, ANDREW C, 6, LAPWING CLOSE, HORNDEAN
GOSS, GILLIAN C, 6, LAPWING CLOSE, HORNDEAN
MIDDLETON, AMANDA, 7, LAPWING CLOSE, HORNDEAN
MIDDLETON, GUY J, 7, LAPWING CLOSE, HORNDEAN
SMITH, ALASTAIR J, 8, LAPWING CLOSE, HORNDEAN
SMITH, SUSANNA, 8, LAPWING CLOSE, HORNDEAN
NASH, LOUISE A, 9, LAPWING CLOSE, HORNDEAN
NASH, RUSSELL C, 9, LAPWING CLOSE, HORNDEAN
BREWSTER, DEREK F, 10, LAPWING CLOSE, HORNDEAN
BREWSTER, SAMANTHA, 10, LAPWING CLOSE, HORNDEAN
HINDMARCH, CHARLES H, 149, LOVEDEAN LANE, LOVEDEAN
SKEET, ANDREW V, 151, LOVEDEAN LANE, LOVEDEAN
SKEET, JOANNA G, 151, LOVEDEAN LANE, LOVEDEAN
MILLS, ANDREW P, 153, LOVEDEAN LANE, LOVEDEAN
MILLS, HILARY V, 153, LOVEDEAN LANE, LOVEDEAN
REYNOLDS, DAVID J, 155, LOVEDEAN LANE, LOVEDEAN
PARKER, JAMES E, 157, LOVEDEAN LANE, LOVEDEAN
PARKER, MARY P, 157, LOVEDEAN LANE, LOVEDEAN
MELOY, FREDERICK C, 161, LOVEDEAN LANE, LOVEDEAN
MELOY, JOAN M, 161, LOVEDEAN LANE, LOVEDEAN
HOPER, IAN W, 179, LOVEDEAN LANE, LOVEDEAN
HOPER, PATRICIA M, 179, LOVEDEAN LANE, LOVEDEAN
LINKHORN, JOHN H, 187, LOVEDEAN LANE, LOVEDEAN
SANSOM, CHRISTIAN, 193, LOVEDEAN LANE, LOVEDEAN
TIMBRELL, SALLY, 193, LOVEDEAN LANE, LOVEDEAN
FAIRALL, EDWARD G, 197, LOVEDEAN LANE, LOVEDEAN
FAIRALL, WINIFRED I, 197, LOVEDEAN LANE, LOVEDEAN
ACOTT, BETTY M, 199, LOVEDEAN LANE, LOVEDEAN
ACOTT, ROY F, 199, LOVEDEAN LANE, LOVEDEAN
HALLIDAY, EILEEN M, 203, LOVEDEAN LANE, LOVEDEAN
HALLIDAY, ROBERT I.C, 203, LOVEDEAN LANE, LOVEDEAN
MCLEOD, DORIS L, 209, LOVEDEAN LANE, LOVEDEAN
MCLEOD, STANLEY E, 209, LOVEDEAN LANE, LOVEDEAN
WALTON, GEORGINA M.F, 227, LOVEDEAN LANE, LOVEDEAN
WALTON, ROBERT, 227, LOVEDEAN LANE, LOVEDEAN
JEFFRIES, DOROTHY M, 229, LOVEDEAN LANE, LOVEDEAN
JEFFRIES, MARTIN B, 229, LOVEDEAN LANE, LOVEDEAN
TAYLOR, BRIAN J, 239, LOVEDEAN LANE, LOVEDEAN
TAYLOR, CORRINA H, 239, LOVEDEAN LANE, LOVEDEAN
HERBERT, HEATHER K, 241, LOVEDEAN LANE, LOVEDEAN
HERBERT, JOHN V, 241, LOVEDEAN LANE, LOVEDEAN
HERBERT, KATHERINE J, 241, LOVEDEAN LANE, LOVEDEAN
HERBERT, PAUL D, 241, LOVEDEAN LANE, LOVEDEAN
STROUD, ALAN R, 263, LOVEDEAN LANE, LOVEDEAN
STROUD, IRIS, 263, LOVEDEAN LANE, LOVEDEAN
STROUD, MALCOLM P, 263, LOVEDEAN LANE, LOVEDEAN
KEIFER, JUDITH A, 269, LOVEDEAN LANE, LOVEDEAN
KEIFER, TIMOTHY J, 269, LOVEDEAN LANE, LOVEDEAN
NORMAN, DANIEL F, 152, LOVEDEAN LANE, LOVEDEAN
NORMAN, DONNA T, 152, LOVEDEAN LANE, LOVEDEAN
KNIGHT, AMY, 156, LOVEDEAN LANE, LOVEDEAN
KNIGHT, HELEN M, 156, LOVEDEAN LANE, LOVEDEAN
KNIGHT, SIMON D, 156, LOVEDEAN LANE, LOVEDEAN
KNIGHT, STEVEN, 156, LOVEDEAN LANE, LOVEDEAN
KNIGHT, TREVOR, 156, LOVEDEAN LANE, LOVEDEAN
KNIGHT, VICKI, 156, LOVEDEAN LANE, LOVEDEAN
JACKSON, DEBORAH A, 170, LOVEDEAN LANE, LOVEDEAN
JACKSON, NORMAN C, 170, LOVEDEAN LANE, LOVEDEAN
JACKSON, SUSAN E, 170, LOVEDEAN LANE, LOVEDEAN
JACKSON, VICTORIA J, 170, LOVEDEAN LANE, LOVEDEAN
MCELHINNEY, JOSEPH, 172, LOVEDEAN LANE, LOVEDEAN
MCELHINNEY, SARAH E, 172, LOVEDEAN LANE, LOVEDEAN
MCELHINNEY, VALERIE J, 172, LOVEDEAN LANE, LOVEDEAN
RAMSAY, ALAN L, 174, LOVEDEAN LANE, LOVEDEAN
SAXBY, ANN R, 174, LOVEDEAN LANE, LOVEDEAN
SAXBY, KIM W, 174, LOVEDEAN LANE, LOVEDEAN
HUGHES, JENNIFER M, 176, LOVEDEAN LANE, LOVEDEAN
HUGHES, NICOLA J, 176, LOVEDEAN LANE, LOVEDEAN
HUGHES, ROBERT D, 176, LOVEDEAN LANE, LOVEDEAN
PRILL, CHRISTINE M, 178, LOVEDEAN LANE, LOVEDEAN
PRILL, TERENCE W, 178, LOVEDEAN LANE, LOVEDEAN
HATCH, ALAN, 180, LOVEDEAN LANE, LOVEDEAN
HATCH, GRAHAM J, 180, LOVEDEAN LANE, LOVEDEAN
HATCH, MARGARET, 180, LOVEDEAN LANE, LOVEDEAN
HATCH, REBECCA, 180, LOVEDEAN LANE, LOVEDEAN
HUDSON, CHRISTOPHER S, 182, LOVEDEAN LANE, LOVEDEAN
HUDSON, JULIE A, 182, LOVEDEAN LANE, LOVEDEAN
STACEY, FLORENCE G, 184, LOVEDEAN LANE, LOVEDEAN
NORTHEAST, ALISON R, 186, LOVEDEAN LANE, LOVEDEAN
NORTHEAST, MATTHEW, 186, LOVEDEAN LANE, LOVEDEAN
JONES, BRIAN P, 188, LOVEDEAN LANE, LOVEDEAN
JONES, DERYL A, 188, LOVEDEAN LANE, LOVEDEAN
ROYLE, DEAN M, 190, LOVEDEAN LANE, LOVEDEAN
ROYLE, JACQUELINE A.G, 190, LOVEDEAN LANE, LOVEDEAN
ROYLE, MICHAEL, 190, LOVEDEAN LANE, LOVEDEAN
PITMAN, LESLIE S, 192, LOVEDEAN LANE, LOVEDEAN
PITMAN, MARY A, 192, LOVEDEAN LANE, LOVEDEAN
REYNOLDS, LESLEY L, 224, LOVEDEAN LANE, LOVEDEAN
REYNOLDS, WILLIAM J, 224, LOVEDEAN LANE, LOVEDEAN
ROBINSON, IAN, 226, LOVEDEAN LANE, LOVEDEAN
ROBINSON, JOANNE, 226, LOVEDEAN LANE, LOVEDEAN
RUTTLE, DORIS A, 246, LOVEDEAN LANE, LOVEDEAN
RUTTLE, JOHN W, 246, LOVEDEAN LANE, LOVEDEAN
GRIFFITHS, DAVID M, 282, LOVEDEAN LANE, LOVEDEAN
GRIFFITHS, KATIE J, 282, LOVEDEAN LANE, LOVEDEAN
GRIFFITHS, LYNDA E, 282, LOVEDEAN LANE, LOVEDEAN
HEATH, BARBARA J, KINGSWOOD FARM, LOVEDEAN LANE,
HEATH, FREDERICK W, KINGSWOOD FARM, LOVEDEAN LANE, LOVEDEAN
LARKING, ADELE J, STABLE COTTAGE, LOVEDEAN FARM, LOVEDEAN LANE, LOVEDEAN
POWELL, GILLIAN M, STABLE COTTAGE, LOVEDEAN FARM, LOVEDEAN LANE, LOVEDEAN
ROGERS, NICHOLAS J, STABLE COTTAGE, LOVEDEAN FARM, LOVEDEAN LANE, LOVEDEAN
SHERWARD, JANET A, 1, LOXWOOD ROAD, LOVEDEAN
SHERWARD, MICHAEL P, 1, LOXWOOD ROAD, LOVEDEAN
HOLMES, ALISON J, 3, LOXWOOD ROAD, LOVEDEAN
HOLMES, CHRISTOPHER D, 3, LOXWOOD ROAD, LOVEDEAN
MARSHALL, GARRY, 5, LOXWOOD ROAD, LOVEDEAN
MARSHALL, PAULINE E, 5, LOXWOOD ROAD, LOVEDEAN
MABEY, DOREEN O, 7, LOXWOOD ROAD, LOVEDEAN
MABEY, PETER R, 7, LOXWOOD ROAD, LOVEDEAN
HAYES, JULIAN R.R, 9, LOXWOOD ROAD, LOVEDEAN
HAYES, JUSTIN, 9, LOXWOOD ROAD, LOVEDEAN
HAYES, KIM S, 9, LOXWOOD ROAD, LOVEDEAN
ADAMS, CLAIRE A, 11, LOXWOOD ROAD, LOVEDEAN
ADAMS, JAMES C.H, 11, LOXWOOD ROAD, LOVEDEAN
FORBES, ANDREW G, 15, LOXWOOD ROAD, LOVEDEAN
FORBES, ROSEMARY A, 15, LOXWOOD ROAD, LOVEDEAN
CRABTREE, STEPHEN J, 17, LOXWOOD ROAD, LOVEDEAN
CRABTREE, SYLVIA R, 17, LOXWOOD ROAD, LOVEDEAN
MORGAN, DEREK T, 19, LOXWOOD ROAD, LOVEDEAN
MORGAN, JULIE, 19, LOXWOOD ROAD, LOVEDEAN
MORGAN, NICOLETTE, 19, LOXWOOD ROAD, LOVEDEAN
MORGAN, VERONICA, 19, LOXWOOD ROAD, LOVEDEAN
WHITAKER, ANNE B, 21, LOXWOOD ROAD, LOVEDEAN
WHITAKER, GORDON A, 21, LOXWOOD ROAD, LOVEDEAN
SPILLANE, MICHAEL D, 23, LOXWOOD ROAD, LOVEDEAN
SPILLANE, WENDY, 23, LOXWOOD ROAD, LOVEDEAN
JONES, JOAN M, 27, LOXWOOD ROAD, LOVEDEAN
JONES, STEPHEN A, 27, LOXWOOD ROAD, LOVEDEAN
FORD, JILLIAN F, 29, LOXWOOD ROAD, LOVEDEAN
FORD, JUSTIN K.W, 29, LOXWOOD ROAD, LOVEDEAN
FORD, KENNETH, 29, LOXWOOD ROAD, LOVEDEAN
SHAVE, PEARL C, 31, LOXWOOD ROAD, LOVEDEAN
SHAVE, RALPH E.J, 31, LOXWOOD ROAD, LOVEDEAN
GOATER, COLIN B.L, 33, LOXWOOD ROAD, LOVEDEAN
GOATER, MARY, 33, LOXWOOD ROAD, LOVEDEAN
BRAMBLE, DENNIS, 35, LOXWOOD ROAD, LOVEDEAN
BRAMBLE, JUDITH, 35, LOXWOOD ROAD, LOVEDEAN
WILLEY, GORDON R, 37, LOXWOOD ROAD, LOVEDEAN
WILLEY, ZENA M, 37, LOXWOOD ROAD, LOVEDEAN
BRYANT, JULIE A, 39, LOXWOOD ROAD, LOVEDEAN

Electoral Roll

BRYANT, STEVEN J, 39, LOXWOOD ROAD, LOVEDEAN
WEIGHT, ALBERT R, 41, LOXWOOD ROAD, LOVEDEAN
WEIGHT, SHEILA R, 41, LOXWOOD ROAD, LOVEDEAN
LIDDELL, BRIAN W.J, 43, LOXWOOD ROAD, LOVEDEAN
LIDDELL, LISA J, 43, LOXWOOD ROAD, LOVEDEAN
LIDDELL, SUSAN, 43, LOXWOOD ROAD, LOVEDEAN
CLEMENT, ANITA R, 45, LOXWOOD ROAD, LOVEDEAN
CLEMENT, KEITH J, 45, LOXWOOD ROAD, LOVEDEAN
BURROWES, ANDREW D, 47, LOXWOOD ROAD, LOVEDEAN
BURROWES, JEAN P, 47, LOXWOOD ROAD, LOVEDEAN
SYMONDS, MARGARET R, 49, LOXWOOD ROAD, LOVEDEAN
SYMONDS, RONALD G, 49, LOXWOOD ROAD, LOVEDEAN
COHEN, ANDREW E, 51, LOXWOOD ROAD, LOVEDEAN
COHEN, YVONNE C, 51, LOXWOOD ROAD, LOVEDEAN
THOMAS, MATTHEW N, 53, LOXWOOD ROAD, LOVEDEAN
BAULF, HELEN C, 55, LOXWOOD ROAD, LOVEDEAN
BAULF, MARTIN G, 55, LOXWOOD ROAD, LOVEDEAN
DAYSH, BRIAN L.F, 57, LOXWOOD ROAD, LOVEDEAN
DAYSH, WINIFRED E, 57, LOXWOOD ROAD, LOVEDEAN
JEFFRIES, RAYMOND D, 59, LOXWOOD ROAD, LOVEDEAN
KAVANAGH, EDNA J, 59, LOXWOOD ROAD, LOVEDEAN
SUMMERFIELD, ROBIN N, 61, LOXWOOD ROAD, LOVEDEAN
SUMMERFIELD, VALERIE M, 61, LOXWOOD ROAD, LOVEDEAN
FARRER, RUBY I, 63, LOXWOOD ROAD, LOVEDEAN
MILES, GORDON W, 65, LOXWOOD ROAD, LOVEDEAN
MILES, WINIFRED M, 65, LOXWOOD ROAD, LOVEDEAN
BARTLETT, LISA J, 2, LOXWOOD ROAD, LOVEDEAN
BARTLETT, TERRY, 2, LOXWOOD ROAD, LOVEDEAN
REID, JASON W, 4, LOXWOOD ROAD, LOVEDEAN
REID, KARAN P, 4, LOXWOOD ROAD, LOVEDEAN
REID, ROBERT W, 4, LOXWOOD ROAD, LOVEDEAN
REID, SIMON R, 4, LOXWOOD ROAD, LOVEDEAN
SOLWAY, GEOFFREY F, 6, LOXWOOD ROAD, LOVEDEAN
SOLWAY, JENNIFER A, 6, LOXWOOD ROAD, LOVEDEAN
SOLWAY, REBECCA L, 6, LOXWOOD ROAD, LOVEDEAN
BLAKE, IAN D, 8, LOXWOOD ROAD, LOVEDEAN
BLAKE, PACHARA, 8, LOXWOOD ROAD, LOVEDEAN
GLADDING, DAVID S, 10, LOXWOOD ROAD, LOVEDEAN
GLADDING, JENNIFER R, 10, LOXWOOD ROAD, LOVEDEAN
FITCH, ANTHONY C, 12, LOXWOOD ROAD, LOVEDEAN
FITCH, CHRISTINA J, 12, LOXWOOD ROAD, LOVEDEAN
LARMER, BARRY R, 14, LOXWOOD ROAD, LOVEDEAN
LARMER, ELIZABETH S, 14, LOXWOOD ROAD, LOVEDEAN
LARMER, SUSAN E, 14, LOXWOOD ROAD, LOVEDEAN
MASTERS, ETHEL F, 14, LOXWOOD ROAD, LOVEDEAN
BARNETT, COLIN D, 16, LOXWOOD ROAD, LOVEDEAN
BARNETT, LARRAINE, 16, LOXWOOD ROAD, LOVEDEAN
RICHARDSON, FRANK L, 18, LOXWOOD ROAD, LOVEDEAN
RICHARDSON, JUNE D, 18, LOXWOOD ROAD, LOVEDEAN
FRYER, CAROL M, 20, LOXWOOD ROAD, LOVEDEAN
FRYER, NICHOLAS J, 20, LOXWOOD ROAD, LOVEDEAN
FRYER, TREVOR V, 20, LOXWOOD ROAD, LOVEDEAN
SMITH, BRIAN F, 22, LOXWOOD ROAD, LOVEDEAN
SMITH, JOAN, 22, LOXWOOD ROAD, LOVEDEAN
ROBINSON, COLIN L, 24, LOXWOOD ROAD, LOVEDEAN
ROBINSON, MAUREEN J, 24, LOXWOOD ROAD, LOVEDEAN
EMERY, GARY J, 26, LOXWOOD ROAD, LOVEDEAN
EMERY, JULIE A, 26, LOXWOOD ROAD, LOVEDEAN
GANFIELD, ELIZABETH A, 28, LOXWOOD ROAD, LOVEDEAN
GANFIELD, PETER P, 28, LOXWOOD ROAD, LOVEDEAN
GANFIELD, SARAH, 28, LOXWOOD ROAD, LOVEDEAN
GANFIELD, STEPHEN, 28, LOXWOOD ROAD, LOVEDEAN
BROWN, CHERYL A, 30, LOXWOOD ROAD, LOVEDEAN
BROWN, GORDON J, 30, LOXWOOD ROAD, LOVEDEAN
BROWN, HANNAH K, 30, LOXWOOD ROAD, LOVEDEAN
PETHYBRIDGE, DAVID B, 32, LOXWOOD ROAD, LOVEDEAN
PREW, DAVID M, 34, LOXWOOD ROAD, LOVEDEAN
PREW, SALLY J, 34, LOXWOOD ROAD, LOVEDEAN
HOLDEN, SHIRLEY M, 36, LOXWOOD ROAD, LOVEDEAN
HOLDEN, TREVOR J, 36, LOXWOOD ROAD, LOVEDEAN
BURN, ROBERT N, 38, LOXWOOD ROAD, LOVEDEAN
DE CARTE, BERNARD F, 40, LOXWOOD ROAD, LOVEDEAN
DE CARTE, ELEANOR, 40, LOXWOOD ROAD, LOVEDEAN
BOYLE, NICOLA Y, 42, LOXWOOD ROAD, LOVEDEAN
BOYLE, PAUL J, 42, LOXWOOD ROAD, LOVEDEAN
ELVIN, LESLIE T, 44, LOXWOOD ROAD, LOVEDEAN
ELVIN, PAMELA R, 44, LOXWOOD ROAD, LOVEDEAN
FELL, DARREN J, 46, LOXWOOD ROAD, LOVEDEAN
FELL, DAVID T, 46, LOXWOOD ROAD, LOVEDEAN
FELL, JOAN B, 46, LOXWOOD ROAD, LOVEDEAN
FELL, JOHN A, 46, LOXWOOD ROAD, LOVEDEAN
HULKS, ROLAND, 48, LOXWOOD ROAD, LOVEDEAN
JONES, PAULINE A, 48, LOXWOOD ROAD, LOVEDEAN
GIDDINGS, DAVID, 50, LOXWOOD ROAD, LOVEDEAN
GIDDINGS, SYLVIA P, 50, LOXWOOD ROAD, LOVEDEAN
MUNDAY, BARBARA A, 52, LOXWOOD ROAD, LOVEDEAN
MUNDAY, CORRINE A, 52, LOXWOOD ROAD, LOVEDEAN
MUNDAY, MICHAEL A, 52, LOXWOOD ROAD, LOVEDEAN
COCKETT, ALBERT D.J, 54, LOXWOOD ROAD, LOVEDEAN
COCKETT, EILEEN, 54, LOXWOOD ROAD, LOVEDEAN
BLAIR, ALEXANDER R, 56, LOXWOOD ROAD, LOVEDEAN
BLAIR, DEBRA K, 56, LOXWOOD ROAD, LOVEDEAN
ASHFIELD, CAROLINE F, 58, LOXWOOD ROAD, LOVEDEAN
BAILEY, MARK R, 58, LOXWOOD ROAD, LOVEDEAN
FOWLER, MAUREEN, 60, LOXWOOD ROAD, LOVEDEAN
FOWLER, ROBERT V, 60, LOXWOOD ROAD, LOVEDEAN
MORTIMORE, BEVERLEY M, 62, LOXWOOD ROAD, LOVEDEAN
MOTH, JOHN P, 62, LOXWOOD ROAD, LOVEDEAN
DAWSON, EMMA J, 64, LOXWOOD ROAD, LOVEDEAN
DAWSON, LIS, 64, LOXWOOD ROAD, LOVEDEAN
DAWSON, MARTIN J, 64, LOXWOOD ROAD, LOVEDEAN
DAWSON, STEPHEN J.H, 64, LOXWOOD ROAD, LOVEDEAN
REX, ANNE-MARIE, 66, LOXWOOD ROAD, LOVEDEAN
REX, RAYMOND H, 66, LOXWOOD ROAD, LOVEDEAN
CHAPLAIN, KENNETH R, 68, LOXWOOD ROAD, LOVEDEAN
CHAPLAIN, SALLY A, 68, LOXWOOD ROAD, LOVEDEAN
WILLIAMS, PAMELA S, 70, LOXWOOD ROAD, LOVEDEAN
WILLIAMS, PAUL H, 70, LOXWOOD ROAD, LOVEDEAN
BATCHELER, CHERIFA A, 72, LOXWOOD ROAD, LOVEDEAN
BATCHELER, LINDSAY R, 72, LOXWOOD ROAD, LOVEDEAN
WHITE, ADRIAN P, 74, LOXWOOD ROAD, LOVEDEAN
WHITE, LISA A, 74, LOXWOOD ROAD, LOVEDEAN
TUSLER, KATHLEEN M, 76, LOXWOOD ROAD, LOVEDEAN
TUSLER, PHILIP D, 76, LOXWOOD ROAD, LOVEDEAN
CUMMINGS, DAVID C, 78, LOXWOOD ROAD, LOVEDEAN
LAWRENCE, DAVID J, 80, LOXWOOD ROAD, LOVEDEAN
LAWRENCE, MICHELE L, 80, LOXWOOD ROAD, LOVEDEAN
WHITTINGHAM, GREGORY M, 82, LOXWOOD ROAD,
WOOD, ELIZABETH G, 82, LOXWOOD ROAD, LOVEDEAN
COLLINS, MARK A, 84, LOXWOOD ROAD, LOVEDEAN
COLLINS, SANDRA C, 84, LOXWOOD ROAD, LOVEDEAN
MCILWRAITH, ANTONIA B.H, 86, LOXWOOD ROAD,
THOMAS, ANNELORE G.M, 86, LOXWOOD ROAD, LOVEDEAN
THOMAS, PETER N, 86, LOXWOOD ROAD, LOVEDEAN
JOHNSON, JOHN, 88, LOXWOOD ROAD, LOVEDEAN
SCOUSE, KAREN J, 88, LOXWOOD ROAD, LOVEDEAN
EYNON, GARETH, 90, LOXWOOD ROAD, LOVEDEAN
EYNON, GLYN, 90, LOXWOOD ROAD, LOVEDEAN
EYNON, JANET, 90, LOXWOOD ROAD, LOVEDEAN
EYNON, REBECCA, 90, LOXWOOD ROAD, LOVEDEAN
WELLINGS, CATHERINE M, 92, LOXWOOD ROAD, LOVEDEAN
WELLINGS, PAUL, 92, LOXWOOD ROAD, LOVEDEAN
WELLINGS, RYAN P, 92, LOXWOOD ROAD, LOVEDEAN
BLAYDES, ANGELA J, 94, LOXWOOD ROAD, LOVEDEAN
BLAYDES, MARK H, 94, LOXWOOD ROAD, LOVEDEAN
BLAYDES, SALLY E, 94, LOXWOOD ROAD, LOVEDEAN
KNIGHT, CAROL, 96, LOXWOOD ROAD, LOVEDEAN
KNIGHT, JAMES G, 96, LOXWOOD ROAD, LOVEDEAN
JAMES, ANNA, 98, LOXWOOD ROAD, LOVEDEAN
JAMES, JANE, 98, LOXWOOD ROAD, LOVEDEAN
JAMES, MICHAEL D, 98, LOXWOOD ROAD, LOVEDEAN
JAMES, TOM, 98, LOXWOOD ROAD, LOVEDEAN
HOHL, DAVID, 100, LOXWOOD ROAD, LOVEDEAN
SMITH, HELEN, 100, LOXWOOD ROAD, LOVEDEAN
WARREN, JAMES M, 102, LOXWOOD ROAD, LOVEDEAN
WARREN, MICHAEL D, 102, LOXWOOD ROAD, LOVEDEAN
WARREN, SUSAN J, 102, LOXWOOD ROAD, LOVEDEAN
PENNERY, JOHN P, 104, LOXWOOD ROAD, LOVEDEAN
PENNERY, KAREN J, 104, LOXWOOD ROAD, LOVEDEAN
MEREDITH, ALAN E, 1, LYNE PLACE, HORNDEAN
MEREDITH, ROBERT, 1, LYNE PLACE, HORNDEAN
MEREDITH, SUSAN, 1, LYNE PLACE, HORNDEAN
MEREDITH, VIVIENNE, 1, LYNE PLACE, HORNDEAN
NEWELL, JOAN E, 2, LYNE PLACE, HORNDEAN
NEWELL, KENNETH B, 2, LYNE PLACE, HORNDEAN
PHILLIPS, MICHAEL G, 3, LYNE PLACE, HORNDEAN
PHILLIPS, SANDRA G, 3, LYNE PLACE, HORNDEAN
SAWYER, KEVIN M, 4, LYNE PLACE, HORNDEAN
SAWYER, NICOLA L, 4, LYNE PLACE, HORNDEAN
MARSHALL, IAN K, 5, LYNE PLACE, HORNDEAN
MARSHALL, JOANNE C, 5, LYNE PLACE, HORNDEAN
MARSHALL, PAMELA A, 5, LYNE PLACE, HORNDEAN
GROVES, JANET, 6, LYNE PLACE, HORNDEAN
GROVES, PETER A, 6, LYNE PLACE, HORNDEAN
COLTON, JUNE R, 7, LYNE PLACE, HORNDEAN
COLTON, ROBERT L, 7, LYNE PLACE, HORNDEAN
THATCHER, ALBERT R, 1, CAUSEWAY FARM, LYNE PLACE,
THATCHER, ROSEMARY F, 1, CAUSEWAY FARM, LYNE PLACE,
SMITH, VERA D, 2, CAUSEWAY FARM, LYNE PLACE,
CONSIDINE, IRENE V, 3, CAUSEWAY FARM, LYNE PLACE,
PULLEN, LESLIE E, 4, CAUSEWAY FARM, LYNE PLACE,
BIGSWORTH, EDITH N, 5, CAUSEWAY FARM, LYNE PLACE,
GARDNER, EMILY D.E, 6, CAUSEWAY FARM, LYNE PLACE,
YOULDON, PHYLLIS R, 8, CAUSEWAY FARM, LYNE PLACE,
SMITH, MAUDE, 9, CAUSEWAY FARM, LYNE PLACE,
HARRIS, GWYNETH Q.E, 10, CAUSEWAY FARM, LYNE PLACE,
SANDALLS, CONSTANCE M, 11, CAUSEWAY FARM, LYNE PLACE, HORNDEAN
LEWIS, VIOLET E, 12, CAUSEWAY FARM, LYNE PLACE,
COOKE, CHARLES O, 13, CAUSEWAY FARM, LYNE PLACE,
JENKIN, KENNETH H, 14, CAUSEWAY FARM, LYNE PLACE,
COCKS, JESSIE B, 15, CAUSEWAY FARM, LYNE PLACE,
PERKINS, AGNES E, 16, CAUSEWAY FARM, LYNE PLACE,
PHILLIPS, IRENE M, 17, CAUSEWAY FARM, LYNE PLACE,
SHILHAM, EDNA E, 18, CAUSEWAY FARM, LYNE PLACE,
WORWOOD, GERTRUDE F.E, 19, CAUSEWAY FARM, LYNE PLACE, HORNDEAN
RUSSELL, ELSIE J, 20, CAUSEWAY FARM, LYNE PLACE,
RUSSELL, GEORGE W, 20, CAUSEWAY FARM, LYNE PLACE,
WHITING, GLADYS L, 22, CAUSEWAY FARM, LYNE PLACE,
SANDERSON, ROSINA J, 23, CAUSEWAY FARM, LYNE PLACE,
NICHOLAS, ESME V, 24, CAUSEWAY FARM, LYNE PLACE,
HALL, MARY, 25, CAUSEWAY FARM, LYNE PLACE,
GRAYER, MINNIE, 26, CAUSEWAY FARM, LYNE PLACE,
PLEDGER, NELLIE, 27, CAUSEWAY FARM, LYNE PLACE,
JACKETT, ENA L, 28, CAUSEWAY FARM, LYNE PLACE,
PHILLIPS, ETHEL P, 29, CAUSEWAY FARM, LYNE PLACE,
TESTER, OLIVE C, 30, CAUSEWAY FARM, LYNE PLACE,
AMPHLETT, DOROTHY L.P, 31, CAUSEWAY FARM, LYNE PLACE,
HUSKINSON, SARAH J, 32, CAUSEWAY FARM, LYNE PLACE,
MAKEPEACE, ALICE E, 33, CAUSEWAY FARM, LYNE PLACE,
GOTHERIDGE, EVELINE, 34, CAUSEWAY FARM, LYNE PLACE,
SHEAFF, EDWARD C, 35, CAUSEWAY FARM, LYNE PLACE,
LEMON, MARION O, 36, CAUSEWAY FARM, LYNE PLACE,
SMITH, VIOLET L, 37, CAUSEWAY FARM, LYNE PLACE,
SNAITH, GEORGE S, 38, CAUSEWAY FARM, LYNE PLACE,
ROBERTS, JANET L, 39, CAUSEWAY FARM, LYNE PLACE,
ROGERS, IRIS, 40, CAUSEWAY FARM, LYNE PLACE,
ROGERS, MOLLIE, 40, CAUSEWAY FARM, LYNE PLACE,
ALLSOP, CHRISTINA C, 41, CAUSEWAY FARM, LYNE PLACE,
BALCHIN, FREDERICK G, 42, CAUSEWAY FARM, LYNE PLACE,
BALCHIN, PATRICIA E, 42, CAUSEWAY FARM, LYNE PLACE,
HAMMOND, JEAN G, 43, CAUSEWAY FARM, LYNE PLACE,
BEAGLEY, DOROTHY M, 44, CAUSEWAY FARM, LYNE PLACE,
BEAGLEY, MONTAGUE W, 44, CAUSEWAY FARM, LYNE PLACE,
GRAYLAND, PATRICIA E, 45, CAUSEWAY FARM, LYNE PLACE,
HELLIER, JOYCE F, 46, CAUSEWAY FARM, LYNE PLACE,
MILES, GERALD R, 47, CAUSEWAY FARM, LYNE PLACE,
SAUNDERS, EDNA G, 48, CAUSEWAY FARM, LYNE PLACE,
MARDEL, IVY F, 49, CAUSEWAY FARM, LYNE PLACE,
MAY, FLORENCE A, 50, CAUSEWAY FARM, LYNE PLACE,
NICHOLSON, CYRIL V.J, 51, CAUSEWAY FARM, LYNE PLACE,
DRIVER, MARGARET E, 52, CAUSEWAY FARM, LYNE PLACE,
BRYANT, BERENICE M, 53, CAUSEWAY FARM, LYNE PLACE,
BRYANT, JAMES P, 53, CAUSEWAY FARM, LYNE PLACE,
BRACK, MARGARET A, 54, CAUSEWAY FARM, LYNE PLACE,
BLABER, ALICE, 55, CAUSEWAY FARM, LYNE PLACE,
HURST, FLORENCE E, 56, CAUSEWAY FARM, LYNE PLACE,
WILSON, PATRICIA J, 57, CAUSEWAY FARM, LYNE PLACE,
VAILE, FLORENCE L, 58, CAUSEWAY FARM, LYNE PLACE,
ROGERS, PERCY A, 59, CAUSEWAY FARM, LYNE PLACE,
ROGERS, PHYLLIS M, 59, CAUSEWAY FARM, LYNE PLACE,
KOUGHAN, ANNE K, 60, CAUSEWAY FARM, LYNE PLACE,
WHITLOCK, MONICA J, 61, CAUSEWAY FARM, LYNE PLACE,
CLARK, REGINALD E, 62, CAUSEWAY FARM, LYNE PLACE,
CLARK, WINIFRED E, 62, CAUSEWAY FARM, LYNE PLACE,
DUNFORD, SYBIL M, 63, CAUSEWAY FARM, LYNE PLACE,
LEE, MABEL, 64, CAUSEWAY FARM, LYNE PLACE, HORNDEAN
LEE, ETTIE, 65, CAUSEWAY FARM, LYNE PLACE, HORNDEAN
ROBERTS, WILLIAM A, 66, CAUSEWAY FARM, LYNE PLACE,
SHERBOURNE, GRACE H, 66, CAUSEWAY FARM, LYNE PLACE,
BRANDOM, IVY K, 67, CAUSEWAY FARM, LYNE PLACE,
BARKER, ROSIE E, 68, CAUSEWAY FARM, LYNE PLACE,
BURKETT, ARTHUR J, 69, CAUSEWAY FARM, LYNE PLACE,
BURKETT, AVRIL B, 69, CAUSEWAY FARM, LYNE PLACE,
HILLS, FREDERICK J.R, 70, CAUSEWAY FARM, LYNE PLACE,
HILLS, PATRICIA M, 70, CAUSEWAY FARM, LYNE PLACE,
ARNOLD, DOROTHY A.M, 71, CAUSEWAY FARM, LYNE PLACE,
ARNOLD, WILLIAM J, 71, CAUSEWAY FARM, LYNE PLACE,
TOWNER, CHRISTINE A, 18, NEW ROAD, LOVEDEAN
TOWNER, KATRINA E, 18, NEW ROAD, LOVEDEAN
TOWNER, ROGER R.D, 18, NEW ROAD, LOVEDEAN
SMITH, BETTY E, 19, NEW ROAD, LOVEDEAN
GIBBON, BARBARA L, 20, NEW ROAD, LOVEDEAN
GIBBON, GORDON W.A, 20, NEW ROAD, LOVEDEAN
TRAVISS, GORDON P, 21, NEW ROAD, LOVEDEAN
TRAVISS, SUSANNE, 21, NEW ROAD, LOVEDEAN
RAND, GILLIAN M, 22, NEW ROAD, LOVEDEAN
RAND, KENNETH, 22, NEW ROAD, LOVEDEAN
RAND, MICHAEL A, 22, NEW ROAD, LOVEDEAN
HAYWARD-CRISP, RITA L, 23, NEW ROAD, LOVEDEAN
HAYWARD-CRISP, ROY A, 23, NEW ROAD, LOVEDEAN
ELLIOTT, DAVID J, 24, NEW ROAD, LOVEDEAN
ELLIOTT, HAZEL M, 24, NEW ROAD, LOVEDEAN
DAVIES, GLORIA P, 25, NEW ROAD, LOVEDEAN
DAVIES, STUART M, 25, NEW ROAD, LOVEDEAN
PHILLIPS, AGNES J, 25, NEW ROAD, LOVEDEAN
SCOTT, ANDREW P, 26, NEW ROAD, LOVEDEAN
SCOTT, CHRISTINE M, 26, NEW ROAD, LOVEDEAN
FIFIELD, KEVIN, 27, NEW ROAD, LOVEDEAN
GOODWIN, TONI L, 27, NEW ROAD, LOVEDEAN
HUCKLEBRIDGE, DAVID W, 27, NEW ROAD, LOVEDEAN
HUCKLEBRIDGE, JUDITH M, 27, NEW ROAD, LOVEDEAN
BARNARD, ELVA A, 28, NEW ROAD, LOVEDEAN
BARNARD, HARRY, 28, NEW ROAD, LOVEDEAN
KEMP, RUPERT R, 29, NEW ROAD, LOVEDEAN
HUDSON, GRAHAM E, 30, NEW ROAD, LOVEDEAN
HUDSON, KAY M, 30, NEW ROAD, LOVEDEAN
HUDSON, LISA A, 30, NEW ROAD, LOVEDEAN
TURNILL, AMBER C.J, 31, NEW ROAD, LOVEDEAN
CORNWELL, SUSAN A, 32, NEW ROAD, LOVEDEAN
TURNILL, EVAN, 33, NEW ROAD, LOVEDEAN
TURNILL, MARGARET T, 33, NEW ROAD, LOVEDEAN
TURNILL, PETER R, 33, NEW ROAD, LOVEDEAN
DIXON, COLIN A, 34, NEW ROAD, LOVEDEAN
SUMNERS, ANTHONY J, 35, NEW ROAD, LOVEDEAN
SUMNERS, SHEILA, 35, NEW ROAD, LOVEDEAN
GORSHKOV, DAVID, 36, NEW ROAD, LOVEDEAN
GORSHKOV, KAREN E, 36, NEW ROAD, LOVEDEAN
SWIFT, ANGELA M, 37, NEW ROAD, LOVEDEAN
SWIFT, ANNEKE K.M, 37, NEW ROAD, LOVEDEAN
SWIFT, GEORGIA J.K, 37, NEW ROAD, LOVEDEAN
SWIFT, JOAN K, 37, NEW ROAD, LOVEDEAN
SWIFT, RAYMOND W, 37, NEW ROAD, LOVEDEAN
SWIFT, SJOKE P.A, 37, NEW ROAD, LOVEDEAN
SWIFT, WILLIAM H, 37, NEW ROAD, LOVEDEAN
SHAKESPEAR, JOHN G.W, 38, NEW ROAD, LOVEDEAN
SHAKESPEAR, MARION L, 38, NEW ROAD, LOVEDEAN
SHAKESPEAR, TIMOTHY J.W, 38, NEW ROAD, LOVEDEAN
KNIGHT, BERNARD A, 41, NEW ROAD, LOVEDEAN
KNIGHT, EILEEN D, 41, NEW ROAD, LOVEDEAN
MEREDITH, MARGARET E, 43, NEW ROAD, LOVEDEAN
MEREDITH, RONALD W, 43, NEW ROAD, LOVEDEAN
MEREDITH, STEVEN C, 43, NEW ROAD, LOVEDEAN
ROBERTS, JEANETTE, 1, NIGHTJAR CLOSE, LOVEDEAN
ROBERTS, PAUL H, 1, NIGHTJAR CLOSE, LOVEDEAN
O'LEARY, BARRIE P, 2, NIGHTJAR CLOSE, LOVEDEAN
O'LEARY, LESLEY J, 2, NIGHTJAR CLOSE, LOVEDEAN
ARNOLD, BARRY S, 3, NIGHTJAR CLOSE, LOVEDEAN

WEEKS, HELEN C, 3, NIGHTJAR CLOSE, LOVEDEAN
BORROW, ALAN S, 4, NIGHTJAR CLOSE, LOVEDEAN
LONGDEN-THURGOOD, CLIFFORD J, 5, NIGHTJAR CLOSE,
LONGDEN-THURGOOD, PATRICIA A, 5, NIGHTJAR CLOSE,
HEATH, ANN D, 6, NIGHTJAR CLOSE, LOVEDEAN
HEATH, STANLEY V, 6, NIGHTJAR CLOSE, LOVEDEAN
HALL, ALISON J, 7, NIGHTJAR CLOSE, LOVEDEAN
HALL, DEREK A, 7, NIGHTJAR CLOSE, LOVEDEAN
ROBSON, CAROLINE M, 8, NIGHTJAR CLOSE, LOVEDEAN
ROBSON, CHARLES J, 8, NIGHTJAR CLOSE, LOVEDEAN
POOLE, HEATHER I, 9, NIGHTJAR CLOSE, LOVEDEAN
POOLE, MICHAEL, 9, NIGHTJAR CLOSE, LOVEDEAN
LOCKE, DAVID H, 10, NIGHTJAR CLOSE, LOVEDEAN
NICHOLSON, BEVERLY J, 10, NIGHTJAR CLOSE, LOVEDEAN
MASON, KATHLEEN M, 14, NIGHTJAR CLOSE, LOVEDEAN
MASON, PHILIP J, 14, NIGHTJAR CLOSE, LOVEDEAN
ROBINSON, JAMES W, 15, NIGHTJAR CLOSE, LOVEDEAN
ROBINSON, MAVIS A, 15, NIGHTJAR CLOSE, LOVEDEAN
HATCH, CHRISTOPHER R, 16, NIGHTJAR CLOSE, LOVEDEAN
HATCH, JOANNE, 16, NIGHTJAR CLOSE, LOVEDEAN
GENT, MARY H, 17, NIGHTJAR CLOSE, LOVEDEAN
WORLEY, CLARE L, 18, NIGHTJAR CLOSE, LOVEDEAN
WORLEY, JONATHAN R, 18, NIGHTJAR CLOSE, LOVEDEAN
MANLEY, MARIE J, 19, NIGHTJAR CLOSE, LOVEDEAN
MANLEY, PETER G, 19, NIGHTJAR CLOSE, LOVEDEAN
BEZZANT, KRISTIAN, 20, NIGHTJAR CLOSE, LOVEDEAN
KERRIDGE, JAQUELINE C, 21, NIGHTJAR CLOSE, LOVEDEAN
FREEMAN, THOMAS A, 1, NURSERY GARDENS, HORNDEAN
LAGUE, SHEILA M, 1A, NURSERY GARDENS, HORNDEAN
GARDNER, LAURA, 2, NURSERY GARDENS, HORNDEAN
FOWLER, GRAHAM J, 2A, NURSERY GARDENS, HORNDEAN
FOWLER, LINDA A, 2A, NURSERY GARDENS, HORNDEAN
JONES, MICHAEL R, 3, NURSERY GARDENS, HORNDEAN
JONES, SHIRLEY A, 3, NURSERY GARDENS, HORNDEAN
LILLEY, ANDREW M, 4, NURSERY GARDENS, HORNDEAN
LILLEY, DIANA F, 4, NURSERY GARDENS, HORNDEAN
LILLEY, PETER E.S, 4, NURSERY GARDENS, HORNDEAN
LILLEY, RICHARD S.S, 4, NURSERY GARDENS, HORNDEAN
HAXELL, CHRISTOPHER P, 5, NURSERY GARDENS,
HAXELL, DENNIS A, 5, NURSERY GARDENS, HORNDEAN
HAXELL, WENDY E, 5, NURSERY GARDENS, HORNDEAN
BARRETT, SHEILA D, 6, NURSERY GARDENS, HORNDEAN
WILLARD, ROBINA H, 7, NURSERY GARDENS, HORNDEAN
WILLARD, STEPHEN H, 7, NURSERY GARDENS, HORNDEAN
BRISTOW, JOAN K, 8, NURSERY GARDENS, HORNDEAN
DINNIS, JESSIE H, 8, NURSERY GARDENS, HORNDEAN
HEWITT, JENNIFER J, 9, NURSERY GARDENS, HORNDEAN
HEWITT, JOHN J, 9, NURSERY GARDENS, HORNDEAN
HEWITT, MARJORIE P, 9, NURSERY GARDENS, HORNDEAN
BROCKMAN, JONATHAN P, 10, NURSERY GARDENS,
BROCKMAN, MARK J, 10, NURSERY GARDENS, HORNDEAN
LEGG, GILLIAN M, 10, NURSERY GARDENS, HORNDEAN
LEGG, JOHN A, 10, NURSERY GARDENS, HORNDEAN
COOKE, DAVID, 11, NURSERY GARDENS, HORNDEAN
COOKE, DEBORAH A, 11, NURSERY GARDENS, HORNDEAN
COOKE, MATTHEW A, 11, NURSERY GARDENS, HORNDEAN
COOKE, ROSEMARY A, 11, NURSERY GARDENS, HORNDEAN
PEABODY-ROLF, HELEN R, 12, NURSERY GARDENS,
PEABODY-ROLF, JOHN P, 12, NURSERY GARDENS, HORNDEAN
ROLISON, REBECCA J, 14, NURSERY GARDENS, HORNDEAN
ROLISON, SALLY J, 14, NURSERY GARDENS, HORNDEAN
HUGHES, ANTHONY A, 15, NURSERY GARDENS, HORNDEAN
HUGHES, KIRSTY J, 15, NURSERY GARDENS, HORNDEAN
FRANCIS, STEPHEN J, 16, NURSERY GARDENS, HORNDEAN
PETTIFER, SUSAN J, 16, NURSERY GARDENS, HORNDEAN
EYRES, KAREN, 17, NURSERY GARDENS, HORNDEAN
SMITH, MARTIN J, 18, NURSERY GARDENS, HORNDEAN
RODGERS, ADRIAN, 1, OAKS COPPICE, HORNDEAN
RODGERS, HELEN, 1, OAKS COPPICE, HORNDEAN
CLARKE, JOHN, 2, OAKS COPPICE, HORNDEAN
CLARKE, MARY A, 2, OAKS COPPICE, HORNDEAN
BECK, JOANNA, 3, OAKS COPPICE, HORNDEAN
BECK, PAUL, 3, OAKS COPPICE, HORNDEAN
WEST, HAYLEY N, 4, OAKS COPPICE, HORNDEAN
WEST, PETER D, 4, OAKS COPPICE, HORNDEAN
WEST, SHARON M, 4, OAKS COPPICE, HORNDEAN
CHARD, DEREK R, 5, OAKS COPPICE, HORNDEAN
CHARD, JANET, 5, OAKS COPPICE, HORNDEAN
WHITE, KATY J, 6, OAKS COPPICE, HORNDEAN
WHITE, LUCY J, 6, OAKS COPPICE, HORNDEAN
WHITE, PETER C, 6, OAKS COPPICE, HORNDEAN
WHITE, SYLVIA C, 6, OAKS COPPICE, HORNDEAN
HARLEY, GRAHAM L, 7, OAKS COPPICE, HORNDEAN
HARMER, ALLAN A.G, 8, OAKS COPPICE, HORNDEAN
HARMER, SUSAN C, 8, OAKS COPPICE, HORNDEAN
BEALE, ANDREW A.J, 9, OAKS COPPICE, HORNDEAN
BEALE, ANGELA M, 9, OAKS COPPICE, HORNDEAN
BEALE, RACHEL M, 9, OAKS COPPICE, HORNDEAN
BEALE, ROBERT J, 9, OAKS COPPICE, HORNDEAN
SHEPPERD, MARK I, 10, OAKS COPPICE, HORNDEAN
SHEPPERD, RACHEL J, 10, OAKS COPPICE, HORNDEAN
HAY, JOHN, 11, OAKS COPPICE, HORNDEAN
SPARROW, ANITA M, 11, OAKS COPPICE, HORNDEAN
COCKING, MARINA E, 15, OAKS COPPICE, HORNDEAN
COCKING, PETER W, 15, OAKS COPPICE, HORNDEAN
MARSH, ALAN, 17, OAKS COPPICE, HORNDEAN
MARSH, LOUISE A, 17, OAKS COPPICE, HORNDEAN
MARSH, PATRICIA I, 17, OAKS COPPICE, HORNDEAN
COX, CHRISTINE R, 19, OAKS COPPICE, HORNDEAN
COX, COLIN J, 19, OAKS COPPICE, HORNDEAN
COX, CONSTANCE L, 19, OAKS COPPICE, HORNDEAN
BARRON, EILEEN M, 21, OAKS COPPICE, HORNDEAN
BARRON, ROBERT M, 21, OAKS COPPICE, HORNDEAN
STAFFORD, LOUIS G, 23, OAKS COPPICE, HORNDEAN
MCKAY, ELAINE C, 24, OAKS COPPICE, HORNDEAN
MCKAY, IAN R, 24, OAKS COPPICE, HORNDEAN
MCKAY, LINDA S, 24, OAKS COPPICE, HORNDEAN
WOODCOCK, PAUL A, 24, OAKS COPPICE, HORNDEAN
KNIGHT, CHRISTOPHER R, 25, OAKS COPPICE, HORNDEAN
KNIGHT, JULIE A, 25, OAKS COPPICE, HORNDEAN
BUTTERS, BRIAN C, 26, OAKS COPPICE, HORNDEAN
BUTTERS, JOAN M, 26, OAKS COPPICE, HORNDEAN
MITCHARD, ALISON L, 28, OAKS COPPICE, HORNDEAN
MITCHARD, DAVID J, 28, OAKS COPPICE, HORNDEAN
KEMP, ANNETTE Y, 30, OAKS COPPICE, HORNDEAN
KEMP, RICHARD J, 30, OAKS COPPICE, HORNDEAN
KEMP, SARAH L, 30, OAKS COPPICE, HORNDEAN
ETHERINGTON, DAVID A, 1, PENTERE ROAD, LOVEDEAN
ETHERINGTON, JULIE E, 1, PENTERE ROAD, LOVEDEAN
ETHERINGTON, LOUISE J, 1, PENTERE ROAD, LOVEDEAN
RASELL, JANE D, 2, PENTERE ROAD, LOVEDEAN
WHITE, PAUL L, 2, PENTERE ROAD, LOVEDEAN
WOODCOCK, JACQUELINE, 3, PENTERE ROAD, LOVEDEAN
WOODCOCK, JOHN, 3, PENTERE ROAD, LOVEDEAN
STAPLEY, DAVID T, 4, PENTERE ROAD, LOVEDEAN
STAPLEY, MARIE, 4, PENTERE ROAD, LOVEDEAN
STAPLEY, PAUL D, 4, PENTERE ROAD, LOVEDEAN
GANNON, CHRISTOPHER A, 6, PENTERE ROAD, LOVEDEAN
HART, SUSIE, 6, PENTERE ROAD, LOVEDEAN
JAMES, ELIZABETH, 7, PENTERE ROAD, LOVEDEAN
WITHEY, EILEEN M, 8, PENTERE ROAD, LOVEDEAN
WITHEY, SIMON B, 8, PENTERE ROAD, LOVEDEAN
PERRY, BRENDA K, 9, PENTERE ROAD, LOVEDEAN
PERRY, HOWARD A, 9, PENTERE ROAD, LOVEDEAN
RIDGES, JONATHAN P, 10, PENTERE ROAD, LOVEDEAN
RIDGES, MARGARET, 10, PENTERE ROAD, LOVEDEAN
O'SHEA, BENJAMIN M, 11, PENTERE ROAD, LOVEDEAN
O'SHEA, MICHAEL G, 11, PENTERE ROAD, LOVEDEAN
O'SHEA, PATRICIA J, 11, PENTERE ROAD, LOVEDEAN
SMITH, IAN D, 12, PENTERE ROAD, LOVEDEAN
SMITH, ZOE, 12, PENTERE ROAD, LOVEDEAN
WOODWARD, CATHERINE, 14, PENTERE ROAD, LOVEDEAN
WOODWARD, MERVYN E, 14, PENTERE ROAD, LOVEDEAN
WOODWARD, MICHELLE L, 14, PENTERE ROAD, LOVEDEAN
MILES, CAROLE Y, 15, PENTERE ROAD, LOVEDEAN
MILES, GEORGINA C, 15, PENTERE ROAD, LOVEDEAN
MILES, GERALD H, 15, PENTERE ROAD, LOVEDEAN
TYE, RICHARD K, 16, PENTERE ROAD, LOVEDEAN
TYE, SANDRA A, 16, PENTERE ROAD, LOVEDEAN
TYE, SONJA M, 16, PENTERE ROAD, LOVEDEAN
TYE, TAMARA M, 16, PENTERE ROAD, LOVEDEAN
ROWE, JOANNE L, 17, PENTERE ROAD, LOVEDEAN
ROWE, PHILIP J, 17, PENTERE ROAD, LOVEDEAN
KEARSEY, GAIL A, 18, PENTERE ROAD, LOVEDEAN
KEARSEY, RICHARD J, 18, PENTERE ROAD, LOVEDEAN
JOLLIFFE, ANTHONY N, 19, PENTERE ROAD, LOVEDEAN
JOLLIFFE, JULIE E, 19, PENTERE ROAD, LOVEDEAN
NOBLE, DAVID, 20, PENTERE ROAD, LOVEDEAN
NOBLE, EILEEN B, 20, PENTERE ROAD, LOVEDEAN
BURNS, MARGARET-MARY, 21, PENTERE ROAD, LOVEDEAN
YOUENS, PETER H, 21, PENTERE ROAD, LOVEDEAN
MCKENNA, BRIAN R, 22, PENTERE ROAD, LOVEDEAN
MCKENNA, CLAIRE L, 22, PENTERE ROAD, LOVEDEAN
MCKENNA, HAYLEY A.C, 22, PENTERE ROAD, LOVEDEAN
MCCUE, GWYNETH S, 23, PENTERE ROAD, LOVEDEAN
MCCUE, ROGER V, 23, PENTERE ROAD, LOVEDEAN
CROWLEY, JUDITH M, 24, PENTERE ROAD, LOVEDEAN
PYLE, DANIEL M, 25, PENTERE ROAD, LOVEDEAN
PYLE, GAIL D, 25, PENTERE ROAD, LOVEDEAN
PYLE, NICOLA-MARIE, 25, PENTERE ROAD, LOVEDEAN
PYLE, RICHARD M, 25, PENTERE ROAD, LOVEDEAN
GODDARD, JANE E, 26, PENTERE ROAD, LOVEDEAN
GODDARD, JERRY R, 26, PENTERE ROAD, LOVEDEAN
LAMB, CHARLES P, 27, PENTERE ROAD, LOVEDEAN
LAMB, MAUREEN, 27, PENTERE ROAD, LOVEDEAN
MORGAN, DAVID J.C, 28, PENTERE ROAD, LOVEDEAN
MORGAN, JACQUELINE A, 28, PENTERE ROAD, LOVEDEAN
MARINACCIO, JENNIFER, 29, PENTERE ROAD, LOVEDEAN
MARINACCIO, LUCIANO, 29, PENTERE ROAD, LOVEDEAN
ELLIS, SUSANNAH, 30, PENTERE ROAD, LOVEDEAN
REYNOLDS, PHILIP J, 30, PENTERE ROAD, LOVEDEAN
WILSON, COLIN J, 31, PENTERE ROAD, LOVEDEAN
WILSON, JULIE, 31, PENTERE ROAD, LOVEDEAN
TREW, KERINA J, 1, PEPER HAROW, HORNDEAN
TREW, RICKY, 1, PEPER HAROW, HORNDEAN
ENEFER, WALTER D, 3, PEPER HAROW, HORNDEAN
PAVITT, KEITH B, 5, PEPER HAROW, HORNDEAN
PAVITT, RITA, 5, PEPER HAROW, HORNDEAN
BRYANT, AUDREY J, 7, PEPER HAROW, HORNDEAN
HALLS, ANDREW F, 9, PEPER HAROW, HORNDEAN
HALLS, FRANK, 9, PEPER HAROW, HORNDEAN
HALLS, JOYCE M, 9, PEPER HAROW, HORNDEAN
MUNDELL, LOUISE, 1, PIPIT CLOSE, HORNDEAN
MUNDELL, WILLIAM L, 1, PIPIT CLOSE, HORNDEAN
DEAN, ANTHONY, 2, PIPIT CLOSE, HORNDEAN
DEAN, JOAN, 2, PIPIT CLOSE, HORNDEAN
DEAN, KAREN, 2, PIPIT CLOSE, HORNDEAN
DEAN, TRACY, 2, PIPIT CLOSE, HORNDEAN
BARNES, SUZANNE M, 3, PIPIT CLOSE, HORNDEAN
SLARK, ALBERT A.P, 4, PIPIT CLOSE, HORNDEAN
SLARK, CHLOE J, 4, PIPIT CLOSE, HORNDEAN
SLANE, HELEN A, 5, PIPIT CLOSE, HORNDEAN
SLANE, NICHOLAS P, 5, PIPIT CLOSE, HORNDEAN
KELLEHER, CLARE A, 6, PIPIT CLOSE, HORNDEAN
KELLEHER, WILLIAM A, 6, PIPIT CLOSE, HORNDEAN
HARRIS, DEBRA, 7, PIPIT CLOSE, HORNDEAN
HARRIS, MARK J, 7, PIPIT CLOSE, HORNDEAN
LOVEGROVE, SUZANNE, 8, PIPIT CLOSE, HORNDEAN
EATON, MARTIN G, 9, PIPIT CLOSE, HORNDEAN
EDWARDS, JULIE E, 9, PIPIT CLOSE, HORNDEAN
ELMER, CHRISTOPHER D, 10, PIPIT CLOSE, HORNDEAN
ELMER, DAVID M, 10, PIPIT CLOSE, HORNDEAN
ELMER, JANET C, 10, PIPIT CLOSE, HORNDEAN
HUME, GLEN J, 11, PIPIT CLOSE, HORNDEAN
HUME, JANE E, 11, PIPIT CLOSE, HORNDEAN
FAULKNER, LORRAINE E, 1, PLOVERS ROAD, HORNDEAN
FAULKNER, MICHAEL, 1, PLOVERS ROAD, HORNDEAN
STUBBS, MARK, 2, PLOVERS ROAD, HORNDEAN
WORDEN, CLAIRE L, 2, PLOVERS ROAD, HORNDEAN
DUNLOP, WILLIAM J, 4, PLOVERS ROAD, HORNDEAN
EDWARDS, SANDRA J, 4, PLOVERS ROAD, HORNDEAN
PHILLIPS, ANDREA D, 6, PLOVERS ROAD, HORNDEAN
DITCHBURN, NICHOLA C, 8, PLOVERS ROAD, HORNDEAN
DITCHBURN, STEPHEN P, 8, PLOVERS ROAD, HORNDEAN
HYLAND, MARIE T, 6, PUMP LANE, HORNDEAN
HYLAND, MICHAEL J, 6, PUMP LANE, HORNDEAN
SHAW, CHRISTOPHER M, 7, PUMP LANE, HORNDEAN
SHAW, EVELYN R, 7, PUMP LANE, HORNDEAN
PALMER, DAVID W, 8, PUMP LANE, HORNDEAN
PALMER, SUSAN P, 8, PUMP LANE, HORNDEAN
HENNING, KENNETH F, 9, PUMP LANE, HORNDEAN
MAILES, BELINDA J, 10, PUMP LANE, HORNDEAN
MEEK, JOHN C, 10, PUMP LANE, HORNDEAN
BRODERICK, DEBORAH J, 11, PUMP LANE, HORNDEAN
BRODERICK, LIAM D, 11, PUMP LANE, HORNDEAN
CLEGG, MARGARET H, 12, PUMP LANE, HORNDEAN
CLEGG, PETER L, 12, PUMP LANE, HORNDEAN
POTTER, STEVEN A, 12, PUMP LANE, HORNDEAN
BUDD, BARBARA A, 1, QUAIL WAY, HORNDEAN
BUDD, NIGEL J, 1, QUAIL WAY, HORNDEAN
MONAHAN, DAWN P, 2, QUAIL WAY, HORNDEAN
MONAHAN, PETER, 2, QUAIL WAY, HORNDEAN
WILSON, ANDREW R, 3, QUAIL WAY, HORNDEAN
WILSON, JAYNE M, 3, QUAIL WAY, HORNDEAN
DODSWORTH, CHARMAINE L, 4, QUAIL WAY, HORNDEAN
DODSWORTH, MARTIN J, 4, QUAIL WAY, HORNDEAN
DODSWORTH, SUZANNE P, 4, QUAIL WAY, HORNDEAN
PHILLIPS, MARTIN J, 5, QUAIL WAY, HORNDEAN
PHILLIPS, TONI I, 5, QUAIL WAY, HORNDEAN
GREEN, GLENIS M, 7, QUAIL WAY, HORNDEAN
GREEN, JOHN R, 7, QUAIL WAY, HORNDEAN
HIGGINS, JOHN B, 8, QUAIL WAY, HORNDEAN
HIGGINS, SALLY B, 8, QUAIL WAY, HORNDEAN
LEROY, GEMMA J, 9, QUAIL WAY, HORNDEAN
LEROY, MARTYN J, 9, QUAIL WAY, HORNDEAN
LEROY, SUSAN A, 9, QUAIL WAY, HORNDEAN
WELLS, ADRIAN H, 10, QUAIL WAY, HORNDEAN
WELLS, MARYANNE J, 10, QUAIL WAY, HORNDEAN
TAYLOR, MARK G, 11, QUAIL WAY, HORNDEAN
TAYLOR, SANDRA D, 11, QUAIL WAY, HORNDEAN
BENNETT, PAUL D, 12, QUAIL WAY, HORNDEAN
PATTERSON, SUSAN M, 12, QUAIL WAY, HORNDEAN
CROOKS, JANICE H, 14, QUAIL WAY, HORNDEAN
CROOKS, RICHARD A, 14, QUAIL WAY, HORNDEAN
MCBRIDE, LISA L, 15, QUAIL WAY, HORNDEAN
MCBRIDE, MICHAEL E, 15, QUAIL WAY, HORNDEAN
MCBRIDE, SHONA, 15, QUAIL WAY, HORNDEAN
ROMAN, DOREEN, 16, QUAIL WAY, HORNDEAN
ROMAN, NEIL W.M, 16, QUAIL WAY, HORNDEAN
ROMAN, TREVOR W.M, 16, QUAIL WAY, HORNDEAN
O'CARROLL, AMANDA J, 17, QUAIL WAY, HORNDEAN
O'CARROLL, PAUL C, 17, QUAIL WAY, HORNDEAN
MILLER, GRAEME S, 18, QUAIL WAY, HORNDEAN
MILLER, JANE M, 18, QUAIL WAY, HORNDEAN
BARRETT, DAVID A, 19, QUAIL WAY, HORNDEAN
BARRETT, SAMANTHA M, 19, QUAIL WAY, HORNDEAN
SAWFORD, COLIN A, 20, QUAIL WAY, HORNDEAN
SAWFORD, DAWN L, 20, QUAIL WAY, HORNDEAN
GRAY, EDWARD, 21, QUAIL WAY, HORNDEAN
GRAY, PAMELA, 21, QUAIL WAY, HORNDEAN
SIM, KENNETH A, 22, QUAIL WAY, HORNDEAN
SIM, LESLEY A, 22, QUAIL WAY, HORNDEAN
MCLINN, CAROL A, 23, QUAIL WAY, HORNDEAN
FLYNN, ISOBEL M, 24, QUAIL WAY, HORNDEAN
FLYNN, PATRICK J, 24, QUAIL WAY, HORNDEAN
NOYCE, KEVIN S, 25, QUAIL WAY, HORNDEAN
NOYCE, NICOLA J, 25, QUAIL WAY, HORNDEAN
THOMPSON, DEREK, 26, QUAIL WAY, HORNDEAN
MATTHEWS, FAITH A, 27, QUAIL WAY, HORNDEAN
MATTHEWS, GARETH W, 27, QUAIL WAY, HORNDEAN
MATTHEWS, JANICE A, 27, QUAIL WAY, HORNDEAN
MATTHEWS, JOHN W, 27, QUAIL WAY, HORNDEAN
CREAMER, MARK R, 28, QUAIL WAY, HORNDEAN
CREAMER, SUSANNAH A, 28, QUAIL WAY, HORNDEAN
REARDON, DANIEL R, 29, QUAIL WAY, HORNDEAN
REARDON, JANE B, 29, QUAIL WAY, HORNDEAN
BLOCK, JEAN, 1, REDSHANK ROAD, HORNDEAN
BLOCK, KENNETH F, 1, REDSHANK ROAD, HORNDEAN
COLLINGWOOD, GAYNOR L, 2, REDSHANK ROAD,
SMITH, SUSAN M, 3, REDSHANK ROAD, HORNDEAN
GOLDUP, AUDREY B, 4, REDSHANK ROAD, HORNDEAN
SEAGER, BRIAN C, 5, REDSHANK ROAD, HORNDEAN
CONNOLLY, MARGARET, 6, REDSHANK ROAD, HORNDEAN
WARNER, ANTHONY D, 7, REDSHANK ROAD, HORNDEAN
GALE, SHAUN M, 8, REDSHANK ROAD, HORNDEAN
PALMER, BRIAN M, 9, REDSHANK ROAD, HORNDEAN
PALMER, JULIE E, 9, REDSHANK ROAD, HORNDEAN
UNDERWOOD, DEBRA A, 10, REDSHANK ROAD, HORNDEAN
UNDERWOOD, JAMES F, 10, REDSHANK ROAD, HORNDEAN

Electoral Roll

TAYLOR, NICOLA J, 11, REDSHANK ROAD, HORNDEAN
TAYLOR, PAUL N, 11, REDSHANK ROAD, HORNDEAN
LONG, CHRISTINE, 12, REDSHANK ROAD, HORNDEAN
SCOTT, ALBAN, 14, REDSHANK ROAD, HORNDEAN
SCOTT, JOYCE, 14, REDSHANK ROAD, HORNDEAN
CHAPMAN, JULIA S, 15, REDSHANK ROAD, HORNDEAN
SEARLE, CHRISTOPHER A, 16, REDSHANK ROAD, HORNDEAN
SEARLE, JULIE A, 16, REDSHANK ROAD, HORNDEAN
CHAPLIN, MICHAEL J, 17, REDSHANK ROAD, HORNDEAN
CHAPLIN, SUSAN N, 17, REDSHANK ROAD, HORNDEAN
KEENE, NICOLA J, 18, REDSHANK ROAD, HORNDEAN
KEENE, STEPHEN O, 18, REDSHANK ROAD, HORNDEAN
GRAVES, BRIAN A, 19, REDSHANK ROAD, HORNDEAN
GRAVES, JUNE R, 19, REDSHANK ROAD, HORNDEAN
MULLINS, MARTIN J, 20, REDSHANK ROAD, HORNDEAN
MULLINS, SUSAN J, 20, REDSHANK ROAD, HORNDEAN
PILKINGTON, GRAHAM K, 21, REDSHANK ROAD, HORNDEAN
PILKINGTON, SUSAN D, 21, REDSHANK ROAD, HORNDEAN
MAY, CHRISTOPHER J, 22, REDSHANK ROAD, HORNDEAN
MAY, WENDY A, 22, REDSHANK ROAD, HORNDEAN
BARTON, ANDREW D, 23, REDSHANK ROAD, HORNDEAN
BARTON, DAVID A, 23, REDSHANK ROAD, HORNDEAN
BARTON, PENELOPE J, 23, REDSHANK ROAD, HORNDEAN
HOUGHTON, PAUL, 24, REDSHANK ROAD, HORNDEAN
STOUSE, ELAINE R, 24, REDSHANK ROAD, HORNDEAN
EVELEIGH, JOHN V, 26, REDSHANK ROAD, HORNDEAN
EVELEIGH, SHIRLEY A, 26, REDSHANK ROAD, HORNDEAN
PARKS, ANDREW N, 28, REDSHANK ROAD, HORNDEAN
PARKS, JUDITH D, 28, REDSHANK ROAD, HORNDEAN
LANE, CHERYL A.W, 30, REDSHANK ROAD, HORNDEAN
LANE, PETER A.R, 30, REDSHANK ROAD, HORNDEAN
DUNN, JEREMY P, 32, REDSHANK ROAD, HORNDEAN
COLLIER, GARRY E, 34, REDSHANK ROAD, HORNDEAN
COLLIER, LINDA C, 34, REDSHANK ROAD, HORNDEAN
TRICKETT, JILL M, CARAVAN 1, VIOLA, ROADS HILL, CATHERINGTON
TRICKETT, WILLIAM D, CARAVAN 1, VIOLA, ROADS HILL,
TRICKETT, WILLIAM H, CARAVAN 1, VIOLA, ROADS HILL,
TRICKETT, SCOTT A.C, CARAVAN 2, VIOLA, ROADS HILL,
TRICKETT, SYLVIA J, CARAVAN 2, VIOLA, ROADS HILL,
BURNETT, ARTHUR R, 1, FAIRFIELDS, ROADS HILL,
BURNETT, ROSE, 1, FAIRFIELDS, ROADS HILL,
BURNETT, PETER, 2, FAIRFIELDS, ROADS HILL,
DAY, FREDERICK, 4, FAIRFIELDS, ROADS HILL,
TRICKETT, JOHN, 4, FAIRFIELDS, ROADS HILL,
TRICKETT, LOUISE, 4, FAIRFIELDS, ROADS HILL,
TRICKETT, MICHAEL, 4, FAIRFIELDS, ROADS HILL,
TRICKETT, PATRICIA, 4, FAIRFIELDS, ROADS HILL,
HUNT, DAVID, FOUR WINDS, ROADS HILL, CATHERINGTON
HUNT, MABS E, FOUR WINDS, ROADS HILL, CATHERINGTON
BRAUNTON, HENRY, WHITEGATE FARM, ROADS HILL,
BRAUNTON, MARGARET E, WHITEGATE FARM, ROADS HILL,
BROWN, MARGERET B, 5, ROSE HILL, LOVEDEAN
ROBINSON, DOROTHY I, 5, ROSE HILL, LOVEDEAN
ROBINSON, RONALD R, 5, ROSE HILL, LOVEDEAN
GRIFFITHS, CHERYL L, 7, ROSE HILL, LOVEDEAN
GRIFFITHS, DAVID M, 7, ROSE HILL, LOVEDEAN
GRIFFITHS, OWEN C, 7, ROSE HILL, LOVEDEAN
GRIFFITHS, VALERIE E, 7, ROSE HILL, LOVEDEAN
BARFOOT, GEORGE E, 9, ROSE HILL, LOVEDEAN
GOWIN, BARBARA D, ESTANCIA, ROSE HILL, LOVEDEAN
GOWIN, RONALD W, ESTANCIA, ROSE HILL, LOVEDEAN
GODDARD, JUDITH M, KILINDINI, ROSE HILL, LOVEDEAN
GODDARD, PETER F.V, KILINDINI, ROSE HILL, LOVEDEAN
ATKIN, ROBERT J, LANE END, ROSE HILL, LOVEDEAN
KEMP, DOROTHY, PEEL COTTAGE, ROSE HILL, LOVEDEAN
KEMP, TONY E, PEEL COTTAGE, ROSE HILL, LOVEDEAN
BROWN, SEAN W, TAMARISK, ROSE HILL, LOVEDEAN
KNIGHT, DANIEL J, TAMARISK, ROSE HILL, LOVEDEAN
PRICE, GARRY A, TAMARISK, ROSE HILL, LOVEDEAN
SINGLETON, MARGARET, TAMARISK, ROSE HILL, LOVEDEAN
SINGLETON, MICHAEL J, TAMARISK, ROSE HILL, LOVEDEAN
MARTIN, MICHAEL F, THE WOODLANDS, ROSE HILL,
MARTIN, SHEILA E, THE WOODLANDS, ROSE HILL,
GALYER, KATHLEEN, WELLESLEY, ROSE HILL, LOVEDEAN
HAMMOND, AUDREY E, 1, ROSELANDS, LOVEDEAN
FRANCIS, MARK J, 2, ROSELANDS, LOVEDEAN
FRANCIS, RACHEL A, 2, ROSELANDS, LOVEDEAN
HARRISON, SARA M, 3, ROSELANDS, LOVEDEAN
NICHOLSON, DEBORAH J, 4, ROSELANDS, LOVEDEAN
CONNOR, ALISON M, 5, ROSELANDS, LOVEDEAN
CONNOR, IAN G, 5, ROSELANDS, LOVEDEAN
MARTIN, ALAN R, 6, ROSELANDS, LOVEDEAN
MARTIN, HEATHER J, 6, ROSELANDS, LOVEDEAN
MARTIN, JOHN A, 6, ROSELANDS, LOVEDEAN
MARTIN, MARY, 6, ROSELANDS, LOVEDEAN
PRICE, GLYNIS, 7, ROSELANDS, LOVEDEAN
PRICE, KEITH, 7, ROSELANDS, LOVEDEAN
PETTITT, BARRIE D, 8, ROSELANDS, LOVEDEAN
PETTITT, JULIE, 8, ROSELANDS, LOVEDEAN
PETTITT, MARIE F, 8, ROSELANDS, LOVEDEAN
SANSOM, ANDREW J, 9, ROSELANDS, LOVEDEAN
SANSOM, PAULINE W, 9, ROSELANDS, LOVEDEAN
FOSTER, PETER, 10, ROSELANDS, LOVEDEAN
READ, ADA, 11, ROSELANDS, LOVEDEAN
READ, SIDNEY C, 11, ROSELANDS, LOVEDEAN
HOLE, NIGEL A, 12, ROSELANDS, LOVEDEAN
HOLE, TERESA M, 12, ROSELANDS, LOVEDEAN
FINDLAY, JOHN D, 13, ROSELANDS, LOVEDEAN
FINDLAY, KAREN S, 13, ROSELANDS, LOVEDEAN
CARTER, BRONWIN M, 14, ROSELANDS, LOVEDEAN
CARTER, PAUL B, 14, ROSELANDS, LOVEDEAN
MCDONALD, ANGELA L, 15, ROSELANDS, LOVEDEAN
MCDONALD, KEITH, 15, ROSELANDS, LOVEDEAN
BAWDEN, SARAH, 16, ROSELANDS, LOVEDEAN
ROGERS, KEVIN C, 17, ROSELANDS, LOVEDEAN
ROGERS, MARILYN E, 17, ROSELANDS, LOVEDEAN
BURGE, FRANCIS, 18, ROSELANDS, LOVEDEAN
BURGE, SUZANNA, 18, ROSELANDS, LOVEDEAN
WEBBER, BARBARA, 19, ROSELANDS, LOVEDEAN
WEBBER, MELVIN, 19, ROSELANDS, LOVEDEAN
WEBBER, VICTORIA L, 19, ROSELANDS, LOVEDEAN
ATKINSON, COLIN, 20, ROSELANDS, LOVEDEAN
ATKINSON, MADALENE M, 20, ROSELANDS, LOVEDEAN
MILLICAN, PHILIP D, 21, ROSELANDS, LOVEDEAN
CAUSLEY, PETER W, 22, ROSELANDS, LOVEDEAN
CAUSLEY, VIVIENNE Y, 22, ROSELANDS, LOVEDEAN
PERKINS, BRYAN A, 23, ROSELANDS, LOVEDEAN
KILLICK, BRIAN A, 24, ROSELANDS, LOVEDEAN
KILLICK, SUZANNE, 24, ROSELANDS, LOVEDEAN
ARMSTRONG, LINDA J, 25, ROSELANDS, LOVEDEAN
ARMSTRONG, ROBIN, 25, ROSELANDS, LOVEDEAN
TAYLOR, JANICE F, 25A, ROSELANDS, LOVEDEAN
WOODMAN, JULIE A, 25B, ROSELANDS, LOVEDEAN
WOODMAN, TERRY J, 25B, ROSELANDS, LOVEDEAN
BEACHER, ANTHONY W, 26, ROSELANDS, LOVEDEAN
BEACHER, LORNA J, 26, ROSELANDS, LOVEDEAN
BEACHER, SIMON D, 26, ROSELANDS, LOVEDEAN
DOCKERTY, FRANCES M, 27, ROSELANDS, LOVEDEAN
DRAKE, DAVID J, 30, ROSELANDS, LOVEDEAN
DRAKE, LYNN M, 30, ROSELANDS, LOVEDEAN
DILLON, CHRISTOPHER J, 31, ROSELANDS, LOVEDEAN
DILLON, JACQUELINE P, 31, ROSELANDS, LOVEDEAN
DANCE, TINA M, 32, ROSELANDS, LOVEDEAN
RAMSAY, MAIDIE E, 33, ROSELANDS, LOVEDEAN
BILLINGTON, AMANDA L, 34, ROSELANDS, LOVEDEAN
GREEN, DAWN C, 35, ROSELANDS, LOVEDEAN
GREEN, LEONARD D, 35, ROSELANDS, LOVEDEAN
STOREY, JAMES W, 36, ROSELANDS, LOVEDEAN
STOREY, JULIE A, 36, ROSELANDS, LOVEDEAN
CLAVEY, KELLY, 1, SANDPIPER CLOSE, HORNDEAN
REEVES, KEVIN A.G, 2, SANDPIPER CLOSE, HORNDEAN
DUNNE, MARK P, 3, SANDPIPER CLOSE, HORNDEAN
DUNNE, WENDY A, 3, SANDPIPER CLOSE, HORNDEAN
COOPER, IAN, 4, SANDPIPER CLOSE, HORNDEAN
COOPER, JOANNA K, 4, SANDPIPER CLOSE, HORNDEAN
EDWARDS, DAVID P, 5, SANDPIPER CLOSE, HORNDEAN
RAINE, VICTORIA E, 5, SANDPIPER CLOSE, HORNDEAN
ASCHERL, TIMOTHY A, 6, SANDPIPER CLOSE, HORNDEAN
SHERLOW, MATTHEW J, 7, SANDPIPER CLOSE, HORNDEAN
DOWDELL, MARK A, 8, SANDPIPER CLOSE, HORNDEAN
STONE, KERRY-ANNE, 8, SANDPIPER CLOSE, HORNDEAN
OWEN, KEITH R, 9, SANDPIPER CLOSE, HORNDEAN
WILLIAMS, KAREN, 10, SANDPIPER CLOSE, HORNDEAN
PERRY, GAVIN S, 11, SANDPIPER CLOSE, HORNDEAN
EISMORE, RAYMOND A, 12, SANDPIPER CLOSE, HORNDEAN
WHITE, KAY, 14, SANDPIPER CLOSE, HORNDEAN
PHIPPS, EDNA M, 15, SANDPIPER CLOSE, HORNDEAN
GREEN, SARAH J, 16, SANDPIPER CLOSE, HORNDEAN
WOOLGAR, ANTHONY J, 16, SANDPIPER CLOSE, HORNDEAN
CROSS, KEVIN T, 17, SANDPIPER CLOSE, HORNDEAN
WHATLEY, GILLIAN, 18, SANDPIPER CLOSE, HORNDEAN
WHATLEY, JONATHAN K, 18, SANDPIPER CLOSE, HORNDEAN
DAY, IAN J, 1, SHEPPARD CLOSE, LOVEDEAN
NORMAN, JULIE A, 1, SHEPPARD CLOSE, LOVEDEAN
BIDDULPH, DAVID J, 3, SHEPPARD CLOSE, LOVEDEAN
COUZENS, STEPHEN R, 4, SHEPPARD CLOSE, LOVEDEAN
KEATING, LESLEY M.F, 5, SHEPPARD CLOSE, LOVEDEAN
KEATING, MICHAEL J.D, 5, SHEPPARD CLOSE, LOVEDEAN
JONES, PATRICIA M, 6, SHEPPARD CLOSE, LOVEDEAN
HALL, NICOLA J, 7, SHEPPARD CLOSE, LOVEDEAN
RALPH, DEREK G, 8, SHEPPARD CLOSE, LOVEDEAN
WARNER, SARAH J, 8, SHEPPARD CLOSE, LOVEDEAN
EARL, ANDREW C, 9, SHEPPARD CLOSE, LOVEDEAN
EARL, LORRAYNE E, 9, SHEPPARD CLOSE, LOVEDEAN
CONRAN, CARINA L, 10, SHEPPARD CLOSE, LOVEDEAN
CONRAN, PATRICIA J, 10, SHEPPARD CLOSE, LOVEDEAN
PORTER, JOHN, 10, SHEPPARD CLOSE, LOVEDEAN
LIU, MINCHUN, 11, SHEPPARD CLOSE, LOVEDEAN
ZHANG, JI, 11, SHEPPARD CLOSE, LOVEDEAN
NUGENT, CYRIL W, 12, SHEPPARD CLOSE, LOVEDEAN
NUGENT, FREDA K, 12, SHEPPARD CLOSE, LOVEDEAN
STURT, IRIS M, 14, SHEPPARD CLOSE, LOVEDEAN
MORCOMBE, SUSAN J, 15, SHEPPARD CLOSE, LOVEDEAN
MORCOMBE, VERNON J, 15, SHEPPARD CLOSE, LOVEDEAN
GREEN, KAREN J, 16, SHEPPARD CLOSE, LOVEDEAN
GREEN, MARTIN C, 16, SHEPPARD CLOSE, LOVEDEAN
WISE, ANDREW M, 17, SHEPPARD CLOSE, LOVEDEAN
CLARK, DEBORAH L, 18, SHEPPARD CLOSE, LOVEDEAN
CLARK, STEVEN R, 18, SHEPPARD CLOSE, LOVEDEAN
CORNISH, DAVID A, 19, SHEPPARD CLOSE, LOVEDEAN
CORNISH, LISA, 19, SHEPPARD CLOSE, LOVEDEAN
MALLINSON-MALVERN, JOHANNE S, 20, SHEPPARD CLOSE,
MALLINSON-MALVERN, PAUL, 20, SHEPPARD CLOSE,
DOIGNIE, LINDA C, 21, SHEPPARD CLOSE, LOVEDEAN
SERGEANT, JAMES A, 21, SHEPPARD CLOSE, LOVEDEAN
COPPING, HAZEL M, 22, SHEPPARD CLOSE, LOVEDEAN
BOWMAN, PIERS B, 23, SHEPPARD CLOSE, LOVEDEAN
TUDOR, DONNA M, 23, SHEPPARD CLOSE, LOVEDEAN
CHAPMAN, KAREN J, 24, SHEPPARD CLOSE, LOVEDEAN
CHAPMAN, MARK D, 24, SHEPPARD CLOSE, LOVEDEAN
ARNOLD, CHRISTOPHER M, 25, SHEPPARD CLOSE,
PRIVETT, BARBARA A, 26, SHEPPARD CLOSE, LOVEDEAN
DURMAN, KERRY A, 27, SHEPPARD CLOSE, LOVEDEAN
DURMAN, TIM, 27, SHEPPARD CLOSE, LOVEDEAN
RUDD, NICHOLAS I, 28, SHEPPARD CLOSE, LOVEDEAN
MARSH, ALEXANDER M, 29, SHEPPARD CLOSE, LOVEDEAN
MARSH, HANNAH R, 29, SHEPPARD CLOSE, LOVEDEAN
PODGER, DAVID G, 30, SHEPPARD CLOSE, LOVEDEAN
PODGER, ELIZABETH A, 30, SHEPPARD CLOSE, LOVEDEAN
MCMAHON, DIANE, 31, SHEPPARD CLOSE, LOVEDEAN
DEBENHAM, EVE M, 32, SHEPPARD CLOSE, LOVEDEAN
DEBENHAM, SABRINA A, 32, SHEPPARD CLOSE, LOVEDEAN
HERBERT, ALEXANDRA, 33, SHEPPARD CLOSE, LOVEDEAN
CARPENTER, PAUL, 34, SHEPPARD CLOSE, LOVEDEAN
FARROW, HAYLEY, 34, SHEPPARD CLOSE, LOVEDEAN
PARISH, ADRIAN R, 35, SHEPPARD CLOSE, LOVEDEAN
PARISH, MANDY J, 35, SHEPPARD CLOSE, LOVEDEAN
MERTON, DOREEN M, 1, THE SPINNEY, HORNDEAN
MERTON, PETER G.F, 1, THE SPINNEY, HORNDEAN
KEENAN, PAUL A, 2, THE SPINNEY, HORNDEAN
KEENAN, SUSAN J, 2, THE SPINNEY, HORNDEAN
KNIGHT, GLENN C, 3, THE SPINNEY, HORNDEAN
KNIGHT, VANESSA, 3, THE SPINNEY, HORNDEAN
DYER, CHRISTOPHER A, 4, THE SPINNEY, HORNDEAN
DYER, KAREN L, 4, THE SPINNEY, HORNDEAN
HORNE, ANDREW, 5, THE SPINNEY, HORNDEAN
BARLOW, ALISON P, 6, THE SPINNEY, HORNDEAN
BARLOW, GRAHAM, 6, THE SPINNEY, HORNDEAN
BARLOW, MICHELLE L, 6, THE SPINNEY, HORNDEAN
SPENCER, CAROLE A.A, 7, THE SPINNEY, HORNDEAN
SPENCER, EDWARD A, 7, THE SPINNEY, HORNDEAN
SPENCER, STEPHEN G.C, 7, THE SPINNEY, HORNDEAN
HUNT, JANE, 8, THE SPINNEY, HORNDEAN
HUNT, RICHARD J, 8, THE SPINNEY, HORNDEAN
MARTIN, ALEXIS D, 10, THE SPINNEY, HORNDEAN
MARTIN, LIZA R, 10, THE SPINNEY, HORNDEAN
MARSHMAN, KEITH R, 12, THE SPINNEY, HORNDEAN
MARSHMAN, TINA L, 12, THE SPINNEY, HORNDEAN
DANIELS, GRAHAM A, 34, THE SPINNEY, HORNDEAN
DANIELS, MICHELLE P, 34, THE SPINNEY, HORNDEAN
NORTH, LOUISE E, 35, THE SPINNEY, HORNDEAN
NORTH, MICHAEL H, 35, THE SPINNEY, HORNDEAN
LEWINGTON, CATHERINE L.G, 36, THE SPINNEY, HORNDEAN
WOOD, FIONA S.M, 37, THE SPINNEY, HORNDEAN
BENNETT, ANTHONY G, 38, THE SPINNEY, HORNDEAN
TODD, MARILYN B, 38, THE SPINNEY, HORNDEAN
JAMES, DARREN P, 39, THE SPINNEY, HORNDEAN
JAMES, SONIA M.J, 39, THE SPINNEY, HORNDEAN
WALSH, ANITA C, 40, THE SPINNEY, HORNDEAN
WALSH, MICHAEL W.J, 40, THE SPINNEY, HORNDEAN
WALSH, SYLVIA A, 40, THE SPINNEY, HORNDEAN
LEWIS, BRIAN H, 41, THE SPINNEY, HORNDEAN
LEWIS, MARGARET A, 41, THE SPINNEY, HORNDEAN
LEWIS, SAMANTHA, 41, THE SPINNEY, HORNDEAN
CLARK, ANDREA E, 42, THE SPINNEY, HORNDEAN
CLARK, MICHAEL J, 42, THE SPINNEY, HORNDEAN
CLARK, SUSAN V, 42, THE SPINNEY, HORNDEAN
JONES, CLEO, 43, THE SPINNEY, HORNDEAN
JONES, REGINALD G, 43, THE SPINNEY, HORNDEAN
KIRBY, EDWARD H, 44, THE SPINNEY, HORNDEAN
KIRBY, EILEEN M, 44, THE SPINNEY, HORNDEAN
CULBERTSON, GEOFFREY M.J, 46, THE SPINNEY, HORNDEAN
CULBERTSON, SHEILA, 46, THE SPINNEY, HORNDEAN
SADLER, AMANDA J, 48, THE SPINNEY, HORNDEAN
SADLER, JAMES C, 48, THE SPINNEY, HORNDEAN
RICE, MOIRA C, 1, STONECHAT ROAD, HORNDEAN
RICE, WILLIAM C, 1, STONECHAT ROAD, HORNDEAN
DIXON, ALISON J, 3, STONECHAT ROAD, HORNDEAN
DIXON, TARQUIN A, 3, STONECHAT ROAD, HORNDEAN
SMITH, DAVID A, 5, STONECHAT ROAD, HORNDEAN
SMITH, JULIET M, 5, STONECHAT ROAD, HORNDEAN
ANTHONY, PAULA J, 7, STONECHAT ROAD, HORNDEAN
CLARKE, JENNIFER, 9, STONECHAT ROAD, HORNDEAN
WAINWRIGHT, PETER P, 11, STONECHAT ROAD, HORNDEAN
PHELAN, HELEN J, 14, STONECHAT ROAD, HORNDEAN
WEBB, ROBIN P, 15, STONECHAT ROAD, HORNDEAN
BEAUCHAMP, AMANDA J, 16, STONECHAT ROAD, HORNDEAN
BEAUCHAMP, MICHAEL D, 16, STONECHAT ROAD, HORNDEAN
CARTER, ANGELA M, 17, STONECHAT ROAD, HORNDEAN
ROBINSON, ALWYMN J, 19, STONECHAT ROAD, HORNDEAN
SIMS, JENNIFER A, 19, STONECHAT ROAD, HORNDEAN
MOORE, ROGER J, 21, STONECHAT ROAD, HORNDEAN
ROBERTSON, CLAIRE, 21, STONECHAT ROAD, HORNDEAN
LUCAS, JOANNA E, 1, SWIFT CLOSE, HORNDEAN
LUCAS, ROBERT C, 1, SWIFT CLOSE, HORNDEAN
WEBSTER, FADLINA, 1A, SWIFT CLOSE, HORNDEAN
WEBSTER, GRAHAM C, 1A, SWIFT CLOSE, HORNDEAN
DAVIES, NICHOLAS G, 2, SWIFT CLOSE, HORNDEAN
DAVIES, VANESSA C, 2, SWIFT CLOSE, HORNDEAN
COLES, ADRIAN M, 3, SWIFT CLOSE, HORNDEAN
COLES, LESLEY S, 3, SWIFT CLOSE, HORNDEAN
OLIVER, MARTIN P, 4, SWIFT CLOSE, HORNDEAN
OLIVER, SUSAN, 4, SWIFT CLOSE, HORNDEAN
BODKIN, DAVID C, 5, SWIFT CLOSE, HORNDEAN
MARTIN, GILLIAN C, 5, SWIFT CLOSE, HORNDEAN
MARTIN, HARVEY G, 5, SWIFT CLOSE, HORNDEAN
CROSS, VANESSA E, 6, SWIFT CLOSE, HORNDEAN
BRYDEN, KAREN J, 7, SWIFT CLOSE, HORNDEAN
BRYDEN, PETER D, 7, SWIFT CLOSE, HORNDEAN
HARDIMENT, ELIZABETH H, 1, TILFORD ROAD, LOVEDEAN
HARDIMENT, ROBERT W, 1, TILFORD ROAD, LOVEDEAN
HEBENTON, ALAN S, 2, TILFORD ROAD, LOVEDEAN
HEBENTON, GINA M, 2, TILFORD ROAD, LOVEDEAN
HEBENTON, VERONICA A, 2, TILFORD ROAD, LOVEDEAN
YOUNGER, BONITA L, 3, TILFORD ROAD, LOVEDEAN
YOUNGER, PETER J, 3, TILFORD ROAD, LOVEDEAN
KNIGHT, JONATHAN S, 4, TILFORD ROAD, LOVEDEAN
KNIGHT, KAY G, 4, TILFORD ROAD, LOVEDEAN

KNIGHT, KEVIN H, 4, TILFORD ROAD, LOVEDEAN
KNIGHT, MICHAEL D, 4, TILFORD ROAD, LOVEDEAN
OAKSHOTT, JENNIFER A, 4, TILFORD ROAD, LOVEDEAN
JONES, ANDREA E, 5, TILFORD ROAD, LOVEDEAN
JONES, CAROL J, 5, TILFORD ROAD, LOVEDEAN
JONES, CHRISTOPHER R, 5, TILFORD ROAD, LOVEDEAN
JONES, KEITH A, 5, TILFORD ROAD, LOVEDEAN
OATLEY, JAMES F, 6, TILFORD ROAD, LOVEDEAN
OATLEY, JENNIFER G, 6, TILFORD ROAD, LOVEDEAN
OATLEY, PAUL G, 6, TILFORD ROAD, LOVEDEAN
SPENCER, TIMOTHY A, 7, TILFORD ROAD, LOVEDEAN
GRAHAM, LISA D, 8, TILFORD ROAD, LOVEDEAN
GRAHAM, MATTHEW J, 8, TILFORD ROAD, LOVEDEAN
GRAHAM, SHARON Y, 8, TILFORD ROAD, LOVEDEAN
GRAHAM, STUART, 8, TILFORD ROAD, LOVEDEAN
BRIDGES, DAVID R, 9, TILFORD ROAD, LOVEDEAN
BRIDGES, JENNIFER A, 9, TILFORD ROAD, LOVEDEAN
GARDNER, ALAN J, 10, TILFORD ROAD, LOVEDEAN
GARDNER, DOROTHY, 10, TILFORD ROAD, LOVEDEAN
MONK, MARY M, 11, TILFORD ROAD, LOVEDEAN
DESBOIS, GUDRUN, 12, TILFORD ROAD, LOVEDEAN
DESBOIS, LEON A, 12, TILFORD ROAD, LOVEDEAN
LACEY, STEPHEN B, 1, VICTORY AVENUE, HORNDEAN
EVANS, STEPHEN R, 2A, VICTORY AVENUE, HORNDEAN
TAYLOR, WENDY A, 2A, VICTORY AVENUE, HORNDEAN
WILSON, SUZANNE D, 3, VICTORY AVENUE, HORNDEAN
WILSON, TONY, 3, VICTORY AVENUE, HORNDEAN
LEPPARD, TONIA C, 4, VICTORY AVENUE, HORNDEAN
PALLETT, SIMON A, 4, VICTORY AVENUE, HORNDEAN
MINCHIN, BARRY J, 5, VICTORY AVENUE, HORNDEAN
MINCHIN, LINDA C, 5, VICTORY AVENUE, HORNDEAN
FARUGIA, HELENA, 6, VICTORY AVENUE, HORNDEAN
SPEAR, JANICE L, 7, VICTORY AVENUE, HORNDEAN
SPEAR, PETER D, 7, VICTORY AVENUE, HORNDEAN
SHARRATT, RICHARD M, 8, VICTORY AVENUE, HORNDEAN
SHARRATT, SUSAN, 8, VICTORY AVENUE, HORNDEAN
SHARRATT, VICTORIA, 8, VICTORY AVENUE, HORNDEAN
ARNOLD, CATHERINE E, 9, VICTORY AVENUE, HORNDEAN
ARNOLD, MARK S, 9, VICTORY AVENUE, HORNDEAN
ARNOLD, MICHAEL E, 9, VICTORY AVENUE, HORNDEAN
ARNOLD, NADINE E, 9, VICTORY AVENUE, HORNDEAN
LOTINGA, DAVID A, 10, VICTORY AVENUE, HORNDEAN
LOTINGA, GWENDOLINE A, 10, VICTORY AVENUE,
LOTINGA, RUTH E, 10, VICTORY AVENUE, HORNDEAN
LOTINGA, STEPHEN A, 10, VICTORY AVENUE, HORNDEAN
CLUNIE, LESLEY A, 11, VICTORY AVENUE, HORNDEAN
CLUNIE, RODNEY A, 11, VICTORY AVENUE, HORNDEAN
CLUNIE, STEVEN S, 11, VICTORY AVENUE, HORNDEAN
BEECH, LYNN J, 12, VICTORY AVENUE, HORNDEAN
BEECH, MARK J, 12, VICTORY AVENUE, HORNDEAN
VANNER, JAYNE K, 13, VICTORY AVENUE, HORNDEAN
VANNER, LEON R, 13, VICTORY AVENUE, HORNDEAN
VANNER, RAYMOND J, 13, VICTORY AVENUE, HORNDEAN
VANNER, SAMANTHA J, 13, VICTORY AVENUE, HORNDEAN
VIGAY, JOHN F, 14, VICTORY AVENUE, HORNDEAN
VIGAY, MAVIS R, 14, VICTORY AVENUE, HORNDEAN
ROBINSON, PHILIP N, 15, VICTORY AVENUE, HORNDEAN
ROBINSON, SUSAN, 15, VICTORY AVENUE, HORNDEAN
MCLENNAN, ALAN J, 16, VICTORY AVENUE, HORNDEAN
MCLENNAN, AUDREY V, 16, VICTORY AVENUE, HORNDEAN
PARKHURST, RICHARD K, 17, VICTORY AVENUE, HORNDEAN
PARKHURST, SANDRA E, 17, VICTORY AVENUE, HORNDEAN
HUNN, BERTHA I, 18, VICTORY AVENUE, HORNDEAN
HUNN, RACHEL, 18, VICTORY AVENUE, HORNDEAN
HUNN, STEPHEN A, 18, VICTORY AVENUE, HORNDEAN
PRESS, BRIAN J, 19, VICTORY AVENUE, HORNDEAN
PRESS, JOSEPHINE F, 19, VICTORY AVENUE, HORNDEAN
BALL, ANTHONY K, 20, VICTORY AVENUE, HORNDEAN
BALL, ERIC A, 20, VICTORY AVENUE, HORNDEAN
FERRAND, ANDREW, 21, VICTORY AVENUE, HORNDEAN
FERRAND, SALLY A, 21, VICTORY AVENUE, HORNDEAN
BROAD, JAMES E, 22, VICTORY AVENUE, HORNDEAN
BROAD, MARY A, 22, VICTORY AVENUE, HORNDEAN
WILLIAMS, DAWN L, 23, VICTORY AVENUE, HORNDEAN
WILLIAMS, JAMES E, 23, VICTORY AVENUE, HORNDEAN
WILLIAMS, PAUL, 23, VICTORY AVENUE, HORNDEAN
MILLER, DIANE L, 23A, VICTORY AVENUE, HORNDEAN
MILLER, MICHAEL J, 23A, VICTORY AVENUE, HORNDEAN
TAYLOR, EDWARD A, 24, VICTORY AVENUE, HORNDEAN
TAYLOR, HEATHER, 24, VICTORY AVENUE, HORNDEAN
CLEIFE, DAVID M, 25, VICTORY AVENUE, HORNDEAN
TILLER, FREDA M, 26, VICTORY AVENUE, HORNDEAN
BEST, DEBRA L, 27, VICTORY AVENUE, HORNDEAN
NASH, PETER L, 28, VICTORY AVENUE, HORNDEAN
NASH, SUSAN G, 28, VICTORY AVENUE, HORNDEAN
CONWAY, JONATHAN L, 29, VICTORY AVENUE, HORNDEAN
SKINNER, DANIELE J, 30, VICTORY AVENUE, HORNDEAN
SKINNER, STEPHEN C, 30, VICTORY AVENUE, HORNDEAN
STOKOE, PAUL M, 31, VICTORY AVENUE, HORNDEAN
STOKOE, SANDRA L, 31, VICTORY AVENUE, HORNDEAN
WILKES, HAZEL A, 32, VICTORY AVENUE, HORNDEAN
WILKES, KENNETH, 32, VICTORY AVENUE, HORNDEAN
PARKHOUSE, JOYCE, 33, VICTORY AVENUE, HORNDEAN
PARKHOUSE, RONALD E.W, 33, VICTORY AVENUE,
HOPGOOD, DAVID J, 34, VICTORY AVENUE, HORNDEAN
HOPGOOD, EVA, 34, VICTORY AVENUE, HORNDEAN
COLLIER, GEORGE E, 35A, VICTORY AVENUE, HORNDEAN
COLLIER, JESSIE A, 35A, VICTORY AVENUE, HORNDEAN
FIELD, CHRISTINE A, 36, VICTORY AVENUE, HORNDEAN
FIELD, TERENCE E, 36, VICTORY AVENUE, HORNDEAN
STAFF, BARBARA I, 37, VICTORY AVENUE, HORNDEAN
EMMS, MICHAEL J, 38, VICTORY AVENUE, HORNDEAN
EMMS, SARAH, 38, VICTORY AVENUE, HORNDEAN
LYNES, DAVID B, 39, VICTORY AVENUE, HORNDEAN
LYNES, FRANCIS C, 39, VICTORY AVENUE, HORNDEAN
LYNES, SANDRA A.M, 39, VICTORY AVENUE, HORNDEAN
STEVENS, GLORIA J, 40, VICTORY AVENUE, HORNDEAN
STEVENS, ROBERT F, 40, VICTORY AVENUE, HORNDEAN
GREGORI, GREGORY, 41, VICTORY AVENUE, HORNDEAN
GREGORI, SUSAN K.M, 41, VICTORY AVENUE, HORNDEAN
ASTRAND, CLIFFORD T, 42, VICTORY AVENUE, HORNDEAN
ASTRAND, SUSAN A, 42, VICTORY AVENUE, HORNDEAN
BENNEYWORTH, MOLLY B, 42, VICTORY AVENUE,
FROST, JENNIFER J, 44, VICTORY AVENUE, HORNDEAN
FROST, RALPH E, 44, VICTORY AVENUE, HORNDEAN
FINNIGAN, BRIAN, 45, VICTORY AVENUE, HORNDEAN
FINNIGAN, SYLVIA, 45, VICTORY AVENUE, HORNDEAN
HAMPSON, NEIL R, 46, VICTORY AVENUE, HORNDEAN
HAMPSON, SHARRON L, 46, VICTORY AVENUE, HORNDEAN
CROSSMAN, JOAN L, 47, VICTORY AVENUE, HORNDEAN
CROSSMAN, STAN E, 47, VICTORY AVENUE, HORNDEAN
PARTRIDGE, PAULA J, 47, VICTORY AVENUE, HORNDEAN
BLACK, GEORGINA, 48, VICTORY AVENUE, HORNDEAN
SMITH, CAROLE E, 49, VICTORY AVENUE, HORNDEAN
SMITH, GEOFFREY H, 49, VICTORY AVENUE, HORNDEAN
TAYLOR, AMY E, 50, VICTORY AVENUE, HORNDEAN
TAYLOR, GEORGE W, 50, VICTORY AVENUE, HORNDEAN
PIGGOTT, JAMES W, 51, VICTORY AVENUE, HORNDEAN
PIGGOTT, SANDRA D, 51, VICTORY AVENUE, HORNDEAN
MILES, DEBRA J, 52, VICTORY AVENUE, HORNDEAN
MILES, DENNIS A, 52, VICTORY AVENUE, HORNDEAN
MILES, PHILLIP D, 52, VICTORY AVENUE, HORNDEAN
MCEWAN, GRAHAM J.D, 53, VICTORY AVENUE, HORNDEAN
MCEWAN, SARAH J, 53, VICTORY AVENUE, HORNDEAN
BUICK, MARTIN J, 54, VICTORY AVENUE, HORNDEAN
EVANS, PHILIP M, 55, VICTORY AVENUE, HORNDEAN
EVANS, SIMONE, 55, VICTORY AVENUE, HORNDEAN
ROWLANDS, KERRY C, 56, VICTORY AVENUE, HORNDEAN
ROWLANDS, LISA C, 56, VICTORY AVENUE, HORNDEAN
ROWLANDS, RICHARD J, 56, VICTORY AVENUE, HORNDEAN
ROWLANDS, ROBERT J, 56, VICTORY AVENUE, HORNDEAN
GOODRIDGE, BRYAN T.L, 57, VICTORY AVENUE, HORNDEAN
GOODRIDGE, TESS P, 57, VICTORY AVENUE, HORNDEAN
WOOD, KIM J, 59, VICTORY AVENUE, HORNDEAN
WOOD, STEPHEN J, 59, VICTORY AVENUE, HORNDEAN
MUGRIDGE, SYLVIA G, 60, VICTORY AVENUE, HORNDEAN
BAKER, GRAHAM R, 61, VICTORY AVENUE, HORNDEAN
BAKER, JAMES G, 61, VICTORY AVENUE, HORNDEAN
BAKER, MARION G.H, 61, VICTORY AVENUE, HORNDEAN
MARSH, DAVID J.B, 62, VICTORY AVENUE, HORNDEAN
MARSH, DAVID W, 62, VICTORY AVENUE, HORNDEAN
MARSH, DOROTHY M, 62, VICTORY AVENUE, HORNDEAN
MARSH, SARAH J, 62, VICTORY AVENUE, HORNDEAN
CALVERLEY, MELITA, 63, VICTORY AVENUE, HORNDEAN
CALVERLEY, SIMON G, 63, VICTORY AVENUE, HORNDEAN
OUSBY, MICHAEL J, 65, VICTORY AVENUE, HORNDEAN
OUSBY, RACHEL K, 65, VICTORY AVENUE, HORNDEAN
KIRK, KATRINA C, 1, WAGTAIL ROAD, HORNDEAN
ANDERSON, SHAUN M, 3, WAGTAIL ROAD, HORNDEAN
ANDERSON, TRACEY J, 3, WAGTAIL ROAD, HORNDEAN
PERRY, PHILLIP R, 5, WAGTAIL ROAD, HORNDEAN
LUCKETT, DOROTHY A, 7, WAGTAIL ROAD, HORNDEAN
ROBERTS, VANESSA E, 9, WAGTAIL ROAD, HORNDEAN
CUMMINGS, ISOBEL, 11, WAGTAIL ROAD, HORNDEAN
MOORE, SAMANTHA, 15, WAGTAIL ROAD, HORNDEAN
WHEELER, MARIA A, 17, WAGTAIL ROAD, HORNDEAN
BARWIS, DEBORAH E, 19, WAGTAIL ROAD, HORNDEAN
MARSHALL, KIRSTY L, 21, WAGTAIL ROAD, HORNDEAN
RAYMENT, ADRIAN, 21, WAGTAIL ROAD, HORNDEAN
KNIGHT, JOHN W, 2, WAGTAIL ROAD, HORNDEAN
KNIGHT, MARIE E, 2, WAGTAIL ROAD, HORNDEAN
KNIGHT, RICHARD P, 2, WAGTAIL ROAD, HORNDEAN
KNIGHT, STEPHEN P, 2, WAGTAIL ROAD, HORNDEAN
PARRETT-HARRIS, ANITA V, 4, WAGTAIL ROAD, HORNDEAN
PARRETT-HARRIS, STUART G, 4, WAGTAIL ROAD, HORNDEAN
CHEWTER, ANNETTE, 6, WAGTAIL ROAD, HORNDEAN
CHEWTER, KATIE L, 6, WAGTAIL ROAD, HORNDEAN
STARMORE, MARCUS, 6, WAGTAIL ROAD, HORNDEAN
OWEN, CHRISTOPHER J, 8, WAGTAIL ROAD, HORNDEAN
PENTNEY, ASHLEY G, 8, WAGTAIL ROAD, HORNDEAN
PENTNEY, EILEEN A, 8, WAGTAIL ROAD, HORNDEAN
MARSHALL, LOUISE, 4, WARBLER CLOSE, HORNDEAN
STEPHENS, KATHRYN J, 5, WARBLER CLOSE, HORNDEAN
STEPHENS, NEVILLE D, 5, WARBLER CLOSE, HORNDEAN
STEPHENS, NICOLA J, 5, WARBLER CLOSE, HORNDEAN
STEPHENS, SAMANTHA M, 5, WARBLER CLOSE, HORNDEAN
HARFORD, VANESSA G, 6, WARBLER CLOSE, HORNDEAN
MACNEE, RICHARD J, 6, WARBLER CLOSE, HORNDEAN
BRICE, JOHN E, 1, WESTBROOKE CLOSE, HORNDEAN
BRICE, VERONICA A, 1, WESTBROOKE CLOSE, HORNDEAN
MERRITT, JOHNATHAN J, 2, WESTBROOKE CLOSE,
MERRITT, SAMANTHA D, 2, WESTBROOKE CLOSE,
MCFARLANE, ALEXANDER, 3, WESTBROOKE CLOSE,
MCFARLANE, SUSAN J, 3, WESTBROOKE CLOSE, HORNDEAN
TIPPING, CLAIR D, 4, WESTBROOKE CLOSE, HORNDEAN
TIPPING, JULIA K, 4, WESTBROOKE CLOSE, HORNDEAN
TIPPING, PETER N, 4, WESTBROOKE CLOSE, HORNDEAN
FOSTER, CHRISTINE M, 5, WESTBROOKE CLOSE, HORNDEAN
ALVAREZ CARAMAZANA, PABLO, 6, WESTBROOKE CLOSE,
COOPER, KEVIN J, 6, WESTBROOKE CLOSE, HORNDEAN
PALFREY, JOAN M, 6, WESTBROOKE CLOSE, HORNDEAN
PALFREY, STEPHEN J, 6, WESTBROOKE CLOSE, HORNDEAN
GIBBONS, PAUL W, 7, WESTBROOKE CLOSE, HORNDEAN
SINCLAIR, MARGARET D, 8, WESTBROOKE CLOSE,
SINCLAIR, PETER O, 8, WESTBROOKE CLOSE, HORNDEAN
CRAGHILL, ANNETTE, 9, WESTBROOKE CLOSE, HORNDEAN
CRAGHILL, PETER D, 9, WESTBROOKE CLOSE, HORNDEAN
BAILEY, ANITA L, 10, WESTBROOKE CLOSE, HORNDEAN
BAILEY, NIGEL, 10, WESTBROOKE CLOSE, HORNDEAN
SMITH, ALLAN E, 11, WESTBROOKE CLOSE, HORNDEAN
SMITH, CAROLINE L, 11, WESTBROOKE CLOSE, HORNDEAN
SMITH, STEPHEN M, 11, WESTBROOKE CLOSE, HORNDEAN
SMITH, VALERIE M, 11, WESTBROOKE CLOSE, HORNDEAN
ALLISON, CHRISTINE M, 2, WILTON DRIVE, HORNDEAN
ALLISON, DAVID, 2, WILTON DRIVE, HORNDEAN
MARSH, ANNE F, 4, WILTON DRIVE, HORNDEAN
MARSH, LOUISE C, 4, WILTON DRIVE, HORNDEAN
WRIGHT, ANDREW J, 6, WILTON DRIVE, HORNDEAN
WRIGHT, DAVID L, 6, WILTON DRIVE, HORNDEAN
WRIGHT, KATHERINE B, 6, WILTON DRIVE, HORNDEAN
BEAUMONT, CAROL, 7, WILTON DRIVE, HORNDEAN
BEAUMONT, DANIEL W, 7, WILTON DRIVE, HORNDEAN
BEAUMONT, MICHAEL, 7, WILTON DRIVE, HORNDEAN
JONES, LISA A, 7, WILTON DRIVE, HORNDEAN
OLIVER, MARILYN R, 8, WILTON DRIVE, HORNDEAN
OLIVER, NIGEL A, 8, WILTON DRIVE, HORNDEAN
GLEDHILL, BESSIE C, 9, WILTON DRIVE, HORNDEAN
GLEDHILL, DENNIS R, 9, WILTON DRIVE, HORNDEAN
THOMPSON, DAVID S, 10, WILTON DRIVE, HORNDEAN
THOMPSON, SARAH-JANE, 10, WILTON DRIVE, HORNDEAN
ENEFER, MARY-JANE R, 11, WILTON DRIVE, HORNDEAN
REEVES, ANNE G, 11, WILTON DRIVE, HORNDEAN
REEVES, VICTOR A, 11, WILTON DRIVE, HORNDEAN
BUIST, ROBERT S.R, 12, WILTON DRIVE, HORNDEAN
JAMIESON, ANNE R, 12, WILTON DRIVE, HORNDEAN
JAMIESON, IAN, 12, WILTON DRIVE, HORNDEAN
PARISH, GRAHAM M, 14, WILTON DRIVE, HORNDEAN
PARISH, LINDA R, 14, WILTON DRIVE, HORNDEAN
PARISH, LOUISE K, 14, WILTON DRIVE, HORNDEAN
MCGOFF, ARTHUR M, 15, WILTON DRIVE, HORNDEAN
HOWE, ASHLEY B, 16, WILTON DRIVE, HORNDEAN
HOWE, LINDA, 16, WILTON DRIVE, HORNDEAN
NORRIS, LESLEY A, 18, WILTON DRIVE, HORNDEAN
NORRIS, TONY, 18, WILTON DRIVE, HORNDEAN
STEVENS, GARETH L, 18, WILTON DRIVE, HORNDEAN
DUNN, CAROLE A, 20, WILTON DRIVE, HORNDEAN
DUNN, JOHN R, 20, WILTON DRIVE, HORNDEAN
DUNN, KERRY L, 20, WILTON DRIVE, HORNDEAN
DUNN, ROY A, 20, WILTON DRIVE, HORNDEAN
SCHOFIELD, MARK N, 22, WILTON DRIVE, HORNDEAN
HILL, BARBARA M, 24, WILTON DRIVE, HORNDEAN
HILL, WILLIAM, 24, WILTON DRIVE, HORNDEAN
NAVARATNE, DHARINI A.S, 25, WILTON DRIVE, HORNDEAN
FEWINGS, JOANNE E, 26, WILTON DRIVE, HORNDEAN
FEWINGS, MARK A, 26, WILTON DRIVE, HORNDEAN
CAMPBELL, ADRIAN, 27, WILTON DRIVE, HORNDEAN
CAMPBELL, JULIE, 27, WILTON DRIVE, HORNDEAN
MCINTOSH, ANITA, 28, WILTON DRIVE, HORNDEAN
KING, DOUGLAS J, 29, WILTON DRIVE, HORNDEAN
KING, HILARY J, 29, WILTON DRIVE, HORNDEAN
BATEMAN, KIM, 30, WILTON DRIVE, HORNDEAN
BATEMAN, WILLIAM H, 30, WILTON DRIVE, HORNDEAN
POWELL, ANN C, 31, WILTON DRIVE, HORNDEAN
POWELL, TERENCE H, 31, WILTON DRIVE, HORNDEAN
CLAUS, GERBEN T, 32, WILTON DRIVE, HORNDEAN
CLAUS, KAREN L, 32, WILTON DRIVE, HORNDEAN
CORNS, JENNA M, 33, WILTON DRIVE, HORNDEAN
CORNS, MATTHEW A, 33, WILTON DRIVE, HORNDEAN
CORNS, PETER, 33, WILTON DRIVE, HORNDEAN
CORNS, SUSAN M, 33, WILTON DRIVE, HORNDEAN
WATTS, ALISON J, 34, WILTON DRIVE, HORNDEAN
WATTS, LESLEY, 34, WILTON DRIVE, HORNDEAN
WATTS, MELANIE K, 34, WILTON DRIVE, HORNDEAN
WATTS, ROBERT H.J, 34, WILTON DRIVE, HORNDEAN
FOSTER, GILLIAN H, 35, WILTON DRIVE, HORNDEAN
FOSTER, VICTOR T, 35, WILTON DRIVE, HORNDEAN
TUCKER, JOHN A, 36, WILTON DRIVE, HORNDEAN
WHITE, JOHN G, 37, WILTON DRIVE, HORNDEAN
PARSONS, ELIZABETH, 38, WILTON DRIVE, HORNDEAN
PARSONS, GRAHAM J, 38, WILTON DRIVE, HORNDEAN
FARMER, DENISE, 40, WILTON DRIVE, HORNDEAN
FARMER, PETER A.N, 40, WILTON DRIVE, HORNDEAN
RAYMENT, DAVID A, 1, WINKFIELD ROW, HORNDEAN
RAYMENT, WENDY E, 1, WINKFIELD ROW, HORNDEAN
CANNINGS, IRIS M, 3, WINKFIELD ROW, HORNDEAN
CANNINGS, RICHARD H, 3, WINKFIELD ROW, HORNDEAN
CHAMBERLAIN, EILEEN M, 5, WINKFIELD ROW, HORNDEAN
PEARCE, PAULINE E, 7, WINKFIELD ROW, HORNDEAN
PEARCE, ROBERT J, 7, WINKFIELD ROW, HORNDEAN
BRETTELL, DAWN M, 9, WINKFIELD ROW, HORNDEAN
BRETTELL, TONY J, 9, WINKFIELD ROW, HORNDEAN
BURTON, KEITH W, 11, WINKFIELD ROW, HORNDEAN
BURTON, STELLA M, 11, WINKFIELD ROW, HORNDEAN
CONWAY, ROSE L, 13, WINKFIELD ROW, HORNDEAN
CARTER, SARAH J, 15, WINKFIELD ROW, HORNDEAN
WILKINS, NIGEL R, 15, WINKFIELD ROW, HORNDEAN
MERRY, OSWALD T, 16, WINKFIELD ROW, HORNDEAN
LAMBERT, DOROTHY R, 17, WINKFIELD ROW, HORNDEAN
PARSONS, BRIAN, 18, WINKFIELD ROW, HORNDEAN
PARSONS, CAROLE A, 18, WINKFIELD ROW, HORNDEAN
ANTCLIFF, GEOFFREY B, 19, WINKFIELD ROW, HORNDEAN
RUSSELL, DAVID, 20, WINKFIELD ROW, HORNDEAN
RUSSELL, DIANE, 20, WINKFIELD ROW, HORNDEAN
BORLAND, DOROTHY W, 21, WINKFIELD ROW, HORNDEAN
BORLAND, IAIN J, 21, WINKFIELD ROW, HORNDEAN
MARSHALL, ANDREW R, 22, WINKFIELD ROW, HORNDEAN
MARSHALL, HEATHER A, 22, WINKFIELD ROW, HORNDEAN
LOCKWOOD, JOSEPH A, 23, WINKFIELD ROW, HORNDEAN
KNIGHT, VIOLET M, 24, WINKFIELD ROW, HORNDEAN

Electoral Roll

WHITE, IAN A.J, 25, WINKFIELD ROW, HORNDEAN
WHITE, JANICE B, 25, WINKFIELD ROW, HORNDEAN
BAILEY, DORIS P, 26, WINKFIELD ROW, HORNDEAN
BAILEY, PATRICK, 26, WINKFIELD ROW, HORNDEAN
FURSE, ADRIAN, 27, WINKFIELD ROW, HORNDEAN
FURSE, JACQUELINE A, 27, WINKFIELD ROW, HORNDEAN
FURSE, JAMES, 27, WINKFIELD ROW, HORNDEAN
FURSE, STEWART R, 27, WINKFIELD ROW, HORNDEAN
WEARN, FREDERICK G, 28, WINKFIELD ROW, HORNDEAN
WEARN, IRENE, 28, WINKFIELD ROW, HORNDEAN
LABRUM, KENA I, 29, WINKFIELD ROW, HORNDEAN
LABRUM, MARK W, 29, WINKFIELD ROW, HORNDEAN
LABRUM, ROGER W, 29, WINKFIELD ROW, HORNDEAN
CAREY, SOPHIE T, 30, WINKFIELD ROW, HORNDEAN
GOODACRE, PAUL R, 32, WINKFIELD ROW, HORNDEAN
GOODACRE, SUSAN C, 32, WINKFIELD ROW, HORNDEAN
SOUZA, ISABELL, 33, WINKFIELD ROW, HORNDEAN
SOUZA, PHILIP J, 33, WINKFIELD ROW, HORNDEAN
EDENS, JAMES O, 34, WINKFIELD ROW, HORNDEAN
EDENS, LESLEY A, 34, WINKFIELD ROW, HORNDEAN
JENKINS, KAREN, 35, WINKFIELD ROW, HORNDEAN
JENKINS, STANLEY, 35, WINKFIELD ROW, HORNDEAN
WAKEFORD, BRIAN W, 36, WINKFIELD ROW, HORNDEAN
WAKEFORD, JUNE V, 36, WINKFIELD ROW, HORNDEAN
HOLLOWAY, VICTOR G, 37, WINKFIELD ROW, HORNDEAN
SMITH, DAVID W, 38, WINKFIELD ROW, HORNDEAN
SMITH, SUZANNE E, 38, WINKFIELD ROW, HORNDEAN
COTTON, KEITH W, 39, WINKFIELD ROW, HORNDEAN
COTTON, ROSE, 39, WINKFIELD ROW, HORNDEAN
JONES, BETTY A, 40, WINKFIELD ROW, HORNDEAN
JONES, HARLEY J.D, 40, WINKFIELD ROW, HORNDEAN
HUNT, EDWARD C, 41, WINKFIELD ROW, HORNDEAN
HUNT, SHEILA M.A, 41, WINKFIELD ROW, HORNDEAN
GOBLE, CICELY P, 42, WINKFIELD ROW, HORNDEAN
GOBLE, JOHN R, 42, WINKFIELD ROW, HORNDEAN
TUCKER, DOROTHY A, 43, WINKFIELD ROW, HORNDEAN
TUCKER, PETER D, 43, WINKFIELD ROW, HORNDEAN
HARRISON, GLADYS J, 44, WINKFIELD ROW, HORNDEAN
HARRISON, HERBERT H, 44, WINKFIELD ROW, HORNDEAN
HARRISON, KEITH H, 44, WINKFIELD ROW, HORNDEAN
REEVES, ELSIE, 45, WINKFIELD ROW, HORNDEAN
REEVES, MAITLAND W, 45, WINKFIELD ROW, HORNDEAN
CARPENTER, BETTY, 47, WINKFIELD ROW, HORNDEAN
CARPENTER, ERNEST C, 47, WINKFIELD ROW, HORNDEAN
RAYNER, HOWARD D, 49, WINKFIELD ROW, HORNDEAN
RAYNER, MYRA, 49, WINKFIELD ROW, HORNDEAN
WEIGHELL, FRANCES E, 51, WINKFIELD ROW, HORNDEAN
WEIGHELL, RONALD P, 51, WINKFIELD ROW, HORNDEAN
SNOW, PETER J, 55, WINKFIELD ROW, HORNDEAN
SNOW, SANDRA A, 55, WINKFIELD ROW, HORNDEAN
JONES, ADA J, 57, WINKFIELD ROW, HORNDEAN
ROXBURGH, JOHN, 59, WINKFIELD ROW, HORNDEAN
ROXBURGH, JUNE P, 59, WINKFIELD ROW, HORNDEAN
ASHTON, JOHN K, 61, WINKFIELD ROW, HORNDEAN
ASHTON, ROSEMARIE, 61, WINKFIELD ROW, HORNDEAN
LONG, KATINA J, 1, WITLEY ROAD, LOVEDEAN
WILLIAMS, BARBARA F, 1, WITLEY ROAD, LOVEDEAN
MARTIN, CAROL A, 2, WITLEY ROAD, LOVEDEAN
MARTIN, COLIN, 2, WITLEY ROAD, LOVEDEAN
MARTIN, SARAH L, 2, WITLEY ROAD, LOVEDEAN
MCEWEN, EDNA O, 3, WITLEY ROAD, LOVEDEAN
MCEWEN, ROBERT J, 3, WITLEY ROAD, LOVEDEAN
THOMAS, JANET C, 4, WITLEY ROAD, LOVEDEAN
THOMAS, VAUGHAN G, 4, WITLEY ROAD, LOVEDEAN
MINAY, IAN F, 5, WITLEY ROAD, LOVEDEAN
MINAY, PENNY-ANNE, 5, WITLEY ROAD, LOVEDEAN
FAIRINGSIDE, BARRY M, 6, WITLEY ROAD, LOVEDEAN
FAIRINGSIDE, SUSAN H, 6, WITLEY ROAD, LOVEDEAN
MOORE, NELLY, 7, WITLEY ROAD, LOVEDEAN
MERCER, ANDREW J, 8, WITLEY ROAD, LOVEDEAN
MERCER, JANE L, 8, WITLEY ROAD, LOVEDEAN
SMITH, DEREK J, 9, WITLEY ROAD, LOVEDEAN
JOSS, JACQUELINE A, 10, WITLEY ROAD, LOVEDEAN
JOSS, KATHLEEN R, 10, WITLEY ROAD, LOVEDEAN
JOSS, RAOUL, 10, WITLEY ROAD, LOVEDEAN
HAWKINS, CHRISTINA D, 12, WITLEY ROAD, LOVEDEAN
HAWKINS, ERNEST G, 12, WITLEY ROAD, LOVEDEAN
HOGGETT, BETTY E, 14, WITLEY ROAD, LOVEDEAN
COOPER, JUDITH A, 2, WOODLAND VIEW, HORNDEAN
COOPER, RICHARD A, 2, WOODLAND VIEW, HORNDEAN
LEE, JULIE C, 4, WOODLAND VIEW, HORNDEAN
NEW, ADRIAN P, 4, WOODLAND VIEW, HORNDEAN
THOMAS, DAVID L, 6, WOODLAND VIEW, HORNDEAN
THOMAS, GWAWR, 6, WOODLAND VIEW, HORNDEAN
BLEWDEN, PETER R, 8, WOODLAND VIEW, HORNDEAN
BLEWDEN, SUSAN M, 8, WOODLAND VIEW, HORNDEAN
LAMBSHEAD, CLIVE L, 9, WOODLAND VIEW, HORNDEAN
LAMBSHEAD, PAMELA C, 9, WOODLAND VIEW, HORNDEAN
ISAAC, ALISON A, 10, WOODLAND VIEW, HORNDEAN
ISAAC, JONATHAN, 10, WOODLAND VIEW, HORNDEAN
BEALE, GEOFFREY J, 11, WOODLAND VIEW, HORNDEAN
SMITH, GILLIAN A, 12, WOODLAND VIEW, HORNDEAN
SMITH, MARTIN D, 12, WOODLAND VIEW, HORNDEAN
GRANGER-BROWN, NICHOLAS J, 14, WOODLAND VIEW,
TAW, GARY E, 15, WOODLAND VIEW, HORNDEAN
TAW, PENELOPE A, 15, WOODLAND VIEW, HORNDEAN
GREENSMITH, AMANDA J, 16, WOODLAND VIEW, HORNDEAN
GREENSMITH, MICHAEL T, 16, WOODLAND VIEW, HORNDEAN
MORGAN, MARY, 16, WOODLAND VIEW, HORNDEAN
JOLLIFFE, HELEN A, 17, WOODLAND VIEW, HORNDEAN
JOLLIFFE, IAN, 17, WOODLAND VIEW, HORNDEAN
DASGUPTA, ASIM K, 18, WOODLAND VIEW, HORNDEAN
DASGUPTA, RUMELLA, 18, WOODLAND VIEW, HORNDEAN
DASGUPTA, SUPTA, 18, WOODLAND VIEW, HORNDEAN
DASGUPTA, TANYA, 18, WOODLAND VIEW, HORNDEAN
DANCE, GILLIAN I, 19, WOODLAND VIEW, HORNDEAN
HARRIS, BERTRAM L, 1, WOODSTOCK AVENUE, HORNDEAN
HARRIS, DOROTHY A, 1, WOODSTOCK AVENUE, HORNDEAN
WARROW, DAVID M, 5, WOODSTOCK AVENUE, HORNDEAN
WARROW, SARAH L, 5, WOODSTOCK AVENUE, HORNDEAN
CULLIMORE, JEAN L, 7, WOODSTOCK AVENUE, HORNDEAN
CULLIMORE, PATRICK B, 7, WOODSTOCK AVENUE,
BARRIE, WENDY F, 9, WOODSTOCK AVENUE, HORNDEAN
POWER, JOSEPH S, 9, WOODSTOCK AVENUE, HORNDEAN
AUGER, DAPHNE I, 11, WOODSTOCK AVENUE, HORNDEAN
AUGER, DAVID R, 11, WOODSTOCK AVENUE, HORNDEAN
CANNON, BERNARD J, 13, WOODSTOCK AVENUE, HORNDEAN
CANNON, PAULINE, 13, WOODSTOCK AVENUE, HORNDEAN
BEAN, GRAHAM S, 15, WOODSTOCK AVENUE, HORNDEAN
BEAN, JUDITH L, 15, WOODSTOCK AVENUE, HORNDEAN
BRIXEY, ANDREW P, 17, WOODSTOCK AVENUE, HORNDEAN
BRIXEY, PATRICIA L, 17, WOODSTOCK AVENUE, HORNDEAN
PALMER, BRENDA B, 19, WOODSTOCK AVENUE, HORNDEAN
PALMER, JOHN B, 19, WOODSTOCK AVENUE, HORNDEAN
PALMER, YVONNE K, 19, WOODSTOCK AVENUE, HORNDEAN
MAHLER, FRANCES E, 21, WOODSTOCK AVENUE, HORNDEAN
MAHLER, JOHN V.E, 21, WOODSTOCK AVENUE, HORNDEAN
RANDALL, KAREN L, 25, WOODSTOCK AVENUE, HORNDEAN
RANDALL, TONY, 25, WOODSTOCK AVENUE, HORNDEAN
MILLARD, DAVID F, 27, WOODSTOCK AVENUE, HORNDEAN
MILLARD, VALERIE, 27, WOODSTOCK AVENUE, HORNDEAN
CHURCHER, PHILIP R, 29, WOODSTOCK AVENUE,
LEWIN, JEAN A, 31, WOODSTOCK AVENUE, HORNDEAN
LIST, JANE A, 33, WOODSTOCK AVENUE, HORNDEAN
LIST, JOHN R, 33, WOODSTOCK AVENUE, HORNDEAN
LIST, WILLIAM J, 33, WOODSTOCK AVENUE, HORNDEAN
RICKETTS, JENNIFER D, 35, WOODSTOCK AVENUE,
RICKETTS, REGINALD C, 35, WOODSTOCK AVENUE,
COOK, JONATHAN H.B, 37, WOODSTOCK AVENUE,
COOK, KATHLEEN J.H, 37, WOODSTOCK AVENUE,
WEBB, ALAN J, 39, WOODSTOCK AVENUE, HORNDEAN
WEBB, ANNE J, 39, WOODSTOCK AVENUE, HORNDEAN
PERRY, GORDON L, 41, WOODSTOCK AVENUE, HORNDEAN
PERRY, WINIFRED C.M, 41, WOODSTOCK AVENUE,
JOLLIFFE, LIONEL J, 43, WOODSTOCK AVENUE, HORNDEAN
JOLLIFFE, SANDRA J, 43, WOODSTOCK AVENUE, HORNDEAN
PETERS, CATHERINE A, 45, WOODSTOCK AVENUE,
PETERS, KEITH G, 45, WOODSTOCK AVENUE, HORNDEAN
CHAMBERS, JANINE N.A, 47, WOODSTOCK AVENUE,
CHAMBERS, KIRSTIE A, 47, WOODSTOCK AVENUE,
PARSONS, ELAINE, 49, WOODSTOCK AVENUE, HORNDEAN
PARSONS, MARTIN A, 49, WOODSTOCK AVENUE, HORNDEAN
FINCH, KENNETH J, 51, WOODSTOCK AVENUE, HORNDEAN
FINCH, MAVIS P, 51, WOODSTOCK AVENUE, HORNDEAN
ATHERTON, NORMAN L, 53, WOODSTOCK AVENUE,
CROUCH, ANITA L, 55, WOODSTOCK AVENUE, HORNDEAN
SANDERS, BRENDA M, 57, WOODSTOCK AVENUE, HORNDEAN
SANDERS, DONALD H, 57, WOODSTOCK AVENUE,
LEWINS, ELIZABETH M, 59, WOODSTOCK AVENUE,
LEWINS, MATTHEW, 59, WOODSTOCK AVENUE, HORNDEAN
DOWNE, ALAN C, 61, WOODSTOCK AVENUE, HORNDEAN
DOWNE, GEORGINA, 61, WOODSTOCK AVENUE, HORNDEAN
TUMBER, JOYCE R, 63, WOODSTOCK AVENUE, HORNDEAN
GREENWOOD, DORIS, 65, WOODSTOCK AVENUE, HORNDEAN
LITTLEWOOD, MARGARET, 65, WOODSTOCK AVENUE,
ASLETT, CATHERINE, 67, WOODSTOCK AVENUE, HORNDEAN
ASLETT, ERIC S, 67, WOODSTOCK AVENUE, HORNDEAN
JOLLIFFE, BETTY, 6, WOODSTOCK AVENUE, HORNDEAN
REED, IAN, 8, WOODSTOCK AVENUE, HORNDEAN
REED, JANET M, 8, WOODSTOCK AVENUE, HORNDEAN
GRAY, DORIS I, 10, WOODSTOCK AVENUE, HORNDEAN
GRAY, VALERIE J, 10, WOODSTOCK AVENUE, HORNDEAN
PARSONS, AUGUSTUS R, 12, WOODSTOCK AVENUE,
PARSONS, MAISIE E, 12, WOODSTOCK AVENUE, HORNDEAN
WHITE, CLIVE E, 14, WOODSTOCK AVENUE, HORNDEAN
WHITE, PAMELA E.A, 14, WOODSTOCK AVENUE, HORNDEAN
HEADLAND, PAULINE D, 24, WOODSTOCK AVENUE,
HEADLAND, PETER A, 24, WOODSTOCK AVENUE, HORNDEAN
KERSLAKE, FREDA E, 26, WOODSTOCK AVENUE, HORNDEAN
KERSLAKE, PHILIP H, 26, WOODSTOCK AVENUE, HORNDEAN
HOWARD, CHRISTOPHER A, 28, WOODSTOCK AVENUE,
HOWARD, DOREEN F, 28, WOODSTOCK AVENUE, HORNDEAN
KEMP, MAUREEN M, 30, WOODSTOCK AVENUE, HORNDEAN
FOWLES, PATRICIA A, 56, WOODSTOCK AVENUE, HORNDEAN
FOWLES, RICHARD G, 56, WOODSTOCK AVENUE, HORNDEAN
FOWLES, STUART A, 56, WOODSTOCK AVENUE, HORNDEAN
DAY, ANTHONY P, 58, WOODSTOCK AVENUE, HORNDEAN
DAY, CHRISTINE E, 58, WOODSTOCK AVENUE, HORNDEAN
LOWE, DEREK J, 60, WOODSTOCK AVENUE, HORNDEAN
LOWE, KIM, 60, WOODSTOCK AVENUE, HORNDEAN
ORKIBI, GWYNETH, 62, WOODSTOCK AVENUE, HORNDEAN
ORKIBI, MORRIS, 62, WOODSTOCK AVENUE, HORNDEAN
BUNDEY, PAUL, 64, WOODSTOCK AVENUE, HORNDEAN
BUNDEY, PAULINE S, 64, WOODSTOCK AVENUE, HORNDEAN
BUNDEY, RACHEL, 64, WOODSTOCK AVENUE, HORNDEAN
BUNDEY, STEPHEN, 64, WOODSTOCK AVENUE, HORNDEAN
ROBINSON, KENNETH J, 66, WOODSTOCK AVENUE,
DENNIS, ELIZABETH S, 1, YOELLS LANE, LOVEDEAN
DENNIS, SHANE, 1, YOELLS LANE, LOVEDEAN
WARBURTON, JOYCE, 3, YOELLS LANE, LOVEDEAN
WARBURTON, ROY, 3, YOELLS LANE, LOVEDEAN
SHUTTLEWORTH, LORAINE, 5, YOELLS LANE, LOVEDEAN
SHUTTLEWORTH, ROBERT D, 5, YOELLS LANE, LOVEDEAN
ADAMSON, GRAHAM R, 7, YOELLS LANE, LOVEDEAN
ADAMSON, JOYCE V.D, 7, YOELLS LANE, LOVEDEAN
ADAMSON, LAWRENCE A, 7, YOELLS LANE, LOVEDEAN
SCOWEN, ZENA M, 9, YOELLS LANE, LOVEDEAN
WHITAKER, MARTIN B, 11, YOELLS LANE, LOVEDEAN
WHITAKER, SHIRLEY V, 11, YOELLS LANE, LOVEDEAN
MOORES, JENNIFER A, 15, YOELLS LANE, LOVEDEAN
MOSS, PETER, 15, YOELLS LANE, LOVEDEAN
BURNHAM, SHIRLEY A, 17, YOELLS LANE, LOVEDEAN
BURNHAM, STUART G.F, 17, YOELLS LANE, LOVEDEAN
WILKINS, CAROLYN A, 19, YOELLS LANE, LOVEDEAN
WILKINS, PAUL N, 19, YOELLS LANE, LOVEDEAN
DUNMORE, LEONARD S, 21, YOELLS LANE, LOVEDEAN
DUNMORE, MARIE L, 21, YOELLS LANE, LOVEDEAN
NEWSTEAD, GLADYS L.M, 21, YOELLS LANE, LOVEDEAN
BROWN, HELEN S, 23, YOELLS LANE, LOVEDEAN
SANDERSON, JENNIFER A, 25, YOELLS LANE, LOVEDEAN
MOORE, IVAN, 25A, YOELLS LANE, LOVEDEAN
MOORE, PENELOPE A, 25A, YOELLS LANE, LOVEDEAN
BLABER, ANNE-LOUISE, 25B, YOELLS LANE, LOVEDEAN
BLABER, GEOFFREY L.K, 25B, YOELLS LANE, LOVEDEAN
INGS, ROBIN L, 27, YOELLS LANE, LOVEDEAN
INGS, SYLVIA G, 27, YOELLS LANE, LOVEDEAN
HOPKINS, KATHLEEN M, 29, YOELLS LANE, LOVEDEAN
HOPKINS, LEONARD G, 29, YOELLS LANE, LOVEDEAN
POUND, STEPHEN J, 31, YOELLS LANE, LOVEDEAN
PANG, CHI WAI, 33, YOELLS LANE, LOVEDEAN
ANDERSON, ANTHONY J, 35, YOELLS LANE, LOVEDEAN
ANDERSON, KATIE L, 35, YOELLS LANE, LOVEDEAN
ANDERSON, SEAN A, 35, YOELLS LANE, LOVEDEAN
ANDERSON, THERESA F.P, 35, YOELLS LANE, LOVEDEAN
THOMAS, RAYMOND M, 37, YOELLS LANE, LOVEDEAN
TYDEMAN, TANYA M, 37, YOELLS LANE, LOVEDEAN
VOLLER, CHRISTOPHER B, 39, YOELLS LANE, LOVEDEAN
VOLLER, VIVIENNE E, 39, YOELLS LANE, LOVEDEAN
PERKINS, ALISON C, 41, YOELLS LANE, LOVEDEAN
PERKINS, CELIA D, 41, YOELLS LANE, LOVEDEAN
PERKINS, DARREN J, 41, YOELLS LANE, LOVEDEAN
PERKINS, DAVID J, 41, YOELLS LANE, LOVEDEAN
BARNES, ANDREW, 43, YOELLS LANE, LOVEDEAN
BARNES, LINDA T, 43, YOELLS LANE, LOVEDEAN
SMITH, BETTY I, 43, YOELLS LANE, LOVEDEAN
SMITH, EDWARD L, 43, YOELLS LANE, LOVEDEAN
JOHNSON, KAREN, 47, YOELLS LANE, LOVEDEAN
JOHNSON, ROGER D, 47, YOELLS LANE, LOVEDEAN
ANDREWS, STEPHEN G,,
CHILD, KIETH A.B,,
CHILD, SARAH E,,
DEVITT, ANTHONY W,,
FORBES, SALLY E,,
GOSS, CHRISTOPHER H,,
GOSS, SALLY
HOLLAND, DAVID
JACKSON, NORMAN C,,
LAND, MATTHEW J,,
LEWIS, PETER R,,
LEWIS, VENA E,,
REEVES, RICHARD C,,
THOMAS, STEPHEN R,,
WAISTER, BETTY E,,
WAISTER, MICHAEL

HORNDEAN (CATHERINGTON)
DAUGHTRY, ADAM J, 1, BELMONT CLOSE, HORNDEAN
DAUGHTRY, GILLIAN L, 1, BELMONT CLOSE, HORNDEAN
DAUGHTRY, GRAHAME K, 1, BELMONT CLOSE, HORNDEAN
HAGGIS, ROSS H, 2, BELMONT CLOSE, HORNDEAN
STRUDWICK, EMMA J, 3, BELMONT CLOSE, HORNDEAN
GILBERT, DAVID J, 4, BELMONT CLOSE, HORNDEAN
GILBERT, SHEILA D, 4, BELMONT CLOSE, HORNDEAN
MORGAN, BARRY M, 5, BELMONT CLOSE, HORNDEAN
MORGAN, LAURA, 5, BELMONT CLOSE, HORNDEAN
PETTY, CLARENCE E, 6, BELMONT CLOSE, HORNDEAN
PETTY, NELLIE G, 6, BELMONT CLOSE, HORNDEAN
PAY, ALBERT H, 7, BELMONT CLOSE, HORNDEAN
PAY, ETHEL V, 7, BELMONT CLOSE, HORNDEAN
BARTON, GEORGE W, 8, BELMONT CLOSE, HORNDEAN
BARTON, SYBIL I, 8, BELMONT CLOSE, HORNDEAN
COLE, EDNA G, 9, BELMONT CLOSE, HORNDEAN
COLE, JACK L, 9, BELMONT CLOSE, HORNDEAN
SHELDON, KATHLEEN M, 10, BELMONT CLOSE, HORNDEAN
RAINE, CARLA J, 11, BELMONT CLOSE, HORNDEAN
RAINE, IAN E, 11, BELMONT CLOSE, HORNDEAN
RAINE, JANET R, 11, BELMONT CLOSE, HORNDEAN
MURRANT, SARAH M, 187, CATHERINGTON LANE, CATHERINGTON
SCHILLEMORE, BRIAN C, 201, CATHERINGTON LANE, CATHERINGTON
SCHILLEMORE, MOLLY J, 201, CATHERINGTON LANE,
STEVENSON, PATRICIA A, 203, CATHERINGTON LANE,
STEVENSON, ROBERT F, 203, CATHERINGTON LANE,
STEVENSON, HELEN, 205, CATHERINGTON LANE,
STEVENSON, KEITH J, 205, CATHERINGTON LANE,
HOWARD, ANNE, 207, CATHERINGTON LANE,
HOWARD, JOHN L, 207, CATHERINGTON LANE,
WILSON, DIANA J, 209, CATHERINGTON LANE,
WILSON, IAN, 209, CATHERINGTON LANE,
SPARKS, MARGARET F, 213, CATHERINGTON LANE,
SPARKS, RONALD J, 213, CATHERINGTON LANE,
DEEKS, DORIS L, 215, CATHERINGTON LANE,
DEEKS, FREDERIC H, 215, CATHERINGTON LANE,
HOPCRAFT, BARRY, 219, CATHERINGTON LANE,
HOPCRAFT, DIANE, 219, CATHERINGTON LANE,
CROWTHER, GEORGE N, 221, CATHERINGTON LANE,
RIGSBY, DOREEN A, 223, CATHERINGTON LANE,
RIGSBY, ERNEST A, 223, CATHERINGTON LANE,

YOUNG, CHRISTOPHER J, 227, CATHERINGTON LANE,
YOUNG, KATHRYN, 227, CATHERINGTON LANE,
COLLINS, LYDIA J, 229, CATHERINGTON LANE,
COLLINS, PETER D, 229, CATHERINGTON LANE,
HELE, MICHEL J, 233, CATHERINGTON LANE,
HELE, RENATE M, 233, CATHERINGTON LANE,
ROBERTS, DONALD E, 233, CATHERINGTON LANE,
ROBERTS, ERIKA A, 233, CATHERINGTON LANE,
CANNON, BARRY A, 281, CATHERINGTON LANE,
CANNON, FRANCES S, 281, CATHERINGTON LANE,
CANNON, PAUL E, 281, CATHERINGTON LANE,
TAYLOR, ANTHONY F, 283, CATHERINGTON LANE,
TAYLOR, DOREEN E, 283, CATHERINGTON LANE,
BURTON, JOHN D, 285, CATHERINGTON LANE,
BURTON, OLIVIA J, 285, CATHERINGTON LANE,
STONE, JAMES W, 287, CATHERINGTON LANE,
STONE, SHARON, 287, CATHERINGTON LANE,
HARWOOD, JULIA G, 301, CATHERINGTON LANE,
HARWOOD, STEPHEN C.P, 301, CATHERINGTON LANE,
WOODWARD, KATHY A, 305, CATHERINGTON LANE,
WOODWARD, KIT J, 305, CATHERINGTON LANE,
WOODWARD, MALCOLM J, 305, CATHERINGTON LANE,
WOODWARD, PETER M, 305, CATHERINGTON LANE,
SAGE, LEE, 307, CATHERINGTON LANE, CATHERINGTON
SAGE, SARAH L, 307, CATHERINGTON LANE, CATHERINGTON
BUCKWELL, AMANDA, 309, CATHERINGTON LANE,
BUCKWELL, HELEN W, 309, CATHERINGTON LANE,
BUCKWELL, JOHN C, 309, CATHERINGTON LANE,
NAPPER, PAULINE M, 313, CATHERINGTON LANE,
NAPPER, TERRY, 313, CATHERINGTON LANE, CATHERINGTON
GOODYEAR, DELLA C, 315, CATHERINGTON LANE,
GOODYEAR, ROBERT, 315, CATHERINGTON LANE,
SHAW, MELANIE J, 329, CATHERINGTON LANE,
SHAW, SIMON J, 329, CATHERINGTON LANE,
HODGENS, DAVID A, 341, CATHERINGTON LANE,
HODGENS, SUSAN P, 341, CATHERINGTON LANE,
GRAHAM, BARBARA A, 343, CATHERINGTON LANE,
GRAHAM, BRUCE W, 343, CATHERINGTON LANE,
KNIGHT, ROBERT G, 345, CATHERINGTON LANE,
KNIGHT, SYLVIA D, 345, CATHERINGTON LANE,
SEAWARD, FREDERICK J, 214, CATHERINGTON LANE,
SEAWARD, JOSEPHINE M, 214, CATHERINGTON LANE,
ALLEN, STEPHEN D, 240, CATHERINGTON LANE,
O'BRIEN, KIM M, 240, CATHERINGTON LANE,
DALTON, RICHARD C, 284, CATHERINGTON LANE,
DALTON (LADY), JANE H, 284, CATHERINGTON LANE,
DALTON (SIR), GEOFFREY T.J, 284, CATHERINGTON LANE,
DUNNING, HELEN A, 286, CATHERINGTON LANE,
DUNNING, MALCOLM B, 286, CATHERINGTON LANE,
TAYLOR, JULIA, 290, CATHERINGTON LANE, CATHERINGTON
DORNER, CLARISSA O, 292, CATHERINGTON LANE,
DORNER, PETER S, 292, CATHERINGTON LANE,
CARR, HAZEL Y, 300, CATHERINGTON LANE,
CARR, JOSEPH W, 300, CATHERINGTON LANE,
BEARDSLEY, CHRISTOPHER, 330, CATHERINGTON LANE,
EVERSHED, PENELOPE S, 344, CATHERINGTON LANE,
EVERSHED, WILLIAM A, 344, CATHERINGTON LANE,
SCOTT, JOYCE E, 350, CATHERINGTON LANE,
SCOTT, LEONARD, 350, CATHERINGTON LANE,
CLARKE, ROSEMARY S, 352, CATHERINGTON LANE,
CLARKE, SIDNEY, 352, CATHERINGTON LANE,
JOHN, CRAIG B, 360, CATHERINGTON LANE, CATHERINGTON
JOHN, DEE M, 360, CATHERINGTON LANE, CATHERINGTON
PYLE, KATHERINE R, 362, CATHERINGTON LANE,
PYLE, MARY J, 362, CATHERINGTON LANE, CATHERINGTON
PYLE, ROGER J, 362, CATHERINGTON LANE, CATHERINGTON
MOORE, RICHARD J, 364, CATHERINGTON LANE,
MOORE, SARAH-JANE, 364, CATHERINGTON LANE,
WEEKS, BETTY B, 1, CHALK RIDGE, HORNDEAN
WEEKS, EDWIN J, 1, CHALK RIDGE, HORNDEAN
THAYER, GEORGE W, 3, CHALK RIDGE, HORNDEAN
THAYER, VERA M, 3, CHALK RIDGE, HORNDEAN
CUTLER, ALEC A, 5, CHALK RIDGE, HORNDEAN
CUTLER, ZENA H, 5, CHALK RIDGE, HORNDEAN
KETTLE, KENNETH, 7, CHALK RIDGE, HORNDEAN
KETTLE, MARJORIE O, 7, CHALK RIDGE, HORNDEAN
DUNFORD, IRENE E, 2/4, CHALK RIDGE, HORNDEAN
GREGORY, PATRICK J, 2/4, CHALK RIDGE, HORNDEAN
SIMS, CAROLINE F, 6, CHALK RIDGE, HORNDEAN
SIMS, EDWIN J, 6, CHALK RIDGE, HORNDEAN
SAWKINS, PATRICIA C, 8, CHALK RIDGE, HORNDEAN
SAWKINS, ROBERT W, 8, CHALK RIDGE, HORNDEAN
THOMS, RICHARD, 10, CHALK RIDGE, HORNDEAN
THOMS, SUSAN B, 10, CHALK RIDGE, HORNDEAN
HAWKES, DENYSE K, 1, CHERVIL CLOSE, HORNDEAN
HAWKES, DUNCAN R, 1, CHERVIL CLOSE, HORNDEAN
SADLER, CAROL A, 2, CHERVIL CLOSE, HORNDEAN
SADLER, RICHARD T, 2, CHERVIL CLOSE, HORNDEAN
SADLER, TREVOR J, 2, CHERVIL CLOSE, HORNDEAN
BAILEY, DAVID R, 3, CHERVIL CLOSE, HORNDEAN
BAILEY, KAREN, 3, CHERVIL CLOSE, HORNDEAN
BRISTOW, MARY E, 4, CHERVIL CLOSE, HORNDEAN
BRISTOW, MICHAEL A, 4, CHERVIL CLOSE, HORNDEAN
PEMBERTON, MICHAEL, 5, CHERVIL CLOSE, HORNDEAN
PEMBERTON, SAMUEL T, 5, CHERVIL CLOSE, HORNDEAN
PEMBERTON, VALERIE, 5, CHERVIL CLOSE, HORNDEAN
TEDSTONE, CARVER J, 6, CHERVIL CLOSE, HORNDEAN
BELGRANO, KYLE L, 7, CHERVIL CLOSE, HORNDEAN
HUDSON, JO A.M, 7, CHERVIL CLOSE, HORNDEAN
WARDROP, RICHARD G, 8, CHERVIL CLOSE, HORNDEAN
WARDROP, VANESSA L, 8, CHERVIL CLOSE, HORNDEAN
ROLFE, BERYL M, 9, CHERVIL CLOSE, HORNDEAN
ROLFE, GARY J, 9, CHERVIL CLOSE, HORNDEAN
ROLFE, PETER J, 9, CHERVIL CLOSE, HORNDEAN
DORAN, MARIA A, 10, CHERVIL CLOSE, HORNDEAN
DORAN, MICHAEL J, 10, CHERVIL CLOSE, HORNDEAN
VAUGHAN, LESLEY J, 11, CHERVIL CLOSE, HORNDEAN
VAUGHAN, TERRY R, 11, CHERVIL CLOSE, HORNDEAN
DOWN, MARGARET R, 12, CHERVIL CLOSE, HORNDEAN
JACKSON, MICHAEL J, 14, CHERVIL CLOSE, HORNDEAN
JACKSON, TINA K, 14, CHERVIL CLOSE, HORNDEAN
BURNETT, LINDA, 15, CHERVIL CLOSE, HORNDEAN
PURSGLOVE, CHRISTOPHER H, 15, CHERVIL CLOSE,
KENWORTHY, MICH'LL C, 16, CHERVIL CLOSE, HORNDEAN
KENWORTHY, SUSAN V, 16, CHERVIL CLOSE, HORNDEAN
SINCLAIR, JULIE A, 17, CHERVIL CLOSE, HORNDEAN
SINCLAIR, MARK A, 17, CHERVIL CLOSE, HORNDEAN
EDWARDS, IAN D, 18, CHERVIL CLOSE, HORNDEAN
EDWARDS, SUSAN J, 18, CHERVIL CLOSE, HORNDEAN
TENNENT, KATRINA G, 20, CHERVIL CLOSE, HORNDEAN
TENNENT, PAUL M, 20, CHERVIL CLOSE, HORNDEAN
SMITH, JAMES W, 21, CHERVIL CLOSE, HORNDEAN
SMITH, JOAN M, 21, CHERVIL CLOSE, HORNDEAN
SMITH, NICKY M, 21, CHERVIL CLOSE, HORNDEAN
SMITH, PAUL J, 21, CHERVIL CLOSE, HORNDEAN
COOPER, HELEN, 22, CHERVIL CLOSE, HORNDEAN
COOPER, MARK N, 22, CHERVIL CLOSE, HORNDEAN
BARNEY, PAUL R, 23, CHERVIL CLOSE, HORNDEAN
PLEDGE, PATRICIA, 23, CHERVIL CLOSE, HORNDEAN
SHOOBRIDGE, PATRICK, 24, CHERVIL CLOSE, HORNDEAN
O'CARROLL, JULIE D, 25, CHERVIL CLOSE, HORNDEAN
O'CARROLL, LIAM J, 25, CHERVIL CLOSE, HORNDEAN
MUSSELL, ANDREW R, 26, CHERVIL CLOSE, HORNDEAN
MUSSELL, SUZANNE J, 26, CHERVIL CLOSE, HORNDEAN
FEREDAY, VINCENT P, 27, CHERVIL CLOSE, HORNDEAN
JUBB, ANITA M, 27, CHERVIL CLOSE, HORNDEAN
CROSS, ANDREA E, 28, CHERVIL CLOSE, HORNDEAN
CROSS, LEE, 28, CHERVIL CLOSE, HORNDEAN
LEVERETT, NICHOLAS V, 29, CHERVIL CLOSE, HORNDEAN
TOWNSEND, MATTHEW D, 30, CHERVIL CLOSE, HORNDEAN
TOWNSEND, RAYMOND E, 30, CHERVIL CLOSE, HORNDEAN
TOWNSEND, SAMUEL J, 30, CHERVIL CLOSE, HORNDEAN
STONEMAN, MARY V, 31, CHERVIL CLOSE, HORNDEAN
STONEMAN, TIMOTHY J, 31, CHERVIL CLOSE, HORNDEAN
ALBON, AMANDA, 1, CLAIRE GARDENS, HORNDEAN
ALBON, JENNIFER, 1, CLAIRE GARDENS, HORNDEAN
ALBON, KATHERINE R, 1, CLAIRE GARDENS, HORNDEAN
ALBON, PAULINE, 1, CLAIRE GARDENS, HORNDEAN
ALBON, RICHARD E, 1, CLAIRE GARDENS, HORNDEAN
ALBON, SALLY A, 1, CLAIRE GARDENS, HORNDEAN
ALBON, SARAH J, 1, CLAIRE GARDENS, HORNDEAN
DENBY, GARETH J, 2, CLAIRE GARDENS, HORNDEAN
DENBY, JANET M, 2, CLAIRE GARDENS, HORNDEAN
HOLDER, MATTHEW J, 3, CLAIRE GARDENS, HORNDEAN
HOLDER, RICHARD J, 3, CLAIRE GARDENS, HORNDEAN
HOLDER, ROSEMARY J, 3, CLAIRE GARDENS, HORNDEAN
HALLETT, ANGELA E, 4, CLAIRE GARDENS, HORNDEAN
HALLETT, PETER W, 4, CLAIRE GARDENS, HORNDEAN
THOMPSON, GEORGE M, 5, CLAIRE GARDENS, HORNDEAN
THOMPSON, JULIE A, 5, CLAIRE GARDENS, HORNDEAN
BUTTON, CAROL A, 6, CLAIRE GARDENS, HORNDEAN
BUTTON, NIGEL P, 6, CLAIRE GARDENS, HORNDEAN
BUTTON, ROBERT A, 6, CLAIRE GARDENS, HORNDEAN
CAREY, ALISON M, 7, CLAIRE GARDENS, HORNDEAN
CAREY, COLLETTE G, 7, CLAIRE GARDENS, HORNDEAN
CAREY, JANINE M, 7, CLAIRE GARDENS, HORNDEAN
CAREY, MOIRA H, 7, CLAIRE GARDENS, HORNDEAN
CAREY, THOMAS, 7, CLAIRE GARDENS, HORNDEAN
MANN, KAREN J, 8, CLAIRE GARDENS, HORNDEAN
MANN, PAUL A, 8, CLAIRE GARDENS, HORNDEAN
MANN, ROSALIND H, 8, CLAIRE GARDENS, HORNDEAN
MANN, SARAH E, 8, CLAIRE GARDENS, HORNDEAN
SHORT, JOHN M, 9, CLAIRE GARDENS, HORNDEAN
SHORT, MARY E, 9, CLAIRE GARDENS, HORNDEAN
DEAN, COLIN E, 10, CLAIRE GARDENS, HORNDEAN
DEAN, GLYNIS A, 10, CLAIRE GARDENS, HORNDEAN
DEAN, PETER N, 10, CLAIRE GARDENS, HORNDEAN
DEAN, SHARON A, 10, CLAIRE GARDENS, HORNDEAN
BOYD, DOROTHY G, 11, CLAIRE GARDENS, HORNDEAN
DOCKER, CATHERINE M, 12, CLAIRE GARDENS, HORNDEAN
DOCKER, COLIN A, 12, CLAIRE GARDENS, HORNDEAN
DOCKER, STEPHEN P, 12, CLAIRE GARDENS, HORNDEAN
STYLES, MICHAEL J, 13, CLAIRE GARDENS, HORNDEAN
STYLES, SYLVIE, 13, CLAIRE GARDENS, HORNDEAN
HEMMINGS, BERYL P, 14, CLAIRE GARDENS, HORNDEAN
HEMMINGS, GEORGE T, 14, CLAIRE GARDENS, HORNDEAN
BEALE, DAPHNE E, 15, CLAIRE GARDENS, HORNDEAN
BEALE, ELOISE A, 15, CLAIRE GARDENS, HORNDEAN
BEALE, WILLIAM J, 15, CLAIRE GARDENS, HORNDEAN
ANNETT, DAVID M, 16, CLAIRE GARDENS, HORNDEAN
ANNETT, MAUREEN, 16, CLAIRE GARDENS, HORNDEAN
ANNETT, PAUL, 16, CLAIRE GARDENS, HORNDEAN
BROWN, DAVID J, 18, CLAIRE GARDENS, HORNDEAN
BROWN, LISA K, 18, CLAIRE GARDENS, HORNDEAN
O'FEE, ROBERT, 20, CLAIRE GARDENS, HORNDEAN
O'FEE, SANDRA D, 20, CLAIRE GARDENS, HORNDEAN
TODD, DEREK C, 21A, CLAIRE GARDENS, HORNDEAN
WELLS, GAYNOR E, 21B, CLAIRE GARDENS, HORNDEAN
WELLS, KEITH C, 21B, CLAIRE GARDENS, HORNDEAN
SAUNDERS, KEVIN J, 22A, CLAIRE GARDENS, HORNDEAN
PENN, JENNIFER J, 22B, CLAIRE GARDENS, HORNDEAN
MCGILVARY, GORDON M, 23A, CLAIRE GARDENS, HORNDEAN
MCGILVARY, MAUREEN L.M, 23A, CLAIRE GARDENS,
MERRELL, LESLIE F, 23B, CLAIRE GARDENS, HORNDEAN
MERRELL, PAMELA B, 23B, CLAIRE GARDENS, HORNDEAN
FANCY, ELIZABETH A, 24A, CLAIRE GARDENS, HORNDEAN
HEPWORTH, ZOE L, 24B, CLAIRE GARDENS, HORNDEAN
MOYNAN, HAZEL J, 25B, CLAIRE GARDENS, HORNDEAN
WILLIAMS, ALAN R, 26A, CLAIRE GARDENS, HORNDEAN
BONNER, CORNELIUS C, 26B, CLAIRE GARDENS, HORNDEAN
BONNER, MARGARET, 26B, CLAIRE GARDENS, HORNDEAN
MATTHEWS, PAUL B, 27, CLAIRE GARDENS, HORNDEAN
MCDONALD, IAN, 27, CLAIRE GARDENS, HORNDEAN
MCDONALD, RITA M, 27, CLAIRE GARDENS, HORNDEAN
LINGHAM, DENISE A.C, 28, CLAIRE GARDENS, HORNDEAN
LINGHAM, PETER, 28, CLAIRE GARDENS, HORNDEAN
JACKSON, BRIDGET C, 29, CLAIRE GARDENS, HORNDEAN
JACKSON, LOUISE A, 29, CLAIRE GARDENS, HORNDEAN
JACKSON, PETER R, 29, CLAIRE GARDENS, HORNDEAN
BISHOP, NORMAN F, 30, CLAIRE GARDENS, HORNDEAN
REED, HAZEL C, 30, CLAIRE GARDENS, HORNDEAN
REED, RUSSELL J, 30, CLAIRE GARDENS, HORNDEAN
WHITE, GRAHAM, 31, CLAIRE GARDENS, HORNDEAN
WHITE, MARK A, 31, CLAIRE GARDENS, HORNDEAN
BERESFORD, TREVOR, 32, CLAIRE GARDENS, HORNDEAN
THATCHER, IAN L, 32, CLAIRE GARDENS, HORNDEAN
THATCHER, KATIE L, 32, CLAIRE GARDENS, HORNDEAN
THATCHER, SANDRA L, 32, CLAIRE GARDENS, HORNDEAN
BOYDEN, GLYNN T, 33, CLAIRE GARDENS, HORNDEAN
BOYDEN, TREVOR G, 33, CLAIRE GARDENS, HORNDEAN
THORNHILL, DEAN L, 34, CLAIRE GARDENS, HORNDEAN
THORNHILL, GARY A, 34, CLAIRE GARDENS, HORNDEAN
THORNHILL, JOAN E, 34, CLAIRE GARDENS, HORNDEAN
THORNHILL, LEONARD W, 34, CLAIRE GARDENS, HORNDEAN
COMPTON, EMMA M, 1, COMFREY CLOSE, HORNDEAN
POPE, JASON, 1, COMFREY CLOSE, HORNDEAN
CROSS, MAX D, 2, COMFREY CLOSE, HORNDEAN
CROSS, SUSAN B, 2, COMFREY CLOSE, HORNDEAN
SWIFT, ANN E, 3, COMFREY CLOSE, HORNDEAN
SWIFT, ROBERT G, 3, COMFREY CLOSE, HORNDEAN
DUNN, DAVINA C, 4, COMFREY CLOSE, HORNDEAN
DUNN, TERENCE J, 4, COMFREY CLOSE, HORNDEAN
FLATMAN, CHRISTOPHER A, 5, COMFREY CLOSE, HORNDEAN
FLATMAN, LAURA C, 5, COMFREY CLOSE, HORNDEAN
FLATMAN, PATRICIA A, 5, COMFREY CLOSE, HORNDEAN
LAVERY, ALAN, 6, COMFREY CLOSE, HORNDEAN
LAVERY, IRENE D, 6, COMFREY CLOSE, HORNDEAN
SAMSON, BARBARA K, 7, COMFREY CLOSE, HORNDEAN
SAMSON, DENIS W, 7, COMFREY CLOSE, HORNDEAN
COOMBES, ANTHONY P, 8, COMFREY CLOSE, HORNDEAN
COOMBES, JUDITH A, 8, COMFREY CLOSE, HORNDEAN
MEW, CLAIRE L, 10, COMFREY CLOSE, HORNDEAN
MEW, KEVIN P, 10, COMFREY CLOSE, HORNDEAN
PARR, ELIZABETH K, 1, COOMBS CLOSE, HORNDEAN
PARR, EMMA R.H, 1, COOMBS CLOSE, HORNDEAN
PARR, GRAHAM J.F, 1, COOMBS CLOSE, HORNDEAN
DARVILLE, ALAN, 2, COOMBS CLOSE, HORNDEAN
DARVILLE, JEAN A, 2, COOMBS CLOSE, HORNDEAN
COLE, ADRIAN R, 3, COOMBS CLOSE, HORNDEAN
ASHTON, CAROLE D, 4, COOMBS CLOSE, HORNDEAN
ASHTON, NIGEL G, 4, COOMBS CLOSE, HORNDEAN
BAKER, MALCOLM R.K, 6, COOMBS CLOSE, HORNDEAN
BAKER, PENELOPE J, 6, COOMBS CLOSE, HORNDEAN
GREENWOOD, ALBERT E, 7, COOMBS CLOSE, HORNDEAN
GREENWOOD, IRIS E.M, 7, COOMBS CLOSE, HORNDEAN
BATTY, COLIN J, 8, COOMBS CLOSE, HORNDEAN
CATO, DAWN R, 8, COOMBS CLOSE, HORNDEAN
WILSON, JULIE L, 10, COOMBS CLOSE, HORNDEAN
WILSON, KEVIN M, 10, COOMBS CLOSE, HORNDEAN
BAILEY, CHRISTINE E, 12, COOMBS CLOSE, HORNDEAN
BAILEY, DEREK R, 12, COOMBS CLOSE, HORNDEAN
BAILEY, MELANIE A, 12, COOMBS CLOSE, HORNDEAN
TOMLINSON, JOHN, 14, COOMBS CLOSE, HORNDEAN
TOMLINSON, WENDY J, 14, COOMBS CLOSE, HORNDEAN
RUSSELL, ROBERT K, 16, COOMBS CLOSE, HORNDEAN
RUSSELL, SUSAN J, 16, COOMBS CLOSE, HORNDEAN
PAVEY, CLAIRE M, 18, COOMBS CLOSE, HORNDEAN
SELLERS, DENISE J, 20, COOMBS CLOSE, HORNDEAN
SELLERS, ROGER G, 20, COOMBS CLOSE, HORNDEAN
TOMLINSON, FAYE J, 22, COOMBS CLOSE, HORNDEAN
TOMLINSON, GRAHAM R, 22, COOMBS CLOSE, HORNDEAN
TOMLINSON, JEAN P, 22, COOMBS CLOSE, HORNDEAN
TOMLINSON, MICHELLE D, 22, COOMBS CLOSE, HORNDEAN
YOUNG, SADIE, 24, COOMBS CLOSE, HORNDEAN
GILCHRIST, CLAIRE M, 26, COOMBS CLOSE, HORNDEAN
GILCHRIST, KEITH, 26, COOMBS CLOSE, HORNDEAN
LAMBERT, CHRISTOPHER P, 28, COOMBS CLOSE, HORNDEAN
LAMBERT, DOREEN M, 28, COOMBS CLOSE, HORNDEAN
LAMBERT, WILLIAM G.E, 28, COOMBS CLOSE, HORNDEAN
WRIGHT, COLIN A, 1, DERWENT CLOSE, HORNDEAN
WRIGHT, JANET C, 1, DERWENT CLOSE, HORNDEAN
FRASER, DEBORAH L, 2, DERWENT CLOSE, HORNDEAN
HALLIWELL, MALCOLM A.K, 3, DERWENT CLOSE,
HALLIWELL, PATRICIA D, 3, DERWENT CLOSE, HORNDEAN
COULSON, CATHERINE A, 4, DERWENT CLOSE, HORNDEAN
COULSON, DIANE M, 4, DERWENT CLOSE, HORNDEAN
BENNETT, MICHAEL D, 5, DERWENT CLOSE, HORNDEAN
CANTINI, MARCELLO V, 5, DERWENT CLOSE, HORNDEAN
CANTINI, SAMANTHA, 5, DERWENT CLOSE, HORNDEAN
GIDDINGS, ALISON, 6, DERWENT CLOSE, HORNDEAN
GIDDINGS, ANNETTE D, 6, DERWENT CLOSE, HORNDEAN
GIDDINGS, ROBIN C, 6, DERWENT CLOSE, HORNDEAN
HANSON, GUY F, 7, DERWENT CLOSE, HORNDEAN
HOPPER, JENNY C, 7, DERWENT CLOSE, HORNDEAN
BENN, GRAHAME A, 8, DERWENT CLOSE, HORNDEAN
STILL, CAROLYN J, 8, DERWENT CLOSE, HORNDEAN
CRASSWELLER, PENELOPE J, 9, DERWENT CLOSE,
CRASSWELLER, TONY J, 9, DERWENT CLOSE, HORNDEAN
COSTELLO, LESLEY A, 11, DERWENT CLOSE, HORNDEAN

Electoral Roll

COBB, SANDRA A, 12, DERWENT CLOSE, HORNDEAN
BALL, CATHRIN M.E, 14, DERWENT CLOSE, HORNDEAN
BALL, PAUL A, 14, DERWENT CLOSE, HORNDEAN
DAVIES, MARK P, 15, DERWENT CLOSE, HORNDEAN
DAVIES, SANDRA E, 15, DERWENT CLOSE, HORNDEAN
KNOTT, ROSEMARY, 16, DERWENT CLOSE, HORNDEAN
BOTTLE, RICHARD D, 17, DERWENT CLOSE, HORNDEAN
POPE, KAREN L, 17, DERWENT CLOSE, HORNDEAN
COOPER, IRIS J, 18, DERWENT CLOSE, HORNDEAN
COOPER, JOHN D, 18, DERWENT CLOSE, HORNDEAN
WARE, ABIGAIL J, 19, DERWENT CLOSE, HORNDEAN
HOWES, IAIN, 20, DERWENT CLOSE, HORNDEAN
LANGDON, SALLY L, 20, DERWENT CLOSE, HORNDEAN
LEGGETT, LINDA A, 22, DERWENT CLOSE, HORNDEAN
LEGGETT, SEAN, 22, DERWENT CLOSE, HORNDEAN
PAINE, ADAM D, 23, DERWENT CLOSE, HORNDEAN
PAINE, DAVID G, 23, DERWENT CLOSE, HORNDEAN
PAINE, DENISE M.F, 23, DERWENT CLOSE, HORNDEAN
PAINE, MATTHEW J, 23, DERWENT CLOSE, HORNDEAN
LOVICK, DARREN B, 24, DERWENT CLOSE, HORNDEAN
LOVICK, JAY D, 24, DERWENT CLOSE, HORNDEAN
LOVICK, LYNDA M, 24, DERWENT CLOSE, HORNDEAN
SNEDDEN, BENJAMIN J, 25, DERWENT CLOSE, HORNDEAN
SNEDDEN, MARGARET S, 25, DERWENT CLOSE, HORNDEAN
DOYLE, MARK A, 26, DERWENT CLOSE, HORNDEAN
DOYLE, SUSAN J, 26, DERWENT CLOSE, HORNDEAN
WOODCOCK, COLIN E, 27, DERWENT CLOSE, HORNDEAN
WOODCOCK, SANDRA M, 27, DERWENT CLOSE, HORNDEAN
BURFORD, JANE M, 28, DERWENT CLOSE, HORNDEAN
BURFORD, THOMAS J.J, 28, DERWENT CLOSE, HORNDEAN
JOHNSON, JOHN D, 29, DERWENT CLOSE, HORNDEAN
JOHNSON, ROSEMARY A, 29, DERWENT CLOSE, HORNDEAN
CLARKE, CELIA J, 30, DERWENT CLOSE, HORNDEAN
DUNFORD, DAVID K, 31, DERWENT CLOSE, HORNDEAN
DUNFORD, KEVIN J, 31, DERWENT CLOSE, HORNDEAN
DUNFORD, LINDA A, 31, DERWENT CLOSE, HORNDEAN
INKER, DAVID J, 32, DERWENT CLOSE, HORNDEAN
INKER, SANDRA L, 32, DERWENT CLOSE, HORNDEAN
BREWSTER, LYNNE P, 34, DERWENT CLOSE, HORNDEAN
BREWSTER, MATTHEW J, 34, DERWENT CLOSE, HORNDEAN
BREWSTER, STEPHEN, 34, DERWENT CLOSE, HORNDEAN
ROBINSON, ALAN V.R, 35, DERWENT CLOSE, HORNDEAN
ROBINSON, GREG A, 35, DERWENT CLOSE, HORNDEAN
ROBINSON, JULIE L, 35, DERWENT CLOSE, HORNDEAN
FULCHER, NICOLA M, 36, DERWENT CLOSE, HORNDEAN
FULCHER, PETER J, 36, DERWENT CLOSE, HORNDEAN
LEWIS, CARLA L, 37, DERWENT CLOSE, HORNDEAN
LEWIS, GILLIAN A, 37, DERWENT CLOSE, HORNDEAN
LEWIS, JOHN, 37, DERWENT CLOSE, HORNDEAN
STREET, JAMES R, 37, DERWENT CLOSE, HORNDEAN
LE CLERCQ, BELINDA J, 38, DERWENT CLOSE, HORNDEAN
LE CLERCQ, PHILIP A, 38, DERWENT CLOSE, HORNDEAN
ANGUS, JOAN H, 39, DERWENT CLOSE, HORNDEAN
ANGUS, WILLIAM F, 39, DERWENT CLOSE, HORNDEAN
MAHLER, GERALD V.E, 40, DERWENT CLOSE, HORNDEAN
MAHLER, HAZEL P, 40, DERWENT CLOSE, HORNDEAN
MAHLER, LUCETTA H, 40, DERWENT CLOSE, HORNDEAN
KELLY, CLAIRE T, 41, DERWENT CLOSE, HORNDEAN
KELLY, ROLAND M, 41, DERWENT CLOSE, HORNDEAN
EDWARDS, CHRISTINA, 42, DERWENT CLOSE, HORNDEAN
EDWARDS, GEORGE R, 42, DERWENT CLOSE, HORNDEAN
HOBBS, NICHOLAS D, 43, DERWENT CLOSE, HORNDEAN
HOBBS, PAMELA A, 43, DERWENT CLOSE, HORNDEAN
HAWKINS, JOHN C, 44, DERWENT CLOSE, HORNDEAN
WHITE, DANNIELLE J, 44, DERWENT CLOSE, HORNDEAN
WHITE, MARTINA E, 44, DERWENT CLOSE, HORNDEAN
WHITE, ROSEMARIE E.P, 44, DERWENT CLOSE, HORNDEAN
ASHTON, MARILYN, 45, DERWENT CLOSE, HORNDEAN
ASHTON, RODERICK, 45, DERWENT CLOSE, HORNDEAN
MARTIN, ADAM D.A, 46, DERWENT CLOSE, HORNDEAN
MARTIN, MARGARET C, 46, DERWENT CLOSE, HORNDEAN
MARTIN, PETER R, 46, DERWENT CLOSE, HORNDEAN
LEWIS, GAVIN A, 47, DERWENT CLOSE, HORNDEAN
LEWIS, GORDON G.P, 47, DERWENT CLOSE, HORNDEAN
LEWIS, JEAN, 47, DERWENT CLOSE, HORNDEAN
LEWIS, TIMOTHY M, 47, DERWENT CLOSE, HORNDEAN
HAWES, DAVID J, 48, DERWENT CLOSE, HORNDEAN
HAWES, SAMANTHA J, 48, DERWENT CLOSE, HORNDEAN
HAWES, SCOTT J, 48, DERWENT CLOSE, HORNDEAN
HAWES, SHEILA J, 48, DERWENT CLOSE, HORNDEAN
GREY, ANTHONY R, 49, DERWENT CLOSE, HORNDEAN
GREY, ELIZABETH J, 49, DERWENT CLOSE, HORNDEAN
GREY, JESSICA A, 49, DERWENT CLOSE, HORNDEAN
MANT, CATHERINE M, 50, DERWENT CLOSE, HORNDEAN
MANT, NEIL F, 50, DERWENT CLOSE, HORNDEAN
KNIGHT, JOHN, 51, DERWENT CLOSE, HORNDEAN
FOSTER, JAMES W, 52, DERWENT CLOSE, HORNDEAN
FOSTER, MARGARET A, 52, DERWENT CLOSE, HORNDEAN
HAGGARTY, STUART J.L, 52, DERWENT CLOSE, HORNDEAN
COWELL, PAUL B, 53, DERWENT CLOSE, HORNDEAN
PALMER, JULIETTE C, 53, DERWENT CLOSE, HORNDEAN
DICKS, RENA A, 54, DERWENT CLOSE, HORNDEAN
DICKS, ROGER F, 54, DERWENT CLOSE, HORNDEAN
CALLAGHAN, GORDON J, 55, DERWENT CLOSE, HORNDEAN
CALLAGHAN, JOAN M, 55, DERWENT CLOSE, HORNDEAN
CORNEY, HILLARY J, 56, DERWENT CLOSE, HORNDEAN
COLDRICK, STEVEN A, 57, DERWENT CLOSE, HORNDEAN
COLDRICK, SUSAN T, 57, DERWENT CLOSE, HORNDEAN
AMEY, DAVID A, 1, DOWN FARM PLACE, HORNDEAN
CHALMERS, TRACEY J, 1, DOWN FARM PLACE, HORNDEAN
DULAKE, REBECCA M, 2, DOWN FARM PLACE, HORNDEAN
STOWERS, LISA J, 3, DOWN FARM PLACE, HORNDEAN
HAMM, GAVIN J, 4, DOWN FARM PLACE, HORNDEAN
HAMM, PAULINE, 4, DOWN FARM PLACE, HORNDEAN
PRATER, LAUREN J, 5, DOWN FARM PLACE, HORNDEAN
GRANT, LISA M, 6, DOWN FARM PLACE, HORNDEAN
JURY, SUZANNE E, 7, DOWN FARM PLACE, HORNDEAN
PHILLIPS, JOHN D, 8, DOWN FARM PLACE, HORNDEAN
PHILLIPS, SUSAN C, 8, DOWN FARM PLACE, HORNDEAN
EDNEY, PATRICK M, 9, DOWN FARM PLACE, HORNDEAN
MCMEEKIN, KAREN M, 9, DOWN FARM PLACE, HORNDEAN
DOWNIE, NATASHA, 10, DOWN FARM PLACE, HORNDEAN
BUNDAY, JOHN, 14, DOWN FARM PLACE, HORNDEAN
RACKETT, BRENDA M, 15, DOWN FARM PLACE, HORNDEAN
WELLING, GEORGE R, 16, DOWN FARM PLACE, HORNDEAN
WELLING, MARY I, 16, DOWN FARM PLACE, HORNDEAN
SPICER, AMY B, CAMPDOWN, DOWN ROAD, HORNDEAN
ODEY, JENNIFER A, DOWNLANDS, DOWN ROAD, HORNDEAN
ODEY, THOMAS H, DOWNLANDS, DOWN ROAD, HORNDEAN
SAVAGE, ANTHONY G, MILKWOOD, DOWN ROAD, HORNDEAN
BODDY, CAROL M, NEYOR GADING, DOWN ROAD,
BODDY, DONALD J, NEYOR GADING, DOWN ROAD,
BODDY, JOANNE K, NEYOR GADING, DOWN ROAD,
WEBB, JACQUELINE M, ROSE VILLA, DOWN ROAD,
WEBB, MAURICE A, ROSE VILLA, DOWN ROAD, HORNDEAN
PAYNE, MICHAEL J, ST. MARKS, DOWN ROAD, HORNDEAN
PAYNE, RICHARD M, ST. MARKS, DOWN ROAD, HORNDEAN
PAYNE, YVONNE A, ST. MARKS, DOWN ROAD, HORNDEAN
HILL, FRANCES E, THE HAVEN, DOWN ROAD, HORNDEAN
KNIGHT, LESLIE C, THE RAMBLERS, DOWN ROAD,
KNIGHT, SHEILA E, THE RAMBLERS, DOWN ROAD,
PETERS, DAVID F, WINDY RIDGE, DOWN ROAD, HORNDEAN
GREEN, LEONARD, 2, DOWNHOUSE ROAD, CATHERINGTON
SMITH, ALAN J, 4, DOWNHOUSE ROAD, CATHERINGTON
SMITH, BEN J, 4, DOWNHOUSE ROAD, CATHERINGTON
SMITH, HEATHER, 4, DOWNHOUSE ROAD, CATHERINGTON
BOXALL, AMANDA, 6, DOWNHOUSE ROAD, CATHERINGTON
BOXALL, PETER, 6, DOWNHOUSE ROAD, CATHERINGTON
WEARN, JAMES, 8, DOWNHOUSE ROAD, CATHERINGTON
WEARN, KERI A, 8, DOWNHOUSE ROAD, CATHERINGTON
PERRY, MARIA D.D, 10, DOWNHOUSE ROAD, CATHERINGTON
SCHOFIELD, ELIZABETH A.D, 10, DOWNHOUSE ROAD,
WHITE, KEITH G, 12/14, DOWNHOUSE ROAD,
WHITE, LORRAINE A, 12/14, DOWNHOUSE ROAD,
SLIGHT, MARILYN E, 16, DOWNHOUSE ROAD,
SLIGHT, STEPHEN W, 16, DOWNHOUSE ROAD,
COLES, ANDREW L, 20, DOWNHOUSE ROAD, CATHERINGTON
COLES, JAMIE, 20, DOWNHOUSE ROAD, CATHERINGTON
COLES, VIOLET P, 20, DOWNHOUSE ROAD, CATHERINGTON
WILTON, MARY A, 22, DOWNHOUSE ROAD, CATHERINGTON
WILTON, STEPHEN A, 22, DOWNHOUSE ROAD,
SWEENEY, ANN M, 26, DOWNHOUSE ROAD, CATHERINGTON
SWEENEY, THOMAS C, 26, DOWNHOUSE ROAD,
RATCLIFFE, PETER J, 28, DOWNHOUSE ROAD,
RATCLIFFE, RITA K, 28, DOWNHOUSE ROAD, CATHERINGTON
GRAINGER, ANTHONY R, 30, DOWNHOUSE ROAD,
GRAINGER, RUTH, 30, DOWNHOUSE ROAD, CATHERINGTON
STANLEY, GEORGE M, 34, DOWNHOUSE ROAD,
STANLEY, LINDA, 34, DOWNHOUSE ROAD, CATHERINGTON
DAINES, MARGARET E, 36, DOWNHOUSE ROAD,
DAINES, PHILIP A, 36, DOWNHOUSE ROAD, CATHERINGTON
CANTRILL, MARGARET R, 38, DOWNHOUSE ROAD,
CANTRILL, PETER J, 38, DOWNHOUSE ROAD,
KIDD, BRIAN P, 40, DOWNHOUSE ROAD, CATHERINGTON
MYLES, PATRICK N.J, 40, DOWNHOUSE ROAD,
YOUNG, AMY A.W, 42, DOWNHOUSE ROAD, CATHERINGTON
THORNTON, JOANNE, 44, DOWNHOUSE ROAD,
THORNTON, SCOTT, 44, DOWNHOUSE ROAD,
THORNTON, STEPHEN, 44, DOWNHOUSE ROAD,
THORNTON, VICKY, 44, DOWNHOUSE ROAD,
NICHOLAS, MAUREEN G, 50, DOWNHOUSE ROAD,
NICHOLAS, RICHARD A, 50, DOWNHOUSE ROAD,
LANGWORTHY, HARRY V, 52, DOWNHOUSE ROAD,
LANGWORTHY, PATRICIA E, 52, DOWNHOUSE ROAD,
KINGSFORD, CARYL A, 54, DOWNHOUSE ROAD,
KINGSFORD, DAMIAN J.C, 54, DOWNHOUSE ROAD,
KINGSFORD, DEREK C, 54, DOWNHOUSE ROAD,
WINTER, CHRISTOPHER C, 56, DOWNHOUSE ROAD,
WINTER, JEAN L, 56, DOWNHOUSE ROAD, CATHERINGTON
STACE, EILEEN M, 58, DOWNHOUSE ROAD, CATHERINGTON
CANN, GRAHAM C, 60, DOWNHOUSE ROAD, CATHERINGTON
CANN, PATRICIA, 60, DOWNHOUSE ROAD, CATHERINGTON
INKPEN, ALAN M, 62, DOWNHOUSE ROAD, CATHERINGTON
INKPEN, JENNIFER A, 62, DOWNHOUSE ROAD,
INKPEN, MICHAEL J, 62, DOWNHOUSE ROAD,
JONES, SIDNEY B, 62, DOWNHOUSE ROAD, CATHERINGTON
MEW, ERNEST B, 64, DOWNHOUSE ROAD, CATHERINGTON
MEW, MAUREEN B, 64, DOWNHOUSE ROAD, CATHERINGTON
BONNER, DEREK, 68, DOWNHOUSE ROAD, CATHERINGTON
BONNER, GLADYS I, 68, DOWNHOUSE ROAD, CATHERINGTON
BONNER, JENNIFER, 68, DOWNHOUSE ROAD,
BONNER, NICOLE M, 68, DOWNHOUSE ROAD,
PERRY, OWEN R, 70, DOWNHOUSE ROAD, CATHERINGTON
PERRY, RITA J, 70, DOWNHOUSE ROAD, CATHERINGTON
PERRY, SAMANTHA D, 70, DOWNHOUSE ROAD,
BRIDGEMAN, EDWARD, 72, DOWNHOUSE ROAD,
BRIDGEMAN, IRIS E, 72, DOWNHOUSE ROAD,
NORMAN, DAVE J, 74, DOWNHOUSE ROAD, CATHERINGTON
NORMAN, MARK J, 74, DOWNHOUSE ROAD, CATHERINGTON
NORMAN, PATRICIA M, 74, DOWNHOUSE ROAD,
MASON, JAMES, 76, DOWNHOUSE ROAD, CATHERINGTON
READ, ALAN E.T, 78, DOWNHOUSE ROAD, CATHERINGTON
READ, JOHNATHON L, 78, DOWNHOUSE ROAD,
READ, MARY P, 78, DOWNHOUSE ROAD, CATHERINGTON
READ, ROBERT J, 78, DOWNHOUSE ROAD, CATHERINGTON
WHITEHEAD, MARK C, 80, DOWNHOUSE ROAD,
WHITEHEAD, SANDRA Y, 80, DOWNHOUSE ROAD,
BUTLER, GLORIA, 82, DOWNHOUSE ROAD, CATHERINGTON
BUTLER, REGINALD D, 82, DOWNHOUSE ROAD,
WALSH, BRIAN A, 84, DOWNHOUSE ROAD, CATHERINGTON
WALSH, CAROLINE I, 84, DOWNHOUSE ROAD,
GRAY, JANETTE E, 86, DOWNHOUSE ROAD, CATHERINGTON
GRAY, PAUL R, 86, DOWNHOUSE ROAD, CATHERINGTON
GRAY, KATHLEEN D, 88, DOWNHOUSE ROAD,
JOHNSON, ANGELA C.L, 90, DOWNHOUSE ROAD,
JOHNSON, BRIAN D, 90, DOWNHOUSE ROAD, CATHERINGTON
JOHNSON, LOUISE A, 90, DOWNHOUSE ROAD,
HILLS, HEATHER M, 92, DOWNHOUSE ROAD,
HILLS, SIMON P, 92, DOWNHOUSE ROAD, CATHERINGTON
PARSONS, CYRIL O, 94, DOWNHOUSE ROAD, CATHERINGTON
DALEY, JONATHAN P, 96, DOWNHOUSE ROAD,
DALEY, SARAH, 96, DOWNHOUSE ROAD, CATHERINGTON
BISHOPP, RICHARD J, 98, DOWNHOUSE ROAD,
LE GOUBIN, JULIEN C, 98, DOWNHOUSE ROAD,
LE GOUBIN, MARY E, 98, DOWNHOUSE ROAD,
GAME, COLIN J, 100, DOWNHOUSE ROAD, CATHERINGTON
GAME, JENNIFER, 100, DOWNHOUSE ROAD, CATHERINGTON
GORDON, ANDREW, 102, DOWNHOUSE ROAD,
WHITTAKER, JOYCE A, 120, DOWNHOUSE ROAD,
WHITTAKER, MICHAEL J, 120, DOWNHOUSE ROAD,
BROWNE, FREDA V, 122, DOWNHOUSE ROAD, CATHERINGTON
BROWNE, MALCOLM R, 122, DOWNHOUSE ROAD,
AIKEN, TERENCE C, 124, DOWNHOUSE ROAD,
AIKEN, VALERIE I, 124, DOWNHOUSE ROAD, CATHERINGTON
WOODS, LINDA, 128, DOWNHOUSE ROAD, CATHERINGTON
WOODS, LISA, 128, DOWNHOUSE ROAD, CATHERINGTON
WOODS, MICHAEL, 128, DOWNHOUSE ROAD,
WOODS, SARAH, 128, DOWNHOUSE ROAD, CATHERINGTON
HADFIELD, LILIAN M, 130, DOWNHOUSE ROAD,
HADFIELD, PETER, 130, DOWNHOUSE ROAD, CATHERINGTON
PRIDHAM, DAVID G, 132, DOWNHOUSE ROAD,
PRIDHAM, LINDA O, 132, DOWNHOUSE ROAD,
PIERCE, CAROL A, 134, DOWNHOUSE ROAD, CATHERINGTON
AYLING, BRENDA J, 136, DOWNHOUSE ROAD, CATHERINGTON
AYLING, TOBY, 136, DOWNHOUSE ROAD, CATHERINGTON
AYLING, TONY J, 136, DOWNHOUSE ROAD, CATHERINGTON
BONIFACE, JONATHAN, 1, DRAYCOTE ROAD, HORNDEAN
GOODE, JANE A, 1, DRAYCOTE ROAD, HORNDEAN
TURNER, ANTHONY K, 3, DRAYCOTE ROAD, HORNDEAN
TURNER, RITA M, 3, DRAYCOTE ROAD, HORNDEAN
TURNER, STEWART L, 3, DRAYCOTE ROAD, HORNDEAN
TURNER, TRACEY J, 3, DRAYCOTE ROAD, HORNDEAN
ROSE, JOHN W, 5, DRAYCOTE ROAD, HORNDEAN
ROSE, JOSEPHINE, 5, DRAYCOTE ROAD, HORNDEAN
DODDS, CHRISTINE M, 7, DRAYCOTE ROAD, HORNDEAN
DODDS, PAUL A, 7, DRAYCOTE ROAD, HORNDEAN
PAYNE, FREDA E, 9, DRAYCOTE ROAD, HORNDEAN
SPREADBURY, DAPHNE L, 11, DRAYCOTE ROAD, HORNDEAN
SPREADBURY, STUART I, 11, DRAYCOTE ROAD, HORNDEAN
LANDER, CLAIRE A, 13, DRAYCOTE ROAD, HORNDEAN
EDIN, HUSSEYIN, 15, DRAYCOTE ROAD, HORNDEAN
EDIN, TULAY, 15, DRAYCOTE ROAD, HORNDEAN
TAIT, CHRISTOPHER E, 2, DRAYCOTE ROAD, HORNDEAN
TAIT, EDWARD F, 2, DRAYCOTE ROAD, HORNDEAN
TAIT, MARION, 2, DRAYCOTE ROAD, HORNDEAN
QUINEY, DAPHNE E, 4, DRAYCOTE ROAD, HORNDEAN
COUZENS, IAN G, 6, DRAYCOTE ROAD, HORNDEAN
COUZENS, VIRGINIA M, 6, DRAYCOTE ROAD, HORNDEAN
GALYER, FREDERICK J, 8, DRAYCOTE ROAD, HORNDEAN
ROYCE, SYLVIA R, 10, DRAYCOTE ROAD, HORNDEAN
NICOLL, ALISON J, 12, DRAYCOTE ROAD, HORNDEAN
NICOLL, PAUL, 12, DRAYCOTE ROAD, HORNDEAN
PICKLES, ANDREW, 14, DRAYCOTE ROAD, HORNDEAN
PICKLES, PHYLLIS L, 14, DRAYCOTE ROAD, HORNDEAN
PICKLES, RICHARD H, 14, DRAYCOTE ROAD, HORNDEAN
COLE, ELSIE M, 16, DRAYCOTE ROAD, HORNDEAN
CHURCH, CLARE L, 18, DRAYCOTE ROAD, HORNDEAN
WILMAN, JONATHAN F, 20, DRAYCOTE ROAD, HORNDEAN
WILMAN, LESLEY J, 20, DRAYCOTE ROAD, HORNDEAN
HILLMAN, DEBRA J, 22, DRAYCOTE ROAD, HORNDEAN
HILLMAN, NICHOLAS A.T, 22, DRAYCOTE ROAD, HORNDEAN
VISSER, MARK J, 24, DRAYCOTE ROAD, HORNDEAN
VISSER, SANDRA M, 24, DRAYCOTE ROAD, HORNDEAN
NEWSOME, LAURENCE, 26, DRAYCOTE ROAD, HORNDEAN
NEWSOME, TERESA H, 26, DRAYCOTE ROAD, HORNDEAN
MCINTOSH, ANDREW R, 28, DRAYCOTE ROAD, HORNDEAN
MCINTOSH, COLLIN, 28, DRAYCOTE ROAD, HORNDEAN
MCINTOSH, JUDITH A, 28, DRAYCOTE ROAD, HORNDEAN
SODHA, ASHOK A, 30, DRAYCOTE ROAD, HORNDEAN
SODHA, NILA, 30, DRAYCOTE ROAD, HORNDEAN
PRATT, ANDREW C, 32, DRAYCOTE ROAD, HORNDEAN
PRATT, SUSAN F, 32, DRAYCOTE ROAD, HORNDEAN
BROCKWAY, JOAN M, 1, DRIFT ROAD, HORNDEAN
MONNERY, BRENDA M, 1A, DRIFT ROAD, HORNDEAN
MONNERY, GILBERT D, 1A, DRIFT ROAD, HORNDEAN
MONNERY, RICHARD H, 1A, DRIFT ROAD, HORNDEAN
BROCKWAY, ALICE P, 3, DRIFT ROAD, HORNDEAN
DEVINE, NATASHA T, 7, DRIFT ROAD, HORNDEAN
ROGERS, DAVID, 7, DRIFT ROAD, HORNDEAN
ROGERS, JANICE P, 7, DRIFT ROAD, HORNDEAN
ROGERS, TIMOTHY J, 7, DRIFT ROAD, HORNDEAN
PORTER, JOHN R, 11, DRIFT ROAD, HORNDEAN
PORTER, RITA N, 11, DRIFT ROAD, HORNDEAN
HALE, MARY W, 15, DRIFT ROAD, HORNDEAN
WHITEHOUSE, JAMES, 17, DRIFT ROAD, HORNDEAN
WHITEHOUSE, PAMELA, 17, DRIFT ROAD, HORNDEAN
WELLS, ELLA D, 31, DRIFT ROAD, HORNDEAN
THOMAS, ROY B, 33, DRIFT ROAD, HORNDEAN
EVANS, ELIZABETH A, 35, DRIFT ROAD, HORNDEAN

EVANS, TERENCE P, 35, DRIFT ROAD, HORNDEAN
KELLY, ROBERT J, 37, DRIFT ROAD, HORNDEAN
KELLY, RUTH H, 37, DRIFT ROAD, HORNDEAN
DUNFORD, IAN, 51, DRIFT ROAD, HORNDEAN
DUNFORD, TERESA J, 51, DRIFT ROAD, HORNDEAN
FUDGE, BRIAN W, 99, DRIFT ROAD, HORNDEAN
FUDGE, PHYLLIS G, 99, DRIFT ROAD, HORNDEAN
CARPENTER, JUNE M, 101, DRIFT ROAD, HORNDEAN
CARPENTER, RONALD F, 101, DRIFT ROAD, HORNDEAN
HAIMES, FLORENCE B, 103, DRIFT ROAD, HORNDEAN
HAIMES, RAYMOND C, 103, DRIFT ROAD, HORNDEAN
PASSELLS, MARY B, 105, DRIFT ROAD, HORNDEAN
HEAD, KAREN D, 107, DRIFT ROAD, HORNDEAN
KNIGHT, MATTHEW J, 107, DRIFT ROAD, HORNDEAN
CARVER, VERA M, 109, DRIFT ROAD, HORNDEAN
MOORE, DIANA J, 109, DRIFT ROAD, HORNDEAN
MOORE, JAMES T, 109, DRIFT ROAD, HORNDEAN
MOORE, JASON, 109, DRIFT ROAD, HORNDEAN
MOORE, STEPHEN, 109, DRIFT ROAD, HORNDEAN
MOORE, TERENCE, 109, DRIFT ROAD, HORNDEAN
PENTENEY, JEAN, 111, DRIFT ROAD, HORNDEAN
PENTENEY, PETER R, 111, DRIFT ROAD, HORNDEAN
BLAND, CAROLINE A, 113, DRIFT ROAD, HORNDEAN
BLAND, LIAM F, 113, DRIFT ROAD, HORNDEAN
BLAND, MICHAEL E, 113, DRIFT ROAD, HORNDEAN
TAYLOR, JULIE A, 115, DRIFT ROAD, HORNDEAN
THORNTON, CLIVE N, 115, DRIFT ROAD, HORNDEAN
GILES, DEREK N, 117, DRIFT ROAD, HORNDEAN
GILES, MARGARET A, 117, DRIFT ROAD, HORNDEAN
GILES, NORMAN R, 117A, DRIFT ROAD, HORNDEAN
GILES, VIOLET N.D, 117A, DRIFT ROAD, HORNDEAN
LIPSCOMBE, BRYAN F, 119, DRIFT ROAD, HORNDEAN
COUPLAND, LEE D, 121, DRIFT ROAD, HORNDEAN
COUPLAND, NIGEL F, 121, DRIFT ROAD, HORNDEAN
COUPLAND, PAULINE V, 121, DRIFT ROAD, HORNDEAN
DENNETT, EDMUND, 123, DRIFT ROAD, HORNDEAN
DENNETT, HELENA J, 123, DRIFT ROAD, HORNDEAN
HEDGES, JENNIFER, 125, DRIFT ROAD, HORNDEAN
HEDGES, MICHAEL R, 125, DRIFT ROAD, HORNDEAN
MATTHEWS, BETTY A, 127, DRIFT ROAD, HORNDEAN
GOTHARD, HELEN C, 129, DRIFT ROAD, HORNDEAN
GOTHARD, RALPH, 129, DRIFT ROAD, HORNDEAN
BURNETT, CLIFFORD M, 131, DRIFT ROAD, HORNDEAN
BURNETT, ROMA C, 131, DRIFT ROAD, HORNDEAN
ROGERS, MICHELLE, 133, DRIFT ROAD, HORNDEAN
SPIERS, HAZEL P, 133, DRIFT ROAD, HORNDEAN
HILLMAN, MYRTLE A, 135, DRIFT ROAD, HORNDEAN
HILLMAN, TREVOR G, 135, DRIFT ROAD, HORNDEAN
HART, PAMELA J, 139, DRIFT ROAD, HORNDEAN
HART, WILLIAM L, 139, DRIFT ROAD, HORNDEAN
JEFFRIES, VALERIE D, 141, DRIFT ROAD, HORNDEAN
PAYNE, HEATHER J, 141A, DRIFT ROAD, HORNDEAN
PAYNE, ROGER T, 141A, DRIFT ROAD, HORNDEAN
BLYTHE, CAROLE, 143, DRIFT ROAD, HORNDEAN
MARTIN, MALCOLM L, 143, DRIFT ROAD, HORNDEAN
DONALD, BRIAN, 145, DRIFT ROAD, HORNDEAN
PULSFORD, DEBORAH A, 145, DRIFT ROAD, HORNDEAN
LAGUE, PETER J, 1, ENNERDALE CLOSE, HORNDEAN
LAGUE, SANDRA, 1, ENNERDALE CLOSE, HORNDEAN
ATKINSON, SHANE R, 2, ENNERDALE CLOSE, HORNDEAN
ATKINSON, SUSAN D, 2, ENNERDALE CLOSE, HORNDEAN
CHERRINGTON, KEITH D, 3, ENNERDALE CLOSE, HORNDEAN
CHERRINGTON, SALLY F, 3, ENNERDALE CLOSE, HORNDEAN
INSKIP, MATTHEW F, 4, ENNERDALE CLOSE, HORNDEAN
ROBERTS, JANE, 4, ENNERDALE CLOSE, HORNDEAN
HENDERSON, THOMAS M.P, 5, ENNERDALE CLOSE,
HENDERSON, VIRGINIA M, 5, ENNERDALE CLOSE,
WRIGHT, ELIZABETH M, 6, ENNERDALE CLOSE, HORNDEAN
GORDON, JAMES A, 7, ENNERDALE CLOSE, HORNDEAN
GORDON, ROBERT J, 7, ENNERDALE CLOSE, HORNDEAN
GYNGELL, MARGARET M, 8, ENNERDALE CLOSE, HORNDEAN
KENYON, ALAN J, 9, ENNERDALE CLOSE, HORNDEAN
KENYON, KAREN E, 9, ENNERDALE CLOSE, HORNDEAN
NORMAN, ROGER, 10, ENNERDALE CLOSE, HORNDEAN
NORMAN, VICKI J, 10, ENNERDALE CLOSE, HORNDEAN
HADOW, CHRISTOPHER V, 11, ENNERDALE CLOSE,
HADOW, STELLA A, 11, ENNERDALE CLOSE, HORNDEAN
STODDART, HEATHER L, 12, ENNERDALE CLOSE, HORNDEAN
STODDART, LEE H, 12, ENNERDALE CLOSE, HORNDEAN
STODDART, SHEILA, 12, ENNERDALE CLOSE, HORNDEAN
DYKE, NICHOLAS D, 14, ENNERDALE CLOSE, HORNDEAN
WOODALL, TRACY A, 14, ENNERDALE CLOSE, HORNDEAN
DANN, KEVIN J, 15, ENNERDALE CLOSE, HORNDEAN
UNDERHAY, PAUL M, 15, ENNERDALE CLOSE, HORNDEAN
WATT, SALLY C, 15, ENNERDALE CLOSE, HORNDEAN
WISEMAN, STEPHEN R, 15, ENNERDALE CLOSE, HORNDEAN
JUBIN, ROGER, 16, ENNERDALE CLOSE, HORNDEAN
BACKSHALL, JULIE E, 17, ENNERDALE CLOSE, HORNDEAN
BACKSHALL, PAUL S, 17, ENNERDALE CLOSE, HORNDEAN
DALY, DENISE M, 18, ENNERDALE CLOSE, HORNDEAN
DALY, GERALD C, 18, ENNERDALE CLOSE, HORNDEAN
GRADDON, CHRISTINE A, 19, ENNERDALE CLOSE,
GRADDON, DAVID J, 19, ENNERDALE CLOSE, HORNDEAN
HEWINSON, IAN M, 20, ENNERDALE CLOSE, HORNDEAN
HEWINSON, SANDRA E, 20, ENNERDALE CLOSE, HORNDEAN
PRIME, DEBORAH A, 21, ENNERDALE CLOSE, HORNDEAN
PRIME, IAN C, 21, ENNERDALE CLOSE, HORNDEAN
MCGREEVY, HELEN, 22, ENNERDALE CLOSE, HORNDEAN
MCGREEVY, MARK, 22, ENNERDALE CLOSE, HORNDEAN
HUNT, CAROL, 23, ENNERDALE CLOSE, HORNDEAN
HUNT, CHLOE D, 23, ENNERDALE CLOSE, HORNDEAN
VEITCH, RICHARD J, 23, ENNERDALE CLOSE, HORNDEAN
STEVENS, ALISON M, 24, ENNERDALE CLOSE, HORNDEAN
STEVENS, MICHAEL L, 24, ENNERDALE CLOSE, HORNDEAN
PIKE, DOUGLAS G, 25, ENNERDALE CLOSE, HORNDEAN
PIKE, MARGARET I, 25, ENNERDALE CLOSE, HORNDEAN
PIKE, NICHOLAS G, 25, ENNERDALE CLOSE, HORNDEAN
JACOBS, CAROLINE, 1, ESKDALE CLOSE, HORNDEAN
JACOBS, PETER J, 1, ESKDALE CLOSE, HORNDEAN
JACOBS, SAMANTHA R, 1, ESKDALE CLOSE, HORNDEAN
BREMNER, ANDREW S, 2, ESKDALE CLOSE, HORNDEAN
BREMNER, ANNE, 2, ESKDALE CLOSE, HORNDEAN
MELLOR, KAREN E, 3, ESKDALE CLOSE, HORNDEAN
MELLOR, LEIGH, 3, ESKDALE CLOSE, HORNDEAN
HARPIN, CHRISTINE A, 4, ESKDALE CLOSE, HORNDEAN
HARPIN, LEONARD, 4, ESKDALE CLOSE, HORNDEAN
HARPIN, MANDY L, 4, ESKDALE CLOSE, HORNDEAN
HARPIN, SAMANTHA A, 4, ESKDALE CLOSE, HORNDEAN
LUCAS, CHERYL Y, 4, ESKDALE CLOSE, HORNDEAN
RUDDELL, JOCELYN, 5, ESKDALE CLOSE, HORNDEAN
RUDDELL, NATHAN J.D, 5, ESKDALE CLOSE, HORNDEAN
RUDDELL, THOMAS C, 5, ESKDALE CLOSE, HORNDEAN
IRELAND, BARBARA M, 6, ESKDALE CLOSE, HORNDEAN
IRELAND, MICHAEL J, 6, ESKDALE CLOSE, HORNDEAN
LANGLEY, KAY S, 7, ESKDALE CLOSE, HORNDEAN
LANGLEY, WILLIAM E, 7, ESKDALE CLOSE, HORNDEAN
STACEY, MABEL A, 8, ESKDALE CLOSE, HORNDEAN
STACEY, ROBIN E, 8, ESKDALE CLOSE, HORNDEAN
HARVEY, MICHAEL R, 9, ESKDALE CLOSE, HORNDEAN
HARVEY, SHARON M, 9, ESKDALE CLOSE, HORNDEAN
HARVEY, STUART J, 9, ESKDALE CLOSE, HORNDEAN
BURNETT, CAMPBELL, 10, ESKDALE CLOSE, HORNDEAN
LE POIDEVIN, GLENYS A, 11, ESKDALE CLOSE, HORNDEAN
LE POIDEVIN, JOHN A, 11, ESKDALE CLOSE, HORNDEAN
MOBBS, ALISON J, 12, ESKDALE CLOSE, HORNDEAN
MOBBS, ANTHONY J, 12, ESKDALE CLOSE, HORNDEAN
MILLER, CARLY J, 13, ESKDALE CLOSE, HORNDEAN
SAVAGE-BROOKES, LEE, 13, ESKDALE CLOSE, HORNDEAN
BYFIELD, KEVIN C, 14, ESKDALE CLOSE, HORNDEAN
BYFIELD, SARAH J, 14, ESKDALE CLOSE, HORNDEAN
BAILEY, ANN M, 15, ESKDALE CLOSE, HORNDEAN
BAILEY, NICHOLAS E.J, 15, ESKDALE CLOSE, HORNDEAN
REEVE, ALAN H, 16, ESKDALE CLOSE, HORNDEAN
REEVE, KAREN J, 16, ESKDALE CLOSE, HORNDEAN
SHIPP, BRIAN G, 17, ESKDALE CLOSE, HORNDEAN
SHIPP, GILLIAN T, 17, ESKDALE CLOSE, HORNDEAN
BONE, DAVID J, 18, ESKDALE CLOSE, HORNDEAN
ROWLES, KATHRYN E, 18, ESKDALE CLOSE, HORNDEAN
FIELD-FIDLER, AMANDA C.F, 19, ESKDALE CLOSE, HORNDEAN
FIELD-FIDLER, JEAN W.F, 19, ESKDALE CLOSE, HORNDEAN
BIRD-NEWELL, DAVID M, 20, ESKDALE CLOSE, HORNDEAN
BIRD-NEWELL, DENISE S, 20, ESKDALE CLOSE, HORNDEAN
SILLS, COLIN J, 21, ESKDALE CLOSE, HORNDEAN
SILLS, LYNDA K, 21, ESKDALE CLOSE, HORNDEAN
SELBY, JANE C, 22, ESKDALE CLOSE, HORNDEAN
SELBY, PETER F, 22, ESKDALE CLOSE, HORNDEAN
FOSTER, JACQUELINE G, 23, ESKDALE CLOSE, HORNDEAN
FOSTER, KEVIN G, 23, ESKDALE CLOSE, HORNDEAN
ARMOUR, STUART P, 24, ESKDALE CLOSE, HORNDEAN
ARMOUR, SUSAN E, 24, ESKDALE CLOSE, HORNDEAN
ARMOUR, WILLIAM, 24, ESKDALE CLOSE, HORNDEAN
EAVES, JOANNA E, 25, ESKDALE CLOSE, HORNDEAN
EAVES, PAULINE E, 25, ESKDALE CLOSE, HORNDEAN
EAVES, PHILIP H, 25, ESKDALE CLOSE, HORNDEAN
FOX, DAVID L, 26, ESKDALE CLOSE, HORNDEAN
FOX, NITA C, 26, ESKDALE CLOSE, HORNDEAN
FOX, PAUL D, 26, ESKDALE CLOSE, HORNDEAN
MARSHMAN, GEOFFREY P, 28, ESKDALE CLOSE, HORNDEAN
MARSHMAN, SONIA, 28, ESKDALE CLOSE, HORNDEAN
BURKE, IAN, 29, ESKDALE CLOSE, HORNDEAN
BURKE, JACQUELINE, 29, ESKDALE CLOSE, HORNDEAN
WARD, KEVEN R, 30, ESKDALE CLOSE, HORNDEAN
WARD, VALERIE E, 30, ESKDALE CLOSE, HORNDEAN
BELL, DAPHNE J, 31, ESKDALE CLOSE, HORNDEAN
BELL, KENNETH A, 31, ESKDALE CLOSE, HORNDEAN
KING, MICHAEL J, 32, ESKDALE CLOSE, HORNDEAN
KING, PAMELA I, 32, ESKDALE CLOSE, HORNDEAN
BROWN, DEREK, 33, ESKDALE CLOSE, HORNDEAN
BROWN, JANET A, 33, ESKDALE CLOSE, HORNDEAN
BROWN, MICHELLE, 33, ESKDALE CLOSE, HORNDEAN
CAWTHRON, PAULETTE, 35, ESKDALE CLOSE, HORNDEAN
CAWTHRON, VINCENT, 35, ESKDALE CLOSE, HORNDEAN
SHEPPARD, ANNE, 36, ESKDALE CLOSE, HORNDEAN
SHEPPARD, PATRICK M, 36, ESKDALE CLOSE, HORNDEAN
DENT, MARION E, 37, ESKDALE CLOSE, HORNDEAN
DENT, VICTOR S, 37, ESKDALE CLOSE, HORNDEAN
DIXON, CHRISTINE, 38, ESKDALE CLOSE, HORNDEAN
DIXON, JOHN A, 38, ESKDALE CLOSE, HORNDEAN
DIXON, SAMANTHA J, 38, ESKDALE CLOSE, HORNDEAN
HEATH, PATRICIA A, 1, FIRST AVENUE, HORNDEAN
HAYWARD, JESSIE, 3, FIRST AVENUE, HORNDEAN
WEAVING, EVELYN M, 5, FIRST AVENUE, HORNDEAN
GRANT, WINIFRED E, 7, FIRST AVENUE, HORNDEAN
STEVENS, PERCY J, 9, FIRST AVENUE, HORNDEAN
HELLYER, ANGELINA M, 11, FIRST AVENUE, HORNDEAN
HELLYER, CHARLES R, 11, FIRST AVENUE, HORNDEAN
MESSAGE, RUBY M, 13, FIRST AVENUE, HORNDEAN
BARWELL, HELEN, 15, FIRST AVENUE, HORNDEAN
BARWELL, IAN, 15, FIRST AVENUE, HORNDEAN
MARSH, MARY L, 17, FIRST AVENUE, HORNDEAN
STACEY, PAMELA J, 19, FIRST AVENUE, HORNDEAN
BUISSON, MARK A, 21, FIRST AVENUE, HORNDEAN
COTTINGHAM, ROSEMARY A, 21, FIRST AVENUE, HORNDEAN
ALLAN, LORRAINE G, 23, FIRST AVENUE, HORNDEAN
STYLES, NICHOLAS J, 23, FIRST AVENUE, HORNDEAN
SHAW, MARGARET, 25, FIRST AVENUE, HORNDEAN
CATES, STEPHEN, 27, FIRST AVENUE, HORNDEAN
STACEY, PAULA L, 29, FIRST AVENUE, HORNDEAN
HAYWARD, PERCY, 31, FIRST AVENUE, HORNDEAN
SHARRETT, DAVID M, 33, FIRST AVENUE, HORNDEAN
CHAMBERLAIN, ROBERT J, 37, FIRST AVENUE, HORNDEAN
MURRANT, ROSEMARY A, 39, FIRST AVENUE, HORNDEAN
CATHRAE, MALCOLM, 41, FIRST AVENUE, HORNDEAN
MCCALL, DORIS J, 41, FIRST AVENUE, HORNDEAN
STANLEY, SHELLEY-MARIE, 43, FIRST AVENUE, HORNDEAN
GINNS, ANN-MARIE, 45, FIRST AVENUE, HORNDEAN
COTTINGHAM, CAROLINE, 47, FIRST AVENUE, HORNDEAN
GIDDINGS, DAPHNE J, 2, FIRST AVENUE, HORNDEAN
GIDDINGS, FREDERICK C, 2, FIRST AVENUE, HORNDEAN
CULLUM, SYDNEY M, 4, FIRST AVENUE, HORNDEAN
BEECH, ISIAH R, 6, FIRST AVENUE, HORNDEAN
BEECH, KATHLEEN E, 6, FIRST AVENUE, HORNDEAN
BOSWELL, NANCY L, 8, FIRST AVENUE, HORNDEAN
HALL, ADA H, 10, FIRST AVENUE, HORNDEAN
TURNER, KAREN V, 12, FIRST AVENUE, HORNDEAN
TURNER, LAURENCE J, 12, FIRST AVENUE, HORNDEAN
HARRIS, MARIAN, 14, FIRST AVENUE, HORNDEAN
HARRIS, STEPHEN M, 14, FIRST AVENUE, HORNDEAN
FINN, ELIZABETH S, 16, FIRST AVENUE, HORNDEAN
FINN, GLEN T, 16, FIRST AVENUE, HORNDEAN
PARKER, ANNE E, 18, FIRST AVENUE, HORNDEAN
HURD, FREDERICK J, 20, FIRST AVENUE, HORNDEAN
HURD, KATHLEEN, 20, FIRST AVENUE, HORNDEAN
WORDEN, KENNETH R, FLAT 1, 22, FIRST AVENUE,
GARDNER, KIM, FLAT 2, 22, FIRST AVENUE, HORNDEAN
MCPHILLIPS, GARY R, FLAT 2, 22, FIRST AVENUE, HORNDEAN
ROBERTS, MARCUS P, FLAT 3, 22, FIRST AVENUE, HORNDEAN
MULLIS, MELVIN D, FLAT 4, 22, FIRST AVENUE, HORNDEAN
JAY, GARY, FLAT 5, 22, FIRST AVENUE, HORNDEAN
KENNETT, SARAH E, FLAT 5, 22, FIRST AVENUE, HORNDEAN
CARRUTHERS, JOHN S, FLAT 6, 22, FIRST AVENUE,
CARRUTHERS, SHARON L, FLAT 6, 22, FIRST AVENUE,
HINTZE, MARY B, 24, FIRST AVENUE, HORNDEAN
HINTZE, STEPHEN J, 24, FIRST AVENUE, HORNDEAN
DEAKIN, KAREN J.R, 26, FIRST AVENUE, HORNDEAN
CAMPBELL SMITH, FLORA M, 28, FIRST AVENUE, HORNDEAN
CAMPBELL-SMITH, KAREN, 28, FIRST AVENUE, HORNDEAN
GARD, MAUREEN D, 30, FIRST AVENUE, HORNDEAN
GARD, NEVILLE I, 30, FIRST AVENUE, HORNDEAN
WELCH, ROBERT W, 32, FIRST AVENUE, HORNDEAN
WELCH, SHIRLEY C, 32, FIRST AVENUE, HORNDEAN
GAUNT, GEOFFREY S, 34, FIRST AVENUE, HORNDEAN
GAUNT, SUSANNE M, 34, FIRST AVENUE, HORNDEAN
LUFF, ANTHONY A, 36, FIRST AVENUE, HORNDEAN
LUFF, JENNIFER S, 36, FIRST AVENUE, HORNDEAN
MITCHELL, MICHELLE A, 40, FIRST AVENUE, HORNDEAN
COSTELLO, MARY E, 42, FIRST AVENUE, HORNDEAN
COSTELLO, THOMAS, 42, FIRST AVENUE, HORNDEAN
ADLAM, DORIS E, 44, FIRST AVENUE, HORNDEAN
LANCASTER, LEWIS C, 46, FIRST AVENUE, HORNDEAN
LANCASTER, SUSAN A, 46, FIRST AVENUE, HORNDEAN
NORRIS, EDWARD G, 48, FIRST AVENUE, HORNDEAN
OATES, ELSIE J, 50, FIRST AVENUE, HORNDEAN
DICKINSON, NIGEL R, 52, FIRST AVENUE, HORNDEAN
ROSS, TRACY L, 52, FIRST AVENUE, HORNDEAN
MURRANT, LISA, 54, FIRST AVENUE, HORNDEAN
MILLS, MEDINA, 56, FIRST AVENUE, HORNDEAN
EDNEY, PETER J, 58, FIRST AVENUE, HORNDEAN
EDNEY, SARAH D, 58, FIRST AVENUE, HORNDEAN
NELSON-TOMSEN, JOHN A, 65, FIVE HEADS ROAD,
NELSON-TOMSEN, JULIA K, 65, FIVE HEADS ROAD,
BERRY, ERICH A, 74, FIVE HEADS ROAD, HORNDEAN
BERRY, GLADYS D, 74, FIVE HEADS ROAD, HORNDEAN
BERRY, HAROLD G, 74, FIVE HEADS ROAD, HORNDEAN
GREVES, PAUL A, 76, FIVE HEADS ROAD, HORNDEAN
GREVES, PAULINE J, 76, FIVE HEADS ROAD, HORNDEAN
GARLICK, LESLIE A, 78, FIVE HEADS ROAD, HORNDEAN
GARLICK, MABEL J, 78, FIVE HEADS ROAD, HORNDEAN
LENNOX, ELIZABETH L, 79, FIVE HEADS ROAD, HORNDEAN
LENNOX, IAN G, 79, FIVE HEADS ROAD, HORNDEAN
ALLINGHAM, REBECCA B, 80, FIVE HEADS ROAD, HORNDEAN
BAKER, NIGEL J.C, 81, FIVE HEADS ROAD, HORNDEAN
BAKER, URSULA A, 81, FIVE HEADS ROAD, HORNDEAN
FLETCHER, CHERYL D, 82, FIVE HEADS ROAD, HORNDEAN
FLETCHER, GILES W, 82, FIVE HEADS ROAD, HORNDEAN
FLETCHER, WILLIAM E, 82, FIVE HEADS ROAD, HORNDEAN
SCARCE, ALISON, 82, FIVE HEADS ROAD, HORNDEAN
EDNEY, ANGELA J, 83, FIVE HEADS ROAD, HORNDEAN
EDNEY, BARRY, 83, FIVE HEADS ROAD, HORNDEAN
EDNEY, CHRISTOPHER J, 83, FIVE HEADS ROAD, HORNDEAN
MOULD, PAULINE E, 84, FIVE HEADS ROAD, HORNDEAN
MOULD, WILLIAM A, 84, FIVE HEADS ROAD, HORNDEAN
MUMBY, RONALD M, 86, FIVE HEADS ROAD, HORNDEAN
MILLER, EILEEN M, 90, FIVE HEADS ROAD, HORNDEAN
PRYOR, DAVID C, 94, FIVE HEADS ROAD, HORNDEAN
PRYOR, DEBRA E, 94, FIVE HEADS ROAD, HORNDEAN
EASTON, BARRY E, FLAT 1, CATHERINGTON HOUSE, 182, FIVE HEADS ROAD, HORNDEAN
EASTON, JACQUELINE L, FLAT 1, CATHERINGTON HOUSE, 182, FIVE HEADS ROAD, HORNDEAN
ROBINSON, CHARLES D, FLAT 2, CATHERINGTON HOUSE, 182, FIVE HEADS ROAD, HORNDEAN
ROBINSON, FIONA E, FLAT 2, CATHERINGTON HOUSE, 182, FIVE HEADS ROAD, HORNDEAN
BAKER, ALISON, 1, FRANCIS ROAD, HORNDEAN
BAKER, GAVIN L, 1, FRANCIS ROAD, HORNDEAN
LOWE, JOY H.J, 2, FRANCIS ROAD, HORNDEAN
EVERETT, GEOFFREY A, 3, FRANCIS ROAD, HORNDEAN
EVERETT, JOAN M, 3, FRANCIS ROAD, HORNDEAN

Electoral Roll

PRIGG, DERRICK V, 4, FRANCIS ROAD, HORNDEAN
TRODD, MARLANE D, 4, FRANCIS ROAD, HORNDEAN
HAWKINS, EDMUND G, 5, FRANCIS ROAD, HORNDEAN
HAWKINS, YVONNE M, 5, FRANCIS ROAD, HORNDEAN
STEDMAN, GLADYS E, 6, FRANCIS ROAD, HORNDEAN
STEDMAN, LESLIE A, 6, FRANCIS ROAD, HORNDEAN
STEDMAN, STANLEY E, 6, FRANCIS ROAD, HORNDEAN
AUSTIN, BRETT L, 7, FRANCIS ROAD, HORNDEAN
AUSTIN, SUSAN J, 7, FRANCIS ROAD, HORNDEAN
EDLESTON, CHRISTOPHER, 7, FRANCIS ROAD, HORNDEAN
SNOW, KENNETH G, 8, FRANCIS ROAD, HORNDEAN
SNOW, PATRICIA R, 8, FRANCIS ROAD, HORNDEAN
BARTLETT, GRAHAM J, 9, FRANCIS ROAD, HORNDEAN
BARTLETT, LETITIA E, 9, FRANCIS ROAD, HORNDEAN
WATSON, GWENLLIAN M, 10, FRANCIS ROAD, HORNDEAN
CASTLE, JENNIFER M, 11, FRANCIS ROAD, HORNDEAN
BORRETT, BRIAN M, 12, FRANCIS ROAD, HORNDEAN
BORRETT, SYLVIA J, 12, FRANCIS ROAD, HORNDEAN
TAAFFE, GEORGE J, 13, FRANCIS ROAD, HORNDEAN
COLLIER, WALTER H, 14, FRANCIS ROAD, HORNDEAN
PYATT, DAPHNE Z, 15, FRANCIS ROAD, HORNDEAN
LEWCOCK, ELIZABETH E, 16, FRANCIS ROAD, HORNDEAN
LEWCOCK, SIDNEY G, 16, FRANCIS ROAD, HORNDEAN
BEAMISH, ELSIE M, 18, FRANCIS ROAD, HORNDEAN
DEASLEY, JOHN D, 19, FRANCIS ROAD, HORNDEAN
DEASLEY, MURIEL K, 19, FRANCIS ROAD, HORNDEAN
WAY, AMANDA F, 20, FRANCIS ROAD, HORNDEAN
WAY, STEPHEN R, 20, FRANCIS ROAD, HORNDEAN
GRAYLEN, ANTHONY M, 21, FRANCIS ROAD, HORNDEAN
GRAYLEN, SHIRLEY H, 21, FRANCIS ROAD, HORNDEAN
CAMERON, HELEN E, 22, FRANCIS ROAD, HORNDEAN
FORWARD, TREVOR C, 23, FRANCIS ROAD, HORNDEAN
FORWARD, VERONICA S, 23, FRANCIS ROAD, HORNDEAN
DAVIES, GLYNN, 24, FRANCIS ROAD, HORNDEAN
DAVIES, SANDRA J, 24, FRANCIS ROAD, HORNDEAN
DAVIES, STEPHEN R, 24, FRANCIS ROAD, HORNDEAN
JOHNSON, SIDNEY C, 25, FRANCIS ROAD, HORNDEAN
JOHNSON, YVONNE M.E, 25, FRANCIS ROAD, HORNDEAN
LEWIS, LESLIE A, 26, FRANCIS ROAD, HORNDEAN
LEWIS, VANESSA J, 26, FRANCIS ROAD, HORNDEAN
PURVIS, GRAHAM R, 27, FRANCIS ROAD, HORNDEAN
BROWN, AUDREY F, 28, FRANCIS ROAD, HORNDEAN
BROWN, RONALD G, 28, FRANCIS ROAD, HORNDEAN
HARTLEY, BRIAN K, 30, FRANCIS ROAD, HORNDEAN
BACON, MICHAEL E, 1, GLAMORGAN ROAD, CATHERINGTON
BACON, VIOLET P, 1, GLAMORGAN ROAD, CATHERINGTON
BREWER, ALAN D, 3, GLAMORGAN ROAD, CATHERINGTON
BREWER, JACQUELINE, 3, GLAMORGAN ROAD,
BLACKSHAW, ANGELA E, 5, GLAMORGAN ROAD,
BLACKSHAW, CHARLES E, 5, GLAMORGAN ROAD,
BENNETT, CLAIRE M, 7, GLAMORGAN ROAD,
HEALEY, CHRISTOPHER S, 9, GLAMORGAN ROAD,
HEALEY, PAULINE J, 9, GLAMORGAN ROAD, CATHERINGTON
HEALEY, RUSSELL S, 9, GLAMORGAN ROAD, CATHERINGTON
COUGHTREY, RAYMOND M, 11, GLAMORGAN ROAD,
COUGHTREY, VALERIE M, 11, GLAMORGAN ROAD,
FOSTER, NIGEL R, 13, GLAMORGAN ROAD, CATHERINGTON
FOSTER, ROSEMARY S, 13, GLAMORGAN ROAD,
WESTCOTT, JULIE A, 15, GLAMORGAN ROAD,
WESTCOTT, MARK D, 15, GLAMORGAN ROAD,
FLINT, ADRIENNE E, 19, GLAMORGAN ROAD, CATHERINGTON
FLINT, DAVID W, 19, GLAMORGAN ROAD, CATHERINGTON
PHELPS, ARTHUR F, 21, GLAMORGAN ROAD, CATHERINGTON
PHELPS, DAISY, 21, GLAMORGAN ROAD, CATHERINGTON
SPARKS, ROGER, 23, GLAMORGAN ROAD, CATHERINGTON
SPARKS, SUZANNE V, 23, GLAMORGAN ROAD,
DRIDGE, BRIAN A, 25, GLAMORGAN ROAD, CATHERINGTON
DRIDGE, VALERIE J, 25, GLAMORGAN ROAD, CATHERINGTON
ASCHERL, ANGELA G, 27, GLAMORGAN ROAD,
ASCHERL, LISA C, 27, GLAMORGAN ROAD, CATHERINGTON
ASCHERL, VICTOR, 27, GLAMORGAN ROAD, CATHERINGTON
BLACKWOOD, ANDREW A, 29, GLAMORGAN ROAD,
HARFIELD, THALIA J, 29, GLAMORGAN ROAD,
WILLSHIRE, JOHN W, 29A, GLAMORGAN ROAD,
BYLETT, VICKI A, 31, GLAMORGAN ROAD, CATHERINGTON
WILSON, GEOFFREY R, 31, GLAMORGAN ROAD,
WILSON, ROBERT A, 31, GLAMORGAN ROAD, CATHERINGTON
PHELPS, CLIFFORD F, 33, GLAMORGAN ROAD,
PHELPS, MARGARET, 33, GLAMORGAN ROAD,
JARVIS, ANDREW B, 35, GLAMORGAN ROAD, CATHERINGTON
JARVIS, BARRY D, 35, GLAMORGAN ROAD, CATHERINGTON
JARVIS, ELAINE A, 35, GLAMORGAN ROAD, CATHERINGTON
GRAY, ANNIE, 37, GLAMORGAN ROAD, CATHERINGTON
GRAY, CHARLES P, 37, GLAMORGAN ROAD, CATHERINGTON
GRAY, CHARLES W, 37, GLAMORGAN ROAD, CATHERINGTON
WALTERS, GEORGE H, 39, GLAMORGAN ROAD,
WALTERS, SHEILA A, 39, GLAMORGAN ROAD,
CRAWFORD, JOHN G, 41, GLAMORGAN ROAD,
CRAWFORD, PATRICIA, 41, GLAMORGAN ROAD,
DURRANT, DAVID A, 43, GLAMORGAN ROAD, CATHERINGTON
DURRANT, ELIZABETH R.A, 43, GLAMORGAN ROAD,
DURRANT, KENNETH, 43, GLAMORGAN ROAD,
DOE, LESLIE S, 45, GLAMORGAN ROAD, CATHERINGTON
SAUNDERS, AUDREY W.A, 45, GLAMORGAN ROAD,
SAUNDERS, RAYMOND J, 45, GLAMORGAN ROAD,
NELSON, DENISE E, 47, GLAMORGAN ROAD, CATHERINGTON
NELSON, DONALD M, 47, GLAMORGAN ROAD,
DUFFIELD, MAY E, 49, GLAMORGAN ROAD, CATHERINGTON
STEADMAN, GLORIA A, 63, GLAMORGAN ROAD,
STEADMAN, JOHN E, 63, GLAMORGAN ROAD,
STEADMAN, MARK J, 63, GLAMORGAN ROAD,
HANLON, CAROLINE V, 2, GLAMORGAN ROAD,
HANLON, CHRISTOPHER P, 2, GLAMORGAN ROAD,
SMITH, IAN D, 10, GLAMORGAN ROAD, CATHERINGTON
PUTNAM, IVY R, 12, GLAMORGAN ROAD, CATHERINGTON
THOMPSON, RAYMOND B, 14, GLAMORGAN ROAD,
THOMPSON, SHIRLEY A, 14, GLAMORGAN ROAD,
SMITH, CAROL A, 16, GLAMORGAN ROAD, CATHERINGTON
SMITH, JOHN A, 16, GLAMORGAN ROAD, CATHERINGTON
CHILDS, JOAN E, 18, GLAMORGAN ROAD, CATHERINGTON
SAIT, MARION B.L, 20, GLAMORGAN ROAD, CATHERINGTON
ATCHERLEY, DONNA L, 22, GLAMORGAN ROAD,
CLARK, CHRISTOPHER I, 22, GLAMORGAN ROAD,
HAMILTON, CHRISTINA M, 24, GLAMORGAN ROAD,
HAMILTON, IAIN P, 24, GLAMORGAN ROAD, CATHERINGTON
BURCHELL, EMMA V, 26, GLAMORGAN ROAD,
BURCHELL, GARY J, 26, GLAMORGAN ROAD, CATHERINGTON
HARRIS, DONALD J, 26, GLAMORGAN ROAD, CATHERINGTON
HARRIS, JANET, 26, GLAMORGAN ROAD, CATHERINGTON
BYERLEY, DAVID J, 28, GLAMORGAN ROAD, CATHERINGTON
BYERLEY, JANE E, 28, GLAMORGAN ROAD, CATHERINGTON
SEARLE, NIGEL, 30, GLAMORGAN ROAD, CATHERINGTON
SEARLE, TRACEY J, 30, GLAMORGAN ROAD, CATHERINGTON
CLARK, JACQUELINE S, 32, GLAMORGAN ROAD,
FRANCIS, JACQUELINE M, 34, GLAMORGAN ROAD,
FRANCIS, JOSEPH G, 34, GLAMORGAN ROAD, CATHERINGTON
COLE, DOREEN A, 36, GLAMORGAN ROAD, CATHERINGTON
COLE, LIONEL C, 36, GLAMORGAN ROAD, CATHERINGTON
PRICE, EVELYN M, 38, GLAMORGAN ROAD, CATHERINGTON
RICHARDSON, JANET E, 40, GLAMORGAN ROAD,
RICHARDSON, PAUL, 40, GLAMORGAN ROAD,
WRIGHT, SIMON C, 42, GLAMORGAN ROAD, CATHERINGTON
WRIGHT, SUSAN, 42, GLAMORGAN ROAD, CATHERINGTON
VACHER, GRAHAM, 48, GLAMORGAN ROAD, CATHERINGTON
VACHER, JANET, 48, GLAMORGAN ROAD, CATHERINGTON
CLARK, ROBERT I, 50, GLAMORGAN ROAD, CATHERINGTON
DRAKE, HILDA C, 50, GLAMORGAN ROAD, CATHERINGTON
SCHNICHELS, KARIN M, 1, GODWIN CRESCENT, HORNDEAN
WESTON, ANNE, 2, GODWIN CRESCENT, HORNDEAN
WESTON, GERALD J, 2, GODWIN CRESCENT, HORNDEAN
STONES, JOHN C, 3, GODWIN CRESCENT, HORNDEAN
STONES, PATRICIA J, 3, GODWIN CRESCENT, HORNDEAN
UPFIELD, CHRISTOPHER M, 4, GODWIN CRESCENT,
UPFIELD, MICHELLE, 4, GODWIN CRESCENT, HORNDEAN
WISE, CLARE L, 5, GODWIN CRESCENT, HORNDEAN
WISE, MALCOLM J, 5, GODWIN CRESCENT, HORNDEAN
JONES, MANDY, 6, GODWIN CRESCENT, HORNDEAN
JONES, MICHAEL, 6, GODWIN CRESCENT, HORNDEAN
KINSLEY, BRIAN, 7, GODWIN CRESCENT, HORNDEAN
KINSLEY, NICOLA J, 7, GODWIN CRESCENT, HORNDEAN
SHEELEY, DOREEN R, 8, GODWIN CRESCENT, HORNDEAN
SHEELEY, JOHN D, 8, GODWIN CRESCENT, HORNDEAN
BRATTY, DAPHNE, 9, GODWIN CRESCENT, HORNDEAN
BRATTY, GEORGE A, 9, GODWIN CRESCENT, HORNDEAN
BEVERIDGE, ALISTAIR N, 10, GODWIN CRESCENT,
BEVERIDGE, ELAINE, 10, GODWIN CRESCENT,
BEVERIDGE, JAMES W, 10, GODWIN CRESCENT, HORNDEAN
GRENFELL, ANDREW C, 12, GODWIN CRESCENT, HORNDEAN
GRAHAM, STEVEN K.E, 14, GODWIN CRESCENT, HORNDEAN
GRAHAM, TRACY, 14, GODWIN CRESCENT, HORNDEAN
NORMAN, CLAIRE, 15, GODWIN CRESCENT, HORNDEAN
NORMAN, RICHARD J, 15, GODWIN CRESCENT, HORNDEAN
MASON, CAROLINE M, 16, GODWIN CRESCENT, HORNDEAN
POTTER, MICHAEL J, 16, GODWIN CRESCENT, HORNDEAN
PHILLIPS, MARGARET R, 17, GODWIN CRESCENT, HORNDEAN
PHILLIPS, RICHARD J, 17, GODWIN CRESCENT, HORNDEAN
ROBINSON, NICHOLAS D, 18, GODWIN CRESCENT,
ROBINSON, SHARON D, 18, GODWIN CRESCENT, HORNDEAN
BROWN, BEVERLEY A, 19, GODWIN CRESCENT, HORNDEAN
BROWN, ROY C, 19, GODWIN CRESCENT, HORNDEAN
WILSON, ANN M, 20, GODWIN CRESCENT, HORNDEAN
ANDREW, JANE G, 21, GODWIN CRESCENT, HORNDEAN
ANDREW, KENNETH A, 21, GODWIN CRESCENT, HORNDEAN
ROBERTSON, GORDON J, 22, GODWIN CRESCENT,
ILLINGWORTH, JANET E, 23, GODWIN CRESCENT,
FISHER, GLENN R, 24, GODWIN CRESCENT, HORNDEAN
FISHER, KELLY, 24, GODWIN CRESCENT, HORNDEAN
STORR, ANTHONY M, 25, GODWIN CRESCENT, HORNDEAN
STORR, CAROL K, 25, GODWIN CRESCENT, HORNDEAN
VICKERS, JASON M, 26, GODWIN CRESCENT, HORNDEAN
VICKERS, TANYA J, 26, GODWIN CRESCENT, HORNDEAN
BOUCHER, ANNIE W.F, 27, GODWIN CRESCENT, HORNDEAN
BOUCHER, CAROL A, 27, GODWIN CRESCENT, HORNDEAN
KEMPSON, HELEN L, 28, GODWIN CRESCENT, HORNDEAN
WEST, WILLIAM M, 29, GODWIN CRESCENT, HORNDEAN
DAVISON, CLIFFORD R, 30, GODWIN CRESCENT, HORNDEAN
SPONG, MAUREEN A, 31, GODWIN CRESCENT, HORNDEAN
PENROSE, DENISE, 32, GODWIN CRESCENT, HORNDEAN
ALLARD, LORRAINE, 33, GODWIN CRESCENT, HORNDEAN
WILLIAMS, DAVID, 33, GODWIN CRESCENT, HORNDEAN
OLDREIVE, STEPHEN R, 34, GODWIN CRESCENT, HORNDEAN
OLDREIVE, SUSAN H, 34, GODWIN CRESCENT, HORNDEAN
NOBLE, HEATHER J, 35, GODWIN CRESCENT, HORNDEAN
NOBLE, PAUL D, 35, GODWIN CRESCENT, HORNDEAN
JONES, JEAN K, 1, HAWTHORN ROAD, HORNDEAN
JONES, ROY, 1, HAWTHORN ROAD, HORNDEAN
TOWLER, DIANA, 1A, HAWTHORN ROAD, HORNDEAN
TOWLER, MARTIN, 1A, HAWTHORN ROAD, HORNDEAN
TOWLER, NEIL, 1A, HAWTHORN ROAD, HORNDEAN
BLACKWELL, PAMELA W, 2, HAWTHORN ROAD, HORNDEAN
RAYNER, BARRY G, 3, HAWTHORN ROAD, HORNDEAN
RAYNER, BERYL J, 3, HAWTHORN ROAD, HORNDEAN
CHILDS, HELEN A, 4, HAWTHORN ROAD, HORNDEAN
CHILDS, MICHAEL J, 4, HAWTHORN ROAD, HORNDEAN
BEVAN, CHRISTOPHER A, 5, HAWTHORN ROAD, HORNDEAN
BEVAN, PAMELA M, 5, HAWTHORN ROAD, HORNDEAN
BEVAN, PATRICK A.M, 5, HAWTHORN ROAD, HORNDEAN
COYNE, MARIE, 6, HAWTHORN ROAD, HORNDEAN
STACEY, DENNIS E, 6A, HAWTHORN ROAD, HORNDEAN
BEST, MARILYN, 7, HAWTHORN ROAD, HORNDEAN
GOODSON, PHILIP A, 7, HAWTHORN ROAD, HORNDEAN
DAVIS, JOAN, 8, HAWTHORN ROAD, HORNDEAN
DAVIS, ROBERT K, 8, HAWTHORN ROAD, HORNDEAN
GREEN, ANGELA, 9, HAWTHORN ROAD, HORNDEAN
STEVENS, HENRY E.P, 15, HAWTHORN ROAD, HORNDEAN
COPE, JULIE A, 16, HAWTHORN ROAD, HORNDEAN
SHAVE, DEIRDRE S, 17, HAWTHORN ROAD, HORNDEAN
SHAVE, PAUL D, 17, HAWTHORN ROAD, HORNDEAN
SHAVE, STUART T, 17, HAWTHORN ROAD, HORNDEAN
CRABBE, HELENE S, 18, HAWTHORN ROAD, HORNDEAN
CRABBE, IAN M.A, 18, HAWTHORN ROAD, HORNDEAN
GREENWOOD, BASIL S, 19, HAWTHORN ROAD, HORNDEAN
GREENWOOD, HILDA E.L, 19, HAWTHORN ROAD, HORNDEAN
TURNER, DAVINA K, 20, HAWTHORN ROAD, HORNDEAN
TURNER, JAMIE R, 20, HAWTHORN ROAD, HORNDEAN
JACKMAN, BRENDA N, 21, HAWTHORN ROAD, HORNDEAN
JACKMAN, CHRISTINE, 21, HAWTHORN ROAD, HORNDEAN
JACKMAN, MICHAEL, 21, HAWTHORN ROAD, HORNDEAN
HEWETT, BARBARA O, 22, HAWTHORN ROAD, HORNDEAN
HEWETT, DAVID W, 22, HAWTHORN ROAD, HORNDEAN
HEWETT, TIMOTHY J, 22, HAWTHORN ROAD, HORNDEAN
COWDREY, LAWRENCE G, 23, HAWTHORN ROAD, HORNDEAN
COWDREY, MARION, 23, HAWTHORN ROAD, HORNDEAN
YOUNG, RITA J.M, 24, HAWTHORN ROAD, HORNDEAN
TURNER, KIM M, 25, HAWTHORN ROAD, HORNDEAN
TURNER, RICHARD S, 25, HAWTHORN ROAD, HORNDEAN
PILE, JOSEPHINE J, 26, HAWTHORN ROAD, HORNDEAN
PILE, MICHAEL T, 26, HAWTHORN ROAD, HORNDEAN
LEWENDON, CHRISTINA G, 46, HAWTHORN ROAD,
RYALL, IAN M, 46, HAWTHORN ROAD, HORNDEAN
STANISTREET, ADAM N.F, 47, HAWTHORN ROAD, HORNDEAN
STANISTREET, FREDERICK G, 47, HAWTHORN ROAD,
STANISTREET, RIA D.J, 47, HAWTHORN ROAD, HORNDEAN
STANISTREET, SALLY J, 47, HAWTHORN ROAD, HORNDEAN
LEACH, RONALD J, 48, HAWTHORN ROAD, HORNDEAN
HELLIER, JUNE, 2, HILLSIDE CLOSE, HORNDEAN
PRICE, JAMIE, 3, HILLSIDE CLOSE, HORNDEAN
PRICE, SELINA M, 3, HILLSIDE CLOSE, HORNDEAN
RIPPON, KAREN, 4, HILLSIDE CLOSE, HORNDEAN
RIPPON, KELLY-MARIE, 4, HILLSIDE CLOSE, HORNDEAN
RIPPON, MATTHEW J, 4, HILLSIDE CLOSE, HORNDEAN
LEE, AUDREY L, 5, HILLSIDE CLOSE, HORNDEAN
LEE, ERIC N.J, 5, HILLSIDE CLOSE, HORNDEAN
SINGLETON, BADEN B, 6, HILLSIDE CLOSE, HORNDEAN
SINGLETON, ROSANNA, 6, HILLSIDE CLOSE, HORNDEAN
TALBOT, JOAN E, 7, HILLSIDE CLOSE, HORNDEAN
DAVIS, EDWIN J, 8, HILLSIDE CLOSE, HORNDEAN
ADLAM, DOUGLAS A, 9, HILLSIDE CLOSE, HORNDEAN
ADLAM, JEAN S, 9, HILLSIDE CLOSE, HORNDEAN
RIDOUT, MARY J, 10, HILLSIDE CLOSE, HORNDEAN
HALEWOOD, ALAN, 11, HILLSIDE CLOSE, HORNDEAN
CONWAY, MARGARET E, 12, HILLSIDE CLOSE, HORNDEAN
RENDLE, JACQUELINE A, 13, HILLSIDE CLOSE, HORNDEAN
HARLEY, PAMELA M, 14, HILLSIDE CLOSE, HORNDEAN
HARLEY, ROBERT A, 14, HILLSIDE CLOSE, HORNDEAN
BURCHELL, NICOLAS W, 15, HILLSIDE CLOSE, HORNDEAN
BURGES, KAREN A, 15, HILLSIDE CLOSE, HORNDEAN
DAVIS, LINDA V, 16, HILLSIDE CLOSE, HORNDEAN
HOBBS, ANN R.F, 1, HILLTOP GARDENS, HORNDEAN
HOBBS, JAMES M, 1, HILLTOP GARDENS, HORNDEAN
HOBBS, JOANNE S, 1, HILLTOP GARDENS, HORNDEAN
HOBBS, JOHN E, 1, HILLTOP GARDENS, HORNDEAN
PAGE, KAREN M, 2, HILLTOP GARDENS, HORNDEAN
PAGE, PHILIP E, 2, HILLTOP GARDENS, HORNDEAN
MORGAN, BRIAN J, 3, HILLTOP GARDENS, HORNDEAN
MORGAN, SHEILA A, 3, HILLTOP GARDENS, HORNDEAN
BARTER, HELEN V, 4, HILLTOP GARDENS, HORNDEAN
BARTER, TERENCE, 4, HILLTOP GARDENS, HORNDEAN
DOWLING, JEAN E, 4, HILLTOP GARDENS, HORNDEAN
HULBERT, CALA L, 5, HILLTOP GARDENS, HORNDEAN
HULBERT, DAVID J, 5, HILLTOP GARDENS, HORNDEAN
HICKS, DAVID J, 6, HILLTOP GARDENS, HORNDEAN
HICKS, SUSAN R, 6, HILLTOP GARDENS, HORNDEAN
HEMINGWAY, MARGARET J, 7, HILLTOP GARDENS,
JONES, PAUL, 1, HOLDENHURST CLOSE, HORNDEAN
JONES, SHARON J, 1, HOLDENHURST CLOSE, HORNDEAN
LEJASMEIERS, ROSEMARY A, 2, HOLDENHURST CLOSE,
LEJASMEIERS, VICTOR P, 2, HOLDENHURST CLOSE,
MUSCATO, CRAIG R, 3, HOLDENHURST CLOSE, HORNDEAN
MUSCATO, DEBORAH A, 3, HOLDENHURST CLOSE,
MAIN, ANDREW, 4, HOLDENHURST CLOSE, HORNDEAN
MAIN, BRIDGIT, 4, HOLDENHURST CLOSE, HORNDEAN
FLETCHER, JO-ANNE, 5, HOLDENHURST CLOSE, HORNDEAN
FLETCHER, STEFAN, 5, HOLDENHURST CLOSE, HORNDEAN
NORRIS, DEBORAH M, 6, HOLDENHURST CLOSE, HORNDEAN
NORRIS, GRAHAM A, 6, HOLDENHURST CLOSE, HORNDEAN
VOLLER, CLARE J, 7, HOLDENHURST CLOSE, HORNDEAN
MENAGE, ANNE, 8, HOLDENHURST CLOSE, HORNDEAN
TURNER, CAROL A, 9, HOLDENHURST CLOSE, HORNDEAN
TURNER, LOUISE C, 9, HOLDENHURST CLOSE, HORNDEAN
TURNER, PETER R, 9, HOLDENHURST CLOSE, HORNDEAN
TURNER, SHARON L, 9, HOLDENHURST CLOSE, HORNDEAN
BAMPTON, DEREK A, 10, HOLDENHURST CLOSE, HORNDEAN
COLLINS, SANDRA, 10, HOLDENHURST CLOSE, HORNDEAN
PRICE, JANET M, 12, HOLDENHURST CLOSE, HORNDEAN
PRICE, STEPHEN P.M, 12, HOLDENHURST CLOSE, HORNDEAN
BRUMHILL, JOAN P, 14, HOLDENHURST CLOSE, HORNDEAN
BRUMHILL, RONALD D, 14, HOLDENHURST CLOSE,
TODD, ADAM T, 15, HOLDENHURST CLOSE, HORNDEAN

TODD, KEITH T, 15, HOLDENHURST CLOSE, HORNDEAN
TODD, SHORA A, 15, HOLDENHURST CLOSE, HORNDEAN
OWEN, MARK P, 16, HOLDENHURST CLOSE, HORNDEAN
OWEN, SUSAN M, 16, HOLDENHURST CLOSE, HORNDEAN
SLEEMAN, BLANCHE M, 17, HOLDENHURST CLOSE,
SLEEMAN, PATRICIA A, 17, HOLDENHURST CLOSE,
DOREY, SARAH L, 18, HOLDENHURST CLOSE, HORNDEAN
GOUGH, GRAHAM R, 18, HOLDENHURST CLOSE, HORNDEAN
PITT, ELAINE F, 19, HOLDENHURST CLOSE, HORNDEAN
PITT, MICHAEL L, 19, HOLDENHURST CLOSE, HORNDEAN
PITT, SALLY C, 19, HOLDENHURST CLOSE, HORNDEAN
PITT, STEPHEN J, 19, HOLDENHURST CLOSE, HORNDEAN
BATCHELOR, HILARY A, 1, THE HOLLIES, HORNDEAN
BATCHELOR, RICHARD T, 1, THE HOLLIES, HORNDEAN
BATCHELOR, TIMOTHY R, 1, THE HOLLIES, HORNDEAN
AWFORD, AMANDA J, 2, THE HOLLIES, HORNDEAN
AWFORD, ANDREW T, 2, THE HOLLIES, HORNDEAN
MURPHY, DECLAN P.D, 3, THE HOLLIES, HORNDEAN
MURPHY, IRENA M, 3, THE HOLLIES, HORNDEAN
BRENNAN, MICHELLE, 1, JUNIPER ROAD, HORNDEAN
BRENNAN, STEPHEN M, 1, JUNIPER ROAD, HORNDEAN
LEVERETT, DOROTHY, 1, JUNIPER ROAD, HORNDEAN
LEVERETT, EDWARD W, 1, JUNIPER ROAD, HORNDEAN
TULLEY, JOHN R, 2, JUNIPER ROAD, HORNDEAN
TULLEY, LYNNE J, 2, JUNIPER ROAD, HORNDEAN
HATHAWAY, COLIN T, 3, JUNIPER ROAD, HORNDEAN
VICARY, BARBARA, 3, JUNIPER ROAD, HORNDEAN
RIDDLES, ELISABETH M, 4, JUNIPER ROAD, HORNDEAN
RIDDLES, IAN D, 4, JUNIPER ROAD, HORNDEAN
JACKSON, NINA E, 5, JUNIPER ROAD, HORNDEAN
CANN, ADRIAN J, 6, JUNIPER ROAD, HORNDEAN
CANN, MARION, 6, JUNIPER ROAD, HORNDEAN
WESTON, DAVID, 7, JUNIPER ROAD, HORNDEAN
WESTON, TERESA M, 7, JUNIPER ROAD, HORNDEAN
KNAPP, HAZEL D, 9, JUNIPER ROAD, HORNDEAN
KNAPP, PETER C, 9, JUNIPER ROAD, HORNDEAN
COLE, TREVOR W, 10, JUNIPER ROAD, HORNDEAN
KING, EILEAN M, 11, JUNIPER ROAD, HORNDEAN
KING, SIMON, 11, JUNIPER ROAD, HORNDEAN
STANISLAWSKI, ANDRE, 12, JUNIPER ROAD, HORNDEAN
COLESHILL, JACQUELYN A, 14, JUNIPER ROAD, HORNDEAN
COLESHILL, MICHAEL E, 14, JUNIPER ROAD, HORNDEAN
JOBSON, LINDA B.J, 15, JUNIPER ROAD, HORNDEAN
PEARSON, ALAN, 15, JUNIPER ROAD, HORNDEAN
PARR, NEAL D, 16, JUNIPER ROAD, HORNDEAN
PARR, SAMAMTHA J, 16, JUNIPER ROAD, HORNDEAN
MONTGOMERY, NIGEL W, 17, JUNIPER ROAD, HORNDEAN
MONTGOMERY, SANDRA D, 17, JUNIPER ROAD, HORNDEAN
CARTMELL, JAYNE, 18, JUNIPER ROAD, HORNDEAN
CARTMELL, TIMOTHY J, 18, JUNIPER ROAD, HORNDEAN
MANN, DOREEN C, 19, JUNIPER ROAD, HORNDEAN
MOORE, BERYL E, 20, JUNIPER ROAD, HORNDEAN
HADWEN, LINDA, 21, JUNIPER ROAD, HORNDEAN
WOOTTON, MARGARET, 23, JUNIPER ROAD, HORNDEAN
WOOTTON, PETER J, 23, JUNIPER ROAD, HORNDEAN
HALL, CAROLE A, HEREWARD, LITH AVENUE, HORNDEAN
JORDAN, SYDNEY A, HEREWARD, LITH AVENUE, HORNDEAN
KNIPE, ANDREW M, LUCKY BREAK, LITH AVENUE,
KNIPE, LESLIE J, LUCKY BREAK, LITH AVENUE, HORNDEAN
KNIPE, MOLLIE P, LUCKY BREAK, LITH AVENUE, HORNDEAN
KNIPE, PHILIP J, LUCKY BREAK, LITH AVENUE, HORNDEAN
DENNIS, MARILYN, MEADOWSWEET, LITH AVENUE,
DENNIS, STEPHEN J, MEADOWSWEET, LITH AVENUE,
BONES, RONALD E, MOHILL, LITH AVENUE, HORNDEAN
MCHUGH, ANTHONY G, MOHILL, LITH AVENUE, HORNDEAN
MCHUGH, DEBORAH, MOHILL, LITH AVENUE, HORNDEAN
MCHUGH, GERRY, MOHILL, LITH AVENUE, HORNDEAN
MCHUGH, TERESA J, MOHILL, LITH AVENUE, HORNDEAN
ROBINSON, ANDREW P, NYEWOOD, LITH AVENUE,
ROBINSON, ROSAMUND M, NYEWOOD, LITH AVENUE,
PARKER, BARBARA M, SUNRISE, LITH AVENUE, HORNDEAN
PARKER, PAUL, SUNRISE, LITH AVENUE, HORNDEAN
PARKER, ROSS A, SUNRISE, LITH AVENUE, HORNDEAN
MAY, LOUISE, WOODLAND COTTAGE, LITH AVENUE,
MAY, SALLY, WOODLAND COTTAGE, LITH AVENUE,
MAY, TIMOTHY, WOODLAND COTTAGE, LITH AVENUE,
HALL, JANICE R.D, DEERLEAP, LITH CRESCENT, HORNDEAN
HALL, RICHARD T, DEERLEAP, LITH CRESCENT, HORNDEAN
ALDRIDGE, JOHN A, HOLLYBANK, LITH LANE, HORNDEAN
HOLMES, ERNEST E, THREE BEARS BUNGALOW, LITH LANE,
HOLMES, ROSEMARY E, THREE BEARS BUNGALOW, LITH LANE, HORNDEAN
MAY, CHERYL, 95, LONDON ROAD, HORNDEAN
NOLAN, DEIDRE L, 95, LONDON ROAD, HORNDEAN
HARROWELL, GILBERT W, 133, LONDON ROAD, HORNDEAN
ELDRICGE, TREVOR R, 1, MOBILE HOME PARK, LONDON ROAD, HORNDEAN
NORTHCOTT, LEEANA R, 1, MOBILE HOME PARK, LONDON ROAD, HORNDEAN
HEATH, DESMOND H, 2, MOBILE HOME PARK, LONDON ROAD, HORNDEAN
HAYWARD, FRANK E, 3, MOBILE HOME PARK, LONDON ROAD, HORNDEAN
LINFORD, DORIS N.E, 3, MOBILE HOME PARK, LONDON ROAD, HORNDEAN
TAIT, ANN-MARIE, 4, MOBILE HOME PARK, LONDON ROAD,
ORRISS, NICOLA J, 5, MOBILE HOME PARK, LONDON ROAD,
CHALCOTT, IRENE, 6, MOBILE HOME PARK, LONDON ROAD,
BISHOP, RAYMOND, 7, MOBILE HOME PARK, LONDON ROAD,
BISHOP, ROSEMARY E.M, 7, MOBILE HOME PARK, LONDON ROAD, HORNDEAN
KNIGHT, CHRISTOPHER S, 8, MOBILE HOME PARK, LONDON ROAD, HORNDEAN
O'LOUGHLIN, CAROLE A, 8, MOBILE HOME PARK, LONDON ROAD, HORNDEAN
TAYLOR, JAMES, 9, MOBILE HOME PARK, LONDON ROAD,
CALLARD, PAUL, 10, MOBILE HOME PARK, LONDON ROAD,
YALDEN, KENNETH J, 11, MOBILE HOME PARK, LONDON ROAD, HORNDEAN
CARTER, FRED, 13, MOBILE HOME PARK, LONDON ROAD,
CARTER, MARGARET, 13, MOBILE HOME PARK, LONDON ROAD, HORNDEAN
POWELL, MARK A, 13, MOBILE HOME PARK, LONDON ROAD,
CLISSETT, LEONARD, 14, MOBILE HOME PARK, LONDON ROAD, HORNDEAN
SAWKINS, SARITA, 15, MOBILE HOME PARK, LONDON ROAD,
RHAM, CHRISTOPHER, 16, MOBILE HOME PARK, LONDON ROAD, HORNDEAN
ABBINNETT, TRACEY E, 18, MOBILE HOME PARK, LONDON ROAD, HORNDEAN
HAHN-GRIFFITHS, WILLIAM P, 18, MOBILE HOME PARK, LONDON ROAD, HORNDEAN
MCKEOWN, NEIL, 19, MOBILE HOME PARK, LONDON ROAD,
PALMER, JAMES B, 20, MOBILE HOME PARK, LONDON ROAD,
GILLAN, BEVERLEY, 21, MOBILE HOME PARK, LONDON ROAD,
PICKETT, CHRISTOPHER J, 137, LONDON ROAD, HORNDEAN
PICKETT, VANESSA J, 137, LONDON ROAD, HORNDEAN
STEWARD, JUDITH A, 139, LONDON ROAD, HORNDEAN
STEWARD, LISA J, 139, LONDON ROAD, HORNDEAN
STEWARD, THOMAS J, 139, LONDON ROAD, HORNDEAN
TAYLOR, ANNA M, 141, LONDON ROAD, HORNDEAN
TAYLOR, MALCOLM R, 141, LONDON ROAD, HORNDEAN
LANE, LYNDA, 143, LONDON ROAD, HORNDEAN
LANE, STEPHEN, 143, LONDON ROAD, HORNDEAN
PETTIFOR, ROBERT, 149, LONDON ROAD, HORNDEAN
PENKETH, ROSEMARY L, 151, LONDON ROAD, HORNDEAN
MASON, MARTIN G, 153, LONDON ROAD, HORNDEAN
MASON, PETER, 153, LONDON ROAD, HORNDEAN
BENNETT, JOAN M, 155, LONDON ROAD, HORNDEAN
BENNETT, STEPHEN D, 155, LONDON ROAD, HORNDEAN
DEW, DAVID C, 157, LONDON ROAD, HORNDEAN
DEW, SHIRLEY M, 157, LONDON ROAD, HORNDEAN
WIGLEY, CAROL J, 159, LONDON ROAD, HORNDEAN
WIGLEY, DEREK R, 159, LONDON ROAD, HORNDEAN
WIGLEY, SIMON D, 159, LONDON ROAD, HORNDEAN
BEACH, MARTIN R, 161, LONDON ROAD, HORNDEAN
BEACH, MICHELLE C, 161, LONDON ROAD, HORNDEAN
MCTAVISH, CAROLINE, 163, LONDON ROAD, HORNDEAN
MCTAVISH, PHILIP G, 163, LONDON ROAD, HORNDEAN
MOTH, NICHOLAS, 165, LONDON ROAD, HORNDEAN
WEST, WILLIAM H, 167, LONDON ROAD, HORNDEAN
TAYLOR, LUKE M, 169, LONDON ROAD, HORNDEAN
TAYLOR, SHEILA V, 169, LONDON ROAD, HORNDEAN
PERRY, GORDON J, 171, LONDON ROAD, HORNDEAN
PERRY, PATRICIA J, 171, LONDON ROAD, HORNDEAN
BARLOW, DAVID J, 173, LONDON ROAD, HORNDEAN
BARLOW, ERICA L, 173, LONDON ROAD, HORNDEAN
CLARKE, AMBER J, 175, LONDON ROAD, HORNDEAN
CLARKE, PAMELA A, 175, LONDON ROAD, HORNDEAN
CLARKE, ROGER M, 175, LONDON ROAD, HORNDEAN
ABLITT, BARBARA F, 177, LONDON ROAD, HORNDEAN
ANSELL, MICHAEL R, 177, LONDON ROAD, HORNDEAN
ANSELL, WENDY L, 177, LONDON ROAD, HORNDEAN
BENTLEY, JEANNETTE I, 179, LONDON ROAD, HORNDEAN
BENTLEY, MICHAEL N, 179, LONDON ROAD, HORNDEAN
BENTLEY, PAUL S, 179, LONDON ROAD, HORNDEAN
CHRISTOPHERSON, CHRISTINE M, 187, LONDON ROAD,
CHRISTOPHERSON, KEVIN J, 187, LONDON ROAD,
CHRISTOPHERSON, PATRICK, 187, LONDON ROAD,
VOWLES, ROBIN A, 189, LONDON ROAD, HORNDEAN
COOPER, MANDY M, 191, LONDON ROAD, HORNDEAN
COOPER, STEVEN G, 191, LONDON ROAD, HORNDEAN
TABNER, EVELYN R, 195, LONDON ROAD, HORNDEAN
TABNER, ROBERT, 195, LONDON ROAD, HORNDEAN
WEST, BERTRAM, 197, LONDON ROAD, HORNDEAN
TIPPER, DARREN S.P, 199, LONDON ROAD, HORNDEAN
TIPPER, DAVID E.J, 199, LONDON ROAD, HORNDEAN
TIPPER, DOROTHY M, 199, LONDON ROAD, HORNDEAN
GREEN, JANET M, 201, LONDON ROAD, HORNDEAN
GREEN, JOHN, 201, LONDON ROAD, HORNDEAN
STURGESS, IDA R, 201, LONDON ROAD, HORNDEAN
ASTLE, DONALD L, 203A, LONDON ROAD, HORNDEAN
MARTIN, FREDERICK J, 205, LONDON ROAD, HORNDEAN
MARTIN, MARILYN M, 205, LONDON ROAD, HORNDEAN
ELLIOTT, ELSIE E, 205A, LONDON ROAD, HORNDEAN
SKINNER, ELEANOR M, 207, LONDON ROAD, HORNDEAN
SKINNER, GRAHAM J, 207, LONDON ROAD, HORNDEAN
ETHERINGTON, RAYMOND, 207A, LONDON ROAD,
HEWITT, EAIN R, 209, LONDON ROAD, HORNDEAN
WILSON, NATASHA M, 209, LONDON ROAD, HORNDEAN
WADE-PALMER, AUBREY R, 209A, LONDON ROAD, HORNDEAN
WADE-PALMER, EILEEN M, 209A, LONDON ROAD, HORNDEAN
MOORE, FREDERICK T, 211, LONDON ROAD, HORNDEAN
HOUGHTON, ALEXANDER J, 213, LONDON ROAD, HORNDEAN
HOUGHTON, RITA M, 213, LONDON ROAD, HORNDEAN
WATTS, ALLISON, 213A, LONDON ROAD, HORNDEAN
WATTS, CLIFFORD J, 213A, LONDON ROAD, HORNDEAN
WATTS, DAVID J, 213A, LONDON ROAD, HORNDEAN
MCLOUGHLIN, HAZEL E, 215, LONDON ROAD, HORNDEAN
SMITH, ALEXANDRA M, 217, LONDON ROAD, HORNDEAN
SMITH, CLIFFORD J, 217, LONDON ROAD, HORNDEAN
SMITH, HOWARD M, 217, LONDON ROAD, HORNDEAN
SMITH, JACQUELINE M, 217, LONDON ROAD, HORNDEAN
MEDLICOTT, JOHN B, 219, LONDON ROAD, HORNDEAN
BEVERLEY, DAVID J, 221, LONDON ROAD, HORNDEAN
BEVERLEY, MIRANDA B.E, 221, LONDON ROAD, HORNDEAN
TATCHELL, EUPHEMIA M, 223, LONDON ROAD, HORNDEAN
BURRETT, FRANK R, 225, LONDON ROAD, HORNDEAN
BURRETT, SONIA M, 225, LONDON ROAD, HORNDEAN
COTTON, JANET A, 227, LONDON ROAD, HORNDEAN
COTTON, RAYMOND R, 227, LONDON ROAD, HORNDEAN
BENDY, ANDREW, 229, LONDON ROAD, HORNDEAN
BENDY, ANGELA C, 229, LONDON ROAD, HORNDEAN
STOKER, FRANCES W, 231, LONDON ROAD, HORNDEAN
WILSON, ELSIE, 233, LONDON ROAD, HORNDEAN
HATCHER, KEVIN F, 235, LONDON ROAD, HORNDEAN
PAYNE, SALLY A, 237, LONDON ROAD, HORNDEAN
PAYNE, STEPHEN, 237, LONDON ROAD, HORNDEAN
WATKYNS, JOHN P, 237A, LONDON ROAD, HORNDEAN
WATKYNS, MARILYN D, 237A, LONDON ROAD, HORNDEAN
WATKYNS, STEPHEN, 237A, LONDON ROAD, HORNDEAN
DEACON, STANLEY A, 239, LONDON ROAD, HORNDEAN
COLDRICK, MARGARET M, 241, LONDON ROAD, HORNDEAN
COLDRICK, RONALD J.W, 241, LONDON ROAD, HORNDEAN
MASON, LILY J, 243, LONDON ROAD, HORNDEAN
OSGOOD, BERYL M, 245, LONDON ROAD, HORNDEAN
OSGOOD, GILBERT R, 245, LONDON ROAD, HORNDEAN
LAKE, AMANDA J, 247, LONDON ROAD, HORNDEAN
LAKE, SIMON R, 247, LONDON ROAD, HORNDEAN
FELLINGHAM, RICHARD A, 2, ST.CHRISTOPHERS MOBILE HOME PK, LONDON ROAD, HORNDEAN
SCOTT, MELANIE, 3, ST.CHRISTOPHERS MOBILE HOME PK, LONDON ROAD, HORNDEAN
SCOTT, MICHAEL, 3, ST.CHRISTOPHERS MOBILE HOME PK, LONDON ROAD, HORNDEAN
HASKETT, JANE L, 4, ST.CHRISTOPHERS MOBILE HOME PK, LONDON ROAD, HORNDEAN
MACLEOD, ALAN S, 5, ST.CHRISTOPHERS MOBILE HOME PK, LONDON ROAD, HORNDEAN
WALTERS, JOANNE, 5, ST.CHRISTOPHERS MOBILE HOME PK, LONDON ROAD, HORNDEAN
BAXENDALE, JOSEPH, 6, ST.CHRISTOPHERS MOBILE HOME PK, LONDON ROAD, HORNDEAN
BLAMIRE, SARAH L, 6, ST.CHRISTOPHERS MOBILE HOME PK, LONDON ROAD, HORNDEAN
BISHOP, DAVID A.M, 7, ST.CHRISTOPHERS MOBILE HOME PK, LONDON ROAD, HORNDEAN
SPENCER, ANDREA P, 8, ST.CHRISTOPHERS MOBILE HOME PK, LONDON ROAD, HORNDEAN
SPENCER, DEREK J, 8, ST.CHRISTOPHERS MOBILE HOME PK, LONDON ROAD, HORNDEAN
CHATTERTON, JOAN B, 9, ST.CHRISTOPHERS MOBILE HOME PK, LONDON ROAD, HORNDEAN
ELLIS, JOHN, 10, ST.CHRISTOPHERS MOBILE HOME PK, LONDON ROAD, HORNDEAN
ELLIS, VERA, 10, ST.CHRISTOPHERS MOBILE HOME PK, LONDON ROAD, HORNDEAN
BILES, BARRY M, 12, ST.CHRISTOPHERS MOBILE HOME PK, LONDON ROAD, HORNDEAN
BILES, JEANNE E, 12, ST.CHRISTOPHERS MOBILE HOME PK, LONDON ROAD, HORNDEAN
KNIGHT, PETER J, FLAT 1, 253, LONDON ROAD, HORNDEAN
KNIGHT, SHARON, FLAT 1, 253, LONDON ROAD, HORNDEAN
PORRITT, MALCOLM A, FLAT 2, 253, LONDON ROAD,
OTHEN, KENNETH, 255, LONDON ROAD, HORNDEAN
PUTTOCK, ROSEMARY, 255, LONDON ROAD, HORNDEAN
MOORE, JULIE V, 257, LONDON ROAD, HORNDEAN
MOORE, MELVYN R, 257, LONDON ROAD, HORNDEAN
STANLEY, GILES A, 259, LONDON ROAD, HORNDEAN
ISGAR, SHEILA, 267, LONDON ROAD, HORNDEAN
ISGAR, THOMAS B, 267, LONDON ROAD, HORNDEAN
MARSHALL, PEGGY K, 269, LONDON ROAD, HORNDEAN
HORNIBLOW, ARCHIBALD E, 271, LONDON ROAD, HORNDEAN
UZZELL, BRYAN, 273, LONDON ROAD, HORNDEAN
UZZELL, JEAN, 273, LONDON ROAD, HORNDEAN
CHAPMAN, JOHN P, 275, LONDON ROAD, HORNDEAN
CHAPMAN, ROSEMARY E, 275, LONDON ROAD, HORNDEAN
MARTIN, GREGORY R, 277, LONDON ROAD, HORNDEAN
MARTIN, TRACEY E, 277, LONDON ROAD, HORNDEAN
MAIN, ALISON R, 277A, LONDON ROAD, HORNDEAN
TOMKINS, ELAINE J.M, 279, LONDON ROAD, HORNDEAN
TOMKINS, ROBERT W, 279, LONDON ROAD, HORNDEAN
READ, JOHN A, 281, LONDON ROAD, HORNDEAN
READ, SYLVIA J, 281, LONDON ROAD, HORNDEAN
POLWIN, ANDREW S, 283, LONDON ROAD, HORNDEAN
POLWIN, JANE C, 283, LONDON ROAD, HORNDEAN
HOOPER, LILIAN M, 285, LONDON ROAD, HORNDEAN
NORRIS, JOHN, 1, BUTSER COURT, LONDON ROAD, HORNDEAN
WALLIS, EDITH E, 3, BUTSER COURT, LONDON ROAD,
WALLIS, GEORGE, 3, BUTSER COURT, LONDON ROAD,
HAYTER, PETER B.T, 4, BUTSER COURT, LONDON ROAD,
HAYTER, RACHEL M, 4, BUTSER COURT, LONDON ROAD,
NORRIS, JILL, 5, BUTSER COURT, LONDON ROAD, HORNDEAN
HICKMAN, ROSEMARY A, 6, BUTSER COURT, LONDON ROAD, HORNDEAN
WALSH, CHRISTOPHER S, 8, BUTSER COURT, LONDON ROAD,
TILT, MICHAEL S, 9, BUTSER COURT, LONDON ROAD,
MCCALL, ELLEN G, 10, BUTSER COURT, LONDON ROAD,
MCCALL, WILLIAM A, 10, BUTSER COURT, LONDON ROAD,
BRITTON, MARGARET J, 287, LONDON ROAD, HORNDEAN
BRITTON, RONALD A.G, 287, LONDON ROAD, HORNDEAN
WESTCOTT, CHRISTINE, 289, LONDON ROAD, HORNDEAN
WESTCOTT, JOHN R, 289, LONDON ROAD, HORNDEAN
WESTCOTT, KESTER J, 289, LONDON ROAD, HORNDEAN
DICKINSON, JEAN W, 291, LONDON ROAD, HORNDEAN
GOULD, MARY E, 293, LONDON ROAD, HORNDEAN
SWAINSON, ANN, 293, LONDON ROAD, HORNDEAN
SWAINSON, DEREK E, 293, LONDON ROAD, HORNDEAN

Electoral Roll

TEE, ANTHONY M, 295, LONDON ROAD, HORNDEAN
TEE, BRENDA J, 295, LONDON ROAD, HORNDEAN
LAMB, SUSAN A, 1, LOVAGE WAY, HORNDEAN
WHEELER, ROGER H, 2, LOVAGE WAY, HORNDEAN
MCSHEA, HAYLEY L, 3, LOVAGE WAY, HORNDEAN
MCSHEA, PATRICK R, 3, LOVAGE WAY, HORNDEAN
CARTMELL, DEBORAH, 4, LOVAGE WAY, HORNDEAN
CARTMELL, NICHOLAS S, 4, LOVAGE WAY, HORNDEAN
FORD, DONNA M, 6, LOVAGE WAY, HORNDEAN
FORD, SHANE C, 6, LOVAGE WAY, HORNDEAN
TURNER, ELAINE A, 7, LOVAGE WAY, HORNDEAN
ENTICKNAP, SANDRA L, 8, LOVAGE WAY, HORNDEAN
ENTICKNAP, STEPHEN, 8, LOVAGE WAY, HORNDEAN
SMITH, PAUL R, 9, LOVAGE WAY, HORNDEAN
BOWLES, ANDREW S, 10, LOVAGE WAY, HORNDEAN
BOWLES, THERESA J, 10, LOVAGE WAY, HORNDEAN
HARRISON, CLIFFORD, 11, LOVAGE WAY, HORNDEAN
HARRISON, MARJORIE, 11, LOVAGE WAY, HORNDEAN
PRATT, KAREN J, 12, LOVAGE WAY, HORNDEAN
PRATT, KEVIN N, 12, LOVAGE WAY, HORNDEAN
CHAPMAN, MANISHA, 14, LOVAGE WAY, HORNDEAN
CHAPMAN, VICTOR B, 14, LOVAGE WAY, HORNDEAN
WOOD, KIM E, 15, LOVAGE WAY, HORNDEAN
WOOD, SEAN W, 15, LOVAGE WAY, HORNDEAN
DANCE, TONY D, 16, LOVAGE WAY, HORNDEAN
HATCH, LOUISE, 17, LOVAGE WAY, HORNDEAN
HATCH, MARTIN J, 17, LOVAGE WAY, HORNDEAN
KELLY, SYLVIA M.K, 18, LOVAGE WAY, HORNDEAN
HANSLER, EILEEN M, 19, LOVAGE WAY, HORNDEAN
SHIELDS, STUART A, 19, LOVAGE WAY, HORNDEAN
SHIELDS, WENDY J, 19, LOVAGE WAY, HORNDEAN
FISHER, JULIE I, 20, LOVAGE WAY, HORNDEAN
FISHER, STEPHEN J, 20, LOVAGE WAY, HORNDEAN
MCLAVERTY, VICTORIA J, 20, LOVAGE WAY, HORNDEAN
HEWETT, CLAUDIA, 21, LOVAGE WAY, HORNDEAN
HEWETT, MATTHEW L, 21, LOVAGE WAY, HORNDEAN
BARLOW-BROWN, JOHN, 22, LOVAGE WAY, HORNDEAN
BARLOW-BROWN, PAMELA R, 22, LOVAGE WAY, HORNDEAN
HORDER, JANE L, 23, LOVAGE WAY, HORNDEAN
MASLEN, LISA A, 24, LOVAGE WAY, HORNDEAN
MASLEN, TIMOTHY J, 24, LOVAGE WAY, HORNDEAN
MILDENHALL, DONALD E, 25, LOVAGE WAY, HORNDEAN
MILDENHALL, GWENDOLINE, 25, LOVAGE WAY, HORNDEAN
NEVILLE, KIM M, 27, LOVAGE WAY, HORNDEAN
CROUCH, CATHERINE F, 29, LOVAGE WAY, HORNDEAN
CROUCH, TONY A.B, 29, LOVAGE WAY, HORNDEAN
RIDGE, CHRISTOPHER J, 31, LOVAGE WAY, HORNDEAN
RIDGE, LYNN, 31, LOVAGE WAY, HORNDEAN
SYKES, DAVID, 33, LOVAGE WAY, HORNDEAN
SYKES, KAREN J, 33, LOVAGE WAY, HORNDEAN
HARMS, BARRY J, 35, LOVAGE WAY, HORNDEAN
HARMS, REBECCA J, 35, LOVAGE WAY, HORNDEAN
HARMS, WENDY C, 35, LOVAGE WAY, HORNDEAN
TAYLOR, JACQUELINE E, 37, LOVAGE WAY, HORNDEAN
WHITE, CHRISTOPHER J, 39, LOVAGE WAY, HORNDEAN
WHITE, EDWINA I, 39, LOVAGE WAY, HORNDEAN
CLARK, PAULINE, 41, LOVAGE WAY, HORNDEAN
CLARK, ROBERT W, 41, LOVAGE WAY, HORNDEAN
GRACE, STEPHEN A, 43, LOVAGE WAY, HORNDEAN
GRACE, VICTORIA J, 43, LOVAGE WAY, HORNDEAN
CRIPPS, ALLISON E, 45, LOVAGE WAY, HORNDEAN
PALMER, ANDREW P, 47, LOVAGE WAY, HORNDEAN
PALMER, DOREEN, 47, LOVAGE WAY, HORNDEAN
WRIGHT, BERNARD A, 49, LOVAGE WAY, HORNDEAN
WRIGHT, PATRICIA J.G, 49, LOVAGE WAY, HORNDEAN
PARR, PETER J, 51, LOVAGE WAY, HORNDEAN
BALL, HELEN D, 53, LOVAGE WAY, HORNDEAN
WOODWARD, HELEN E.C, 55, LOVAGE WAY, HORNDEAN
WOODWARD, JAMES S, 55, LOVAGE WAY, HORNDEAN
DAVIS, ROBERT J, 57, LOVAGE WAY, HORNDEAN
WILSON, JOANNE M, 57, LOVAGE WAY, HORNDEAN
BRAGG, MICHELLE, 59, LOVAGE WAY, HORNDEAN
BRAGG, PHILIP, 59, LOVAGE WAY, HORNDEAN
CUMBERS, CHARLES I, 61, LOVAGE WAY, HORNDEAN
CUMBERS, MANDY, 61, LOVAGE WAY, HORNDEAN
ELPHICK, MICHAEL J, 63, LOVAGE WAY, HORNDEAN
ELPHICK, WINIFRED A, 63, LOVAGE WAY, HORNDEAN
CULLIMORE, NICOLA J, 65, LOVAGE WAY, HORNDEAN
ROGERS, SIMON J, 65, LOVAGE WAY, HORNDEAN
WOOL, RUTH B, 67, LOVAGE WAY, HORNDEAN
CROSS, JULIA S, 69, LOVAGE WAY, HORNDEAN
CROSS, PETER M, 69, LOVAGE WAY, HORNDEAN
HUTCHINGS, ANTONY J, 1, MUNDAYS ROW, HORNDEAN
HUTCHINGS, JACQUELINE B, 1, MUNDAYS ROW, HORNDEAN
ANCELL, CRAIG L, 3, MUNDAYS ROW, HORNDEAN
NEWSON, ANNA L, 3, MUNDAYS ROW, HORNDEAN
CRONSHAW, DOUGLAS O, 5, MUNDAYS ROW, HORNDEAN
WEEKS, CHRISTINE S, 7, MUNDAYS ROW, HORNDEAN
WEEKS, LESLIE R, 7, MUNDAYS ROW, HORNDEAN
CANN, KAREN, 9, MUNDAYS ROW, HORNDEAN
CANN, STUART R, 9, MUNDAYS ROW, HORNDEAN
TILLER, GARY J, 11, MUNDAYS ROW, HORNDEAN
TILLER, SALLY, 11, MUNDAYS ROW, HORNDEAN
LANGAN, DENISE, 15, MUNDAYS ROW, HORNDEAN
LANGAN, WILLIAM, 15, MUNDAYS ROW, HORNDEAN
HAMMOND, BEVERLEY, 17, MUNDAYS ROW, HORNDEAN
HAMMOND, STEVEN R, 17, MUNDAYS ROW, HORNDEAN
DYKES, HEATHER A, 19, MUNDAYS ROW, HORNDEAN
DYKES, IAN R, 19, MUNDAYS ROW, HORNDEAN
WALLIS, KEITH C, 21, MUNDAYS ROW, HORNDEAN
WALLIS, PENELOPE A.M, 21, MUNDAYS ROW, HORNDEAN
GOODYER, TERENCE, 23, MUNDAYS ROW, HORNDEAN
GOODYER, ZOE C, 23, MUNDAYS ROW, HORNDEAN
GRIGGS, JOCASTA H, 25, MUNDAYS ROW, HORNDEAN
GRIGGS, PHILLIP A, 25, MUNDAYS ROW, HORNDEAN
PARKER, WILLIAM D, 27, MUNDAYS ROW, HORNDEAN
SMITH, JILL M, 29, MUNDAYS ROW, HORNDEAN
SMITH, RONALD E, 29, MUNDAYS ROW, HORNDEAN
CALLOW, CAROL E, 31, MUNDAYS ROW, HORNDEAN
CALLOW, MICHAEL J, 31, MUNDAYS ROW, HORNDEAN
WEST, CHERYL M.A, 33, MUNDAYS ROW, HORNDEAN
WINGETT, ANGELA J, 35, MUNDAYS ROW, HORNDEAN
WINGETT, JOHN, 35, MUNDAYS ROW, HORNDEAN
WINGETT, MATTHEW J, 35, MUNDAYS ROW, HORNDEAN
GILL, LAWRENCE, 1, NORTH ROAD, HORNDEAN
GILL, NELLIE, 1, NORTH ROAD, HORNDEAN
KENYON, DOREEN E, 3, NORTH ROAD, HORNDEAN
BAKER, DOREEN E, 5, NORTH ROAD, HORNDEAN
BAKER, KENNETH P, 5, NORTH ROAD, HORNDEAN
FLIS, HELENA E, 7, NORTH ROAD, HORNDEAN
FLIS, ZENON A, 7, NORTH ROAD, HORNDEAN
MANN, BRENDA M, 9, NORTH ROAD, HORNDEAN
SALMONS, ANN B, 15, NORTH ROAD, HORNDEAN
HARVEY, CHARLES H, 17, NORTH ROAD, HORNDEAN
HARVEY, JEAN G, 17, NORTH ROAD, HORNDEAN
ADAMSON, IRIS R, 19, NORTH ROAD, HORNDEAN
BIRD, GRAHAM A, 21, NORTH ROAD, HORNDEAN
BIRD, LINDA J, 21, NORTH ROAD, HORNDEAN
NICHOLS, FRANCES J, 23, NORTH ROAD, HORNDEAN
NICHOLS, JOANNA E, 23, NORTH ROAD, HORNDEAN
NICHOLS, JONATHAN E, 23, NORTH ROAD, HORNDEAN
NICHOLS, MALCOLM E.V, 23, NORTH ROAD, HORNDEAN
LAWSON, ANDREA, 25, NORTH ROAD, HORNDEAN
LAWSON, BENJAMIN J, 25, NORTH ROAD, HORNDEAN
CHRISTIAN, BARBARA H, 33, NORTH ROAD, HORNDEAN
CHRISTIAN, BRUCE W.F, 33, NORTH ROAD, HORNDEAN
GRAY, DOREEN E, 35, NORTH ROAD, HORNDEAN
GRAY, LOWRY, 35, NORTH ROAD, HORNDEAN
LOVETT, IVY V, 37, NORTH ROAD, HORNDEAN
ALBON, ARTHUR S, 39, NORTH ROAD, HORNDEAN
ALBON, EIRENE M, 39, NORTH ROAD, HORNDEAN
SNELGROVE, SHEILA, 41, NORTH ROAD, HORNDEAN
QUINN, LILIAN L, 43, NORTH ROAD, HORNDEAN
MCKINLEY, CECILIA B, 45, NORTH ROAD, HORNDEAN
BARROW, LESLIE S, 51, NORTH ROAD, HORNDEAN
BARROW, MARY G, 51, NORTH ROAD, HORNDEAN
GUY, IVAN E, 53, NORTH ROAD, HORNDEAN
SHERGOLD, JOHN H, 55, NORTH ROAD, HORNDEAN
SHERGOLD, SYLVIA A, 55, NORTH ROAD, HORNDEAN
HATCH, IRENE D.M, 67, NORTH ROAD, HORNDEAN
HATCH, PETER R, 67, NORTH ROAD, HORNDEAN
STALLARD, MARJORIE L, 69, NORTH ROAD, HORNDEAN
STALLARD, REGINALD A, 69, NORTH ROAD, HORNDEAN
TIMMS, DIERDRE B, 71, NORTH ROAD, HORNDEAN
SHARPLING, MARGARET, 73, NORTH ROAD, HORNDEAN
POYNER, PHYLLIS M, 79, NORTH ROAD, HORNDEAN
POYNER, WILLIAM F, 79, NORTH ROAD, HORNDEAN
BUXEY, PAUL J, 81, NORTH ROAD, HORNDEAN
BUXEY, SUSAN, 81, NORTH ROAD, HORNDEAN
ELVIN, FREDERICK R, 83, NORTH ROAD, HORNDEAN
ELVIN, SHEILA L, 83, NORTH ROAD, HORNDEAN
MITCHELL, AMOS, 93, NORTH ROAD, HORNDEAN
MITCHELL, MARGARET F, 93, NORTH ROAD, HORNDEAN
THOMSON, ANDREW G, 2, NORTH ROAD, HORNDEAN
THOMSON, DAVID A, 2, NORTH ROAD, HORNDEAN
THOMSON, PAUL J, 2, NORTH ROAD, HORNDEAN
THOMSON, VALERIE A, 2, NORTH ROAD, HORNDEAN
DAVIDGE, BERYL L, 2A, NORTH ROAD, HORNDEAN
SCOTT, PETER T, 4, NORTH ROAD, HORNDEAN
LOCKYER, CHERIE E, 6, NORTH ROAD, HORNDEAN
LOCKYER, EDWARD W, 6, NORTH ROAD, HORNDEAN
TRIM, DAVID V, 8, NORTH ROAD, HORNDEAN
TRIM, HEATHER J, 8, NORTH ROAD, HORNDEAN
TRIM, MICHAEL D, 8, NORTH ROAD, HORNDEAN
WEALD, ELAINE J, 10, NORTH ROAD, HORNDEAN
WEALD, GRAHAM, 10, NORTH ROAD, HORNDEAN
BRADSTREET, DOROTHY, 12, NORTH ROAD, HORNDEAN
BRADSTREET, WILLIAM H, 12, NORTH ROAD, HORNDEAN
ARMITAGE, FLORENCE, 14, NORTH ROAD, HORNDEAN
ARMITAGE, JOHN, 14, NORTH ROAD, HORNDEAN
JORDAN, AMANDA L, 16, NORTH ROAD, HORNDEAN
JORDAN, LOUIS, 16, NORTH ROAD, HORNDEAN
JORDAN, SUSAN P, 16, NORTH ROAD, HORNDEAN
SPICER, PETER D, 18, NORTH ROAD, HORNDEAN
SMITH, RACHEL C, 20, NORTH ROAD, HORNDEAN
SMITH, RICHARD J, 20, NORTH ROAD, HORNDEAN
SMITH, RICHARD T, 20, NORTH ROAD, HORNDEAN
SMITH, YVONNE, 20, NORTH ROAD, HORNDEAN
MILLS, RUBY M, 22, NORTH ROAD, HORNDEAN
PAYNE, MARGARET B.M, 22, NORTH ROAD, HORNDEAN
HEAD, GRAHAM L, 24, NORTH ROAD, HORNDEAN
HEAD, MAUREEN J, 24, NORTH ROAD, HORNDEAN
BRANDOM, JANET E, 26, NORTH ROAD, HORNDEAN
BRANDOM, SALLY D, 26, NORTH ROAD, HORNDEAN
MALBY, ADAM D, 28, NORTH ROAD, HORNDEAN
TAYLOR, SALLY P, 28, NORTH ROAD, HORNDEAN
WINTLE, JANICE M.A, 30, NORTH ROAD, HORNDEAN
WINTLE, MARC D, 30, NORTH ROAD, HORNDEAN
WINTLE, ROBERT J, 30, NORTH ROAD, HORNDEAN
SNELLGROVE, JEAN V, 32, NORTH ROAD, HORNDEAN
SNELLGROVE, MICHAEL F, 32, NORTH ROAD, HORNDEAN
VALENTINE, DAVID, 34, NORTH ROAD, HORNDEAN
VALENTINE, ROSEMARY A, 34, NORTH ROAD, HORNDEAN
WRIGHT, AUDREY G, 36, NORTH ROAD, HORNDEAN
WRIGHT, EDWARD T, 36, NORTH ROAD, HORNDEAN
CRIDDLE, JAMES A, 38, NORTH ROAD, HORNDEAN
CRIDDLE, JANE L, 38, NORTH ROAD, HORNDEAN
BAIRSTOW, AMY H, 40, NORTH ROAD, HORNDEAN
WHITE, GARRY C, 42, NORTH ROAD, HORNDEAN
TREAGUS, EILEEN J, 44, NORTH ROAD, HORNDEAN
TREAGUS, NORMAN, 44, NORTH ROAD, HORNDEAN
MARSHALL, PHILIPPA A, 46, NORTH ROAD, HORNDEAN
MARSHALL, ROSS T, 46, NORTH ROAD, HORNDEAN
JORDAN, DENIS W, 48, NORTH ROAD, HORNDEAN
JORDAN, PATRICIA, 48, NORTH ROAD, HORNDEAN
FULL, META E, 50, NORTH ROAD, HORNDEAN
FAIRBROTHER, JENNY P, 52, NORTH ROAD, HORNDEAN
FIDLER, JAMES, 54, NORTH ROAD, HORNDEAN
FIDLER, SANDRA E, 54, NORTH ROAD, HORNDEAN
HOBBS, MARK A, 56, NORTH ROAD, HORNDEAN
HOBBS, NICOLETTE L, 56, NORTH ROAD, HORNDEAN
PARKIN, ROBERT J, 58, NORTH ROAD, HORNDEAN
PARKIN, YOLANDE E, 58, NORTH ROAD, HORNDEAN
LEADBEATER, DOROTHY J, 60, NORTH ROAD, HORNDEAN
LYNES, SUSAN J, 62, NORTH ROAD, HORNDEAN
COOPER, NATALIE M, 64, NORTH ROAD, HORNDEAN
MCGLYNN, MATTHEW, 64, NORTH ROAD, HORNDEAN
FUDGE, PHYLLIS G, 66, NORTH ROAD, HORNDEAN
RAMSAY, ANDREW F, 68, NORTH ROAD, HORNDEAN
WARREN, LOUIS, 68, NORTH ROAD, HORNDEAN
GRAHAM, GILLIAN R, 70, NORTH ROAD, HORNDEAN
GRAHAM, MAXINE, 70, NORTH ROAD, HORNDEAN
GRAHAM, NORMAN L, 70, NORTH ROAD, HORNDEAN
FAIRALL, RAYMOND W, 72, NORTH ROAD, HORNDEAN
FAIRALL, ROBERT E, 72, NORTH ROAD, HORNDEAN
FAIRALL, YVONNE B, 72, NORTH ROAD, HORNDEAN
EASTMAN, NANCY B, 74, NORTH ROAD, HORNDEAN
BROOM, ANDREW G, 76, NORTH ROAD, HORNDEAN
BROOM, DAVID A, 76, NORTH ROAD, HORNDEAN
BROOM, FLORENCE J, 76, NORTH ROAD, HORNDEAN
HALL, ELENA I, 78, NORTH ROAD, HORNDEAN
HALL, RICHARD A.J, 78, NORTH ROAD, HORNDEAN
GIBSON, IAN C, 80, NORTH ROAD, HORNDEAN
GIBSON, JENNIFER J, 80, NORTH ROAD, HORNDEAN
MCINTYRE, KEITH M, 82, NORTH ROAD, HORNDEAN
MCINTYRE, MICHAEL T, 82, NORTH ROAD, HORNDEAN
MCINTYRE, PATRICIA A, 82, NORTH ROAD, HORNDEAN
MCINTYRE, TERENCE M, 82, NORTH ROAD, HORNDEAN
MOREMAN, BRIAN J, 84, NORTH ROAD, HORNDEAN
MOREMAN, MURIEL Y, 84, NORTH ROAD, HORNDEAN
MCDONALD, IAN, 86, NORTH ROAD, HORNDEAN
MCDONALD, MARGARET, 86, NORTH ROAD, HORNDEAN
OSGOOD, WINIFRED R, 86, NORTH ROAD, HORNDEAN
BEESON, BRIAN, 88, NORTH ROAD, HORNDEAN
BEESON, REBECCA, 88, NORTH ROAD, HORNDEAN
ANDERS, PHYLLIS M, 90, NORTH ROAD, HORNDEAN
NIGHTINGALE, AUDREY, 92, NORTH ROAD, HORNDEAN
NIGHTINGALE, JOHN, 92, NORTH ROAD, HORNDEAN
WRIGHT, ARTHUR M, 94, NORTH ROAD, HORNDEAN
WRIGHT, WINIFRED M, 94, NORTH ROAD, HORNDEAN
VIGGERS, BERYL I, 1, NORTHFIELD CLOSE, HORNDEAN
VIGGERS, SIDNEY A, 1, NORTHFIELD CLOSE, HORNDEAN
FAY, VICTORIA, 2, NORTHFIELD CLOSE, HORNDEAN
KOSTOVIC, MICKEY, 2, NORTHFIELD CLOSE, HORNDEAN
POULSON, CHRISTOPHER P, 3, NORTHFIELD CLOSE,
POULSON, KATIE, 3, NORTHFIELD CLOSE, HORNDEAN
POULSON, LESLEY L.E, 3, NORTHFIELD CLOSE, HORNDEAN
POULSON, NORMAN, 3, NORTHFIELD CLOSE, HORNDEAN
REITH, CLAIRE H, 4, NORTHFIELD CLOSE, HORNDEAN
REITH, MALCOLM S, 4, NORTHFIELD CLOSE, HORNDEAN
REITH, STUART, 4, NORTHFIELD CLOSE, HORNDEAN
REITH, SUSAN J, 4, NORTHFIELD CLOSE, HORNDEAN
FENTIMAN, VIDA F, 5, NORTHFIELD CLOSE, HORNDEAN
NASH, DAVID M, 6, NORTHFIELD CLOSE, HORNDEAN
NASH, LOUISE A, 6, NORTHFIELD CLOSE, HORNDEAN
PAPE, KENNETH J, 7, NORTHFIELD CLOSE, HORNDEAN
CHIPPS, STEPHEN E, 8, NORTHFIELD CLOSE, HORNDEAN
CHIPPS, TERESA J, 8, NORTHFIELD CLOSE, HORNDEAN
REDDING, ANDREW M, 9, NORTHFIELD CLOSE, HORNDEAN
REDDING, HELEN E, 9, NORTHFIELD CLOSE, HORNDEAN
LYNN, ANDREW M, 10, NORTHFIELD CLOSE, HORNDEAN
LYNN, ANNETTE P, 10, NORTHFIELD CLOSE, HORNDEAN
WIFFEN, FRANCIS G, 11, NORTHFIELD CLOSE, HORNDEAN
WIFFEN, JUDITH A, 11, NORTHFIELD CLOSE, HORNDEAN
WIFFEN, KARYN A, 11, NORTHFIELD CLOSE, HORNDEAN
WIFFEN, SIMON M, 11, NORTHFIELD CLOSE, HORNDEAN
MOSS, RUSSELL H, 12, NORTHFIELD CLOSE, HORNDEAN
MOSS, SUSAN M, 12, NORTHFIELD CLOSE, HORNDEAN
AYRES, WILLIAM R, 13, NORTHFIELD CLOSE, HORNDEAN
BURNARD, GEOFFREY L, 13, NORTHFIELD CLOSE,
PENNEY, JOHN P, 14, NORTHFIELD CLOSE, HORNDEAN
PENNEY, JOHN P (JNR), 14, NORTHFIELD CLOSE, HORNDEAN
PENNEY, MARY B, 14, NORTHFIELD CLOSE, HORNDEAN
HUGHES, JENNIFER M, 15, NORTHFIELD CLOSE, HORNDEAN
HUGHES, ROBIN, 15, NORTHFIELD CLOSE, HORNDEAN
RUSSELL, PAUL A, 16, NORTHFIELD CLOSE, HORNDEAN
IDE, TINA S, 17, NORTHFIELD CLOSE, HORNDEAN
STRANGEWAY, MICHAEL, 17, NORTHFIELD CLOSE,
COOMBS, STEPHEN W, 18, NORTHFIELD CLOSE, HORNDEAN
TYLER, JANICE C, 18, NORTHFIELD CLOSE, HORNDEAN
MELLA, JENNIFER, 19, NORTHFIELD CLOSE, HORNDEAN
MELLA, MARTIN, 19, NORTHFIELD CLOSE, HORNDEAN
CARLOS-PERKINS, DOREEN S, SPENCERS, OLD LANE,
HOSKINS, EDNA J, 1, ROMSEY ROAD, HORNDEAN
HOSKINS, GEOFFREY A, 1, ROMSEY ROAD, HORNDEAN
PRINCE, MAVIS J, 2, ROMSEY ROAD, HORNDEAN
OSBORN, KENNETH R, 3, ROMSEY ROAD, HORNDEAN
OSBORN, SHEILA M, 3, ROMSEY ROAD, HORNDEAN
BROOKES, NORMAN, 4, ROMSEY ROAD, HORNDEAN

DOBA, BENJAMIN, 5, ROMSEY ROAD, HORNDEAN
DOBA, LINDA J, 5, ROMSEY ROAD, HORNDEAN
DOBA, SHAUN B, 5, ROMSEY ROAD, HORNDEAN
HILLS, ANDREA C, 6, ROMSEY ROAD, HORNDEAN
ROMP, DARRIN M, 6, ROMSEY ROAD, HORNDEAN
MARSH, CHRISTINA A, 7, ROMSEY ROAD, HORNDEAN
MARSH, ROBERT F, 7, ROMSEY ROAD, HORNDEAN
DALE, CHRISTINE, 8, ROMSEY ROAD, HORNDEAN
DALE, VICTOR H, 8, ROMSEY ROAD, HORNDEAN
SUTHERLAND, JOAN L, 9, ROMSEY ROAD, HORNDEAN
SUTHERLAND, JOHN E.G, 9, ROMSEY ROAD, HORNDEAN
COWEN, MICHAEL, 10, ROMSEY ROAD, HORNDEAN
COWEN, TINA C, 10, ROMSEY ROAD, HORNDEAN
ISGAR, HILDA C, 11, ROMSEY ROAD, HORNDEAN
WARD, LESLIE J.C, 12, ROMSEY ROAD, HORNDEAN
WARD, VALERIE J, 12, ROMSEY ROAD, HORNDEAN
LEGGAT, GRAHAM Y, 13, ROMSEY ROAD, HORNDEAN
STEVENS, IAN G, 14, ROMSEY ROAD, HORNDEAN
DOWLING, THOMAS, 15, ROMSEY ROAD, HORNDEAN
DOWLING, VIOLET A, 15, ROMSEY ROAD, HORNDEAN
FEGREDO, IVAN D, 16, ROMSEY ROAD, HORNDEAN
FEGREDO, JACQUELINE E, 16, ROMSEY ROAD, HORNDEAN
LANE, ALAN C, 17, ROMSEY ROAD, HORNDEAN
LANE, MAUREEN E, 17, ROMSEY ROAD, HORNDEAN
HAYNES, ANTHONY G, 18, ROMSEY ROAD, HORNDEAN
HAYNES, MAUREEN, 18, ROMSEY ROAD, HORNDEAN
CROSS, LILIAN D, 19, ROMSEY ROAD, HORNDEAN
OWEN, DOROTHY J, 20, ROMSEY ROAD, HORNDEAN
OWEN, ROBERT G, 20, ROMSEY ROAD, HORNDEAN
BROWNE, EDITH M, 1, ST. ANDREW CLOSE, HORNDEAN
BROWNE, THOMAS A, 1, ST. ANDREW CLOSE, HORNDEAN
SHAW, ALAN P, 2, ST. ANDREW CLOSE, HORNDEAN
SHAW, AMANDA, 2, ST. ANDREW CLOSE, HORNDEAN
SHAW, KAREN E, 2, ST. ANDREW CLOSE, HORNDEAN
SHAW, KELLY J, 2, ST. ANDREW CLOSE, HORNDEAN
SHAW, PETER W, 2, ST. ANDREW CLOSE, HORNDEAN
COZENS, KENNETH J, 3, ST. ANDREW CLOSE, HORNDEAN
COZENS, MOYA E, 3, ST. ANDREW CLOSE, HORNDEAN
PEACOCK, BRENDAN, 4, ST. ANDREW CLOSE, HORNDEAN
PEACOCK, DIANE H, 4, ST. ANDREW CLOSE, HORNDEAN
THOMPSON, DEREK P.W, 5, ST. ANDREW CLOSE, HORNDEAN
THOMPSON, FRANCES, 5, ST. ANDREW CLOSE, HORNDEAN
CUMMING, ADRIAN, 6, ST. ANDREW CLOSE, HORNDEAN
CUMMING, JACQUELINE F, 6, ST. ANDREW CLOSE,
CUMMING, MATTHEW F, 6, ST. ANDREW CLOSE, HORNDEAN
KERR, ALEXANDER R, 7, ST. ANDREW CLOSE, HORNDEAN
KERR, LINDA R, 7, ST. ANDREW CLOSE, HORNDEAN
KERR, SUZANNAH L, 7, ST. ANDREW CLOSE, HORNDEAN
BOSLEY, PETA A, 8, ST. ANDREW CLOSE, HORNDEAN
BOSLEY, STEPHEN R, 8, ST. ANDREW CLOSE, HORNDEAN
LEWIS, BRYAN F, 9, ST. ANDREW CLOSE, HORNDEAN
LEWIS, JASON S, 9, ST. ANDREW CLOSE, HORNDEAN
LEWIS, SUZANNE, 9, ST. ANDREW CLOSE, HORNDEAN
SMITH, JOAN, 10, ST. ANDREW CLOSE, HORNDEAN
SMITH, ROBERT S, 10, ST. ANDREW CLOSE, HORNDEAN
PEARSON, PHYLLIS L, 11, ST. ANDREW CLOSE, HORNDEAN
PEARSON, RONALD W, 11, ST. ANDREW CLOSE, HORNDEAN
HASSELL, HORACE W, 1, ST. GILES WAY, HORNDEAN
HASSELL, VALERIE R, 1, ST. GILES WAY, HORNDEAN
GARRARD, SHIRLEY W, 2, ST. GILES WAY, HORNDEAN
GARRARD, WILLIAM J, 2, ST. GILES WAY, HORNDEAN
COX, BRIAN, 3, ST. GILES WAY, HORNDEAN
DOYLE, SHEILA R, 3, ST. GILES WAY, HORNDEAN
HAYTER, DEREK J, 4, ST. GILES WAY, HORNDEAN
HAYTER, LYNN T, 4, ST. GILES WAY, HORNDEAN
CLARKE, COLIN N, 5, ST. GILES WAY, HORNDEAN
CLARKE, JANETTE, 5, ST. GILES WAY, HORNDEAN
DAUGHTRY, ANTHONY R.J, 6, ST. GILES WAY, HORNDEAN
DAUGHTRY, JEANETTE L, 6, ST. GILES WAY, HORNDEAN
DAUGHTRY, MICHELLE L, 6, ST. GILES WAY, HORNDEAN
HOBBINS, BARRY R, 7, ST. GILES WAY, HORNDEAN
HOBBINS, DARREN R, 7, ST. GILES WAY, HORNDEAN
HOBBINS, DENNIS R, 7, ST. GILES WAY, HORNDEAN
HOBBINS, ROSALIND P, 7, ST. GILES WAY, HORNDEAN
RENCOURT, RICHARD M, 8, ST. GILES WAY, HORNDEAN
RENCOURT, SHEILA J, 8, ST. GILES WAY, HORNDEAN
OLIVER, DOROTHY F, 9, ST. GILES WAY, HORNDEAN
OLIVER, MARGARET, 9, ST. GILES WAY, HORNDEAN
ROE, JOHN A, 10, ST. GILES WAY, HORNDEAN
NEWHAM, CHRISTOPHER J, 12, ST. GILES WAY, HORNDEAN
NEWHAM, RICHARD E, 12, ST. GILES WAY, HORNDEAN
NEWHAM, SUSAN M, 12, ST. GILES WAY, HORNDEAN
JOHNSTONE, DUNCAN, 1, ST. HILDA AVENUE, HORNDEAN
JOHNSTONE, LESLEY, 1, ST. HILDA AVENUE, HORNDEAN
WALKER, JOHN A, 2, ST. HILDA AVENUE, HORNDEAN
WALKER, TERESA, 2, ST. HILDA AVENUE, HORNDEAN
COLDRICK, ROBERT J, 3, ST. HILDA AVENUE, HORNDEAN
COLDRICK, TRACY A, 3, ST. HILDA AVENUE, HORNDEAN
COOK, DEBORAH J, 4, ST. HILDA AVENUE, HORNDEAN
COOK, KEVIN N, 4, ST. HILDA AVENUE, HORNDEAN
CRISP, ALISON L, 5, ST. HILDA AVENUE, HORNDEAN
CRISP, PAUL J, 5, ST. HILDA AVENUE, HORNDEAN
MATHERS, KEVIN A, 6, ST. HILDA AVENUE, HORNDEAN
MATHERS, SAMANTHA T, 6, ST. HILDA AVENUE, HORNDEAN
MULLINS, MARGARET A, 7, ST. HILDA AVENUE, HORNDEAN
MULLINS, NICOLA M, 7, ST. HILDA AVENUE, HORNDEAN
MIHELL, PAUL S, 8, ST. HILDA AVENUE, HORNDEAN
WILSON, LAURA, 8, ST. HILDA AVENUE, HORNDEAN
TOWNS, EVELINE M, 9, ST. HILDA AVENUE, HORNDEAN
TOWNS, JOHN W.E, 9, ST. HILDA AVENUE, HORNDEAN
TOWNS, MATTHEW J, 9, ST. HILDA AVENUE, HORNDEAN
TOWNS, RUSSELL J, 9, ST. HILDA AVENUE, HORNDEAN
HADDOW, ANTONY J, 10, ST. HILDA AVENUE, HORNDEAN
HADDOW, BARBARA A, 10, ST. HILDA AVENUE, HORNDEAN
JOHNSON, ANTONY M, 11, ST. HILDA AVENUE, HORNDEAN
JOHNSON, JULIE M, 11, ST. HILDA AVENUE, HORNDEAN
COLE, JULIE L, 12, ST. HILDA AVENUE, HORNDEAN
COLE, JUSTIN P, 12, ST. HILDA AVENUE, HORNDEAN
PARHAM, CAROL D, 13, ST. HILDA AVENUE, HORNDEAN
PARHAM, DAVID A, 13, ST. HILDA AVENUE, HORNDEAN
TAYLOR, COLIN E, 14, ST. HILDA AVENUE, HORNDEAN
TAYLOR, LEWIS C, 14, ST. HILDA AVENUE, HORNDEAN
TAYLOR, LYNDA J, 14, ST. HILDA AVENUE, HORNDEAN
TAYLOR, WESLEY J, 14, ST. HILDA AVENUE, HORNDEAN
SHERRINGTON, JAN, 15, ST. HILDA AVENUE, HORNDEAN
SHERRINGTON, PEGGY J, 15, ST. HILDA AVENUE, HORNDEAN
SMITH, GARY J, 16, ST. HILDA AVENUE, HORNDEAN
SMITH, SUZANNE J, 16, ST. HILDA AVENUE, HORNDEAN
LONG, LUCINDA G, 17, ST. HILDA AVENUE, HORNDEAN
LONG, PETER J, 17, ST. HILDA AVENUE, HORNDEAN
HALE, MANDY L, 18, ST. HILDA AVENUE, HORNDEAN
HALE, PAUL A, 18, ST. HILDA AVENUE, HORNDEAN
GREIG, DAVID P, 19, ST. HILDA AVENUE, HORNDEAN
HIOM, LINDA A, 19, ST. HILDA AVENUE, HORNDEAN
CHANT, CONSTANCE H, 20, ST. HILDA AVENUE, HORNDEAN
CHANT, DARREN J, 20, ST. HILDA AVENUE, HORNDEAN
THOMPSAL, JEAN C, 20, ST. HILDA AVENUE, HORNDEAN
HOWLETT, KEVIN, 21, ST. HILDA AVENUE, HORNDEAN
BRAMWELL, STEPHEN J, 22, ST. HILDA AVENUE, HORNDEAN
HIOM, DAVID H, 22, ST. HILDA AVENUE, HORNDEAN
HIOM, JACQUELINE A, 22, ST. HILDA AVENUE, HORNDEAN
BROWN, ALAN K, 23, ST. HILDA AVENUE, HORNDEAN
BROWN, FAY M, 23, ST. HILDA AVENUE, HORNDEAN
BROWN, LINDA A, 23, ST. HILDA AVENUE, HORNDEAN
BROWN, THOMAS E, 23, ST. HILDA AVENUE, HORNDEAN
FELTHAM, JAYNE, 24, ST. HILDA AVENUE, HORNDEAN
FELTHAM, WAYNE, 24, ST. HILDA AVENUE, HORNDEAN
ROWNEY, IAN T, 25, ST. HILDA AVENUE, HORNDEAN
ROWNEY, JANE E, 25, ST. HILDA AVENUE, HORNDEAN
ROSE, BEVERLY M, 26, ST. HILDA AVENUE, HORNDEAN
HAMILTON, CLIFFORD J, 27, ST. HILDA AVENUE, HORNDEAN
HAMILTON, MAUREEN V, 27, ST. HILDA AVENUE, HORNDEAN
MARDLE, DAVID E, 28, ST. HILDA AVENUE, HORNDEAN
MARDLE, PATRICIA M, 28, ST. HILDA AVENUE, HORNDEAN
HARVEY, DAVID G, 29, ST. HILDA AVENUE, HORNDEAN
HARVEY, DREENA E.A, 29, ST. HILDA AVENUE, HORNDEAN
HARVEY, STUART V, 29, ST. HILDA AVENUE, HORNDEAN
CUNNAH, DAVID L, 1, ST. HUBERT ROAD, HORNDEAN
CUNNAH, MARGARET A, 1, ST. HUBERT ROAD, HORNDEAN
LEWIS, DAVID C, 3, ST. HUBERT ROAD, HORNDEAN
LEWIS, SHIRLEY A, 3, ST. HUBERT ROAD, HORNDEAN
WOODS, CHRISTINE E, 5, ST. HUBERT ROAD, HORNDEAN
WOODS, DAVID A, 5, ST. HUBERT ROAD, HORNDEAN
WILLIAMS, MARY C, 7, ST. HUBERT ROAD, HORNDEAN
WILLIAMS, PETER D, 7, ST. HUBERT ROAD, HORNDEAN
PICKFORD, KATHLEEN M, 9, ST. HUBERT ROAD, HORNDEAN
PICKFORD, SUSAN M, 9, ST. HUBERT ROAD, HORNDEAN
CAPELING, HILDA M, 2, ST. HUBERT ROAD, HORNDEAN
MCVEIGH, IDA, 2, ST. HUBERT ROAD, HORNDEAN
GAMBLE, MARTYN S, 4, ST. HUBERT ROAD, HORNDEAN
GAMBLE, TERESA F, 4, ST. HUBERT ROAD, HORNDEAN
EVISON, JOHN D, 6, ST. HUBERT ROAD, HORNDEAN
EVISON, JOYCE M, 6, ST. HUBERT ROAD, HORNDEAN
MORRIS, ROBERT G.C, 8, ST. HUBERT ROAD, HORNDEAN
EDWARDS, JOSEPH M, 10, ST. HUBERT ROAD, HORNDEAN
EDWARDS, VANESSA A, 10, ST. HUBERT ROAD, HORNDEAN
HAYTER, ANDREW P, 1, ST. MICHAELS WAY, HORNDEAN
STONELAKE, KATHRINE, 1, ST. MICHAELS WAY, HORNDEAN
ROGERS, JULIE A, 2, ST. MICHAELS WAY, HORNDEAN
ROGERS, STEPHEN J, 2, ST. MICHAELS WAY, HORNDEAN
BRAY, FREDERICK G, 3, ST. MICHAELS WAY, HORNDEAN
BRAY, MAUREEN J, 3, ST. MICHAELS WAY, HORNDEAN
STALLARD, RONALD K, 4, ST. MICHAELS WAY, HORNDEAN
HUDSON, DEREK C, 5, ST. MICHAELS WAY, HORNDEAN
WATTS, SHIRLEY R, 5, ST. MICHAELS WAY, HORNDEAN
REEVES, ANTHONY R, 6, ST. MICHAELS WAY, HORNDEAN
REEVES, NONA M, 6, ST. MICHAELS WAY, HORNDEAN
CHILDS, WILLIAM J, 7, ST. MICHAELS WAY, HORNDEAN
MUNFORD, EVELYN M, 8, ST. MICHAELS WAY, HORNDEAN
MUNFORD, MICHAEL L, 8, ST. MICHAELS WAY, HORNDEAN
MUNFORD, TRACEY R, 8, ST. MICHAELS WAY, HORNDEAN
SKINNER, DONALD H, 9, ST. MICHAELS WAY, HORNDEAN
SKINNER, TERESA, 9, ST. MICHAELS WAY, HORNDEAN
STARES, ARTHUR T.W, 10, ST. MICHAELS WAY, HORNDEAN
STARES, MAUREEN R, 10, ST. MICHAELS WAY, HORNDEAN
DENNIS, JOHN E, 11, ST. MICHAELS WAY, HORNDEAN
DENNIS, MARIE A, 11, ST. MICHAELS WAY, HORNDEAN
PENDLE, JOAN K, 12, ST. MICHAELS WAY, HORNDEAN
PENDLE, JOHN H.D, 12, ST. MICHAELS WAY, HORNDEAN
SEARLE, HAROLD, 13, ST. MICHAELS WAY, HORNDEAN
SEARLE, JEANNE K, 13, ST. MICHAELS WAY, HORNDEAN
BATCHELER, ANDREW, 14, ST. MICHAELS WAY, HORNDEAN
BATCHELER, SIMON R, 14, ST. MICHAELS WAY, HORNDEAN
KYNASTON, LINDA C, 14, ST. MICHAELS WAY, HORNDEAN
BIGGS, JAMES E, 15, ST. MICHAELS WAY, HORNDEAN
BIGGS, KEITH M, 15, ST. MICHAELS WAY, HORNDEAN
BIGGS, SHEILA J, 15, ST. MICHAELS WAY, HORNDEAN
PROBERT, ANTHONY P, 16, ST. MICHAELS WAY, HORNDEAN
PROBERT, ROSEMARY K, 16, ST. MICHAELS WAY, HORNDEAN
BODELL, KEVIN J, 17, ST. MICHAELS WAY, HORNDEAN
BROWNE, FIONA C, 18, ST. MICHAELS WAY, HORNDEAN
RICHARDSON, DAVID P, 18, ST. MICHAELS WAY, HORNDEAN
BURNS, ALEXANDER J, 19, ST. MICHAELS WAY, HORNDEAN
BURNS, VIOLET, 19, ST. MICHAELS WAY, HORNDEAN
LANCASTER, ALAN, 20, ST. MICHAELS WAY, HORNDEAN
LANCASTER, MARY, 20, ST. MICHAELS WAY, HORNDEAN
HAYTER, DENISE V, 1, SAXON CLOSE, HORNDEAN
HAYTER, LEE P, 1, SAXON CLOSE, HORNDEAN
PAYNE, ELAINE M, 2, SAXON CLOSE, HORNDEAN
SMITH, PAUL T, 3, SAXON CLOSE, HORNDEAN
SMITH, REBECCA A, 3, SAXON CLOSE, HORNDEAN
SMITH, TARINA A, 3, SAXON CLOSE, HORNDEAN
MURDOCH, PAULA, 4, SAXON CLOSE, HORNDEAN
BLYTH, CHRISTINE J, 5, SAXON CLOSE, HORNDEAN
KINGE, TINA R, 5, SAXON CLOSE, HORNDEAN
EVANS, SUSAN M, 6, SAXON CLOSE, HORNDEAN
JERRUM, JOHN, 7, SAXON CLOSE, HORNDEAN
JERRUM, SHEILA F, 7, SAXON CLOSE, HORNDEAN
WOOD, DAVID, 9, SAXON CLOSE, HORNDEAN
WOOD, LINDA M, 9, SAXON CLOSE, HORNDEAN
WOOD, PAUL M, 9, SAXON CLOSE, HORNDEAN
STREET, LESLIE S, 10, SAXON CLOSE, HORNDEAN
CARPENTER, KEITH, 11, SAXON CLOSE, HORNDEAN
HELLIER, MARK J, 11, SAXON CLOSE, HORNDEAN
POLLARD, GEORGE A, 12, SAXON CLOSE, HORNDEAN
BARROW, BRIAN L, 13, SAXON CLOSE, HORNDEAN
BARROW, SHIRLEY E, 13, SAXON CLOSE, HORNDEAN
JERRUM, JEAN M, 15, SAXON CLOSE, HORNDEAN
JOLLEY, DOROTHY M, 16, SAXON CLOSE, HORNDEAN
CURTIS, NICHOLA, 18, SAXON CLOSE, HORNDEAN
SMALL, MICHELLE J, 19, SAXON CLOSE, HORNDEAN
ROBINSON, AMANDA, 20, SAXON CLOSE, HORNDEAN
MIROY, MARY R, 21, SAXON CLOSE, HORNDEAN
COLWILL, MAXINE M, 22, SAXON CLOSE, HORNDEAN
SMITH, JULIA M, 23, SAXON CLOSE, HORNDEAN
SMITH, LESLIE G, 23, SAXON CLOSE, HORNDEAN
DEAR, ADRIAN P, 1, SOUTH ROAD, HORNDEAN
DEAR, MOLLY A, 1, SOUTH ROAD, HORNDEAN
MUSTCHIN, DEREK G, 3, SOUTH ROAD, HORNDEAN
MUSTCHIN, JEAN A, 3, SOUTH ROAD, HORNDEAN
LEIGH, MARTYN D, 5, SOUTH ROAD, HORNDEAN
LEIGH, SUSAN L, 5, SOUTH ROAD, HORNDEAN
WILLIAMSON, MARTIN K, 7, SOUTH ROAD, HORNDEAN
BAMBROUGH, JOHN A, 9, SOUTH ROAD, HORNDEAN
WIGLEY, RONALD C, 11, SOUTH ROAD, HORNDEAN
BARNETT, DESMOND J, 13, SOUTH ROAD, HORNDEAN
BARNETT, TERESA K, 13, SOUTH ROAD, HORNDEAN
WELLSTEAD, CHRISTOPHER T, 15, SOUTH ROAD, HORNDEAN
WELLSTEAD, JANE E, 15, SOUTH ROAD, HORNDEAN
HARPER, JAMES P, 17, SOUTH ROAD, HORNDEAN
HARPER, SUSANNE M, 17, SOUTH ROAD, HORNDEAN
VAN WIJK, CHRISTINE, 19, SOUTH ROAD, HORNDEAN
VAN WIJK, JENNI M, 19, SOUTH ROAD, HORNDEAN
VAN WIJK, JOEY, 19, SOUTH ROAD, HORNDEAN
FAIRBROTHER, CHRISTOPHER O, 21, SOUTH ROAD,
SANDERCOCK, DAPHNE E, 21, SOUTH ROAD, HORNDEAN
YOUNG, CATHERINE M, 23, SOUTH ROAD, HORNDEAN
YOUNG, DAVID P, 23, SOUTH ROAD, HORNDEAN
WRIGHT, ANGELA M, 25, SOUTH ROAD, HORNDEAN
WRIGHT, DEREK R, 25, SOUTH ROAD, HORNDEAN
GREEN, CAROL, 31A, SOUTH ROAD, HORNDEAN
GREEN, MICHAEL, 31A, SOUTH ROAD, HORNDEAN
BASSETT, ANNALESA C, 33, SOUTH ROAD, HORNDEAN
BASSETT, ELEONOR M, 33, SOUTH ROAD, HORNDEAN
BASSETT, MARTYN C, 33, SOUTH ROAD, HORNDEAN
BASSETT, MATTHEW J, 33, SOUTH ROAD, HORNDEAN
BASSETT, SUSAN A, 33, SOUTH ROAD, HORNDEAN
SHAW, ANN W, 35, SOUTH ROAD, HORNDEAN
SHAW, SIMON K, 35, SOUTH ROAD, HORNDEAN
FREEMAN, ALISON L, 35A, SOUTH ROAD, HORNDEAN
FREEMAN, SIMON R, 35A, SOUTH ROAD, HORNDEAN
BARNES, JOSEPH, 37, SOUTH ROAD, HORNDEAN
BARNES, VERA N, 37, SOUTH ROAD, HORNDEAN
KNIGHT, PETER G, 39, SOUTH ROAD, HORNDEAN
KNIGHT, ROGER G, 39, SOUTH ROAD, HORNDEAN
KNIGHT, VALERIE K, 39, SOUTH ROAD, HORNDEAN
ROSS, IAN M.G, 41, SOUTH ROAD, HORNDEAN
ROSS, SHAUN M, 41, SOUTH ROAD, HORNDEAN
ROSS, SUSAN P, 41, SOUTH ROAD, HORNDEAN
SULLIVAN, LISA M, 47, SOUTH ROAD, HORNDEAN
SULLIVAN, MICHAEL, 47, SOUTH ROAD, HORNDEAN
SULLIVAN, PAULA V, 47, SOUTH ROAD, HORNDEAN
SULLIVAN, RACHEL P, 47, SOUTH ROAD, HORNDEAN
BOLTON, MARK C, 51, SOUTH ROAD, HORNDEAN
EVANS, VIOLET, 51, SOUTH ROAD, HORNDEAN
WALKER, CHRISTINE A, 53, SOUTH ROAD, HORNDEAN
WALKER, ROLAND B, 53, SOUTH ROAD, HORNDEAN
GREGOR, MICHELLE R, 55, SOUTH ROAD, HORNDEAN
PERRY, GEORGE, 55, SOUTH ROAD, HORNDEAN
PERRY, SUSAN, 55, SOUTH ROAD, HORNDEAN
FLEMING, MARY D, 57, SOUTH ROAD, HORNDEAN
RINGROSE, BARBARA A, 59, SOUTH ROAD, HORNDEAN
RINGROSE, BRIAN S, 59, SOUTH ROAD, HORNDEAN
COMPTON, ANDREW M, 61, SOUTH ROAD, HORNDEAN
COMPTON, HELEN S, 61, SOUTH ROAD, HORNDEAN
EDWARDS, RODNEY K, 63, SOUTH ROAD, HORNDEAN
PARKES, DAKSHA, 63, SOUTH ROAD, HORNDEAN
SNELGROVE, ROBERT J, 65, SOUTH ROAD, HORNDEAN
SUMMERS, JOHN A, 67, SOUTH ROAD, HORNDEAN
SUMMERS, LUCY M, 67, SOUTH ROAD, HORNDEAN
SQUIRES, DAVID F, 69, SOUTH ROAD, HORNDEAN
SQUIRES, JUDITH, 69, SOUTH ROAD, HORNDEAN
BARRY, SHARON E, 71, SOUTH ROAD, HORNDEAN
BARRY, TIMOTHY J, 71, SOUTH ROAD, HORNDEAN
BALDWIN, DARREN C, 73, SOUTH ROAD, HORNDEAN
WYATT, JOANNE S, 73, SOUTH ROAD, HORNDEAN
TILLER, LORAYNE M, 75, SOUTH ROAD, HORNDEAN
TILLER, LOUISE, 75, SOUTH ROAD, HORNDEAN
TILLER, NATALIE, 75, SOUTH ROAD, HORNDEAN

Electoral Roll

TILLER, WILLIAM R, 75, SOUTH ROAD, HORNDEAN
HIGHAM, KAY M, 77, SOUTH ROAD, HORNDEAN
HIGHAM, STEPHEN K, 77, SOUTH ROAD, HORNDEAN
IREDALE, ALBERT, 79, SOUTH ROAD, HORNDEAN
IREDALE, MOLLIE N, 79, SOUTH ROAD, HORNDEAN
IREDALE, ROBERT J, 79, SOUTH ROAD, HORNDEAN
MAIDMENT, RICHARD J, 81, SOUTH ROAD, HORNDEAN
MAIDMENT, TERRY I, 81, SOUTH ROAD, HORNDEAN
WINGATE, CARLY A, 83, SOUTH ROAD, HORNDEAN
WINGATE, LISA A, 83, SOUTH ROAD, HORNDEAN
WINGATE, STEPHEN, 83, SOUTH ROAD, HORNDEAN
SWIERS, ANNETTE M, 85, SOUTH ROAD, HORNDEAN
SWIERS, STEPHEN J, 85, SOUTH ROAD, HORNDEAN
KIRBY, JANET H, 87, SOUTH ROAD, HORNDEAN
KIRBY, JASON A, 87, SOUTH ROAD, HORNDEAN
WILKINS, FRANCES J, 89, SOUTH ROAD, HORNDEAN
WILKINS, JOHN, 89, SOUTH ROAD, HORNDEAN
HUTCHINGS, MADELAINE D, 91, SOUTH ROAD, HORNDEAN
BRIDLE, JOHN L, 93, SOUTH ROAD, HORNDEAN
BRIDLE, SANDRA H, 93, SOUTH ROAD, HORNDEAN
SOUTEN, ALBERT E, 95, SOUTH ROAD, HORNDEAN
SOUTEN, PAMELA H.D, 95, SOUTH ROAD, HORNDEAN
LEE, ANTHONY J, 97, SOUTH ROAD, HORNDEAN
LEE, PATRICIA A, 97, SOUTH ROAD, HORNDEAN
FOSTER, ANTON K, 99, SOUTH ROAD, HORNDEAN
FOSTER, DEBERA C, 99, SOUTH ROAD, HORNDEAN
COOMBES, CLAIR L, 101, SOUTH ROAD, HORNDEAN
SKINNER, TREVOR G, 101, SOUTH ROAD, HORNDEAN
MUNT, GAIL, 103, SOUTH ROAD, HORNDEAN
MUNT, TREVOR C, 103, SOUTH ROAD, HORNDEAN
HART, JOHN, 103A, SOUTH ROAD, HORNDEAN
HART, PATRICIA, 103A, SOUTH ROAD, HORNDEAN
WHITE, CAREY J, 105, SOUTH ROAD, HORNDEAN
WHITE, PAUL S, 105, SOUTH ROAD, HORNDEAN
HYDE, LILIAN E, 107, SOUTH ROAD, HORNDEAN
HYDE, PETER R, 107, SOUTH ROAD, HORNDEAN
INGRAM, DAVID N, 109, SOUTH ROAD, HORNDEAN
INGRAM, VICTORIA A, 109, SOUTH ROAD, HORNDEAN
HARRIS, ALEXANDER R, 111, SOUTH ROAD, HORNDEAN
HARRIS, ALMA J, 111, SOUTH ROAD, HORNDEAN
HUGHES, GREGORY M, 113, SOUTH ROAD, HORNDEAN
HUGHES, SARAH H, 113, SOUTH ROAD, HORNDEAN
WALKER, CORROL A, 115, SOUTH ROAD, HORNDEAN
WALKER, LOUIS T, 115, SOUTH ROAD, HORNDEAN
KERBY, DEREK L, 117, SOUTH ROAD, HORNDEAN
RAINES, ALISON F, 119, SOUTH ROAD, HORNDEAN
RAINES, STEPHEN W, 119, SOUTH ROAD, HORNDEAN
STREVETT, JEAN M, 129, SOUTH ROAD, HORNDEAN
STREVETT, KEITH J, 129, SOUTH ROAD, HORNDEAN
HOWARD-HARWOOD, IAN P, 131, SOUTH ROAD, HORNDEAN
HOWARD-HARWOOD, LUKE I, 131, SOUTH ROAD, HORNDEAN
HOWARD-HARWOOD, SUSAN E, 131, SOUTH ROAD,
STEEL, JOAN M, 133, SOUTH ROAD, HORNDEAN
STEEL, RALPH R, 133, SOUTH ROAD, HORNDEAN
MINKER, DEBORAH, 135, SOUTH ROAD, HORNDEAN
MINKER, GARY R, 135, SOUTH ROAD, HORNDEAN
PHIPPS, DAVID N, 137, SOUTH ROAD, HORNDEAN
RYDER, GWENDOLINE, 2, SOUTH ROAD, HORNDEAN
JOHNSON, DAPHNE V, 4, SOUTH ROAD, HORNDEAN
LONGCROFT-WHEATON, GAIUS R, 6, SOUTH ROAD,
LONGCROFT-WHEATON, OCTAVIUS R, 6, SOUTH ROAD,
WHEATON, RICHARD J, 6, SOUTH ROAD, HORNDEAN
WHEATON, SANDRA J, 6, SOUTH ROAD, HORNDEAN
COLE, ANNA, 8, SOUTH ROAD, HORNDEAN
BOYDEN, EDITH G, 10, SOUTH ROAD, HORNDEAN
BOYDEN, GEORGE R, 10, SOUTH ROAD, HORNDEAN
HAIMES, DAVID I.F, 12, SOUTH ROAD, HORNDEAN
HAIMES, SANDRA J, 12, SOUTH ROAD, HORNDEAN
WEBBER, BRYAN H.J, 14, SOUTH ROAD, HORNDEAN
WEBBER, JOSEPHINE M, 14, SOUTH ROAD, HORNDEAN
COX, HARRY M.G, 16, SOUTH ROAD, HORNDEAN
COX, MARGARET B, 16, SOUTH ROAD, HORNDEAN
COX, PETER, 16, SOUTH ROAD, HORNDEAN
SYMON, AMANDA D, 18, SOUTH ROAD, HORNDEAN
SYMON, DAVID C, 18, SOUTH ROAD, HORNDEAN
WHELAN, OLIVIA, 18, SOUTH ROAD, HORNDEAN
STEWART, JEAN A.L, 20, SOUTH ROAD, HORNDEAN
STEWART, WILLIAM, 20, SOUTH ROAD, HORNDEAN
UNDERWOOD, SYLVIA E, 22, SOUTH ROAD, HORNDEAN
UNDERWOOD, THOMAS A, 22, SOUTH ROAD, HORNDEAN
MCDOWELL, ERIC J, 34, SOUTH ROAD, HORNDEAN
MCDOWELL, KATHLEEN M, 34, SOUTH ROAD, HORNDEAN
HUNTER, PAULA D, 36, SOUTH ROAD, HORNDEAN
TREVELLICK, JASON P, 38, SOUTH ROAD, HORNDEAN
TREVELLICK, PETER B, 38, SOUTH ROAD, HORNDEAN
TREVELLICK, SUSAN M, 38, SOUTH ROAD, HORNDEAN
BROWN, PETER A, 40, SOUTH ROAD, HORNDEAN
CARPENTER, SHIRLEY A, 40, SOUTH ROAD, HORNDEAN
BOTT, CHARIS A, 42, SOUTH ROAD, HORNDEAN
BOTT, JOY E, 42, SOUTH ROAD, HORNDEAN
BOTT, ROBYN K, 42, SOUTH ROAD, HORNDEAN
BALCHIN, JANETTE, 44, SOUTH ROAD, HORNDEAN
BALCHIN, STANLEY R, 44, SOUTH ROAD, HORNDEAN
MERRETT, LINDA H, 46, SOUTH ROAD, HORNDEAN
WAY, STEPHEN R, 46, SOUTH ROAD, HORNDEAN
CHANNING, JOSEPHINE A, 48, SOUTH ROAD, HORNDEAN
CHANNING, MICHAEL S, 48, SOUTH ROAD, HORNDEAN
CHANNING, REGINALD M.J, 48, SOUTH ROAD, HORNDEAN
THURGOOD, EILEEN, 50, SOUTH ROAD, HORNDEAN
THURGOOD, HENRY J, 50, SOUTH ROAD, HORNDEAN
THURGOOD, RODERICK E, 50, SOUTH ROAD, HORNDEAN
RIDLEY, RUTH A, 52, SOUTH ROAD, HORNDEAN
CARTER, WILLIAM A, 56, SOUTH ROAD, HORNDEAN
LONG, SYBIL K, 58, SOUTH ROAD, HORNDEAN
FURLONGER, DEREK T, 60, SOUTH ROAD, HORNDEAN
FURLONGER, RUTH, 60, SOUTH ROAD, HORNDEAN
HARPER, KARALYN J, 62, SOUTH ROAD, HORNDEAN
HARPER, NICHOLAS P, 62, SOUTH ROAD, HORNDEAN
HARPER, PETER B, 62, SOUTH ROAD, HORNDEAN
CLEAR, BARBARA M, 62A, SOUTH ROAD, HORNDEAN
CLEAR, JOHN G, 62A, SOUTH ROAD, HORNDEAN
HALES, EILEEN G, 64, SOUTH ROAD, HORNDEAN
HALES, FREDERICK R, 64, SOUTH ROAD, HORNDEAN
COOPER, PAMELA I, 64A, SOUTH ROAD, HORNDEAN
COWTAN, BRIAN M, 66, SOUTH ROAD, HORNDEAN
COWTAN, JULIEN M, 66, SOUTH ROAD, HORNDEAN
COWTAN, RICHARD J, 66, SOUTH ROAD, HORNDEAN
LIBBY, GRAHAM J, 68, SOUTH ROAD, HORNDEAN
PAGE, MARIA H, 68, SOUTH ROAD, HORNDEAN
HEALEY, MICHAEL J, 70, SOUTH ROAD, HORNDEAN
HEALEY, WINIFREDE M, 70, SOUTH ROAD, HORNDEAN
SMITH, IAN S, 2, SOUTHDOWN ROAD, HORNDEAN
SMITH, SANDRA, 2, SOUTHDOWN ROAD, HORNDEAN
FERGUSON, RICHARD S, 4, SOUTHDOWN ROAD, HORNDEAN
FERGUSON, ROBERT, 4, SOUTHDOWN ROAD, HORNDEAN
FERGUSON, SUSAN G, 4, SOUTHDOWN ROAD, HORNDEAN
STARK, HILARY M, 6, SOUTHDOWN ROAD, HORNDEAN
CURRY, DEBORAH S, 7, SOUTHDOWN ROAD, HORNDEAN
CURRY, MARTIN A, 7, SOUTHDOWN ROAD, HORNDEAN
SMITH, ANNE E, 8, SOUTHDOWN ROAD, HORNDEAN
SMITH, STEPHEN R, 8, SOUTHDOWN ROAD, HORNDEAN
COCKBURN, ANDREW E, 9, SOUTHDOWN ROAD, HORNDEAN
COCKBURN, KERRY A, 9, SOUTHDOWN ROAD, HORNDEAN
COCKBURN, LYNETTE, 9, SOUTHDOWN ROAD, HORNDEAN
COCKBURN, PATRICIA A, 9, SOUTHDOWN ROAD, HORNDEAN
COCKBURN, VICTORIA, 9, SOUTHDOWN ROAD, HORNDEAN
ALLEN, GORDON T, 9A, SOUTHDOWN ROAD, HORNDEAN
ALLEN, PATRICIA I, 9A, SOUTHDOWN ROAD, HORNDEAN
EVANS, DAVID E, 10, SOUTHDOWN ROAD, HORNDEAN
EVANS, JONATHON, 10, SOUTHDOWN ROAD, HORNDEAN
EVANS, MARY L, 10, SOUTHDOWN ROAD, HORNDEAN
NICHOLSON, PETER, 11, SOUTHDOWN ROAD, HORNDEAN
NICHOLSON, SARAH, 11, SOUTHDOWN ROAD, HORNDEAN
REHR, ALISON A, 12, SOUTHDOWN ROAD, HORNDEAN
REHR, GEOFFREY D, 12, SOUTHDOWN ROAD, HORNDEAN
SIMMONDS, RALPH W, 13, SOUTHDOWN ROAD, HORNDEAN
HAYTER, LYNNE, 14, SOUTHDOWN ROAD, HORNDEAN
HAYTER, TERENCE, 14, SOUTHDOWN ROAD, HORNDEAN
HOLLAND, DAPHNE I, 15, SOUTHDOWN ROAD, HORNDEAN
OSBORNE, BRUCE E, 15, SOUTHDOWN ROAD, HORNDEAN
JUPP, JENNIFER S, 16, SOUTHDOWN ROAD, HORNDEAN
JUPP, PHILIP R, 16, SOUTHDOWN ROAD, HORNDEAN
WILLIAMS, ALAN J, 17, SOUTHDOWN ROAD, HORNDEAN
WILLIAMS, ALISON J, 17, SOUTHDOWN ROAD, HORNDEAN
DUDLEY, MARILYN A, 18, SOUTHDOWN ROAD, HORNDEAN
DUDLEY, MARTIN C, 18, SOUTHDOWN ROAD, HORNDEAN
DUDLEY, STELLA J, 18, SOUTHDOWN ROAD, HORNDEAN
BALDWIN, PHILIP J, 19, SOUTHDOWN ROAD, HORNDEAN
HOWE, PATRICIA M, 19, SOUTHDOWN ROAD, HORNDEAN
MILNE, RICHARD E, 20, SOUTHDOWN ROAD, HORNDEAN
MILNE, SUSAN M, 20, SOUTHDOWN ROAD, HORNDEAN
MILNE, VICTORIA J, 20, SOUTHDOWN ROAD, HORNDEAN
TICKELL, ELAINE P, 21, SOUTHDOWN ROAD, HORNDEAN
TICKELL, JAMES R, 21, SOUTHDOWN ROAD, HORNDEAN
PLOWRIGHT, DAVID F, 22, SOUTHDOWN ROAD, HORNDEAN
PLOWRIGHT, EMMA L, 22, SOUTHDOWN ROAD, HORNDEAN
PLOWRIGHT, FRANCES R, 22, SOUTHDOWN ROAD,
PLOWRIGHT, HONOR, 22, SOUTHDOWN ROAD, HORNDEAN
KIMBER, JAYNE C, 23, SOUTHDOWN ROAD, HORNDEAN
KIMBER, STEVEN B, 23, SOUTHDOWN ROAD, HORNDEAN
HAYWARD, AUDREY, 24, SOUTHDOWN ROAD, HORNDEAN
HAYWARD, PETER J, 24, SOUTHDOWN ROAD, HORNDEAN
COTSELL, CHARLOTTE, 25, SOUTHDOWN ROAD, HORNDEAN
COTSELL, JULIE B, 25, SOUTHDOWN ROAD, HORNDEAN
COTSELL, LUCY B, 25, SOUTHDOWN ROAD, HORNDEAN
COTSELL, TREVOR F, 25, SOUTHDOWN ROAD, HORNDEAN
DICKIE, DEIDRE, 26, SOUTHDOWN ROAD, HORNDEAN
DICKIE, ROBERT J, 26, SOUTHDOWN ROAD, HORNDEAN
BALLARD, JACQUELINE D, 27, SOUTHDOWN ROAD,
BALLARD, TREVOR R, 27, SOUTHDOWN ROAD, HORNDEAN
GREEN, ADAM O, 27A, SOUTHDOWN ROAD, HORNDEAN
GREEN, ALEXANDER W.E, 27A, SOUTHDOWN ROAD,
GREEN, JENNIFER, 27A, SOUTHDOWN ROAD, HORNDEAN
GREEN, THOMAS C, 27A, SOUTHDOWN ROAD, HORNDEAN
GREEN, WILLIAM E.C, 27A, SOUTHDOWN ROAD, HORNDEAN
HEYES, PAUL T, 28, SOUTHDOWN ROAD, HORNDEAN
HEYES, SHEILA E, 28, SOUTHDOWN ROAD, HORNDEAN
GREEN, BARBARA A, 29, SOUTHDOWN ROAD, HORNDEAN
GREEN, TREVOR J, 29, SOUTHDOWN ROAD, HORNDEAN
EASTON, PETER, 30, SOUTHDOWN ROAD, HORNDEAN
EASTON, SARAH E, 30, SOUTHDOWN ROAD, HORNDEAN
DEVEREUX, JENNIFER M, 31A, SOUTHDOWN ROAD,
JONES, CHRISTOPHER I, 31A, SOUTHDOWN ROAD,
HILL, HELEN M, 32, SOUTHDOWN ROAD, HORNDEAN
DRUMMOND, JOAN M, 33, SOUTHDOWN ROAD, HORNDEAN
ROBERTS, ANN M, 33, SOUTHDOWN ROAD, HORNDEAN
ROBERTS, BRIAN A, 33, SOUTHDOWN ROAD, HORNDEAN
ROBERTS, JENNIFER M, 33, SOUTHDOWN ROAD, HORNDEAN
SNOWDEN, DAVID J, 35, SOUTHDOWN ROAD, HORNDEAN
SNOWDEN, KATHRYN L, 35, SOUTHDOWN ROAD, HORNDEAN
SNOWDEN, SUSAN L, 35, SOUTHDOWN ROAD, HORNDEAN
LAPAGE, CHRISTOPHER M, 100, SOUTHDOWN ROAD,
LAPAGE, JUDITH A, 100, SOUTHDOWN ROAD, HORNDEAN
LAPAGE, STEPHEN M, 100, SOUTHDOWN ROAD, HORNDEAN
THOMPSON, ARTHUR R, 102, SOUTHDOWN ROAD,
THOMPSON, JOSEPHINE M, 102, SOUTHDOWN ROAD,
PEAT, ANDREW D, 104, SOUTHDOWN ROAD, HORNDEAN
PEAT, HAYLEY M, 104, SOUTHDOWN ROAD, HORNDEAN
COCHRANE, ANNIE G, 106, SOUTHDOWN ROAD, HORNDEAN
SHONS, ALAN P, 108, SOUTHDOWN ROAD, HORNDEAN
SHONS, BERNICE A, 108, SOUTHDOWN ROAD, HORNDEAN
SHONS, VICTORIA, 108, SOUTHDOWN ROAD, HORNDEAN
STUBBS, SHIRLEY, 110, SOUTHDOWN ROAD, HORNDEAN
STUBBS, TREVOR J, 110, SOUTHDOWN ROAD, HORNDEAN
FLOREY, PETER J, 112, SOUTHDOWN ROAD, HORNDEAN
LITTLE, BETTY, 114, SOUTHDOWN ROAD, HORNDEAN
SWAINSBURY, LEONARD F, 116, SOUTHDOWN ROAD,
SWAINSBURY, RUTH S.A, 116, SOUTHDOWN ROAD,
BROOKS, DENNIS E.A, 118, SOUTHDOWN ROAD, HORNDEAN
BROOKS, MAUD F.E, 118, SOUTHDOWN ROAD, HORNDEAN
GENTRY, CHRISTINE S, 118, SOUTHDOWN ROAD, HORNDEAN
LEE, STEPHEN G, 120, SOUTHDOWN ROAD, HORNDEAN
COURTNEY, EDNA J, 122, SOUTHDOWN ROAD, HORNDEAN
COURTNEY, RONALD L, 122, SOUTHDOWN ROAD, HORNDEAN
STEVENS, ESTHER, 124, SOUTHDOWN ROAD, HORNDEAN
HADLEY, ANNE, 126, SOUTHDOWN ROAD, HORNDEAN
HADLEY, JOHN C, 126, SOUTHDOWN ROAD, HORNDEAN
HADLEY, RICHARD, 126, SOUTHDOWN ROAD, HORNDEAN
LEE, ANN H.J, 128, SOUTHDOWN ROAD, HORNDEAN
LEE, MICHAEL D, 128, SOUTHDOWN ROAD, HORNDEAN
MCGRATH, AUDREY M, 130, SOUTHDOWN ROAD, HORNDEAN
SHARDLOW, DIANE, 1, THORNFIELD CLOSE, HORNDEAN
BROCKWAY, MARY L, 2, THORNFIELD CLOSE, HORNDEAN
BROCKWAY, STEPHEN R, 2, THORNFIELD CLOSE, HORNDEAN
SUMMERS, PAUL J, 3, THORNFIELD CLOSE, HORNDEAN
SUMMERS, TRACY, 3, THORNFIELD CLOSE, HORNDEAN
WATKINS, KATIE A, 4, THORNFIELD CLOSE, HORNDEAN
WATKINS, LINDA A, 4, THORNFIELD CLOSE, HORNDEAN
WATKINS, MICHAEL J, 4, THORNFIELD CLOSE, HORNDEAN
WATKINS, PETER J, 4, THORNFIELD CLOSE, HORNDEAN
FIELDS, ELAINE V, 6, THORNFIELD CLOSE, HORNDEAN
GANDER, DAWN E, 7, THORNFIELD CLOSE, HORNDEAN
GANDER, MALCOLM A, 7, THORNFIELD CLOSE, HORNDEAN
SMITH, CHARLES D, 8, THORNFIELD CLOSE, HORNDEAN
SMITH, JANICE I, 8, THORNFIELD CLOSE, HORNDEAN
MOULSON, CHRISTINE M, 9, THORNFIELD CLOSE,
MOULSON, EDWARD J, 9, THORNFIELD CLOSE, HORNDEAN
MOULSON, JOHN L, 9, THORNFIELD CLOSE, HORNDEAN
BOXALL, ROSEMARY A, 10, THORNFIELD CLOSE, HORNDEAN
NEHVE, PETER, 10, THORNFIELD CLOSE, HORNDEAN
KING, EMMA, 11, THORNFIELD CLOSE, HORNDEAN
KING, NAOMI, 11, THORNFIELD CLOSE, HORNDEAN
KING, RHONDA C, 11, THORNFIELD CLOSE, HORNDEAN
KING, ROGER, 11, THORNFIELD CLOSE, HORNDEAN
SUMMERS, DAVID J, 12, THORNFIELD CLOSE, HORNDEAN
SUMMERS, EVELYN A.M, 12, THORNFIELD CLOSE,
DAY, ANDREW R, 13, THORNFIELD CLOSE, HORNDEAN
DAY, SANDRA V, 13, THORNFIELD CLOSE, HORNDEAN
PARKER, ELIZABETH M, 14, THORNFIELD CLOSE, HORNDEAN
PARKER, IAN C, 14, THORNFIELD CLOSE, HORNDEAN
PARKER, MATTHEW, 14, THORNFIELD CLOSE, HORNDEAN
PARKER, OLIVER, 14, THORNFIELD CLOSE, HORNDEAN
NASH, CAROL A, 15, THORNFIELD CLOSE, HORNDEAN
NASH, JOHN A, 15, THORNFIELD CLOSE, HORNDEAN
SESSIONS, MARY L, 15, THORNFIELD CLOSE, HORNDEAN
HARPUR, BRIAN J, 2, THE VALE, HORNDEAN
HARPUR, MICHELE F, 2, THE VALE, HORNDEAN
STOTT, IAN J, 4, THE VALE, HORNDEAN
STOTT, NICOLA C, 4, THE VALE, HORNDEAN
ROGERS, JAYNE E, 6, THE VALE, HORNDEAN
ROGERS, RICHARD C, 6, THE VALE, HORNDEAN
ADAM, DEBORAH J, 8, THE VALE, HORNDEAN
ADAM, JOHN, 8, THE VALE, HORNDEAN
DREW, SYLVIA M, 10, THE VALE, HORNDEAN
WORRELL, BERNARD W, 10, THE VALE, HORNDEAN
KELLY, BRIAN A, 11, THE VALE, HORNDEAN
KELLY, WAYNE A, 11, THE VALE, HORNDEAN
EYLES, SHIRLEY, 12, THE VALE, HORNDEAN
EYLES, WILLIAM T, 12, THE VALE, HORNDEAN
DENNISON, GEOFFREY, 14, THE VALE, HORNDEAN
DENNISON, LINDA, 14, THE VALE, HORNDEAN
MIDGLEY, COLIN R, 16, THE VALE, HORNDEAN
MIDGLEY, KATHARINE L, 16, THE VALE, HORNDEAN
MIDGLEY, MONICA, 16, THE VALE, HORNDEAN
MULHOLLAND, BRIAN, 17, THE VALE, HORNDEAN
MULHOLLAND, TRACY A, 17, THE VALE, HORNDEAN
GRIFFITHS, ANTHONY J, 18, THE VALE, HORNDEAN
GRIFFITHS, JOANNE T, 18, THE VALE, HORNDEAN
LYNE, CHARLES A, 19, THE VALE, HORNDEAN
LYNE, DORINDA, 19, THE VALE, HORNDEAN
SUTTON, DUDLEY J, 20, THE VALE, HORNDEAN
SUTTON, SHIRLEY V, 20, THE VALE, HORNDEAN
MILLER, PHILIP J, 21, THE VALE, HORNDEAN
MILLER, ROBYN V, 21, THE VALE, HORNDEAN
HUGHES, ANGELA, 22, THE VALE, HORNDEAN
HUGHES, SIMON M, 22, THE VALE, HORNDEAN
DEACON, BARRY, 3, VIKING WAY, HORNDEAN
DEACON, SIMON, 3, VIKING WAY, HORNDEAN
DEACON, VALERIE E, 3, VIKING WAY, HORNDEAN
RIGBY, AMANDA J, 5, VIKING WAY, HORNDEAN
RIGBY, MICHAEL, 5, VIKING WAY, HORNDEAN
GLEDHILL, JOHN W.J, 7, VIKING WAY, HORNDEAN
GLEDHILL, VIVIEN J, 7, VIKING WAY, HORNDEAN
TITE, BERYL R F, 9, VIKING WAY, HORNDEAN
TITE, PETER A, 9, VIKING WAY, HORNDEAN
WITHERDEN, DORIS W, 11, VIKING WAY, HORNDEAN
ASKWITH, JANE, 19, VIKING WAY, HORNDEAN
ASKWITH, OLIVE A, 19, VIKING WAY, HORNDEAN
CRAIG, ALEXANDER M, 29, VIKING WAY, HORNDEAN

CRAIG, SUSAN J, 29, VIKING WAY, HORNDEAN
BUTCHER, DOREEN, 31, VIKING WAY, HORNDEAN
BUTCHER, RONALD C, 31, VIKING WAY, HORNDEAN
PETTITT, SUSAN M, 33, VIKING WAY, HORNDEAN
DENNY, ALICE M, 3, NORDIC COURT, VIKING WAY,
DENNY, JOHN S.T, 3, NORDIC COURT, VIKING WAY,
ATKEY, GEOFFREY, 37, VIKING WAY, HORNDEAN
ATKEY, NUALA M, 37, VIKING WAY, HORNDEAN
GILCHRIST, CELESTE P, 39, VIKING WAY, HORNDEAN
GILCHRIST, DAVID G, 39, VIKING WAY, HORNDEAN
HAYMAN, MARGARET A, 41, VIKING WAY, HORNDEAN
HAYMAN, MICHAEL L, 41, VIKING WAY, HORNDEAN
HAYMAN, PHILIP, 41, VIKING WAY, HORNDEAN
MORGAN, ALICE E, 43, VIKING WAY, HORNDEAN
MORGAN, CHARLES A, 43, VIKING WAY, HORNDEAN
CLARK, PETER, 45, VIKING WAY, HORNDEAN
CLARK, VALERIE A, 45, VIKING WAY, HORNDEAN
HESKETH, DOROTHY A, 47, VIKING WAY, HORNDEAN
JAMES, ERNEST A, 49, VIKING WAY, HORNDEAN
LINKHORN, AMANDA J, 51, VIKING WAY, HORNDEAN
LINKHORN, MARCUS J, 51, VIKING WAY, HORNDEAN
BAYLISS, CAROL L, 53, VIKING WAY, HORNDEAN
BAYLISS, CLARE S, 53, VIKING WAY, HORNDEAN
BAYLISS, RAYMOND W, 53, VIKING WAY, HORNDEAN
JAFKINS, ALAN R, 55, VIKING WAY, HORNDEAN
JAFKINS, CAROL A, 55, VIKING WAY, HORNDEAN
DUNKLEY, MAUREEN D, 57, VIKING WAY, HORNDEAN
DUNKLEY, ROBERT C, 57, VIKING WAY, HORNDEAN
HASKETT, ANN B, 59, VIKING WAY, HORNDEAN
HASKETT, KENNETH J, 59, VIKING WAY, HORNDEAN
HASKETT, LISA A, 59, VIKING WAY, HORNDEAN
HASKETT, WAYNE K, 59, VIKING WAY, HORNDEAN
WOOD, FREDERICK T.W, 61, VIKING WAY, HORNDEAN
WOOD, MARGHERITA D, 61, VIKING WAY, HORNDEAN
SKINNER, SUSAN, 63, VIKING WAY, HORNDEAN
SKINNER, WILLIAM G, 63, VIKING WAY, HORNDEAN
MASON, BRENDA M, 65, VIKING WAY, HORNDEAN
MASON, DAVID W, 65, VIKING WAY, HORNDEAN
BOAST, JON P, 67, VIKING WAY, HORNDEAN
BOAST, RACHELL, 67, VIKING WAY, HORNDEAN
CREESE, FREDERICK, 69, VIKING WAY, HORNDEAN
CREESE, JOY, 69, VIKING WAY, HORNDEAN
MILWARD, JOANN E, 71, VIKING WAY, HORNDEAN
MILWARD, LYNN E, 71, VIKING WAY, HORNDEAN
HATTON, JOAN A.A, 2, VIKING WAY, HORNDEAN
CORNFOOT, BERTHA L, 4, VIKING WAY, HORNDEAN
DAVID, CHRISTINE K, 6, VIKING WAY, HORNDEAN
DAVID, WILLIAM R, 6, VIKING WAY, HORNDEAN
ANDERSON, ALEX J, 8, VIKING WAY, HORNDEAN
ANDERSON, NICOLA J, 8, VIKING WAY, HORNDEAN
HORTON, JOHN, 10, VIKING WAY, HORNDEAN
DOLLERY, NORMAN R, 12, VIKING WAY, HORNDEAN
DOLLERY, RENEE E, 12, VIKING WAY, HORNDEAN
GRAHAM, HANNAH, 14, VIKING WAY, HORNDEAN
GRAHAM, MAUREEN, 14, VIKING WAY, HORNDEAN
ROGERS, DENNIS A, 16, VIKING WAY, HORNDEAN
ROGERS, EILEEN A, 16, VIKING WAY, HORNDEAN
DOLAN, JOHN P, 18, VIKING WAY, HORNDEAN
DOLAN, JULIA M, 18, VIKING WAY, HORNDEAN
MAYNARD, DORIS R, 20, VIKING WAY, HORNDEAN
COZENS-THOMPSON, DOREEN J, 22, VIKING WAY,
COZENS-THOMPSON, THOMAS, 22, VIKING WAY, HORNDEAN
WATTS-PLUMPKIN, FAITH C, 24, VIKING WAY, HORNDEAN
WATTS-PLUMPKIN, MERVYN D, 24, VIKING WAY, HORNDEAN
WOODS, FREDERICK G, 26, VIKING WAY, HORNDEAN
WOODS, IRIS D, 26, VIKING WAY, HORNDEAN
LINES, DENNIS R, 28, VIKING WAY, HORNDEAN
LINES, DOROTHY M, 28, VIKING WAY, HORNDEAN
NUNDY, JOHN A, 30, VIKING WAY, HORNDEAN
NUNDY, PATRICIA E, 30, VIKING WAY, HORNDEAN
FIRTH, ANN S, 32, VIKING WAY, HORNDEAN
FIRTH, GORDON, 32, VIKING WAY, HORNDEAN
JONES, DERRICK F, 34, VIKING WAY, HORNDEAN
JONES, SHIRLEY T.D, 34, VIKING WAY, HORNDEAN
ELLINOR, RONALD S.A, 36, VIKING WAY, HORNDEAN
FRASER, SHIRLEY A, 36, VIKING WAY, HORNDEAN
BURTON, STEPHEN A, 38, VIKING WAY, HORNDEAN
WILKINSON, PATRICK, 40, VIKING WAY, HORNDEAN
WILKINSON, SARAH A.E, 40, VIKING WAY, HORNDEAN
BRYANT, DEBORAH, 42, VIKING WAY, HORNDEAN
BRYANT, ROLAND J, 42, VIKING WAY, HORNDEAN
THOMAS, CAROL, 44, VIKING WAY, HORNDEAN
THOMAS, MICHAEL R, 44, VIKING WAY, HORNDEAN
THOMAS, WILLIAM R, 44, VIKING WAY, HORNDEAN
OAKES, DAVID R, 46, VIKING WAY, HORNDEAN
OAKES, FRANCES J, 46, VIKING WAY, HORNDEAN
BODY, CHRISTINE E, 48, VIKING WAY, HORNDEAN
BODY, MALCOLM, 48, VIKING WAY, HORNDEAN
BODY, MATTHEW C, 48, VIKING WAY, HORNDEAN
BROOKES, JILL M, 50, VIKING WAY, HORNDEAN
BROOKES, TREVOR E, 50, VIKING WAY, HORNDEAN
BRAY, GAYLE A, 54, VIKING WAY, HORNDEAN
BRAY, MURRAY, 54, VIKING WAY, HORNDEAN
SERTIN, DAVID, 70, VIKING WAY, HORNDEAN
SERTIN, MATTHEW, 70, VIKING WAY, HORNDEAN
SERTIN, YVETTE, 70, VIKING WAY, HORNDEAN
SMITH, RUBY D, 72, VIKING WAY, HORNDEAN
SMITH, TIMOTHY J, 72, VIKING WAY, HORNDEAN
MARTINDALE, JANET J, 1, WASDALE CLOSE, HORNDEAN
FULLER, GRAHAM R, 2, WASDALE CLOSE, HORNDEAN
FULLER, JOY B, 2, WASDALE CLOSE, HORNDEAN
SPARROW, GHISLAINE G, 3, WASDALE CLOSE, HORNDEAN
SPARROW, TERENCE, 3, WASDALE CLOSE, HORNDEAN
WATTON, LEIGH, 4, WASDALE CLOSE, HORNDEAN
WATTON, LESLEY M, 4, WASDALE CLOSE, HORNDEAN
HORDER, IAN, 5, WASDALE CLOSE, HORNDEAN
ARTHUR, ANDREA N, 6, WASDALE CLOSE, HORNDEAN
ARTHUR, LINDA J, 6, WASDALE CLOSE, HORNDEAN
CLANCY, MARGARET B, 6, WASDALE CLOSE, HORNDEAN
NICHOLS, KATHRYN J, 7, WASDALE CLOSE, HORNDEAN
NICHOLS, PAUL D, 7, WASDALE CLOSE, HORNDEAN
WRIGHT, PHILIPPA M, 8, WASDALE CLOSE, HORNDEAN
WRIGHT, SIMON W, 8, WASDALE CLOSE, HORNDEAN
TAYLOR, BARBARA E, 9, WASDALE CLOSE, HORNDEAN
TAYLOR, GREGORY N, 9, WASDALE CLOSE, HORNDEAN
HARDS, CAROL A, 10, WASDALE CLOSE, HORNDEAN
HARDS, JOHN M, 10, WASDALE CLOSE, HORNDEAN
STANTON, JANET O, 11, WASDALE CLOSE, HORNDEAN
STANTON, JOHN R, 11, WASDALE CLOSE, HORNDEAN
BEACH, JULIE, 12, WASDALE CLOSE, HORNDEAN
BEACH, JULIE (JNR), 12, WASDALE CLOSE, HORNDEAN
BEACH, ROBERT W, 12, WASDALE CLOSE, HORNDEAN
BERRY, DOUGLAS E, 12, WASDALE CLOSE, HORNDEAN
BENNETT, MARY A, 13, WASDALE CLOSE, HORNDEAN
BROWN, PETER G, 13, WASDALE CLOSE, HORNDEAN
MEWES, ALBERT W, 14, WASDALE CLOSE, HORNDEAN
MEWES, JOYCE C, 14, WASDALE CLOSE, HORNDEAN
STROUD, KEITH, 15, WASDALE CLOSE, HORNDEAN
STROUD, STEPHANIE A, 15, WASDALE CLOSE, HORNDEAN
GREENE, ANGELA J, 16, WASDALE CLOSE, HORNDEAN
GREENE, DAVID J, 16, WASDALE CLOSE, HORNDEAN
GREENE, MARIA A, 16, WASDALE CLOSE, HORNDEAN
MEAKIN, ANN, 17, WASDALE CLOSE, HORNDEAN
MEAKIN, BRIAN, 17, WASDALE CLOSE, HORNDEAN
BARNETT, LAURENCE G, 18, WASDALE CLOSE, HORNDEAN
BARNETT, RUTH M, 18, WASDALE CLOSE, HORNDEAN
PAWSON, MICHAEL T, 19, WASDALE CLOSE, HORNDEAN
PAWSON, SYLVIA M, 19, WASDALE CLOSE, HORNDEAN
CHURCHER, JOHN W, 20, WASDALE CLOSE, HORNDEAN
CHURCHER, JULIE H, 20, WASDALE CLOSE, HORNDEAN
RAY, DAVID G, 21, WASDALE CLOSE, HORNDEAN
RAY, HELEN A, 21, WASDALE CLOSE, HORNDEAN
POWELL, JANET, 22, WASDALE CLOSE, HORNDEAN
POWELL, KEITH A.T, 22, WASDALE CLOSE, HORNDEAN
BAILEY, GRAHAM W, 23, WASDALE CLOSE, HORNDEAN
BAILEY, LYNNE, 23, WASDALE CLOSE, HORNDEAN
KIMBER, SHEILA A, 24, WASDALE CLOSE, HORNDEAN
KIMBER, WILLIAM A, 24, WASDALE CLOSE, HORNDEAN
FOSTER, DENISE H, 25, WASDALE CLOSE, HORNDEAN
FOSTER, PAUL A, 25, WASDALE CLOSE, HORNDEAN
SWANN, RONALD D, 26, WASDALE CLOSE, HORNDEAN
SWANN, SALLY-JANE, 26, WASDALE CLOSE, HORNDEAN
WILSON, DEBRA, 27, WASDALE CLOSE, HORNDEAN
WILSON, STEVEN M, 27, WASDALE CLOSE, HORNDEAN
HOPKINS, DUNCAN, 28, WASDALE CLOSE, HORNDEAN
HOPKINS, LAYLA, 28, WASDALE CLOSE, HORNDEAN
HOPKINS, MAUREEN J, 28, WASDALE CLOSE, HORNDEAN
ANDREWS, JOHN E, 29, WASDALE CLOSE, HORNDEAN
ANDREWS, LINDA L, 29, WASDALE CLOSE, HORNDEAN
HOCKIN, DAVID I, 30, WASDALE CLOSE, HORNDEAN
HOCKIN, LYNN, 30, WASDALE CLOSE, HORNDEAN
LYNES, SHAUN S, 31, WASDALE CLOSE, HORNDEAN
LYNES, TRACEY A, 31, WASDALE CLOSE, HORNDEAN
TAYLOR, JANET M, 32, WASDALE CLOSE, HORNDEAN
TAYLOR, MARK W, 32, WASDALE CLOSE, HORNDEAN
KEMP, CHRISTOPHER I, 33, WASDALE CLOSE, HORNDEAN
KEMP, WENDY M, 33, WASDALE CLOSE, HORNDEAN
LAND, CHARLOTTE L, 34, WASDALE CLOSE, HORNDEAN
LAND, GILLIAN, 34, WASDALE CLOSE, HORNDEAN
LAND, JOHN, 34, WASDALE CLOSE, HORNDEAN
LAND, PENELOPE J, 34, WASDALE CLOSE, HORNDEAN
JACKSON, DAVID J, 36, WASDALE CLOSE, HORNDEAN
JACKSON, ELIZABETH A, 36, WASDALE CLOSE, HORNDEAN
HARRIS, BEVERLY, 37, WASDALE CLOSE, HORNDEAN
HARRIS, CHRISTOPHER M, 37, WASDALE CLOSE, HORNDEAN
JEFFERY, KAREN L, 38, WASDALE CLOSE, HORNDEAN
JEFFERY, MARK K, 38, WASDALE CLOSE, HORNDEAN
KENNY, BARBARA, 39, WASDALE CLOSE, HORNDEAN
KENNY, CHRISTOPHER, 39, WASDALE CLOSE, HORNDEAN
WOODLAND, DAPHNE M, 40, WASDALE CLOSE, HORNDEAN
WOODLAND, PETER E, 40, WASDALE CLOSE, HORNDEAN
SPARKS, DEBORAH J, 41, WASDALE CLOSE, HORNDEAN
SPARKS, HUGH P, 41, WASDALE CLOSE, HORNDEAN
SPARKS, JAMES, 41, WASDALE CLOSE, HORNDEAN
CHALLINOR, GAIL I, 42, WASDALE CLOSE, HORNDEAN
CHALLINOR, IRIS K, 42, WASDALE CLOSE, HORNDEAN
CHALLINOR, JOHN T.R, 42, WASDALE CLOSE, HORNDEAN
CHALLINOR, MARK R.G, 42, WASDALE CLOSE, HORNDEAN
HUMPHRIES, ANDREW, 1, WELL COPSE CLOSE, HORNDEAN
HUMPHRIES, GENETTE A, 1, WELL COPSE CLOSE,
PRIOR, GRAHAM J, 3, WELL COPSE CLOSE, HORNDEAN
PRIOR, VICTORIA, 3, WELL COPSE CLOSE, HORNDEAN
WALLACE, HILARY, 5, WELL COPSE CLOSE, HORNDEAN
WALLACE, ROBERT J, 5, WELL COPSE CLOSE, HORNDEAN
TAYLOR, JENNIFER G, 7, WELL COPSE CLOSE, HORNDEAN
BROWN, AMANDA J, 9, WELL COPSE CLOSE, HORNDEAN
SOLTANI, ALANA, 15, WELL COPSE CLOSE, HORNDEAN
SOLTANI, HAMID, 15, WELL COPSE CLOSE, HORNDEAN
SOLTANI, KIM T, 15, WELL COPSE CLOSE, HORNDEAN
MURRAY, ANDREA, 17, WELL COPSE CLOSE, HORNDEAN
TENNANT, GEORGE A, 19, WELL COPSE CLOSE, HORNDEAN
TENNANT, JULIA O, 19, WELL COPSE CLOSE, HORNDEAN
BAILEY, JULIE M, 21, WELL COPSE CLOSE, HORNDEAN
BAILEY, TREVOR J, 21, WELL COPSE CLOSE, HORNDEAN
RICHARDS, NICHOLAS P, 23, WELL COPSE CLOSE,
RICHARDS, NORMA E, 23, WELL COPSE CLOSE, HORNDEAN
RODGERS, ANITA D, 25, WELL COPSE CLOSE, HORNDEAN
RODGERS, DAVID, 25, WELL COPSE CLOSE, HORNDEAN
HAWKINS, DAVID P, 27, WELL COPSE CLOSE, HORNDEAN
HAWKINS, PAULA S, 27, WELL COPSE CLOSE, HORNDEAN
STEPHENS, GRACE M, 29, WELL COPSE CLOSE, HORNDEAN
STEPHENS, HOLLY R, 29, WELL COPSE CLOSE, HORNDEAN
PRIOR, PAMELA R, 31, WELL COPSE CLOSE, HORNDEAN
PRIOR, ROBERT J, 31, WELL COPSE CLOSE, HORNDEAN
REDHOUSE, ANTHONY K, 2, WELL COPSE CLOSE,
REDHOUSE, CLAIRE H, 2, WELL COPSE CLOSE, HORNDEAN
REDHOUSE, JENNIFER, 2, WELL COPSE CLOSE, HORNDEAN
HARRIS, ANNE, 4, WELL COPSE CLOSE, HORNDEAN
WALLING, NICOLA L, 6, WELL COPSE CLOSE, HORNDEAN
WALLING, PAUL, 6, WELL COPSE CLOSE, HORNDEAN
BOYD, JEAN M, 8, WELL COPSE CLOSE, HORNDEAN
WARNER, BARBARA A, 10, WELL COPSE CLOSE, HORNDEAN
WARNER, NINA, 10, WELL COPSE CLOSE, HORNDEAN
WARNER, TERENCE A, 10, WELL COPSE CLOSE, HORNDEAN
MARR, CHRISTINE J, 12, WELL COPSE CLOSE, HORNDEAN
MARR, PAUL, 12, WELL COPSE CLOSE, HORNDEAN
WEST, GARY, 14, WELL COPSE CLOSE, HORNDEAN
HUMMERSTONE, IAN D, 16, WELL COPSE CLOSE, HORNDEAN
DUFFY, LAWRENCE, 18, WELL COPSE CLOSE, HORNDEAN
DUFFY, MARGARET, 18, WELL COPSE CLOSE, HORNDEAN
MATHERS, KEITH, 20, WELL COPSE CLOSE, HORNDEAN
MATHERS, NORMA, 20, WELL COPSE CLOSE, HORNDEAN
PALMER, LAUREEN E, 22, WELL COPSE CLOSE, HORNDEAN
PERRY, ALAN J, 22, WELL COPSE CLOSE, HORNDEAN
PERRY, CHRISTOPHER M, 22, WELL COPSE CLOSE,
DAVIES, ERIC J, 24, WELL COPSE CLOSE, HORNDEAN
GRACE, MELONIE J, 24, WELL COPSE CLOSE, HORNDEAN
GREEN, BRIAN N, 1, WESSEX ROAD, HORNDEAN
GREEN, MARION J, 1, WESSEX ROAD, HORNDEAN
GREEN, SIMON C, 1, WESSEX ROAD, HORNDEAN
DUGGAN, ALEXANDER R, 3, WESSEX ROAD, HORNDEAN
DUGGAN, CHRISTOPHER P, 3, WESSEX ROAD, HORNDEAN
DUGGAN, MATTHEW S, 3, WESSEX ROAD, HORNDEAN
DUGGAN, SUSAN J, 3, WESSEX ROAD, HORNDEAN
PARR, ALAN J, 5, WESSEX ROAD, HORNDEAN
PARR, DENISE W, 5, WESSEX ROAD, HORNDEAN
HANNEY, IAN L, 7, WESSEX ROAD, HORNDEAN
HANNEY, PAULINE, 7, WESSEX ROAD, HORNDEAN
WHITEHEAD, NUALA J, 9, WESSEX ROAD, HORNDEAN
WHITEHEAD, ROBERT M, 9, WESSEX ROAD, HORNDEAN
CAPON, PHILIP L, 11, WESSEX ROAD, HORNDEAN
WOODHOUSE, CAROL, 11, WESSEX ROAD, HORNDEAN
DYER, PHILIP P, 13, WESSEX ROAD, HORNDEAN
DYER, SUSAN L, 13, WESSEX ROAD, HORNDEAN
PARKER, JOHN A, 15, WESSEX ROAD, HORNDEAN
DUFF, DIANE E, 17, WESSEX ROAD, HORNDEAN
SMYTH, MARK M, 17, WESSEX ROAD, HORNDEAN
THOMPSON, DAVID J, 19, WESSEX ROAD, HORNDEAN
THOMPSON, JACQUELINE D, 19, WESSEX ROAD, HORNDEAN
DAY, JOHN P, 29, WESSEX ROAD, HORNDEAN
DAY, MURIEL R, 29, WESSEX ROAD, HORNDEAN
GIBSON, ALISON C, 31, WESSEX ROAD, HORNDEAN
GIBSON, PAUL A, 31, WESSEX ROAD, HORNDEAN
BAILEY, MARK R, 33, WESSEX ROAD, HORNDEAN
WEBB, JOANNE C, 33, WESSEX ROAD, HORNDEAN
RANSON, MARK A, 35, WESSEX ROAD, HORNDEAN
RANSON, SAMANTHA A, 35, WESSEX ROAD, HORNDEAN
LEWIS, FREDERICK G, 2, WESSEX ROAD, HORNDEAN
LEWIS, OLIVE V, 2, WESSEX ROAD, HORNDEAN
FRENCH, ELSPETH A, 4, WESSEX ROAD, HORNDEAN
DICKINSON, PETER A, 6, WESSEX ROAD, HORNDEAN
DICKINSON, SARAH L, 6, WESSEX ROAD, HORNDEAN
HAMILTON, ANN R, 8, WESSEX ROAD, HORNDEAN
HAMILTON, JOHN W, 8, WESSEX ROAD, HORNDEAN
DAGNELL, ADAM J, 10, WESSEX ROAD, HORNDEAN
DAGNELL, CRAIG J, 10, WESSEX ROAD, HORNDEAN
DAGNELL, KEVIN J, 10, WESSEX ROAD, HORNDEAN
DAGNELL, VALERIE A, 10, WESSEX ROAD, HORNDEAN
MANSLEY, CHRISTINE T, 12, WESSEX ROAD, HORNDEAN
MANSLEY, DAVID S, 12, WESSEX ROAD, HORNDEAN
MANSLEY, HELEN M, 12, WESSEX ROAD, HORNDEAN
MANSLEY, JOANNE T, 12, WESSEX ROAD, HORNDEAN
MACEY, DAVID T, 14, WESSEX ROAD, HORNDEAN
MACEY, MARGARET, 14, WESSEX ROAD, HORNDEAN
WITHEY, FRANK K, 16, WESSEX ROAD, HORNDEAN
WITHEY, PEGGY, 16, WESSEX ROAD, HORNDEAN
GRANT, DIANA H, 18, WESSEX ROAD, HORNDEAN
GRANT, ROLAND H, 18, WESSEX ROAD, HORNDEAN
LEWIS, CHRISTOPHER D, 20, WESSEX ROAD, HORNDEAN
LEWIS, SANDRA J, 20, WESSEX ROAD, HORNDEAN
HEWLAND, BRIAN W, 22, WESSEX ROAD, HORNDEAN
HEWLAND, PATRICIA M, 22, WESSEX ROAD, HORNDEAN
QUINN, KATHREN, 24, WESSEX ROAD, HORNDEAN
HAMMOND, JOSEPH L, 26, WESSEX ROAD, HORNDEAN
HAMMOND, MENNA, 26, WESSEX ROAD, HORNDEAN
CHATFIELD, SYLVIA J, 28, WESSEX ROAD, HORNDEAN
SPENCER, HEATHER A, 30, WESSEX ROAD, HORNDEAN
SPENCER, JONATHAN C, 30, WESSEX ROAD, HORNDEAN
SPEARING, JANET A, 32, WESSEX ROAD, HORNDEAN
SPEARING, PETER D, 32, WESSEX ROAD, HORNDEAN
UNDERWOOD, CHRISTINE, 34, WESSEX ROAD, HORNDEAN
UNDERWOOD, GARRY B, 34, WESSEX ROAD, HORNDEAN
UNDERWOOD, PAUL M, 34, WESSEX ROAD, HORNDEAN
HOLLAND, CLAIRE L, 36, WESSEX ROAD, HORNDEAN
HOLLAND, PAUL W, 36, WESSEX ROAD, HORNDEAN
WEARN, GEMMA M, 38, WESSEX ROAD, HORNDEAN
WEARN, KERRY A, 38, WESSEX ROAD, HORNDEAN
WEARN, MYRA P, 38, WESSEX ROAD, HORNDEAN
WEARN, ROGER F, 38, WESSEX ROAD, HORNDEAN

Electoral Roll

HOWE, CARON, 40, WESSEX ROAD, HORNDEAN
HOWE, DAVID J, 40, WESSEX ROAD, HORNDEAN
ELLIS, JONATHAN D, 42, WESSEX ROAD, HORNDEAN
ELLIS, LORAYNE D, 42, WESSEX ROAD, HORNDEAN
DAVIDSON, JAMES D, 44, WESSEX ROAD, HORNDEAN
DAVIDSON, MATTHEW V, 44, WESSEX ROAD, HORNDEAN
DAVIDSON, VALERIE A, 44, WESSEX ROAD, HORNDEAN
ROGERS, LORRAINE, 46, WESSEX ROAD, HORNDEAN
ROGERS, ROY J, 46, WESSEX ROAD, HORNDEAN
ACHESON, ALLAN, 48, WESSEX ROAD, HORNDEAN
ACHESON, VICKI L, 48, WESSEX ROAD, HORNDEAN
RIDLEY-ELLIS, HANNAH T, 50, WESSEX ROAD, HORNDEAN
RIDLEY-ELLIS, TERENCE J, 50, WESSEX ROAD, HORNDEAN
RIDLEY-ELLIS, TERESA A, 50, WESSEX ROAD, HORNDEAN
DIGGLES, IAN R, 52, WESSEX ROAD, HORNDEAN
DIGGLES, MARILYN A, 52, WESSEX ROAD, HORNDEAN
COOPER, ANGELA M, 1, WHITE DIRT LANE, HORNDEAN
COOPER, BASIL C, 1, WHITE DIRT LANE, HORNDEAN
MONNERY, CAROL A, 3, WHITE DIRT LANE, HORNDEAN
MONNERY, CLAIRE E, 3, WHITE DIRT LANE, HORNDEAN
MONNERY, ERNEST W, 3, WHITE DIRT LANE, HORNDEAN
GUFFICK, ALFRED, 3A, WHITE DIRT LANE, HORNDEAN
GUFFICK, CHRISTINE H, 3A, WHITE DIRT LANE, HORNDEAN
GUFFICK, PENELOPE J, 3A, WHITE DIRT LANE, HORNDEAN
SMITH, JOHN W, 5, WHITE DIRT LANE, HORNDEAN
STUEBS, KLAUS-PETER, 7, WHITE DIRT LANE, HORNDEAN
STUEBS, PAULINE B, 7, WHITE DIRT LANE, HORNDEAN
ASHWELL, FIONA S, 9, WHITE DIRT LANE, HORNDEAN
WINTER, EDITH L, 11, WHITE DIRT LANE, HORNDEAN
WINTER, MARY C, 11, WHITE DIRT LANE, HORNDEAN
ROBOTHAM, KATHRYN A, 13, WHITE DIRT LANE, HORNDEAN
ROBOTHAM, LYNN P, 13, WHITE DIRT LANE, HORNDEAN
DARNLEY-SMITH, HUGH W.W, 15, WHITE DIRT LANE,
DARNLEY-SMITH, SUSANNAH L, 15, WHITE DIRT LANE,
BRYDON, JANE E, 17, WHITE DIRT LANE, HORNDEAN
BRYDON, KEVIN J, 17, WHITE DIRT LANE, HORNDEAN
BRYDON, SARAH, 17, WHITE DIRT LANE, HORNDEAN
BOURTON, AMANDA L, 19, WHITE DIRT LANE, HORNDEAN
BOURTON, DAVID E, 19, WHITE DIRT LANE, HORNDEAN
CAME, ANDREW D, 21, WHITE DIRT LANE, HORNDEAN
CAME, ANGELA R, 21, WHITE DIRT LANE, HORNDEAN
CURRY, CHRISTOPHER R, 23, WHITE DIRT LANE, HORNDEAN
CURRY, NICOLA A, 23, WHITE DIRT LANE, HORNDEAN
LAWES, ELISABETH M, 25, WHITE DIRT LANE, HORNDEAN
GOLDSMITH, BRIAN D, 27, WHITE DIRT LANE, HORNDEAN
DAVIES, EILEEN J, 29, WHITE DIRT LANE, HORNDEAN
DAVIES, IEUAN C, 29, WHITE DIRT LANE, HORNDEAN
DAVIES, ROBERT M, 29, WHITE DIRT LANE, HORNDEAN
BLUNDEN, CATHERINE A, 31, WHITE DIRT LANE, HORNDEAN
BLUNDEN, LESLIE A, 31, WHITE DIRT LANE, HORNDEAN
BLUNDEN, SHEILA, 31, WHITE DIRT LANE, HORNDEAN
JOEL, DAVID, 33, WHITE DIRT LANE, HORNDEAN
JOEL, LYNDA, 33, WHITE DIRT LANE, HORNDEAN
ROWE, ALEXANDER D, 39, WHITE DIRT LANE, HORNDEAN
ROWE, ANTOINETTE C.V, 39, WHITE DIRT LANE, HORNDEAN
ROWE, DAVID F, 39, WHITE DIRT LANE, HORNDEAN
ROWE, TRACEY-ANN, 39, WHITE DIRT LANE, HORNDEAN
BOUTELL, JOHN A, 41, WHITE DIRT LANE, HORNDEAN
LONG, ANDREW S, 43, WHITE DIRT LANE, HORNDEAN
LONG, JENNIFER C, 43, WHITE DIRT LANE, HORNDEAN
CLISSETT, DIANA, 45, WHITE DIRT LANE, HORNDEAN
CLISSETT, KEVIN, 45, WHITE DIRT LANE, HORNDEAN
PEARSE, CHRISTOPHER D, 45, WHITE DIRT LANE,
PEARSE, SAMANTHA C, 45, WHITE DIRT LANE, HORNDEAN
WARRIOR, JOHN, 47, WHITE DIRT LANE, HORNDEAN
WARRIOR, JULIET J, 47, WHITE DIRT LANE, HORNDEAN
PINHORN, HELEN P, 81, WHITE DIRT LANE, HORNDEAN
PINHORN, MARK K, 81, WHITE DIRT LANE, HORNDEAN
NASH, ALAN E, 125, WHITE DIRT LANE, HORNDEAN
NASH, ANDREW R, 125, WHITE DIRT LANE, HORNDEAN
NASH, SARAH L, 125, WHITE DIRT LANE, HORNDEAN
NASH, VALERIE A, 125, WHITE DIRT LANE, HORNDEAN
SMITH, DIANA H, 131, WHITE DIRT LANE, HORNDEAN
SMITH, MICHAEL J, 131, WHITE DIRT LANE, HORNDEAN
JONES, HAROLD R, 133, WHITE DIRT LANE, HORNDEAN
JONES, IRENE C, 133, WHITE DIRT LANE, HORNDEAN
ANDREWS, DAPHNE J, 141, WHITE DIRT LANE, HORNDEAN
ANDREWS, MICHAEL I.J, 141, WHITE DIRT LANE, HORNDEAN
WILLIAMS, ANDREW N, 145, WHITE DIRT LANE, HORNDEAN
WILLIAMS, ISABEL R, 145, WHITE DIRT LANE, HORNDEAN
WILLIAMS, SALLY E, 145, WHITE DIRT LANE, HORNDEAN
BROWN, DOROTHY I, 149, WHITE DIRT LANE, HORNDEAN
DODSWORTH, ANDREW, 153, WHITE DIRT LANE, HORNDEAN
DODSWORTH, DARREN A, 153, WHITE DIRT LANE,
GREEN, DAVID S, 6, WHITE DIRT LANE, HORNDEAN
LOMAX, HANNAH, 8, WHITE DIRT LANE, HORNDEAN
WILLIS, ROBIN, 8, WHITE DIRT LANE, HORNDEAN
HARPER, LUCY J, 10, WHITE DIRT LANE, HORNDEAN
OROSZ, MARK S.J, 10, WHITE DIRT LANE, HORNDEAN
BROOME, PAUL A, 12, WHITE DIRT LANE, HORNDEAN
HILLS, EDWARD M, 120, WHITE DIRT LANE, HORNDEAN
HILLS, PATRICIA J, 120, WHITE DIRT LANE, HORNDEAN
HARVEY-WHITING, SHIRLEY A, 124, WHITE DIRT LANE,
WHITING, DAVID J, 124, WHITE DIRT LANE, HORNDEAN
TOTIS, GIAN F, 126, WHITE DIRT LANE, HORNDEAN
TOTIS, MARION J, 126, WHITE DIRT LANE, HORNDEAN
HARDING, FELICITY I, 128, WHITE DIRT LANE, HORNDEAN
HARDING, PETER B, 128, WHITE DIRT LANE, HORNDEAN
COLLIER, JACQUELINE C, 130, WHITE DIRT LANE,
SNELLING, ALFRED H.W, 134, WHITE DIRT LANE, HORNDEAN
SNELLING, JANNICE, 134, WHITE DIRT LANE, HORNDEAN
BROWNING, BRENDA E, 142, WHITE DIRT LANE, HORNDEAN
BROWNING, VERNON I, 142, WHITE DIRT LANE, HORNDEAN
THOMAS, ANNETTE M, 144, WHITE DIRT LANE, HORNDEAN
THOMAS, JOHN E.K, 144, WHITE DIRT LANE, HORNDEAN
SHELTON, MIRANDA M, 146, WHITE DIRT LANE, HORNDEAN
ROWNEY, JENNIFER, 148, WHITE DIRT LANE, HORNDEAN
ROWNEY, MARK R, 148, WHITE DIRT LANE, HORNDEAN
ROWNEY, ROBERT R, 148, WHITE DIRT LANE, HORNDEAN
PATRICK, ALAN J, 152, WHITE DIRT LANE, HORNDEAN
PATRICK, JACQUELINE C, 152, WHITE DIRT LANE,
PATRICK, LOUISE J, 152, WHITE DIRT LANE, HORNDEAN
HORSFALL, BARBARA A.M., 154, WHITE DIRT LANE,
HORSFALL, CARLY J, 154, WHITE DIRT LANE, HORNDEAN
HORSFALL, CHRISTOPHER D, 154, WHITE DIRT LANE,
HORSFALL, JONATHAN L, 154, WHITE DIRT LANE,
HORSFALL, REBECCA L, 154, WHITE DIRT LANE, HORNDEAN
JERMYN, ROGER, 1, WODE CLOSE, HORNDEAN
WHEATLEY, BARBARA L, 1, WODE CLOSE, HORNDEAN
WHEATLEY, MATTHEW J, 1, WODE CLOSE, HORNDEAN
ATHA, DAVID J, 2, WODE CLOSE, HORNDEAN
ATHA, JACQUELINE A, 2, WODE CLOSE, HORNDEAN
SEDDON, ARTHUR, 2, WODE CLOSE, HORNDEAN
SEDDON, MARELYN, 2, WODE CLOSE, HORNDEAN
TANNER, MICHAEL J, 3, WODE CLOSE, HORNDEAN
WILSON, VERA E, 4, WODE CLOSE, HORNDEAN
REGAN, BRIAN R, 5, WODE CLOSE, HORNDEAN
BARNS, GWENDOLINE, 6, WODE CLOSE, HORNDEAN
BARNS, JACK R, 6, WODE CLOSE, HORNDEAN
PARSONS, CHERI M, 7, WODE CLOSE, HORNDEAN
PARSONS, RONALD J, 7, WODE CLOSE, HORNDEAN
JENKINS, BARBARA L, 8, WODE CLOSE, HORNDEAN
JENKINS, PETER J.G, 8, WODE CLOSE, HORNDEAN
BOWEN, CAROLINE M, 9, WODE CLOSE, HORNDEAN
TURNER, CONSTANCE M, 10, WODE CLOSE, HORNDEAN
BATEMAN, ARTHUR J, 11, WODE CLOSE, HORNDEAN
BATEMAN, AUDREY I, 11, WODE CLOSE, HORNDEAN
ROGERS, ALAN G, 12, WODE CLOSE, HORNDEAN
ROGERS, MARGARET R, 12, WODE CLOSE, HORNDEAN
ROGERS, PAUL T, 12, WODE CLOSE, HORNDEAN
SPENCER, JACK, 13, WODE CLOSE, HORNDEAN
SPENCER, MAVIS V, 13, WODE CLOSE, HORNDEAN
COLE, BRIAN, 14, WODE CLOSE, HORNDEAN
COLE, GRACE M, 14, WODE CLOSE, HORNDEAN
ADAMS, COLIN, 15, WODE CLOSE, HORNDEAN
ADAMS, RITA A, 15, WODE CLOSE, HORNDEAN
CASSAR, ALFRED A, 16, WODE CLOSE, HORNDEAN
CASSAR, ANNA V, 16, WODE CLOSE, HORNDEAN
ROBINSON, NICHOLAS J, 17, WODE CLOSE, HORNDEAN
WATERMAN, CAROL A, 17, WODE CLOSE, HORNDEAN
TURNBULL, ABBIGAIL J, 18, WODE CLOSE, HORNDEAN
TURNBULL, ANNA L, 18, WODE CLOSE, HORNDEAN
TURNBULL, JOHN J, 18, WODE CLOSE, HORNDEAN
TURNBULL, LOUISE, 18, WODE CLOSE, HORNDEAN
PETLEY, BARBARA J, 19, WODE CLOSE, HORNDEAN
PETLEY, DAVID J, 19, WODE CLOSE, HORNDEAN
WALTON, GLADYS C.L, 1, WREXHAM GROVE, HORNDEAN
WILLIAMSON, AMY, 2, WREXHAM GROVE, HORNDEAN
WILLIAMSON, HEATHER A.B, 2, WREXHAM GROVE,
WILLIAMSON, KATHERINE, 2, WREXHAM GROVE,
WILLIAMSON, TIMOTHY, 2, WREXHAM GROVE, HORNDEAN
WINSLADE, VERA L, 2A, WREXHAM GROVE, HORNDEAN
BEARD, STEPHEN A, 3, WREXHAM GROVE, HORNDEAN
KIMBER, SALLY A, 3, WREXHAM GROVE, HORNDEAN
BONE, MALCOLM J,,
CAPELING, JOHN
CAPELING, MARIETTA
LINEKER, ELIZABETH F,,
LINEKER, ROBERT J,,
MCKERNAN, JAMES
MOLYNEAUX, DEAN G,,
PESKETT, DAWN
SHELLEY, DAVID J,,
THOMAS, EMMA M,,
THOMAS, ROBERT P,,

HORNDEAN (HAZLETON) ,
KERR, DIANNE, 1, ACACIA GARDENS, HORNDEAN
KERR, EMILY, 1, ACACIA GARDENS, HORNDEAN
KERR, GEORGE, 1, ACACIA GARDENS, HORNDEAN
KERR, GRAEME, 1, ACACIA GARDENS, HORNDEAN
KERR, KIRSTIN, 1, ACACIA GARDENS, HORNDEAN
DOPSON, COLIN R, 2, ACACIA GARDENS, HORNDEAN
DOPSON, DEBORAH J, 2, ACACIA GARDENS, HORNDEAN
THOMAS, ARCHIBALD E, 3, ACACIA GARDENS, HORNDEAN
MANCHIP, ANTONY W, 4, ACACIA GARDENS, HORNDEAN
MANCHIP, JULIE S, 4, ACACIA GARDENS, HORNDEAN
MORRIS, KEITH, 5, ACACIA GARDENS, HORNDEAN
MORRIS, MARTIN A, 5, ACACIA GARDENS, HORNDEAN
MORRIS, SHIRLEY L, 5, ACACIA GARDENS, HORNDEAN
BATHE, IAN P, 6, ACACIA GARDENS, HORNDEAN
DAWE, CLAIRE R, 7, ACACIA GARDENS, HORNDEAN
DAWE, MARCUS W, 7, ACACIA GARDENS, HORNDEAN
PIPER, COLIN M, 8, ACACIA GARDENS, HORNDEAN
PIPER, TRACY L, 8, ACACIA GARDENS, HORNDEAN
BAKER, JONATHAN W, 9, ACACIA GARDENS, HORNDEAN
DAVIS, PHILIP, 9, ACACIA GARDENS, HORNDEAN
DAVIS, SUSAN J, 9, ACACIA GARDENS, HORNDEAN
SYDENHAM, SUZANNE, 10, ACACIA GARDENS, HORNDEAN
KELLETT, JULIA A, 11, ACACIA GARDENS, HORNDEAN
KELLETT, NEIL H, 11, ACACIA GARDENS, HORNDEAN
ROGERS, ALAN F, 13, ACACIA GARDENS, HORNDEAN
ROGERS, KATE L, 13, ACACIA GARDENS, HORNDEAN
ROGERS, LISA A, 13, ACACIA GARDENS, HORNDEAN
ROGERS, SHIRLEY P, 13, ACACIA GARDENS, HORNDEAN
RICHARDSON, MARGARET T.E, 1, ALMOND CLOSE,
CROWDY, DUDLEY G, 2, ALMOND CLOSE, HORNDEAN
YATES, EILEEN, 2, ALMOND CLOSE, HORNDEAN
HOLE, LORNA M, 3, ALMOND CLOSE, HORNDEAN
HOLE, RAYMOND G, 3, ALMOND CLOSE, HORNDEAN
TAIT, ANTHONY P, 4, ALMOND CLOSE, HORNDEAN
TAIT, SHARON, 4, ALMOND CLOSE, HORNDEAN
CHUDASAMA, INDIRA, 5, ALMOND CLOSE, HORNDEAN
RICHES, JACK R, 5, ALMOND CLOSE, HORNDEAN
RICHES, LEONORA, 5, ALMOND CLOSE, HORNDEAN
SMITH, ADRIAN A, 6, ALMOND CLOSE, HORNDEAN
THOMPSON, ARNOLD J, 7, ALMOND CLOSE, HORNDEAN
THOMPSON, DOROTHY W, 7, ALMOND CLOSE, HORNDEAN
GRAY, MALCOLM J, 8, ALMOND CLOSE, HORNDEAN
GRAY, TINA L, 8, ALMOND CLOSE, HORNDEAN
GALE, LINDA M, 9, ALMOND CLOSE, HORNDEAN
GALE, PETER G, 9, ALMOND CLOSE, HORNDEAN
MAHONEY, CAROL P, 1, BEECH WAY, HORNDEAN
MAHONEY, ROSINA M, 1, BEECH WAY, HORNDEAN
MAHONEY, WILLIAM H, 1, BEECH WAY, HORNDEAN
HART, AMANDA L, 2, BEECH WAY, HORNDEAN
STEERE, BERTRAM G, 2, BEECH WAY, HORNDEAN
CRAWFORD, SHEILA G, 3, BEECH WAY, HORNDEAN
HAYNES, CLAIRE L, 4, BEECH WAY, HORNDEAN
HAYNES, VIVIAN J, 4, BEECH WAY, HORNDEAN
DIXON, DORIS E, 5, BEECH WAY, HORNDEAN
TUCKER, BRIAN P, 6, BEECH WAY, HORNDEAN
TUCKER, DORIS E, 6, BEECH WAY, HORNDEAN
EVANS, MARJORIE A, 7, BEECH WAY, HORNDEAN
LING, JEAN M, 8, BEECH WAY, HORNDEAN
LING, LESLIE P, 8, BEECH WAY, HORNDEAN
LING, PETER D, 8, BEECH WAY, HORNDEAN
ARNOLD, DENNIS F, 9, BEECH WAY, HORNDEAN
ARNOLD, DORIS B, 9, BEECH WAY, HORNDEAN
ARNOLD, MARK D, 9, BEECH WAY, HORNDEAN
GATES, ANNE, 10, BEECH WAY, HORNDEAN
GATES, JAMES A, 10, BEECH WAY, HORNDEAN
SHARP, IRENE J, 11, BEECH WAY, HORNDEAN
DEVERILL, CHARLES A, 12, BEECH WAY, HORNDEAN
DEVERILL, JOYCE D, 12, BEECH WAY, HORNDEAN
RODDIS, KATHLEEN M.J, 13, BEECH WAY, HORNDEAN
LUFF, ANGELA M, 15, BEECH WAY, HORNDEAN
LUFF, BARRY W, 15, BEECH WAY, HORNDEAN
BUDD, ALAN R, 17, BEECH WAY, HORNDEAN
BUDD, ANN, 17, BEECH WAY, HORNDEAN
BALL, ANDY, 19, BEECH WAY, HORNDEAN
HOLMES, TRACEY, 19, BEECH WAY, HORNDEAN
DAVIES, JOHN G, NOBLES BARN, BLENDWORTH
EVANS, HENRY J, NOBLES FARM, BLENDWORTH
EVANS, PAUL A, NOBLES FARM, BLENDWORTH
EVANS, SUSAN R, NOBLES FARM, BLENDWORTH
SIMCOX, ALAN J, 1, BRIAR CLOSE, HORNDEAN
SIMCOX, KENDEL M, 1, BRIAR CLOSE, HORNDEAN
LANE, NEIL P, 3, BRIAR CLOSE, HORNDEAN
LANE, SHARON D, 3, BRIAR CLOSE, HORNDEAN
FLYNN, THOMAS J, 5, BRIAR CLOSE, HORNDEAN
FLYNN, VALERIE D, 5, BRIAR CLOSE, HORNDEAN
BATHO, ALAN G, 7, BRIAR CLOSE, HORNDEAN
BATHO, BRENDA S, 7, BRIAR CLOSE, HORNDEAN
TAYLOR, ANGELA, 9, BRIAR CLOSE, HORNDEAN
TAYLOR, MARK S, 9, BRIAR CLOSE, HORNDEAN
PRATER, LORRAINE A, 10, BRIAR CLOSE, HORNDEAN
PRATER, SOPHIE L, 10, BRIAR CLOSE, HORNDEAN
COATES, NATALIE, 11, BRIAR CLOSE, HORNDEAN
SMITH, ROY, 11, BRIAR CLOSE, HORNDEAN
SMITH, SHEENA P, 11, BRIAR CLOSE, HORNDEAN
PYMONT, LINDA, 12, BRIAR CLOSE, HORNDEAN
PYMONT, ROGER K, 12, BRIAR CLOSE, HORNDEAN
O'CONNELL, EMMA K, 13, BRIAR CLOSE, HORNDEAN
O'CONNELL, JONATHON A, 13, BRIAR CLOSE, HORNDEAN
O'CONNELL, KEVIN R.C, 13, BRIAR CLOSE, HORNDEAN
O'CONNELL, LAURA V, 13, BRIAR CLOSE, HORNDEAN
GOLDING, JONATHON J, 14, BRIAR CLOSE, HORNDEAN
GOLDING, SUSAN E.A, 14, BRIAR CLOSE, HORNDEAN
FLYNN, JOAN L, 15, BRIAR CLOSE, HORNDEAN
FLYNN, VICTOR A.H, 15, BRIAR CLOSE, HORNDEAN
MOORE, PETER J, 16, BRIAR CLOSE, HORNDEAN
MOORE, THELMA J, 16, BRIAR CLOSE, HORNDEAN
PALMER, JEAN, 17, BRIAR CLOSE, HORNDEAN
TURNBULL, JOAN, 18, BRIAR CLOSE, HORNDEAN
EATON, DAVID G, 19, BRIAR CLOSE, HORNDEAN
EATON, DIANA B, 19, BRIAR CLOSE, HORNDEAN
VINCENT-SPALL, ANDREW, 20, BRIAR CLOSE, HORNDEAN
VINCENT-SPALL, MAXINE, 20, BRIAR CLOSE, HORNDEAN
TIPPER, BRIDGET S, 21, BRIAR CLOSE, HORNDEAN
TIPPER, JOHN E.J, 21, BRIAR CLOSE, HORNDEAN
MARTIN, ANNE L, 22, BRIAR CLOSE, HORNDEAN
MARTIN, BRETT J, 22, BRIAR CLOSE, HORNDEAN
MARTIN, JOHN S, 22, BRIAR CLOSE, HORNDEAN
WATSON-COWEN, DEREK, 23, BRIAR CLOSE, HORNDEAN
WATSON-COWEN, PAMELA F.M, 23, BRIAR CLOSE, HORNDEAN
CANNINGS, HANNAH M, 24, BRIAR CLOSE, HORNDEAN
CANNINGS, LINDA E, 24, BRIAR CLOSE, HORNDEAN
CANNINGS, PETER J, 24, BRIAR CLOSE, HORNDEAN
JIGGINS, BRIAN J, 25, BRIAR CLOSE, HORNDEAN
JIGGINS, WENDY M, 25, BRIAR CLOSE, HORNDEAN
MERCER, ALAN, 26, BRIAR CLOSE, HORNDEAN
MERCER, GARY J, 26, BRIAR CLOSE, HORNDEAN
MERCER, SANDRA E, 26, BRIAR CLOSE, HORNDEAN
CUNNAH, JULIE A, 27, BRIAR CLOSE, HORNDEAN
CUNNAH, MARK D, 27, BRIAR CLOSE, HORNDEAN
BRUMMELL, PEGGY, 28, BRIAR CLOSE, HORNDEAN
BRUMMELL, RONALD C, 28, BRIAR CLOSE, HORNDEAN
SCOTT, GORDON C, 29, BRIAR CLOSE, HORNDEAN

SCOTT, KIM, 29, BRIAR CLOSE, HORNDEAN
PRIEST, STEVEN J, 30, BRIAR CLOSE, HORNDEAN
PRIEST, YVONNE L, 30, BRIAR CLOSE, HORNDEAN
JENKINS, IRENE I, 31, BRIAR CLOSE, HORNDEAN
JENKINS, SIDNEY F, 31, BRIAR CLOSE, HORNDEAN
RASON, ADAM L, 32, BRIAR CLOSE, HORNDEAN
RASON, JULIE A, 32, BRIAR CLOSE, HORNDEAN
MCINNES, JAMES S, 33, BRIAR CLOSE, HORNDEAN
PURDEY, ANDREW B, 35, BRIAR CLOSE, HORNDEAN
PURDEY, DENISE E, 35, BRIAR CLOSE, HORNDEAN
MONTGOMERY, AMY A, 1, CEDAR CRESCENT, HORNDEAN
MONTGOMERY, GEORGE, 1, CEDAR CRESCENT, HORNDEAN
O'LEARY, RUEBELLE A, 1, CEDAR CRESCENT, HORNDEAN
CRAPNELL, EDNA B, 2, CEDAR CRESCENT, HORNDEAN
CRAPNELL, GERALD E, 2, CEDAR CRESCENT, HORNDEAN
WILDISH, ALAN J, 4, CEDAR CRESCENT, HORNDEAN
WILDISH, KRISTOPHER A, 4, CEDAR CRESCENT, HORNDEAN
WILDISH, PHILIPPA, 4, CEDAR CRESCENT, HORNDEAN
ROWLAND, BETTY J, 6, CEDAR CRESCENT, HORNDEAN
ROWLAND, FREDERICK E, 6, CEDAR CRESCENT, HORNDEAN
BEDFORD, KENNETH H, 8, CEDAR CRESCENT, HORNDEAN
BEDFORD, LYNN, 8, CEDAR CRESCENT, HORNDEAN
BEDFORD, RICHARD A, 8, CEDAR CRESCENT, HORNDEAN
BEDFORD, ROBERT L, 8, CEDAR CRESCENT, HORNDEAN
HARRIS, JANET R, 10, CEDAR CRESCENT, HORNDEAN
HARRIS, JOHN P, 10, CEDAR CRESCENT, HORNDEAN
MASSEY, FRANCES D, 11, CEDAR CRESCENT, HORNDEAN
MASSEY, NORMAN E, 11, CEDAR CRESCENT, HORNDEAN
KING, MARTIN E, 12, CEDAR CRESCENT, HORNDEAN
KING, WENDY M, 12, CEDAR CRESCENT, HORNDEAN
LONGYEAR, CYRIL F, 13, CEDAR CRESCENT, HORNDEAN
LONGYEAR, JOSEPHINE M, 13, CEDAR CRESCENT,
KATTENHORN, DONALD, 14, CEDAR CRESCENT, HORNDEAN
KATTENHORN, EDNA S, 14, CEDAR CRESCENT, HORNDEAN
EASTON, ANGELA M, 15, CEDAR CRESCENT, HORNDEAN
EASTON, GEOFFREY M, 15, CEDAR CRESCENT, HORNDEAN
EASTON, KATRINA V, 15, CEDAR CRESCENT, HORNDEAN
MOSS, BARBARA, 16, CEDAR CRESCENT, HORNDEAN
LOCKIE, FREDERICK A, 17, CEDAR CRESCENT, HORNDEAN
LOCKIE, PAULINE A, 17, CEDAR CRESCENT, HORNDEAN
LOCKIE, SAMANTHA C, 17, CEDAR CRESCENT, HORNDEAN
SHAW, JOAN I, 18, CEDAR CRESCENT, HORNDEAN
SHAW, RONALD W, 18, CEDAR CRESCENT, HORNDEAN
BERRYMAN, IAN, 19, CEDAR CRESCENT, HORNDEAN
ROWDEN, CAROLE A, 19, CEDAR CRESCENT, HORNDEAN
ROWDEN, VICTORIA C, 19, CEDAR CRESCENT, HORNDEAN
MOORE, ANTHONY J, 20, CEDAR CRESCENT, HORNDEAN
MOORE, ROSLYN M, 20, CEDAR CRESCENT, HORNDEAN
JELLEY, DAVID G, 21, CEDAR CRESCENT, HORNDEAN
JELLEY, DOROTHY J, 21, CEDAR CRESCENT, HORNDEAN
KING, MARY P, 22, CEDAR CRESCENT, HORNDEAN
KING, PHYLLIS M, 22, CEDAR CRESCENT, HORNDEAN
KING, WALTER G.E, 22, CEDAR CRESCENT, HORNDEAN
TAYLOR, BRYAN E, 23, CEDAR CRESCENT, HORNDEAN
TAYLOR, PAUL M, 23, CEDAR CRESCENT, HORNDEAN
TAYLOR, SHEILA E, 23, CEDAR CRESCENT, HORNDEAN
CHRISTIE, ANNETTE G, 24, CEDAR CRESCENT, HORNDEAN
CHRISTIE, KENNETH, 24, CEDAR CRESCENT, HORNDEAN
POWELL, JOAN, 25, CEDAR CRESCENT, HORNDEAN
SHEAFF, GRAHAM C, 26, CEDAR CRESCENT, HORNDEAN
SHEAFF, PATRICIA E, 26, CEDAR CRESCENT, HORNDEAN
PAICE, DENISE B.J, 27, CEDAR CRESCENT, HORNDEAN
SOFFE, PETER J, 27, CEDAR CRESCENT, HORNDEAN
COX, EDNA J, 28, CEDAR CRESCENT, HORNDEAN
COX, MICHELLE D, 28, CEDAR CRESCENT, HORNDEAN
TARRANT, BRIDGET J, 29, CEDAR CRESCENT, HORNDEAN
TARRANT, RONALD W, 29, CEDAR CRESCENT, HORNDEAN
FROST, CHRISTOPHER R, 30, CEDAR CRESCENT, HORNDEAN
FROST, HILARY M, 30, CEDAR CRESCENT, HORNDEAN
CLARKE, JAMES E, 31, CEDAR CRESCENT, HORNDEAN
CLARKE, PETER T, 31, CEDAR CRESCENT, HORNDEAN
COLLYER, JOYCE E, 32, CEDAR CRESCENT, HORNDEAN
WAY, GLADYS, 32, CEDAR CRESCENT, HORNDEAN
EAMES, HAZEL B, 33, CEDAR CRESCENT, HORNDEAN
EAMES, MICHAEL J, 33, CEDAR CRESCENT, HORNDEAN
GOULD, CHRISTINE P, 34, CEDAR CRESCENT, HORNDEAN
GOULD, ROBERT B, 34, CEDAR CRESCENT, HORNDEAN
SOUTHGATE, MARY M, 35, CEDAR CRESCENT, HORNDEAN
SOUTHGATE, WILLIAM C, 35, CEDAR CRESCENT, HORNDEAN
KIMBER, JOHN R, 36, CEDAR CRESCENT, HORNDEAN
KIMBER, YVONNE A, 36, CEDAR CRESCENT, HORNDEAN
BRAY, DOROTHY, 37, CEDAR CRESCENT, HORNDEAN
BRAY, ROBERT, 37, CEDAR CRESCENT, HORNDEAN
DERRETT, GRAHAM J, 38, CEDAR CRESCENT, HORNDEAN
DERRETT, JUDITH A, 38, CEDAR CRESCENT, HORNDEAN
THURBON, ALAN W, 39, CEDAR CRESCENT, HORNDEAN
THURBON, JEAN C, 39, CEDAR CRESCENT, HORNDEAN
WOODGATE, LESLEY A, 40, CEDAR CRESCENT, HORNDEAN
WOODGATE, PAUL E, 40, CEDAR CRESCENT, HORNDEAN
HAWKINS, CAROL R, 41, CEDAR CRESCENT, HORNDEAN
HAWKINS, CHRISTOPHER J, 41, CEDAR CRESCENT,
HAWKINS, DANNY J, 41, CEDAR CRESCENT, HORNDEAN
HAWKINS, MARK C, 41, CEDAR CRESCENT, HORNDEAN
HOWE, ANNE L, 42, CEDAR CRESCENT, HORNDEAN
HOWE, COLIN F, 42, CEDAR CRESCENT, HORNDEAN
COLE, FIONA A, 43, CEDAR CRESCENT, HORNDEAN
COLE, PETER L, 43, CEDAR CRESCENT, HORNDEAN
STREET, ALICE C, 44, CEDAR CRESCENT, HORNDEAN
STREET, MICHAEL E, 44, CEDAR CRESCENT, HORNDEAN
HARPER, ANNE, 45, CEDAR CRESCENT, HORNDEAN
HARPER, CHRISTOPHER T, 45, CEDAR CRESCENT, HORNDEAN
CLARKSON, DOROTHY, 46, CEDAR CRESCENT, HORNDEAN
WATSON, JOHN, 46, CEDAR CRESCENT, HORNDEAN
BROWN, DARREN J, 47, CEDAR CRESCENT, HORNDEAN
BROWN, DEREK G, 47, CEDAR CRESCENT, HORNDEAN
BROWN, DRENA C.S, 47, CEDAR CRESCENT, HORNDEAN
WARD, PATRICIA M, 48, CEDAR CRESCENT, HORNDEAN
WARD, RUSSELL S, 48, CEDAR CRESCENT, HORNDEAN
PURL, ARTHUR R, 49, CEDAR CRESCENT, HORNDEAN
PURL, EILEEN L, 49, CEDAR CRESCENT, HORNDEAN
PURL, RACHAEL M, 49, CEDAR CRESCENT, HORNDEAN
TURNER, DOROTHY F, 50, CEDAR CRESCENT, HORNDEAN
TURNER, ROBERT W, 50, CEDAR CRESCENT, HORNDEAN
CROSSLEY, MAXINE T, 51, CEDAR CRESCENT, HORNDEAN
O'BOYLE, DAVID J, 51, CEDAR CRESCENT, HORNDEAN
WORRALL, MATTHEW J.J, 51, CEDAR CRESCENT, HORNDEAN
SIMPSON, ESME C, 52, CEDAR CRESCENT, HORNDEAN
SIMPSON, JOE, 52, CEDAR CRESCENT, HORNDEAN
DORAN, EILEEN J, 53, CEDAR CRESCENT, HORNDEAN
DORAN, MICHAEL W, 53, CEDAR CRESCENT, HORNDEAN
DORAN, PAUL R, 53, CEDAR CRESCENT, HORNDEAN
WILKINS, ROY C, 54, CEDAR CRESCENT, HORNDEAN
WILKINS, RUTH G, 54, CEDAR CRESCENT, HORNDEAN
BUTTERS, ALEXANDER, 56, CEDAR CRESCENT, HORNDEAN
BUTTERS, ELSIE, 56, CEDAR CRESCENT, HORNDEAN
BUTTERS, FIONA I, 56, CEDAR CRESCENT, HORNDEAN
STRUTT, DAVID T, 1, CHESTNUT AVENUE, HORNDEAN
STRUTT, VALERIE H, 1, CHESTNUT AVENUE, HORNDEAN
GARLAND, IRENE C, 2, CHESTNUT AVENUE, HORNDEAN
GARLAND, RONALD W, 2, CHESTNUT AVENUE, HORNDEAN
GARDINER, MOLLIE L, 3, CHESTNUT AVENUE, HORNDEAN
GARDINER, OSWALD B, 3, CHESTNUT AVENUE, HORNDEAN
MAIDMENT, MARGARET M, 4, CHESTNUT AVENUE,
MAIDMENT, TERENCE R, 4, CHESTNUT AVENUE, HORNDEAN
COLLINS, PATRICIA B, 5, CHESTNUT AVENUE, HORNDEAN
COLLINS, PETER N, 5, CHESTNUT AVENUE, HORNDEAN
PAYNE, KATHLEEN W, 7, CHESTNUT AVENUE, HORNDEAN
PAYNE, RONALD G, 7, CHESTNUT AVENUE, HORNDEAN
MASSEY, BARBARA A, 8, CHESTNUT AVENUE, HORNDEAN
MASSEY, JACK F, 8, CHESTNUT AVENUE, HORNDEAN
ALLEN, GWENDOLINE N, 9, CHESTNUT AVENUE, HORNDEAN
WIGGINS, PETER R, 10, CHESTNUT AVENUE, HORNDEAN
CARTMAN, JAMES P, 11, CHESTNUT AVENUE, HORNDEAN
CARTMAN, MICHELLE A, 11, CHESTNUT AVENUE, HORNDEAN
OWEN, CAROLE A, 11, CHESTNUT AVENUE, HORNDEAN
OWEN, DAVID, 11, CHESTNUT AVENUE, HORNDEAN
BRYANT, CHRISTINA C, STARLINGS, CHURCH PATH,
KYTE, GEORGE R, OWL COTTAGE, CHURCH PATH,
PETERS, WENDY, OWL COTTAGE, CHURCH PATH, HORNDEAN
DENTON, WAYNE J, DOWNACRE, CHURCH PATH, HORNDEAN
ADIE, SUSAN J, ELLARONA, CHURCH PATH, HORNDEAN
BOOTH, HAZEL O, GREENSLEEVES, CHURCH PATH,
GRAY, CLARE, GREENSLEEVES, CHURCH PATH, HORNDEAN
GRAY, GARRY M, GREENSLEEVES, CHURCH PATH,
MERWOOD, ALISON J, HOLLY DENE, CHURCH PATH,
MERWOOD, TIMOTHY J, HOLLY DENE, CHURCH PATH,
KENT, CLIVE E, OLD ORCHARD, CHURCH PATH, HORNDEAN
PEREIRA, SYLVIA R, OLD ORCHARD, CHURCH PATH,
STEWART, STEPHEN A, THE PADDOCK, CHURCH PATH,
STEWART, VIVIENNE, THE PADDOCK, CHURCH PATH,
WHITTAKER, GEORGE H, TREETOPS, CHURCH PATH,
EILFIELD, ROSEMARY E, TROVE HOUSE, CHURCH PATH,
EILFIELD, THOMAS R, TROVE HOUSE, CHURCH PATH,
LAWS, RUBY D, THE YEWS, CHURCH PATH,
WILSON, ADRIENNE L, WESTWARD HOUSE, CHURCH PATH,
WILSON, GRAHAM D, WESTWARD HOUSE, CHURCH PATH,
BONGIBLAUT, CHRISTELLE, BLENDWORTH LODGE, CHURCH PATH, HORNDEAN
CHANCELLOR, MURRAY H, BLENDWORTH LODGE, CHURCH PATH, HORNDEAN
CHANCELLOR, RACHEL S, BLENDWORTH LODGE, CHURCH PATH, HORNDEAN
BATT, BRUCE N, LANE END, CHURCH PATH, HORNDEAN
COHMAN, SAMUEL L, LANE END, CHURCH PATH, HORNDEAN
MANNERING, JOHN T, 1, DEEP DELL, HORNDEAN
MANNERING, MARJORIE, 1, DEEP DELL, HORNDEAN
GULLIVER, JACQUELINE D, 2, DEEP DELL, HORNDEAN
GULLIVER, JOHN F, 2, DEEP DELL, HORNDEAN
WHITE, NORMA, 3, DEEP DELL, HORNDEAN
WHITE, ROBIN, 3, DEEP DELL, HORNDEAN
GARLAND, LEONARD P, 4, DEEP DELL, HORNDEAN
GARLAND, PAUL L, 4, DEEP DELL, HORNDEAN
GARLAND, RUSSELL E, 4, DEEP DELL, HORNDEAN
GARLAND, SUSAN E, 4, DEEP DELL, HORNDEAN
DADDS, JOY A, 5, DEEP DELL, HORNDEAN
DADDS, MERVYN S, 5, DEEP DELL, HORNDEAN
DADDS, NICOLA J, 5, DEEP DELL, HORNDEAN
DADDS, SEAN S, 5, DEEP DELL, HORNDEAN
MORTIMER, KATE E, 6, DEEP DELL, HORNDEAN
MORTIMER, PAUL M, 6, DEEP DELL, HORNDEAN
SHEPHARD, GEORGINA F, 7, DEEP DELL, HORNDEAN
WADDINGHAM, LAWRENCE K, 7, DEEP DELL, HORNDEAN
SKINNER, ANDREW J, 8, DEEP DELL, HORNDEAN
SKINNER, ELAINE E, 8, DEEP DELL, HORNDEAN
MOORE, GARY, 9, DEEP DELL, HORNDEAN
MOORE, VIVIENNE, 9, DEEP DELL, HORNDEAN
LLOYD-PAYNE, BRETT, 11, DEEP DELL, HORNDEAN
WHITEHEAD, MICHAEL J, 17, ELDERBERRY WAY, HORNDEAN
WHITEHEAD, MICHELLE J, 17, ELDERBERRY WAY, HORNDEAN
WHITEHEAD, ROSEMARY A, 17, ELDERBERRY WAY,
KING, DANIEL J, 19, ELDERBERRY WAY, HORNDEAN
KING, ROSEMARY J, 19, ELDERBERRY WAY, HORNDEAN
DALLAS, DAVID, 21, ELDERBERRY WAY, HORNDEAN
DALLAS, JACQUELINE A, 21, ELDERBERRY WAY, HORNDEAN
DALLAS, MICHAEL P, 21, ELDERBERRY WAY, HORNDEAN
DALLAS, WENDY R, 21, ELDERBERRY WAY, HORNDEAN
STAMPER, RALPH C, 23, ELDERBERRY WAY, HORNDEAN
STAMPER, STACEY D, 23, ELDERBERRY WAY, HORNDEAN
DAY, ARTHUR P, 1, FIR TREE GARDENS, HORNDEAN
DAY, MARGARET R, 1, FIR TREE GARDENS, HORNDEAN
VINCENT, ANDREW C, 2, FIR TREE GARDENS, HORNDEAN
VINCENT, JACQUELINE C, 2, FIR TREE GARDENS, HORNDEAN
GIDDINGS, FRANCIS J, 3, FIR TREE GARDENS, HORNDEAN
PEARSON, LOUISE, 3, FIR TREE GARDENS, HORNDEAN
STOTHARD, STEPHANIE J, 4, FIR TREE GARDENS, HORNDEAN
MOORE, KIM, 5, FIR TREE GARDENS, HORNDEAN
MOORE, MARK, 5, FIR TREE GARDENS, HORNDEAN
SMART, FIONA C, 6, FIR TREE GARDENS, HORNDEAN
SMART, KENNETH J, 6, FIR TREE GARDENS, HORNDEAN
STEPHENSON, PETER A, 7, FIR TREE GARDENS, HORNDEAN
MILES, SUSAN A, 8, FIR TREE GARDENS, HORNDEAN
PRICE, MICHAEL P, 10, FIR TREE GARDENS, HORNDEAN
SAURIN, TRACY, 10, FIR TREE GARDENS, HORNDEAN
MANN, GEOFFREY M, 11, FIR TREE GARDENS, HORNDEAN
MANN, JUDITH L, 11, FIR TREE GARDENS, HORNDEAN
AVERY, KAREN, 13, FIR TREE GARDENS, HORNDEAN
AVERY, PAUL, 13, FIR TREE GARDENS, HORNDEAN
POWELL, CLAIRE L, 14, FIR TREE GARDENS, HORNDEAN
POWELL, DAVID, 14, FIR TREE GARDENS, HORNDEAN
POWELL, VICTOR A, 14, FIR TREE GARDENS, HORNDEAN
DENSTON, DOROTHY K, 15, FIR TREE GARDENS, HORNDEAN
SPENCER, DAVID J, 16, FIR TREE GARDENS, HORNDEAN
SPENCER, SUSAN M, 16, FIR TREE GARDENS, HORNDEAN
BONE, HELEN J, 17, FIR TREE GARDENS, HORNDEAN
BONE, MARGARET, 17, FIR TREE GARDENS, HORNDEAN
BONE, PETER W, 17, FIR TREE GARDENS, HORNDEAN
ROWLANDS, CHRISTINE, 18, FIR TREE GARDENS, HORNDEAN
ROWLANDS, DARREN J, 18, FIR TREE GARDENS, HORNDEAN
ROWLANDS, MALCOLM E, 18, FIR TREE GARDENS,
ROWLANDS, SCOTT A, 18, FIR TREE GARDENS, HORNDEAN
CORREA, HELEN R, 19, FIR TREE GARDENS, HORNDEAN
CORREA, ROBERT J, 19, FIR TREE GARDENS, HORNDEAN
CROW, ELEANOR J, 20, FIR TREE GARDENS, HORNDEAN
CROW, JAMES R, 20, FIR TREE GARDENS, HORNDEAN
CROW, JULIA E, 20, FIR TREE GARDENS, HORNDEAN
CROW, ROBERT J, 20, FIR TREE GARDENS, HORNDEAN
MORING, KAREN J, 21, FIR TREE GARDENS, HORNDEAN
MORING, PAMELA M, 21, FIR TREE GARDENS, HORNDEAN
MORING, ROBERT B, 21, FIR TREE GARDENS, HORNDEAN
DUNCAN, BRIAN C, 22, FIR TREE GARDENS, HORNDEAN
DUNCAN, TERESA M, 22, FIR TREE GARDENS, HORNDEAN
DUNLAN, LOUISE E, 22, FIR TREE GARDENS, HORNDEAN
SKEET, ANDREW, 23, FIR TREE GARDENS, HORNDEAN
SKEET, CLIVE L.S, 23, FIR TREE GARDENS, HORNDEAN
SKEET, SHIRLEY J, 23, FIR TREE GARDENS, HORNDEAN
BUTCHER, MATTHEW, 24, FIR TREE GARDENS, HORNDEAN
BUTCHER, SAMANTHA, 24, FIR TREE GARDENS, HORNDEAN
MORRISON-CHAPMAN, MEGAN, 152, GREENFIELD CRESCENT,
SAVAGE, KARL P, 154, GREENFIELD CRESCENT, HORNDEAN
SAVAGE, KIM L, 154, GREENFIELD CRESCENT, HORNDEAN
BUCKIE, DONNA F, 156, GREENFIELD CRESCENT, HORNDEAN
BUCKIE, IAN E, 156, GREENFIELD CRESCENT, HORNDEAN
GILSON, ROSS M, 156, GREENFIELD CRESCENT, HORNDEAN
JOHNSON, NIGEL, 158, GREENFIELD CRESCENT, HORNDEAN
JOHNSON, ROSIE J, 158, GREENFIELD CRESCENT, HORNDEAN
EADE, ALAN D, 160, GREENFIELD CRESCENT, HORNDEAN
EADE, WENDY J, 160, GREENFIELD CRESCENT, HORNDEAN
BURGHAM-WILSON, ALAN, 161, GREENFIELD CRESCENT,
BURGHAM-WILSON, DOREEN A, 161, GREENFIELD CRESCENT,
BURGHAM-WILSON, KEITH D, 161, GREENFIELD CRESCENT,
BURGHAM-WILSON, PAUL, 161, GREENFIELD CRESCENT,
ROY, ANDREW W, 162, GREENFIELD CRESCENT, HORNDEAN
ROY, SUSAN L, 162, GREENFIELD CRESCENT, HORNDEAN
FRANCIS, JEAN, 163, GREENFIELD CRESCENT, HORNDEAN
WEST, BRIAN, 164, GREENFIELD CRESCENT, HORNDEAN
WILLIAMS, ELIZABETH A, 164, GREENFIELD CRESCENT,
CHISHOLM, DAVID R, 165, GREENFIELD CRESCENT,
CHISHOLM, JULIET R, 165, GREENFIELD CRESCENT,
BROWN, EDWARD J, 166, GREENFIELD CRESCENT, HORNDEAN
READ, MARGARET, 166, GREENFIELD CRESCENT, HORNDEAN
CROWHURST, LESLIE E, 167, GREENFIELD CRESCENT,
CROWHURST, MAUREEN L, 167, GREENFIELD CRESCENT,
BLANCHARD, NEIL, 168, GREENFIELD CRESCENT, HORNDEAN
BLANCHARD, SHARON E, 168, GREENFIELD CRESCENT,
SANDY, CHARLENE D, 170, GREENFIELD CRESCENT,
SANDY, JOHN C, 170, GREENFIELD CRESCENT, HORNDEAN
SANDY, LOUISE J, 170, GREENFIELD CRESCENT, HORNDEAN
SANDY, RITA I, 170, GREENFIELD CRESCENT, HORNDEAN
JOHNSON, AMANDA C, 172, GREENFIELD CRESCENT,
JOHNSON, NOEL K, 172, GREENFIELD CRESCENT, HORNDEAN
JOHNSON, SEAN T, 172, GREENFIELD CRESCENT, HORNDEAN
BAKER, RUSSELL J, 174, GREENFIELD CRESCENT, HORNDEAN
REES, NICOLA J, 174, GREENFIELD CRESCENT, HORNDEAN
DAWE, NORMA M, 176, GREENFIELD CRESCENT, HORNDEAN
DAWE, TIMOTHY J, 176, GREENFIELD CRESCENT, HORNDEAN
FARRELL, KATIE E, 178, GREENFIELD CRESCENT, HORNDEAN
FARRELL, MICHAEL, 178, GREENFIELD CRESCENT,
VANDOME, ELIZABETH Y, 179, GREENFIELD CRESCENT,
VANDOME, WALTER J, 179, GREENFIELD CRESCENT,
HULETT, ALAN R, 180, GREENFIELD CRESCENT, HORNDEAN
HULETT, ANGELA V, 180, GREENFIELD CRESCENT,
HULETT, CHRISTINE E, 180, GREENFIELD CRESCENT,
HULETT, MARY A, 180, GREENFIELD CRESCENT, HORNDEAN
GODDARD, HILDA M, 181, GREENFIELD CRESCENT,
GODDARD, WALTER A, 181, GREENFIELD CRESCENT,
STEWART, ANDREW T, 182, GREENFIELD CRESCENT,
STEWART, ELIZABETH A, 182, GREENFIELD CRESCENT,
STEWART, JOANNE E, 182, GREENFIELD CRESCENT,
WARWICKER, AILEEN D, 183, GREENFIELD CRESCENT,

Electoral Roll

BLACKMAN, PETER L, 184, GREENFIELD CRESCENT,
BLACKMAN, SHIRLEY, 184, GREENFIELD CRESCENT,
WILLIS, JEAN M, 185, GREENFIELD CRESCENT, HORNDEAN
WILLIS, JOHN H, 185, GREENFIELD CRESCENT, HORNDEAN
RUSSELL, BRIAN M, 186, GREENFIELD CRESCENT, HORNDEAN
RUSSELL, NICHOLA J, 186, GREENFIELD CRESCENT,
RUSSELL, VICKY, 186, GREENFIELD CRESCENT, HORNDEAN
MURDOCH, HILDA V, 187, GREENFIELD CRESCENT,
SHERIDAN, WILLIAM R, 188, GREENFIELD CRESCENT,
RUDGE, CHARLES H, 190, GREENFIELD CRESCENT,
RUDGE, HEATHER, 190, GREENFIELD CRESCENT, HORNDEAN
GODDEN, KEITH S, 192, GREENFIELD CRESCENT, HORNDEAN
GODDEN, MARJORIE J, 192, GREENFIELD CRESCENT,
MORRISON, KEITH A.J, 193, GREENFIELD CRESCENT,
MORRISON, MARIANNE, 193, GREENFIELD CRESCENT,
LITTLE, BARRIE, 194, GREENFIELD CRESCENT, HORNDEAN
LITTLE, SUSAN M, 194, GREENFIELD CRESCENT, HORNDEAN
BACK, ESTHER P, 195, GREENFIELD CRESCENT, HORNDEAN
BACK, MICHAEL D, 195, GREENFIELD CRESCENT, HORNDEAN
PEARCE, MARY A.L, 196, GREENFIELD CRESCENT, HORNDEAN
BRODIE, ALFRED R, 197, GREENFIELD CRESCENT,
BRODIE, PATRICIA J, 197, GREENFIELD CRESCENT,
HADAWAY, DOREEN F, 198, GREENFIELD CRESCENT,
WILEY, CAROL A, 199, GREENFIELD CRESCENT, HORNDEAN
WILEY, JOHN R, 199, GREENFIELD CRESCENT, HORNDEAN
WILEY, SHAUN J, 199, GREENFIELD CRESCENT, HORNDEAN
MERRETT, GILLIAN, 200, GREENFIELD CRESCENT,
MERRETT, HELEN O.N, 200, GREENFIELD CRESCENT,
MERRETT, JAMES M.N, 200, GREENFIELD CRESCENT,
MERRETT, JOHN N, 200, GREENFIELD CRESCENT, HORNDEAN
LAWRY, DELIA S, 201, GREENFIELD CRESCENT, HORNDEAN
LAWRY, REBECCA, 201, GREENFIELD CRESCENT, HORNDEAN
LAWRY, SAMUEL, 201, GREENFIELD CRESCENT, HORNDEAN
TAYLOR, PATRICIA D, 202, GREENFIELD CRESCENT,
YOUNG, BETTY H, 203, GREENFIELD CRESCENT, HORNDEAN
PINK, JUNE C, 204, GREENFIELD CRESCENT, HORNDEAN
ANDREWS, KATHLEEN M, 205, GREENFIELD CRESCENT,
ANDREWS, ROBERT G, 205, GREENFIELD CRESCENT,
NICHOLLS, NATALIE A, 206, GREENFIELD CRESCENT,
SMITH, IAN T, 206, GREENFIELD CRESCENT, HORNDEAN
SMITH, JENNIFER A, 206, GREENFIELD CRESCENT,
SIBLEY, JAMES, 207, GREENFIELD CRESCENT, HORNDEAN
SIBLEY, JAMES T.W, 207, GREENFIELD CRESCENT, HORNDEAN
SIBLEY, YVONNE M, 207, GREENFIELD CRESCENT,
JACKSON, BRENDA A, 208, GREENFIELD CRESCENT,
JACKSON, PAUL R, 208, GREENFIELD CRESCENT, HORNDEAN
UNWIN, CHARLES C, 209, GREENFIELD CRESCENT,
O'NEILL, BRENDA K, 210, GREENFIELD CRESCENT,
O'NEILL, BRENDAN P, 210, GREENFIELD CRESCENT,
O'NEILL, RORY P.F, 210, GREENFIELD CRESCENT, HORNDEAN
O'NEILL, STEPHEN R, 210, GREENFIELD CRESCENT,
O'NEILL, TERRENCE J, 210, GREENFIELD CRESCENT,
KEARNS, ROBERT D, 211, GREENFIELD CRESCENT,
RANGER, IRENE F, 211, GREENFIELD CRESCENT, HORNDEAN
PETTITT, BERYL E, 212, GREENFIELD CRESCENT, HORNDEAN
KELLY, ALAN S, 214, GREENFIELD CRESCENT, HORNDEAN
KELLY, CHERYL S, 214, GREENFIELD CRESCENT, HORNDEAN
WADE, CHRISTINE, 216, GREENFIELD CRESCENT, HORNDEAN
HOMER, DEREK B, 218, GREENFIELD CRESCENT, HORNDEAN
HOMER, VIOLET A, 218, GREENFIELD CRESCENT, HORNDEAN
CROPPER, PENELOPE J, 220, GREENFIELD CRESCENT,
HUSTON, BRIAN, 220, GREENFIELD CRESCENT, HORNDEAN
BOURNE, PETER C, 222, GREENFIELD CRESCENT, HORNDEAN
BOURNE, SHEILA E, 222, GREENFIELD CRESCENT,
TAYLOR, GEORGE A, 224, GREENFIELD CRESCENT,
TAYLOR, JACQUELINE J, 224, GREENFIELD CRESCENT,
PALER, EVELYN J, 226, GREENFIELD CRESCENT, HORNDEAN
PALER, GERALD J, 226, GREENFIELD CRESCENT, HORNDEAN
HOLT, JANET L, 227, GREENFIELD CRESCENT, HORNDEAN
HOLT, JOANNE L, 227, GREENFIELD CRESCENT, HORNDEAN
HOLT, RAYMOND P, 227, GREENFIELD CRESCENT, HORNDEAN
WEARN, JOHN P, 228, GREENFIELD CRESCENT, HORNDEAN
WEARN, PATRICIA A, 228, GREENFIELD CRESCENT,
ANDREWS, ROY F, 229, GREENFIELD CRESCENT, HORNDEAN
ANDREWS, VERA O.A, 229, GREENFIELD CRESCENT,
JEFFERIES, MONTAGUE G.H, 5, HAVANT ROAD, HORNDEAN
REYNOLDS, ALAN, 7, HAVANT ROAD, HORNDEAN
REYNOLDS, JEAN B, 7, HAVANT ROAD, HORNDEAN
CLARK, MONICA, 9, HAVANT ROAD, HORNDEAN
RASON, CLIFFORD T, 11, HAVANT ROAD, HORNDEAN
RASON, GRAINNE M, 11, HAVANT ROAD, HORNDEAN
PAYNE, HAZEL A, 13, HAVANT ROAD, HORNDEAN
PAYNE, HEATHER E, 13, HAVANT ROAD, HORNDEAN
PAYNE, ROGER D, 13, HAVANT ROAD, HORNDEAN
LOUGHER, DAVID A, 15, HAVANT ROAD, HORNDEAN
LOUGHER, JOSEPHINE, 15, HAVANT ROAD, HORNDEAN
HALL, ERNEST A, 17, HAVANT ROAD, HORNDEAN
HALL, PAMELA B, 17, HAVANT ROAD, HORNDEAN
HALL, WENDY D, 17, HAVANT ROAD, HORNDEAN
GREGORY, LILIAN E, 19, HAVANT ROAD, HORNDEAN
DRY, CAROLINE L, 21, HAVANT ROAD, HORNDEAN
DRY, JOHN D, 21, HAVANT ROAD, HORNDEAN
DRY, SANDRA P, 21, HAVANT ROAD, HORNDEAN
HOLDHAM, JAMIE L, 23, HAVANT ROAD, HORNDEAN
HOLDHAM, JANETTE R, 23, HAVANT ROAD, HORNDEAN
HOLDHAM, JOHN P, 23, HAVANT ROAD, HORNDEAN
ALLERY, JESSIE E, 1, ROSECOTT, HAVANT ROAD, HORNDEAN
FENTON, MAVIS A, 2, ROSECOTT, HAVANT ROAD, HORNDEAN
BORROW, BETTY I, 3, ROSECOTT, HAVANT ROAD, HORNDEAN
KIRK, BARBARA, 4, ROSECOTT, HAVANT ROAD, HORNDEAN
WHITE, JOAN M, 5, ROSECOTT, HAVANT ROAD, HORNDEAN
WHITE, RONALD W, 5, ROSECOTT, HAVANT ROAD,
SUFF, DORIS A, 7, ROSECOTT, HAVANT ROAD, HORNDEAN
ADAMS, GWENNYTH C, 8, ROSECOTT, HAVANT ROAD,
HATHAWAY, EDWIN J, 9, ROSECOTT, HAVANT ROAD,
RICHARDS, KATHLEEN M, 10, ROSECOTT, HAVANT ROAD,
CARTER, VERA M, 11, ROSECOTT, HAVANT ROAD,
DAVIS, HILDA, 12, ROSECOTT, HAVANT ROAD, HORNDEAN
WILLIAMSON, IRENE E, 13, ROSECOTT, HAVANT ROAD,
TAYLOR, MARGARET L, 14, ROSECOTT, HAVANT ROAD,
PILE, MARGARET I.M, 16, ROSECOTT, HAVANT ROAD,
MUNN, DORIS E, 17, ROSECOTT, HAVANT ROAD, HORNDEAN
SADLER, LAURENCE A.J, 18, ROSECOTT, HAVANT ROAD,
LIBBY, IDA M, 19, ROSECOTT, HAVANT ROAD, HORNDEAN
THAIR, WINIFRED A, 20, ROSECOTT, HAVANT ROAD,
MURPHY, FREDA E, 21, ROSECOTT, HAVANT ROAD,
JONES, AUDREY M, 22, ROSECOTT, HAVANT ROAD,
JONES, DESMOND R, 22, ROSECOTT, HAVANT ROAD,
PAYNE, WINIFRED R, 23, ROSECOTT, HAVANT ROAD,
MOYS, FLORENCE I, 24, ROSECOTT, HAVANT ROAD,
MOYS, WILLIAM R, 24, ROSECOTT, HAVANT ROAD,
TAVENDER, JOAN, 25, ROSECOTT, HAVANT ROAD, HORNDEAN
BURGESS, MARGARET D, 26, ROSECOTT, HAVANT ROAD,
FROUD, THOMAS R.W, 27, ROSECOTT, HAVANT ROAD,
JUBBER, KATHLEEN M, 28, ROSECOTT, HAVANT ROAD,
WRIGHT, JOAN, 29, ROSECOTT, HAVANT ROAD, HORNDEAN
JARRETT, KATHLEEN M, 30, ROSECOTT, HAVANT ROAD,
MCCARTHY, EDITH M, 31, ROSECOTT, HAVANT ROAD,
MCCARTHY, MARGARET, 31, ROSECOTT, HAVANT ROAD,
SANDLE, GRACE E.B, 32, ROSECOTT, HAVANT ROAD,
STEWARD, FREDERICK J.F, 33, ROSECOTT, HAVANT ROAD,
STEWARD, JOAN C, 33, ROSECOTT, HAVANT ROAD,
DAVIES, MURIEL F, 34, ROSECOTT, HAVANT ROAD,
DAVIES, THOMAS A, 34, ROSECOTT, HAVANT ROAD,
HUGHES, MARJORIE R, 35, ROSECOTT, HAVANT ROAD,
DOBLE, MURIEL, 36, ROSECOTT, HAVANT ROAD, HORNDEAN
REED, ARTHUR J, 37, ROSECOTT, HAVANT ROAD, HORNDEAN
REED, JOYCE E, 37, ROSECOTT, HAVANT ROAD, HORNDEAN
NEWELL, JESSIE E, 38, ROSECOTT, HAVANT ROAD,
FISHER, JOHN W, 39, ROSECOTT, HAVANT ROAD, HORNDEAN
SEDGWICK, GEOFFREY W, 40, ROSECOTT, HAVANT ROAD,
SEDGWICK, MARJORIE A, 40, ROSECOTT, HAVANT ROAD,
DRINKWATER-LUNN, MINNIE E, 41, ROSECOTT, HAVANT ROAD, HORNDEAN
HIGLETT, KATHLEEN A, 42, ROSECOTT, HAVANT ROAD,
REYNOLDS, CLARE C, 25, HAVANT ROAD, HORNDEAN
REYNOLDS, SPENCER J, 25, HAVANT ROAD, HORNDEAN
GRAHAM, KAREN M, 31, HAVANT ROAD, HORNDEAN
GRAHAM, SARAH J, 31, HAVANT ROAD, HORNDEAN
GRAHAM, STEVEN B, 31, HAVANT ROAD, HORNDEAN
WARREN, GEORGE W, 33, HAVANT ROAD, HORNDEAN
WARREN, MAUREEN P, 33, HAVANT ROAD, HORNDEAN
WINTERBURN, DERICK A, 35, HAVANT ROAD, HORNDEAN
WINTERBURN, DOREEN M, 35, HAVANT ROAD, HORNDEAN
MALIN, PHILIP G, 37, HAVANT ROAD, HORNDEAN
WINN, JOANNE P, 37, HAVANT ROAD, HORNDEAN
WILSON, DEBORAH, 37A, HAVANT ROAD, HORNDEAN
WILSON, MARK, 37A, HAVANT ROAD, HORNDEAN
RINES, ALAN M, 39, HAVANT ROAD, HORNDEAN
RINES, LEAH K, 39, HAVANT ROAD, HORNDEAN
RINES, MARC A, 39, HAVANT ROAD, HORNDEAN
RINES, PENELOPE D, 39, HAVANT ROAD, HORNDEAN
CORNICK, BENJAMIN, 41, HAVANT ROAD, HORNDEAN
CORNICK, ELIZABETH J, 41, HAVANT ROAD, HORNDEAN
CORNICK, LISA, 41, HAVANT ROAD, HORNDEAN
CORNICK, ROBERT G, 41, HAVANT ROAD, HORNDEAN
CORNICK, TIMOTHY, 41, HAVANT ROAD, HORNDEAN
HATHERLY, PETER M, 43, HAVANT ROAD, HORNDEAN
HATHERLY, ROSALEEN M, 43, HAVANT ROAD, HORNDEAN
WALLER, DAVID S, 45, HAVANT ROAD, HORNDEAN
WALLER, ELIZABETH P, 45, HAVANT ROAD, HORNDEAN
WALLER, EMMA L, 45, HAVANT ROAD, HORNDEAN
WALLER, STEPHEN A, 45, HAVANT ROAD, HORNDEAN
JACOBS, MADELINE P, 47, HAVANT ROAD, HORNDEAN
DAVIS, ANNA M, 47A, HAVANT ROAD, HORNDEAN
DAVIS, KERRY A, 47A, HAVANT ROAD, HORNDEAN
DAVIS, PAUL A, 47A, HAVANT ROAD, HORNDEAN
RUNALLS, MARJORIE G, 49, HAVANT ROAD, HORNDEAN
RUNALLS, STANLEY A.J, 49, HAVANT ROAD, HORNDEAN
GROOME, ANNA J, 51, HAVANT ROAD, HORNDEAN
GROOME, PETER J, 51, HAVANT ROAD, HORNDEAN
BALL, ANN, 53, HAVANT ROAD, HORNDEAN
BALL, ERIC R, 53, HAVANT ROAD, HORNDEAN
BUDGEN, DAVID J, 53A, HAVANT ROAD, HORNDEAN
BUDGEN, JANIS, 53A, HAVANT ROAD, HORNDEAN
BUDGEN, LEE, 53A, HAVANT ROAD, HORNDEAN
WINTERS, ROSALIE A, 55, HAVANT ROAD, HORNDEAN
BENFORD, GRETA C, 57, HAVANT ROAD, HORNDEAN
MCGUIRE, JANET, 59, HAVANT ROAD, HORNDEAN
MCGUIRE, PAUL J, 59, HAVANT ROAD, HORNDEAN
JERRETT, ANDREW D, 61, HAVANT ROAD, HORNDEAN
JERRETT, SUSAN M, 61, HAVANT ROAD, HORNDEAN
PETERS, KENNETH, 63, HAVANT ROAD, HORNDEAN
PETERS, RITA M, 63, HAVANT ROAD, HORNDEAN
PURNELL, MOLLY P, 65, HAVANT ROAD, HORNDEAN
PURNELL, WILLIAM G, 65, HAVANT ROAD, HORNDEAN
MORGAN, ROY C, 67, HAVANT ROAD, HORNDEAN
OGILVIE, DEBORAH J, 67, HAVANT ROAD, HORNDEAN
GRANT, MARJORIE, 67A, HAVANT ROAD, HORNDEAN
COLEMAN, CEDRIC E, 69/71, HAVANT ROAD, HORNDEAN
COLEMAN, JOSEPH J.C, 69/71, HAVANT ROAD, HORNDEAN
COLEMAN, PENELOPE J, 69/71, HAVANT ROAD, HORNDEAN
CROMWELL, KATHLEEN J, 73, HAVANT ROAD, HORNDEAN
CROMWELL, STEPHEN, 73, HAVANT ROAD, HORNDEAN
MACDUFF, AVERIL M, 77, HAVANT ROAD, HORNDEAN
MACDUFF, DONALD A, 77, HAVANT ROAD, HORNDEAN
BLOFELD, MICHAEL R.E, 79, HAVANT ROAD, HORNDEAN
BLOFELD, VIOLET L, 79, HAVANT ROAD, HORNDEAN
SPITTLES, ANN H, 81, HAVANT ROAD, HORNDEAN
SPITTLES, HELEN R, 81, HAVANT ROAD, HORNDEAN
SPITTLES, TREVOR W, 81, HAVANT ROAD, HORNDEAN
BRYANT, RAYMOND R, 83, HAVANT ROAD, HORNDEAN
WATERFIELD, MARY R, 83, HAVANT ROAD, HORNDEAN
COLES, ERIC, 85, HAVANT ROAD, HORNDEAN
COLES, WENDY P, 85, HAVANT ROAD, HORNDEAN
GREGG, TERENCE D, 87, HAVANT ROAD, HORNDEAN
HOGAN, AMANDA J, 89, HAVANT ROAD, HORNDEAN
HOGAN, DAVID A, 89, HAVANT ROAD, HORNDEAN
LITTERA, ALISON J, 89, HAVANT ROAD, HORNDEAN
EATON-MILLER, DAWN L, 12, HAVANT ROAD, HORNDEAN
MILLER, ROBERT P.G, 12, HAVANT ROAD, HORNDEAN
ROBERTS, BRIDGET M, 16, HAVANT ROAD, HORNDEAN
ROBERTS, JOHN, 16, HAVANT ROAD, HORNDEAN
NOAKES, BARBARA, 18, HAVANT ROAD, HORNDEAN
NOAKES, PATRICK, 18, HAVANT ROAD, HORNDEAN
RAY, CAROL E, 20, HAVANT ROAD, HORNDEAN
RAY, JOHN E, 20, HAVANT ROAD, HORNDEAN
SULLIVAN, DAVID C, 20A, HAVANT ROAD, HORNDEAN
SULLIVAN, NIGEL R, 20A, HAVANT ROAD, HORNDEAN
SULLIVAN, SCOTT N, 20A, HAVANT ROAD, HORNDEAN
SULLIVAN, SUSAN M, 20A, HAVANT ROAD, HORNDEAN
GREEN, BARBARA A, 22, HAVANT ROAD, HORNDEAN
GREEN, EILEEN, 22, HAVANT ROAD, HORNDEAN
MACDONALD, ANDREW, 24, HAVANT ROAD, HORNDEAN
MACDONALD, IRENE, 24, HAVANT ROAD, HORNDEAN
MACDONALD, MICHAEL J, 24, HAVANT ROAD, HORNDEAN
MACDONALD, NEIL, 24, HAVANT ROAD, HORNDEAN
RAMSKILL, JEAN P, 26, HAVANT ROAD, HORNDEAN
RAMSKILL, MICHAEL B, 26, HAVANT ROAD, HORNDEAN
RAMSKILL, SHAYNE B, 26, HAVANT ROAD, HORNDEAN
OLIVER, IAN P, 28, HAVANT ROAD, HORNDEAN
OLIVER, JACQUELINE, 28, HAVANT ROAD, HORNDEAN
HOWARD, CELIA R, 30, HAVANT ROAD, HORNDEAN
HOWARD, EDWIN J, 30, HAVANT ROAD, HORNDEAN
BELSEY, CATHERINE E, 32, HAVANT ROAD, HORNDEAN
BELSEY, OWEN A, 32, HAVANT ROAD, HORNDEAN
PEARSON, DAVID J.A, 34, HAVANT ROAD, HORNDEAN
PEARSON, KIRSTEN M, 34, HAVANT ROAD, HORNDEAN
PEARSON, MARY K, 34, HAVANT ROAD, HORNDEAN
HILL, MATTHEW D, HAZLETON FARM, HAVANT ROAD,
WREN, BRENDA D, HAZLETON FARM, HAVANT ROAD,
WREN, NIGEL E, HAZLETON FARM, HAVANT ROAD,
SURRY, JOHN F, 93, HAZLETON WAY, HORNDEAN
WETHERELL, PAULINE, 93, HAZLETON WAY, HORNDEAN
BOND, ROY W, 95, HAZLETON WAY, HORNDEAN
BIGNELL, ADAM D, 97, HAZLETON WAY, HORNDEAN
BIGNELL, DAVID T, 97, HAZLETON WAY, HORNDEAN
BIGNELL, JENNIFER H, 97, HAZLETON WAY, HORNDEAN
EDWARDS, ARRON, 99, HAZLETON WAY, HORNDEAN
EDWARDS, DALE, 99, HAZLETON WAY, HORNDEAN
EDWARDS, DAVID J, 99, HAZLETON WAY, HORNDEAN
EDWARDS, IRENE, 99, HAZLETON WAY, HORNDEAN
TUTT, GREGORY J, 101, HAZLETON WAY, HORNDEAN
TUTT, JACQUELINE A, 101, HAZLETON WAY, HORNDEAN
BURT, RODERICK J, 103, HAZLETON WAY, HORNDEAN
BURT, SHIRLEY, 103, HAZLETON WAY, HORNDEAN
PHILLIPS, CLIVE G, 105, HAZLETON WAY, HORNDEAN
PHILLIPS, JANET E, 105, HAZLETON WAY, HORNDEAN
MARTELL, IVY M, 107, HAZLETON WAY, HORNDEAN
ELSEY, JOYCE A, 109, HAZLETON WAY, HORNDEAN
MUNDIN, DEREK I, 111, HAZLETON WAY, HORNDEAN
MUNDIN, ROSEMARY, 111, HAZLETON WAY, HORNDEAN
FRYER, DENNIS F, 113, HAZLETON WAY, HORNDEAN
FRYER, PAULINE J, 113, HAZLETON WAY, HORNDEAN
ALMOND, AGNES H, 115, HAZLETON WAY, HORNDEAN
HOLLOWAY, EDWARD J, 115, HAZLETON WAY, HORNDEAN
STANLEY, IRIS E, 117, HAZLETON WAY, HORNDEAN
STANLEY, ROY C, 117, HAZLETON WAY, HORNDEAN
HUNT, BARBARA, 119, HAZLETON WAY, HORNDEAN
HUNT, WILLIAM E, 119, HAZLETON WAY, HORNDEAN
WESTON, DORIS M, 121, HAZLETON WAY, HORNDEAN
WESTON, WILLIAM A, 121, HAZLETON WAY, HORNDEAN
THOMPSON, LOUISE A, 123, HAZLETON WAY, HORNDEAN
THOMPSON, RONALD P, 123, HAZLETON WAY, HORNDEAN
THOMPSON, TERESA A, 123, HAZLETON WAY, HORNDEAN
RILEY, KENNETH S.J, 125, HAZLETON WAY, HORNDEAN
FAIRLESS, DAVID C, 127, HAZLETON WAY, HORNDEAN
JAY, BELYNDA, 127, HAZLETON WAY, HORNDEAN
HOBBS, JOAN B, 129, HAZLETON WAY, HORNDEAN
RICHARDS, BRIAN, 131, HAZLETON WAY, HORNDEAN
RICHARDS, JEAN L, 131, HAZLETON WAY, HORNDEAN
AINSLIE-HOOPER, HILARY J, 133, HAZLETON WAY,
AINSLIE-HOOPER, LESLIE F, 133, HAZLETON WAY, HORNDEAN
VINCENT, BRIAN F, 135, HAZLETON WAY, HORNDEAN
VINCENT, SARAH L, 135, HAZLETON WAY, HORNDEAN
ATWELL, CHRISTOPHER, 139, HAZLETON WAY, HORNDEAN
ATWELL, DENISE, 139, HAZLETON WAY, HORNDEAN
DARAZ, LEE, 141, HAZLETON WAY, HORNDEAN
WALKER, SHELLIE A, 141, HAZLETON WAY, HORNDEAN
WALKER, SUSAN, 141, HAZLETON WAY, HORNDEAN
WALKER, TAMSIN S, 141, HAZLETON WAY, HORNDEAN
ALLEN, MICHAEL, 143, HAZLETON WAY, HORNDEAN
CLARK, PAUL A, 145, HAZLETON WAY, HORNDEAN
CLARK, SHEREE, 145, HAZLETON WAY, HORNDEAN
YOUNG, ALBERT H, 147, HAZLETON WAY, HORNDEAN
YOUNG, BRENDA A, 147, HAZLETON WAY, HORNDEAN
SARGEANT, DOROTHY M, 149, HAZLETON WAY, HORNDEAN
SARGEANT, KENNETH W.C, 149, HAZLETON WAY, HORNDEAN
LOW, BEATRICE A, 151, HAZLETON WAY, HORNDEAN

OLIVER, MARGARET, 151, HAZLETON WAY, HORNDEAN
OLIVER, MICHAEL J, 151, HAZLETON WAY, HORNDEAN
ALLEN, PEGGY, 153, HAZLETON WAY, HORNDEAN
POLLACCO, JOSEPHINE, 155, HAZLETON WAY, HORNDEAN
POLLACCO, LOUIS, 155, HAZLETON WAY, HORNDEAN
PALMER, HEATHER E, 157, HAZLETON WAY, HORNDEAN
SMITH, NIGEL D, 157, HAZLETON WAY, HORNDEAN
GODFREY, MANTON R, 159, HAZLETON WAY, HORNDEAN
SMITH, RODNEY W, 161, HAZLETON WAY, HORNDEAN
SMITH, ROSEMARY A, 161, HAZLETON WAY, HORNDEAN
KEOGH, LYNDA B, 163, HAZLETON WAY, HORNDEAN
GRAY, HELEN E.M, 165, HAZLETON WAY, HORNDEAN
GRAY, JANICE E, 165, HAZLETON WAY, HORNDEAN
ANGUS, STEPHANIE R, 167, HAZLETON WAY, HORNDEAN
COX, SUSAN, 169, HAZLETON WAY, HORNDEAN
BUSHELL, SHARON M, 171, HAZLETON WAY, HORNDEAN
BUSHELL, STEPHEN G, 171, HAZLETON WAY, HORNDEAN
FOLEY-GREAVES, ADAM B, 173, HAZLETON WAY, HORNDEAN
FOLEY-GREAVES, ALAN F, 173, HAZLETON WAY, HORNDEAN
FOLEY-GREAVES, JANE A, 173, HAZLETON WAY, HORNDEAN
BURNETT, DAWN C, 175, HAZLETON WAY, HORNDEAN
BURNETT, KEVIN J, 175, HAZLETON WAY, HORNDEAN
WORRALL, KEVIN N.P, 177, HAZLETON WAY, HORNDEAN
WORRALL, VICTORIA C, 177, HAZLETON WAY, HORNDEAN
HARDING, CATHERINE E, 179, HAZLETON WAY, HORNDEAN
HARDING, MARGARET S, 179, HAZLETON WAY, HORNDEAN
HARDING, PETER B, 179, HAZLETON WAY, HORNDEAN
HELM, COLIN, 183, HAZLETON WAY, HORNDEAN
HELM, WENDY, 183, HAZLETON WAY, HORNDEAN
ALCOCK, CONSTANCE V, 185, HAZLETON WAY, HORNDEAN
ALCOCK, MARGARET J, 185, HAZLETON WAY, HORNDEAN
ALCOCK, SAMANTHA C, 185, HAZLETON WAY, HORNDEAN
ALCOCK, STEWART C, 185, HAZLETON WAY, HORNDEAN
ALCOCK, VICTOR J, 185, HAZLETON WAY, HORNDEAN
KELLETT, MICHAEL K, 82, HAZLETON WAY, HORNDEAN
SHARMA, MAYA D, 82, HAZLETON WAY, HORNDEAN
MALINS, JOAN P, 84, HAZLETON WAY, HORNDEAN
MALINS, THOMAS, 84, HAZLETON WAY, HORNDEAN
BUTLER, EDNA A, 86, HAZLETON WAY, HORNDEAN
GOOCH, CHARLES S, 88, HAZLETON WAY, HORNDEAN
RICKARD, DOROTHY A, 88, HAZLETON WAY, HORNDEAN
JEREMY, ANGELA P, 90, HAZLETON WAY, HORNDEAN
JEREMY, GORDON R, 90, HAZLETON WAY, HORNDEAN
WILLIAMS, CORA A.G, 92, HAZLETON WAY, HORNDEAN
LAURIE, KENNETH C, 94, HAZLETON WAY, HORNDEAN
LAURIE, KEVIN C, 94, HAZLETON WAY, HORNDEAN
LAURIE, MOIRA, 94, HAZLETON WAY, HORNDEAN
LAURIE, STEVEN A, 94, HAZLETON WAY, HORNDEAN
SCANLON, SYLVIA J, 96, HAZLETON WAY, HORNDEAN
PRICE, ALICE H, 100, HAZLETON WAY, HORNDEAN
HURST, CHRISTINE, 102, HAZLETON WAY, HORNDEAN
HURST, DEREK A.G, 102, HAZLETON WAY, HORNDEAN
ATTFIELD, CATHERINE, 106, HAZLETON WAY, HORNDEAN
ATTFIELD, RACHEL D, 106, HAZLETON WAY, HORNDEAN
SMALLMAN, CLARE B.S, 108, HAZLETON WAY, HORNDEAN
SMALLMAN, HAROLD, 108, HAZLETON WAY, HORNDEAN
CARTER, HEIDI J, 110, HAZLETON WAY, HORNDEAN
CARTER, ROBERT V, 110, HAZLETON WAY, HORNDEAN
SHRIMPTON, JOAN H, 112, HAZLETON WAY, HORNDEAN
SHRIMPTON, ROBERT E, 112, HAZLETON WAY, HORNDEAN
WEDD, ANN R, 114, HAZLETON WAY, HORNDEAN
WEDD, RICHARD, 114, HAZLETON WAY, HORNDEAN
HUTTON, BRENDA D, 116, HAZLETON WAY, HORNDEAN
HUTTON, RALPH, 116, HAZLETON WAY, HORNDEAN
JENKINS, ERNEST J, 118, HAZLETON WAY, HORNDEAN
HECTOR, PETER, 120, HAZLETON WAY, HORNDEAN
BAKER, NIGEL D, 122, HAZLETON WAY, HORNDEAN
BAKER, SYLVIA A, 122, HAZLETON WAY, HORNDEAN
ANDERSON, ELIZABETH K, 124, HAZLETON WAY, HORNDEAN
GRIFFITHS, GILLIAN M, 126, HAZLETON WAY, HORNDEAN
GRIFFITHS, RUTH F, 126, HAZLETON WAY, HORNDEAN
WESTON, CATHERINE E, 128, HAZLETON WAY, HORNDEAN
WESTON, SIDNEY E, 128, HAZLETON WAY, HORNDEAN
COX, ANNE M, 130, HAZLETON WAY, HORNDEAN
MOSS, KATHLEEN J, 130, HAZLETON WAY, HORNDEAN
MOSS, STEPHEN, 130, HAZLETON WAY, HORNDEAN
LACY, LUCY E, 132, HAZLETON WAY, HORNDEAN
CLUE, MARGARET M, 134, HAZLETON WAY, HORNDEAN
CLUE, RAYMOND S, 134, HAZLETON WAY, HORNDEAN
JEFFERIES, BARBARA M, 138, HAZLETON WAY, HORNDEAN
JEFFERIES, STEPHEN, 138, HAZLETON WAY, HORNDEAN
JEFFERIES, WILLIAM C, 138, HAZLETON WAY, HORNDEAN
DAVIES, WINIFRED M, 140, HAZLETON WAY, HORNDEAN
MILLETT, MARGARET J, 142, HAZLETON WAY, HORNDEAN
HARRIS, JOHN A, 144, HAZLETON WAY, HORNDEAN
HARRIS, JOSEPHINE M, 144, HAZLETON WAY, HORNDEAN
REYNOLDS, BRUCE W, 146, HAZLETON WAY, HORNDEAN
REYNOLDS, SUSAN J, 146, HAZLETON WAY, HORNDEAN
GOFF, CYRIL J, 148, HAZLETON WAY, HORNDEAN
GOFF, GILLIAN R, 148, HAZLETON WAY, HORNDEAN
HARFIELD, VALERIE B, 150, HAZLETON WAY, HORNDEAN
LANDER, DANIEL P, 152, HAZLETON WAY, HORNDEAN
LANDER, MATTHEW L, 152, HAZLETON WAY, HORNDEAN
MIRZA, FAROOQ R, 152, HAZLETON WAY, HORNDEAN
ROBERTS, JEFFERY, 154, HAZLETON WAY, HORNDEAN
ROBERTS, MALCOLM, 154, HAZLETON WAY, HORNDEAN
ROBERTS, VALERIE, 154, HAZLETON WAY, HORNDEAN
JONES, NELLIE, 156, HAZLETON WAY, HORNDEAN
JONES, ROBERT, 156, HAZLETON WAY, HORNDEAN
JAMES, DAVID S, 158, HAZLETON WAY, HORNDEAN
JAMES, KEVIN, 158, HAZLETON WAY, HORNDEAN
JAMES, LESLEY C, 158, HAZLETON WAY, HORNDEAN
KRUSTINS, HILDA, 160, HAZLETON WAY, HORNDEAN
KRUSTINS, JANIS O, 160, HAZLETON WAY, HORNDEAN
MAIDEN, IAN R, 162, HAZLETON WAY, HORNDEAN
MAIDEN, JACQUELINE A, 162, HAZLETON WAY, HORNDEAN
MAIDEN, THOMAS A, 162, HAZLETON WAY, HORNDEAN
LE MARQUER, BRIAN R, 168, HAZLETON WAY, HORNDEAN
LE MARQUER, LESLEY J, 168, HAZLETON WAY, HORNDEAN
BRISTOW, ARTHUR D, 170, HAZLETON WAY, HORNDEAN
BRISTOW, DOUGLAS K, 170, HAZLETON WAY, HORNDEAN
MANSELL, DAVID S, 172, HAZLETON WAY, HORNDEAN
MANSELL, KAREN L, 172, HAZLETON WAY, HORNDEAN
HOLLAND, ANNALIE S, 174, HAZLETON WAY, HORNDEAN
HOLLAND, RITA, 174, HAZLETON WAY, HORNDEAN
HOLLAND, ROBERT, 174, HAZLETON WAY, HORNDEAN
KNIGHT, ROBERT J, 176, HAZLETON WAY, HORNDEAN
KNIGHT, SUMALA, 176, HAZLETON WAY, HORNDEAN
REED, CLAUDIE S, 178, HAZLETON WAY, HORNDEAN
REED, JOANNA L, 178, HAZLETON WAY, HORNDEAN
REED, NIGEL D, 178, HAZLETON WAY, HORNDEAN
JONES, PETER, 1, HILL VIEW, HORNDEAN
IGLESIAS, HILARY L, 2, HILL VIEW, HORNDEAN
IGLESIAS, RACQUEL, 2, HILL VIEW, HORNDEAN
BOWRING, PATRICK N, 3, HILL VIEW, HORNDEAN
LILLEMAN, CHRISTINE E, 3, HILL VIEW, HORNDEAN
DICKENS, NINA J, 4, HILL VIEW, HORNDEAN
DICKENS, ROBERT, 4, HILL VIEW, HORNDEAN
RULE, JEAN M, 5, HILL VIEW, HORNDEAN
RULE, JOHN E, 5, HILL VIEW, HORNDEAN
AMBLER, MARJORIE, 6, HILL VIEW, HORNDEAN
WATTS, MARGARET, 6, HILL VIEW, HORNDEAN
RUDMAN, DEREK W, 7, HILL VIEW, HORNDEAN
RUDMAN, MARION A, 7, HILL VIEW, HORNDEAN
EVANS, DEREK A, 8, HILL VIEW, HORNDEAN
DICKINSON, JOHN G, 1, HOLLYBANK CLOSE, HORNDEAN
DICKINSON, VALERIE A, 1, HOLLYBANK CLOSE, HORNDEAN
CREEVY, JOHN, 2, HOLLYBANK CLOSE, HORNDEAN
POTTER, EDWINA C, 2, HOLLYBANK CLOSE, HORNDEAN
TAYLOR, CHRISTOPHER E, 3, HOLLYBANK CLOSE,
TAYLOR, KENNETH E, 3, HOLLYBANK CLOSE, HORNDEAN
WOODGATE, JOHN S, 4, HOLLYBANK CLOSE, HORNDEAN
WOODGATE, JULIE A, 4, HOLLYBANK CLOSE, HORNDEAN
HOLDEN, ANN, 5, HOLLYBANK CLOSE, HORNDEAN
REEVES, CHARLES H, 6, HOLLYBANK CLOSE, HORNDEAN
GLENISTER, FREDERICK A, 7, HOLLYBANK CLOSE,
GLENISTER, JOYCE M, 7, HOLLYBANK CLOSE, HORNDEAN
FORTH, CRAIG A, 1, IDSWORTH CLOSE, HORNDEAN
FORTH, JULIAN H, 1, IDSWORTH CLOSE, HORNDEAN
FORTH, LEE J, 1, IDSWORTH CLOSE, HORNDEAN
FORTH, MARJORIE B, 1, IDSWORTH CLOSE, HORNDEAN
DARLING, DAVID, 2, IDSWORTH CLOSE, HORNDEAN
DARLING, JEAN C, 2, IDSWORTH CLOSE, HORNDEAN
HUGHES, LEONARD, 3, IDSWORTH CLOSE, HORNDEAN
HUGHES, LINDSAY A, 3, IDSWORTH CLOSE, HORNDEAN
GARDINER, ROBERT J, 4, IDSWORTH CLOSE, HORNDEAN
GARDINER, VALERIE J, 4, IDSWORTH CLOSE, HORNDEAN
SIMPSON, ROBERT M, 5, IDSWORTH CLOSE, HORNDEAN
SIMPSON, SALLY L, 5, IDSWORTH CLOSE, HORNDEAN
LEWIS, DAVID H, 7, IDSWORTH CLOSE, HORNDEAN
LEWIS, PHYLLIS, 7, IDSWORTH CLOSE, HORNDEAN
NEAVE, LAXMI S, 8, IDSWORTH CLOSE, HORNDEAN
NEAVE, RICHARD S, 8, IDSWORTH CLOSE, HORNDEAN
COLE, NIGEL J, 9, IDSWORTH CLOSE, HORNDEAN
HOWARTH, ANDREW J, 9, IDSWORTH CLOSE, HORNDEAN
HOWARTH, LORNA M, 9, IDSWORTH CLOSE, HORNDEAN
MASON, DUNCAN, 10, IDSWORTH CLOSE, HORNDEAN
MASON, JANETTE E, 10, IDSWORTH CLOSE, HORNDEAN
STIRZAKER, ALLISON J, 11, IDSWORTH CLOSE, HORNDEAN
STIRZAKER, IAN D, 11, IDSWORTH CLOSE, HORNDEAN
MALMQUIST, KATARINA, 12, IDSWORTH CLOSE, HORNDEAN
MALMQUIST, PETER, 12, IDSWORTH CLOSE, HORNDEAN
DAVEY, DAVID K, 2, LARCHFIELD WAY, HORNDEAN
DAVEY, SANDRA A, 2, LARCHFIELD WAY, HORNDEAN
BENHAM, ALAN C, 4, LARCHFIELD WAY, HORNDEAN
BENHAM, BRENDA R, 4, LARCHFIELD WAY, HORNDEAN
FORD, JENNIFER M, 6, LARCHFIELD WAY, HORNDEAN
FORD, MICHAEL T, 6, LARCHFIELD WAY, HORNDEAN
ALLEBONE, DERRICK, 8, LARCHFIELD WAY, HORNDEAN
ALLEBONE, GLORIA B, 8, LARCHFIELD WAY, HORNDEAN
SMITH, PATRICIA G, 9, LARCHFIELD WAY, HORNDEAN
SMITH, WALLACE F, 9, LARCHFIELD WAY, HORNDEAN
SMITH, JUNE R, 10, LARCHFIELD WAY, HORNDEAN
SMITH, WILLIAM H, 10, LARCHFIELD WAY, HORNDEAN
GREEN, MOLLY G, 11, LARCHFIELD WAY, HORNDEAN
DAVIS, TREVOR R, 12, LARCHFIELD WAY, HORNDEAN
DAVIS, VALERIE J, 12, LARCHFIELD WAY, HORNDEAN
FOSSEY, FREDERICK A, 13, LARCHFIELD WAY, HORNDEAN
FOSSEY, OLWEN M, 13, LARCHFIELD WAY, HORNDEAN
STREVENS, ANN, 14, LARCHFIELD WAY, HORNDEAN
STREVENS, ANTHONY V, 14, LARCHFIELD WAY, HORNDEAN
STREVENS, JULIA C, 14, LARCHFIELD WAY, HORNDEAN
STREVENS, PHILIPPA J, 14, LARCHFIELD WAY, HORNDEAN
JEWELL, SHEILA D, 15, LARCHFIELD WAY, HORNDEAN
RODGERS, CHRISTINE M, 16, LARCHFIELD WAY, HORNDEAN
GEORGE, JEFFREY R, 3, LAUREL ROAD, HORNDEAN
GEORGE, MARGARET, 3, LAUREL ROAD, HORNDEAN
BURT, MARVIN J, 6, LAUREL ROAD, HORNDEAN
SAWFORD, DOREEN E, 6, LAUREL ROAD, HORNDEAN
ROGERS, JOSEPH, 7, LAUREL ROAD, HORNDEAN
ROGERS, JOSEPHINE, 7, LAUREL ROAD, HORNDEAN
MCILROY, DAVID E, 8, LAUREL ROAD, HORNDEAN
MCILROY, JUNE, 8, LAUREL ROAD, HORNDEAN
SOLLIS, IRENE E, 9, LAUREL ROAD, HORNDEAN
SOLLIS, WILFRED G, 9, LAUREL ROAD, HORNDEAN
PIPER, ROSE, 10, LAUREL ROAD, HORNDEAN
LAMPARD, TERRY J, 11, LAUREL ROAD, HORNDEAN
LAMPARD, VIOLET M, 11, LAUREL ROAD, HORNDEAN
HUSSELBY, KATHLEEN A, 12, LAUREL ROAD, HORNDEAN
HUSSELBY, ROY W, 12, LAUREL ROAD, HORNDEAN
KIRBY, BRIAN, 13, LAUREL ROAD, HORNDEAN
KIRBY, GILLIAN D, 13, LAUREL ROAD, HORNDEAN
KIRBY, TINA L, 13, LAUREL ROAD, HORNDEAN
BAKER, CYRIL, 14, LAUREL ROAD, HORNDEAN
BAKER, MOLLY E, 14, LAUREL ROAD, HORNDEAN
KELLY, PHYLL, 15, LAUREL ROAD, HORNDEAN
POLLARD, GEORGE A, 17, LAUREL ROAD, HORNDEAN
POLLARD, PEGGY B, 17, LAUREL ROAD, HORNDEAN
LOCK, ANDREW J, 1, LINDEN WAY, HORNDEAN
LOCK, ANGELA M, 1, LINDEN WAY, HORNDEAN
LOCK, JOHN E, 1, LINDEN WAY, HORNDEAN
LOCK, RICHARD W, 1, LINDEN WAY, HORNDEAN
JOLLEY, PAMELA E, 2, LINDEN WAY, HORNDEAN
MATTINGLY, ERNEST W.F, 3, LINDEN WAY, HORNDEAN
REES, ANN E, 3, LINDEN WAY, HORNDEAN
REES, CLIFFORD F, 3, LINDEN WAY, HORNDEAN
REES, SYLVIA J, 3, LINDEN WAY, HORNDEAN
WHITE, MICHAEL R, 4, LINDEN WAY, HORNDEAN
HAINES, ANITA J, 5, LINDEN WAY, HORNDEAN
HAINES, ROBERT A, 5, LINDEN WAY, HORNDEAN
NORRIS, JANET B, 6, LINDEN WAY, HORNDEAN
NORRIS, STEPHEN S, 6, LINDEN WAY, HORNDEAN
BROOKS, ELLEN M, 7/8, LINDEN WAY, HORNDEAN
COATES, FLORENCE M, 7/8, LINDEN WAY, HORNDEAN
FOSTER, BRIDGET M, 7/8, LINDEN WAY, HORNDEAN
HORN, IRIS, 7/8, LINDEN WAY, HORNDEAN
LOCKE, KATHLEEN, 7/8, LINDEN WAY, HORNDEAN
NANCARROW, BEATRICE, 7/8, LINDEN WAY, HORNDEAN
SULLIVAN, EDNA M, 7/8, LINDEN WAY, HORNDEAN
URRY, MARJORIE, 7/8, LINDEN WAY, HORNDEAN
WHITE, MINNIE, 7/8, LINDEN WAY, HORNDEAN
YEOMANS, CATHERINE, 7/8, LINDEN WAY, HORNDEAN
SHIELDS, HENRY D, 9, LINDEN WAY, HORNDEAN
SHIELDS, KAY L, 9, LINDEN WAY, HORNDEAN
ATHA, GILLIAN M, 10, LINDEN WAY, HORNDEAN
ATHA, NEVILLE W, 10, LINDEN WAY, HORNDEAN
COCHRAN, ROGER, 11, LINDEN WAY, HORNDEAN
COCHRAN, SUSAN W, 11, LINDEN WAY, HORNDEAN
O'CONNELL, JOHN M, 12, LINDEN WAY, HORNDEAN
O'CONNELL, PEGGY, 12, LINDEN WAY, HORNDEAN
BUTLER, JULIE D, 13, LINDEN WAY, HORNDEAN
CROUD, ALISON L, 14, LINDEN WAY, HORNDEAN
SHEA, ANNA, 2, MAPLETREE AVENUE, HORNDEAN
SHEA, BERNARD J, 2, MAPLETREE AVENUE, HORNDEAN
DEWIS, ANTONY N, 3, MAPLETREE AVENUE, HORNDEAN
DEWIS, JACK R.D, 3, MAPLETREE AVENUE, HORNDEAN
DEWIS, SUSAN M, 3, MAPLETREE AVENUE, HORNDEAN
NOBES, JOAN E, 3, MAPLETREE AVENUE, HORNDEAN
SPIERS, FIONA L, 3, MAPLETREE AVENUE, HORNDEAN
DE REDING, IVAN J, 4, MAPLETREE AVENUE, HORNDEAN
DE REDING, JOCELYN L, 4, MAPLETREE AVENUE, HORNDEAN
VICKERS, BRENDA, 5, MAPLETREE AVENUE, HORNDEAN
VICKERS, GEOFFREY E, 5, MAPLETREE AVENUE, HORNDEAN
JONES, VALERIE, 6, MAPLETREE AVENUE, HORNDEAN
AKEHURST, DONALD N, 7, MAPLETREE AVENUE, HORNDEAN
WATSON, GEOFFREY R, 8, MAPLETREE AVENUE, HORNDEAN
WATSON, IRENE A, 8, MAPLETREE AVENUE, HORNDEAN
LYONS, MARTIN J, 9, MAPLETREE AVENUE, HORNDEAN
LYONS, MICHAEL, 9, MAPLETREE AVENUE, HORNDEAN
LYONS, STELLA M, 9, MAPLETREE AVENUE, HORNDEAN
ASH, YVONNE B, 10, MAPLETREE AVENUE, HORNDEAN
DAVIDGE, ARTHUR C, 11, MAPLETREE AVENUE, HORNDEAN
DAVIDGE, DOROTHY, 11, MAPLETREE AVENUE, HORNDEAN
RAYMOND, ANTHONY H, 13, MAPLETREE AVENUE,
RAYMOND, JANET R, 13, MAPLETREE AVENUE, HORNDEAN
GOULD, JAMES A, 15, MAPLETREE AVENUE, HORNDEAN
GOULD, LISA M, 15, MAPLETREE AVENUE, HORNDEAN
GOULD, MARION P, 15, MAPLETREE AVENUE, HORNDEAN
GALIPEAU, EMILE O, 17, MAPLETREE AVENUE, HORNDEAN
CURTIS, ALBERT E, 19, MAPLETREE AVENUE, HORNDEAN
CURTIS, LILIAN A.M, 19, MAPLETREE AVENUE, HORNDEAN
BURTON, CATHERINE P, 20, MAPLETREE AVENUE,
BURTON, FRANK E, 20, MAPLETREE AVENUE, HORNDEAN
BALDOCK, ALFRED G, 21, MAPLETREE AVENUE, HORNDEAN
MOORE, ALISON E, 21, MAPLETREE AVENUE, HORNDEAN
MOORE, GILLIAN E, 21, MAPLETREE AVENUE, HORNDEAN
MOORE, SARAH-JANE, 21, MAPLETREE AVENUE, HORNDEAN
SHEPHERD, GEORGE P, 22, MAPLETREE AVENUE, HORNDEAN
SHEPHERD, WINIFRED V.M, 22, MAPLETREE AVENUE,
SKINNER, JULIE E, 23, MAPLETREE AVENUE, HORNDEAN
SKINNER, KEITH M, 23, MAPLETREE AVENUE, HORNDEAN
HISCUTT, ALAN D, 24, MAPLETREE AVENUE, HORNDEAN
HISCUTT, RICHARD J, 24, MAPLETREE AVENUE, HORNDEAN
HISCUTT, TERENCE, 24, MAPLETREE AVENUE, HORNDEAN
HISCUTT, WENDY M, 24, MAPLETREE AVENUE, HORNDEAN
RIALL, PETER J, 24, MAPLETREE AVENUE, HORNDEAN
HOWITT, AVERIL E, 25, MAPLETREE AVENUE, HORNDEAN
HOWITT, DERRICK, 25, MAPLETREE AVENUE, HORNDEAN
EDMUNDS, KEITH A, 26, MAPLETREE AVENUE, HORNDEAN
EDMUNDS, MARY, 26, MAPLETREE AVENUE, HORNDEAN
MORRIS, JOAN F.G, 27, MAPLETREE AVENUE, HORNDEAN
KEAY, KEITH J, 28, MAPLETREE AVENUE, HORNDEAN
KEAY, PATRICIA, 28, MAPLETREE AVENUE, HORNDEAN
KEAY, VINCENT J, 28, MAPLETREE AVENUE, HORNDEAN
FERGUSON, GORDON S, 29, MAPLETREE AVENUE,
FERGUSON, VALERIE S, 29, MAPLETREE AVENUE, HORNDEAN
GIBBINS, HARRY W, 30, MAPLETREE AVENUE, HORNDEAN
GIBBINS, JOAN K, 30, MAPLETREE AVENUE, HORNDEAN
HERRING, ANNA J, 31, MAPLETREE AVENUE, HORNDEAN

Electoral Roll

HERRING, DAVID J, 31, MAPLETREE AVENUE, HORNDEAN
JONES, LINDA J, 32, MAPLETREE AVENUE, HORNDEAN
JONES, PETER R, 32, MAPLETREE AVENUE, HORNDEAN
JONES, ROBERT P, 32, MAPLETREE AVENUE, HORNDEAN
HUTSON, GERALD R, 33, MAPLETREE AVENUE, HORNDEAN
HUTSON, SHEILA M, 33, MAPLETREE AVENUE, HORNDEAN
STONE, ROSEMARY, 34, MAPLETREE AVENUE, HORNDEAN
NOYE, ADRIAN P, 35, MAPLETREE AVENUE, HORNDEAN
NOYE, JILL F, 35, MAPLETREE AVENUE, HORNDEAN
NOYE, ROBERT J, 35, MAPLETREE AVENUE, HORNDEAN
NOYE, TIMOTHY P, 35, MAPLETREE AVENUE, HORNDEAN
FELTHAM, BERNARD M, 36, MAPLETREE AVENUE,
FELTHAM, PEARL I, 36, MAPLETREE AVENUE, HORNDEAN
TOPLEY, ANYA M, 37, MAPLETREE AVENUE, HORNDEAN
TOPLEY, BARBARA A, 37, MAPLETREE AVENUE, HORNDEAN
TOPLEY, JOHN, 37, MAPLETREE AVENUE, HORNDEAN
TOPLEY, NATASHA S, 37, MAPLETREE AVENUE, HORNDEAN
GILLARD, MELANIE J, 38, MAPLETREE AVENUE, HORNDEAN
GILLARD, ROBERT N, 38, MAPLETREE AVENUE, HORNDEAN
COLQUHOUN, JOSEPH G, 39, MAPLETREE AVENUE,
MUNNS, BARRY G, 40, MAPLETREE AVENUE, HORNDEAN
MUNNS, ELAINE, 40, MAPLETREE AVENUE, HORNDEAN
MUNNS, JOAN M, 40, MAPLETREE AVENUE, HORNDEAN
MUNNS, KEVIN, 40, MAPLETREE AVENUE, HORNDEAN
MUNNS, NEIL, 40, MAPLETREE AVENUE, HORNDEAN
BYWATER, JOYCE, 41, MAPLETREE AVENUE, HORNDEAN
BYWATER, KEITH W, 41, MAPLETREE AVENUE, HORNDEAN
ROUTLEDGE, GEORGE A, 42, MAPLETREE AVENUE,
CASEY, ARLINE M, 43, MAPLETREE AVENUE, HORNDEAN
CASEY, JAMES D, 43, MAPLETREE AVENUE, HORNDEAN
COOPER, ANDREW E.J, 44, MAPLETREE AVENUE, HORNDEAN
COOPER, JEANETTE P, 44, MAPLETREE AVENUE, HORNDEAN
MEGGISON, BRENDA J, 45, MAPLETREE AVENUE, HORNDEAN
MEGGISON, ROY F, 45, MAPLETREE AVENUE, HORNDEAN
ROGERS, KEVIN P, 1, ORCHARD CLOSE, HORNDEAN
ROGERS, TRACEY J, 1, ORCHARD CLOSE, HORNDEAN
SCHUELER, GOTZ M, 2, ORCHARD CLOSE, HORNDEAN
SCHUELER, MAUREEN M, 2, ORCHARD CLOSE, HORNDEAN
LOCK, KEVIN A, 3, ORCHARD CLOSE, HORNDEAN
LOCK, MICHELLE J, 3, ORCHARD CLOSE, HORNDEAN
MORISON, ELIZABETH A, 4, ORCHARD CLOSE, HORNDEAN
MORISON, GILES R, 4, ORCHARD CLOSE, HORNDEAN
MORISON, STEWART R, 4, ORCHARD CLOSE, HORNDEAN
FLINN, LAWRENCE, 5, ORCHARD CLOSE, HORNDEAN
ROSE, FRANCES A, 2, DEAN COURT, PORTSMOUTH ROAD, HORNDEAN
HOARE, WINIFRED D, 6, DEAN COURT, PORTSMOUTH ROAD, HORNDEAN
BAUM, FLORENCE L, 23, DEAN COURT, PORTSMOUTH ROAD, HORNDEAN
STRATFORD, DOROTHY I, 25, DEAN COURT, PORTSMOUTH ROAD, HORNDEAN
MOSELY, JOHN E, 2, PORTSMOUTH ROAD, HORNDEAN
MOSELY, SANDRA S.D, 2, PORTSMOUTH ROAD, HORNDEAN
SYKES, LEZLEY B, 8, PORTSMOUTH ROAD, HORNDEAN
SYKES, ROBERT S, 8, PORTSMOUTH ROAD, HORNDEAN
WATT, DIANNE L, 27, PORTSMOUTH ROAD, HORNDEAN
SAWLEY, KEVIN E, 29, PORTSMOUTH ROAD, HORNDEAN
BROWN, NORA, 33, PORTSMOUTH ROAD, HORNDEAN
DREW, DOROTHY M, 33, PORTSMOUTH ROAD, HORNDEAN
HICKMAN, CHRISTOPHER P, 35, PORTSMOUTH ROAD,
HICKMAN, SUSAN J, 35, PORTSMOUTH ROAD, HORNDEAN
LOVETT, ANDREW G, 37, PORTSMOUTH ROAD, HORNDEAN
LOVETT, JULIE A, 37, PORTSMOUTH ROAD, HORNDEAN
TURNER, BARBARA H, 39, PORTSMOUTH ROAD, HORNDEAN
TURNER, DAVID A, 39, PORTSMOUTH ROAD, HORNDEAN
TURNER, IAN, 39, PORTSMOUTH ROAD, HORNDEAN
TURNER, PAUL, 39, PORTSMOUTH ROAD, HORNDEAN
CLEMENTS, ELIZABETH L.A, 49, PORTSMOUTH ROAD,
CLEMENTS, GEOFFREY R, 49, PORTSMOUTH ROAD,
CLEMENTS, LISA A, 49, PORTSMOUTH ROAD, HORNDEAN
WINGHAM, BARRY E, 51, PORTSMOUTH ROAD, HORNDEAN
THOMAS, KATHLEEN M, 53, PORTSMOUTH ROAD,
WELCH, ROBIN, 53, PORTSMOUTH ROAD, HORNDEAN
ABBINETT, SHARRON L, 54, PORTSMOUTH ROAD, HORNDEAN
TAYLOR, DEAN M, 54, PORTSMOUTH ROAD, HORNDEAN
AMBIA, GULAM, 65A, PORTSMOUTH ROAD, HORNDEAN
AMBIA, GULAM E, 65A, PORTSMOUTH ROAD, HORNDEAN
AMBIA, SHOPNA, 65A, PORTSMOUTH ROAD, HORNDEAN
KHAN, MOHAMMED I, 65A, PORTSMOUTH ROAD, HORNDEAN
BALL, ALASTAIR G, 67, PORTSMOUTH ROAD, HORNDEAN
JONES, COLIN, 69, PORTSMOUTH ROAD, HORNDEAN
RAYMOND, KAY M, 69, PORTSMOUTH ROAD, HORNDEAN
PHELAN, AMANDA C, 71, PORTSMOUTH ROAD, HORNDEAN
PHELAN, PAUL A, 71, PORTSMOUTH ROAD, HORNDEAN
MELROSE, ABIGAIL F, 73, PORTSMOUTH ROAD, HORNDEAN
MELROSE, GRAHAM, 73, PORTSMOUTH ROAD, HORNDEAN
GUIDOBONI, ANTHONY M, 75, PORTSMOUTH ROAD,
GUIDOBONI, GIOVANNI E, 75, PORTSMOUTH ROAD,
GUIDOBONI, PATRICIA A, 75, PORTSMOUTH ROAD,
GUIDOBONI, WINIFRED, 75, PORTSMOUTH ROAD,
PONSFORD, PHYLLIS A, 77, PORTSMOUTH ROAD, HORNDEAN
KING, PHYLLIS, 79, PORTSMOUTH ROAD, HORNDEAN
KING, TERENCE R, 79, PORTSMOUTH ROAD, HORNDEAN
CRUMP, AUDREY R, 81, PORTSMOUTH ROAD, HORNDEAN
MARTIN, DOROTHY E, 83, PORTSMOUTH ROAD, HORNDEAN
FLEWIN, IRIS, 85, PORTSMOUTH ROAD, HORNDEAN
TROY, SHEENA M, 85A, PORTSMOUTH ROAD, HORNDEAN
MARTIN, JOYCE W, 87, PORTSMOUTH ROAD, HORNDEAN
EWENS, JACK G.C, 89, PORTSMOUTH ROAD, HORNDEAN
EWENS, PATRICIA F, 89, PORTSMOUTH ROAD, HORNDEAN
ASHTON, REBECCA A, 91, PORTSMOUTH ROAD, HORNDEAN
GARROD, JANE A, 91, PORTSMOUTH ROAD, HORNDEAN
GARROD, ROBERT N, 91, PORTSMOUTH ROAD, HORNDEAN
WALLAGE, WILLIAM F, 91, PORTSMOUTH ROAD, HORNDEAN
WHITBOURNE, CAROL R, 93, PORTSMOUTH ROAD,
WHITBOURNE, DAVID W, 93, PORTSMOUTH ROAD,
WHITBOURNE, MATTHEW D, 93, PORTSMOUTH ROAD,
SYKES, HENRY, 95, PORTSMOUTH ROAD, HORNDEAN
SYKES, MAY, 95, PORTSMOUTH ROAD, HORNDEAN
CROUCH, BRENT M, 129, PORTSMOUTH ROAD, HORNDEAN
CROUCH, ROSEMARIE L, 129, PORTSMOUTH ROAD,
VITLER, HAZEL A, 131, PORTSMOUTH ROAD, HORNDEAN
VITLER, JOHN H, 131, PORTSMOUTH ROAD, HORNDEAN
MELLISH, CHARLES T, 133, PORTSMOUTH ROAD, HORNDEAN
MELLISH, CYNTHIA, 133, PORTSMOUTH ROAD, HORNDEAN
SARGEANT, GILBERT E, 135, PORTSMOUTH ROAD,
SARGEANT, JOAN K, 135, PORTSMOUTH ROAD, HORNDEAN
GOODGER, JOY B, 137, PORTSMOUTH ROAD, HORNDEAN
GOODGER, RONALD E, 137, PORTSMOUTH ROAD,
KATTENHORN, ALISON M, 141, PORTSMOUTH ROAD,
KATTENHORN, DAVID L, 141, PORTSMOUTH ROAD,
KATTENHORN, CAROLE Y, 143, PORTSMOUTH ROAD,
KATTENHORN, LESLIE A, 143, PORTSMOUTH ROAD,
CAMERON, FREDERICK D, 145, PORTSMOUTH ROAD,
CAMERON, JANE W, 145, PORTSMOUTH ROAD, HORNDEAN
HULME, KAREN M, 147, PORTSMOUTH ROAD, HORNDEAN
SALERO, MAUREEN, 149, PORTSMOUTH ROAD, HORNDEAN
SALERO, PETER V, 149, PORTSMOUTH ROAD, HORNDEAN
PEARSON, ALAN F, 151, PORTSMOUTH ROAD, HORNDEAN
PEARSON, SANDRA I, 151, PORTSMOUTH ROAD, HORNDEAN
ALLEN, EDWARD, 153, PORTSMOUTH ROAD, HORNDEAN
CLEGG, ETHEL, 153, PORTSMOUTH ROAD, HORNDEAN
FORDHAM, HILDA, 153, PORTSMOUTH ROAD, HORNDEAN
GAYLARD, EDWARD, 153, PORTSMOUTH ROAD, HORNDEAN
GUY, FLORENCE, 153, PORTSMOUTH ROAD, HORNDEAN
HONOUR, ANNIE, 153, PORTSMOUTH ROAD, HORNDEAN
HOWARD, GLADYS, 153, PORTSMOUTH ROAD, HORNDEAN
JENKINS, SARAH, 153, PORTSMOUTH ROAD, HORNDEAN
JEWELL, JANE, 153, PORTSMOUTH ROAD, HORNDEAN
JOLLY, DORIS, 153, PORTSMOUTH ROAD, HORNDEAN
LAVENDER, MARGARET, 153, PORTSMOUTH ROAD,
MACLEAN, DOREEN, 153, PORTSMOUTH ROAD, HORNDEAN
MARTIN, ESTHER, 153, PORTSMOUTH ROAD, HORNDEAN
NASH, CATALINA, 153, PORTSMOUTH ROAD, HORNDEAN
PALFREYMAN, LILIAN, 153, PORTSMOUTH ROAD, HORNDEAN
RILEY, ELLEN, 153, PORTSMOUTH ROAD, HORNDEAN
RUMBOLD, WILLIAM, 153, PORTSMOUTH ROAD, HORNDEAN
SAMMARS, MINNIE, 153, PORTSMOUTH ROAD, HORNDEAN
STARKS, WINIFRED, 153, PORTSMOUTH ROAD, HORNDEAN
STOKES, FRANCES, 153, PORTSMOUTH ROAD, HORNDEAN
THOMAS, VIOLET, 153, PORTSMOUTH ROAD, HORNDEAN
WILLIAMS, ALEC, 153, PORTSMOUTH ROAD, HORNDEAN
WRIGHT, WILLIAM, 153, PORTSMOUTH ROAD, HORNDEAN
YORSTON, GERTRUDE, 153, PORTSMOUTH ROAD,
BARLOW, JOYCE J, 155, PORTSMOUTH ROAD, HORNDEAN
BARLOW, RAYMOND J, 155, PORTSMOUTH ROAD, HORNDEAN
HARKINS, JOHN, 157, PORTSMOUTH ROAD, HORNDEAN
HARKINS, KAY A, 157, PORTSMOUTH ROAD, HORNDEAN
TURVEY, DESNI, 159, PORTSMOUTH ROAD, HORNDEAN
TURVEY, PETER, 159, PORTSMOUTH ROAD, HORNDEAN
TURVEY, STEVEN P, 159, PORTSMOUTH ROAD, HORNDEAN
TUCKER, DEREK W, 161, PORTSMOUTH ROAD, HORNDEAN
TUCKER, ROSEMARY, 161, PORTSMOUTH ROAD, HORNDEAN
POOLE, EVELYN E, 163, PORTSMOUTH ROAD, HORNDEAN
BARNES, GRANT L, 164, PORTSMOUTH ROAD, HORNDEAN
BARNES, HENRY G, 164, PORTSMOUTH ROAD, HORNDEAN
BARNES, KIMBERLEY S, 164, PORTSMOUTH ROAD,
SALMON, DEBRA A, 165, PORTSMOUTH ROAD, HORNDEAN
SALMON, JAMES K, 165, PORTSMOUTH ROAD, HORNDEAN
COLE, DIANA J, 166, PORTSMOUTH ROAD, HORNDEAN
COLE, SIMON A, 166, PORTSMOUTH ROAD, HORNDEAN
YOUNG, EDWARD C, 167, PORTSMOUTH ROAD, HORNDEAN
YOUNG, JOAN M, 167, PORTSMOUTH ROAD, HORNDEAN
HAYWARD, JOHN S, 168, PORTSMOUTH ROAD, HORNDEAN
HAYWARD, JULIA E.B, 168, PORTSMOUTH ROAD, HORNDEAN
HAYWARD, REBECCA J, 168, PORTSMOUTH ROAD, HORNDEAN
GRUNDY, KATHARINE A.R, 169, PORTSMOUTH ROAD,
PRIOR, ALEXANDER G, 170, PORTSMOUTH ROAD,
PRIOR, GERALD L, 170, PORTSMOUTH ROAD, HORNDEAN
PRIOR, RACHEL B, 170, PORTSMOUTH ROAD, HORNDEAN
PRIOR, STEPHEN H, 170, PORTSMOUTH ROAD, HORNDEAN
PRIOR, VALERIE C, 170, PORTSMOUTH ROAD, HORNDEAN
TIPPINS, ALVIN D, 171, PORTSMOUTH ROAD, HORNDEAN
TIPPINS, MARJORIE G, 171, PORTSMOUTH ROAD, HORNDEAN
COURSE, BARBARA M, 172, PORTSMOUTH ROAD, HORNDEAN
COURSE, TREVOR G, 172, PORTSMOUTH ROAD, HORNDEAN
PRIVETT, BETTY M, 172, PORTSMOUTH ROAD, HORNDEAN
PRIVETT, LILIAN M, 172, PORTSMOUTH ROAD, HORNDEAN
SEATON, CHRISTINE T, 173, PORTSMOUTH ROAD,
SEATON, LAWRENCE W, 173, PORTSMOUTH ROAD,
COLLINS, DERRIAN G, 174, PORTSMOUTH ROAD, HORNDEAN
COLLINS, JONATHAN Z, 174, PORTSMOUTH ROAD,
COLLINS, MICHAEL P, 174, PORTSMOUTH ROAD, HORNDEAN
MAXWELL, CATHERINE, 174, PORTSMOUTH ROAD,
PETERS, PATRICIA G, 174A, PORTSMOUTH ROAD, HORNDEAN
LEONARD, JANICE C, 176, PORTSMOUTH ROAD, HORNDEAN
LEONARD, KEITH C, 176, PORTSMOUTH ROAD, HORNDEAN
BAKER, DAVID G, 178, PORTSMOUTH ROAD, HORNDEAN
BAKER, JOYCE E, 178, PORTSMOUTH ROAD, HORNDEAN
BAKER, KAREN F, 178, PORTSMOUTH ROAD, HORNDEAN
BAKER, VINCENT P, 178, PORTSMOUTH ROAD, HORNDEAN
BATEMAN, JANICE E, 180, PORTSMOUTH ROAD, HORNDEAN
BATEMAN, PETER S, 180, PORTSMOUTH ROAD, HORNDEAN
PATEL, SYLVIA J, 182, PORTSMOUTH ROAD, HORNDEAN
FLYNN, ANNE E, 184, PORTSMOUTH ROAD, HORNDEAN
FLYNN, LIESLOTTE M, 184, PORTSMOUTH ROAD, HORNDEAN
METCALF, JEAN A, 186, PORTSMOUTH ROAD, HORNDEAN
BARTHOLOMEW, BRIDGET E, 188, PORTSMOUTH ROAD,
BARTHOLOMEW, STEPHEN J, 188, PORTSMOUTH ROAD,
MARCHANT, MAUREEN J, 190, PORTSMOUTH ROAD,
MARCHANT, PETER, 190, PORTSMOUTH ROAD, HORNDEAN
HARTT, ALAN J, 192, PORTSMOUTH ROAD, HORNDEAN
HARTT, ANDREW M, 192, PORTSMOUTH ROAD, HORNDEAN
HARTT, MARGARET, 192, PORTSMOUTH ROAD, HORNDEAN
CROSS, MICHAEL J, 194, PORTSMOUTH ROAD, HORNDEAN
CROSS, SHERIDAN A, 194, PORTSMOUTH ROAD, HORNDEAN
ALLAND, BRIAN, 196, PORTSMOUTH ROAD, HORNDEAN
ALLAND, PAULINE A, 196, PORTSMOUTH ROAD, HORNDEAN
COSTER, BETTY B, 198, PORTSMOUTH ROAD, HORNDEAN
COSTER, GEORGE A, 198, PORTSMOUTH ROAD, HORNDEAN
BACON, THELMA I.M, 200, PORTSMOUTH ROAD, HORNDEAN
BRUTNELL, DERRICK M, 200, PORTSMOUTH ROAD,
BRUTNELL, JACQUELINE A, 200, PORTSMOUTH ROAD,
BRANSCOMBE, GORDON, 202, PORTSMOUTH ROAD,
BRANSCOMBE, RENIRA M, 202, PORTSMOUTH ROAD,
SIMONS, DAVID E, 204, PORTSMOUTH ROAD, HORNDEAN
SIMONS, SHEILA M, 204, PORTSMOUTH ROAD, HORNDEAN
JUPE, MATTHEW P, 206, PORTSMOUTH ROAD, HORNDEAN
JUPE, STEPHEN D, 206, PORTSMOUTH ROAD, HORNDEAN
JUPE, SUSAN A, 206, PORTSMOUTH ROAD, HORNDEAN
SANDWELL, DAVID O, 208, PORTSMOUTH ROAD, HORNDEAN
SANDWELL, EILEEN, 208, PORTSMOUTH ROAD, HORNDEAN
RUSSELL-SMITH, DUNCAN, 210, PORTSMOUTH ROAD,
RUSSELL-SMITH, ELSBETH, 210, PORTSMOUTH ROAD,
RUSSELL-SMITH, JANET M, 210, PORTSMOUTH ROAD,
RUSSELL-SMITH, JOHN H, 210, PORTSMOUTH ROAD,
TATLOW, ALAN R, 212, PORTSMOUTH ROAD, HORNDEAN
TATLOW, MARILYN R, 212, PORTSMOUTH ROAD, HORNDEAN
HANFREY, AMANDA, 214, PORTSMOUTH ROAD, HORNDEAN
POTTER, DEAN L, 214, PORTSMOUTH ROAD, HORNDEAN
CARR, CHRISTOPHER J, 214A, PORTSMOUTH ROAD,
CARR, JACQUELINE E, 214A, PORTSMOUTH ROAD,
COLLINS, KEITH F, 218, PORTSMOUTH ROAD, HORNDEAN
COLLINS, MARGARET J, 218, PORTSMOUTH ROAD,
RANDALL, JANET A, 220, PORTSMOUTH ROAD, HORNDEAN
RANDALL, NICHOLAS S, 220, PORTSMOUTH ROAD,
ELLIFF, CYNTHIA B, 222, PORTSMOUTH ROAD, HORNDEAN
ELLIFF-GLENNON, CLARE A, 222, PORTSMOUTH ROAD,
GAGE, ELEANOR M, 224, PORTSMOUTH ROAD, HORNDEAN
CREAMER, MARGARET J, 226, PORTSMOUTH ROAD,
CREAMER, MICHAEL R, 226, PORTSMOUTH ROAD,
BURTON, MARK A, 228, PORTSMOUTH ROAD, HORNDEAN
STILES, LINDA S, 228, PORTSMOUTH ROAD, HORNDEAN
PINKNEY, AVRIL S, 232, PORTSMOUTH ROAD, HORNDEAN
PINKNEY, BRUCE I, 232, PORTSMOUTH ROAD, HORNDEAN
PINKNEY, NIGEL A, 232, PORTSMOUTH ROAD, HORNDEAN
BOXER, PHYLLIS D, 234, PORTSMOUTH ROAD, HORNDEAN
MITCHELL, JANE M, 236, PORTSMOUTH ROAD, HORNDEAN
MITCHELL, ROBERT, 236, PORTSMOUTH ROAD, HORNDEAN
ALLEN, PAUL, 1, PUMP LANE, HORNDEAN
ALLEN, SHIRLEY, 1, PUMP LANE, HORNDEAN
LACEY, BRENDA A, 2, PUMP LANE, HORNDEAN
LACEY, JAMES C, 2, PUMP LANE, HORNDEAN
LACEY, PAUL A, 2, PUMP LANE, HORNDEAN
MCLEOD, IAN, 3, PUMP LANE, HORNDEAN
MCLEOD, JACQUELINE M, 3, PUMP LANE, HORNDEAN
MCLEOD, MALCOLM W, 3, PUMP LANE, HORNDEAN
MCCLELLAND, DONALD D, 4, PUMP LANE, HORNDEAN
BOWDEN, DAVID A, 5, PUMP LANE, HORNDEAN
BOWDEN, LISA, 5, PUMP LANE, HORNDEAN
WILLIAMS, MAUREEN M, 14, PUMP LANE, HORNDEAN
WILLIAMS, MICHAEL J, 14, PUMP LANE, HORNDEAN
LE MANQUAIS, KAREN C, 15, PUMP LANE, HORNDEAN
LE MANQUAIS, PAUL G, 15, PUMP LANE, HORNDEAN
BLACKBURN, PATRICIA J, 16, PUMP LANE, HORNDEAN
BLACKBURN, PETER, 16, PUMP LANE, HORNDEAN
CAPEL, ROBERT C, 16, PUMP LANE, HORNDEAN
MOSS, ANNE M, 17, PUMP LANE, HORNDEAN
MOSS, RICHARD G, 17, PUMP LANE, HORNDEAN
HALL, DAVID I, 18, PUMP LANE, HORNDEAN
HALL, JENNIFER, 18, PUMP LANE, HORNDEAN
MUNDEN, BEVERLY T, 19, PUMP LANE, HORNDEAN
MUNDEN, BRIAN L, 19, PUMP LANE, HORNDEAN
BARRINGER, EDWARD, 20, PUMP LANE, HORNDEAN
BARRINGER, SUSAN M, 20, PUMP LANE, HORNDEAN
GAUDION, MARTIN D, 21, PUMP LANE, HORNDEAN
GAUDION, NADINE, 21, PUMP LANE, HORNDEAN
SMITH, AUDREY M, 22, PUMP LANE, HORNDEAN
LAWRIE, ALICE C, 23, PUMP LANE, HORNDEAN
LAWRIE, GEORGINA M, 23, PUMP LANE, HORNDEAN
LAWRIE, GRAHAME A, 23, PUMP LANE, HORNDEAN
LAWRIE, JESSICA M, 23, PUMP LANE, HORNDEAN
HART, JANE A, 24, PUMP LANE, HORNDEAN
HART, MICHAEL R, 24, PUMP LANE, HORNDEAN
GRAY, ELIZABETH S, 25, PUMP LANE, HORNDEAN
GRAY, NICOLA J, 25, PUMP LANE, HORNDEAN
GRAY, STEPHEN M, 25, PUMP LANE, HORNDEAN
AYLAND, MALCOLM, 26, PUMP LANE, HORNDEAN
ELGHEITHY, CHRISTINE, 27, PUMP LANE, HORNDEAN
ELGHEITHY, MOHAMED S, 27, PUMP LANE, HORNDEAN
AWCOCK, ADRIAN R, 28, PUMP LANE, HORNDEAN
AWCOCK, EDWARD O.G, 28, PUMP LANE, HORNDEAN
AWCOCK, MARK R, 28, PUMP LANE, HORNDEAN
AWCOCK, PAUL O, 28, PUMP LANE, HORNDEAN
AWCOCK, RITA M, 28, PUMP LANE, HORNDEAN
PERMAN, CHRISTOPHER M, 29, PUMP LANE, HORNDEAN
PERMAN, CLAIRE L, 29, PUMP LANE, HORNDEAN
PERMAN, DIANE E, 29, PUMP LANE, HORNDEAN

PERMAN, MATTHEW D, 29, PUMP LANE, HORNDEAN
FOSTER, GLORIA A, 31, PUMP LANE, HORNDEAN
FOSTER, STEPHEN, 31, PUMP LANE, HORNDEAN
BUTLER, ELIZABETH, 32, PUMP LANE, HORNDEAN
BUTLER, RICHARD K, 32, PUMP LANE, HORNDEAN
LANGRISH, MADELINE J, PYLE FARM, PYLE LANE, HORNDEAN
LANGRISH, PETER G, PYLE FARM, PYLE LANE, HORNDEAN
LANGRISH, SYDNEY K, BLANCHARDS, PYLE LANE,
JONES, ALLAN C, 30, ROSEMARY WAY, HORNDEAN
JONES, KEITH C, 30, ROSEMARY WAY, HORNDEAN
JONES, MAUREEN L, 30, ROSEMARY WAY, HORNDEAN
HOBBS, MICHAEL W, 32, ROSEMARY WAY, HORNDEAN
ROOKE, EDWARD C, 34, ROSEMARY WAY, HORNDEAN
ROOKE, JOAN M, 34, ROSEMARY WAY, HORNDEAN
SMITHERS, ADRIAN H.L, 36, ROSEMARY WAY, HORNDEAN
SMITHERS, MAUREEN A, 36, ROSEMARY WAY, HORNDEAN
ATLEE, JOHN A, 38, ROSEMARY WAY, HORNDEAN
ATLEE, MARY E, 38, ROSEMARY WAY, HORNDEAN
DOUGLAS, DENNIS K.B, 39, ROSEMARY WAY, HORNDEAN
DOUGLAS, DOROTHY B, 39, ROSEMARY WAY, HORNDEAN
JOYCE, DORA A.P, 40, ROSEMARY WAY, HORNDEAN
JOYCE, JACK F, 40, ROSEMARY WAY, HORNDEAN
HICKMAN, DEREK A, 41, ROSEMARY WAY, HORNDEAN
HICKMAN, RITA, 41, ROSEMARY WAY, HORNDEAN
KEYFORD, MICHAEL J, 42, ROSEMARY WAY, HORNDEAN
PETCHEY, ZENA A, 42, ROSEMARY WAY, HORNDEAN
COLLETT, BRIAN D, 43, ROSEMARY WAY, HORNDEAN
COLLETT, JOYCE, 43, ROSEMARY WAY, HORNDEAN
DAVIES, MARGARET E.R, 44, ROSEMARY WAY, HORNDEAN
DAVIES, NORMAN D, 44, ROSEMARY WAY, HORNDEAN
DEXTER, DAPHNE E, 45, ROSEMARY WAY, HORNDEAN
DEXTER, GEORGE V, 45, ROSEMARY WAY, HORNDEAN
STONE, JOY, 46, ROSEMARY WAY, HORNDEAN
STONE, MICHAEL, 46, ROSEMARY WAY, HORNDEAN
MANCEY, COLIN B, 47, ROSEMARY WAY, HORNDEAN
MANCEY, DEBRA A, 47, ROSEMARY WAY, HORNDEAN
HARRIS, ALAN R, 48, ROSEMARY WAY, HORNDEAN
HARRIS, DAPHNE, 48, ROSEMARY WAY, HORNDEAN
HARRIS, ROSS P, 48, ROSEMARY WAY, HORNDEAN
HELLIER, JOAN U.M, 49, ROSEMARY WAY, HORNDEAN
HELLIER, WALTER, 49, ROSEMARY WAY, HORNDEAN
HARDY, BERYL, 50, ROSEMARY WAY, HORNDEAN
HARDY, GEORGE E, 50, ROSEMARY WAY, HORNDEAN
MORGAN, JACQUELINE A, 51, ROSEMARY WAY, HORNDEAN
COUSINS, CHRISTENA M, 52, ROSEMARY WAY, HORNDEAN
COUSINS, NIGEL J, 52, ROSEMARY WAY, HORNDEAN
CLARK, CLIVE R, 53, ROSEMARY WAY, HORNDEAN
INGS, SUSANNE L, 53, ROSEMARY WAY, HORNDEAN
NEWMAN, CRAIG E, 55, ROSEMARY WAY, HORNDEAN
NEWMAN, SUSAN A, 55, ROSEMARY WAY, HORNDEAN
CHURCHILL, BRIAN A, 57, ROSEMARY WAY, HORNDEAN
CHURCHILL, DEBRA J, 57, ROSEMARY WAY, HORNDEAN
CHURCHILL, PATRICIA A, 57, ROSEMARY WAY, HORNDEAN
MAYNE, STEPHEN, 58, ROSEMARY WAY, HORNDEAN
UPTON, FRANK R, 59, ROSEMARY WAY, HORNDEAN
UPTON, MARGARET R, 59, ROSEMARY WAY, HORNDEAN
SUDDON, STUART, 60, ROSEMARY WAY, HORNDEAN
JENKINS, ALAN A, 61, ROSEMARY WAY, HORNDEAN
JENKINS, YVONNE I, 61, ROSEMARY WAY, HORNDEAN
ELLIS, ELLEN J, 62, ROSEMARY WAY, HORNDEAN
BATTEN, PAMELA M, 63, ROSEMARY WAY, HORNDEAN
CALLABY, ROBERT M, 63, ROSEMARY WAY, HORNDEAN
PAYNE, CECIL F, 64, ROSEMARY WAY, HORNDEAN
PAYNE, EDNA J, 64, ROSEMARY WAY, HORNDEAN
FURMEDGE, JAMES V, 65, ROSEMARY WAY, HORNDEAN
VINCENT, BRIAN C, 66, ROSEMARY WAY, HORNDEAN
VINCENT, MARCIA A, 66, ROSEMARY WAY, HORNDEAN
BERRIMAN, BARBARA, 67, ROSEMARY WAY, HORNDEAN
BERRIMAN, MICHAEL G, 67, ROSEMARY WAY, HORNDEAN
FRESHWATER, DAVID, 68, ROSEMARY WAY, HORNDEAN
FRESHWATER, PATRICIA M, 68, ROSEMARY WAY, HORNDEAN
SCHULTE, JOHANNA, 69, ROSEMARY WAY, HORNDEAN
HUNT, ALAN D, 71, ROSEMARY WAY, HORNDEAN
HUNT, JONOTHAN J, 71, ROSEMARY WAY, HORNDEAN
HUNT, SUSAN J, 71, ROSEMARY WAY, HORNDEAN
STEWART, CLAIRE L, 71, ROSEMARY WAY, HORNDEAN
THOMAS, ANTHONY J, 73, ROSEMARY WAY, HORNDEAN
THOMAS, CATHERINE J, 73, ROSEMARY WAY, HORNDEAN
PAYNTER-HART, MARGARET, 75, ROSEMARY WAY, HORNDEAN
PAYNTER-HART, RACHAEL E, 75, ROSEMARY WAY, HORNDEAN
ASHDOWN, MARJORIE E, 77, ROSEMARY WAY, HORNDEAN
WALLIS, DUNCAN L, 1, ROWLANDS CASTLE ROAD, HORNDEAN
HALLETT, ANGELA J, 3, ROWLANDS CASTLE ROAD,
HALLETT, TERENCE W, 3, ROWLANDS CASTLE ROAD,
BRITTAIN, DEREK F, 7, ROWLANDS CASTLE ROAD,
BRITTAIN, JOAN, 7, ROWLANDS CASTLE ROAD, HORNDEAN
CLARK, MONICA, 9, ROWLANDS CASTLE ROAD, HORNDEAN
WITHERS, GILLIAN, 11, ROWLANDS CASTLE ROAD,
WITHERS, TONY, 11, ROWLANDS CASTLE ROAD, HORNDEAN
KIDD, DEBORAH J, 21, ROWLANDS CASTLE ROAD,
TEMPLEMAN, ANN R, 39, ROWLANDS CASTLE ROAD,
TEMPLEMAN, GRAHAM P, 39, ROWLANDS CASTLE ROAD,
TEMPLEMAN, JOANNE M, 39, ROWLANDS CASTLE ROAD,
TEMPLEMAN, NICOLA A, 39, ROWLANDS CASTLE ROAD,
DREW, AMY L, 8, ROWLANDS CASTLE ROAD, HORNDEAN
DREW, KEITH R, 8, ROWLANDS CASTLE ROAD, HORNDEAN
DREW, LESLEY M, 8, ROWLANDS CASTLE ROAD, HORNDEAN
DREW, RICHARD K, 8, ROWLANDS CASTLE ROAD,
LITTLEFIELD, JOAN, 18, ROWLANDS CASTLE ROAD,
LITTLEFIELD, JOHN A, 18, ROWLANDS CASTLE ROAD,
LEE, FREDERICK J, 20, ROWLANDS CASTLE ROAD,
LEE, JOYCE M, 20, ROWLANDS CASTLE ROAD, HORNDEAN
CREES, BARRY J, 34, ROWLANDS CASTLE ROAD, HORNDEAN
CREES, VICTORIA E, 34, ROWLANDS CASTLE ROAD,
PALMER, GARRICK S, 38, ROWLANDS CASTLE ROAD,
VINCENT-SPALL, IAN, 42, ROWLANDS CASTLE ROAD,
VINCENT-SPALL, WENDY M, 42, ROWLANDS CASTLE ROAD,
HIRE, RACHEL O, 44, ROWLANDS CASTLE ROAD, HORNDEAN
HOLDFORTH, SYLVIA A, 44, ROWLANDS CASTLE ROAD,
HORSTED, DOROTHY M, 46, ROWLANDS CASTLE ROAD,
HORSTED, FREDERIC C, 46, ROWLANDS CASTLE ROAD,
PESCOTT, GRACE K, 48, ROWLANDS CASTLE ROAD,
TURNER, GEORGE D, 50, ROWLANDS CASTLE ROAD,
TURNER, LAURA, 50, ROWLANDS CASTLE ROAD, HORNDEAN
STRANGE, JOHN J, 1, POND COTTAGES, SHEEPWASH ROAD,
STRANGE, JULIE M, 1, POND COTTAGES, SHEEPWASH ROAD,
STRANGE, AMOS J, 2, POND COTTAGES, SHEEPWASH ROAD,
STRANGE, WENDY D, 2, POND COTTAGES, SHEEPWASH ROAD,
JAGO, ETHEL V, 44, SPRING VALE, HORNDEAN
EADES, CAROL A, 46, SPRING VALE, HORNDEAN
EADES, TIMOTHY G, 46, SPRING VALE, HORNDEAN
BALCOMBE, EDITH C.J, 47, SPRING VALE, HORNDEAN
BALCOMBE, RONALD W, 47, SPRING VALE, HORNDEAN
CHINN, RICHARD, 48, SPRING VALE, HORNDEAN
CHINN, SUSAN M, 48, SPRING VALE, HORNDEAN
WEBSTER, FRANCES, 49, SPRING VALE, HORNDEAN
WEBSTER, KENNETH J, 49, SPRING VALE, HORNDEAN
RICKETTS, FREDA P, 50, SPRING VALE, HORNDEAN
TICKNER, CHRISTINE L, 51, SPRING VALE, HORNDEAN
WATKINS, CAROL L, 51, SPRING VALE, HORNDEAN
HUNT, LUCY C, 52, SPRING VALE, HORNDEAN
HUNT, MICHAEL A, 52, SPRING VALE, HORNDEAN
HUNT, PAUL E, 52, SPRING VALE, HORNDEAN
HUNT, WILLIAM E, 52, SPRING VALE, HORNDEAN
GREENWAY, ADAM, 53, SPRING VALE, HORNDEAN
GREENWAY, LORRAINE, 53, SPRING VALE, HORNDEAN
METHERELL, PETER C, 54, SPRING VALE, HORNDEAN
METHERELL, SHEILA A, 54, SPRING VALE, HORNDEAN
COLLINS, IRENE N, 55, SPRING VALE, HORNDEAN
VOYSEY, ALAN M, 56, SPRING VALE, HORNDEAN
VOYSEY, LYNN, 56, SPRING VALE, HORNDEAN
VOYSEY, SAMANTHA, 56, SPRING VALE, HORNDEAN
LOWE, COLIN F, 57, SPRING VALE, HORNDEAN
LOWE, JEAN, 57, SPRING VALE, HORNDEAN
SANDHAM, DORA E, 58, SPRING VALE, HORNDEAN
BEDFORD, IAN, 59, SPRING VALE, HORNDEAN
THOMAS, MARK D.E, 60, SPRING VALE, HORNDEAN
THOMAS, VANESSA N, 60, SPRING VALE, HORNDEAN
WILLIAMS, CAROLE A, 61, SPRING VALE, HORNDEAN
WILLIAMS, PETER L, 61, SPRING VALE, HORNDEAN
WRIGHT, MARGARET, 62, SPRING VALE, HORNDEAN
WRIGHT, ROBERT, 62, SPRING VALE, HORNDEAN
NORRIS, ALBERT W, 63, SPRING VALE, HORNDEAN
NORRIS, EDNA M, 63, SPRING VALE, HORNDEAN
HEWITT, DENNIS G, 64, SPRING VALE, HORNDEAN
HEWITT, IVY S, 64, SPRING VALE, HORNDEAN
KENT, BRIAN E.G, 66, SPRING VALE, HORNDEAN
KENT, EDWARD S, 66, SPRING VALE, HORNDEAN
KENT, JEANNETTE P, 66, SPRING VALE, HORNDEAN
WHEATLEY, JANET P, 68, SPRING VALE, HORNDEAN
WHEATLEY, KAREN J, 68, SPRING VALE, HORNDEAN
WHEATLEY, RONALD B, 68, SPRING VALE, HORNDEAN
DAVIDSON, ALISTAIR R, 70, SPRING VALE, HORNDEAN
DAVIDSON, ROSEMARY A, 70, SPRING VALE, HORNDEAN
MITCHELL, LORRAINE M, 70, SPRING VALE, HORNDEAN
MITCHELL, ROBERT D, 70, SPRING VALE, HORNDEAN
PRICE, JEAN S, 25, VERBENA CRESCENT, HORNDEAN
RICHARDS, WILLIAM F.C, 26, VERBENA CRESCENT,
RICHARDS, WINIFRED M, 26, VERBENA CRESCENT,
HARRIS, JOHN P, 27, VERBENA CRESCENT, HORNDEAN
HARRIS, VALERIE A, 27, VERBENA CRESCENT, HORNDEAN
STACEY, ANNE E, 28, VERBENA CRESCENT, HORNDEAN
WILSON, BERYL S, 29, VERBENA CRESCENT, HORNDEAN
HUDSON, DOROTHY P, 30, VERBENA CRESCENT, HORNDEAN
HUDSON, JOHN T, 30, VERBENA CRESCENT, HORNDEAN
SMITH, ANN, 31, VERBENA CRESCENT, HORNDEAN
SMITH, ROGER W, 31, VERBENA CRESCENT, HORNDEAN
MCILROY, DEBBIE N, 32, VERBENA CRESCENT, HORNDEAN
STEAD, VALERIE A, 32, VERBENA CRESCENT, HORNDEAN
STEVENS, JONATHAN T, 33, VERBENA CRESCENT, HORNDEAN
STEVENS, KEITH D, 33, VERBENA CRESCENT, HORNDEAN
STEVENS, MATTHEW D.C, 33, VERBENA CRESCENT,
WHITE, DAVID F, 34, VERBENA CRESCENT, HORNDEAN
WHITE, JUNE A, 34, VERBENA CRESCENT, HORNDEAN
BRITTON, SALLY-ANNE C, 36, VERBENA CRESCENT,
HANDLEY, PETER, 36, VERBENA CRESCENT, HORNDEAN
WRIGHT, BRENDA, 1, WELLINGTON CLOSE, HORNDEAN
WRIGHT, STANLEY, 1, WELLINGTON CLOSE, HORNDEAN
SMART, DAVID J, 2, WELLINGTON CLOSE, HORNDEAN
SMART, SARAH J, 2, WELLINGTON CLOSE, HORNDEAN
PHIPPS, ELLEN F, 3, WELLINGTON CLOSE, HORNDEAN
PHIPPS, LESLIE W, 3, WELLINGTON CLOSE, HORNDEAN
GILLESPIE, ROSEMARY, 4, WELLINGTON CLOSE, HORNDEAN
STONER, DIANE S.M, 5, WELLINGTON CLOSE, HORNDEAN
STONER, OLIVER M.R, 5, WELLINGTON CLOSE, HORNDEAN
HADOW, KEITH V, 6, WELLINGTON CLOSE, HORNDEAN
HADOW, MARJORIE L, 6, WELLINGTON CLOSE, HORNDEAN
WATTS, PHYLLIS M, 1, WHITEBEAM CLOSE, HORNDEAN
WATTS, RAYMOND A, 1, WHITEBEAM CLOSE, HORNDEAN
WRIGHT, DENNIS W, 2, WHITEBEAM CLOSE, HORNDEAN
WRIGHT, FREDA, 2, WHITEBEAM CLOSE, HORNDEAN
SATCHWELL, JANICE A, 3, WHITEBEAM CLOSE, HORNDEAN
SATCHWELL, MICHAEL D, 3, WHITEBEAM CLOSE, HORNDEAN
MADGE, FERNLEIGH R, 4, WHITEBEAM CLOSE, HORNDEAN
MADGE, MAUREEN C, 4, WHITEBEAM CLOSE, HORNDEAN
HUNTER, BARBARA D, 5, WHITEBEAM CLOSE, HORNDEAN
HUNTER, HENRY E, 5, WHITEBEAM CLOSE, HORNDEAN
HUBBARD, ALLAN, 6, WHITEBEAM CLOSE, HORNDEAN
HUBBARD, BETTY J, 6, WHITEBEAM CLOSE, HORNDEAN
HUBBARD, THOMAS R, 6, WHITEBEAM CLOSE, HORNDEAN
DRAPER, DEREK D, 7, WHITEBEAM CLOSE, HORNDEAN
DRAPER, PAMELA J, 7, WHITEBEAM CLOSE, HORNDEAN
LEO, EDMUND J, 7, WHITEBEAM CLOSE, HORNDEAN
GAY, CHRISTINE M, 8, WHITEBEAM CLOSE, HORNDEAN
GAY, CHRISTOPHER W, 8, WHITEBEAM CLOSE, HORNDEAN
HARRISON, DAVID W, 9, WHITEBEAM CLOSE, HORNDEAN
HARRISON, JOAN, 9, WHITEBEAM CLOSE, HORNDEAN
FRYATT, ANN, 1, WHITEHAVEN, HORNDEAN
FRYATT, PAUL R, 1, WHITEHAVEN, HORNDEAN
SMITH, IRENE B, 2, WHITEHAVEN, HORNDEAN
HARLEY, JACQUELINE M, 2A, WHITEHAVEN, HORNDEAN
HARLEY, LESLIE J, 2A, WHITEHAVEN, HORNDEAN
BOWERS, AMANDA, 3, WHITEHAVEN, HORNDEAN
LEONARD, GARY E, 3, WHITEHAVEN, HORNDEAN
WILDSMITH, MARIENETTE A, 4, WHITEHAVEN, HORNDEAN
WILSON, DAVID R, 4, WHITEHAVEN, HORNDEAN
MILLER, DAVID J, 5, WHITEHAVEN, HORNDEAN
MILLER, PAMELA J, 5, WHITEHAVEN, HORNDEAN
OAKLAND, JULIE, 6, WHITEHAVEN, HORNDEAN
OAKLAND, NIGEL, 6, WHITEHAVEN, HORNDEAN
WHITE, CHLOE U, 7, WHITEHAVEN, HORNDEAN
WHITE, DANIEL J, 7, WHITEHAVEN, HORNDEAN
WHITE, DIANA R, 7, WHITEHAVEN, HORNDEAN
WHITE, JOHN G, 7, WHITEHAVEN, HORNDEAN
HALL, JANE, 8, WHITEHAVEN, HORNDEAN
ROSS, PAUL J, 8, WHITEHAVEN, HORNDEAN
STALEY, ALAN J, 9, WHITEHAVEN, HORNDEAN
STALEY, ANN, 9, WHITEHAVEN, HORNDEAN
FOSTER, EDWIN C, 10, WHITEHAVEN, HORNDEAN
FOSTER, ELIZABETH, 10, WHITEHAVEN, HORNDEAN
DRAPER, CHRISTINA D, 11, WHITEHAVEN, HORNDEAN
DRAPER, DIANA E, 11, WHITEHAVEN, HORNDEAN
HARTLEY, RAYMOND E, 11, WHITEHAVEN, HORNDEAN
HISCOCK, KENNETH J, 12, WHITEHAVEN, HORNDEAN
HISCOCK, ROSEMARY G, 12, WHITEHAVEN, HORNDEAN
BROWN, MARY, 13, WHITEHAVEN, HORNDEAN
BROWN, ROBERT J, 13, WHITEHAVEN, HORNDEAN
LANG, VALMAI B, 14, WHITEHAVEN, HORNDEAN
PALMER, FRANCES R, 15, WHITEHAVEN, HORNDEAN
PALMER, NICOLAS S, 15, WHITEHAVEN, HORNDEAN
LOVEGROVE, JOHN B, 15A, WHITEHAVEN, HORNDEAN
LOVEGROVE, KATHARINE J, 15A, WHITEHAVEN, HORNDEAN
ATKINSON, JANET M, 16, WHITEHAVEN, HORNDEAN
ATKINSON, NEIL, 16, WHITEHAVEN, HORNDEAN
ANTHONY, MAVIS E, 17, WHITEHAVEN, HORNDEAN
BAKER, HAZEL, 18, WHITEHAVEN, HORNDEAN
BAKER, VERNON K, 18, WHITEHAVEN, HORNDEAN
KEENE, DOUGLAS M, 20, WHITEHAVEN, HORNDEAN
ARTHUR, HILDA A, 22, WHITEHAVEN, HORNDEAN
BOULTER, VERA, 22, WHITEHAVEN, HORNDEAN
BRITTAIN, BLANCHE, 22, WHITEHAVEN, HORNDEAN
GARNER, GLADYS D, 22, WHITEHAVEN, HORNDEAN
GEOGHGAN, KATHLEEN M, 22, WHITEHAVEN, HORNDEAN
GOODALL, WALTER C, 22, WHITEHAVEN, HORNDEAN
HAYWARD, LILY A, 22, WHITEHAVEN, HORNDEAN
HORNE, WINIFRED, 22, WHITEHAVEN, HORNDEAN
JONES, IRENE J, 22, WHITEHAVEN, HORNDEAN
LONG, EDNA M, 22, WHITEHAVEN, HORNDEAN
MORING, THELMA, 22, WHITEHAVEN, HORNDEAN
NEWTON, FRANCES E, 22, WHITEHAVEN, HORNDEAN
BARCHAM, ROBERT J, 24, WHITEHAVEN, HORNDEAN
BOWEN, DAVID W,,
BOWEN, KATHLEEN M.R,,
COOLING, HELEN M,,
GILLESPIE, SIMON M,,
HARRIS, PHILIP N,,
HULME, LAON S.G,,
PINHORN, JEFFREY A,,
WOODS, SHIRLEY

Index

agriculture (see farming)
agricultural depression, 49, 50, 54
agricultural output, 31, 33, 45
Anchor, 36
Andover, 31
Angles, 16
Anglo-Saxons, 17, 19
Anglo-Saxon village, 16, 19
Appleford Charity, 43, 56
archery butts, 28
arrows, flint, 12
arthritis, 17
assarts, 22
axe, hand, 11
axe, Cornish, 12

barrow, round, 12
Bat and Ball Inn, 13
Beaufort, Duke of, 36, 43, 45
Belgic jars, 13
Birinus, Bishop, 17
Bishop of Winchester's estates, 21–23
Bishop's Waltham manor, 21
Bitterne, 15
Black Death, 22–23
Blendworth, *passim*
Blendworth Centre, New, 78
Blendworth Church built, 42, 55
Blendworth Common, 50
Blendworth Down, 11, 13, 45, 50
Blendworth Lodge, 46, 52, 55, 58, 63, 65–6, 69
Blendworth School, 56, 57, 67–8, 72, 73, 75
blitz, 72
Bowyer, Herbert F., 54, 70
Brett, Humphrey, 29
Brett, Roberts, 36
Broadhalfpenny Down, 12
Bronze Age, 12
bronze implements, 12, 17
buildings, brick, 16, 34, 40, 54

buildings, timber-framed, 16, 34
burials, Anglo-Saxon, 17
burials, Iron-Age, 13
burials, Romano-British, 16
Butser Hill, 11–12, 15

Cadlington House, 55, 63, 66, 72, 74, 78
Catherington, *passim*
Catherington Church, 19, 43, 55
Catherington Common, 50
Catherington Down, 50, 77
Catherington House, 46
Catherington Lith, 73, 79
Catherington School, 56–7, 67, 72–3, 75
Catholic Church, 75
Causeway Farm, 13, 15, 36, 61, 62
Celtic fields, 12, 20
census, 51–4, 57–8, 61, 75–6
Ceptune manor, 19, 20
Chalton, 12, 15–7, 19, 21, 23, 26, 29, 34, 36, 42, 45, 49, 55
charcoal, 16, 17, 22
Cheriton gold stater, 13
Chichester, 15, 21, 32, 50
Christianity, 17
churchwardens, 42–3
Clanfield, 12, 16, 19, 49, 77
Clarke-Jervoise, Jervoise, 43–4, 49, 50, 52, 55
clock, 40–1
coach services, 41–2
coinage, 13, 16, 52
Community Association, 74
Compton Census, 33
copyhold, 36, 44–6, 50
Corn Laws, 49
Cosham, 63–4, 73
Cowplain, 12, 16, 69, 72, 74–5, 77
Crookhorn, 15
crops, 27–32, 35, 40, 45

demesne lands, 20–1
Denmead, 16
disease, 26, 57, 67–9
Dockyard, Portsmouth, 36, 39, 49, 50
Domesday Book, 19
Down House, 12
Drill Hall, 66, 75
Droxford, 20
Droxford deanery, 22

early man, 11
Earl Godwin, 19
East Meon, 35
education, 43, 56–7, 67–9, 72
Edward the Confessor, 19
electricity, 70, 74–5
Elizabeth I, 26
Elizabeth II, 73
employment, 50, 54–5, 66, 77–8
Emsworth, 21, 50, 52, 61, 69
enclosure, 12, 13, 15, 22–3, 39, 43, 49, 50

famine, 22, 26
Fareham, 17, 23
Farmer Inn, 35, 63, 69
farming, 12, 20–1, 23, 27–31, 44–5, 49, 53–4
feudal system, 20, 23
Fifhide, William de, 20–1
fire station, 76
Five Heads Farm, 36, 45, 50, 63, 69, 71
Five Heads Manor, 21, 23, 29, 43–4
food riots, 27, 45, 49
Forest of Bere, 10, 15–6, 20, 22, 27–9, 31, 34–5, 39, 51, 65, 71
freehold, 36, 44

Gale family, 54
Gales Brewery, 54, 61–2, 66, 69, 70, 76, 78–9
geology, 10
Good Intent, 53, 64, 66, 69, 70
Gosport, 36
Gravel Hill, 15, 70
Gravel Hill Bottom, 12
Great Depression, 70
Great Famine, 22
Guildford, 55

Hambledon, 16–7, 20–1, 52
Harold Godwinson, Earl, 19
harvests, 12, 15, 22–3, 26, 49, 50
Havant, 15, 17, 20–1, 34, 50, 63, 69
Hayling Island, 22
Hearth Tax, 30, 34–6
highwaymen, 51
Hilliard, Nicholas, 26
hill fort, 12, 17
Hinton Burrant, 23, 28
Hinton Daubney, 15, 20, 29, 30, 43, 50, 63
Hinton Markaunt, 23, 31
Hinton Manor, 15, 30, 63
Hog's Lodge, 12–13
holiday resort, 64
homo sapiens, 11
Hood, Lord Samuel, 46, 52
Horndean, 34–5, 40–2, 46, 50, *passim*
Horndean Infants School, 75–6
Horndean School, 56, 73, 75, 77
Horndean Secondary School, 75, 77
horse racing, 52
house contents, 27–33
household size, 19
housing development, 74–9
Hugh de Port, 19
hunter-gatherers, 11
hurricane, 78
husbandman, 28–31, 35
hut sites, 12, 16
Hyde Chapel, 29
Hyde, Sir Nicholas, 29

ice age, 11, 12
Idsworth, 19, 49, 69
Idesworth Down, 13
industrial estate, 77–9
Industrial Revolution, 23, 39, 47, 54
inflation, 23, 50
influenza, 23
Iron Age, 12, 16
Iron Age implements, 12
Isle of Wight, 41
Isolation Hospital, 64, 67

Jutes, 16

Index

Katryngton Inne, 35
Kean, Edmund, 52, 56
Keydell House, 52, 56, 63, 72, 74
Keydell Nurseries, 78
Kilns, brick, 10
　　　pottery, 15
Knighton, Sir William, 52, 55, 58

labourers, agricultural, 29, 30, 46, 50
labour services, 22–3
land hunger, 21
Langstone Harbour, 29
lead-bronze alloy, 12
Library, 78
Light Railway, 63–4, 67, 70–2, 79
livestock, 27–33, 35, 40, 45
living standards, 22–3, 26, 58
London, 34, 36, 51
London clay, 15
loom weight, 12, 15, 17
Lovedean, 30, 43–4, 55–6, 64
Lovedean Mission, 55–6
Lovedean, Thomas, 30
Ludmore, 30

mains drainage, 70
mains water, 70, 73–4
manorial court, 45
markets, 21
Marlowe, Christopher, 26
Merchistoun Estate, 74–6
Merchistoun Hall, 35, 46, 63, 69, 72, 74–5
Mesolithic, 11
Methodist Chapel, 55, 61, 64, 79
Middle Stone Age, 11
mill, 20–1, 36, 40, 44, 46
money lending, 39
motorway (A3M), 77, 80
Motley's Copse, 19
Murray, Admiral, 74, 78

Napier, Sir Charles, 69
Nash Hall, 73, 78
Neanderthal man, 11
Neolithic, 11
Netherly Down, 12, 16,
　　　Farm, 13, 15

New Stone Age, 11–12

Odiham, 31
oil exploration, 78
Old Stone Age, 11
open fields, 22–3, 39
overseers of the poor, 42–3
Oxenbourne Down, 11–12

Padnell, 10, 34
pagans, 17
Palaeolithic, 11
Parish Council, 58, 69, 71, 75–6, 80
Parish Hall, 61, 65–6, 68–9, 75, 78–9
parish system, 17
pasture, 20–2, 27–9, 31, 50
Peasants Revolt, 23
Pepys, Samuel, 34
Petersfield, 31, 34, 41, 51, 61, 63, 68–9, 73
plague, 22–3, 26
Poor House (Workhouse) 43, 47, 51, 64, 68, 71, 78
Poor Law, 26, 30, 42, 49, 51
poor rate, 49
population, 19–23, 26–7, 33, 39, 45, 47, 49, 53–4,
　　　72, 75–7, 79
Portchester, 17, 21, 26
Portchester Castle, 16
Portsdown Hill, 12, 21, 52, 63
Portsea Island, 20, 39
Portsmouth, 21, 32, 34, 36, 39, 41, 49, 50, 52, 54,
　　　61, 64, 67, 77
pottery, 12–3, 17, 21
pottery, Roman, 5
poverty, 26–7, 47, 49, 51, 57–8, 64
prices, 22, 26, 28, 33, 45, 47, 49
probate inventory, 27, 34, 40
probate records, 30, 35
Pyle Farm, 36, 45, 69, 70

Quallett's Grove, 35, 46, 52, 69
quern, 15, 17

rationing, 73
Reading beds, 10, 15
recreation ground, 71
Red Lion, 36, 44, 61, 63–6, 69
rents, 23, 36

Rifle Club, 66
Roger de Belesme, Earl of Arundel and Shrewsbury, 19
Roger de Montgomery, Earl of Shrewsbury, 19, 20
Roman discoveries, 15
Roman Empire, 15, 16
'rough music', 66
Rowlands Castle, 10, 15–6, 34
R.C. on Crown Woods & Forests, 22, 39
rural society, 29, 30, 46
Rushmore Pond, 17, 71, 78

St. Catherines House, 35–6, 63
salt, 29
Sandys, Lord, 29
servants, domestic, 43, 53–4
Shakespeare, William, 26
Sheepwash Pond, 11, 15, 71
Ship and Bell, 36, 41, 44, 52, 54, 58, 64, 69
shops, 32–3, 40, 44, 52–3, 61, 70, 80
Snell's Corner, 11, 13, 15, 17
social attitudes, 42, 46, 67–8
social life, 52, 58, 63, 71
South Downs, 12, 21
Southwick Priory, 21
Spanish Armada, 26
Speenhamland System, 47
Spenser, Edmund, 26
Statute of Labourers, 23
Stone Age, 12
strip lynchets, 20
Stubbins Down, 16
sumptuary legislation, 23
supermarket, 80
surveyors of highways, 42
Swing Riots, 50–1

taxation, 16, 22, 27, 30
telephone exchange, 65, 75–6

Titchfield, 22
Titchfield Abbey, 21, 23
Titchfield Church, 17
Tithe Commutation Act, 55
transport, 63–5, 70–1, 74, 76–7, 80
trade, 12–3, 15–6, 21, 32–3, 58
treadwheel, 35
Turbery field, 17
turnpike road, 39, 41

unemployment, 26, 47, 49, 71

VE Day, 73
VJ Day, 73

wages, 22, 23, 26, 50
Wait Lane End, 41
war, 41, 45, 49–51, 67
    First World, 68–9, 71
    Second World, 69, 71–4
Warblington, 26
war memorial, 69, 71, 73, 77
Waterlooville, 12, 41, 61, 63, 73, 77, 79
weather, 22, 42, 45, 49, 57, 68, 78
wells, 10, 16, 35–6, 63
Wellington, Duke of, 50, 52
Weston, Richard, 31
Wickham, 17, 21, 26
William I, Duke of Normandy, 19
Winchester, 15
Windmill Hill, 11, 12, 13, 15
wool textile industry, 31–2
Worcester, Earl of, 29, 43
Worlidge, John, 31

yeomen, 27–8, 30–31, 35, 39, 40
Yoells, 20